Basic Principles of
American Government

BASIC PRINCIPLES OF AMERICAN GOVERNMENT

(1983 Edition)

William R. Sanford, Ph.D.

Carl R. Green, Ph.D.

AMSCO SCHOOL PUBLICATIONS, INC.

315 Hudson Street / New York, N.Y. 10013

When ordering this book, please specify:
either **R 193 H** *or*
AMERICAN GOVERNMENT, HARDBOUND EDITION

(1983 Edition)

ISBN 0–87720–622–8

Copyright © 1979, 1977 by Amsco School Publications, Inc.

No part of this book may be reproduced in any form
without written permission from the publisher.

Printed in the United States of America

PREFACE

The Constitution of the United States is a document that British Prime Minister William Gladstone once hailed as "the most wonderful work ever struck off at a given time by the brain and purpose of man." *Basic Principles of American Government* is a book about the system of government established by that Constitution and about how that system has evolved to meet modern needs.

As authors and teachers, we believe that young people retain a deep and vigorous interest in their country and in the *how* and *why* of its operations. There we have placed our emphasis: on *how* our government works, in all its frustrating but marvelous complexity; and on *why* it works the way it does, sometimes smoothly and sometimes haltingly.

The twenty-one chapters that lie ahead contain a wide variety of learning aids: headings and subheadings in generous numbers, mid-chapter and end-of-chapter summaries, review and discussion questions, suggestions for activities, and vocabulary lists. *Basic Principles of American Government* also draws on our long acquaintance with the needs and interests of students. Each chapter begins with an account of a dramatic incident related to the chapter's topic; these episodes range in time from the hiding of Connecticut's colonial charter (which introduces Chapter 2, on the origins of the United States' system of government) to John Kennedy's handling of the Cuban missile crisis (which opens Chapter 7, on the presidency). Learning objectives for each chapter grow out of these incidents, and are posed in the form of questions which serve as headings for the eight or more sections into which every chapter is divided. At the midpoint of each chapter, the reader is invited to pause briefly to review informally the basic concepts just discussed. Photographs, drawings, tables, and charts—relating closely to the text and keyed to it—provide springboards for further inquiry experiences. Each chapter closes with a variety of review questions and suggested activities designed to review the content of the chapter and to create further awareness of national values and the workings of our system of government.

Basic Principles of American Government offers several chapters not found in most other American government textbooks. The Introduction draws upon the immediacy of students' experiences with their own school government. Chapter 12 gives readers an opportunity to study the growth of the Constitution as reflected in eight landmark Supreme Court decisions.

Chapter 20 reminds young readers that a wide range of career opportunities awaits them in government service. In the same chapter, sound advice on how to take—and pass—civil service examinations is offered, along with a discussion of the advantages and disadvantages of public employment. Finally, Chapter 21 takes a hard, provocative look at the future of government in this country: How will our institutions change to meet the challenges of the next hundred years?

We want to emphasize that even with all these special features, *Basic Principles of American Government* has a traditional orientation. The book is designed to fit within the confines of a one-semester government course, and the table of contents reflects a standard approach to the subject. That is, the text moves from the development of theories of government and the writing of the Constitution to the three branches of the federal government, and then to a careful analysis of state, county, and city governments. Moreover, the reading level has been calculated to keep better readers interested without discouraging those who are still developing their reading skills.

This book's theme may be stated in a single word: *involvement*. Democracy can endure only as long as we are willing to make the sacrifices that a system of self-government demands. We must stay informed, make decisions, vote, hold office, and remain eternally alert to the actions of the public officials to whom we entrust the mechanisms of our government.

William R. Sanford
Carl R. Green

CONTENTS

2 Principles of the American Legislative System

FOUR   The Organization and Power of Congress 82

FIVE   How Laws Are Made: The Congress at Work 104

SIX   Congress and the Control of Fiscal Policy 125

3 Development of the Executive Branch

SEVEN   The Many Jobs of the President 146

INTRODUCTION: STUDENT GOVERNMENT— HOAX OR OPPORTUNITY?

Spring brings to the high schools of the United States the ritual of student government elections. Hand-painted posters crowd walls and lockers. Assemblies reverberate with the sound of political speechmaking. If the school has developed a tradition of lively campaigning, enthusiasm builds day by day as campaigners rally their forces. When election day arrives, small groups of would-be politicians wait impatiently outside the student activities office while election officials count the paper ballots.

Then, as suddenly as it began, the event is over. Baseball games, the prom, and the prospects of graduation compete for student attention. The victorious candidates take their oath of office, gather at their appointed meeting place—and disappear from public sight. Within a few months, the campus begins to complain again about the inactivity of student government.

Perhaps your school does not fit this pattern. Somewhere, the law of averages tells us, a school must exist whose students are satisfied with their elected officials and with the rules that govern their school life. For most students, however, the following complaints may sound familiar:

"What happened to all those promises Bob made during the campaign? I haven't heard a word about open campus or a better break for girls' sports since he took office."

"I give up. We were all set to vote for a student union when Mr. Kellerman stood up and told us that the motion was out of order. That's what he says every time we look into anything important."

"Student government? Do we have one? Nobody ever tells us what goes on in those meetings they have every week."

"Just once, I'd like to see someone run for student office who isn't up there strictly on the basis of personality. How can you choose between Sally Rah-Rah and Ted Sportshero? I'm interested in issues and ideas."

"Did you see the figures from the last election? Less than 20 percent of the kids bothered to vote. So how can they say that the council represents all of us?"

"I ran for office because I thought the job was important, but do you know what we debated at the last meeting? First we voted to send flowers for Mrs. Robinson's funeral. Then we argued for thirty minutes about the theme of the decorations for the fall dance. We never did discuss the new assembly plan."

Still, all these complaints relate only to student government, not to the larger political system—don't they? No, not quite. Millions of Americans feel much the same way about the workings of local, state, and national governments. Some of this unhappiness is based on real weaknesses in the way government works. Other complaints, however, have developed because too many of us don't understand the workings of the elaborate machine we call government.

Each of the six complaints cited above finds its parallels in the larger political world outside school walls. Let's take a closer look.

UNKEPT PROMISES

Politicians, whether running for student body president or President of the United States, make promises when they run for office. Actually, there's nothing wrong with that. People interested enough in public service to become candidates often do so because they have specific goals they want to achieve. On the other hand, politicians also know that they must tell voters what they want to hear. Once in office, many of them operate on the belief that memories are short and that they won't be held accountable for promises made in the heat of a campaign.

Another fact should be noted as well. Even the best-intentioned office-holders discover that their power to bring about change is limited. Lack of money, unforeseen political or social consequences, and legal restrictions combine to restrict their power to deliver on their promises. Unaware of these limitations, the electorate—whether high school seniors or senior citizens—becomes disillusioned.

RESTRICTIONS ON POWER

Just as student representatives often find their wishes frustrated by the power of the faculty advisor, the acts of Congress are subject to veto by the President. American representative government works through a delegation of powers. A state or national legislature has fewer limits on its powers than a student council, of course, but the principle remains the same.

The line of authority in your school begins with the state education code. Local policies and regulations are usually written by an elected board of trustees. These same trustees hire school administrators and teachers, to whom they delegate the authority to run the schools. A few of these powers are further delegated to student government, most often in the form of a constitution. Not many powers are delegated in this way, to be sure. The adults in your community have strong doubts about the wisdom of handing too much control of the schools to young people. This hesitation becomes most evident when students begin to work with an important issue such as teacher evaluations, dress codes, or budget decisions that go counter to established policy. At that point, the faculty advisor steps in with a veto, and council members are forced to accept a firsthand lesson in the limitation of political power.

LACK OF COMMUNICATION

Ask your parents tonight how their senator or representative voted on a recent national issue. In all probability, they won't know—any more than you know what your student council had listed on its agenda at the last meeting. Both situations revolve around the problem of communications. Some schools hear about the council's activities through the newspaper; others have room representatives who report in home rooms. Politicians do much the same. They make speeches, send out newsletters, and hope the press will cover their activities. In most cases, the effort isn't enough. The word doesn't reach everyone—and people drift further and further away from the personal contact needed to make democratic government work.

UNSUITABLE CANDIDATES

An old proverb from traditional politics says, "You can't beat somebody with nobody." Political managers know that people tend to vote for names and faces they recognize—even though that often means celebrities, military heroes, and relatives of well-known officeholders. If your student government is overloaded with athletes, cheerleaders, and the socially "in" group, that's rather like electing members from only one political viewpoint. Finding a candidate who truly represents your thinking—either in your school community or in the larger political arena—has become a major challenge.

VOTER APATHY

Unless your student council was elected by votes cast in the classrooms, it is unlikely that much more than 20 percent of the student body voted. A quick check of any recent election in your community will probably reveal a similarly low turnout. What's wrong? The low figures could represent general discontentment with politics and politicians, whether in student government or in city, state, or national legislatures. More often it represents apathy—a general decline in voter interest and involvement in everyday political affairs. The danger of such nonparticipation should be apparent: no representative government can truly govern without the informed consent of its people. Your school has probably tried special nominating conventions or increased coverage in the daily bulletin or school newspaper, all to no avail. Solutions at the community, state, and national levels remain equally elusive.

INABILITY TO REACH IMPORTANT DECISIONS

Have you ever watched a political body at work? Far from being the high drama of popular imagination, the enactment of legislation more often turns out to be wordy, tedious, and dull. In a democracy everyone must be heard. Unless debate is restricted by special rules or time limits, people tend to present their opinions at great length. The student council that spends an hour reaching a decision on a seemingly insignificant detail such as sending a funeral wreath has its counterparts in your local school board, city government, county board of supervisors, state legislature, and federal government. Most of us lack the patience to endure these talkathons, and we turn away. As a consequence, too many political decisions are made before empty seats.

Is this, then, an obituary for the American political system? Not at all. Despite its weaknesses, your own student government continues to function. At times, it may even rise to heights of unexpected accomplishment. So it is with the larger structure of government outside your school. People continue to step forward, willing to serve with intelligence and dedication in the often thankless task of making our institutions work. Slowly, sometimes painfully, we solve our problems. The complex body of laws, rules, regulations, procedures, and limitations provides a road map toward that goal.

This book hopes to enroll you as a participant in the political process. Change, growth, and the achievement of social justice can be found within the system. After you understand how and why our local, state, and national governments work as they do, you will be ready to vote, attend meetings, debate the issues—and even think about running for public office yourself.

Your own student government would be a good place to begin. Once involved, you may find that the student council works better—and accomplishes more—than most people give it credit for. If it doesn't, then you can attempt to change it. Throughout this book, that vital point is stressed: democratic government cannot endure without the participation of an informed, concerned electorate. Whatever your party, whatever your political philosophy, there's room for you.

Take a hand!

1

THE PRINCIPLES BEHIND AMERICAN GOVERNMENT

CHAPTER ONE

⓪RGANIZING A SOCIETY:
BASIC THEORIES OF GOVERNMENT

Jack spoke. "We've got to decide about being rescued."

There was a buzz. One of the small boys, Henry, said that he wanted to go home.

"Shut up," said Ralph absently. He lifted the conch. "Seems to me we have to have a chief to decide things."

"A chief! A chief!"

"I ought to be chief," said Jack with simple arrogance, "because I'm chapter chorister and head boy. I can sing C sharp."

Another buzz.

"Well then," said Jack, "I—"

He hesitated. The dark boy, Roger, stirred at last and spoke up.

"Let's have a vote."

"Yes!"

"Vote for chief."

"Let's vote—"

This toy of voting was almost as pleasing as the conch. Jack started to protest, but the clamor changed from the general wish for a chief to an election by acclaim of Ralph himself. None of the boys could have found good reason for this; what intelligence had been shown was traceable to Piggy while the most obvious leader was Jack. But there was a stillness about Ralph as he sat that marked him out; there was his size, and attractive appearance; but most obscurely, yet most powerfully, there was the conch. The being that had blown that, had sat waiting for them on the platform with the delicate thing balanced on his knees, was set apart.

"Him with the shell."

"Ralph! Ralph!"

"Let him be the chief with the trumpet-thing."
Ralph raised a hand for silence.
"All right. Who wants Jack for chief?"
With dreary obedience the choir raised their hands.
"Who wants me?"
Every hand outside the choir except Piggy's was raised immediately.
Then Piggy, too, raised his hand grudgingly into the air.
Ralph counted.
"I'm chief then."
The circle of boys broke into applause. Even the choir applauded.*

Readers familiar with William Golding's *Lord of the Flies* will know that Ralph, Jack, Piggy, and the other boys are survivors of a plane crash, stranded on an island without adults around to guide or direct them. Almost immediately, the boys turn for security and organization to a simple form of government. They want someone to be responsible, someone to make the decisions. Other animals may gather together in social groups, but only humans create political structures. Throughout history, *homo sapiens* has recognized that societies work best when rules of conduct are established—and a means found to enforce them.

In the novel, Ralph tries to hold back the savagery that begins to close in on the boys.

"The rules!" shouted Ralph, "you're breaking the rules!"
"Who cares?"
Ralph summoned his wits. "Because the rules are the only thing we've got!"†

Despite Ralph's desperate attempt to keep a sense of organization and purpose alive, the boys' society tumbles headlong into death and disaster. Luckily, most people remain more optimistic than Golding. We believe that reasonable men and women can create governments that allow basic freedom and dignity without sacrificing strength and moral values.

In this chapter you will explore a number of variations on an old theme —the search for an ideal theory of government. The questions that will be discussed are:

1. What is meant by the concept of "nation"?
2. What are the forms of government according to distribution of power?
3. What are the forms of government according to decision-making process?
4. What are the forms of government according to economic philosophy?
5. What type of government existed in the earliest human societies?
6. How did Asiatic despotism set a pattern of government?
7. What contributions did the Greeks and Romans make to a theory of government?

*Reprinted by permission of Coward, McCann & Geoghegan, Inc., from pages 21–22 of *Lord of the Flies* by William Golding. Copyright © 1954 by William Gerald Golding.
†*Ibid.*, p. 106.

8. How did government develop in medieval Europe?
9. What governmental features are found in most modern nation-states?

What is meant by the concept of "nation"?

Take out a sheet of paper. Write the numbers one to five. Then list the first five answers that come to mind when you hear the question, "What are you?"

Look at your list and check the lists written by your family or classmates. Almost invariably, one of the answers will refer to a nationality. It might be "American" or "United States citizen." Less frequently, people will answer in terms of national origin—perhaps Swedish or Mexican. Such a reaction to the question of personal identification is not surprising. Almost everyone takes the ideas of nations and nationality for granted. After all, we have divided the world into nations—167 of them at last count.

NATIONHOOD DEFINED

Yet, through most of human history, nations did not exist. If all of humanity's time on earth could be compressed into a single twenty-four–hour day, civilization and the political divisions called *nations* would occupy only the last few seconds. Before a society can be considered to have reached the status of nationhood, it must meet four requirements:

Figure 1.1
Although the people of the United States represent a multitude of races, nationalities, and religions, they have at least one thing in common: all are equal before the law.
Source: Lynn Landy.

1. *Clearly defined boundaries.* The citizens of a nation know where their boundaries begin and end. The territory enclosed by those borders need meet no standard size: Andorra, high in the Pyrenees mountains, covers only 179 square miles, while Canada's 24 million people are spread out over 3,845,000 square miles (larger by almost one-third than the area of the United States). In today's world, however, fixed land and coastal boundaries are no longer enough. The question of the extent to which a nation controls its offshore waters and the airspace above its territory has generated major international controversy.

2. *Population.* A nation cannot exist without people who identify with its flag, government, and goals. Again, size does not matter. The South Pacific island kingdom of Tonga has only about 100,000 inhabitants, while India stops counting at more than 670 million.

3. *Sovereignty.* A nation possesses *sovereignty* when its people make their own decisions, free of outside interference. A nation makes its own laws, carries on relations with other countries, and sets its own economic goals. By this definition, Monaco cannot claim to be a nation, because France controls many aspects of that tiny principality's political and economic life.

4. *Government.* Every nation has evolved its own form of government. Just as the boys on Golding's island realized that they needed a system for making and enforcing rules of behavior, modern peoples have decided that strong governments are needed to ensure their security and possessions. In this book, the word *state* will be used to refer to the government of either a nation or a particular subdivision of a nation (such as the state of Alaska).

EARLY PHILOSOPHIES OF GOVERNMENT

The nature and origins of government have always occupied the thoughts of philosophers. The Greeks, for example, realized that a strange conflict had developed. In theory, they believed that the state should be the servant of humanity. In practice, they saw everywhere the sad fact that people had become the servants of the state.

Some philosophers have tried to examine the innermost meaning of government. Plato saw the state as the counterpart of the soul, but many times magnified. Aristotle defined the state as an organic whole to which each individual belongs, just as bees belong to a hive; neither hive nor bee can exist without the other. Many years later, the Frenchman Jean Jacques Rousseau agreed with Aristotle when he called the state a "corporate person," possessed of a collective will more perfect than the individual will.

Rousseau also devised a more concrete theory—that of the *social contract.* Humanity once existed in a state of nature, free and content, he wrote. In time, however, these "noble savages" consented to be governed by a state so that the growing population could live peaceably together. But a contract works both ways. When the government does not govern properly, the people retain the right to change it. This theory of government strongly influenced the framers of this nation's Declaration of Independence and Constitution.

What are the forms of government according to distribution of power?

In this and the next two sections, three methods of categorizing systems of government will be used. One of the most common methods classifies governments according to how power is distributed.

UNITARY GOVERNMENT

A unitary government locates an overwhelming concentration of authority in a central government. Small, primitive nations have often used this system, but it also works well for larger, modern countries. In a unitary government, local governing bodies are restricted to serving as administrative arms of the central authority. Counties in Great Britain, for instance, have none of the independence customarily exercised by American states.

Similarly, France is divided into ninety-six departments, which in turn are grouped together into thirty-six provinces—but all are closely administered by the central government in Paris. If a mayor in the Loire valley wants to repair a local bridge, authorization to spend the money must come from the appropriate *bureaucrat* (government official) in the capital. This does not mean that unitary governments are necessarily less democratic than others. Safeguards against misuse of government power may be written into a national constitution and a bill of rights, or developed through long-standing tradition.

CONFEDERATE GOVERNMENT

At the opposite extreme from unitary government lies the confederation. In a confederate government, local government bodies safeguard their own authority by establishing a weak central government. The United States has twice adopted confederate systems of government. The present-day federal system developed in reaction to the weaknesses of the original Articles of Confederation (discussed in Chapter 2). The second experiment with confederation also failed. Eleven Southern states, distrustful of the national government's centralized power, seceded from the Union in 1860 and 1861 and attempted to form their own Confederate States of America. The United Nations, with its weak General Assembly and veto-plagued Security Council, illustrates a typical confederation.

FEDERAL GOVERNMENT

A federal government divides power between a central government and its component states. A supreme law of the land, called a *constitution*, generally defines the duties, rights, and privileges of each level of government. The balance of power between national, state, and local governments is carefully spelled out. The power to change or amend the constitution usually rests with the people or their elected representatives.

What are the forms of government according to decision-making power?

In the give-and-take of daily living, most families work out some sort of decision-making process. Perhaps in one household a dominant parent makes all the major decisions, while in another each family member has a voice in deciding important questions. Whatever the system, these families have done exactly what nations must do. Somehow, a people must find an acceptable way of carrying on the business of government. Ideally, the people make a free choice based on their own history and traditions. In many cases, however, the decisions have been forced on them.

When classified on the basis of decision-making, every nation falls into one of two categories of government (*anarchy*, the absence of organized government, cannot be considered a category of government). Like the family in which one parent makes all the decisions, *totalitarianism* places total power in the hands of a single individual or a small, elite group. In a *democracy*, on the other hand, all citizens take part in decision-making.

TOTALITARIAN GOVERNMENTS

In most cases, no outside force—whether a constitution, elections, or public opinion—exists to limit the actions of a totalitarian nation's rulers. A modern totalitarian system usually follows a definite pattern of restrictions on personal freedom:

1. The government comes to power by violent means.
2. The government uses terror and police power to eliminate all opposition.
3. The single party in power forms an elite, privileged class.
4. The government controls all means of education, information, and expression.
5. A vast propaganda machine continuously "sells" the government program.

Three basic types of totalitarian government can be listed:

1. Monarchy. As the number of people increased in prehistoric times, members of individual tribes began to look to strong warriors, hunters, and priests for leadership. In time, these tribal chieftains came to rule by right of birth, and often claimed kinship with the gods. A government conducted by such a hereditary ruler takes the name of *monarchy*—"rule by one person." While individual monarchs often ruled with compassion and wisdom, they always held life-and-death power over their subjects. Capable rulers like Louis XIV of France and Elizabeth I of England personally supervised the economic, military, and political affairs of their countries.

Monarchy was practically the only form of government for thousands of years. In today's world, however, monarchy has fallen out of favor. The kings and queens who once claimed to rule by God's command have mostly passed from the scene. Even the powerful king of Saudi Arabia listens to counselors and attempts to govern with the best interests of his people in mind. Most monarchs have been reduced to ceremonial status. Great Britain's Queen Elizabeth II still opens each session of Parliament—but she has little control over what goes on there.

2. *Oligarchy.* Your principal might not like to be reminded of the fact, but your school is run by an oligarchy—"rule by a few people." Oligarchy refers to any government—whether that of a school or a city or a nation— in which the decisions are made by a small, privileged group. Renaissance Venice, where the wealthy property owners ran the affairs of the city, is an example of an oligarchy. Unlike monarchies, oligarchies are not necessarily hereditary. Moreover, oligarchies tend to grow more restrictive as time passes. A large corporation seeks to attain a monopoly; a union attempts to expand to take in all workers; school administrators often close ranks to prevent teachers and students from gaining too much influence. In a totalitarian system, the rule of the oligarchy cannot be challenged; in the contemporary phrase, "There's no room at the top."

3. *Dictatorship.* Ancient Rome made constitutional provision for setting up a dictatorship during a military emergency; after the war ended, the dictator returned his absolute authority to the Senate. Modern dictators concentrate absolute power in a single individual and a single political party. If elections are permitted at all, they serve only as rituals designed to glorify the dictator. Dictatorships like Nazi Germany under Hitler and Communist China under Mao Tse-tung place all decision-making power in the hands of a single person.

Dictators often come to power through a revolution, *coup d'état*, or other national emergency. They surround themselves with followers willing to carry out any order "for the good of the state." Once in office, a dictator seldom resigns or retires. Because no orderly means of succession exists in a dictatorship, another revolution or civil war often follows before a new ruler can be installed.

DEMOCRATIC GOVERNMENT

A democracy places final decision-making power in the hands of the people themselves. This authority can be seen in the workings of a democratic system: free elections, limited government, competing political parties, and safeguards for individual freedoms (see the box on page 13 for some thoughts on democracy and totalitarianism). In modern times, democracy has evolved to the point that people expect government to provide social and economic equality along with political equality. Just as in the family that gives every member a vote, democracies often seem noisy and slow-moving in comparison with totalitarian states. Democracy can be either direct or indirect.

Three great men speak on democracy and totalitarianism

PERICLES

N.Y. Public Library

In 431 B.C., a public funeral was held in Athens, Greece, for soldiers killed in a war with Sparta. The Athenian leader Pericles made a famous speech in which he explained the democratic ideals for which the soldiers had died:

Our form of government is called a democracy because it is placed in the hands, not of the few, but of the many. All, moreover, have equal rights under the laws that have to do with disputes between individuals. But in public esteem, each is honored in proportion to his renown in his particular field, his ability being fully as important as his social standing. No poor man, in short, is barred from public service when he can really do the city any good.

CHURCHILL

N.Y. Public Library

Sir Winston Churchill, outstanding World War II leader and one of democracy's great defenders, spoke for Great Britain's form of government:

Many forms of government have been tried in this world of sin and woe. No one pretends that democracy is perfect or all-wise. Indeed, it has been said that democracy is the worst form of government except for all of the other forms which have been tried from time to time.

SAKHAROV

Wide World Photos

Andrei Sakharov, world-renowned as a nuclear physicist, has emerged as a leading critic of Russian communism. In a 1975 essay, he wrote about life under a totalitarian system:

Contemporary Soviet society is based on "state capitalism," a total party-government monopoly over economy, culture, ideology, and the other basic spheres of life. In periods of crisis, such a system engenders rule by terror; in quieter periods, it engenders the dominance of bungling bureaucracy, mediocrity, apathy and dissipation among the people, and the permanent militarization of our economy. . . . Ours is government behind closed doors. Vast, unaccounted-for funds go toward covert and overt expansion in all parts of the world.

1. Direct democracy. When governmental units are small enough, they can practice direct democracy. In this form of government, all citizens take part in decision-making. The New England town meeting, for example, gives voters a chance to approve or disapprove all laws, taxes, and other town business. Direct democracy may also be found in those states where the initiative, referendum, and recall are permitted (see Chapter 16).

2. *Indirect democracy.* In an indirect democracy, the people elect representatives to make political decisions for them. If the representatives do not work in the best interests of the nation, they will be removed from office at the next election. The form of indirect democracy adopted in the United States is called a *republic*, or a *representative democracy.*

Indirect democracies have developed two forms of leadership—presidential and parliamentary.

Presidential leadership. Whatever the title—president, premier, or chief executive—presidential leadership centers administrative authority in a single elected official. As the U.S. example illustrates, presidents are elected by the people for definite terms; constitutions usually limit the president to one or two terms (two four-year terms in the United States, one six-year term in Mexico). Presidential systems make a clear distinction between the administrative powers of the chief executive and the lawmaking powers of the legislature. Out of this division have come two important concepts in U.S. democracy: the separation of powers and the system of checks and balances (discussed in detail in Chapter 3).

Parliamentary leadership. Great Britain's "mother of parliaments" illustrates the basic structure of parliamentary leadership. The nation's chief executive must be a member of the lawmaking body (in Britain, the House of Commons). The leader of the majority party automatically assumes the title of prime minister. In cases where the parliament has more than one house, the prime minister presides over the larger, or popularly elected, house. Unlike the U.S. President, the prime minister is exposed to the daily pressures of writing and voting on legislation, in addition to performing administrative duties. Whenever the majority party loses a vote on a major issue, custom usually demands that the prime minister resign and call new national elections.

Table 1.1 summarizes the contrasting governmental systems in four modern nations.

What are the forms of government according to economic philosophy?

Many of the decisions that a government makes involve money—where to find it and what to spend it on. Anything that government does, from planning space probes to hiring office workers, costs money. Contrary to popular opinion, a government cannot print new money whenever it runs short. Iron laws of economics quickly make such "printing press" money worthless. Financial support for government budgets can be obtained in only five ways. Government can (1) borrow money, at home or abroad; (2) collect taxes from its citizens; (3) go into business for itself, making

Table 1.1

Contrasting systems of government

	United States	Soviet Union	Great Britain	Mexico
Form of government	Presidential leadership. Federal system. Constitution is basic law of the land. Two-party system.	Dictatorship of the proletariat. Constitution has little meaning. In practice, single-party rule has eliminated all opposition.	Parliamentary leadership. Unitary system. Monarchy reduced to ceremonial status. Multiple parties.	Presidential leadership. Constitution serves as goal for the nation. Single party dominates elections.
Economic system	Capitalism, with growing government regulation of business and industry.	Communism —government owns the means of production and makes all economic decisions.	Mixed capitalism and socialism— government controls some basic industries, such as health care and mining.	Regulated capitalism— government's goal is to develop industrial independence.
Personal freedom	Guaranteed by the Constitution.	Limited rights. All citizens subject to Communist party control.	Common law and carefully observed tradition guarantee basic freedoms.	Guaranteed by the Constitution, but police authority sometimes overrides personal rights.
Status of the individual	Emphasis on worth of individual. High standard of living. Well-developed social welfare system.	Individual exists to serve the state. Rising living standards often sacrificed in favor of heavy industry and armaments.	Emphasis on worth of individual. Serious economic problems caused by inflation, labor unrest, and costly imports. Well-developed social welfare system.	Individual rights sometimes sacrificed for rapid economic development. High rate of population growth prevents needed improvement in living standards.

products or providing services; (4) expand the economy by developing new natural resources; or (5) take resources from weaker neighbors through armed aggression.

Most governments today confine themselves to the first three options. Whatever method they choose, some basic questions must be answered: Who should be allowed to own property? Should business operate freely, without restriction? Should the nation's resources be redistributed equally among its citizens? The four main economic systems—capitalism, socialism, communism, and fascism—answer these questions differently. A nation's economic philosophy influences many aspects of national life, including the form of government and the extent of personal freedom.

CAPITALISM

Although the system of capitalism has been both blessed and cursed, capitalism has brought the United States the world's highest standard of living (see Table 1.2). The capitalist believes in four broad principles:

1. Free enterprise. People have the right to choose their own work, business, or profession, and to conduct it with a minimum of government regulation or interference.

2. Private ownership of the means of production. The individual citizen has the right to own and manage farms, factories, mines, railroads, securities, and houses.

3. The profit motive. People are free to enjoy the rewards of their own labor or investment of capital. As economist Adam Smith wrote, "It is not from the benevolence of the butcher or baker . . . that we expect our dinner, but from their regard to their own interest"; in other words, the capitalist's desire to make a profit helps to ensure efficiency and high quality of goods and services.

4. Competition. The struggle between competing companies to sell their goods and services results in lower prices and better products.

Even in the United States, completely free capitalism no longer exists. Under the original *laissez-faire capitalism*, companies and individuals were free to succeed or fail according to their talents. Government kept a strict "hands-off" attitude. (*Laissez-faire* is a French phrase meaning "let people do what they choose.") As corporations grew larger, they used their power to enrich themselves at the expense of workers, farmers, smaller merchants, and consumers. The American people began to demand government regulation to prevent the worst excesses—stock swindles, shoddy merchandise, artificially high prices, adulterated foods. Government responded by slowly assuming greater and greater control over business activity. In the eighteenth century, government contented itself with guaranteeing property rights; in the nineteenth century, it began to regulate capitalist activities; in the twentieth century, government has become a dominant voice in the marketplace.

SOCIALISM

The socialist claims that capitalism can never distribute a country's wealth fairly. Socialism, therefore, believes that all major industries and services (transportation, communications, energy, banking, medicine, steel, and the like) should be owned by the government. Once the *means of production* fall under the control of the state, socialist theory says, the people will

Table 1.2

Living standards under capitalism and communism

Actual prices mean little in comparing standards of living. What really counts is what a worker's paycheck will buy. This table shows how long typical urban workers in the Soviet Union and in the United States must work to buy various items. (It should be noted that expenditures for rent, health care, education, and taxes are much lower in the Soviet Union than in this country.)

Item	Soviet worker	U.S. worker
FOOD		
White bread, 1-lb. loaf	8.5 min.	8 min.
Hamburger, beef, 1 lb.	61 min.	18 min.
Chicken, frozen, 1 lb.	98 min.	12 min.
Cod, frozen, 1 lb.	23 min.	30 min.
Sugar, 1 lb.	29 min.	4 min.
Butter, 1 lb.	110 min.	27 min.
Milk, quart	21 min.	7 min.
Eggs, dozen	73 min.	11 min.
Potatoes, 1 lb.	3 min.	4 min.
Apples, 1 lb.	45 min.	5 min.
Tea, 100 grams	53 min.	10 min.
CLOTHING, PERSONAL NEEDS, SERVICES		
Man's suit	106 hr.	25 hr.
Panty hose, pair	366 min.	18 min.
Toilet soap, bar	20 min.	4 min.
Lipstick	69 min.	30 min.
Cigarettes, 20	15 min.	9 min.
Telephone service, 1 month	154 min.	119 min.
Haircut, men	37 min.	63 min.
Jeans, Levi's	2760 min.	180 min.
Movie	81 min.	42 min.
Dry cleaning, one man's overcoat	92 min.	79 min.
HOUSEHOLD		
Refrigerator, small	155 hr.	44 hr.
Washing machine	432 hr.	52 hr.
Color TV	701 hr.	65 hr.
Light bulb, 100 watts	30 min.	8 min.
Apartment rent, unfurnished, monthly	10 hr.	46 hr.
Household gas, monthly bill	1 hr.	7 hr.
Water, monthly bill	123 min.	32 min.
TRANSPORTATION		
Compact car	53 mo.	5 mo.
Gasoline, regular, 10 gallons	185 min.	32 min.
Bus fare, 2 miles, off-peak hours	3 min.	7 min.
Air fare, 185 miles, economy	505 min.	547 min.

Source: National Federation of Independent Business, Research and Education Foundation, 1982.

benefit from lower prices, improved quality, and a general rise in living standards. Theoretically, the very rich and the very poor will both disappear.

Most modern socialists are willing to accept democratic political processes and constitutional guarantees. Democratic socialist parties in Great Britain and Sweden, for example, have gradually transferred ownership of major industries from private to public hands. Socialist systems generally protect the right of opposing parties to compete freely for power. Except for restrictions on free enterprise and property rights, socialist governments also safeguard personal freedoms.

COMMUNISM

Modern communism combines economic and political beliefs. The essence of communist belief lies in the slogan, "From each according to his abilities, to each according to his needs." Communism attempts to reach that state of equality by prohibiting almost all private ownership of property: the state controls all the means of production, distribution, and exchange. Individual freedoms must sometimes be denied while communism is growing, the theory holds, because it will take time to replace humanity's essential selfishness with a new dedication to the nation and its people. (The unfortunate consequences of the Soviet Union's suppression of freedom of speech are suggested in Figure 1.2.)

Primitive communism began with the first tribe that shared food and living quarters among its members. Modern communism, however, started with the German political economist Karl Marx, whose *Communist Manifesto* attacked the worst excesses of *laissez-faire* capitalism in 1848. Marx's views were later modified by Nikolai Lenin, a leader of the revolution that brought communism to Russia in 1917. Marxist-Leninist theory can be summarized in five basic beliefs:

1. *Economic view of history.* Communist thinkers describe history as a

Figure 1.2
Totalitarian governments cannot afford to allow their citizens the right of free speech. Two winners of the Nobel Prize for Literature, Boris Pasternak and Alexander Solzhenitsyn, and other Russian writers have been persecuted or exiled for criticizing the Soviet regime. Source: Bill Mauldin, Chicago *Sun-Times*.

"I won the Nobel Prize for Literature. What was your crime?"

constant struggle between the "haves" and the "have-nots." The *proletariat* (workers) have always been exploited by the *bourgeoisie* (property owners and capitalists). That situation will continue until communist-led revolutions overthrow the upper and middle classes.

2. *Labor theory of value.* When communists accuse capitalist factory owners of exploiting their workers, they are basing their charge on the labor theory of value. A glass vase, according to this theory, has worth equal to the cost of the raw material (the glass) plus the value of the labor (wages paid to the workers). Any *surplus value* (the capitalist calls it profit) should belong to the workers, without whose labor the vase could not have been made. The theory, while superficially logical, makes no allowance for rewarding the owners for their enterprise in setting up the factory or for the risk they took in investing capital in the project.

3. *Dedication to revolution.* Because the bourgeoisie use government as a tool for the oppression of the working class, noncommunist governments must be overthrown. Peaceful, democratic change is never possible. Communism can come to power only through violent revolution.

4. *Dictatorship of the proletariat.* The true communist state will be run by its workers—a dictatorship of the proletariat. In practice, this means that an elite group of Communist party officials occupy the key party and government positions. In time, the theory suggests, the state will no longer be needed and will "wither away."

5. *Militant atheism.* Communist leaders place heavy political and social pressure on their people to give up all belief in God. In its place, they substitute total dedication to the communist state.

Karl Marx would probably not recognize his theories as they have been put into practice in the Soviet Union, China, and other communist countries. In many respects, the systems developed in those countries come closer to an extreme form of socialism than to the communist ideal he described.

FASCISM

As with modern communism, fascism leads to an all-powerful state that keeps its people under total domination. The basic principles of fascism can be summarized as (1) the leadership principle—the people owe total allegiance to the ruler, the ruler's deputies, and the sole political party; and (2) state socialism—the state represents every aspect of national life. Anyone who opposes a fascist *state* is labeled an enemy of the *people*.

A fascist country may present an agreeable appearance of regular elections, crime-free streets, and a well-managed economy. Private ownership of property—under strict state supervision—is encouraged. In Italy during the 1930's, the fascist dictator Benito Mussolini established a series of "corporations," each of which exercised total control over a segment of Italy's economic life. In reality, therefore, all power lies in the hands of a dictator or an oligarchy. Fascist police authority ignores personal freedoms.

Factory workers and owners alike march to the dictator's drumbeat. Hitler's Germany, Mussolini's Italy, and Franco's Spain are modern examples of fascist governments. An American Nazi party still exists, dedicated to installing a fascist system in this country.

Let's Review For A Moment

What makes a nation? Today 167 countries claim nationhood on the basis of established boundaries, population, national sovereignty, and an independent system of government.

How would you classify a particular government? One method would be to analyze the distribution of power. In a *unitary* system, power is concentrated in a central government; a *confederacy* goes to the opposite extreme, with a weak central government and power retained by the member states; a *federal* government balances authority between the central government and the states.

Another way of classifying governments is by determining who holds the decision-making power. *Totalitarian* states make all decisions for the people; in a *democracy*, this power remains in the hands of the people and their elected representatives. Totalitarian systems may take any of several forms—*monarchy, oligarchy,* or *dictatorship.* Forms of democracy also vary. When your entire class votes on the class colors, that's *direct democracy.* If you elect representatives who make the decision for you, that's *indirect democracy.*

Finally, a third way of classifying a nation's form of government grows out of its economic philosophy. *Capitalism* encourages private ownership of the means of production; profitmaking and competition are encouraged. *Socialism* demands government ownership of the means of production, but accepts peaceful, gradual steps toward that goal. *Communism* also insists upon government ownership, but believes that immediate revolutionary change is the only means of reaching that objective.

How did all these different forms of government develop? Right from the beginning, people seemed determined to set up some system for organizing their developing societies.

What type of government existed in the earliest human societies?

Government probably began with the first human cultures. Archeologists and anthropologists study primitive peoples, past and present, and report that all possess some means of organizing and regulating social and economic relationships. If people are to live together, they must find ways to resolve the conflicts that inevitably occur.

Most primitive societies, by definition, have not progressed to "civilization." Primitive people lead simple, communal lives of hunting and gathering: all members of the group share the meat from the hunt and the produce of the fields. Life is often nomadic. Writing, if it is used, has not developed beyond picture symbols.

Government is an outgrowth of tribal life, an extension of the family or clan structure. No formal body of law exists; the tribe obeys the customs and taboos because failure to do so would endanger everyone. If a formal government structure exists, it grows out of the *extended family*. In contrast to the *nuclear family* found in most industrial nations, several generations live together in the extended family. Everyone is bound together by birth or marriage. An older, wise man or woman usually acts as family leader. In most primitive societies, family members seldom question the decisions of this patriarch or matriarch. The tribal government often consists of a council of these elders, who settle disputes, uphold tribal customs, and supervise religious rites.

In today's world, hundreds of millions of people have come to identify similarly with their nationality, but with an important difference. Americans, for example, can feel a great national pride in an achievement such as the first moon landing—but we can also suppress nationalistic feelings long enough to join with Russia in a joint space venture such as the Apollo-Soyuz project.

How did Asiatic despotism set a pattern of government?

About ten thousand years ago, nomadic tribes began to settle in the great valleys of the Nile, Tigris-Euphrates, Indus, and Yellow rivers (Figure 1.3 shows the areas discussed in this and the following sections). The peoples who built these first civilizations had chanced upon one of history's great discoveries—agriculture. Settling down to till the soil and herd animals did not mean an end to conflict, however. Tribes that were still nomadic swept out of the hills to plunder settlements and carry off livestock. Sometimes, the bandits stayed and forced the conquered farmers to work as slaves or serfs. Class distinctions and a totalitarian form of government began to emerge.

THE CITY–STATE

As civilization grew, the city-state emerged as the basic governmental unit. Strong walls protected the growing class of city dwellers, and trained soldiers guarded farmers in the surrounding fields. Gradually, a class system developed. Most people remained farmers and supported the upper classes with their labor. A small middle class performed skilled labor or ran business enterprises. At the top of the social pyramid, nobles and priests administered political and economic affairs and lived in comparative luxury. The poverty-stricken lower classes were expected to pay heavy taxes and offer total obedience to the ruling classes.

In time, strong city-states extended their authority over larger areas.

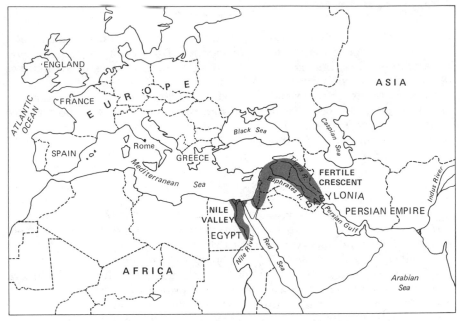

Figure 1.3
Modern systems of government developed around the Mediterranean in ancient times and in medieval Europe

The city-states of the Nile valley of Egypt were unified in this fashion, under the rule of a god-king known as a pharoah. Early rulers found it useful to make themselves into gods; the double authority of state and church easily held large populations under control. Egypt could still not be called a modern nation, however. Little sense of nationality existed among the people, and some cities were kept in the empire only through force. Warfare frequently ravaged the countryside, for most city-states were surrounded by barbarians envious of the rich lands and comfortable life built by these early civilizations.

EARLY NATION–STATES

About 1700 B.C., King Hammurabi of Babylonia carved the world's first code of laws in stone. By setting forth the law for all to see, Hammurabi took the first major step toward guaranteeing equal justice for all. By that time, writing and written records had reached a high degree of efficiency. The new Bronze Age metal technology had increased human mastery of the environment; perhaps it was no coincidence that individual behavior had come under increasing degrees of religious and political control.

Most important, city-states had evolved into nations capable of controlling extensive territories. The Persian Empire stretched from the Mediterranean Sea to the Indus River. The well-administered kingdom of Cyrus and Xerxes maintained internal peace, collected taxes, and carried on international trade. Mighty god-kings met on ill-defined borders to sign treaties and alliances—which often collapsed into wars for land, trade routes, and national resources.

The great empires of this period did not last, for despotic leadership tends to grow corrupt, inefficient, or indifferent. God-kings lose touch with their people; early ambition and dedication give way to luxurious relaxation. Still, the despotic form of government gave two emerging civilizations an example they would try to avoid.

What contributions did the Greeks and Romans make to a theory of government?

Western civilization, to which Americans look for much of their basic world view, began with the marvelous civilizations built by the Greeks and the Romans. Of all the significant advances in government, science, and philosophy that these two cultures gave us, perhaps the most important was a new concept of humanity's place in the universe. Earlier cultures had believed that to pry into the secrets of nature was to risk bringing down the wrath of the gods. The Greeks and Romans came to believe that human beings were important, that the universe was open to rational study. Religion remained significant, but was not regarded as the only reason for existence. Life was to be enjoyed, and government's role was to make the good life possible.

GREEK CONTRIBUTIONS

The city-states of the Greek peninsula never succeeded in joining together into a Greek nation. Instead, they wasted tremendous energy in almost constant warfare with one another. Still, in their proud, independent way, the Greeks were the first culture to break with the Asiatic tradition of despotic royal rule. Many of the Greek city-states (Athens stands out as the best example) developed a system of democratic government still admired today. True, the democracy did not extend to everyone—the Greeks kept slaves, and women were excluded from citizenship—but within these limitations self-government proved itself.

Students of American democracy find many familiar practices in ancient Athens of the fifth century B.C. Athenian men (1) discussed public issues and passed laws as members of the Assembly; (2) elected officials by secret ballot; (3) served on public committees and juries; (4) served in the army or navy. Historians estimate that a third of all Athenian citizens directly served their city in some way each year. This example of direct democracy remains unrivaled.

No less a critic than the great Greek philosopher Plato found the freedom of Athenian democracy excessive. In the *Republic*, Plato described a perfect government as one in which a few wise men ruled for the benefit of all. Plato believed—and the example set by Athens during its wars with Sparta tended to bear him out—that too much freedom would lead to rule by tyrants. In the longer term, the inability of the city-states to cooperate led to their conquest in 338 B.C. by the Macedonians—who themselves were later conquered by the Romans.

ROMAN CONTRIBUTIONS

The history of ancient Rome can be divided into two five-hundred-year eras—the Republic (509–27 B.C.) and the Empire (27 B.C.–A.D. 476). The original Roman city-state grew out of an early monarchy into a representative democracy. True power remained in the hands of the aristocracy, however, for the patrician class controlled the lawmaking body, known as the Senate. In time, the democratic processes gave way to the rule of powerful emperors. Supported by the famous Roman legions, the Empire expanded and prospered. Gradually, however, Roman vitality lessened. Civil wars and civil corruption brought the slow decay that led to the Empire's final downfall at the hands of invading barbarians from Asia and northern Europe.

Rome left Western civilization with two great concepts: (1) a formal system of just laws and (2) the value of citizenship.

1. Codified laws. About 450 B.C., Roman citizens demanded that the city's laws be written out for all to see. Over the centuries, these basic laws grew into a well-organized system based on sound principles of justice. Roman law remains the basis for the legal codes of many European countries.

2. Citizenship. Roman citizenship was one of the most prized of ancient possessions. Such was the power and prestige of Rome that non-Romans willingly placed themselves under Roman domination. Wherever individuals traveled in the Empire, their citizenship guaranteed them the same privileges as the inhabitants of Rome itself received. St. Paul, in fact, used his citizenship to demand that he be tried before Caesar in Rome.

How did government develop in medieval Europe?

For several hundred years after the collapse of the Roman Empire, civilization retreated. Barbarian tribes reduced Europe to a continent of wandering tribes, small city-states, and isolated fortresses. Only the Catholic Church kept alive learning, culture, and memories of a more settled way of life.

THE GROWTH OF FEUDALISM

Gradually, a rough political system grew out of the chaos. Nomadic barbarians accepted Christianity and settled down. Strong warriors gathered people around them in a system of mutual obligations: the weak gave up their freedom and land in return for protection. Monarchy dominated such governments as existed; even the mighty Charlemagne's Holy Roman Empire was held together only by the force of the emperor's personality and sword.

A political-economic system called *feudalism* developed, under which noblemen assumed the functions of government in their own territories. Powerful lords granted tracts of land, called *fiefs*, to loyal nobles; in return, these *vassals* promised to provide knights to fight for their lord when necessary. On each fief, daily life centered in the *manor*, a self-sufficient agricultural community. The *serfs*—peasants who worked on the manor—gave their labor and most of their produce to their lord in exchange for use of the land and protection from attack by invaders. Trade and commerce came to a near standstill.

RETURN TO STRONG CENTRAL GOVERNMENT

After the 1200's, life began to quicken in the almost-forgotten cities. With many nobles gone on the Crusades to recapture the Holy Land from the Moslems, city merchants and artisans gained greater self-government. The Catholic Church became more than ever a dominant political and economic force, a kind of super-government in its own right—only to be stripped of its supremacy by the Protestant Reformation in the 1500's. New coins began to replace barter as a means of settling obligations and paying taxes. City-states like Florence, Venice, and Genoa grew in power. An emerging middle class began to find its voice in political affairs. Even the nature of warfare changed, as guns and cannon replaced the armored knight as master of the battlefield.

What governmental features are found in most modern nation–states?

The new nations that arose in the fifteenth century developed contrasting forms of government. England, for example, began with a totalitarian system (an absolute monarchy), but slowly evolved into a parliamentary democracy. Democratic institutions came much later to France. In Spain, monarchy gave way to the military dictatorship of Francisco Franco, then was restored after he died in 1975. Figure 1.4 provides a graphic look at the modern political spectrum.

GOVERNMENT BODIES

Whatever the system of government, every nation has developed a law-making body, a court system, and a bureaucracy.

1. *Lawmaking body.* Even under a totalitarian system, a lawmaking body provides a useful link between the ruler and the people. The British Parliament began in just that way—as an advisory body to the king. In time, Parliament gained power through its ability to raise taxes. This "power of the purse" gave the lawmakers leverage in their dealings with the monarch.

2. *Court system.* The rough justice of the Middle Ages (when trials for

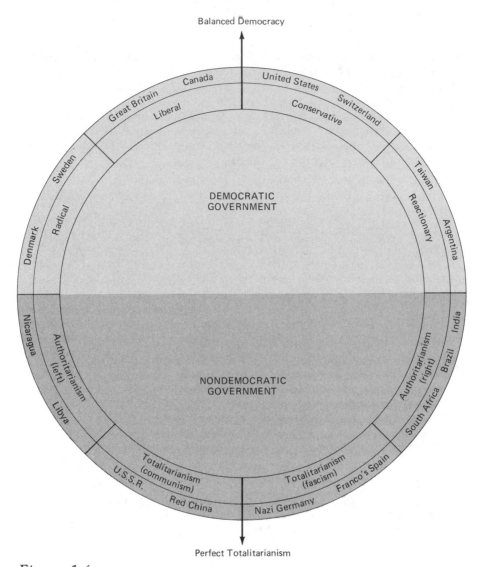

Figure 1.4
The world political spectrum
Source: Adapted from William Ebenstein *et al., American Democracy in World Perspective,* 3rd ed. (New York: Harper & Row, 1973), p. 24.

witchcraft were still common) gradually gave way to organized legal systems. Wise kings adopted uniform law codes, and appointed judges and law enforcement officials to administer them.

3. *Bureaucracy.* As government increased in size and complexity, rulers hired more people to conduct its business. Government *bureaucrats* collected taxes, kept records, ran public services, and did the hundreds of other jobs necessary in even the simplest form of government.

CONSTITUTIONALISM

Modern Western democracy began when England's King John signed the Magna Carta in 1215. For the first time in modern history, a king was forced to accept limitations on his power. Great Britain has never developed a formal constitution; its Petition of Right (1628) and Bill of Rights (1689) remain separate documents, along with the Magna Carta. The United States, by contrast, chose to write down all the rights and limitations of the government in a single document—the Constitution of the United States.

$\mathbb{S}$UMMARY AND CONCLUSIONS

1. As humanity's early tribal societies gave way to cities and then city-states, the concept of the nation gradually emerged. A *nation* has established boundaries and some form of government; its people possess a sense of nationhood; and other states are not free to intrude on its sovereignty.

2. Forms of government may be defined according to the way power is distributed. A *unitary* system keeps power tightly concentrated in a central government; a *confederacy* allows its member states almost total sovereignty; a *federal* system divides power between the central government and the member states.

3. Forms of government may also be classified according to decision-making power into totalitarian governments and democracies. The *totalitarian* state (whether a *monarchy*, *oligarchy*, or *dictatorship*) centers all decision-making in an elite group, often headed by a dictator. By contrast, in a *democracy* the people rule. *Direct* democracies actively involve all citizens in making decisions; *indirect* democracies elect representatives to make laws and administer government affairs.

4. Economic philosophy also influences the form a government will take. *Capitalism* has created a high standard of living for Americans by emphasizing private ownership of the means of production, profitmaking, and competition. *Socialism* normally accepts democratic institutions, but believes in public ownership of transport, mining, communications, heavy industry, and other key economic factors.

5. *Communism* adds the demand for immediate revolution to socialism's insistence on government control of the means of production. In practice, communist leaders like Karl Marx, Nikolai Lenin, and Mao Tse-tung accept dictatorship as the only way government can work efficiently. In the communist view, workers create profits; therefore, only workers should receive the benefits of their labor.

6. *Fascism* shares many techniques of control with communism (strong police authority, strict government control of all phases of economic and political life, a single-party state), but allows private enterprise under tight government supervision. The fascist believes that strong leadership is all-important.

7. Some four thousand years ago, the scattered city-states of the African and Asian river valleys began to form loosely structured nations. The rulers of empires such as Egypt and Persia combined religion and government. Large bureaucracies, extensive contact with other peoples, frequent warfare, and an economy based on slavery also characterized these states.

8. Western civilization began with Greece and Rome. From Greece came the concept that the state exists to serve the people. The Greek city-state of Athens developed civilization's first practicing democracy. Rome built a finely tuned governmental structure that contributed codified laws and a new appreciation for the rights of a nation's citizens.

9. The fall of Rome left Europe locked in the political stagnation of the medieval period. Government reverted to the level of tiny, isolated kingdoms. Feudalism, with its system of mutual obligations, held European society together. In time, commerce revived. Nation-states once again took shape as the Church, the nobles, and hereditary kings struggled for power.

10. Modern governments have grown more and more complex. Lawmaking bodies, a court system, and an extensive bureaucracy are required to handle the tremendous volume of government business. Written constitutions have created limits for government—but beautiful-sounding documents mean little if a people allows its government to violate its basic freedoms.

REVIEW QUESTIONS AND ACTIVITIES

TERMS YOU SHOULD KNOW

anarchy

bourgeoisie

bureaucracy

capitalism

communism

competition

confederate government

constitution

constitutionalism

democracy

direct democracy

extended family

fascism

federal government

feudalism

fief

free enterprise

indirect democracy

laissez-faire *capitalism*

manor

means of production

monarchy

nation

nuclear family

oligarchy

parliamentary leadership

presidential leadership

profit motive

proletariat

representative democracy

republic

serf

social contract
socialism
sovereignty
state

surplus value
totalitarianism
unitary government
vassal

REVIEW QUESTIONS

The following multiple-choice questions are based on the important ideas presented in this chapter. Select the response that best completes each statement.

1. In order for a nation to exist, which of the following must be true? (a) All the people must speak the same language. (b) A single religion must unify the citizens of the country. (c) A strong central government must exercise total power over all local governments. (d) At least a million people must live within the borders of the country. (e) The country must be free to exercise sovereignty in handling its own affairs.

2. The *maximum* amount of personal freedom would be found under a (a) fascist government. (b) communist government. (c) representative democracy. (d) socialist state. (e) all of these equally.

3. Which statement is *least* likely to be true of a totalitarian state? (a) The government maintains strict control over newspapers, radio, and television. (b) School administration and curriculum remain in the hands of local committees. (c) Secret police arrest and imprison individuals without warrant or trial. (d) The government came to power via revolution or *coup d'état*. (e) All political power is held by a single political party.

4. The type of democracy practiced in the United States is properly called (a) direct democracy. (b) parliamentary democracy. (c) socialism. (d) representative democracy. (e) unitary democracy.

5. Which national leader would be forced to call a new election after losing a vote of confidence in the legislature? (a) military dictator. (b) constitutional monarch. (c) president. (d) first secretary of the party. (e) prime minister.

6. The chief difference between modern capitalism and *laissez-faire* capitalism is (a) modern capitalism has done away with private ownership of the means of production. (b) government now regulates business and industry to a great degree. (c) competition has been removed from business practices. (d) *laissez-faire* capitalism produced better, cheaper products. (e) none of these.

7. Which is *not* basic to Marxist-Leninist theory? (a) economic view of history. (b) labor theory of value. (c) dictatorship of the proletariat. (d) militant atheism. (e) all of these are beliefs of modern communism.

8. One of the most important concepts to come out of Greco-Roman civilization was that (a) warfare should never be a part of national life. (b) religion has no place in a people's existence. (c) humans

are important and the universe is knowable. (d) totalitarian governments never work. (e) men and women should share equally in
national life.

9. A place to look for a bureaucrat would be in (a) a government agency
such as the Veterans Administration. (b) a parliamentary form of
government. (c) a communist dictatorship, where government makes
all the decisions. (d) a socialist government, administering major
industries. (e) all of these, for bureaucrats are necessary to every
form of government.

10. The earliest document to which Americans can look as part of their
democratic heritage is the (a) British Constitution. (b) Magna Carta.
(c) Bill of Rights. (d) Mayflower Compact. (e) Declaration of
Independence.

CONCEPT DEVELOPMENT

This chapter has explored a number of significant concepts in the theory
of government. Use your skills in thinking, researching, and writing to
answer the following questions.

1. Contrast the office of the President of the United States with that of the
Prime Minister of Great Britain in terms of (a) election to office, (b)
executive powers, (c) party responsibilities.

2. Patriotism has fallen out of favor with many people in today's world.
Is there anything wrong with loving one's country? Explain what is
good and bad about patriotism and nationalism.

3. Why is a totalitarian government often considered to be more efficient
than a democratic one? What freedoms do a people give up when they
accept totalitarian rule?

4. The British poet Shelley once wrote, "We are all Greeks." He meant,
of course, that Western civilization owes a great debt to classical Greece.
What contributions did those marvelously creative people make to our
modern way of life?

5. What barriers do you see to increased cooperation between nations in
today's world? Are there any factors contributing to better relations?

ACTIVITIES

The following activities are designed to help you use the ideas developed
in this chapter.

1. What is it like to be in business for oneself? One way to find out would
be to ask a local merchant or member of the Chamber of Commerce to
speak to your class on the economic system of the United States. Discuss
what the speaker means by "free enterprise." Ask the speaker to describe the various ways in which business is regulated or restricted by
government action. Can you understand the reasons for such regulation? Visit behind the scenes at a local store to watch "free enterprise"
at work.

2. Find four volunteers to work with you on preparing a round-table
"summit meeting" for the class. Each person would represent a dif-

ferent nation: the United States, Russia, Great Britain, Sweden, and Mexico—each of which represents a different form of government. Have the representatives respond to a series of questions that dramatize the differences among them. The questions might include: "What is your attitude toward free elections, with all political parties participating?" "What economic system do you find most satisfactory?" "Where does the decision-making power lie in your nation's government?" Speakers must research their countries, of course, so that they can reply to these and other questions fully and accurately.

3. Pick several nations that have contrasting political systems. Prepare a poster on each country that illustrates (a) the decision-making process, (b) the economic system, and (c) the degree of personal freedom in each country. A variation on this project would be to make a poster contrasting the United States and the Soviet Union, summarizing their basic similarities and differences.

4. Write a research paper on the subject, "Does modern communism fulfill its promise of 'from each according to his abilities, to each according to his needs'?" In other words, have the communists been able to create the "classless" society their theory describes?

5. The bloody excesses of fascist governments have fascinated people ever since Mussolini, Hitler, and Franco came to power in the 1920's and 1930's. Read one or two of the many books written on these dictatorships, with the purpose of trying to understand what type of personality one must have to rule in this brutal fashion. Could such a government ever take power in the United States? Under what conditions could it happen? Summarize your findings in a brief report, oral or written.

CHAPTER TWO

FREE PEOPLE IN A FREE LAND: BUILDING THE AMERICAN SYSTEM OF GOVERNMENT

Early on Halloween evening, 1687, the newly appointed royal governor of the Confederation of New England rode into Hartford, Connecticut. Behind Sir Edmund Andros marched a troop of British redcoats, bayonets bright in the last light of the setting sun. Andros had been sent to collect—by force if necessary—the colony's charter. With this last legal obstacle out of the way, Connecticut would be governed solely in the name of King James II of England.

King James had ordered this action because he had begun to find the New England colonies increasingly troublesome. The colonists refused to abide by the Acts of Navigation and Trade. Tax revenues arrived late, if they could be collected at all. Andros, as the king's representative in the New World, had been ordered to discipline the unruly colonies, consolidate their governments, and bring them into line as paying members of the British Empire.

Connecticut proved particularly unwilling to accept incorporation into the new Dominion of New England. From Andros' viewpoint, the reason was clear—the colony's charter was far too liberal. Granted by Charles II in 1662, the document provided almost total freedom from royal interference in the colonists' state government. As soon as Andros arrived, therefore, he warned the colony's leaders that they must surrender the charter. Andros must have believed that he had made progress, for the next evening he met with the colony's assembly at the courthouse.

In the king's name, Andros officially annexed Connecticut to the Dominion of New England. The document, secure in a leather-covered box, was carried into the chamber. Governor Treat stood and began a passionate speech opposing the surrender of the charter. Impatiently, Andros reached out to take the box. At that moment, every candle in the room was snuffed out. When tinder was finally found and the candles relighted, the charter had disappeared. Angrily, Andros left the courthouse.

What happened when the lights went out? Lieutenant Joseph Wadsworth, a Connecticut militiaman, grabbed the charter and ran to the nearby Wyllys home. At the suggestion of Ruth Wyllys, he climbed a nearby oak, wrapped the charter in his cloak, and hid it in a hollow of the old tree. The royal governor and the king of England could not be denied that easily, of course. Andros went on to govern Connecticut for the next two years, until King James was overthrown. The Charter Oak (as the tree came to be called) lived 150 years longer, a respected symbol of Connecticut's independence and resistance to tyranny. The thousand-year-old tree stood until 1856, when it fell during a violent storm. Bells tolled all over Hartford the next day, and people draped flags over the great trunk, as if the tree were a fallen hero.

The story has a sequel. Following England's Glorious Revolution of 1688, the hidden charter was restored "in full force" by the new monarchy of William and Mary. Connecticut was allowed to resume its earlier form of government, in which an elected governor shared power with a two-house legislature. The colony's lower chamber represented the population of the various townships in the colony; the upper chamber spoke for the counties. With only minor changes, the charter served as the basic law of Connecticut until 1818.

As this example suggests, America's government was not suddenly "invented" in 1787. The long colonial period—some 180 years—gave the colonists time to experiment extensively with different governmental institutions. During this time, Americans became certain that they wanted personal freedom as well as political self-government. This chapter will explore that important period of the nation's history by answering the following questions:

1. What were the different types of government in the early American colonies?
2. What institutions existed within each colonial government?
3. What was the relationship between the king and the colonies?
4. What British legislative acts led to the Revolution?
5. Did the colonies make any early experiments with union?
6. What did the First Continental Congress accomplish?
7. How did the Second Continental Congress manage the Revolution?
8. What were the strengths and weaknesses of the Articles of Confederation?
9. How did the Constitution come to be written?
10. How was the Constitution adopted and put into effect?

What were the different types of government in the early American colonies?

Late in the 1500's, Queen Elizabeth I authorized one of her court favorites, Sir Walter Raleigh, to establish a colony in America. In keeping with the times, British goals were clear-cut: new territories were considered useful only when they contributed to increased trade or yielded treasures of gold and silver—a concept known as *mercantilism*.

This economic theory was popular from the sixteenth through the eighteenth century. All European nations accepted its teachings: (1) that a colony has value to the extent that it enriches the mother country through creation of a favorable balance of trade; (2) that the colony should export food, timber, furs, and other raw materials inexpensively to the mother country and buy back finished goods, preferably at high prices; (3) that colonial industry should be discouraged and trade with other countries forbidden.

England's first attempt at colonization proved doubly disappointing. Not only did Raleigh's Roanoke colony collapse, but the Indian cultures of the Atlantic seaboard could not duplicate the riches yielded to the Spanish by the Aztecs in Mexico and the Incas in Peru. Optimistic leaders reasoned, however, that the location of the first colony—on a barren island off the coast of North Carolina—had been the cause of the failure and that America was still worth colonizing. Further expeditions were planned, and colonists were recruited. In 1607, a joint-stock venture called the Virginia Company of London sponsored the first permanent British settlement in North America.

CHARTER COLONIES

The settlers who landed at Jamestown, Virginia, carried a charter from King James I giving them the right to colonize, govern themselves, and trade with England. This charter colony quickly began the process of self-government. In 1619 the colonists started their own American parliament, known as the House of Burgesses (a burgess was a delegate from a borough, roughly equal to a county). Thus, a pattern of self-government had been established a year before the Pilgrims sailed from England.

All colonies, charter and otherwise, were ruled by a governor and a two-house legislature. Charter colonies elected their governors, either by popular vote or by vote of the founding company. The upper legislative body was known as the *council*; it was usually made up of the colony's leading citizens. The governor often listened to the council's advice, just as today's President relies on his Cabinet. The lower house, called the *assembly*, seated representatives from each settlement in the colony. Citizens of the charter colonies usually elected both houses by popular vote.

Charter colonies often failed, for either political or economic reasons. Despite the relatively high degree of self-government, many activities (the issuance of paper money, for example) were forbidden. By the mid-1700's, only Connecticut and Rhode Island retained their status as charter colonies.

ROYAL COLONIES

As the name implies, royal colonies remained under the direct control of the British crown. Although the royal colonies had the same three major political institutions found in the charter colonies—governor, council, and assembly—they were selected by different means. The king appointed the royal governor as his personal agent in the New World. The governor's chief task was to collect revenues and send them back to Britain.

In a royal colony, the council was appointed. The governor picked its members from the upper classes, often on recommendation from the monarch. The assembly was popularly elected. All laws passed by the legislatures were subject to review by the king and his ministers, who often vetoed them. By the 1770's, eight of the thirteen colonies were classed as royal (or crown) colonies: Massachusetts, New Hampshire, New York, New Jersey, Virginia, North Carolina, South Carolina, and Georgia.

PROPRIETARY COLONIES

Raleigh's Roanoke colony was a proprietary colony—one that actually belonged to a single person. A powerful Quaker family, the Penns, at one time owned two colonies—Pennsylvania and Delaware. Lord Baltimore was given Maryland by the king in the same fashion as a medieval lord handed out fiefs to his vassals. As with the charter colonies, some proprietary colonies failed and reverted to the crown. When the Carolinas lost their proprietary status, only Maryland, Delaware, and Pennsylvania survived as examples of this unusual practice.

In a proprietary colony, the governor and council were chosen by the proprietor, but the people elected the lower house. That division of interests led to a continuing battle. The assembly struggled with the proprietor and the governor in an effort to obtain legislation favorable to the colony's citizens. The assembly's power to tax gave it a voice that the proprietor could not always ignore.

What institutions existed within each colonial government?

British colonists transplanted many of the forms and traditions of their home government. Most colonists still considered themselves English subjects, even though they had migrated to America. With their English citizenship intact, they reasoned, they possessed all the rights and privileges they formerly enjoyed in Britain—with the single exception that they were no longer represented in Parliament. Soon after the first towns had been laid out, local and colony-wide governments were established, complete with county boundaries, jury trials, sheriffs and justices of the peace, and the first bureaucrats.

Each colony made use of a number of important political institutions: (1) a government limited by a charter or constitution, (2) a royal governor, (3) the governor's council, (4) a popularly elected assembly, and (5) courts and local governments.

GOVERNMENT LIMITED BY CHARTER OR CONSTITUTION

The oldest of the colonial constitutions was the Mayflower Compact (see Figure 2.1). The Pilgrims drew up this simple constitution shortly after they arrived off the coast of Massachusetts in 1620. The Compact stated

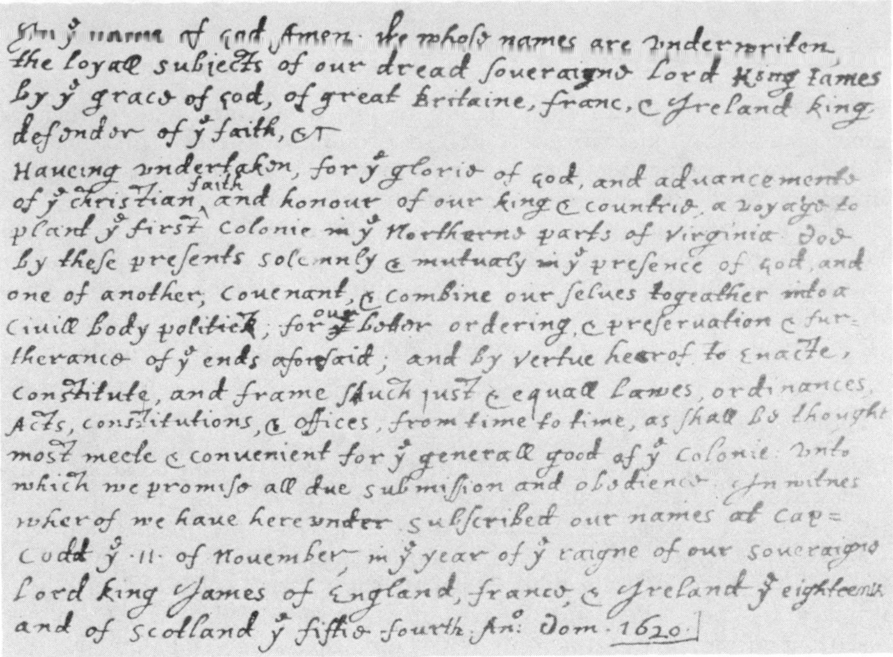
In ye name of God Amen. We whose names are underwriten,
the loyall subjects of our dread soueraigne Lord King James
by ye grace of God, of great Britaine, franc, & Ireland king,
defender of ye faith, &c
Haueing undertaken, for ye glorie of God, and aduancemente
of ye christian faith and honour of our king & countrie, a voyage to
plant ye first Colonie in ye Northerne parts of Virginia. Doe
by these presents solemnly & mutualy in ye presence of God, and
one of another, couenant, & combine our selues togeather into a
ciuill body politick; for our better ordering, & preseruation & fur-
therance of ye ends aforesaid; and by vertue hearof to enacte,
constitute, and frame shuch just & equall lawes, ordinances,
Acts, constitutions, & offices, from time to time, as shall be thought
most meete & conuenient for ye generall good of ye Colonie: unto
which we promise all due submission and obedience. In witnes
wherof we haue hereunder subscribed our names at Cap-
Codd ye ·11· of Nouember, in ye year of ye raigne of our soueraigne
Lord King James of England, france, & Ireland ye eighteenth
and of Scotland ye fiftie fourth. Ano: Dom. 1620.

Figure 2.1
The Mayflower Compact
The American tradition of written constitutions began with the Mayflower Compact, signed by the Pilgrims just before they disembarked to found Plymouth Colony in 1620. Source: Historical Pictures Service, Inc.

that the colonists pledged their submission and obedience to a government that they empowered to make laws for the good of the entire colony. This and all the other early constitutions expressed the colonists' belief in limited government. Even in royal and proprietary colonies, these documents set restrictions on the power of the king and proprietor in the tradition begun by the Magna Carta.

ROYAL GOVERNOR

The royal governors were charged by the crown with an impressive list of duties. They were instructed to (a) send back detailed reports, (b) make a profit for the crown, (c) maintain defense forces against the nearby French and Spanish colonies, and (d) keep the legislatures and courts loyal to the crown. These instructions often led to a running conflict between a royal governor and the people of a colony. The governor looked to Britain and accepted the mercantile theory; the colonists looked to their own farms, businesses, and developing sense of freedom.

Many of the royal governors lived on a grand scale, for their fees and salaries gave them incomes well above the local level. While these officials were not nobility in the European sense, they often modeled their life styles after those of the courts of Europe. This did not endear the governors to the people of the colonies, who had to live simple lives lacking in most luxuries.

COUNCIL

A colonial council combined limited legislative responsibilities with the kinds of duties now given to the U.S. President's Cabinet. Leading political or business figures usually served in the council—just as in the English House of Lords. Only in the charter colonies were the council members elected; in the rest they were appointed by the king or the proprietors. Acts of the assembly required the consent of the council before they could be signed into law. Since the council often failed to give this approval, major problems frequently went unsolved. The council also gave advice to the governor on matters of trade, defense, and political decision-making.

ASSEMBLY

Every colony except Georgia selected its assembly, or lower house, by popular vote (although restrictions on the right to vote drastically limited the number of voters). The assembly held the power to raise money needed to pay the costs of colonial administration (just as all money bills today must originate in the House of Representatives). These local taxes were in addition to the taxes levied on the colonies and their trade by the British Parliament. The assemblies were also responsible for (1) raising local defense forces, (2) maintaining law and order, (3) regulating trade, (4) setting land ownership regulations, and (5) dealing with the Indian problems created by an expanding colonial population.

COURTS AND LOCAL GOVERNMENTS

Local government and the court system followed closely in the tradition of English common law. Direct democracy flourished in the form of the New England town meeting. Juries sat at court trials. These institutions reflected the fact that few of the colonists thought of themselves as building a new or revolutionary system; they demanded from the king only the rights that custom awarded to every English citizen by right of birth.

What was the relationship between the king and the colonies?

No colony was ever as completely regulated by the king of England and his administrators as the written laws would lead one to think. Three factors dominated the relationship between the king and the colonies:

SALUTARY NEGLECT

For well over a hundred years, the main feature of the relationship between Great Britain and America could be termed *salutary* (helpful or beneficial) *neglect*. During the 1600's and early 1700's, England faced constant turmoil at home and conflict overseas. Four wars with France, a civil war, plague and fire in London, a struggle for dominance between the crown and Parliament—all claimed the island nation's attention. As a result of England's distraction, the colonists were free to develop in their own way, to ignore the spirit (and often the letter) of British regulations, and to take responsibility for their own economic well-being and military security.

LACK OF COMMUNICATION

Because of the great distance between England and America, communications between the king and his colonies were slow, irregular, and unreliable. As a consequence, the king had no real feeling for what was happening in the New World. In particular, the British government failed to understand the colonists' changing ideas on government and their relationship to the mother country.

GROWING ROYAL DISSATISFACTION

If the king remained unaware of the new colonial attitudes, one fact did not escape him: the colonies were not fulfilling their original purpose. The costs of colonial administration and defense exceeded the income received. The Acts of Navigation and Trade, along with other tax measures, should have been a major source of revenue for the treasury. But the cost of collecting taxes in the colonies often exceeded the tax money collected. In the 1760's, King George III and his advisors began to think about tightening colonial administration. From their viewpoint, still dominated by the mercantile theory, the colonies were simply not paying their own way.

What British legislative acts led to the Revolution?

The long series of wars between Great Britain and France, known in America as the French and Indian Wars, ended in 1763. Victorious and determined to reap the profits of victory, the British Parliament began work on a series of legislative actions designed to put the colonies on a firm financial footing. Instead, within a dozen years, the various acts brought the colonists to the point of revolt (see Figure 2.2).

THE PROCLAMATION OF 1763

English policymakers saw the Appalachians as a natural frontier between the white colonists and the Indian territories. They wanted to prevent war by keeping the American colonists separated from the Indians; to reserve the Ohio Valley to British land speculators; and to limit the colonists to settlements along the Atlantic seaboard. Therefore they issued the Proclamation of 1763, closing the western lands to further settlement. Many colonists had bought western lands on speculation, however, so the proclamation hit them doubly hard—in the pocketbook as well as in their cherished ideal of freedom of movement.

Figure 2.2
Colonial anger leads to cooperation
Angered by British colonial policies, Americans join together to destroy a statue of
King George III in New York City's Bowling Green. More importantly, colonial leaders
were also laying the foundation for political cooperation among their fiercely in-
dependent local governments. Source: Courtesy of the New-York Historical Society,
New York City.

THE SUGAR ACT OF 1764

The Molasses Act of 1733, which placed a prohibitively high tax on
foreign (non-British) sugar and molasses, had been loosely enforced. The
Sugar Act of 1764 reduced the tax, but was to be strictly enforced. This
law had the double purpose of raising revenue and ending trade with
French colonies in the West Indies. The colonists resisted by stepping up
their smuggling operations. The *triangular trade* (see Figure 2.3) had
become essential to the colonial economy. Without the hard-money profits
from the rum-slaves-sugar exchange, colonists could not afford to buy
essential British manufactured goods.

STAMP ACT OF 1765

This short-lived tax on colonial newspapers, licenses, legal and business
documents, playing cards, diplomas, and other printed material was
intended to help pay the cost of defending the colonies from Indian
attacks. Determined American resistance to the stamp tax centered on the
cry, "No taxation without representation." The colonists claimed that since

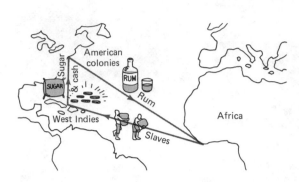

Figure 2.3
A typical triangular trade route
Without profits from their rich three-cornered trade with Africa and the West Indies, the American colonies could not afford to buy the expensive manufactured items they were required to import from England.

they were not represented in Parliament, that body could not tax business and legal transactions within the colonies.

TOWNSHEND DUTIES OF 1767

The British government had run up heavy debts during the wars with France. The Townshend Duties of 1767 tried to raise additional revenues by taxing colonial imports of glass, paper, paint, lead, and tea. The king appointed new officials to enforce the act, and specified that the royal governors' salaries were to come from this source. Colonial legislators realized that the act meant that they could no longer use their control of the governors' pay as a weapon. Stiff resistance to the act forced repeal of all but the tax on tea. Parliament insisted on keeping this one tax as a token of its authority.

OTHER ACTS

Few British actions gained colonial approval in those years. The *Quartering Act* forced townspeople to house British troops in their homes. *Writs of assistance*, or general search warrants, further infringed on colonial liberties by allowing law officers to enter any home, building, or ship in search of smuggled goods. After the Boston Tea Party in 1773, the *Boston Port Act* was passed to close the harbor until the town paid for the lost tea. This and other actions of Parliament, known generally as the *Intolerable Acts*, convinced the colonists that the king's government would never accept colonial freedoms. By 1775, even many of the more conservative leaders had begun to think about independence. The battle of Lexington and Concord loomed on the horizon.

Did the colonies make any early experiments with union?

Despite the increasing oppressiveness of British rule, the colonies were slow to realize that their common interests required cooperative action. A few smaller colonies did merge with larger ones: New Haven Colony, for example, became part of Connecticut, while Plymouth Colony was absorbed by Massachusetts. But in general, differences in population makeup, economic competition, and communication difficulties tended to isolate one colony from another. Most colonies kept an agent in London whose job was to further his own colony's interests. As a result, Georgia had more in common with England than with Massachusetts.

Attempts at union did surface from time to time. Two major efforts were the Albany Plan of Union of 1754 and the Stamp Act Congress of 1765.

ALBANY PLAN OF UNION

In 1754, the threat of attack by the French and their Indian allies hung over the northeastern colonies. As a consequence, the British government called representatives of seven colonies to a conference in Albany. Benjamin Franklin proposed the Albany Plan, under which the colonies would unite in defense of any colony faced with raids or actual invasion. Earlier, for example, Virginia had refused to send troops to help repel an attack on Pennsylvania. The delegates agreed to the plan, which established a grand council whose powers included authority to levy troops, negotiate treaties, declare war, and generally administer the western lands.

The brave beginning signaled by the Albany Plan died as soon as the delegates returned home. No colonial assembly could be convinced that it should ratify the plan. The English also opposed it, but that was a minor factor; most colonists refused to give up even a small degree of their independence.

STAMP ACT CONGRESS

Opposition to the stamp tax led to a more successful effort at cooperation. Delegates from nine colonies met in New York City in 1765 to petition the king for repeal of the hated act. Not only was the tax costly, it proved to be a great nuisance: every sheet of every newspaper had to be stamped. The Stamp Act Congress was echoed by informal groups in the various colonies. Angry colonists began a boycott of British goods, threatened local tax collectors with physical injury, and marched to the harbors to prevent the tax stamps from being unloaded. Faced with severe trade losses, British merchants joined in the protest, and Parliament repealed the Stamp Act in 1766, one year after it had been enacted.

OTHER UNIFIED ACTIONS

Unified action often went beyond such formal meetings as the Albany council and the Stamp Act Congress. The *Committees of Correspondence* circulated letters and papers to keep everyone aware of events happening throughout the colonies. A radical group of middle-class citizens and workers known as the *Sons of Liberty* carried the growing protest movement into the streets, with considerable violence. The *Nonintercourse Agreements* involved Americans throughout the colonies in a boycott of taxed British manufactures. In rebelling against the mercantile theory,

Figure 2.4
**The segmented serpent:
a symbol of growing
colonial resistance to
British domination**
This famous serpent, designed by Benjamin Franklin in 1754, called on the colonies
to unite. To the British, the symbol stood for a "snake in the grass"; but to
Americans, it suggested strength and unity of purpose. The snake symbol appeared
once more in the "Don't Tread on Me" flag. Source: The Bettmann Archive, Inc.

the agreements also encouraged development of American-made products.

By 1775, a new trend toward colonial cooperation had begun to replace
the earlier pattern of individualistic self-interest (see Figure 2.4). The
First Continental Congress was a logical next step in the growing struggle
against British domination.

LET'S REVIEW FOR A MOMENT

The disagreements between Great Britain and its American colonies that
finally led to revolution began with an economic policy called *mercantilism*.
Briefly stated, this theory holds that colonies exist for the enrichment of
the mother country. Various experiments resulted in creation of three types
of colonies in early America—*charter*, *proprietary*, and *royal*.

British parliamentary government served as a model for the colonial
governing bodies. The chief executive was the *royal governor*—elected in
charter colonies, appointed in others. An upper house, the *council*, advised
the governor; its well-to-do members—appointed in royal and proprietary
colonies, elected in charter colonies—held veto power over legislation
passed by the *assembly*. This lower house most clearly represented the
colonists; its elected members held the purse strings and spoke for the
emerging American spirit in the fierce power struggles with Britain.

What would you have done about the colonies if you had been king of
England? Until 1763, you would have been busy with wars and other
troubles. During that period of salutary neglect, the colonies would have
become accustomed to self-government. All too often, you would have felt
that the colonies were more trouble and expense than they were worth.

After 1763, the king and Parliament passed a series of laws designed to
increase tax revenues, limit westward expansion, and generally tighten

imperial control over the restless colonists. Despite the colonists' fierce resentment of British taxes, early efforts at cooperation among the colonies usually collapsed. Most colonies saw in union the exchange of one master for another. The passing of time and new British restrictions— economic as well as political—changed that attitude.

What did the First Continental Congress accomplish?

As was mentioned earlier, the Boston Tea Party of 1773, so popular in the colonies, brought a far different reaction in Great Britain. Parliament passed the Intolerable Acts, which included the closing of the port of Boston—an act of economic execution for that seafaring city. Conflicting opinions shuttled back and forth across the Atlantic in a debate that continued well after war broke out (see the box on page 44). The Massachusetts and Virginia assemblies called for a meeting of all the colonies to discuss the Intolerable Acts. Delegates from twelve colonies (Georgia was not represented) met in Philadelphia on September 5, 1774.

DISCUSSIONS AND DECLARATION

The meetings of the First Continental Congress lasted nearly two months. Men whose names would one day become identified with the new nation joined the discussion—George Washington, Patrick Henry, Samuel Adams. The talks centered on the strained relationship with the mother country. Despite the strong arguments of passionate radicals like Henry and Adams, little sentiment for revolution surfaced at the Congress. Few of the fifty-six delegates would have believed that war was only six months away.

The Congress drafted a petition to the king that explained the viewpoint of the colonies. Many delegates hoped that this *Declaration of Rights and Grievances* would lead to a peaceful solution. The First Continental Congress also took a firmer action: it organized a boycott of all trade with Great Britain until the Intolerable Acts should be repealed. The philosophy of the colonies could not be mistaken; their resolution stated, "The inhabitants of the English colonies in North America are entitled to life, liberty, and property, and they have never ceded these to any power to dispose of without their consent."

SIGNIFICANCE OF THE CONGRESS

The delegates to the First Continental Congress did not attempt to act as a colony-wide government. Instead, their main acomplishment was to prove that the colonies could submerge their differences and work together. The Congress resolved to meet again the following May if the British government had not acted to undo the wrongs inflicted by its repressive laws.

Despite the strong language of the resolution, at that time few people

Not everyone agreed: differing views on the Revolution

Pro-British views

"They must all be subordinate. In all laws relating to trade and navigation especially, this is the mother country, they are the children; they must obey, and we prescribe."
—William Pitt, Earl of Chatham, 1770

"Johnny, you will be hanged, your estate will be forfeited and confiscated, you will leave your excellent wife a widow, and your charming children orphans, beggars and infamous."
—John Adams, reporting what John Dickinson's mother said when she warned him not to join the Revolution, 1775

"Better one tyrant three thousand miles away than three thousand tyrants not a mile away."
—Mather Byles, Boston minister, 1776

"When Jove resolved to send a curse,
And all the woes of life rehearse,
Not plague, not famine, but much worse—
He cursed us with a Congress."
—Tory poem poking fun at the Second Continental Congress, 1776

"Every means of distressing America must meet with my concurrence, as it tends to bring them to feel the necessity of returning to their duty. . . . Nothing but force can bring them to reason."
—George III, 1776

Pro-American views

"If I were an American, as I am an Englishman, while a foreign troop was landed in my country, I never would lay down my arms,—never —never—never!"
—William Pitt, Earl of Chatham, 1777

"An act against the [British] Constitution is void; an act against natural equity is void."
—James Otis, speaking against the writs of assistance, 1761

"You may spread fire, sword, and desolation, but that will not be government. . . . No people can ever be made to submit to a form of government they say they will not receive."
—Duke of Richmond, in a speech to the House of Lords, 1775

"Ye that dare oppose not only the tyranny but the tyrant stand forth! Freedom hath been hunted round the globe. O receive the fugitive, and prepare in time an asylum for mankind."
—Thomas Paine, American propagandist, 1776

"The time is now at hand which must probably determine whether Americans are to be freemen or slaves."
—George Washington, Order of the Day, 1776

"All eyes are open, or opening to the rights of men. The general spread of the light of science [reveals] that the mass of mankind was not born with saddles on their backs."
—Thomas Jefferson, 1776

foresaw independence. But throughout the colonies, an armed militia known as the *Minutemen* had begun to train on village greens. Determined to protect their rights as English citizens, they stockpiled guns and ammunition. Although the First Continental Congress stopped short of calling itself a government, fast-moving events proved that its successor could not evade that responsibility.

How did the Second Continental Congress
manage the Revolution?

By the time the Second Continental Congress met in Philadelphia on May 10, 1775, the British had not only failed to compromise: the first shots of the Revolutionary War had been fired at Lexington and Concord. Almost immediately, the Congress organized a "continental" army, with George Washington as its commander. The delegates agreed that the war in Massachusetts involved all of the colonies; the new army enforced that belief. These men were not totally inexperienced in government, for most of the members of the First Continental Congress of 1774 had been returned in 1775 by their colonial assemblies. However, John Hancock, elected president of the Second Continental Congress, was a new member, as was Benjamin Franklin, recently returned from Europe.

WORK OF THE CONGRESS

The Second Continental Congress linked the colonies together for six years, from 1775 to 1781. No constitution spelled out its powers, and no elections gave popular approval to its membership. Still, the Congress was forced to deal with the multitude of problems brought by the Revolution; only when the Articles of Confederation went into effect in 1781 did the Congress hand over its authority.

The Continental Congress had been in session a year before Richard Henry Lee of Virginia proposed that the events of the battlefield be formally recognized by a Declaration of Independence. A five-member committee, led by Thomas Jefferson, worked on the draft of the document. After extensive debate, delegates approved the substance of the statement on July 2, 1776, but recommended a few additional changes. Two days later, on July 4, 1776, the Declaration of Independence was formally adopted. (The full text of the Declaration is reprinted in the Appendix at the back of this book.)

FOREIGN RELATIONS

The wisdom of allowing the Congress to speak for all thirteen of the new states in foreign affairs was apparent. Aided by the inspired diplomacy of Ben Franklin, the Congress signed a treaty of alliance with France in 1778. Without French assistance, both in money and in military forces, the Americans might well have lost the War of Independence. The Congress also signed trade agreements with Spain and the Netherlands. Like France, these countries supported the Americans by declaring war on Great Britain.

DOMESTIC AFFAIRS

The weaknesses of the Second Continental Congress were most apparent in domestic affairs. The new states remained jealous of one another. No provision for a chief executive to lead the government had been made; a national judiciary did not exist; and no effective taxing system had been developed. Lacking gold to support a currency, the Congress had authorized issuance of over $200 million in paper money, backed largely by the credit of the new republic. As a result, these Continental bills had little actual purchasing power. The phrase "not worth a Continental" was soon being used to describe anything worthless.

DESIGNING A NEW GOVERNMENT

Faced with serious financial and economic problems, the Second Continental Congress realized that the states would have to delegate further powers to a new government. A committee proposed such a government in 1776, but the debate dragged on for a year. Finally, in 1777, the Congress approved a new scheme for uniting the states, called the Articles of Confederation. Before they could go into effect, however, the Articles required the approval of all thirteen states. Eleven states ratified within a year, but Delaware delayed until 1779 and Maryland until 1781.

What were the strengths and weaknesses of the Articles of Confederation?

On first reading, the Articles of Confederation appeared capable of giving the infant republic a working government. The states agreed to a number of cooperative measures, including (1) creation of a national legislative body, scheduled to meet annually and authorized to conduct whatever business was needed; (2) one vote per state, to be cast as instructed by the various state legislatures; and (3) proclamation of a léague of friendship among the states, with the government empowered to provide for the common defense, safeguard individual liberties, and maintain the general welfare. As the name "confederation" suggests, the states retained much of their independence of action.

STRENGTHS OF THE ARTICLES

The Articles of Confederation made a number of useful contributions to the new nation:

1. Most important, the states were able to cooperate in the conduct of the war.

2. By forming a loose union, the individual states became less open to takeover by stronger European nations.

3. Confederation helped Americans to begin thinking of themselves as citizens of a nation, not just of various states.

4. The Confederation dealt wisely with the vast new territories acquired in 1783 north of the Ohio River and between the Allegheny Mountains and the Mississippi River. The Congress of the Confederation passed the *Land Ordinance of 1785*, which set up a system for surveying virgin lands, establishing townships, and holding public land sales. In addition, the *Northwest Ordinance of 1787* not only encouraged settlement but provided

a means by which new states could be admitted on an equal basis with the original thirteen. The principles of the Northwest Ordinance far outlived the Articles of Confederation. Alaska and Hawaii were admitted to the Union under those same rules almost two hundred years later.

WEAKNESSES OF THE ARTICLES

Although the Articles of Confederation created what may have been the best government that could be achieved at the time, they still had glaring weaknesses.

1. No solution was found for the financial problems that plagued the Continental Congress. The government had to operate without the power to tax. Financial support came from the states, which were often slow to meet the central government's requests. Continental currency remained valueless, and the states printed equally worthless money of their own.

2. Unhindered by any regulation of interstate commerce, the individual states erected tariff barriers to one another's goods. The revenues helped pay state bills, but business suffered.

3. Only limited military authority was given to the central government. Most Revolutionary troops were financed, organized, and controlled by the individual state legislatures.

4. No provision was made for a chief executive or for a national bureaucracy. Congressional committees could not properly handle the nation's affairs without executive leadership or the help of full-time employees.

5. The central government lacked police authority; it literally could not punish anyone. Moreover, because no national court system was created, nothing could be done to resolve conflicts between the individual states.

6. Each state was given one vote, regardless of size or population. As a consequence, jealousies and rivalries between states were magnified.

7. Amendments to the Articles of Confederation required a unanimous vote by all thirteen states. This made even the most badly needed changes almost impossible to achieve.

The inefficiency of a government made up of thirteen jealous states soon became obvious. With luck, determination, good leadership, and the help of European allies, the Revolution had ended successfully for the American colonies. Now the challenges of peace called for new directions.

How did the Constitution come to be written?

After Britain agreed to recognize colonial independence in the Treaty of Paris in 1783, the states tackled the problem of regulating interstate commerce. Two meetings in 1785 and 1786 made little progress. Finally, the colonial leadership scheduled a third meeting for the spring of 1787 with the announced purpose of revising the Articles of Confederation.

The *Constitutional Convention* gathered in Philadelphia on May 25, 1787 (see Figure 2.5). Rhode Island was not represented; its legislature

Figure 2.5
**The Constitutional Convention debates
the shape of U.S. government**
George Washington presides over the early debates of the Constitutional Convention,
at which delegates reached the compromises that made our system of government
possible. Source: Free Library of Philadelphia.

opposed the creation of a strong central government. The arrival of New
Hampshire's delegation was delayed by lack of funds until late July. The
fifty-five delegates present included many of the eminent men of the day
—George Washington, James Madison, Benjamin Franklin, Alexander
Hamilton, and others. The convention pledged itself to secrecy (fortunately
for later generations, Madison violated this agreement by keeping a
journal), and unanimously elected Washington as president of the convention. It was agreed that each state would have one vote, and a simple
majority would carry any proposal.

DECISION TO CREATE A NEW GOVERNMENT

Working quickly, the delegates agreed to create a new national government instead of patching up the Articles of Confederation. This first major
decision established a strong central government with three branches—
legislative, executive, and judicial. Unlike the old confederation, the new
government would be federal in nature.

Design of the new national legislature raised the first real controversy.
Soon after the meeting opened, Edmund Randolph of Virginia submitted a
proposal (written largely by Madison) known as the *Virginia Plan*; it
called for a *bicameral* (two-house) *legislature*. Under this plan, the number
of representatives elected to both houses from each state would be based
on the state's population—which would give the larger states a dominant
voice. Within the month, New Jersey countered with a proposal for a
unicameral (one-house) *legislature* based on equal representation for all

states. As in the Congress set up under the Articles of Confederation, this plan gave small states an equal voice with the larger states. The issues of slavery and regulation of interstate commerce also generated controversy.

MAJOR COMPROMISES

Working through the heat of the Philadelphia summer, the convention reached three major compromises.

1. *Bicameral legislature.* The Connecticut Compromise on the federal legislature finally satisfied both sides. The delegates agreed to a bicameral legislature, with a Senate based on equal representation for all the states and a House of Representatives based on the population of each state. The small states were satisfied that their interests would be protected by their equal representation in the Senate. At the same time, the large states could feel secure that their needs would be safeguarded by their greater representation in the House.

2. *Slavery.* Compromise on the slave trade prohibited Congress from interfering with the slave trade until at least 1808. A further compromise permitted each slave to be counted as three-fifths of a person in determining state populations for representation in the House.*

3. *Interstate commerce.* The Southern states feared that the North would cut off the South's profitable cotton trade with England in order to promote its own textile industries. The eventual compromise gave the new government the right to regulate interstate commerce, but forbade the taxation of exports.

OTHER DECISIONS

Even after the Connecticut Compromise, much time and effort went into writing the other provisions of the lengthy Article I. This section of the Constitution established the powers and limitations of the legislative branch. Controversy also arose over Article II—the nature of the presidency, the length of the President's term, and the method of presidential election. The fear of congressional domination of the chief executive, and the fear of popular elections, finally led to a compromise that placed presidential elections in the hands of an electoral college. Voting qualifications were left up to the states.

Finally, on September 17, 1787, the delegates signed the finished product—the Constitution of the United States of America. (The full text of the Constitution is reprinted in the Appendix at the back of this book.) Supported by neither salaries nor expense accounts, the delegates had been called upon to give their best. Benjamin Franklin also expressed his

---

* This provision, so foreign to modern-day belief in racial equality, was nullified by the Thirteenth Amendment in 1865.

approval: "It therefore astonishes me, Sir, to find this system approaching so near to perfection as it does."

How was the Constitution ratified?

As was noted earlier, Maryland had been able to hold up adoption of the Articles of Confederation for three years because approval by all thirteen colonies was required. To prevent a similar delay, the Framers provided that the new Constitution would go into effect when two-thirds of the states—nine of the thirteen—gave their approval.

STRUGGLE FOR RATIFICATION

The debate over ratification speedily divided the nation's citizens into two political factions. Those who favored the new government were called Federalists; those who opposed the Constitution were known as Anti-Federalists. Famous names dotted the list of Anti-Federalists—Patrick Henry, Richard Henry Lee, John Hancock, Samuel Adams. Farmers who needed easy credit opposed the new government. They reasoned that the ban on issuance of paper money by the states would drive up interest rates and make money more expensive.

The main arguments against the Constitution, however, were that it gave the central government enormous power and did not contain guarantees of the traditional British liberties. Patrick Henry spoke for the Anti-Federalists when he said, "I look upon that paper as the most fatal plan that could possibly be conceived to enslave a free people." Supporters were forced to reply. In a series of brilliant newspaper articles called the *Federalist Papers*, Alexander Hamilton, James Madison, and John Jay argued the case for the Constitution line by line. The Federalists also promised that the new government would add a Bill of Rights to the Constitution as soon as it was ratified.

CONSTITUTION RATIFIED

The *Federalist Papers*, along with the influence of men like Washington, Franklin, and Madison, tipped the balance. Three colonies ratified the Constitution before the end of 1787; the ninth state added its approval in late June of 1788 (see Figure 2.6). Still, the federal system would not have worked without the largest, most important states. Only two of these, Pennsylvania and Massachusetts, were among the first nine to ratify. In the summer of 1788, Virginia and New York finally lined up with the others, although by relatively close margins. Even so, the final two states did not rush to make the ratification unanimous: North Carolina joined in 1789, Rhode Island in 1790. (Table 2.1, on page 52, summarizes the major steps leading to formation of the new government.)

The first Congress met in September 1788 in Philadelphia. New York was chosen as the temporary capital. In the first presidential election, the

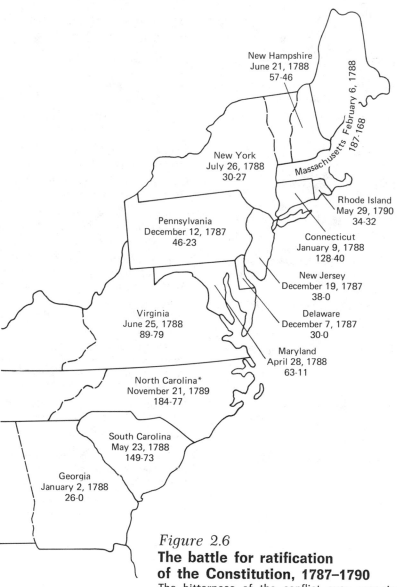

New Hampshire
June 21, 1788
57-46

Massachusetts February 6, 1788
187-168

New York
July 26, 1788
30-27

Rhode Island
May 29, 1790
34-32

Pennsylvania
December 12, 1787
46-23

Connecticut
January 9, 1788
128-40

New Jersey
December 19, 1787
38-0

Virginia
June 25, 1788
89-79

Delaware
December 7, 1787
30-0

Maryland
April 28, 1788
63-11

North Carolina*
November 21, 1789
184-77

South Carolina
May 23, 1788
149-73

Georgia
January 2, 1788
26-0

*North Carolina voted twice. In the
first vote on August 4, 1788, the
ratification resolution was defeated.

Figure 2.6
The battle for ratification of the Constitution, 1787–1790
The bitterness of the conflict over acceptance of a strong central government can be seen in the closeness of the vote in a number of states.

Electoral College voted unanimously for George Washington. The new Congress met in New York on March 4, 1789. On April 30, 1789, Washington recited the oath of office as President of the United States. The new nation at last had a government that would work. It still does.

Table 2.1

The road to union: a summary of key political events leading to the creation of our country

Year	Event	Significance
1600's	*Colonial experiments with various forms of self-government*	*Self-government became an accepted part of American life.*
1643	*New England Confederation*	*Indian threat led to a brief period of colonial cooperation.*
1754	*Albany Plan*	*Not acceptable to the colonies, but served as a model for later efforts.*
1765	*Stamp Act Congress*	*Unified colonial opposition forced repeal of the Stamp Act.*
1770	*Committees of Correspondence*	*Colonial leaders coordinated unified action against British regulations.*
1774	*First Continental Congress*	*Twelve colonies met to petition the king to repeal the Intolerable Acts.*
1775	*Second Continental Congress*	*Provided a government for the colonies during the Revolutionary War.*
1776	*Declaration of Independence*	*Made formal declaration of the separation of the colonies from Great Britain; gave high moral purpose to the Revolution.*
1781	*Articles of Confederation*	*Provided first constitutional government for the new nation.*
1783	*Treaty of Paris*	*Ended the Revolutionary War.*
1787	*Constitutional Convention*	*Rather than revise the Articles, delegates determined to write a new constitution.*
1788	*Constitution ratified*	*The new government came into legal existence after ratification by nine states.*
1789	*Washington inaugurated*	*The nation began its history as the United States of America.*

§UMMARY AND CONCLUSIONS

1. The American colonial period was marked by two currents in British thought. One, the theory of *mercantilism*, insisted that the colonies existed for the benefit of the mother country. The second factor was *salutary neglect*. Wrapped up in its own problems, at least until 1763, Parliament

left the colonies free to develop a tradition of self-government and independence.

2. The colonies can be classified as charter, proprietary, or royal. *Charter colonies* ran their own affairs and elected their own governors; *proprietary colonies* belonged to a company or wealthy individual, who appointed the governor and ran the colony as a money-making enterprise; *royal colonies* were subject to the direct rule of the king.

3. All the colonies developed legislative bodies with two houses. The upper house, or *council*, advised the royal governor and generally represented the colony's upper class. The lower house, or *assembly*, was popularly elected, held the purse strings, and spoke for the colony's middle and lower classes.

4. Only a long series of increasingly restrictive British laws finally drove the colonies together. Since the colonies hadn't been paying their way, the Stamp Act, Sugar Act, restrictions on westward migration, and the Townshend Duties all seemed reasonable enough in London. Colonial resistance led to harsher British action, until the Intolerable Acts of 1773 finally brought the colonies into open resistance.

5. Resistance and thoughts of revolution brought the need for a unified colonial government. At the First Continental Congress in 1774, the colonies pledged mutual cooperation and addressed a Declaration of Rights and Grievances to the king. In 1775, open war with England began at Lexington and Concord.

6. The Second Continental Congress served as a national government from 1775 to 1781. Its members issued the Declaration of Independence and attempted to manage the economic and military problems of the Revolution. The Congress also wrote the Articles of Confederation, signed important treaties of alliance with France and Spain, and issued a quickly devalued paper money to pay for the war.

7. The Articles of Confederation, ratified in 1781, established a weak, confederate form of government. On the positive side, the government gave Americans a chance to work together cooperatively and to present a united front to foreign countries. The weaknesses were many: no executive branch or national bureaucracy; no judicial system; no power to tax; no power to regulate interstate commerce; no satisfactory means of raising an army; and no power to enforce laws or resolve conflicts between the states. The Confederation did deal wisely with the public lands acquired in 1783, preparing the way for their eventual admission as states.

8. In 1787 a convention was called in Philadelphia to revise the Articles of Confederation. Instead, the convention created an entirely new constitution. Major compromises were reached on slavery, interstate commerce, and legislative representation. The present-day Senate, in which each state has an equal voice, and the House of Representatives, with seats allocated according to population, solved the conflict between the large and small states over the question of legislative influence.

9. The ratification process was dominated by campaigns between the Federalists and the Anti-Federalists. The turning point came when the Federalists promised to add a Bill of Rights to the Constitution as soon as the new government met. The last of the required nine states ratified the

document in the summer of 1788. In the spring of 1789, George Washington was sworn in as the first President of the United States of America.

REVIEW QUESTIONS AND ACTIVITIES

TERMS YOU SHOULD KNOW

Albany Plan	*Northwest Ordinance of 1787*
assembly	*Proclamation of 1763*
bicameral legislature	*proprietary colony*
charter colony	*Quartering Act*
Committees of Correspondence	*royal colony*
Constitutional Convention	*salutary neglect*
council	*Second Continental Congress*
Declaration of Rights and Grievances	*Stamp Tax*
Federalist Papers	*Stamp Tax Congress*
First Continental Congress	*Sugar Act*
Intolerable Acts	*Sons of Liberty*
Land Ordinance of 1785	*Townshend Duties*
mercantilism	*unicameral legislature*
Minutemen	*writs of assistance*
Nonintercourse Agreements	

REVIEW QUESTIONS

The following multiple-choice questions are based on the important ideas presented in this chapter. Select the response that best completes each statement.

1. Which of the following statements would *not* be true of the colony of a country which followed mercantilism during the seventeenth century? (a) No manufacturing industries would be permitted in the colony. (b) Gold, silver, and gems would be sent to the mother country. (c) All trade with the mother country would be transported in the mother country's ships. (d) The colony would be encouraged to develop its own form of self-government. (e) Trade between the colony and countries other than the mother country would be forbidden.

2. The colonial governmental institution that most clearly spoke for the average colonist was the (a) royal governor. (b) council. (c) assembly. (d) Dominion of New England. (e) none of these, because all governmental bodies were appointed by the king.

3. Which of the following statements most truly describes the colonial attitude before the 1760's? (a) Most colonists wanted complete independence from Great Britain. (b) The colonists thought that they should be granted more freedoms than British subjects living in England received. (c) Most colonists accepted British rule, but demanded that the monarchy be replaced by a republic. (d) Most col-

onists wanted to transfer their loyalties to the French government. (e) Most colonists wanted only the same rights and privileges enjoyed by British subjects living in England.

4. The existence of "salutary neglect" (a) gave the colonists a chance to develop their own way of life and government. (b) placed the colonists under the strictest possible British control. (c) strengthened the mercantile theory. (d) was a policy of the British government designed to help make the colonies independent. (e) none of these.

5. British revenue-producing acts like the Sugar Act, the Townshend Duties, and the Stamp Tax were resisted by the colonists because (a) the colonists were not represented in the Parliament that passed the taxes. (b) the taxes placed a heavy financial burden on colonial business. (c) paying and collecting the taxes was a costly nuisance. (d) the taxes were considered infringements on colonial freedoms. (e) all of these were reasons for colonial resistance.

6. The *least* successful of early attempts at cooperation among the colonies was (a) the Nonintercourse Agreements. (b) the Committees of Correspondence. (c) the Albany Plan. (d) the Stamp Act Congress. (e) none of these was successful.

7. Which of the following summarizes a major weakness of the Articles of Confederation? (a) No provision was made for an executive branch. (b) The new government had no way of resolving conflicts between the states. (c) The government had no control over interstate commerce. (d) No sound taxing policy was established. (e) All of these.

8. When the Constitutional Convention accepted the Connecticut Compromise on the form of the new legislature, it resolved a conflict between (a) North and South. (b) the two largest states. (c) slaveholders and abolitionists. (d) the large and the small states. (e) the western territories and the original thirteen states.

9. The best description of the new government created under the Constitution is that it was a (a) unitary system with all power concentrated in a central government. (b) federal republic. (c) confederation with a better-organized central government than under the Articles of Confederation. (d) totalitarian system that was democratic in form but dictatorial in operation. (e) modified parliamentary system based on the English model.

10. The states agreed to ratify the Constitution only after the Federalists agreed to return some of the federal government's powers to the states. This statement is (a) true. (b) false; the key issue concerned individual rights and was solved by the promise of a Bill of Rights. (c) false; it was the Anti-Federalists who supported the Constitution.

CONCEPT DEVELOPMENT

This chapter has explored a number of significant concepts relating to the design of American government. Use your skills in thinking, researching, and writing to answer the following questions.

1. Why did the early American colonists create governments that largely duplicated the British system?

2. Summarize the British attitudes toward the American colonies in the 1700's. Why were these policies and feelings logical for the times?

3. The first colonial attempts at union ended largely in failure. Explain why the colonists found it so difficult to cooperate in the early 1700's.

4. What are the strengths and weaknesses of the confederate system of government? Use the Articles of Confederation, the Confederate States of America, and the United Nations as examples in your argument.

5. Many critics attack government secrecy as a prime evil. What arguments can you find to support the need for secrecy? Use the strict secrecy rule imposed at the Constitutional Convention of 1787 as a reference point for your discussion.

ACTIVITIES

The following activities are designed to help you in the ideas developed in this chapter.

1. Americans sometimes assume that revolutionary violence is a recent development. Prepare an oral report for your class on the Sons of Liberty and their activities during the pre-Revolutionary period. An interesting approach would be to compare the Sons of Liberty to present-day revolutionary groups or other organizations that aim at overthrow of an existing government. How are the groups alike? How are they different?

2. Write and perform a skit that presents the British view of the American Revolution. Include the leading politicians of the day—Pitt, Grenville, Lord North, and the others who tried desperately to deal with a situation that quickly escaped their control. Don't forget King George III—what was his role? Remember that from the British viewpoint, the colonists were completely unreasonable in their demands. Excellent sources to draw on are such standard works on the Revolution as: Knollenberg, *Origin of the American Revolution;* Miller, *Origins of the American Revolution;* Commager and Morris, *The Spirit of Seventy-Six;* and Ward, *The War of the Revolution.*

3. If you can locate Richard Morris's interesting book *Seven Who Shaped Our Destiny: The Founding Fathers as Revolutionaries* (New York: Harper & Row, 1973), select one of these seven outstanding Americans as the subject of a multimedia report. Prepare a taped dramatization of your subject's contributions to the new nation, along with visuals for the overhead projector that illustrate the major events discussed on the tape. By using varied voices, sound effects, and a series of fast-changing visuals, you can provide considerable drama along with the factual content of your presentation.

4. The Constitution was written by the fifty-five delegates who met at Philadelphia, and ratified by conventions in the thirteen states. Thus it has never been voted on by the American people. As an experiment, survey a cross-section of your community—people of all ages and occupations—by asking the question, "Do you accept the Constitution of the United States as it now stands, or do you believe that it should be changed?" People who accept the Constitution as it is should be asked what they find most desirable about it; those who ask for change should specify how they want the Constitution revised. Present your findings to the class, along with your interpretation of the results.

CHAPTER THREE

"WISDOM AND GOOD EXAMPLES": THE BROAD PRINCIPLES OF THE CONSTITUTION

The heat lay heavy on Philadelphia that summer of 1787. "A veritable torture," wrote a visiting Frenchman, "is the innumerable flies which constantly light on the face and hands, stinging everywhere. . . . Rooms must be kept closed unless one wishes to be tormented in his bed at the break of day." Another traveler remembered the mosquitos that plagued people even in the daylight.

For the fifty-five delegates to the Constitutional Convention who met in the State House that May, the climate—along with heavy woolen clothes and endless speeches—could only be endured. The young country desperately needed a workable government.

General Washington spoke for the entire convention when he wrote to James Madison: "No morn ever dawned more favorably than ours did; and no day was ever more clouded than the present! Wisdom and good examples are necessary at this time to rescue the political machine from the impending storm."

On September 17, with all their arguments, debates, compromises, and revisions—and most of their doubts—behind them, the Framers of the Constitution stood in line to sign the completed document. Willing hands helped Benjamin Franklin forward to add his signature; some said that the old man wept as he signed. Later, Madison reported that Franklin looked at the back of the chair Washington had occupied, on which a sun was painted, and said, "I have . . . often and often . . . looked at that behind the President without being able to tell whether it was rising or setting: But now at length I have the happiness to know that it is a rising and not a setting sun."

In the months that followed, the country discovered what the Framers of the Constitution had been doing during their secret sessions. Shock, rage, and dismay competed with approval and relief. Certainly, the differences between the Articles of Confederation and the Constitution were great—monstrous, some said. Opponents gathered under the banner of the Anti-Federalists and charged that the spirit of '75 had been destroyed. No one attacked the Constitution more sharply than Patrick Henry. Speaking of the document's authors, the Virginian commented acidly,

> Who authorized them to speak the language of "We, the People," instead of "We, the States"? . . . The people gave them no power to use their name. That they exceeded their power is perfectly clear. . . . Here is a revolution as radical as that which separated us from Great Britain. . . . It is said that eight States have adopted this plan. I declare that if twelve States and a half had adopted it, I would with manly firmness, and in spite of an erring world, reject it.

The Anti-Federalists thrust fiercely at the experimental nature of the new government-to-be. The notion of a Federal City and a national army aroused fear of 100,000 men being sent forth from the capital to enslave the people. Anger was easily aroused. Farmers hated the cities; the back country distrusted the seaboard; and the South feared the commercial power of the North.

Surprisingly, even with the opposition widely mobilized, sentiment gradually swung toward ratification. The noble figure of Washington, and the careful arguments of Madison and Hamilton, began to turn the tide of opinion. The *Federalist Papers*, calm and logical in their explanations, cooled passions. The promise of a bill of rights reassured many doubters. As Washington explained it, the substitution of "We, the People" for "We, the States" exactly summed up the heart of the Constitution:

> The power under the Constitution will always be in the people. It is intrusted for certain defined purposes, and for a certain limited period, to the representatives of their own choosing; and when it is executed contrary to their interests, or not agreeable to their wishes, their servants can and undoubtedly will be recalled.

Thomas Jefferson called the Constitution "the collected wisdom of our country." Time has proven the durability of that document, the oldest written constitution still in effect in the world today. Perhaps, like many other students, you have been asked to memorize the Preamble to the Constitution (see Figure 3.1). Within its single paragraph are contained the basic principles of American democracy. Memorizing it, however, means little unless you understand the meaning of those famous phrases. This chapter will examine the Preamble by considering the first six questions listed below, and then will go on to look at some of the other important constitutional concepts upon which the American system of government has been constructed. The questions to be answered in this chapter include:

1. How did the Constitution create "a more perfect union"?
2. What kind of system was set up to "establish justice"?
3. What is meant by "insuring domestic tranquility"?

The Pennſylvania Packet, *and Daily Advertiſer.*

[Price Four-Pence.]   W E D N E S D A Y, SEPTEMBER 19, 1787.   [No. 2690.]

W E, the People of the United States, in order to form a more perfect Union, eſtabliſh Juſtice, inſure domeſtic Tranquility, provide for the common Defence, promote the General Welfare, and ſecure the Bleſſings of Liberty to Ourſelves and our Poſterity, do ordain and eſtabliſh this Conſtitution for the United States of America.

A R T I C L E I.

Sect. 1. ALL legiſlative powers herein granted ſhall be veſted in a Congreſs of the United States, which ſhall conſiſt of a Senate and Houſe of Repreſentatives.

Sect. 2. The Houſe of Repreſentatives ſhall be compoſed of members choſen every ſecond year by the people of the ſeveral ſtates, and the electors in each ſtate ſhall have the qualifications requiſite for electors of the moſt numerous branch of the ſtate legiſlature.

No perſon ſhall be a repreſentative who ſhall not have attained to the age of twenty-five years, and been ſeven years a citizen of the United States, and who ſhall not, when elected, be an inhabitant of that ſtate in which he ſhall be choſen.

Repreſentatives and direct taxes ſhall be apportioned among the ſeveral ſtates which may be included within this Union, according to their reſpective numbers, which ſhall be determined by adding to the whole number of free perſons, including thoſe bound to ſervice for a term of years, and excluding Indians not taxed, three-fifths of all other perſons. The actual enumeration ſhall be made within three years after the firſt meeting of the Congreſs of the United States, and within every ſubſequent term of ten years, in ſuch manner as they ſhall by law direct. The number of repreſentatives ſhall not exceed one for every thirty thouſand, but each ſtate ſhall have at leaſt one repreſentative; and until ſuch enumeration ſhall be made, the ſtate of New-Hampſhire ſhall be entitled to chuſe three, Maſſachuſetts eight, Rhode-Iſland and Providence Plantations one, Connecticut five, New-York ſix, New-Jerſey four, Pennſylvania eight, Delaware one, Maryland ſix, Virginia ten, North-Carolina five, South-Carolina five, and Georgia three.

When vacancies happen in the repreſentation from any ſtate, the Executive authority thereof ſhall iſſue writs of election to fill ſuch vacancies.

The Houſe of Repreſentatives ſhall chuſe their Speaker and other officers; and ſhall have the ſole power of impeachment.

Sect. 3. The Senate of the United States ſhall be compoſed of two ſenators from each ſtate, choſen by the legiſlature thereof, for ſix years; and each ſenator ſhall have one vote.

Immediately after they ſhall be aſſembled in conſequence of the firſt election, they ſhall be divided as equally as may be into three claſſes. The ſeats of the ſenators of the firſt claſs ſhall be vacated at the expiration of the ſecond year, of the ſecond claſs at the expiration of the fourth year, and of the third claſs at the expiration of the ſixth year, ſo that one-third may be choſen every ſecond year; and if vacancies happen by reſignation, or otherwiſe, during the receſs of the Legiſlature of any ſtate, the Executive thereof may make temporary appointments until the next meeting of the Legiſlature, which ſhall then fill ſuch vacancies.

No perſon ſhall be a ſenator who ſhall not have attained to the age of thirty years, and been nine years a citizen of the United States, and who ſhall not, when elected, be an inhabitant of that ſtate for which he ſhall be choſen.

The Vice-Preſident of the United States ſhall be Preſident of the ſenate, but ſhall have no vote, unleſs they be equally divided.

The Senate ſhall chuſe their other officers, and alſo a Preſident pro tempore, in the abſence of the Vice-Preſident, or when he ſhall exerciſe the office of Preſident of the United States.

The Senate ſhall have the ſole power to try all impeachments. When ſitting for that purpoſe, they ſhall be on oath or affirmation. When the Preſident of the United States is tried, the Chief Juſtice ſhall preſide: And no perſon ſhall be convicted without the concurrence of two-thirds of the members preſent.

Judgment in caſes of impeachment ſhall not extend further than to removal from office, and diſqualification to hold and enjoy any office of honor, truſt or profit under the United States; but the party convicted ſhall nevertheleſs be liable and ſubject to indictment, trial, judgment and puniſhment, according to law.

Sect. 4. The times, places and manner of holding elections for ſenators and repreſentatives, ſhall be preſcribed in each ſtate by the legiſlature thereof; but the Congreſs may at any time by law make or alter ſuch regulations, except as to the places of chuſing Senators.

The Congreſs ſhall aſſemble at leaſt once in every year, and ſuch meeting ſhall be on the firſt Monday in December, unleſs they ſhall by law appoint a different day.

Sect. 5. Each houſe ſhall be the judge of the elections, returns and qualifications of its own members, and a majority of each ſhall conſtitute a quorum to do buſineſs; but a ſmaller number may adjourn from day to day, and may be authorized to compel the attendance of abſent members, in ſuch manner, and under ſuch penalties as each houſe may provide.

Each houſe may determine the rules of its proceedings, puniſh its members for diſorderly behaviour, and, with the concurrence of two-thirds, expel a member.

Each houſe ſhall keep a journal of its proceedings, and from time to time publiſh the ſame, excepting ſuch parts as may in their judgment require ſecrecy; and the yeas and nays of the members of either houſe on any queſtion ſhall, at the deſire of one-fifth of thoſe preſent, be entered on the journal.

Neither houſe, during the ſeſſion of Congreſs, ſhall, without the conſent of the other, adjourn for more than three days, nor to any other place than that in which the two houſes ſhall be ſitting.

Sect. 6. The ſenators and repreſentatives ſhall receive a compenſation for their ſervices, to be aſcertained by law, and paid out of the treaſury of the United States. They ſhall in all caſes, except treaſon, felony and breach of the peace, be privileged from arreſt during their attendance at the ſeſſion of their reſpective houſes, and in going to and returning from the ſame; and for any ſpeech or debate in either houſe, they ſhall not be queſtioned in any other place.

Figure 3.1
The first newspaper printing of the Constitution
Source: Historical Pictures Service, Inc.

4. How can the nation "provide for the common defense"?
5. How far should government go in "promoting the general welfare"?
6. How does government "secure the blessings of liberty" for the American people?
7. Why did the Framers provide for a separation of powers?
8. How does the system of checks and balances work?
9. What makes the Constitution a living, growing document?
10. What assumptions did the Framers start with in writing the Constitution?

How did the Constitution create "a more perfect union"?

A language purist might question the use of a phrase like "more perfect." If something is perfect, how can it be bettered? For the Framers of the Constitution, such a quibble seemed unimportant. The concept of union struck at the heart of the most critical problem created by the Articles of Confederation—the lack of a strong central government. (See Table 3.1 for a summary of the weaknesses corrected by the new Constitution.)

Table 3.1

The Constitution corrects the weaknesses
of the Articles of Confederation

Weaknesses of the Articles	How corrected by the Constitution
1. *No power to collect taxes.*	*Article I, Section 8, empowers Congress to "lay and collect taxes, duties, imports and excises."*
2. *No power over interstate and foreign commerce.*	*Article I, Section 8, gives Congress power to regulate commerce with foreign nations, among the several states, and with Indian tribes.*
3. *States were sovereign.*	*People of the whole nation were made sovereign. A federal union from which secession was impossible was created, and the federal Constitution and laws were made the supreme law of the land.*
4. *No independent executive.*	*Article II provides for President chosen indirectly by the voters. President is given "the executive power"; is made commander-in-chief of the Army and Navy; and may take all steps necessary to see that laws are faithfully executed.*
5. *No federal courts. Federal laws enforced by state courts.*	*Separate system of federal courts provided by Article III with authority to enforce federal laws and annul state laws inconsistent with federal Constitution or laws.*
6. *Congress an assembly of delegates who were chosen by state legislatures, were expected to vote as instructed, and could be recalled. Each state possessed a single vote.*	*Congress composed of representatives who have definite tenure and can act in any manner they choose. House of Representatives chosen by direct vote of people, Senate by state legislatures (now by direct popular vote).*
7. *Articles could be amended only by consent of all the states.*	*Constitution can be amended with approval of three-fourths of states.*
8. *Congress had only specifically delegated powers.*	*Congress given implied, as well as expressed, powers.*

Source: Adapted from John H. Ferguson and Dean E. McHenry, *The American System of Government* (New York: McGraw-Hill, 1973), p. 69. Copyright 1973 McGraw-Hill Book Company. Used with permission of McGraw-Hill Book Company.

FEDERAL SYSTEM ADOPTED

In May 1787, the original thirteen states were acting almost like independent countries. State legislatures passed their own commercial laws, regulated their own military forces, and jealously guarded their own sovereignty. If the new nation were to endure, the central government would need greater powers than those delegated under the Articles of Confederation. Out of the debates at Philadelphia came the answer: a federal government. Federalism would create a proper balance between the individual states and the national government. Under that concept, each level of government was made responsible for the things it could do best.

Several sections of the Constitution (and later amendments) spell out this allocation of powers. Most of the duties specifically delegated to the national government are contained in Article I, Section 8. Those responsibilities described in specific detail are called *expressed powers*. In addition, the Constitution specifies that Congress may make all laws "necessary and proper" to carry out the expressed powers. This "elastic clause" has been affirmed by court decisions and defined by long usage as the *implied powers* of Congress. Together the expressed and implied powers make up the total authority of the federal government. (See Chapter 4, pages 93–94, for further discussion of this important concept.)

FEDERAL–STATE RELATIONSHIP

Two of the Constitution's seven articles (IV and VI), as well as a number of amendments, deal with the relationship between the federal and state governments. Federal treaties and laws passed under the authority of the United States take priority over state laws. Judges in all state courts are bound by such laws, so that equal justice is assured in every state.

STATE–STATE RELATIONSHIP

Anxious to avoid the difficulties caused by the Articles of Confederation, the Framers ordered that each state should give "full faith and credit to the public acts, records, and judicial proceedings of every other state." A marriage in New York, for instance, must be recognized in Ohio; a corporation chartered in Iowa must be allowed to open an office in Oregon. Of course, both the married couple and the corporation must obey the laws of their new state.

Article IV, Section 2, states: "The citizens of each State shall be entitled to all privileges and immunities of citizens in the several States." Simply put, this means that a state may not discriminate against nonresidents, but must give them the full benefits of its laws. This provision does not prevent a state from charging out-of-state fees for use of tax-supported facilities; nor does it stop a state from establishing its own residency requirements for voting in local and state elections.

What kind of system was set up to "establish justice"?

The absence of a judicial system under the Articles of Confederation caused serious problems for the new nation. Although each colony had adopted the British tradition of justice—the common law, the presumption of innocence, and trial by jury—laws and courts varied widely from colony to colony.

COLONIAL COMPLAINTS

Colonial dissatisfaction with the court system helped bring about the Revolution. The British brought some cases to trial in Admiralty Courts, where juries were nc. used. For other crimes the defendants were forced to stand trial in Britain, where they could not benefit from sympathetic colonial juries. It was a challenge for the Constitutional Convention to devise a new system of courts that would calm the fears and gain the respect of the people.

NATIONAL JUDICIARY CREATED

The Framers solved the problem by establishing a national judiciary system (Article III). The Constitution specified only that the federal judiciary would be composed of a Supreme Court and lower federal courts. Congress was assigned the task of designing the lower courts as required to meet the needs of the country. The Judiciary Act of 1789 set up a nationwide system of district courts; in 1891 the federal courts of appeals were added to help cope with the growing tide of appeals to the Supreme Court. (Chapter 11 describes the structure and responsibilities of these courts.)

BILL OF RIGHTS

Most of the Framers believed that the limits on the federal government contained in the seven articles of the Constitution would adequately protect all the traditional freedoms of the American colonists. A people who had just fought a revolution to guarantee certain rights, however, demanded the safeguard of having those rights spelled out in the Constitution. By the end of Washington's first term, the ten amendments that make up the Bill of Rights had been added as promised. (Chapter 13 describes these freedoms in detail.) Furthermore, similar protections were written into the various state constitutions.

AMERICAN JUSTICE AT WORK

American justice depends upon the system itself, of course, but also upon the people who use it. Several key assumptions underlie the workings of the courts and the laws of the land: (1) all people are equal before the law; (2) every person is entitled to treatment that reflects individual dignity and value; and (3) every person accused of a crime is presumed to be innocent until proven guilty. Even with that solid foundation, the system of justice could not work without a widely held belief in the need to obey the laws, to support the work of the courts, and to participate in the making of good, just laws. The Prohibition experience of the 1920's— when the Eighteenth Amendment prohibiting the manufacture and sale of liquor was widely ignored—proves that laws work only when people are willing to accept and obey them.

What is meant by "insuring domestic tranquility"?

A fairly common experience these days begins when a large, noisy party spills into the street. Suddenly, out of the darkness comes the sound of a police bullhorn: "This is an unlawful assembly. You are disturbing the peace. Unless you leave the scene immediately, you will be arrested." The young people who receive these orders believe that their right to assemble peaceably has been violated. In effect, the teenagers' rights have come into conflict with the state's obligation to preserve the "domestic tranquility" for others.

PROTECTION AGAINST DOMESTIC DISTURBANCE

With every freedom comes an equal responsibility. The right of peaceable assembly does not include the right to trespass on other people's property or to disturb their rest. The Constitution requires that the President and his subordinate law enforcement officers ensure domestic peace; state constitutions contain similar provisions.

FEDERAL RESPONSES TO CIVIL DISORDER

Today, the federal government can take any number of actions when faced with civil unrest. The Federal Bureau of Investigation and Treasury agents can be called on to provide highly professional law enforcement services. If state authorities cannot handle a riot situation, the governor can ask for assistance from the National Guard or regular army troops. Federal marshals have been used to enforce civil rights legislation when local officials refused to act. Most disturbances, of course, require only the regular police forces of the city or state to protect the public and restore order.

Natural disasters—tornados, hurricanes, earthquakes, fires, and floods —also upset the domestic tranquility. State and federal governments provide assistance to the victims of such tragedies. Federal law allows the President to declare disaster areas, send emergency aid, and provide for low-interest reconstruction loans.

How can the nation "provide for the common defense"?

To provide for the common defense, the Constitution gives Congress the power to declare war, raise and support an army and navy, regulate the armed forces, and ratify foreign alliances. Muskets have given way to intercontinental missiles, and nuclear-powered submarines prowl where wooden ships once sailed. The United States, long secure behind its ocean barriers, now knows that a strong military establishment provides the most dependable deterrent to a third world war (see Figure 3.2). American Presidents, as commanders-in-chief, believe that national security is their single biggest responsibility. Today, because a nuclear attack could destroy our major cities and military bases on the first day of an all-out war, the price of liberty must be paid in the coin of eternal vigilance.

COSTS OF NATIONAL DEFENSE

Americans are not traditionally a militaristic people. Between wars, the military forces have often been nearly disbanded. In this day of ICBM's and worldwide military alliances, the United States can no longer afford that luxury. In the mid-1970's, a period of relative peace after Vietnam, the armed forces maintain a strength of more than 2 million men and women. The financial burden is also high. The national defense budget requested for 1982 was $188.8 billion—about $770 for every American.

COMPONENTS OF NATIONAL DEFENSE

Modern war, hot or cold, demands more of a country than soldiers in uniform. National defense also requires:

1. *National will.* This country's retreat from Vietnam came only after the American people demanded an end to the struggle there. An informed, patriotic population, proud of their country and its ideals, is the first requirement for an effective national defense. When people lose faith in their leaders, whether because of misguided national policies (many said Vietnam was the wrong war in the wrong place at the wrong time) or the propaganda efforts of their enemies, raw military strength means very little.

2. *Technology.* With technology moving ahead so rapidly, our weapons of today may be surpassed by those of our potential enemies tomorrow. Fortunately, the United States has the scientists, raw materials, facilities, and financial resources to support a vast program of research and development. Only adequate arms control and disarmament treaties with the communist world will enable us to divert resources now used for military purposes to more peaceful and productive ends.

3. *Foreign alliances.* The defense and well-being of the United States rest, at least in part, on access to raw materials and manufactured products obtained outside our borders. Without imports such as oil from Saudi Arabia, copper from Chile, aluminum ore from Jamaica, and electronic components from Japan, the nation's ability to defend itself would quickly decline, as would its high standard of living. This interdependence demands that the United States continue to build economic alliances with other countries.

The United States also needs military alliances. One country, no matter how powerful, cannot singlehandedly defend every corner of the globe—yet our political and economic interests stretch across every continent.

Figure 3.2
Obeying its constitutional mandate to "provide for the common defense," the U.S. government has spent billions of dollars to develop sophisticated weapons like this guided missile, displayed in an Armed Forces Day parade on New York's Fifth Avenue. Source: Wide World Photos.

Should global conflict begin, the United States must be able to rely on the combined military and economic strength of its allies. Our allies, in turn, expect that this country will honor its treaty obligations—even when those commitments are not popular with Congress or the American people.

How far should government go in "promoting the general welfare"?

When the Constitution was written, individual welfare was considered to be a private, local, or state responsibility. In this century, however, the federal government has taken an increasingly active role in "promoting the general welfare." Today, with the government spending ever greater sums for support of medical, educational, and economic needs, one of the country's most critical questions is this: How far should government go in promoting the general welfare of each individual citizen? How much is the nation willing to pay—in taxes and increased government regulation —for these services?

To some degree, the first part of that question has already been answered. Most Americans today look to the federal government as the primary force in maintaining the quality of life in the United States.

Every day, every individual has contact with government agencies; people's health, education, financial security, working conditions, and recreation all depend heavily upon the work of the men and women paid to serve us.

Table 3.2

What social welfare services cost the taxpayers

(In billions cf dollars)

	Old Age and Survivors Insurance	Disability Insurance	Federal Civil Service Retirement	Hospital Insurance	State Unemployment Insurance
1940	$ .6	—	$ .1	—	$ .9
1950	2.1	—	.7	—	1.1
1960	9.8	$ 1.0	1.5	—	2.2
1970	30.0	4.1	3.7	$ 4.9	2.6
1975	56.0	7.4	9.3	11.3	5.3
1980	97.6	16.8	19.5	23.5	11.9

Note: This chart does not list all government social programs. The costs of social welfare programs have increased from under five percent of the gross national product in 1945 to over twenty percent in 1980. Social welfare services now take more than three dollars out of every five collected by the national, state, and local governments.

Source: Table M–4, *Social Security Bulletin* (March 1981), p. 33.

COSTS OF GOVERNMENT SERVICES

A government that is constantly growing in size and influence costs more and more money. (See Table 3.2 for a look at how social services have increased in cost in just four decades.) The average taxpayer in the United States works two days out of five to pay for the services of local, state, and federal government. Of all the areas in the individual American's budget—food, housing, transportation, and the like—taxes have grown faster than any other. A progressive income tax system hits higher incomes more heavily than lower ones. In this way, the wealthy are forced to pay their fair share of the costs of government—unless they can find loopholes in the tax laws.

The cost of public services can also be measured in the increasing influence of the federal government on how Americans live. For example, federal agencies set standards for business activities, regulate working conditions and hours, and protect the environment; federal programs support scientific research, help students attend college, and share new knowledge with both industry and individual citizens. To keep this huge machine running, the government employs more people than any business or industry in the country.

ECONOMIC ASSISTANCE

In this century, "the general welfare" has come to include government economic assistance for those who cannot support themselves. Government welfare programs care for the aged, the handicapped, the unemployed, the poor, the hungry, the sick, the uneducated, and their dependent children. Fifty-one cents out of every federal budget dollar now goes to health, education, and welfare services.

Limits do exist, of course, on what government can do to provide for the general welfare. America's free enterprise system hinges on the idea that the great majority of citizens will provide adequately for themselves. When some people begin to believe that the government owes them a living, individual initiative is discouraged and other people must pay even heavier taxes. In time, the system could collapse of its own weight, with more money being paid out than taxation and borrowing can bring in.

Let's Review for a Moment

In a brief Preamble to the Constitution, the Framers summed up the objectives of American government:

> We, the People of the United States, in Order to form a more perfect Union, establish Justice, insure domestic Tranquility, provide for the common defence, promote the general Welfare, and secure the Blessings of Liberty to ourselves and our Posterity, do ordain and establish this Constitution for the United States of America.

How close has this country come to living up to those goals? Opinions differ, but a consensus might conclude that we've come a long way—but there's still a distance to go.

The Constitution attempted to form a "more perfect union" by establishing a federal system of government. Under that concept, the central government and the individual states share power. Washington has the right to do many things—the *expressed* and *implied powers*—but all other government powers are reserved to the states.

To "insure domestic tranquility," the government is obligated to use its powers to create an environment in which Americans can pursue their daily lives without fear of violence or sudden disaster. On the international level, costly investments in military forces, weapons systems, and research programs must be made in order to "provide for the common defense."

The meaning of "promoting the general welfare" has changed greatly since 1787. The American people today demand more and more services from their government. Some obvious ones are food stamps, Medicare, social security, veterans' benefits, rent subsidies, and environmental protection. Not everyone agrees, however, on how much the federal government should spend on social welfare programs. There's also the problem of government regulation. How much of that are we willing to accept?

Isn't there some conflict between government regulation and that same government's constitutional obligation to "secure the blessings of liberty"?

How does government "secure the blessings of liberty" for the American people?

The prevailing mood of the late 1960's was one of dedication to an expansion of individual liberty. "Do your own thing!" became the slogan of an entire generation. Actually, that spirit was not new to the American scene. Liberty has always captured the passionate attention of Americans; think of Patrick Henry's "Give me liberty or give me death!" and the clear-cut symbolism of the Statue of Liberty and the Liberty Bell.

LIBERTY IS NOT ABSOLUTE

An entire society benefits when its people are free to think and create, free to choose their own occupations, and free to move from one place to another. Too often, however, those who demand liberty for themselves refuse to extend it to others. The colonists who fought for their own freedom from Great Britain saw little reason to extend the full privileges of citizenship to all inhabitants—women, blacks, and Indians, for example. Most Americans now recognize the unfairness of this attitude and have come to think of freedom in relation to social interaction: liberty, they say, is the right to make one's own choices (of life style, occupation, and personal philosophy)—as long as those decisions do not interfere with the right of others to do the same.

To secure the blessings of liberty for the American people, the government has attempted to draw up a series of safeguards. Some of these protect the individual; others limit individual freedoms in order to promote the greater social good. A hermit living on a remote mountain need not worry about other people; a citizen of a heavily populated community must accept many limitations on behavior. Everyone who qualifies for a license has the right to drive a car. No one, however, has the right to drive that car so recklessly that it endangers others.

Surprisingly enough, most people would be uncomfortable if they had total freedom. History shows that the absence of social controls over individual actions can destroy a society. True freedom exists only when every citizen joins the government in acting for the common good.

LIBERTY VERSUS REGULATION

The United States now finds itself caught in a contradiction. On the one hand, the demand for government services grows stronger. On the other hand, many people want more personal freedom. As was noted earlier, with increased government services comes increased government regulation. People find themselves increasingly restricted in the way they run their businesses, the type of house they can build, and the percentage of their paycheck they can spend as they wish.

The dilemma can be seen in the national furor over the busing of children as a means of integrating schools. Is it right to bus children out of their neighborhoods to ensure equal educational opportunities? The nation is still attempting to balance individual liberties against the need for government regulation. The debate is likely to go on for a long time.

Why did the Framers provide for a separation of powers?

The eighteenth-century French philosopher Montesquieu (*MON-tes*-CUE) developed the political theory known as *separation of powers* in a paper called "On the Spirit of the Laws." What Montesquieu said, basically, was that when all power is concentrated in any single government body, tyranny is usually the result. Only when government is divided into separate bodies—executive and legislative, for example—can a people be assured that their political system will remain responsible, limited, and free.

THREE BRANCHES OF GOVERNMENT

Separation of powers was adopted by the First Continental Congress in the Declaration of Rights and Grievances of 1774. State constitutions written during the Revolutionary War also reflected the theory. When the Constitutional Convention assembled, Madison assured the delegates that separation of powers was "a fundamental principle of free government."

As a result of this view, the Constitution placed the power to make laws in the *legislative branch*, the power to enforce the laws in the *executive branch*, and the power to interpret the laws in the *judicial branch*. Critics have argued that only two powers of government are actually involved— policymaking and policy enforcement—with policy interpretation incidental. The American three-part division quickly proved itself effective, however, as the courts soon took on the task of declaring unconstitutional those laws which, when challenged, did not agree with the provisions of the Constitution.

SHIFTING POWERS OF THE THREE BRANCHES

The separation of powers described in the Constitution provides only a rough approximation of the way American government has actually developed. A number of power shifts have occurred, including:

1. The "imperial presidency." Ever since the administration of Franklin Roosevelt, some critics have charged that the modern presidency (the executive branch) has far outstripped the other two branches in its ability both to make and to carry out policy. They believe that in this "imperial presidency" the chief executive has become a kind of American

emperor. Following the unfortunate excesses of the Nixon administration, Congress began to try to restore the old balance, but not always with great success.

2. *The "fourth branch."* Congress has delegated more and more responsibility to independent regulatory agencies, which are sometimes called the "fourth branch" of government (see Chapter 10).

These agencies, such as the Interstate Commerce Commission and the Federal Communications Commission, exercise both legislative and judicial powers over business and private life. Yet their members do not run for election, and not even the President can order them to act.

3. *"Judicial legislation."* The courts have received their share of criticism, particularly for going beyond their task of interpreting the law. The phrase "judicial legislation" refers to attempts by the Supreme Court (particularly under Chief Justice Earl Warren in the 1950's and 1960's) to resolve social issues—school segregation, for example—through its decisions. Many people believe that under the Constitution, such matters should be settled by Congress through legislation.

How does the system of checks and balances work?

Montesquieu's philosophy also contributed the concept of *checks and balances* to the American political system. He believed that although the powers of government should be divided, they should also be so closely interrelated that no one branch would be truly independent of the other two. Because each branch checks, or limits, the powers of the other two, six basic relationships exist under this system (see Figure 3.3).

1. THE PRESIDENT CHECKS THE JUDICIARY

From the Supreme Court down to the district courts, all federal judges are appointed by the President. By choosing judges who reflect his own political philosophy, a President can influence the decisions of those courts for as many years as his appointees remain on the bench. It should be noted, however, that a President may not interfere with judges who are hearing a case. Supreme Court justices never confer with the President before handing down their decisions.

2. THE PRESIDENT CHECKS THE LEGISLATURE

The most dramatic move a President can make to check the actions of Congress is to veto a bill he dislikes (see Chapter 5). Other possible actions include (a) proposing his own legislation to Congress; (b) refusing to use powers delegated by Congress; (c) refusing to spend money appropriated by Congress; (d) influencing congressional elections through personal campaigning; (e) appealing directly to the people for support; and (f) calling special sessions of Congress. Only (a) and (f) are powers provided by the Constitution. The others are informal checks that have developed through usage—and have been subjected to criticism and even

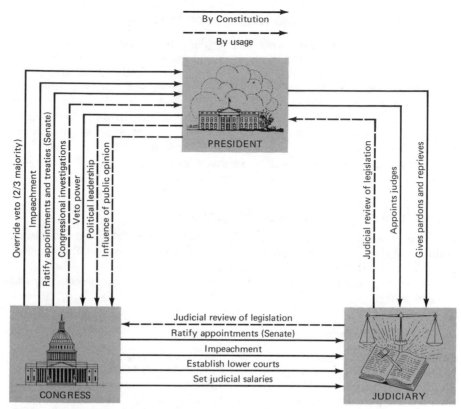

By Constitution

By usage

PRESIDENT

Override veto (2/3 majority)

Impeachment

Ratify appointments and treaties (Senate)

Congressional investigations

Veto power

Political leadership

Influence of public opinion

Judicial review of legislation

Appoints judges

Gives pardons and reprieves

CONGRESS

Judicial review of legislation

Ratify appointments (Senate)

Impeachment

Establish lower courts

Set judicial salaries

JUDICIARY

Figure 3.3
Checks and balances in American government

court tests. The Supreme Court ruled in early 1975, for example, that the Constitution does not give the President specific authority to "impound" funds appropriated by Congress (item c, above). Whether the President has the implied power to do so, however, remains open to court tests.

3. CONGRESS CHECKS THE JUDICIARY

Except for the Supreme Court, the entire federal court system was established by Congress—and could be abolished by Congress if it decided to do so. The Senate must approve the appointment of all federal judges. As a recent example, Congress voted to reject two Supreme Court nominees proposed by President Nixon. Congress also determines the salaries of all federal judges, but may not lower a judge's pay while he or she is on the bench. Congress has the power to impeach a judge whose judicial misconduct violates the public trust.

4. CONGRESS CHECKS THE PRESIDENT

Congress holds a major trump card in its relations with the President—the power of the purse. Only Congress can establish the budget for the executive branch; the yearly parade of administration officials going up to the

Capitol to explain their programs and to plead for more money testifies to the importance of this power. Even a presidential veto is not absolute; by a two-thirds vote of Congress, it may be overturned. Congress also plays a role in foreign policy through its powers to declare war, set limits on foreign aid, determine the size of the military, and (in the Senate) approve treaties. The Senate has the additional right of confirming presidential appointees—Cabinet members, ambassadors, members of commissions, and the like. As an ultimate check on the President, the Constitution gives the legislative branch the power to impeach all civil (nonmilitary) officials in the executive branch.

5. THE COURTS CHECK THE EXECUTIVE BRANCH

The power of *judicial review* gives the judiciary the right to examine all actions of the executive branch. An executive order or regulation that does not meet the test of constitutionality will be set aside by the courts By use of injunctions, federal judges may also forbid some actions and modify others.

6. THE COURTS CHECK THE LEGISLATIVE BRANCH

Judicial review also applies to all federal laws and to state laws that involve federal questions. The review process works slowly. Only after a plaintiff challenges a particular law may the courts take jurisdiction. A court test usually begins in the lower courts and works its way up to the Supreme Court in a series of appeals. Any federal court may declare a law unconstitutional; the decision stands unless appealed. Once a law has been found unconstitutional, it has no legal force anywhere in the United States or its possessions.

What makes the Constitution a living, growing document?

Written almost two hundred years ago, the Constitution has retained a remarkable vigor and freshness. Historian Charles Beard summed up its amazing ability to meet new challenges when he said, "The Constitution . . . is what living men and women think it is." But reaching agreement on what the Constitution is has not always been easy.

STRICT CONSTRUCTION AND LOOSE CONSTRUCTION

Early fears that the Constitution had created too strong a government led the courts to interpret it very strictly. This belief that only those powers specifically granted to the government by the Constitution are lawful is called *strict construction*. Jefferson and Madison led the strict constructionists during the first years of the new government. People who follow that point of view are labeled conservatives, no matter which political party they join.

Over the years, the strict constructionist viewpoint generally gave way to a belief that the federal government should use its implied powers under the Constitution to meet changing social and economic conditions. This *loose construction* of the Constitution led to increased federal authority in many areas of American life. Loose constructionists are called liberals. (In view of the shifts of political thought since the early years of the Republic, it should be remembered that a liberal of the 1800's would be considered extremely conservative today.)

The use of implied powers has enabled Congress to write and pass the laws a changing country needs. For the most part, the courts have accepted this; many court decisions since *McCulloch v. Maryland* (1819) have confirmed the loose constructionist viewpoint. In fact, fears of the strict constructionists that expanded federal regulation would mean lessened personal liberties have not been fully confirmed. Recent court decisions have emphasized the strengthening of individual freedoms against the power of the government (see Chapters 12 and 13).

BREVITY AND CLARITY

Another strength of the Constitution lies in its very brevity. State constitutions often run many hundreds of pages; the Constitution of the United States covers just a few pages and can be read in half an hour. In addition, the language is clear, direct, concise. The Framers did not use confusing phrases or unnecessary words.

Most constitutional questions have arisen because of what the writers left out, not what they put in. For example, the Constitution did not say whether a state could secede from the Union once it had joined. That crucial question helped lead the nation into the Civil War.

UNWRITTEN CONSTITUTION

Custom and usage have created a body of political traditions that form what might be called an *unwritten constitution*. Political parties, conventions, and primaries have been developed even though they are not mentioned anywhere in the Constitution. The President's Cabinet is not mentioned by name, nor is its structure described. When an outgoing President meets with a President-elect, no constitutional provision tells them how to ensure an orderly transition of power.

What assumptions did the Framers start with in writing the Constitution?

As this chapter has shown, the men who wrote the Constitution often rose above the political and economic beliefs of their day. Even so, the government they created took shape on the basis of four important assumptions.

1. CAPITALISM

The Founders believed deeply in capitalism. As Thomas Jefferson explained: "Agriculture, Manufacture, Commerce, and Navigation, the four pillars of our Prosperity, are the most thriving when left to individual Enterprise." Some historians early in this century tried to prove that the Constitution was therefore the work of wealthy men dedicated only to maintaining their own social and economic dominance; but the very flexibility of the government those men created refutes that charge.

Capitalism has grown and matured, and both government and business must now take as much responsibility for curing social ills as for adding up corporate profits. Alexander Hamilton, himself no lover of the common people, spoke to the critics in a way most Americans would still accept today: "It is by this [Constitution], in a great degree, that the rich and the powerful are to be restrained from enterprises against the common liberty."

2. STABILITY

The Framers were not, by today's standards, interested in a broadly based democracy. They attempted to keep the country stable by preserving the existing social values. The vote, they believed, could be entrusted only to those property owners who had a stake in good government. Still, the Constitution did not create a repressive system; the states were left free to define voter qualifications as they desired. Over the years, the American system has adapted well to the demands for greater popular participation in government.

3. OPTIMISM

American government assumes that people are basically rational creatures. Rational men and women, the Framers believed, will keep themselves well informed. They will be concerned about the well-being of both their country and their fellow citizens. The Constitution thus reflects the humanistic beliefs of the late eighteenth century, when optimism about the future of humanity ran high.

4. CHANGE

Even as they wrote the best Constitution they could, the Framers allowed for changes in it. Several methods of amending the basic document were included (see Figure 3.4).

1. An amendment may be proposed by a two-thirds vote in both houses of Congress, and then ratified by three-fourths of the state legislatures. Twenty-five out of twenty-six amendments have been enacted in this way.

2. An amendment may be proposed by a two-thirds vote in both houses of Congress, and then ratified by three-fourths of the states at special conventions called for that purpose. This procedure was used for the Twenty-first Amendment (repeal of Prohibition).

3. If two-thirds of the state legislatures request it, Congress can call a national constitutional convention to propose amendments. Approval by three-fourths of the state legislatures would ratify any amendments proposed by the convention (see Figure 3.5).

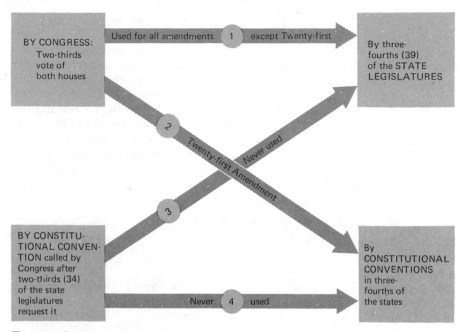

Proposal	When used	Ratification

BY CONGRESS: Two-thirds vote of both houses

Used for all amendments ① except Twenty-first

By three-fourths (39) of the STATE LEGISLATURES

② Twenty-first Amendment

Never used

BY CONSTITUTIONAL CONVENTION called by Congress after two-thirds (34) of the state legislatures request it

③

Never ④ used

By CONSTITUTIONAL CONVENTIONS in three-fourths of the states

Figure 3.4
How do you change the Constitution?
Four paths to amendment

4. A convention similar to that noted in method 3 may also propose amendments—these to be considered by individual state conventions. The amendment would become law if ratified by a three-fourths majority of the state conventions. The Constitution itself was ratified under a similar plan.

Figure 3.5
Should a new Constitutional Convention ever be called, no one knows what proposed amendments might come out of it. This cartoon sums up the worst fears—that a dangerous rewriting of the Constitution would result. Source: From *The Herblock Gallery* (Simon & Schuster, 1968).

Additional change has come from the courts and from Congress—a process sometimes called *informal amendment*. As specific problems arise, the legislature writes new laws to deal with them. As the final interpreter of the law, the Supreme Court often has the opportunity either to restrict or expand federal activities. One obvious example of this type of change has come in the field of civil rights. First, specific amendments to the Constitution helped free black people and guaranteed their basic rights. Later, congressional action extended those rights in specific areas, such as voting. And finally, the courts have ordered the President to provide for strict enforcement of Constitutional guarantees. In this way, all three branches of the federal government have been mobilized in support of the drive for racial equality.

$\mathbb{S}$UMMARY AND CONCLUSIONS

1. In the Preamble to the Constitution, the Framers outlined the basic goals of the new government:

a. *"Create a more perfect union."* By establishing a federal system of government, the Constitution eliminated the weaknesses of the Articles of Confederation. Powers—both expressed and implied—incorporated into the Constitution give Congress and the President the authority they need to govern effectively.

b. *"Establish justice."* The Constitution established a federal judiciary as an equal branch of government in order to ensure the just application of federal law to every American. The Bill of Rights was added to the Constitution in order to provide further specific guarantees of individual rights.

c. *"Insure domestic tranquility."* Limited police powers were written into the Constitution to ensure that government can protect its citizens from domestic disturbances. Since unrest often grows out of social and economic injustice, the government has also attempted to erase these underlying causes of disorder.

d. *"Provide for the common defense."* Despite the heavy costs in money and resources, the United States must maintain strong and alert defense forces. Essential components of this effort include (1) a strong national will, (2) advanced weapons technology, and (3) trustworthy foreign alliances.

e. *"Promote the general welfare."* Most Americans today look to the federal government for assistance in an increasing number of areas. "The general welfare" has come to mean care for the aged, disabled, young, unemployed—anyone who cannot escape poverty or illness without help. The cost of social welfare programs consumes over 50 percent of all government spending.

f. *"Secure the blessings of liberty."* With government services comes government regulation—of both individual and business life. The nation is presently attempting to find a way to balance personal liberties with the need to protect people from the ills and dangers of modern existence— crime, poverty, and an unhealthy environment.

2. The Framers adopted the theory of *separation of powers* in order to prevent any one branch of the government—*legislative, executive,* or *judicial*—from assuming tyrannical control. Some critics believe, however, that the presidency has grown so powerful as to overshadow the other two branches.

3. The idea of *checks and balances* gives each branch of government the responsibility of performing its own duties while also "checking" the activities of the others. For example, the President checks the legislature through the veto power and the judiciary through the power of appointment; the judicial branch exercises the power of *judicial review* over the actions of both Congress and the President; and Congress checks both of the other branches through its control of the federal budget and the power of impeachment.

4. The Constitution remains alive and flexible, thanks largely to what is known as *loose construction* of the powers given to the legislature. An unwritten constitution has also come into existence, made up of customs, practices, and institutions—the President's Cabinet, for example—that have proved workable.

5. Underlying the language of the Constitution are four assumptions held by the Framers: (a) the *capitalistic* system of private enterprise; (b) the preservation of traditional social values; (c) optimism regarding human society; and (d) allowance for amendments to the basic document.

6. Only twenty-six amendments have been added to the Constitution, despite the tremendous changes that have taken place in American society. Flexible, farsighted, and free of excess words and confusing phrases, the Constitution deserves its rank as the world's foremost written document of basic law.

REVIEW QUESTIONS AND ACTIVITIES

TERMS YOU SHOULD KNOW

checks and balances
executive branch
expressed powers
implied powers
informal amendment
judicial branch

judicial review
legislative branch
loose construction
separation of powers
strict construction
unwritten constitution

REVIEW QUESTIONS

The following multiple-choice questions are based on the important ideas presented in this chapter. Select the response that best completes each statement.

1. One state can refuse a family that has just moved there from another state (a) the right to vote in local elections until they have established residency. (b) the right to send their children to state-supported schools. (c) recognition of the legality of their marriage or divorce. (d) the right to run a business in the state if it competes with local businesses. (e) none of these matters can be regulated by a state.

2. Which of the following is *not* true about U.S. justice? (a) An individual is presumed innocent until proven guilty. (b) All people are equal before the law. (c) Every person must be treated with dignity and respect. (d) The law enforcement authorities cannot interfere with matters carried on in the privacy of one's own home. (e) The U.S. legal system allows change to meet new social standards and needs.

3. The largest single share of the federal budget goes toward (a) defense. (b) welfare. (c) government operations. (d) foreign aid. (e) interest on the national debt.

4. Increased government social services lead to (a) higher taxes. (b) more government regulation. (c) lessened individual initiative. (d) a bigger government bureaucracy. (e) all of these.

5. The average taxpayer works how many hours out of each forty-hour work week to pay for the services of local, state, and federal government? (a) Five. (b) Twelve. (c) Sixteen. (d) Twenty. (e) Twenty-four.

6. A useful definition of personal freedom would be the right to (a) make one's own decisions as long as those choices don't interfere with anyone else's rights. (b) do anything one wishes to do. (c) serve the government in the best way possible. (d) take orders without asking questions. (e) do anything one can afford to do.

7. The Constitution makes no provision for the independent regulatory agencies. In creating them, therefore, Congress used its (a) expressed powers. (b) implied powers. (c) veto override power. (d) strict construction approach. (e) power of the purse.

8. The President checks the actions of the legislative branch through the use of formal and informal powers, including (a) the veto. (b) public opinion. (c) influence over congressional election campaigns. (d) refusal to spend money appropriated by Congress. (e) all of these.

9. Once a court has declared a law unconstitutional, the legislative and executive branches (a) can ignore the court decision. (b) can fire the judges and appoint new ones who will agree with their position. (c) can punish the judges by lowering their salaries. (d) must accept the decision as final. (e) can make the law legal by asking the state legislatures to pass it as a state law.

10. Which of the following American traditions would be considered part of the unwritten constitution? (a) Restriction of the President to two terms. (b) Political parties and national conventions. (c) The vice-presidency. (d) Freedom of religion and speech. (e) System of checks and balances.

CONCEPT DEVELOPMENT

This chapter has explored a number of significant concepts relating to the U.S. Constitution. You can use your skills in thinking, researching, and writing to answer the following questions.

1. Imagine that you have been asked to establish a system of government that provides justice to all citizens. What features would you insist on in such a government?

2. What limits on individual liberties are necessary in a modern, urban society?

3. To what degree, if any, should our government put less emphasis on defense spending in favor of more spending for social welfare?

4. Explain the thinking behind our system of checks and balances. Why doesn't this system automatically cause government to come to a standstill, with each branch preventing the others from working?

5. Why did the Framers make the system for amending the Constitution so difficult? Has this complicated process prevented needed amendments from being ratified?

ACTIVITIES

The following activities are designed to help you use the ideas developed in the chapter.

1. The system of checks and balances is one of the keystones of our government. Make a poster or a bulletin board display that illustrates this concept. Figure 3.3 can serve as a guide, but use illustrations (either your own drawings or pictures clipped from magazines) to add interest. The finished display will serve as a quick and dramatic reminder of how this important process works.

2. Two useful books on the Constitutional Convention are Clinton Rossiter, *1787: The Grand Convention,* and Catherine Drinker Bowen, *Miracle at Philadelphia.* Using these books as sources, write a dramatic skit that focuses on one of the major issues faced by the convention. Some sample topics: federation vs. confederation; proportional representation; role of the executive; three-fifths compromise. Find volunteers to put the skit on for your class. (Remember that much of the work of the convention was done in the evenings, when delegates met to talk quietly and informally about the great decisions that lay before them.)

3. Write a short paper comparing the British parliamentary system with the American federal system in relation to the separation of powers. What advantages and disadvantages can you find in each? How have the British resolved the weaknesses in their system that the writers of the American Constitution saw and tried to avoid in 1787?

4. Amending the Constitution of the United States is a long, difficult process. You might find it easier—and interesting—to try your hand at amending the constitution of your student government. Begin by studying the student constitution carefully. How might it be improved? After deciding on appropriate amendments, check the procedure provided for change. With the help of your classmates, complete the necessary papers, organize a campaign, and bring the issue to an election. If you have chosen an area where change is truly needed, your chances of success will be quite high. But even if your amendment is not ratified, you will have experienced the excitement of a real campaign based on issues rather than personalities.

2

PRINCIPLES
OF THE
AMERICAN
LEGISLATIVE
SYSTEM

CHAPTER FOUR

THE ORGANIZATION
AND POWER OF CONGRESS

The newly elected congressman was arguing against the war. Speaking in the House of Representatives, he explained his position:

> When the war began, it was my opinion that all those who . . . could not conscientiously oppose the conduct of the President in the beginning of it because of knowing too much or too little . . . should nevertheless, as good citizens, remain silent on that point, at least till the war should be ended.

This implied criticism, however, was quickly answered by the President. His counterattack, full of partial truths, created a wave of protest against the young congressman in his home district. Political opponents quickly labeled him a traitor.

Undaunted, the congressman persisted: "The President should answer fully, fairly, and candidly. Let him answer with facts and not with arguments." If no explanation of why the country had gone to war was forthcoming, he went on, "then I shall be fully convinced of what I more than suspect already . . . that he feels the blood of this war, like the blood of Abel, crying to heaven against him."

Passionately, he charged that the President must have had some strong motivation for involving the two countries in a war, and that, "trusting to escape scrutiny by fixing the public gaze upon the exceeding brightness of military glory—that attractive rainbow that rises in showers of blood—

he plunged into it, and has swept on and on till, disappointed in his calculations . . . he now finds himself he knows not where."*

Was the young politician talking about the Vietnam conflict? No? Then it must have been the Korean War. Was the President Richard Nixon, or maybe Harry Truman? Those are logical guesses. But the year was 1848. The "enemy" was Mexico. The President under attack was James K. Polk. And the firebrand congressman was none other than Abraham Lincoln.

Opposition to an unpopular war is not unusual in our own era. Lincoln, however, paid a price for his speechmaking. After his term in the House of Representatives ended, his Illinois constituents quickly voted him and his party out of office.

Legally, though, Lincoln had taken his stand on firm constitutional grounds. The Framers of the Constitution gave Congress—not the President—the lawmaking power, including the right to declare war. What Lincoln and later generations of congressional critics of the executive have been exercising is their responsibility to supervise the conduct of government by the executive branch. Under the doctrine of separation of powers, the Constitution spelled out the role of Congress in great detail. More words are devoted to Congress than to the other two branches combined. Far-reaching powers and duties are assigned to legislators like the young Lincoln. With that in mind, you might expect to find answers to the following questions in this chapter:

1. What are the requirements for election to Congress?
2. Why do we have two houses of Congress?
3. What is the term of Congress?
4. How are congressional seats apportioned?
5. How is Congress organized?
6. How is the committee system organized?
7. What is the basis of congressional power?
8. What are the nonlegislative functions of Congress?
9. How has the power of Congress grown?
10. What does it mean to be a member of Congress?

What are the requirements for election to Congress?

As Lincoln's defeat and return to private law practice in 1849 demonstrates, a member of the House of Representatives serves only a two-year term. The entire membership of the House must face the home-district voters in a national election held in November of each even-numbered year.

By contrast, a senator serves a six-year term. Only one-third of the Senate membership stands for election at any one time. Perhaps the pro-

* Quoted in Carl Sandburg, *Abraham Lincoln: The Prairie Years* (New York: Harcourt Brace Jovanovich, 1926), pp. 367–68.

Table 4.1

Constitutional qualifications for election to Congress

Requirement	House of Representatives	Senate
Age	*Twenty-five years or older.*	*Thirty years or older.*
Citizenship	*Must have been a United States citizen for at least seven years.*	*Must have been a United States citizen for at least nine years.*
Residence	*Must be a resident of the state in which he or she is elected. By custom, he or she is also expected to live in the district he or she represents.*	*Must be a resident of the state he or she represents.*

vision for the longer Senate term grew out of a desire to make the Senate a continuing body, capable of giving stability and long-term direction to the legislative process.

QUALIFICATIONS FOR OFFICE

To run for Congress, a candidate must meet a number of qualifications specified by the Constitution. These basic requirements are outlined in Table 4.1.

NOMINATION AND ELECTION PROCEDURES

Candidates for Congress are normally selected by their political parties. Both Republicans and Democrats nominate their candidates in a variety of ways that differ from state to state. One state may use party nominating committees in each congressional district. Another may provide a state convention at which party officials select the candidates. Still other states have developed a primary election process that allows voters to choose their own candidates. Very few congressional candidates can afford to run without the financial and campaigning support of their party.

Both senators and representatives are now elected by all the voters of their states or districts. For most of our history, however, senators were elected indirectly by the legislatures of their home states. This practice did not end until the ratification of the Seventeenth Amendment in 1913. Should a senator resign or die, the governors of many states have the power to appoint a new senator to fill the vacancy until voters can make a new selection in a regular election. By contrast, special elections are usually called to fill vacancies in the House.

Why do we have two houses of Congress?

The Congress of the United States is *bicameral*—that is, composed of two houses. Several historical and practical reasons explain this division. The

British Parliament, with its House of Lords and House of Commons, gave the new country a model. Most of the colonial legislatures contained two houses, and by the time the newly independent Americans met to write the Constitution in 1787, almost all of the state legislatures were bicameral.

However, more pressing reasons than mere tradition led to the selection of a bicameral legislature: (1) A one-house legislature under the Continental Congresses and the Articles of Confederation had not worked well. (2) Several writers of the Constitution wanted the two-house lawmaking body as part of the system of checks and balances they were building into the Constitution. (3) The dispute over representation between the large and small states led to the Connecticut Compromise. As you saw in Chapter 2, each state gained equality in the Senate, with two members apiece; in exchange, the greater economic and political weight of the large states was recognized by basing the number of House members from each state on population.

Most critics believe that the bicameral system has worked well. A number of reasons can be listed in support of a bicameral Congress:

1. *Serves as a brake.* Because a bill must be approved by both houses meeting separately, hasty and unwise legislation can be more effectively prevented. (The passage of a bill into law is the subject of Chapter 5.)

2. *Prevents sectional legislation.* Sectional legislation favoring one region of the country (such as the heavily populated Northeast) can be prevented when such laws would act to the disadvantage of the rest of the country.

3. *Provides differing viewpoints.* Under this system the House, with its entire membership up for reelection every two years, considers itself the vehicle for enacting the immediate wishes of the people. The Senate, on the other hand, with the greater security afforded by its six-year terms, has the opportunity to examine legislation from a longer-range view. Whether or not this works in practice, however, has often been debated.

4. *Provides time for review.* The relatively slow progress of a new bill through two houses provides citizens and the communications media with ample opportunity to review and criticize a bill before it becomes law.

Critics of bicameralism, however, believe that the system often delays the passage of important legislation. They also point out that special interests are given too many chances to delay or defeat the bills they oppose. Despite such criticism, no serious effort has been made to revise the basic system in its almost two hundred years of use.

What is the term of Congress?

The *term of Congress* is the period during which each separate Congress remains in session between elections. Each Congress is numbered consecutively, and has a life span of two years. The first Congress convened in 1788; the Congress that met in January 1981 was the 97th.

Custom divides each term of Congress into two yearly *sessions*. Before

World War II, Congress stayed in session for only four or five months each year, but today's sessions last almost a full calendar year. This complicates matters for members of Congress who are running for reelection, for they must often leave Washington to return home to campaign.

A Congress may be recalled for a special session by the President, even though the regular session has ended and the members have scattered. President Truman used this constitutional power in 1948 when he recalled the legislators to consider a series of bills on education, health, and civil rights, but such sessions are not common.

How are congressional seats apportioned?

By law, the Congress of the United States contains 535 members—100 senators and 435 representatives. The Constitution does not fix the number of representatives; the original House met in 1789 with only sixty-five members. As the population grew, the membership increased to a size that threatened to make the House ineffective. After much debate, Congress passed the Reapportionment Act of 1929 fixing the permanent membership of the House at 435.

As a consequence, population growth has increased the number of people each member of the House represents. Today, each representative speaks for an average of nearly half a million citizens. The number of representatives (out of the 435) that each state sends to the House is determined by the ratio of the state's population to the national population as determined by the census. States with small populations are guaranteed at least one representative. Alaska, Delaware, So. Dakota, No. Dakota, Vermont, and Wyoming each send a single representative to Washington; by contrast, California sends forty-five. In 1978, Congress sent to the states a Constitutional amendment that would give Washington, D.C., full congressional representation (two senators and one representative) for the first time.

REAPPORTIONMENT

The population of the United States continues to grow. More importantly, it moves constantly, shifting from country to city and from state to state. Because of this, House seats are *reapportioned* (redistributed) every ten years following the census, the number for each state being based on the state's current population (see Figure 4.1 for recent changes in representation). The Bureau of the Census prepares the apportionment plan for the President, who forwards it to Congress for action. Unless Congress changes it, the plan becomes law after sixty days.

Each state then begins the tricky task of drawing the lines for its individual congressional districts. As you would imagine, many stormy political battles have developed over the ways in which these boundaries are drawn. Since the state legislature usually has this responsibility, the majority party tries to draw the district lines to favor its own members. This political self-interest has often resulted in the creation of oddly shaped districts in which the majority of voters are registered as members of the party in power—thus providing "safe" seats for the party's candidates. The majority party may also decide to "sacrifice" a district, drawing

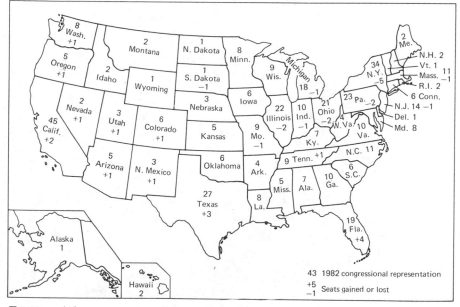

Figure 4.1

Changing patterns of congressional representation: aftermath of reapportionment based on the 1980 census

its boundaries so as to section off as many of the minority party's voters as possible (see Figure 4.2). The name given to this practice is *gerrymandering* (from the name of an early Massachusetts governor, Elbridge Gerry, and the shape of a county he had redistricted in such a way that it vaguely resembled a salamander).

"ONE MAN, ONE VOTE"

The United States Supreme Court ended gerrymandering in a far-reaching decision, *Wesberry v. Sanders*, in 1964. The Court cited the Constitution's "one man, one vote" philosophy, saying that the Framers intended that "as nearly as is practicable, one man's vote in a congressional election is to be worth as much as another's." To achieve this end, the Court demanded (1) that congressional districts be of a reasonably compact shape and (2) that each district in a state contain approximately the same number of people. The courts also reserved the right, under the doctrine of judicial review, to examine all reapportionment plans in order to keep the variations within allowable limits. Of course, this does not prevent a party in power from drawing up a state redistricting plan favorable to its own interests, but it does limit the excesses.

How is Congress organized?

As in any other organization, procedures have been set up within Congress to ensure that "the people's business" (as members of Congress like to call it) is conducted smoothly. The ongoing work of the legislature is supervised by officials of the two houses of Congress.

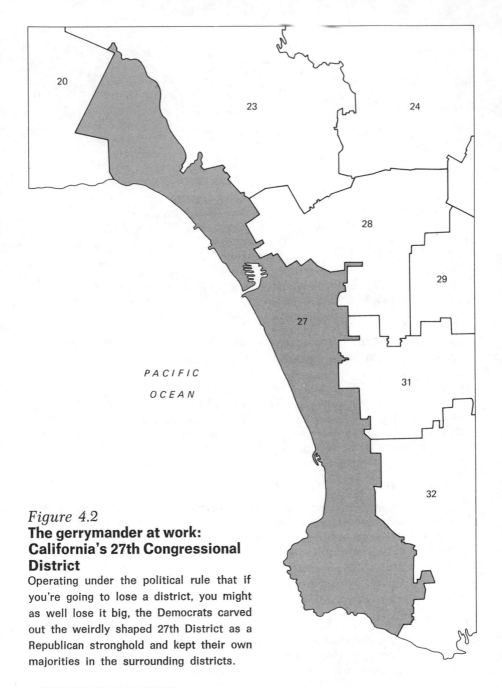

Figure 4.2
The gerrymander at work: California's 27th Congressional District
Operating under the political rule that if you're going to lose a district, you might as well lose it big, the Democrats carved out the weirdly shaped 27th District as a Republican stronghold and kept their own majorities in the surrounding districts.

SPEAKER OF THE HOUSE

The House of Representatives organizes itself under the leadership of a presiding officer known as the Speaker. Unlike the presiding officer of the Senate, the Speaker of the House has real political power. Although he no longer controls appointments to standing committees or decides singlehandedly which bills will reach the floor of the House to be voted on (as he did before the reforms of 1911), the Speaker still works from a position of strength:

1. *Power to recognize members.* The Speaker has the parliamentary authority to *recognize* representatives who wish to speak. Thus the Speaker may remain conveniently blind to an opposing representative, no matter how desperately that legislator signals that he or she wants the floor.

2. *Power to interpret House rules.* The Speaker also interprets and applies the rules of the House. This power enables the Speaker to (1) refer bills to favorable committees, (2) appoint special and conference committee members, and (3) delay or speed up the legislative calendar.

A candidate for Speaker is nominated and then elected at a special party conference, or *caucus*, held by the majority party in the House before a new session of Congress begins. The term of the Speaker runs for two years, the same as the term of the Congress in which he serves. The Speaker may take part in debate only by appointing a temporary presiding officer to fill the chair. He may also vote on any issue, but seldom does so except in the event of a tie. The Speaker stands second in line (behind the Vice President) for succession to the presidency.

PRESIDENT OF THE SENATE

The Vice President of the United States serves as the President of the Senate. This is one of the few specific tasks that the Constitution gives him. In practice, the Vice President delegates to a junior senator the responsibility for presiding over most Senate meetings. The Vice President may not take part in Senate debates, and votes only in the event of a tie.

The Senate also elects a *President pro tempore*, who presides in the absence of the Vice President or when the vice-presidency becomes vacant. The majority party in the Senate chooses one of its leading members for this position (though usually someone other than the party leader).

PARTY LEADERS

Each house has a *majority* and *minority party leader*. These floor leaders do not hold official constitutional positions. Rather, they are party officers who head *steering committees*, which supervise the handling of legislative business in each house—selecting bills for priority consideration, lining up support, overcoming parliamentary obstacles, and the like. Floor leadership positions go to members of Congress whose leadership abilities and powers of persuasion have been recognized by their fellow lawmakers.

The majority and minority party leaders work with the Speaker of the House and the President of the Senate to (1) manage debate on all business before the House or Senate; (2) coordinate the work of the congressional committees; (3) decide on allocation of debate time on the floor; (4) work with the Rules Committee chairman to move bills onto the floor; and (5) organize the party members for crucial votes when unity is essential.

Party whips assist the floor leaders in each house. The whips, usually selected by the party leader, act as assistant floor leaders to line up votes for or against a given bill. The whips must accurately sound out the voting sentiments of the party members. They must also be capable of adding the proper degree of persuasion (from polite debate to political arm-twisting) needed to hold the party position when a vote is taken.

OTHER OFFICIALS

Each house also requires the services of a staff of nonelected officials. These include a Sergeant-at-Arms (maintains order and organizes the security of the house), the legislative counsel (writes and reviews new bills), official reporters, parliamentarians, chaplains, and a number of lesser figures.

How is the committee system organized?

The flood of bills and other business that yearly sweeps over Congress has grown so heavy (a single energy bill submitted by the White House in 1975 ran to four hundred pages) that members cannot stay fully informed on every issue. Members of Congress also tend to become experts in one or two areas of legislation that especially interest them. For these reasons, committees handle the major portion of congressional business.

THREE TYPES OF COMMITTEES

Congressional committees divide into three major categories:

1. Standing committees. Most legislation is examined by standing committees (listed in Table 4.2 according to their relative importance). These permanent committees meet to study all new bills that fall into their special areas of authority, or to investigate matters of congressional concern. Where once the Congress staggered under the weight of eighty-one standing committees, the number has now been streamlined to forty-one —twenty-two in the House and nineteen in the Senate. Each standing committee usually divides itself into several subcommittees that deal with specialized matters within the jurisdiction of the full committee.

2. Special committees. When an unusual situation develops that cannot be handled by normal committee procedures, each house can create a special committee. These "select" committees exist only until their particular task has been accomplished—usually for less than a year. Members of the special committees are appointed by the Speaker of the House or by the President of the Senate. The Senate Select Committee on Intelligence Activities, formed in 1975 to investigate the Central Intelligence Agency, is an example of a special committee.

3. Conference committees. The House and Senate versions of the same bill frequently conflict in language and effect. When this happens, the congressional leadership appoints a temporary conference committee to work out the differences. Because the conference report must be accepted or rejected by the full Congress without further amendment, the committee plays a key role in deciding the final form a bill will take.

Table 4.2 **Standing committees of Congress, 1982**

Ranked by groups in relative order of importance

House of Representatives	Senate
Rules (16 members)	*Appropriations (29 members)*
Appropriations (55)	*Foreign Relations (17)*
Ways and Means (34)	*Finance (20)*
Armed Services (44)	*Armed Services (17)*
Judiciary (28)	*Judiciary (18)*
Agriculture (43)	*Agriculture, Nutrition, and*
Energy and Commerce (42)	*Forestry (17)*
Foreign Affairs (36)	*Commerce, Science, and*
Government Operations (39)	*Transportation (17)*
Banking, Finance, and Urban Affairs (46)	*Banking, Housing, and Urban Affairs (15)*
Budget (30)	*Budget (22)*
Education and Labor (34)	*Labor and Human Resources (16)*
Interior and Insular Affairs (42)	*Energy and Natural Resources (20)*
Science and Technology (40)	*Environment and Public Works (16)*
Public Works and Transportation (46)	
Post Office and Civil Service (26)	*Governmental Affairs (17)*
Merchant Marine and Fisheries (36)	*Veterans' Affairs (12)*
Veterans' Affairs (31)	*Rules and Administration (12)*
Small Business (40)	*Small Business (17)*
District of Columbia (12)	
House Administration (19)	
Standards of Official Conduct (12)	

MEMBERSHIP OF STANDING COMMITTEES

Senate rules allow senators to serve on a maximum of two major committees and one minor committee. House rules permit Democrats to serve on one major and one minor committee *or* two minor committees. House Republicans, with fewer seats to distribute, restrict themselves to a single major or two minor committees. Even with these rules, established by party caucus, exceptions occur. Some senators and representatives content themselves with a single major committee assignment, but a few members of the House hold as many as three committee seats.

In addition, each legislator sits on several subcommittees, some of which rank with full committees in importance. A legislator's committee assignments reflect (1) his or her personal interests; (2) the seniority (length of service) he or she holds in Congress; and (3) the congressional leadership's opinion of his or her abilities. Committee seats are divided between Democrats and Republicans in rough proportion to the strength of each party in the House or Senate as a whole.

The majority party always awards committee chairmanships to its own members. Traditionally, these key posts have gone to the senators or representatives who have the greatest seniority. In 1975, however, the Democratic party caucus voted not to return chairmanships to three senior members because these older conservatives did not reflect the more liberal

Figure 4.3
The work of congressional committees, though often overlooked, does occasionally make headlines. Here, the House Judiciary Committee debates articles of impeachment against President Richard Nixon in July 1974. Source: Wide World Photos.

views of the newly expanded Democratic majority. The revolt did not destroy the seniority system, but the congressional leadership was badly shaken by it.

COMMITTEE FUNCTIONS

Except for the Rules Committee in each house, the standing committees serve as tiny legislatures, each holding hearings on matters related to their area of authority. A bill establishing a new foreign aid program, for example, would be heard before the Senate Committee on Foreign Relations and the House Committee on Foreign Affairs.

Committees also deal with other matters. Many committee hearings take the form of investigations (see Figure 4.3). The information gathered during such sessions may (1) aid in the writing of new laws; (2) spotlight a social problem such as health care; or (3) provide insight into the activities of the executive and judicial branches. Recent hearings on pension problems, organized crime, and Watergate coverup activities have been widely publicized. Such committee investigations yield information necessary to the passage of appropriate legislation and to the proper conduct of government.

LET'S REVIEW FOR A MOMENT

Thus far you've learned some basic facts about Congress. You know that Congress is *bicameral*—divided into two houses. You also know that to run for either the Senate or the House of Representatives, you must meet certain minimum qualifications established by the Constitution, and that you must be elected by the voters of your state or district. If you're a representative, you'll serve for two years; a senator stays in office for six years. All states are equally represented by two senators, while the number of House seats a state receives depends on the size of its population.

Now, as a new member of Congress, to whom would you look for leadership? If you're in the House, the *Speaker* runs the show, while the *Vice President* of the United States presides over the Senate. *Majority* and *minority leaders* and their assistants (the party *whips*) see to the daily flow of business through the two houses.

The various *standing committees* allow Congress to cope with the overload of legislative, investigative, and general supervisory responsibilities given it by law. Can you choose your own committee? Well, you can ask for an assignment, but the congressional leadership has the final voice in such matters. As a new representative from Iowa, you would likely ask for assignment to the Agriculture Committee—but don't be surprised if you find yourself on Merchant Marine and Fisheries. Your *standing committee* will probably be divided into *subcommittees*, so complex are the issues that face Congress. If a "hot" political debate develops, you might be appointed to a *special committee* formed just to investigate that issue. Senior members usually serve on the *conference committees*, which iron out the differences in the bills passed independently by the House and Senate.

Now let's take a closer look at the actual legislative powers of Congress.

What is the basis of congressional power?

One of the earliest political controversies in this country developed between people who supported Alexander Hamilton and those who backed Thomas Jefferson. The question centered on the extent of congressional power. The Hamiltonians formed the Federalist party, which believed in a liberal or *loose construction* of the Constitution. The Jeffersonians (later known as the Democratic-Republicans) stood for a *strict construction*.

A strict interpretation meant that the government—particularly the Congress—was limited to those activities specifically spelled out in the Constitution. Loose constructionists, on the other hand, insisted that the intentions as well as the words of the Constitution's writers should be considered. They also believed that the government could exercise whatever authority was necessary in carrying out the specific powers established by the Constitution. History has seen the victory of the liberal interpretation, with the result that few areas of our national life today escape governmental influence.

EXPRESSED AND IMPLIED POWERS

Congressional powers are either *expressed* (specifically named in Article I, Section 8 of the Constitution) or *implied* (reasonably justifiable as necessary to carry out constitutional duties). Another name for expressed powers is *delegated powers*; a list of them can be found in the box on page 94.

Powers delegated to Congress
by Article I, Section 8 of the Constitution

1. To lay and collect taxes, duties, imposts, and excises for the purpose of paying the debts and providing for the common defense and general welfare of the United States.
2. To borrow money.
3. To regulate foreign and interstate commerce.
4. To formulate rules for bankruptcies and naturalization.
5. To coin money and set standards of weights and measures.
6. To punish counterfeiting.
7. To establish post offices and post roads.
8. To grant copyrights and patents.
9. To set up federal courts below the Supreme Court.
10. To punish piracy and offenses against the law of nations.
11. To declare war.
12. To raise and support armies.
13. To provide and maintain a navy.
14. To enact a code of military law.
15. To call out the national militia.
16. To regulate, arm, and discipline the militia.
17. To govern the District of Columbia.
18. To make all laws necessary and proper for carrying out the foregoing powers (the "elastic clause").

The expressed powers of Congress cover a broad area of governmental control. Congress sets tax rates and regulates interstate commerce. Not only does the legislative branch authorize the spending of our money, it also has the power to borrow it back again. Congress also regulates bankruptcy, oversees the postal system, controls the patent and copyright system, governs territories of the United States, establishes federal courts, declares war, and shares with the President the conduct of foreign affairs.

The battle over the implied powers began as early as 1790. In that year, Hamilton proposed a Bank of the United States to regulate the nation's currency. The Federalists found the constitutional authority they needed to establish such a bank in Article I, Section 8, Clause 18, the *necessary and proper*" clause. This "elastic clause" states that "The Congress shall have power . . . to make all laws which shall be necessary and proper for carrying into execution the foregoing powers . . . ." Congress itself determines what is "necessary and proper" in the course of writing the laws—but such legislation is subject to judicial review by the courts. The Supreme Court confirmed the concept of implied powers in its *McCulloch v. Maryland* decision in 1819 (see Chapter 12).

Expressed powers of a similarly broad nature are the war, judicial, and police powers of Congress.

War powers. During the Vietnam conflict of the 1960's, Congress became concerned that its power to declare war had been taken over by the President. The power to declare war thus clashed with the power of the President, as commander-in-chief of the armed services, to wage war. Congress partially resolved that debate recently by passing legislation that requires the President to gain congressional approval of any emergency military action within ninety days. The President's ability to commit U.S. armed forces to "brushfire" wars has thus been severely limited. In addition, congressional control of the yearly military budget still gives the legislative branch final authority over United States involvement in foreign wars. In 1981, for example, the Reagan administration wished to sell high-technology, airborne-radar planes (AWACS) to Saudi Arabia. The Senate approved the sale, but it took a major effort by the President to line up the necessary votes.

Judicial and police powers. The judicial powers of Congress include the right (1) to establish federal courts; (2) to define federal offenses and prescribe punishments; and (3) to impeach and remove federal officials guilty of violating their oath of office. Laws passed to promote public health, safety, and welfare are part of the police power of Congress. Although the United States does not have a national police force, the Justice Department and the Department of the Treasury provide special marshals and agents to protect the public interest when federal laws are violated.

LIMITS ON CONGRESSIONAL POWER

The elastic clause does not give Congress unlimited power. Restrictions on legislative authority appear at several points in the Constitution. Eight of these *forbidden powers* are listed in Article I, Section 9, and are also included in the Bill of Rights.

In case these limitations should prove insufficient, the Tenth Amendment states that "The powers not delegated to the United States by the Constitution, nor prohibited by it to the States, are reserved to the States respectively, or to the people." Despite this *reserve clause*, however, the federal government's growth in size and power has been steady throughout U.S. history.

What are the nonlegislative functions of Congress?

The complexities of modern life, combined with the increasing size of government itself, have given the federal lawmakers more and more nonlegislative functions.

INVESTIGATION

The House and Senate committees, or their special subcommittees, often investigate (1) the need for new laws; (2) scandalous events or behavior contrary to the public interest; or even (3) the changing patterns of American life. Ever since the Civil War, Congress has kept close watch over the executive branch's conduct of the country's wars. Also, more recently, changes in the organization and methods of the nation's intelligence-gathering agencies came about as a result of such investigations.

During an investigative hearing, the committee summons witnesses to testify under oath. This resemblance to a courtroom trial is misleading, however. Congress never hands down a verdict, nor does it pass sentence. If shortcomings are uncovered, a new law must be written to correct them. Law enforcement agencies may be called in to deal with violations of criminal or civil codes. Public opinion can also be mobilized by such hearings. This educational aspect of congressional hearings has become increasingly important.

SEATING AND CONFIRMATION

Congress possesses final authority over the seating of its own members. The House and Senate use this power most frequently when (1) election results are contested and cannot be resolved at the state level; (2) a member of Congress is accused of improper conduct in office.

More importantly, the Senate must approve White House appointments at many levels. This confirmation process affects officials as varied as the members of the President's Cabinet, federal judges, ambassadors, and the heads of independent agencies such as the Interstate Commerce Commission. This process gives Congress a voice in the selection of the people who interpret and administer our laws.

A nominated official testifies under oath before the appropriate Senate committee. The committee probes the nominee's political philosophy, personal finances, and administrative ability. If the Senate does not approve the nomination—or often if the President foresees an embarrassingly close vote—the candidate's name will be withdrawn.

CONSTITUTIONAL AMENDMENT

Congress plays a key role in amending the Constitution. Any proposed change in that basic law, such as the recent Equal Rights Amendment, must pass both houses by a two-thirds vote before being sent to the states for approval. Three-fourths of the states (thirty-eight in all) must ratify the amendment in their own legislatures before the new law can be put into effect. Congress often sets a time limit for state ratification; if the amendment is not approved in the required number of years, the proposal dies.

If two-thirds of the state legislatures request it, Congress has the power to call a *constitutional convention* to consider further amendments. This situation has never developed, but if it should, Congress has no legal obligation to call the convention. Not even the Supreme Court could make the legislature act if it decided not to do so.

IMPEACHMENT

The House of Representatives possesses one judicial power, that of impeachment of federal officials. This power is rarely employed: articles of impeachment have been voted only a dozen or so times in two hundred years. Americans often forget that impeachment is similar to court indictment; it means only that sufficient evidence exists to justify prosecution of the accused. The trial itself takes place in the Senate. Only four impeached officials, all federal judges, have actually been convicted. and removed from office. The House, of course, also has the constitutional power to impeach the President.

How has the power of Congress grown?

The growth of the influence of Congress can be traced to two important powers given it by the Constitution: (1) *the power to tax* and (2) *the power to regulate interstate commerce.* After their experience with the Continental Congress and the Articles of Confederation, the writers of the Constitution realized the weakness of a national government lacking such powers. Their response to this problem can be read in the first three provisions of Article I, Section 8 (see the box on page 94.)

THROUGH THE POWER TO TAX

American citizens have developed an expanded concept of what government should do for them. They want economic security as well as military security. They insist on old-age benefits, unemployment insurance, health care, and a thousand other services unknown in 1789. The greatly inflated federal budget necessary to pay for these costly services must come, ultimately, from the pockets of the taxpayers themselves.

Today, the federal government collects in taxes approximately twenty-five cents out of every dollar earned by businesses and private citizens. Although Americans pay a large variety of taxes (see Chapter 6), income taxes are the major source of federal dollars. Made possible by the Sixteenth Amendment in 1913, the income tax laws give the government a share of every paycheck, dividend, and capital gain.

With the power to collect money, of course, comes the power to spend it. Even though the President recommends the yearly federal budget, Congress can add a new program (a national health care plan, for example), then raise the money to pay for it by levying new taxes. In other areas, such as defense, it is often the President who pushes for increased spending. (Chapter 6 deals more specifically with how the federal budget affects national life.)

THROUGH THE POWER TO REGULATE INTERSTATE COMMERCE

Congress has enacted many laws that govern the conditions under which both businesses and private individuals live and work. Whether you dig coal, drive a truck, publish a newspaper, or telephone a friend, your activities have been influenced by Congress.

The development of the American transportation system in the nineteenth century brought more and more goods into interstate commerce. Gradually, not only the articles themselves, but the means of transporting and trading them came under regulation. A far-reaching court decision in 1824, *Gibbons v. Ogden*, firmly established federal control of commerce.

It has only been in the second half of this century, however, that

Congress has applied this power to such social issues as racial discrimination. What happens in a small lunchroom in Louisiana, for example, may seem to have little to do with interstate commerce. But the courts have generally agreed that Congress has the authority to force such businesses not to discriminate. The key to this decision lies in the fact that the supplies purchased by even the smallest businesses involve them in interstate commerce.

The interstate commerce regulatory power has also been used against monopolies and other combinations that limit competition. This kind of regulation is intended to protect American prosperity, which has been built on the free flow of goods, services, and people across state lines. Even though the nature of interstate commerce has changed to include air travel and telecommunications, the regulatory powers of Congress remain intact.

LIMITS ON THESE POWERS

Despite what many taxpayers might believe, there are limitations on the power to tax and to regulate commerce. Congress may not tax exports, for example, nor may taxes be levied upon organized religions. Although the Constitution guarantees free passage of goods across state lines, health and safety factors sometimes restrict such movement. This is particularly true of raw agricultural products and dangerous chemicals.

What does it mean to be a member of Congress?

Everyone knows that the duty of a member of Congress is to vote to make new laws. That's true, but a member of Congress is much more than a lawmaker.

SERVICE TO CONSTITUENTS

What do you do if you're upset about pollution, foreign aid, or the new interstate highway? Don't wait—write your senators and representative! After all, you and your community sent them to Washington as personal representatives. They can provide information about any phase of government, its actions or its inactions. Moreover, when enough people make known their opinions about important issues, legislators begin to take action.

What does all this mean? It means, simply, that every member of Congress has a duty to serve as the voice of his or her constituents in Washington. Through that voice, the will of the voters gains expression on a national level, whether the issue affects one person or the entire country.

THE LEGISLATOR'S DILEMMA

Despite this apparently clear-cut mission, the members of Congress face a constant dilemma. When the Clerk of the House or Senate calls for their votes, they must each make a moral decision. Which of the many interests tugging at them should they follow? Their party may demand that they vote one way, while their district or state may want an opposite vote. They may know what will be the most popular decision, but such a stand may violate their own conscience. Whatever the decision, it will be sure to offend someone.

REWARDS AND PRIVILEGES

Members of Congress receive a number of rewards and privileges, outlined in Table 4.3. In addition, election to Congress can be a stepping stone to higher office—perhaps to a governorship or even to the presidency. To encourage freedom of debate, members of Congress may not be sued for what they say in the halls of Congress. They may not be arrested while on congressional business—though this normally amounts to little more than immunity from traffic tickets.

Members of Congress are not paid by the hour. No regulations require their presence on the floor of Congress, or even in Washington, for any specific number of days. Many legends tell about absentee lawmakers who spend long weeks on Bermuda beaches or who run off on junkets to Hong

Table 4.3

Salary and privileges of a member of Congress, 1981

Category	Benefit
Salary	$60,662.50 *(taxable) plus cost-of-living increases.*
Expenses	$40,000 *(taxable).*
Travel	$3,000 *allowance for trips between his or her home and the capital; use of government transport on official business.*
Publications	*Free publication and distribution of his or her speeches and other materials.* *Free copies of the* Congressional Record*: 34 House, 50 Senate.*
Mailing	*Free postage for official mail (known as the franking privilege).*
Offices	*Fully equipped office in House or Senate Office Building.* *One office in home state for a senator, up to three in home district for a representative.*
Staff	*Generous allowance for secretarial assistance and an administrative assistant.*
Communications	*Allowance for stationery and telegrams, plus $6,000 for long-distance telephone calls.*
Pension	*Generous pension after minimum qualifying service in Congress.*
Tax benefits	*Tax exemption based on need to maintain a home in Washington, if occupied less than six months a year.*
Miscellaneous	*Free hospitalization, low-cost personal services (gym, barber, cafeteria, etc.).*

Kong. All members of Congress, however, must divide their time among committee work, service to their home districts, speeches to special-interest groups, and other official business. At election time, members of Congress must be away from Washington for many days at a time while campaigning. For all these reasons, most absences from the floor of Congress are reasonable and expected.

SUMMARY AND CONCLUSIONS

1. The United States Congress is the lawmaking branch of our government. The Constitution spells out its powers and limitations in greater detail than for any other branch. Both the House of Representatives and the Senate are democratically elected, with two-year terms in the House and six-year terms in the Senate. A two-house (*bicameral*) legislature allows new legislation to be considered without unwise haste. Bicameralism also allows representation for the general population (House) and the individual state (Senate).

2. Congress sits for a two-year term, divided into two annual sessions. One hundred senators, two from each state, sit in the upper chamber. The 435 members of the House of Representatives are chosen from individual districts. House districts are reapportioned every ten years, after the national census has determined what shifts in population have taken place.

3. Each house elects a *majority* and *minority leader*, along with other party officials who organize and schedule the work load of Congress. The Constitution provides for a *Speaker of the House* as presiding officer, and custom awards this post to the majority party. The Vice President of the United States serves as *President of the Senate*, but has little real influence except in cases of a tie vote.

4. *Standing committees* and their *subcommittees* perform most of the legislative work done in Congress. Members of Congress receive assignment to these committees, as well as to *special committees*, on the basis of the relative strength of the major political parties. Chairmen are usually selected on the basis of their seniority. Committees hold hearings on new legislation, and also hold investigative hearings when necessary. *Conference committees* meet to iron out differences when the two houses pass different versions of the same bill.

5. Congress operates under a liberal construction of the Constitution, which has given it wide powers. The three main sources of congressional power derive from Article I, Section 8, and include (1) the "elastic clause" of the Constitution, (2) the power to tax, and (3) the power to regulate interstate commerce. In addition, Congress carries out nonlegislative functions, such as confirmation of presidential appointments, investigations, and impeachment proceedings.

6. The pay and privileges given to members of Congress reflect the important role Congress plays in the governing of this country. Our federal

system has seen the presidency emerge as a major force in government. The executive branch, however, can still be checked by Congress, because the legislative branch determines how the billions of dollars collected in taxes will be spent. Congress continues to play a major balancing role in the U.S. system of government—just as planned by the Framers of the Constitution in 1789.

REVIEW QUESTIONS AND ACTIVITIES

TERMS YOU SHOULD KNOW

bicameralism

caucus

conference committee

confirmation process

constitutional convention

elastic clause

expressed powers

forbidden powers

gerrymandering

impeachment

implied powers

judicial powers

loose construction

majority leader

minority leader

"necessary and proper" clause

"one man, one vote"

police powers

party whip

power to recognize

power to regulate interstate commerce

power to tax

President pro tempore

reapportionment

reserve clause

session of Congress

Speaker

special committee

standing committee

steering committee

strict construction

subcommittee

term of Congress

war powers

REVIEW QUESTIONS

The following multiple-choice questions are based on the important ideas presented in this chapter. Select the response that best completes each statement.

1. The Constitution requires that _____ of the membership of the House of Representatives stand for election every two years. (a) one-third. (b) one-half. (c) two-thirds. (d) three-quarters. (e) all.

2. Bicameralism was chosen as the principle for the United States Congress because (a) the British Parliament set the example. (b) one-house legislatures under the Continental Congress and the Articles of Confederation had not proven successful. (c) there was a need to resolve the conflict between the small and large states. (d) colonial legislatures had been bicameral. (e) all of these.

3. Reapportionment serves the necessary purpose of (a) assigning congressional seats according to the wealth of a state. (b) setting the

boundaries of individual congressional districts. (c) rewarding the states that voted for the President in the previous election. (d) assigning seats in the House of Representatives according to changing population patterns. (e) none of these.

4. The "one man, one vote" philosophy would tend to prevent (a) a rural congressional district being drawn the same size as a city district. (b) politicians from "selling out" to special interests. (c) the reelection of the same member of Congress year after year. (d) favored districts from receiving more than their share of defense contracts or federal construction grants. (e) members of Congress from raising their own salaries.

5. The major portion of congressional business is handled (a) by debate on the floor of Congress. (b) through closed-door conferences between White House representatives and the members of Congress. (c) by special investigative committees. (d) by the thirty-six standing committees of the House and Senate. (e) by consultation with the President and his Cabinet.

6. The "elastic clause" in the Constitution has been used to (a) establish the presidency as the dominant branch of government. (b) hold Congress to a strict construction of the Constitution. (c) give Congress the power to make whatever laws are necessary to carry out its responsibilities. (d) allow Congress to increase the national debt. (e) give Congress the power to impeach.

7. The power of Congress to declare war is (a) an expressed power. (b) an implied power. (c) a judicial power. (d) a forbidden power. (e) a reserve power.

8. The confirmation process allows the Senate to (a) propose amendments to the Constitution. (b) sit as a jury to hear charges of impeachment brought by the House. (c) set up investigative committees to probe national problems. (d) judge the abilities of many of the President's appointees to public office. (e) accept or reject the President's yearly budget.

9. Out of every dollar earned by the average citizen, the federal government's share is about (a) ten cents. (b) twenty-five cents. (c) fifty cents. (d) seventy-five cents. (e) ninety cents.

10. *Not* a reward or privilege of a member of Congress is (a) free postage for official mail. (b) travel allowances while on government business. (c) allowances for maintaining an office and staff. (d) tax-free salary and expense account. (e) free hospitalization.

CONCEPT DEVELOPMENT

This chapter has explored a number of significant concepts relating to the organization and power of Congress. You can use your skills in thinking, researching, and writing to answer the following questions.

1. How does one become a member of Congress? Summarize the qualifications required by the Constitution, and the steps that lead to election. Why is the criticism often heard that "only the rich need apply" for election to Congress today?

2. Why do individual representatives or senators need party organizations to help them turn their ideas into legislation?

3. Why does Congress place so much emphasis on the committee system? What changes would you make in it?

4. Are there any limits on the ability of Congress today to pass needed legislation and to fulfill its constitutional duty to check the actions of the executive branch?

5. How has Congress utilized the loose construction of the Constitution? Use the power to tax and the power to regulate interstate commerce as examples to support your argument.

ACTIVITIES

The following activities are designed to help you use the ideas developed in the chapter.

1. Organize a panel discussion or debate on the topic, "Congress should return to a strict construction of the Constitution." Let each side present its argument, then let the class determine whether it would accept the consequences of this decision.

2. Prepare a research report to be given to the class comparing the British parliamentary system with our own Congress. Point out the strengths and weaknesses of each. You'll probably discover that British politicians are envious of our committee system. Why do you think that might be true?

3. Write to your representative or senator and ask for a copy of his or her daily schedule for several weeks. After analyzing it, prepare a chart showing the percentage of time he or she spent on various official duties. Do you feel that he or she is making appropriate and efficient use of time?

4. If this is an election year, invite several local candidates for congressional office—or their campaign managers—to speak to your class. Be prepared to question the speakers on such matters as the candidates' political philosophies, their appraisals of the role of Congress, and their opinions on specific issues that you're interested in.

5. Survey a hundred people at a local shopping center. Ask them (a) to identify their representative and at least one of their two senators, and (b) whether they voted in the last congressional election. Present the results to the class, along with your interpretation of the data.

CHAPTER FIVE

⊞OW LAWS ARE MADE: THE CONGRESS AT WORK

Have you ever argued with a company over a mail-order record that was damaged in the mail? Or perhaps you've wrestled with a traffic bureau clerk who couldn't admit to making an error. Whatever the case, you likely ended up gritting your teeth and muttering, "There ought to be a law!"

Your dilemma, of course, lies in the slow and awkward process by which public concern becomes public law. A 1962 study of abuses in company pension systems, for instance, was not translated into law until 1974. Given a serious emergency, however, the legislative process can occasionally be geared for quick action.

Such was the case in March of 1933, when the shadow of the Great Depression lay dark upon the land. As incoming President Franklin Roosevelt prepared to take his oath of office, some 15 million Americans were unemployed. Wall Street was in panic. Militant farmers fought to prevent the loss of their land through foreclosure. Many banks faced ruin as nervous depositors elbowed each other in their haste to withdraw their savings. By Inauguration Day, a large number of banks had been closed, and others were open only part-time. Despite the optimistic note that Roosevelt struck in his inaugural address—"The only thing we have to fear is fear itself"—the new President knew that he must take positive legislative action to save the banking system from complete collapse.

Given only five days head start, the new Secretary of the Treasury hurriedly drafted an emergency banking bill. Meanwhile, the new President declared a nationwide bank holiday. During this time, all banks were closed to prevent panic withdrawals. The holiday also gave bankers a chance to reassure the public as to the safety of their savings. The country relaxed and caught its breath. A message from the President was waiting for the new Congress when it convened on March 9: "I cannot too strongly urge upon the Congress the clear necessity for immediate action." The legislators needed little urging.

In the House, while newly elected representatives scrambled to find their seats, the Speaker read the text of the emergency bill from the one available draft. Debate was limited to forty minutes, and even before that time had elapsed, the House had shouted the bill through without a roll call. A similar mood prevailed in the Senate. Unwilling to wait for printed copies, the Senate leadership substituted the House version. Despite some heated debate, the bill passed without amendment by a vote of 73 to 7.

By 8:30 that evening, the Emergency Banking Act of 1933 lay on the President's desk. The entire process, from introduction to signature, had taken less than eight hours.

Congress, to be sure, seldom acts with such speed. Of the approximately 20,000 bills and resolutions introduced during each session of Congress, only a handful receive such treatment. As you read this chapter about the deliberate and complex process by which bills normally become law, you will find answers to these basic questions:

1. Who originates new bills?
2. What is the role of congressional committee staffs?
3. What is the role of the lobbyist?
4. What happens when a bill is introduced?
5. What happens when a bill goes before a committee?
6. What is the special role of the House Rules Committee?
7. What happens when a bill reaches the floor?
8. How do the House and Senate iron out their differences?
9. What choices does a President have when a bill reaches his desk?

Who originates new bills?

A proposed new law is called a *bill*. Only a member of Congress can formally introduce a bill for consideration by the House or Senate. Legislators and their staffs may write the bill themselves, or they may be given an already written bill and asked to introduce it by a private individual or special-interest group, by the administration, or by a congressional committee (see Table 5.1).

PREPARING A BILL FOR DEBATE

Many corporations, labor unions, and other special-interest groups retain specialists who write proposed legislation. The Library of Congress provides a Legislative Reference Service for members of Congress who need assistance in researching and writing their bills. Each house of Congress maintains a legislative counsel for the same purpose.

Congressional committees further examine new bills with the help of professional consultants. Committee members also modify the language

Table 5.1

Where bills originate

Source of bills	Description of procedure
Private individuals and special-interest groups	*The largest number of bills are written by these groups, then given to individual members of Congress for introduction. The proposed legislation is intended to promote the cause of the person or group proposing it.*
The administration (the White House and other agencies of the executive branch)	*The executive branch suggests laws and regulations that will assist it in carrying out its constitutional and legislatively ordered responsibilities.*
Congress	*Individual members of Congress write legislation in their areas of specialization and concern. The bills may be introduced on behalf of constituents, or they may reflect the legislator's own assessment of national needs.*
Congressional committees	*A committee or subcommittee, with the aid of its staff, may initiate legislation aimed at solving specific problems uncovered during committee hearings and investigations.*

of bills during their meetings. It is a rare bill indeed that moves on to final enactment without being altered in the process.

As Figure 5.1 illustrates, each line of a bill is numbered so that specific lines can be referred to while the bill is being read, studied, and debated. Copies of all bills, printed by the Government Printing Office (GPO), are available to senators and representatives, their staffs, and the general public.

What is the role of congressional committee staffs?

Each day, by the time members of Congress have attended their committee meetings, greeted their constituents, dealt with their mail, and answered the roll-call bell, they and their personal staffs have little time left for evaluating the flood of bills that come before the House and Senate. Only in this century have funds been provided for professional staffs to serve the *standing committees*. Since every bill must pass through one or more standing committees before it can reach the floor of either house, the value of these often invisible staff members is readily apparent.

MAKEUP OF THE STAFFS

Since 1946, each standing committee has been assigned a minimum of four staff members (including a staff director) and six clerks. The largest and busiest committees, such as the Foreign Relations Committee, require much larger staffs. Without such trained personnel, Congress would be

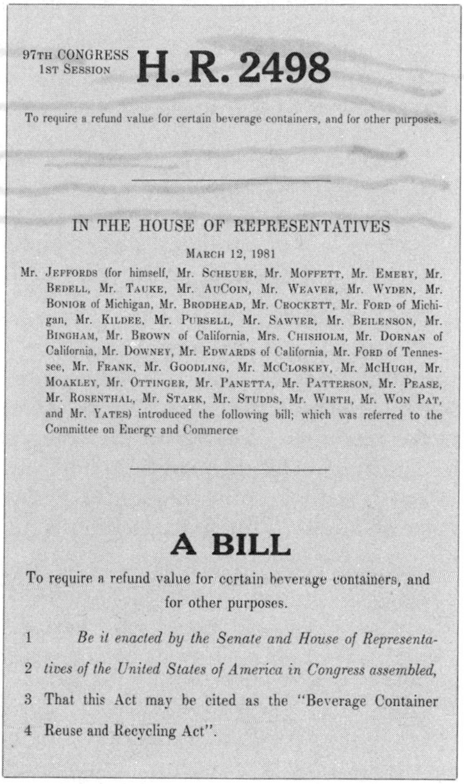
97TH CONGRESS
1ST SESSION
H. R. 2498

To require a refund value for certain beverage containers, and for other purposes.

IN THE HOUSE OF REPRESENTATIVES

MARCH 12, 1981

Mr. JEFFORDS (for himself, Mr. SCHEUER, Mr. MOFFETT, Mr. EMERY, Mr. BEDELL, Mr. TAUKE, Mr. AUCOIN, Mr. WEAVER, Mr. WYDEN, Mr. BONIOR of Michigan, Mr. BRODHEAD, Mr. CROCKETT, Mr. FORD of Michigan, Mr. KILDEE, Mr. PURSELL, Mr. SAWYER, Mr. BEILENSON, Mr. BINGHAM, Mr. BROWN of California, Mrs. CHISHOLM, Mr. DORNAN of California, Mr. DOWNEY, Mr. EDWARDS of California, Mr. FORD of Tennessee, Mr. FRANK, Mr. GOODLING, Mr. MCCLOSKEY, Mr. MCHUGH, Mr. MOAKLEY, Mr. OTTINGER, Mr. PANETTA, Mr. PATTERSON, Mr. PEASE, Mr. ROSENTHAL, Mr. STARK, Mr. STUDDS, Mr. WIRTH, Mr. WON PAT, and Mr. YATES) introduced the following bill; which was referred to the Committee on Energy and Commerce

A BILL

To require a refund value for certain beverage containers, and for other purposes.

Be it enacted by the Senate and House of Representatives of the United States of America in Congress assembled, That this Act may be cited as the "Beverage Container Reuse and Recycling Act".

Figure 5.1
Title page of a typical bill

Would a national law requiring that beverages be sold in refundable cans and bottles cut down on litter and save natural resources? The sponsors of H.R. 2498 thought so, but the bill never became a law.

forced to rely even more heavily on the executive branch for research and evaluation of proposed legislation. Many observers believe, however, that Congress is still understaffed.

The majority party appoints most staff members. According to law, appointment to committee staffs must now be made without regard to political affiliation. Not all committees have become nonpartisan, however, a fact that often leads to political bickering and high staff turnover.

FUNCTIONS OF THE STAFFS

Congressional committee staffs do not establish policy, nor do they initiate legislation. These duties are reserved to the individual members of Congress and to the committees on which they serve. Staff functions, therefore, can be organized under four main headings:

1. *Research.* Staff members collect the data needed by their congressional committees. The Library of Congress, with its huge research facilities, is a prime source of information.

2. *Drafting of bills.* Staff members provide technical writing skills essential to the preparation of legislation. They cooperate in this duty with the Office of Legislative Counsel.

3. *Investigation.* Staff members plan the public hearings that are such an important part of the legislative process. Their investigative role in

these hearings includes (a) interviewing witnesses, (b) assessing the statements of those who testify, and (c) generally doing the legwork that the members of Congress cannot do for themselves.

4. *Expertise.* Staff experts provide the committee with technical analyses of complex matters such as taxation and the budget, new defense projects, and the status of older, ongoing projects such as foreign aid. If staff expertise is not sufficient, specialists from the executive agencies, the universities, business, or organized labor may be called in for consultation on a temporary basis.

The staff director supervises day-to-day staff operations. In addition, the staff director works with the committee chairman to plan committee work, interpret the committee's wishes to the other staff members, and make recommendations to the committee on the basis of studies prepared by the staff. The director also deals with government officials and special-interest groups that frequently besiege the committee with requests for favorable action on matters of special concern to them.

What is the role of the lobbyist?

Americans are persistent joiners of special-interest groups. When any of these groups exerts pressure on Congress (or on other levels of government) for or against legislation, it is called a *pressure group* or *lobby.*

The strongest pressure groups are those which seek to advance a particular economic interest. Lobbyists paid to represent business and professional organizations, labor unions, and farmers' groups can always be found in the halls of Congress. A Teamsters Union lobbyist, of course, does not speak for all of organized labor, nor does an American Medical Association lobbyist represent all doctors.

LOBBYISTS AT WORK

Competent lobbyists push for exceptions, exemptions, subsidies, and other favored treatment for their clients. The lobbyists' role can be summarized as follows:

1. *Drafting of new legislation.* Lobbyists provide expert assistance in drafting bills favorable to their groups' interests. These bills are sometimes labeled as being introduced "by request of" a particular special-interest group.

2. *Expert testimony.* As recognized experts in their special fields, lobbyists may be called to testify before committees considering legislation that affects their clients.

3. *Application of pressure.* Using techniques that have great political effectiveness, lobbyists work to influence debate and voting at each stage of the legislative process. The lobbyists' influence may be felt during initial hearings or in the give-and-take of House and Senate debate. Beaten

in Congress, lobbyists will not give up. By putting pressure on the President, they can still hope to secure a veto that will prevent the bill from becoming law.

LOBBYING TECHNIQUES

The methods lobbyists use to influence legislation are varied:

1. Communications. Letter-writing campaigns, personal visits, telephone calls, and similar communications are used to keep members of Congress informed about the wishes of the lobby.

2. Campaign contributions. "Money is the mother's milk of politics," the saying goes. Lobbyists know where to find contributions to aid friendly lawmakers. Their assistance can take the form of money, campaign work, or personal services.

3. Social contacts. Entertainment has always been a major lobbying technique. Parties, dinners, and "nights on the town" help cement the friendships and obligations that are the stock-in-trade of the lobbyist.

4. Sanctions. Uncooperative members of Congress may find themselves deprived of campaign contributions or facing unexpected opposition at the polls in the next election.

5. Demonstrations. Heavy pressures may be brought to bear through marches and picket lines. Bizarre activities such as the dumping of surplus milk and the slaughter of calves (done to dramatize the low income of farmers) force Congress to pay attention to the needs of particular pressure groups.

6. Formation of alliances. Lobbyists representing different interests may join forces to create an impression of widespread strength in support of or opposition to a particular bill.

Even with all these techniques, however, most lobbyists believe that their most effective weapon is personal contact with members of Congress (see Figure 5.2). In pursuit of this goal, lobbyists must be more than glad-handing distributors of gifts and services. They must cultivate an expertise in their particular fields that makes their opinion valuable. The success of a lobby also depends on its size, prestige, cohesiveness, leadership skills, and financial resources.

IS *LOBBYIST* A BAD WORD?

In U.S. politics, the term *lobbyist* has often been associated with phrases like "corrupt politicians" and "influence-peddling." Whenever a scandal breaks that involves an unethical lobbyist and a weak-willed legislator, lobbying comes under renewed attack. Many examples of corruption have occurred, of course, but the instances we read about in the newspapers do not represent the great majority of lobbying activities.

Clever lobbyists, in fact, do not need to "buy" votes. They know that

Figure 5.2
Lobbyist Clarence Mitchell was the director of the Washington bureau of the NAACP and was sometimes called "the 101st senator" because of his long and active devotion to his cause. He is shown speaking at a press conference called to announce an NAACP lawsuit to block cutbacks in funding for the federal food stamp program. Source: Wide World Photos.

members of Congress from areas with particular economic interests—such as a wheat-growing state or a heavy-industry region—must reflect the wishes of those growers, workers, and factory owners if they want to remain in office. Lobbyists simply arrange for a steady flow of mail, personal visits, and research data to the members of Congress who make up these economic *blocs*—for example, the farm bloc or the steel bloc.

Because blocs often cut across party lines, the lobbyists' task is further simplified. When a vote on a major farm bill is pending, for example, they see to it that all farm bloc lawmakers know how their voters back home feel about the legislation. Then, when election time comes, lobbyists may, within legal limits, assist cooperative politicians with money, facilities, and expert workers for their campaigns.

What happens when a bill is introduced?

Once a bill has been drafted, its introduction into the legislative process is relatively simple. Each draft of proposed legislation is tagged with an identifying number. If introduced in the House of Representatives, it might be called H.R. 1776 (bills are numbered in order of introduction). The Senate version of the same bill might be known as S. 85.

RESOLUTIONS

If a bill merely states the views or opinions of one house, or calls upon the executive branch for information, it is known as a *resolution*. A resolution agreed upon by both houses is called a *joint resolution*, requires the signature of the President, and has the force of law. Both houses may pass a *concurrent resolution* without the President's approval, but these do not carry the weight of law. Concurrent resolutions are used primarily to announce formal decisions, such as setting a date for adjournment or launching a joint investigation.

PROCEDURE FOR INTRODUCING A BILL

In the House, the bill is signed by the representative who is introducing it and dropped into the "hopper" (a box on the desk of the Clerk of the House). A clerk assigns it a number, registers it in the House *Journal*, and sends it to the Government Printing Office. Within a few days, that efficient operation prints enough copies for each member of Congress as well as for other interested agencies and individuals. Senate bills are introduced orally, during the "morning hour"—which lasts from noon until 2:00 P.M.

Major bills are often introduced simultaneously in the House and Senate. In this way, committee work can begin without a delay for the full procedure to take place in the other house.

Printing the number and title of a bill in the *Congressional Record* and the *Journal* technically satisfies the requirement for a *first reading*. This step serves notice on interested parties that legislation which might concern them is under consideration.

REFERRAL TO COMMITTEE

After the introduction and first reading, the bill is almost automatically referred to the appropriate committee. At one time, the Speaker of the House held enormous power through his right to decide which committee would receive a particular bill. If one committee was known to oppose such legislation and another to favor it, the Speaker could ensure its burial or enhance its chance of passage through his choice of committee. Since 1946, committee jurisdiction has been more precisely defined, and assignment of bills is now a routine function of legislative clerks.

LET'S REVIEW FOR A MOMENT

Suppose you believe that there should be a law bringing computers under public control. The first step is to draft a *bill* proposing your new legislation. Writing a bill can be a problem, however. How do you translate everyday language into legislative language? How can you be sure that your new law doesn't conflict with other, existing laws? The legislative experts on the committee staffs of Congress may help—or a special-interest group can provide assistance.

The big step, of course, is finding a sponsor who will introduce your draft bill in the Senate or House of Representatives. In addition to obtaining the cooperation of your senator or representative, you can enlist the help of a *lobbyist* in getting congressional support for your bill. While many people view lobbyists with suspicion, they play a useful role in the complex process of writing, screening, and passing legislation.

Congratulations! Your bill has been introduced and numbered, has received its *first reading*, and has been referred to the appropriate committee. How important is the work of the committee? Let's find out.

What happens when a bill
goes before a committee?

Once a bill is referred to the proper committee, there is no guarantee that it won't die a quick death right there. The legislative process described graphically in Figure 5.3 can take place only after committee (or sub-committee) chairmen decide to schedule *hearings* on a bill. If chairmen believe that a bill does not merit serious consideration, they may quietly "pigeonhole" it—set it aside indefinitely. This action may be influenced by (1) their own evaluation of the bill, (2) the criticism received from interested lobbyists, or (3) the wishes of other committee members.

On the other hand, if hearings are scheduled, a bill will usually receive careful attention. Whether a chairman actively supports the legislation or is only responding to pressure from others, a hearing provides a forum in which to publicize the bill. For the bill's sponsors, this is the time to gather the votes needed to move it out of committee and onto the floor, where it can be considered by the full Senate or House.

THE HEARING PROCESS

A hearing serves primarily as an information-gathering procedure. This fact has sometimes been misunderstood by the American public. The courtroom-like setting, the practice of hearing testimony under oath, and the sharp exchanges between committee members and witnesses often give hearings the appearance of a trial.

Exactly because a hearing is not a courtroom process, balanced judgments may not be heard. Committee members may select only witnesses who will support their own prejudices for or against the bill. Despite this, it is during the hearings that the general public—as well as the ever-present pressure groups—have the most obvious chance to debate the value—or danger—of pending bills.

Legally, all hearings must be open to the public unless the committee votes to move the meeting behind closed doors. In recent years, about one out of three hearings has been closed to the public. Sensitive matters of appropriations and national security are most often heard in secret.

The chairman, with the help of committee staff, schedules the witnesses and sets the time and duration of the meetings. Because most members of Congress belong to several committees, only the most important hearings are fully attended. A typical day's schedule of hearings, as published in the local Washington newspapers, may be seen in Figure 5.4. Witnesses appearing at these hearings usually read a prepared statement before submitting to questioning by those committee members present. A hearing may last only a few hours if the bill is a minor one. On the other hand, hearings on foreign aid bills, which are often complex and controversial, may drag out over several months.

A verbatim record of the hearings is kept, although committee members may edit their remarks before the report on the hearing is printed. The report, which may run to hundreds of pages, is distributed by the GPO to

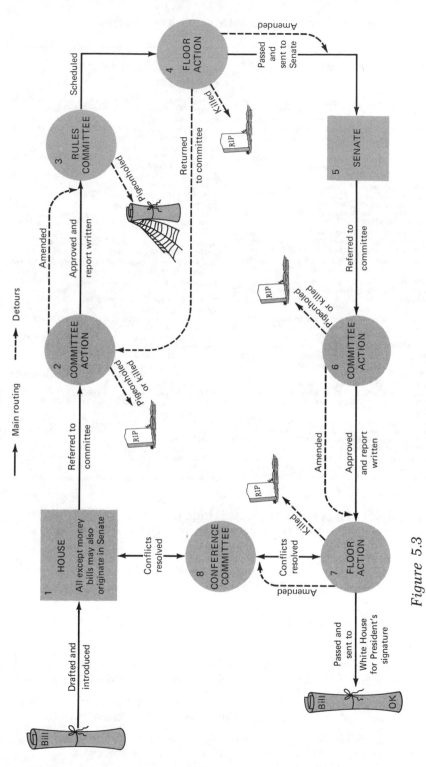

Figure 5.3
The perilous journey of a bill through the U.S. Congress

Senate	House
Meets at 9:30 a.m.	Meets at 10 a.m.
Committees:	Committees:
Appropriations—10 a.m. Open. Mark up leg. appropriating funds for FY82 for the Depts. of Labor, HHS, and Education. 1114 Dirksen Office Building.	**Appropriations**—10:30 a.m. Open. Foreign operations subc. On AID revised budget for FY82 H-302 Capitol.
Armed Services—10 a.m. Open. Testimony on strategic modernization. Sec. of Defense Weinberger. 1318 DOB.	**Appropriations**—2 p.m. Open. Military construction subc. Hrng. on budget revisions & strategic programs. Defense Sec. Weinberger. 2362 RHOB.
Budget—10 a.m. Open. Continue mark-up of proposed second concurrent resl. on the congressional budget for FY82. 6202 DOB.	**Armed Services**—10 a.m. Open (may close). Invest. subc. On progress of Army tank program. 2337 Rayburn House Office Building.
Commerce, Science, and Transportation—9 a.m. Open. Hrng. on leg. requiring a refund value for certain beverage containers, and prohibiting the sale of metal beverage containers with detachable openings. 235 Russell Office Building.	**Armed Services**—10 a.m. Open. Mil. personnel & comp. subc. hrng. on benefits for the former spouse of a military retiree. 2118 RHOB.
Energy and Natural Resources—9 a.m. Open. Oversight hrng. on implementation of Title I of the Natural Gas Policy Act of 1978. 3110 DOB.	**Banking, Finance & Urban Affairs**—9:30 a.m. Open. Intl. trade., invest. & monetary policy subs. Cont. oversight hrngs. on U.S. intl. monetary policies. 2222 RHB.
Environment and Public Works—10 a.m. Open. Mark up amendments to Clean Air Act. 1202 DOB.	**Banking, Finance and Urban Affairs**—10 a.m. Open. Mark-up pending legislation. 2128 RHOB.
Government Affairs—9 a.m. Open. Resume hrngs. to examine the DOD's acquisition process for new major weapons systems and other goods and services. 3302 DOB.	**Budget**—11 a.m. Open. Continue budget. 210 Cannon House Office Building.
Governmental Affairs intergov. relations subc.—10 a.m. Open. Hrng. on state implementation of block grant programs and to examine the impact of further budget reductions of state and local govts. 318 ROB.	**Education & Labor**—9:30 a.m. Open. Jnt. hrng.: elem. secondary & voc. edu. subc. and postsecondary edu. subc. On Educational Testing Act. 2175 RHOB.
Judiciary juvenile justice subc.—9:30 a.m. Open. Oversight hrng. on the exploitation of children. 6226 DOB.	**Education & Labor**—10 a.m. Open. Labor-management rel. subc. On proposed Labor Dept. regulations on the Service Contract Act. 2261 RHOB.
Judiciary Constitution subc.—9:30 a.m. Open. Cont. hrngs. on amending the Constitution to est. leg. authority in the Congress and the states with respect to abortion. 2228 DOB.	**Energy & Commerce**—9:45 a.m. Open. Health & environ. subc. Cont. hrngs. on Clean Air Act: Chlorofluorocarbon provisions. 2322 RHOB.
Veterans Affairs—9:30 a.m. Open. Hrng. on VA Dept. of Medicine and Surgery's implementation of the OMB's circular providing for the contracting out of certain govt services. 412 ROB.	**Energy & Commerce**—9:30 a.m. Open. Fossil & synthetic fuels subc. Mark-up Emergency Petroleum Allocation Act. 2123 RHOB.
Conferees—10 a.m. & 2 p.m. Open. Leg. auth funds for FY82-85 for commodity price support programs	**Foreign Affairs**—9:30 a.m. Open. Intl. operations subc. Hrng. on consular oversight. 2200 RHOB.
	Foreign Affairs—10:30 a.m. Open. Jnt. hrng.: Europe & Mid. East and human rights & intl. organ. subcs. Hrng. on implementation of human rights policy. 2172 RHOB.
	Foreign Affairs—2 p.m. Open. Inter-American aff. subc. Mark-up negotiated settlement in El Salvador. 2255 RHOB.

Figure 5.4
A partial list of a typical day's hearings in Congress
Source: "Today in Congress," Washington *Post*, Nov. 5, 1981, p. A4.

members of the committee. It is then made available to other members of Congress as well as to the general public.

THE PURPOSES OF A HEARING

Hearings serve several purposes:

1. Transmission of information. Information relating to a bill, whether technical, economic, social, or political, may be presented to the committee.

2. Propaganda channel. New or controversial ideas may be "sold" to Congress and the public through exposure in a hearing.

3. Safety valve. A hearing may relieve tensions or adjust conflicts by providing all sides with a means of airing their grievances.

EXECUTIVE SESSIONS

Public hearings do not end in decision-making by the committee. Decisions are made in closed meetings called *executive sessions*. These closed meetings allow the informal give-and-take necessary to produce legislation. Here, committee members can abandon a position or accept a compromise without public embarrassment.

Executive sessions are often referred to as "markups," and, like the formal hearings, are dominated by the committee chairman. The committee staff may also be called on for additional information and analysis during these sessions. Because the bill is examined line-by-line in these markups, the detailed form of the legislation now emerges, ready for presentation to the House and Senate.

Amendments may still be offered on the floor of Congress, but this is not always the case. Some bills come to the floor under special rules which do not allow amendment under any circumstances.

COMMITTEE REPORT

At the end of the executive session, the committee prepares a *report on the bill* which summarizes its recommendations. Evidence considered by the committee is summarized and evaluated. If the committee decides against reporting the bill, its decision is almost always final. Both houses have rules that make it possible to force a bill out of committee, but this procedure is seldom used. Not only is congressional respect for the committee system very great, but the discharge process itself is a difficult one.

Committees seldom report a bill with negative recommendations. When they do, that usually means the committee doesn't want to be blamed for pigeonholing a bill the entire House wants to debate. Committee reports, whether positive or negative, do not usually reveal evidence of division within the committee unless the minority members choose to file a dissenting report.

What is the special role of the House Rules Committee?

When a bill is reported out by a House committee, it is placed on one of three main calendars. Assignment to a calendar theoretically determines the sequence in which Congress will consider new bills—but the Rules Committee often modifies the calendar.

Appropriations bills—bills that will either raise or spend money—go on the Union Calendar. *Public bills*, which affect the country as a whole, are assigned to the House Calendar. *Private bills*, which affect only one person or a few citizens, go on the Private Calendar. Other calendars exist, but they are relatively unimportant.

THE RULES COMMITTEE REGULATES THE FLOW

Despite the existence of the various calendars, in reality they tell very little about the order in which bills will be considered by the House. Bills from a few committees (Ways and Means or Appropriations, for example) receive top priority and will be considered promptly at any time. Conference committee reports and bills vetoed by the President also receive special treatment.

With those few exceptions, legislation reaches the floor of the House only when approved by the Rules Committee. Members of this powerful committee prescribe the conditions under which a bill will be considered. Out of the thousands of bills placed on the calendars, only about a hundred will be judged to be of sufficient importance to warrant debate on the floor of the House. Of these, slightly more than 50 percent will be considered under special resolutions drawn up by the Rules Committee.

Reports that lack privileged status require a ruling before they can be brought to the floor. This Rules Committee "traffic control" makes practical sense, for without it important legislation might be lost in the logjam of earlier bills that clog the calendars. The effect, of course, is to give the Rules Committee substantial control over the major items on the House agenda.

FOUR KINDS OF SPECIAL RULES

In governing the flow of legislation, the Rules Committee grants each bill one of four kinds of special rules:

1. *Open rules.* Most legislation moves to the floor under open rules, which permit the House to amend measures reported out by the standing committees.

2. *Closed rules.* Less commonly, measures may be sent to the floor under closed rules, which limit or even prohibit the offering of amendments.

3. *Waiving points of order.* Seldom used, this rule prevents representatives from making technical "points of order" against certain provisions of what may be a controversial bill.

4. *Arranging a conference.* If the House and Senate have passed different versions of the same bill, a conference is arranged to resolve the conflicts.

As a legitimate part of the "weeding-out" process, the Rules Committee may refuse to grant a hearing to a committee seeking a special rule, or may refuse to grant a special rule following such a hearing. Such refusals are usually equivalent to killing a bill for that session of Congress. The Rules Committee may also bargain with a committee that wants a special rule for one of its bills. The "price" of the special rule is often the addition or subtraction of certain provisions. Because of this power, and because the committee has often been controlled by conservatives, opposition to its power surfaces periodically (see Figure 5.5).

SIDESTEPPING THE RULES COMMITTEE

Not all measures that fail to receive a special rule from the Rules Committee are lost. If sufficient support can be rounded up, such bills may be moved to the floor through *suspension of the rules* or *unanimous consent.*

"Come In — Come In"

Figure 5.5

Although the Rules Committee performs a useful service in scheduling bills for debate on the House floor, its power and generally conservative leadership have often been criticized. Source: From *The Herblock Book* (Beacon Press, 1952).

Also possible is a *discharge procedure*, which forces the Rules Committee to send a pigeonholed bill to the floor.

On *Calendar Wednesday*, the standing committees are permitted to bring to the floor any bills previously reported but lacking privileged status. In practice, however, this option is seldom used as a means of evading the Rules Committee. The majority leader usually requests that Calendar Wednesday for the following week be forgotten—and the motion is almost always accepted by the House.

What happens when a bill reaches the floor?

Many first-time visitors to the House or Senate are shocked to see that most business is conducted with only a small portion of the membership present. The scene of empty desks, casual conversation, and constant movement in and out of the chamber gives the impression that Congress pays little attention to the people's affairs. Such is not the case, however. Other congressional business—hearings, meetings with constituents, and party activities—all make demands on the time of the lawmakers.

DEBATE IN THE HOUSE

Once a bill has cleared the double hurdle of the hearing process and the Rules Committee, it is brought to the floor for debate under specified conditions. It is not unusual for a bill to be presented to the House under a one-hour time limitation. Speakers from the majority and minority parties divide the time equally, as scheduled by their party leaders.

After general debate, the bill receives a section-by-section *second reading*. If amendments are permitted, a five-minute debate limit per amendment may be imposed. Extensions of time—or even suspension of the rules governing debate—are possible, if enough representatives support the motion to grant them.

DEBATE IN THE SENATE

The Senate's smaller membership results in fewer bills and less complicated rules. The one hundred members of this exclusive "club" jealously guard their tradition of unlimited debate on any topic. When a senator or a group of senators use unlimited debate to prevent consideration of a bill, the tactic is known as a *filibuster*. These colorful spectacles sometimes drag on for weeks. In order to keep the floor, senators must remain standing and must speak continuously. At times, faced with the need to fill endless hours, senators have read novels, newspapers, recipes, and other miscellaneous material to their impatient colleagues. A filibuster against the Civil Rights Act of 1964 lasted three months before it was ended; a filibuster against the Tidelands Oil Bill in 1953 stuffed the *Congressional Record* with 1,241,414 extra words.

A filibuster can be ended only by invoking the *closure rule* (often spelled "cloture"). A closure motion requires the signatures of seventeen senators, followed by a vote of three-fifths of the Senate. Despite the frustration caused by filibusters, closure has historically been difficult to achieve, for many senators feel that the next filibuster might be their own.

DELAYING TACTICS

The filibuster is a delaying tactic available only to senators. Other tactics can be used in either house of Congress.

Although amendments have a better chance of being adopted in committee than on the floor, in the Senate they often provide a major opportunity for delaying action on a bill. This is particularly noticeable when a legislator tacks on a *rider*—an amendment having little or no relation to the bill. Members of Congress who might have voted for the bill may withdraw their support because they object to the rider. In addition, the rider itself must be debated, thus further delaying a final vote on the original bill.

Another delaying tactic is the *quorum call*. If a member suggests that less than a quorum—the number of legislators required to conduct business—is present, all debate stops. Bells ring in offices throughout the Capitol, and members scurry in to have their presence recorded. Meanwhile, the side that is losing the debate has a chance to round up additional support.

VOTING ON A BILL

Votes may be cast in a number of ways. Many bills are decided by *voice vote*, particularly if the measure is not controversial. The presiding officer declares for the "ayes" or "nays" according to what he hears. If there is a doubt about the result, a *rising vote*, or head count by the presiding officer, may be demanded. These two forms of voting have the advantage of allowing House and Senate members to cast their votes without making a public record of their position.

On demand of one-fifth of the members present, however, individual votes must be reported on a *roll-call vote*. Most major bills are passed in this manner. In the Senate, a clerk reads each senator's name, and his or her vote is recorded for constituents and other interested observers to check. An electronic system replaced this time-consuming procedure in the House in 1973. Representatives now indicate their votes by inserting personal punch cards into a small box near their seats. When they punch the proper button, a master board at the front of the chamber records each vote.

When members of Congress know that they will be absent during a roll-call vote, they may "pair" their votes. Pairing means that an "aye" voter finds a "nay" voter who will also be absent (or vice versa), thus allowing the two votes to cancel each other.

Even though a bill has been passed by one house, its future remains in doubt. The same procedures must be followed in the other house, with the same potentials for defeat.

How do the House and Senate iron out their differences?

The House and Senate often pass different versions of the same bill. Amendments added in one chamber may not be acceptable to the other. Yet both houses must agree on identical language before the bill may be sent to the President. This conflict becomes the responsibility of a temporary (*ad hoc*) committee known as the *conference committee*.

Membership on the conference committee consists of from three to nine senior members of each house. These designated "managers" or "conferees" are expected to fight for the viewpoint of the house they represent. The chairman and ranking minority member of the committee involved are usually included among the managers. In some cases, the managers are bound by specific instructions as to how much they can compromise.

If the two versions of the bill differ greatly, the conference committee may be required to write what amounts to a new bill. Committee staff members and other experts are often invited in as consultants. Although a total rewrite is rare, a deadlock in the conference committee sometimes does occur. Floor leaders from both parties must then be called in to resolve the problem.

When a final compromise has been hammered out, the bill is reported back to both houses. Evaluation of conference committee legislation shows that both houses are about equally effective in gaining acceptance of their views.

The compromise committee bill may not be amended by either house. Although it is offered on a "take-it-or-leave-it" basis, conference committee recommendations are seldom rejected. Once passed by both houses, the bill is printed on parchment and signed by the Speaker of the House and the President of the Senate. Even after all that study, debate, compromise, and voting, the bill is not yet a law. The President must make the final decision.

What choices does a President have when a bill reaches his desk?

The bills that reach a President's desk are often the result of his own efforts. He may have suggested the original legislation, or he may even have ordered it drafted by his own staff. Once the bill was introduced, he may have used the power of his office to urge its adoption. A favorite technique is to prepare a legislative package containing a number of measures, then tag the whole group with a catchy title, such as "the War on Poverty." Using televised press conferences, the President can label his bills as "must" legislation, hoping for public pressure to aid their passage.

THE PRESIDENT'S CHOICES

Whatever the origins of the bill, the President has four choices once the measure is on his desk:

1. He can sign it. In most cases he will sign the bill, thus making it a law.

2. He can do nothing. He may simply allow the bill to become law without his signature, which it does automatically after ten working days if Congress is still in session.

3. He can "pocket veto" it. If Congress has set a date for adjournment within ten days, the President may let the bill die by "putting it in his pocket." This *pocket veto* has the same effect as a formal veto—it kills the bill—but ducks the need for the President to sustain the veto on the floor of Congress. A court battle over the use of the pocket veto during congressional vacation periods ended in 1976 when President Ford agreed to accept the strict constitutional definition of the procedure. Henceforth, Ford promised, he would use the pocket veto only when Congress was formally adjourned, between sessions.

4. He can veto it. A *veto* is a formal refusal to sign a bill. The President sends the measure back to Congress along with a message explaining his reasons for rejecting it.

One power *not* given the President is that of an *item veto* which would allow him to kill only a certain section of a bill. Lacking this power, the President often uses his veto message to list the portions of the bill he finds objectionable. Once those sections are deleted or modified, he tells Congress, he will be willing to sign the bill into law.

DEALING WITH A VETO

A vetoed bill returns to the house where it originated. If two-thirds of that house approves the bill as it stands, it carries and is sent to the other house for similar action. A second two-thirds vote there completes the *override*, and the bill becomes law without the signature of the President. Should either house fail to override, the veto is said to be sustained and the bill dies—unless it is reintroduced later, to begin the entire process all over again.

Historically, the chances that Congress would override a President's veto have been small. With both presidential and party prestige involved, presidents have usually been able to rally the minimum one-third vote needed to sustain a veto. Dwight Eisenhower, for example, compiled a batting average of .989 (Congress overrode only two vetoes out of 181).

§UMMARY AND CONCLUSIONS

1. The process of enacting a law remains immensely complex, despite all attempts to simplify it. Even newly elected members of Congress must go to "school" to learn the tricks of their demanding trade. Our bicameral (two-house) legislature acts as a safeguard built into the Constitution that (a) guarantees against hasty enactment of legislation and (b) serves as a barrier against passage of laws of narrow purpose.

2. With individual senators and representatives heavily burdened by a long list of political and legislative functions, the *committee system* has become the primary means by which Congress examines new legislation. It is on committees that members of Congress gain expertise, and it is on committees that they make their influence felt. The floor of Congress sometimes serves to focus public attention upon crucial issues or personalities, but it is in the daily grind of committee *hearings* that bills are analyzed, rewritten, and shaped to national needs—or to the realities of political life. *Pressure groups* and *lobbyists*, as well as the *staffs* of the committees, play an important backstage role in the formulation and investigation of prospective laws, or *bills*.

3. The members of Congress themselves depend on the integrity of the legislative system that has evolved. Because they cannot physically cope with the yearly avalanche of bills, they must take guidance from their party leaders, their committee chairmen, and those special-interest groups that offer advice and information. The President and his administration also push for consideration of new legislation. Only members of Congress, however, can actually introduce bills for House and Senate debate.

4. Once approved by the proper committee, a bill is put on a calendar to await its turn for debate on the floor of Congress. At this point, in the House of Representatives, the *Rules Committee* takes over as a kind of "traffic cop," awarding special rules to some bills, denying consideration to

others. Limited means are available to individual members of Congress, to committees, and to the leadership to move bills past the Rules Committee. Despite periodic rebellions against the Rules Committee, the finely balanced procedure generally places the most important bills on the House floor at the proper time.

5. After approval in one house, a bill must also be passed by the other chamber. Any differences are resolved by a *conference committee*, which returns the bill to the House and Senate for final approval. The bill then goes to the President, who can sign it into law, allow it to become law by holding it for ten days, "pocket veto" it by holding it when Congress will be adjourning within ten days, or veto it. Congress can *override* a veto by a two-thirds vote in each house—but the President usually wins the override battle.

6. Over the years, the legislative machinery has been gradually modified. The power of the Speaker of the House and the iron rule of the committee chairmen—particularly the Rules Committee chairman—have been diluted by law as well as by custom. Even though the public is often frustrated by the slow pace of the legislative process, there is little demand for major reform. After all, the present system has worked for two hundred years.

REVIEW QUESTIONS AND ACTIVITIES

TERMS YOU SHOULD KNOW

amendment	*private bill*
appropriations bill	*public bill*
bill	*pocket veto*
Calendar Wednesday	*quorum call*
closure (cloture)	*report on a bill*
concurrent resolution	*resolution*
conference committee	*rider*
discharge procedure	*rising vote*
executive session	*Rules Committee*
filibuster	*standing committee*
hearing	*suspension of the rules*
item veto	*unanimous consent*
joint resolution	*veto*
lobby/lobbyist	*voice vote*
override	

REVIEW QUESTIONS

The following multiple-choice questions are based on the important ideas presented in this chapter. Select the response that best completes each statement.

1. The shortest possible time in which a bill can become law is measured in (a) hours. (b) days. (c) weeks. (d) months. (e) a legislative year.

2. Most bills originate with (a) the administration. (b) Congress. (c) private individuals and pressure groups. (d) congressional committees. (e) the national committee of each political party.

3. Committee staffs provide a number of services to Congress, including (a) investigative services. (b) research. (c) expert testimony. (d) writing proposed bills in proper legislative language. (e) all of these.

4. The most important weapon lobbyists possess is (a) the money they have for buying votes. (b) their ability to organize a letter-writing campaign. (c) the parties they give. (d) the trust and respect they develop with individual members of Congress. (e) their connections with organized crime.

5. The most careful examination of a bill comes during (a) meetings between individual members of Congress and the bill's sponsors. (b) committee hearings. (c) committee staff meetings. (d) debate on the floor of the House or Senate. (e) meetings of the conference committee to iron out differences between two versions of the same bill.

6. Executive sessions of congressional committees are closed to the public so that (a) committee members may make compromises without public embarrassment. (b) secret, illegal deals can be made. (c) lobbyists can join the meeting and speak freely. (d) foreign spies can be kept from learning national secrets. (e) all of these.

7. When a committee reports out a new bill, it is placed on a calendar; the next step is to (a) begin floor debate. (b) pigeonhole the bill. (c) consult the administration to find out the President's wishes. (d) send it to the Rules Committee to establish the bill's priority. (e) read it into the *Congressional Record.*

8. Unlimited floor debate on a bill may take place in (a) the House. (b) the Senate. (c) both houses of Congress. (d) neither house. (e) either house when the rules are suspended.

9. If the vote of a member of Congress is to be recorded for all to see, the type of vote used is the (a) rising vote. (b) roll-call vote. (c) voice vote. (d) "paired" vote. (e) all votes are publicly recorded.

10. The President plays a major role in the legislative process through his ability to (a) recommend new laws. (b) pressure Congress to pass his own bills. (c) veto bills he does not like. (d) appeal to the public for support of his legislation. (e) all of these.

CONCEPT DEVELOPMENT

This chapter has explored the process by which a bill becomes a law. You can use your skills in thinking, researching, and writing to answer the following questions.

1. Why was Congress designed as a bicameral legislature?

2. Trace the progress of a bill from the time it is introduced to the time it lands on the President's desk for signature.

3. Write a plan of action for lobbying for or against a proposed law. How good do you think your chances of success are?

4. Discuss the following statement: The President plays a larger role in creating major new laws than does Congress.

5. Discuss the argument that there are so many laws on the books today that the nation's need is not for more new laws, but for the better application of those already in effect.

ACTIVITIES

The following activities are designed to help you use the ideas developed in the chapter.

1. Today's Speaker of the House possesses great power and influence. But in 1910, it took a "revolution" to cut the Speaker's power down to its present size. Check up on the "Revolution of 1910," and report to the class on the events of that period. How did the old rules compare with today's procedures?

2. Organize a debate on the question: "Resolved, that the Congress of the United States should end all contact with lobbyists, all executive sessions, all compromises of principle."

3. Write to your representative for copies of recently published reports of hearings on a topic that concerns you. After reviewing the reports, discuss with the class such questions as: (a) Were the hearings fair? (b) Did the committee members perform with intelligence and perception? (c) How useful were the hearings in gathering information about the bill under study?

4. Analyze a copy of the *Congressional Record*. Describe to the class the quality and depth of the debate recorded there. What purpose do you find in the material printed under "Extension of Remarks"?

5. Organize a mock committee hearing. Assign class members to various responsibilities, including witnesses, lobbyists, committee members, and committee staff. Write a bill concerning a topic you feel strongly about, such as pollution or student rights, and see what happens to your bill as it is attacked and defended from all sides. You might want to send the resulting bill to your representative and ask for his or her comments.

CHAPTER SIX

ⓒONGRESS AND THE CONTROL OF FISCAL POLICY

Many high school students can tell the exact moment when they begin to take an active interest in the federal government. "Where do all those tax dollars go?" they ask sadly, looking at their first paycheck. Nobody is ever quite prepared for the size of Uncle Sam's big tax bite.

Generally, Americans realize that their taxes pay for "guns and butter" —the national investment in military security, social welfare, and all the programs in between. In your own experience, you may have enjoyed the low prices of a federally subsidized school lunch program, or threaded a new 16mm projector purchased by a federal grant. If the money is spent on such worthwhile services, who can object?

A little digging, however, reveals that federal money finances any number of surprising projects. Chauffered limousines, for example, cost the federal government almost $5 million a year. Dining rooms for the top brass of the Pentagon cost $2 million more. Cabinet secretaries don't miss out on the good food, either. Their personal chefs cost the government $200,000 a year. Uncle Sam also hired 94 elevator operators in Washington, D.C., to push the buttons in automatic elevators. Total cost: $893,000.

The government also sponsors research projects. One study, for example, cost $222,000 to ask if drivers considered large trucks a factor in traffic congestion. (Yes) Another $120,126 was spent to find out whether rear-wheel-steering motorcycles were practical. (No) Finally, $140,000 was spent to survey the number of Samoans living in Orange County, California. The report was lost four months later and hasn't turned up yet.

If such expenditures suggest that no one is minding the store, many members of Congress would agree. In the rush of money bills which move through Congress each year, some *boondoggles* (useless projects) do slip through. Despite the headline-making potential of chauffered limousines and useless elevator operators, the millions spent on such luxuries make up only a tiny part of the money Congress spends each year. The total costs of the programs just mentioned amount to only .00085 percent of the total federal budget. Congress isn't asleep—just busy.

The size and complexity of the federal budget make money matters the largest single concern of each congressional session. The questions about Congress and federal monetary policy that will be examined in this chapter are:

1. How has the federal budget grown over the years?
2. Where does the money come from?
3. What limits the taxes Congress may impose?
4. How does the federal government collect taxes?
5. Where does the federal tax dollar go?
6. Why does the United States have a national debt?
7. How is money appropriated by Congress?
8. How does Congress control the nation's economy?

How has the federal budget grown over the years?

President Washington created the Treasury Department as one of the original Cabinet positions. The first Secretary of the Treasury, Alexander Hamilton, established the federal budget as the cornerstone of national financial stability. The budget, or spending program, would reflect the President's ideas about national needs and priorities. The President would then ask Congress to provide the money necessary to carry out these federal responsibilities.

Not only has government spending increased in dollar amounts since 1789, but the percentage of national income earmarked for federal use has also grown continuously. In 1790, for example, when the population was approximately 4 million, the average federal budget was less than $6 million—about $1.50 per person. By fiscal 1980, the government was spending about $564 billion a year for a population of around 230 million—over $2,450 per person. Table 6.1 traces the steady increase over the decades, broken only by cutbacks following major wars.

Federal spending over the past forty years has grown at an accelerating pace largely because Americans have insisted that government take a more active role in the country's economic and social life. In the 1800s, most people were content if the federal government defended the country, maintained a postal service, and tended to governmental housekeeping. *Tariffs* (taxes on imports) and sales of public lands provided most of the federal revenue (income).

By the 1890's, however, Americans began insisting that the federal

Table 6.1

Increase in the size of the federal budget, 1789–1982

(Yearly averages of federal expenditures in millions of dollars)

Year	Amount	Percent change	Event
1789–1800	$ 5.8		
1801–1810	9.1	+ 56.9	
1811–1820	23.9	+ 162.6	*War of 1812*
1821–1830	16.2	− 32.2	
1831–1840	24.5	+ 51.2	
1841–1850	34.1	+ 39.2	
1851–1860	60.2	+ 76.5	
1861–1865	683.8	+1235.9	*Civil War*
1866–1870	377.6	− 44.8	
1871–1875	287.5	− 23.9	
1876–1880	255.6	− 11.1	
1881–1885	257.7	+ 0.8	
1886–1890	279.1	+ 8.3	
1891–1895	363.6	+ 30.3	
1896–1900	457.5	+ 25.8	
1901–1905	535.6	+ 17.1	
1906–1910	639.2	+ 19.3	
1911–1915	720.3	+ 12.7	
1916–1920	8,065.3	+1019.7	*World War I*
1921–1925	3,579.0	− 55.6	
1926–1930	3,182.2	− 11.1	*Depression begins*
1931–1935	5,214.9	+ 63.8	
1936–1940	10,192.3	+ 95.4	*New Deal*
1941–1945	66,038.0	+ 547.9	*World War II*
1946–1950	42,334.5	− 35.9	
1955	64,570.0	+ 52.5	
1960	76,539.4	+ 18.5	
1965	96,507.0	+ 26.1	
1970	194,968.2	+ 102.0	*Vietnam War*
1979	493,700.0	+ 153.2	
1982	688,800.0	+ 39.5	*Estimated expenditures*

government regulate the large corporations; more importantly, they were also demanding more governmental services of all kinds (see Figure 6.1). These new services required additional public employees, as well as additional dollars. By 1980, over 8 percent of the country's population was working for some level of government. These 18.1 million employees included:

1. Federal: 2.9 million civilian (over 98 percent in the executive branch) and 2.1 million members of the armed forces.
2. State: 3.7 million employees.
3. Local (county, city, town): 9.4 million employees.

Where does the money come from?

In 1979, the total of all goods and services produced by the United States —the *gross national product,* or GNP—reached an astronomical $2.4

Figure 6.1
A long line of people wait to file for unemployment benefits during a recent recession. Unemployment compensation is one of the many social welfare services provided by government. Source: Wide World Photos.

trillion (that's $2,400,000,000,000). The federal budget for that year—$494 billion—represented over 20 percent of the GNP. Add the costs of state and local government, and the growing size of the tax burden at all levels becomes apparent.

With the tariff now capable of supplying only 1 percent of the taxes needed, other federal tax sources have been developed. The federal tax "pie" in 1979 yielded receipts of $465 billion.

As Figure 6.2 shows, the federal government depends on six main sources of income: (1) personal income taxes; (2) Social Security taxes; (3) corporate income taxes; (4) excise taxes; (5) estate and gift taxes; and (6) customs duties. A seventh, minor source of revenue—which includes miscellaneous items such as gifts, land sales, earnings on investments, and the like—accounts for the remaining 2 percent.

PERSONAL INCOME TAXES

By means of the personal income tax, the federal government collects a percentage of each American's earnings. It originally became law in 1894, but the courts declared the law unconstitutional the following year. By 1913 the need for additional tax revenues had grown so pressing that the country ratified the Sixteenth Amendment to the Constitution. This amendment provides that "The Congress shall have power to lay and collect taxes on incomes, from whatever source derived, without apportionment among the several states, and without regard to any census or enumeration."

From the first, the federal income tax system applied *progressive tax rates*. This means that the well-to-do pay a greater proportion of their earnings in taxes than the poor. In recent years, the basic rates have ranged from 12 to 50 percent of taxable personal income.

Not all income is taxable, however. *Exemptions* and *deductions* have been written into the tax laws which allow many personal and business expenses to be subtracted from total earnings before taxes are calculated. Economists believe that tax deductions and exemptions, as long as they reflect the actual cost of doing business, stimulate the economy by encouraging investment.

Because of exemptions and deductions, Americans pay lower taxes than they would if their total gross incomes were taxed at the full 12 to 50 percent rates. A few wealthy citizens, moreover, use special exemptions to greatly reduce their tax bill; others escape taxes altogether by drawing their income from tax-exempt sources, such as municipal bonds. These so-called *loopholes* receive much unfavorable publicity, but Congress has found tax reform a difficult problem to tackle. Most Americans applaud the closing of loopholes—as long as their own special exemptions are not disturbed.

SOCIAL SECURITY TAXES

The Social Security system was established in 1935 to provide old-age benefits for most industrial and commercial workers. Survivors' benefits were added in 1939. Today, Social Security touches the lives of more than nine out of ten Americans. Social Security taxes are withheld from paychecks to cover (1) old-age and survivors' insurance, (2) disability insurance, (3) unemployment insurance, (4) medical insurance, and (5) retirement plans for certain groups of civil servants and railroad workers.

Figure 6.2
Sources of federal income, 1979

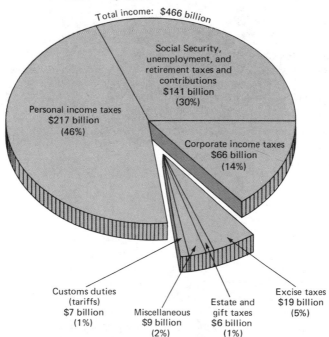

Total income: $466 billion

Social Security, unemployment, and retirement taxes and contributions
$141 billion
(30%)

Personal income taxes
$217 billion
(46%)

Corporate income taxes
$66 billion
(14%)

Customs duties (tariffs)
$7 billion
(1%)

Miscellaneous
$9 billion
(2%)

Estate and gift taxes
$6 billion
(1%)

Excise taxes
$19 billion
(5%)

Estimated figures. Total includes interfund and intragovernmental transactions and receipts, not shown in diagram.

CORPORATE INCOME TAXES

Industries and businesses pay a corporate income tax on profits. These taxes are figured at 17 to 46 percent, after exemptions, but before dividends are paid to investors.

The corporate tax rates have been criticized for drawing off funds that could be used for business expansion and modernization; critics say that increased business profits would create more jobs and higher tax revenues. On the other hand, tax loopholes have enabled some giant corporations to avoid payment of millions of dollars in tax liabilities. The much-debated oil depletion allowance, which gives petroleum companies a tax credit for each barrel of oil they pump out of the ground, is an example of such a special tax exemption.

EXCISE TAXES

Taxes levied on the sale of specific goods and services are known as *excise taxes*. Whenever we pay a telephone bill, buy cosmetics, visit a theater, or buy a bottle of liquor, this tax is included in the price. The excise tax has been labeled a *regressive* tax. That is, when rich and poor pay the same tax on their phone bill, the poor feel the weight of the tax more heavily because each dollar represents a larger share of a poor person's income.

ESTATE AND GIFT TAXES

Whenever one person transfers money or property to someone else, the government collects estate and gift taxes. When a person dies, the heirs receive a lifetime credit against combined estate and gift taxes. This credit was $79,300 in 1983 and will rise to $192,800 in 1987. Once that figure is exceeded, the government collects from 18 to 70 percent of the value of the estate before the heirs receive their share.

Even gifts do not escape taxation. A donor may give up to $10,000 each year to another person without tax. After that limit is reached, the donor must pay the same rates as for estate taxes. Gift taxes are intended to prevent wealthy people from giving away their money in order to avoid estate taxes when they die.

CUSTOMS TAXES

The price of almost every foreign-made item sold in the United States includes a customs tax (also known as a *tariff* or *duty*). Customs inspectors determine the tax rate according to the value of the product imported. A number of items, such as art objects and books, pass through customs duty-free. Many other imports carry only a small customs tax.

United States economic policy featured high tariffs through the 1800's, in order to protect the country's own infant industries. In this century, however, government policy has aimed at continuing tariff reductions. Lower customs taxes stimulated trade between nations, to the benefit of U.S.

exports. Manufacturers who see their products underpriced by imports, however, lobby just as strongly for higher tariffs and other restrictions on imports.

What limits the power of Congress to impose taxes?

Restrictions on the power of Congress to impose taxes come from two main sources: the Constitution and certain court decisions.

The Constitution, for example, forbids the imposition of *export taxes* on goods shipped to other countries. It also provides that *indirect taxes*, the cost of which is ultimately passed on to the consumer, must be uniform throughout the country. For example, federal taxes may not be set higher for a New York manufacturer than for its West Coast counterpart; the employer of a middle-class Chicago salesman must pay the same Social Security tax rate as the employer of a grocery clerk in poverty-stricken Appalachia.

Government has often attempted to use taxes to achieve social goals. The high excise tax on alcoholic beverages not only raises money but also is intended to limit consumption. A major argument in the energy debate of 1974–75 revolved around the use of federal taxes to restrict the use of gasoline. The use of taxes to accomplish social reform cannot be carried to extremes, however. The Supreme Court has ruled on a number of occasions that a tax may not be used to discourage undesirable activities, even an evil like child labor.

How does the federal government collect taxes?

The Treasury Department oversees collection and distribution of the yearly harvest of taxes. The responsibility for actual administration and enforcement of the various tax programs created by Congress has been given to the Internal Revenue Service.

A commissioner, appointed by the President and confirmed by the Senate, directs the Internal Revenue Service (IRS). Fifty-eight IRS districts divide the country geographically. Each district operates under a director, who supervises the collection of taxes in his or her area.

Americans, often to their own surprise, have a worldwide reputation for paying their taxes honestly and promptly—despite the sometimes painful bind created by inflation and high tax rates (see Figure 6.3). The IRS has developed a number of techniques to keep that record of honesty intact. Not only are employers required to withhold taxes from their workers' paychecks, but they must also keep complete records for IRS use. IRS special agents have the power to (1) inspect company books; (2) require witnesses to testify; (3) obtain information on dividend and interest payments; and (4) demand uniform methods of accounting.

All Americans who earn more than a specified minimum amount each year must file an annual tax return. If their employers did not withhold

Figure 6.3
"More than a taxpayer can bear."
Source: Dick Wright, the San Diego *Union.*

sufficient taxes, the taxpayers must pay the difference. If the employers withheld too much, the taxpayers will receive a refund.

When tax evasion does occur, the IRS has the authority to deal effectively with the problem. The service now makes extensive use of computers to check returns and to verify the accuracy of wage, dividend, and interest information. At the least, conviction of tax fraud leads to the payment of heavy fines; judges also hand down prison sentences in more serious cases.

Where does the federal tax dollar go?

As recently as 1900, the federal government was condemned by some for spending $500 million a year. By 1982, with a population three times what it was at the turn of the century, total federal outlays had soared to over a thousand times the earlier figure (see Table 6.1). As demonstrated in Figure 6.4, four major categories account for ninety-seven cents out of each federal dollar.

DEFENSE

Military expenditures have traditionally grabbed the biggest share of the budget, even in peacetime. In recent years, however, the Pentagon's share of the budget has decreased sharply. Between 1960 and 1979, for example, defense costs as a percentage of total government spending fell greatly, from 49 percent to 24 percent. The dollar investment in defense rose from $45 billion in 1960 to $117 billion in 1979; but when inflation is taken into account, this actually represents a slight decrease. Changing relations with the Soviet Union and China, plus the end of direct U.S. military involvement in Vietnam, made this decrease possible. When a renewed arms race began in the 1980's, however, increased military spending once again cut into the federal budget available for investment in human needs (see Figure 6.5).

HUMAN RESOURCES

Government expenditures for education, unemployment compensation, medical care, antipoverty programs, agriculture, and other social welfare projects make up the human resources segment of the budget. These costs jumped from 30 percent to 53 percent of all federal spending in the fifteen years between 1965 and 1980.

Now the largest and fastest-growing budget category, human resources spending reflects a changing emphasis in American priorities. Citizens seem ever more willing to accept a government role in improving the quality of life in the United States.

INTEREST ON THE NATIONAL DEBT

Ever since the Depression of the 1930's, when the government accepted unbalanced budgets as the price of helping jobless and hungry Americans, interest on the national debt has skyrocketed. Basically, this interest is the fee paid for borrowing money to finance activities which the government cannot pay for out of yearly tax revenues.

Eleven percent of the 1979 budget was earmarked for interest payments on the national debt. Higher interest rates and the increasing size of the debt pushed the interest payments from $1 billion in 1939 to $53 billion

Figure 6.4
How the 1979 federal budget dollar was divided

(Total outlays $494 billion)

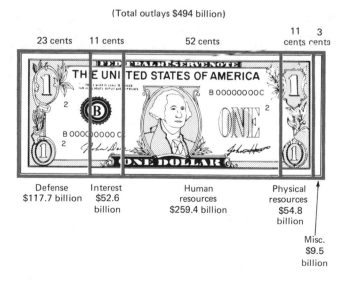

23 cents	11 cents	52 cents	11 cents	3 cents
Defense $117.7 billion	Interest $52.6 billion	Human resources $259.4 billion	Physical resources $54.8 billion	Misc. $9.5 billion

Figure 6.5
"Is nothing sacred any more?"
Source: From *Herblock's State of the Union* (Simon & Schuster, 1972).

in 1979. (A more complete discussion of the national debt will be found on pages 135–37.)

PHYSICAL RESOURCES

Interstate highways, public housing projects, NASA's space shots, agricultural subsidies, and even congressional office space illustrate the varied programs financed by the 11 percent of the 1979 budget devoted to physical resources. As the nation's largest landowner and landlord, the federal government has a yearly housekeeping bill in the billions, even before Congress and the President add new research and construction projects.

MISCELLANEOUS

A miscellaneous collection of expenses made up the last 3 percent of the 1979 budget. Money and arms given as foreign aid, support for the United Nations, disaster relief, and similar items make up this category.

LET'S REVIEW FOR A MOMENT

Can you grasp the full magnitude of government expenditures? If you somehow could spend one million dollars a day for 1,354 years, you would have run through only one year's budget—$494 billion. This remarkable sum of money reflects an ever-increasing demand by the American people for government services.

Most of the money to finance the budget comes from personal and corporate income taxes, Social Security taxes, excise taxes, estate and gift taxes, and customs taxes. Where does it go? Defense, human and physical resources, and interest on the national debt take almost all of your tax dollar.

Congress does not possess unlimited taxing powers. Exports cannot be taxed, for example, and federal tax rates must be equal for all sections of the country. The income tax is a *progressive* tax: the rate of taxation increases with the size of the income. Excise taxes, on the other hand, are examples of *regressive* taxes: the rate of taxation is the same for all.

The Internal Revenue Service, an agency of the Treasury Department, supervises the withholding and collection of income taxes. Despite the complexity of the tax system, and despite a growing need to plug tax loopholes, most Americans pay their taxes honestly—if not happily.

Why does the United States have a national debt?

Revolutions, even those that happened in the 1700's, cost money. The United States was literally born with a *national debt*. By 1900 the debt was $1.3 billion. Because of World War II, the debt ballooned sixfold, from $43 billion in 1940 to $257 billion in 1950. By 1981 the figure stood at $1 trillion—over $4,000 for every man, woman, and child in the United States. (Table 6.2 shows the growth of the debt from 1900 to 1979.)

Table 6.2

The national debt of the United States, 1900–1979

Year	Total debt (billions)	Debt per capita	Interest paid (billions)	Percent of budget for interest
1900	$ 1.3	$ 17	$ *	7.7
1910	1.1	12	*	3.1
1920	24.3	228	1.0	15.9
1930	16.2	132	0.7	19.2
1940	43.0	325	1.0	11.5
1950	257.4	1,697	5.7	14.5
1960	286.3	1,585	9.2	10.0
1970	370.9	1,811	19.3	9.8
1979	826.5	3,740	59.8	11.0

* Less than half a billion dollars.

Note: The national debt passed the trillion dollar mark in the fall of 1981. Interest rates paid by the federal government on the debt also soared upward.

DEFICIT SPENDING AND BALANCED BUDGETS

The federal government creates the national debt by spending more money than it collects. This practice is called *deficit spending*. In 1979, for example, the budget deficit for the year was $27.7 billion. Of course, the President and Congress would prefer to operate under a *balanced budget*, with income equal to outgo. A *budget surplus* would even allow the government to pay off some of the debt, as happened occasionally during the last century.

Debt repayment becomes a luxury, however, when Congress and the President realize that the needs of the American people cannot be met from current income. During a time of high unemployment, for example, the government may borrow money and pump it into the economy. If this practice succeeds, jobs are created—but so is a deficit, which must be added to the national debt to be repaid later.

DEBT CEILING

Congress regularly places a limit on the national debt. When the President realizes that his budget requires borrowing a sum that will push the national debt over the *debt ceiling* established by law, he asks Congress to raise the ceiling. For example, President Gerald Ford asked for a new ceiling of over $600 billion for 1975–76. Even so, the President was forced to ask for an even higher ceiling a year later.

GOVERNMENT SECURITIES

How does anyone, even the U.S. government, go about borrowing a trillion dollars? The Treasury Department issues marketable securities—Treasury bills, notes, certificates, and bonds. Three-quarters of the debt is funded by the sale of securities like these, which can be bought and sold by the public, or by banks, insurance companies, and other lenders, like any corporate bond or trust deed. Nonmarketable securities, such as the savings bonds bought by many Americans, raise the remainder of the money necessary to keep the wheels of government turning. All this Treasury "paper" constitutes a loan of money to the government; eventually the bonds and notes must be redeemed by the Treasury at face value plus interest.

THE EFFECTS OF NATIONAL-DEBT INTEREST

As was mentioned earlier in this chapter, interest payments on the national debt take a big slice of national tax revenues. As the United States pays out more and more money in interest each year, two additional problems result:

1. *The dollar declines in value.* The old cliché "as sound as a dollar" no longer holds true internationally. With the government running far into debt, foreign investors sell off their dollars. This lack of confidence results in a loss of value for the dollar, as compared to stronger currencies such as the West German deutsche mark, the Swiss franc, or the Japanese yen.

2. *Inflation increases.* When the government borrows large sums of money, interest rates soar. Everything in the economy costs more to produce, and the prices of what Americans buy jump upward.

Despite these problems, defenders of deficit spending explain that large corporations borrow to expand and modernize, so why shouldn't the government do the same? They also point out that the ratio between the gross national product and the national debt has improved. In 1950, for example, the debt was equal to one year of the country's GNP; in 1979, it represented only a little more than a four-month share of the GNP.

How is money appropriated by Congress?

The Constitution states that "no money shall be drawn from the Treasury, but in consequence of appropriations made by law." Thus the President may propose a budget, but Congress makes the final decisions as to how much money will be spent. The executive branch has the responsibility of executing the programs mandated by law. Each year, the President sends his requests for budget *appropriations* to Capitol Hill. The year's appropriations must cover continuing programs (veterans' benefits and aid to Latin America, for example) as well as any monies needed to launch new programs. Members of Congress also write legislation that sets up new programs, but until the appropriations process makes funding available, the laws cannot take effect.

THE APPROPRIATIONS PROCEDURE

The annual process of devising and funding the federal budget involves a ten-step procedure (see Figure 6.6 for a graphic summary).

1. Preliminary planning. Each department and agency of the government compiles data on the funding necessary to support both existing and new programs for the coming year. Priorities established by the President and the Office of Management and Budget (OMB) guide the planning during this phase.

2. OMB review. The Office of Management and Budget, which provides federal budgetary control for the executive branch, holds hearings at which each department defends its requests. The OMB then prepares a tentative budget, which the President works out in final detail after conferring with his staff and the department heads. The total proposed cost of government operations for the following year comes out of these conferences. This budget must be completed by the end of the calendar year, at which time the OMB sends it to the Government Printing Office.

3. President's budget message. In January, the President submits his budget to Congress, along with a message outlining his priorities and giving his views on the nation's economy. He explains how the money he is requesting will help solve the country's problems. The budget also includes an estimate of tax revenues expected during the year. If a budget

Figure 6.6
The appropriations process

1. Departments, agencies, and bureaus estimate their needs for the coming year.

2. The Office of Management and Budget works out a budget request for each department with the President.

3. In January of each year, the President submits his budget message to Congress.

4. Subcommittees of the House Appropriations Committee hold hearings; appropriations bills are recommended to the full committee.

5. Appropriations Committee reports to the House, where members debate, amend, and pass the bills.

6. The Senate Appropriations Committee repeats the hearings; reported bills are debated, amended, and passed.

7. A House-Senate conference committee adjusts differences in the two versions.

8. Both houses approve the compromise bills and send them on to the White House.

9. The President either signs or vetoes the bills.

10. Departments operate for the fiscal year on the funds allocated under the appropriations bills.

deficit appears certain, the President must justify the borrowing necessary to balance income and outgo.

4. Committee hearings. Since all appropriations bills (those involving the spending of money) originate in the House of Representatives, subcommittees of the House *Appropriations Committee* hold the first hearings on the budget. (See Chapter 5 for a full discussion of committee procedures.) Once cleared by the Appropriations Committee itself, the bill proceeds to the floor of the House, where the full membership joins in the debate. Most legislators believe that the budget bill is the most important of all the bills Congress considers each year.

5. *House vote.* By now, the budget requests have been broken into a number of individual bills dealing with the defense budget, aid to agriculture, the space program, and the like. The House often changes the amounts requested by the President, thus establishing its own priorities. This independence becomes particularly notable when different parties control Congress and the White House, as occurred in the 1950's and the 1970's.

6. *Senate action.* Once the House has acted, the Senate Appropriations Committee begins work on the appropriations bills. Agencies whose budgets have been cut in the House use the Senate hearings to appeal for restoration of their funds. The Senate often proves sympathetic to such requests. After hearings close, the committee reports the bills to the floor of the Senate, where the dollar amounts are again subject to change. Finally, the full Senate votes on the amended legislation.

7. *Conference committee meetings.* A special House and Senate conference committee meets to work out a compromise on the appropriations voted in the two houses. An old joke has it that the Senate is called the "upper house" of Congress because no matter what the House votes, the Senate "ups" it.

8. *Final congressional action.* Conference committee members return their compromise bills to the House and Senate for final action. Because conference reports cannot be amended, the lawmakers usually accept them. Refusal to approve the report, moreover, would greatly dclay passage of the high-priority appropriations bills. Without such legislation, government operations would cease at the end of the fiscal year.

9. *The President's options.* The President may either sign or veto the bills. He rarely vetoes an appropriations bill, however, preferring not to disrupt the work of the department or agency whose funding depends on that particular bill. Those vetoes that do occur usually relate to an attempt by Congress to change the original budget request drastically. In the battle to override a veto, Congress usually loses.

10. *Using the appropriations.* Each department or agency of government uses its appropriated funds to carry on its activities through the next *fiscal year.* The fiscal year differs from the calendar year in that it runs from October 1 to September 30 of the following year; fiscal 1979 thus began on October 1, 1978. Before 1976, fiscal years began on July 1; the change was made so that Congress would have more time to consider the budget. The General Accounting Office oversees day-to-day government spending once the appropriations have been made.

PROBLEMS CAUSED BY THE APPROPRIATIONS PROCEDURE

A procedure as open to influence as the appropriations process cannot always work smoothly. Three major criticisms are often directed against it.

Short-term commitments. Many executive branch officials believe that appropriations should extend beyond a single year. Long-range programs cannot be developed, they claim, when Congress limits funding to a year at a time. Only military expenditures are constitutionally limited to a maximum two-year period, and a few agencies—notably international operations like the World Bank—receive multi-year funding. Congress, however, does not wish to give up its yearly review of executive branch activities, which the present system provides.

Porkbarreling. Because it is normally impractical for the President to veto an appropriations bill, an unfortunate side effect has developed. Members of Congress often give in to political pressure and add special-interest projects to the general money bills. The total of questionable appropriations is called the legislative session's *porkbarrel.* Many projects involve physical improvements of dubious value (flood control levees on rivers that have never been known to flood, harbor improvements that benefit only a few people, luxurious government office buildings) or financial aid for special interests (subsidies for the merchant marine, bail for interned tuna fishermen). Even a useful porkbarrel project usually represents money spent on a low-priority item.

Members of Congress sometimes guarantee passage of appropriations bills containing their porkbarrel projects by exchanging promises of mutual support—a practice called *logrolling.* Because the President does not have the item veto (see Chapter 5), these special-interest projects tacked onto appropriations bills fill the porkbarrel to overflowing each year.

Complexity of the budget. The printed budget submitted to Congress each year is a document of encyclopedia-like size. Despite improvements over the years, the budget remains difficult to analyze. The Hoover Commission in 1949 did away with the former mass of statistics and tables in order to make the budget focus on the purpose for which the money would be spent. This reform enabled Congress to debate the merits of each program and agency. Since 1968, the White House has submitted a "unified" budget, which lists all moneys expended, including those from special funds such as Social Security and the interstate highway program. Although this enables Congress to see the full impact of federal spending, its job of juggling income and outgo remains complex and demanding.

How does Congress control
the nation's economy?

Skeptics might react to this question by saying, "No one even understands the American economy; how could anyone control it?" Though that statement has an element of truth, Congress does use its power to make fiscal policy for more than paying the bills. By raising or lowering taxes, for example, Congress exerts a direct influence on the course of the economy.

TAXATION TO COMBAT INFLATION

Inflation is often described by economists as "too many dollars chasing too few goods." In other words, if people have too much money and goods are in short supply, then prices will be pushed upward. Traditional economics holds that taxation can be used to stop inflation. The theory is that money taken from the public in taxes is not available to bid for scarce goods, so the prices of those goods go down. The theory does work—but only when government holds on to the excess dollars. If Congress and the President spend the additional tax revenues on new programs, government has simply substituted its own spending for that of the consumer.

TAXATION TO COMBAT RECESSION

Recession is an economic condition typified by high unemployment and lower production of goods and services. In the mid-1970's, recession replaced inflation as the major threat to a stable economy. The government turned to income tax reductions as a means of increasing consumer buying, thus hoping to stimulate business activity and reduce unemployment. Renewed inflation then became a possibility, for the government faced ever-larger deficits caused by the missing tax revenues.

REGULATION OF THE VALUE OF THE CURRENCY

Congress also affects the economy by regulating the value of the currency. Congressional powers in this area include (1) regulation of banking through the Federal Reserve System (see pages 251–52); (2) guarantees of up to $100,000 on individual bank accounts through the Federal Deposit Insurance Corporation; (3) coordination with the President in setting the international value of the dollar; and (4) authorization of U.S. participation in world banking agencies such as the International Monetary Fund.

$\mathbb{S}$UMMARY AND CONCLUSIONS

1. The Congress of the United States raises and spends astronomical sums of money each year. The power to regulate the economy provides Congress with a great challenge, for even as Americans demand more and more services from government, inflation and recession have shaken old economic rules. Despite rising tax rates, the Treasury Department must borrow billions of dollars annually; the accumulation of these billions is called the *national debt*.

2. Four major revenue sources provide over 90 percent of federal income: personal income taxes, Social Security taxes, corporate income

taxes, and excise taxes. Taxes primarily pay for government activities, but Congress also uses them to achieve social goals. The Internal Revenue Service enforces the complex tax laws.

3. The main items in the federal budget are defense, human resources, interest payments on the national debt, and physical resources. The Office of Management and Budget coordinates the preparation of the budget, which the President submits to Congress for approval. Appropriations bills originate in the House of Representatives, where the original requests may be greatly modified by the committee process and floor debate. The Senate conducts its own debates on appropriations bills, after which a conference committee irons out differences between the two houses. Since the President seldom vetoes a money bill, members of Congress often load up the "porkbarrel" with costly and questionable special-interest projects for their constituents.

4. Congress realizes that it can exercise a major influence on the economy through its power to tax. Tax increases have been used as a brake on inflation. Tax reductions have been used as a stimulus during recessions. Congress also attempts to stabilize the value of the dollar through its regulation of the currency and the banking system.

REVIEW QUESTIONS AND ACTIVITIES

TERMS YOU SHOULD KNOW

appropriations
Appropriations Committee
balanced budget
boondoggle
budget
debt ceiling
deficit spending
excise tax
export tax
fiscal year
gross national product (GNP)
human resources
indirect tax
inflation
item veto

logrolling
national debt
patronage
personal income tax
physical resources
porkbarrel
progressive tax
recession
regressive tax
Social Security tax
tariff
tax deduction
tax exemption
tax loophole

OBJECTIVE QUESTIONS

The following multiple-choice questions are based on the important ideas presented in this chapter. Select the response that best completes each statement.

1. Federal spending has grown rapidly because (a) the American people have demanded more and more government services. (b) as the economy has grown, the job of managing big business and big labor has grown more complicated. (c) present-day social philosophy holds that government should help the poor and unemployed. (d) larger expenditures are needed for defense. (e) all of these.

2. The largest single source of federal tax revenues is the (a) corporate income tax. (b) excise tax. (c) Social Security tax. (d) personal income tax. (e) import taxes.

3. An example of a *regressive* tax would be a tax on (a) personal income. (b) corporation profits. (c) cigarettes and liquor. (d) the estate inherited by a person's children. (e) all of these.

4. A *loophole* in the tax laws allows (a) the government a means of collecting extra taxes. (b) the average taxpayer a way of escaping income taxes. (c) Congress a means of changing the President's budget. (d) wealthy corporations and individuals a way of greatly decreasing their tax payments. (e) foreign investors to buy U.S. companies without obeying U.S. laws.

5. Social Security payments for the elderly retired people in this country are intended to (a) provide minimum comfort and security. (b) allow them to enjoy the standard of living they had while they were working. (c) pay only for medical and hospital care. (d) prevent recession by giving older people large amounts of money to spend. (e) keep inflation from getting worse.

6. The government agency established to collect taxes and deal with tax fraud is the (a) GPO. (b) FBI. (c) Secret Service. (d) OMB. (e) IRS.

7. In recent years, federal fiscal policy can best be described as marked by (a) balanced budgets. (b) lowered debt ceilings. (c) closing of tax loopholes. (d) deficit spending. (e) porkbarrel politics.

8. The national debt continues to grow; as a percentage of the GNP it has (a) increased. (b) remained the same. (c) decreased. (d) grown larger than the GNP. (e) the national debt has no relation to the GNP.

9. All federal appropriations bills must originate in (a) the White House. (b) the individual state legislatures. (c) the Senate. (d) the Supreme Court. (e) the House of Representatives.

10. An example of porkbarrel legislation might be (a) an increase in Social Security benefits. (b) establishment of a national health care program. (c) funding of a cancer research project. (d) construction of a breakwater to protect shipping at a Florida resort. (e) funding of a space probe of Mars.

CONCEPT DEVELOPMENT

This chapter has explored a number of significant concepts relating to congressional control of federal fiscal policy. You can use your skills in thinking, researching, and writing to answer the following questions.

1. Why has the federal budget grown so rapidly—much faster than this country's population—over the past fifty years?

2. List the major types of federal taxes. What percentage of government income does each produce?

3. Aside from doing away completely with taxes, what changes would you suggest in the nation's tax structure?

4. Why does government allow the national debt to increase year after year, without making any serious effort to reduce it?

5. Explore the strengths and weaknesses of the civil service system. What, if anything, can be done to make public servants more responsive to the needs of the American people?

ACTIVITIES

The following activities are designed to help you use the ideas developed in the chapter.

1. Obtain a series of tax forms from the IRS, the post office, a bank, or a local tax accountant. Fill out fictitious Form 1040 tax returns for three taxpayers at income levels of (a) $5,000, (b) $20,000, and (c) $100,000. Give each person an equivalent family, but invent expenses in keeping with his or her income. Make overhead transparencies from each return so that you can show them to the class. Discuss the concept of progressive tax rates as it applies to these three returns.

2. Write to your representative and senator asking them for lists of projects they have sponsored which directly benefit your district. Do you believe that any of these can be labeled porkbarrel projects? What, if anything, should be done about such use of tax revenues?

3. The federal bureaucracy is often accused of being slow, inefficient, and uncaring. Interview at least ten people you know who have had direct contact with the federal government (through the Veterans Administration, the Postal Service, the Social Security Administration, the IRS, etc.). What conclusions can you draw from their remarks about the treatment they received?

4. Prepare a bulletin board display in collage form that demonstrates (a) the sources of the federal tax dollar and (b) the uses the government finds for that dollar.

5. Obtain a copy of the federal budget for the current fiscal year. After a brief examination, do you feel that you understand its structure and priorities? Can you discover any equivalents of the bisexual Polish frog study mentioned in the chapter? If you had the authority, where would you begin making cuts in order to eliminate budget deficits?

3

DEVELOPMENT
OF THE
EXECUTIVE
BRANCH

CHAPTER SEVEN

THE MANY JOBS
OF THE PRESIDENT

On Tuesday morning, October 16, 1962, shortly after nine o'clock, President Kennedy called and asked me to come to the White House. He only said that we were facing great trouble. Shortly afterward, in his office, he told me that a U-2 [observation plane] had just finished a photographic mission, and that the intelligence community had become convinced that Russia was placing missiles and atomic weapons in Cuba.

That was the beginning of the Cuban missile crisis—a confrontation between the two giant atomic nations, the U.S. and the U.S.S.R., which brought the world to the abyss of nuclear destruction and the end of mankind.*

These doomsday words came from the pen of Robert Kennedy, the President's brother and the U.S. Attorney General, who played a key advisory role during those near-fatal two weeks. He went on to tell the story of how advice poured into the President's office from military and diplomatic officials. The "hawks" pushed for an immediate air strike to knock out the missiles, or for an air-sea invasion of Cuba. "Doves" pointed out the dangers of armed confrontation, and advised a diplomatic route of compromise and parley. President Kennedy knew he could not permit the missiles to remain eighty miles off the coast of Florida. Those weapons could be used

* Reprinted from page 23 of *Thirteen Days: A Memoir of the Cuban Missile Crisis* by Robert F. Kennedy. By permission of W. W. Norton & Company, Inc. Copyright © 1971, 1969 by W. W. Norton & Company, Inc. Copyright © 1968 by McCall Corporation.

by the Russians to force the United States to back down in other parts of the world. In his own mind, however, Kennedy had already decided that he would not touch off a war with Russia if any possibility of a peaceful settlement remained open. Listening, thinking, questioning, he considered the consequences of each step open to him.

Those hours in the Cabinet Room that Saturday afternoon in October [the 27th] could never be erased from the minds of any of us. We saw as never before the meaning and responsibility involved in the power of the United States, the power of the President, the responsibility we had to people around the globe who had never heard of our country or the men sitting in that room determining their fate, making a decision which would influence whether they would live or die.

"We won't attack tomorrow," the President said. "We shall try again."*

Communication links were opened between Kennedy and the Soviet Premier, Nikita Khrushchev, while the country prepared for any eventuality. The Pentagon placed troops and planes on alert. Panic buying resulted in long lines at grocery stores. Families began digging backyard air raid shelters. Leaders of both countries lived with the terrible knowledge that World War III stood only a decision or two away.

Later that week, Robert Kennedy wrote,

I went immediately to the White House, and there I received a call from Ambassador Dobrynin [Russian ambassador to the United States], saying that he would like to visit with me. I met him in my office at 11:00 a.m. [Sunday, October 28]. He told me that the message was coming through that Khrushchev had agreed to dismantle and withdraw the missiles under adequate supervision and inspection; that everything was going to work out satisfactorily; and that Mr. Khrushchev wanted to send his best wishes to the President and to me.

. . . I believe our deliberations proved conclusively how important it is that the President have recommendations and opinions of more than one individual, of more than one department, and of more than one point of view.

.   .   .

The possibility of the destruction of mankind was always in his [President Kennedy's] mind. Someone once said that World War III would be fought with atomic weapons and the next war with sticks and stones.†

The awesome power that resides in the office of the President of the United States cannot be dramatized any more clearly than in the deadly game of power politics called the Cuban missile crisis. Presidential power does not emerge only in times of emergency, however, as you will learn in this chapter. The qualifications for the presidency, along with the many-

* *Ibid.*, p. 101.
† *Ibid.*, pp 110–11, 127.

sided nature of the job, will be seen as the answers to these questions are discussed:

1. How does a person gain the presidency?
2. What are the duties of the President as chief of state?
3. How does the President serve as chief legislator?
4. What powers does the President exercise as chief executive?
5. How does the President represent us as chief diplomat?
6. How does the President serve as chief politician?
7. Why did the Constitution make the President commander-in-chief of the armed forces?
8. When does the President function as chief jurist?
9. What is the role of the Vice President?
10. What is the job of the President's Executive Office?

How does a person gain the presidency?

Out of the hundreds of millions of Americans who will live and die during your lifetime, fewer than twenty will attain the office of the presidency. The odds on any one of us winning the Irish Sweepstakes are better than the odds on being elected President. Despite the tremendous difficulties to be overcome, however, ambitious politicians still set their sights on the White House and the opportunity to lead the country that goes with election to the Oval Office.

QUALIFICATIONS FOR THE PRESIDENCY

Legal qualifications. Surprisingly, the legal qualifications for being President are very few. The Constitution merely requires that the candidate be thirty-five years of age, a natural-born citizen, and a resident of the United States for at least fourteen years.

Personal qualifications. Tradition has created a second set of unwritten qualifications. No man in his thirties has ever been elected to (or succeeded to) the presidency; the average age at the time of election is more than twenty years older. All presidents have been male, all but two have been married (and only one divorced). Two-thirds have come to the office with law backgrounds. Only one non-Protestant has been elected (an unofficial religious barrier broken by John Kennedy, a Catholic, in 1960).

Political qualifications. A candidate's political background plays a major role in catapulting him into the race for the presidency (see the accompanying box). Most presidents have come out of large states with important blocs of electoral votes. Almost all were well-known public figures before election, as a result of having held high office or commanded troops during a war. On the basis of past history, a would-be President who wanted to serve the most useful apprenticeship would first carve out a career as a state governor, United States senator, or general in the U.S. Army.

Eight "rules" for presidential hopefuls

Any serious candidate for President must play by these "rules" if he hopes to gain his party's nomination. Of course, not all eight rules can ever be applied at one time. Party differences, demands of a particular election, and the personalities of the candidates will all influence the priorities at the convention.

1. The rule of political talent	A candidate should have some successful experience in government, in either an appointed or elected office. Generals can ignore this rule if they choose.
2. The rule of governors	Nominating conventions prefer to choose their candidates from among the state governors. Governors control state delegations; governors do not normally take vote-losing stands on controversial issues, as do members of Congress.
3. The rule of big "swing" states	A candidate from a big state has a better chance, particularly if it is not a one-party state. The hope is that he can carry his own state and that its bloc of convention votes will sway others.
4. The rule of multiple interests	Conventions will choose only candidates who can command support from many different economic interests—agriculture, labor, commerce, and industry.
5. The rule of happy family life	A candidate must seem to lead an ideal family life. A photogenic wife and wholesome-looking children also help.
6. The rule of the small town	Although most Americans live in urban centers, conventions prefer candidates from small towns. Prejudice against big-city candidates is dying, however.
7. The rule of English stock	**Candidates with English ancestors are preferred. Up to 1981, 40 men had held the presidency, and 34 of them** traced their ancestors back to the **British Isles.**
8. The rule of Protestantism	Only one non-Protestant (Kennedy, a Roman Catholic) has held the office, despite the Constitution's ban on religious tests for holding any office.

Source: Adapted from Sidney Hyman, "Nine Tests for Presidential Hopefuls," *The New York Times Magazine*, January 4, 1959. © 1959 by The New York Times Company. Reprinted by permission.

ELECTORAL COLLEGE

The Framers of the Constitution did not foresee mass communications and national political parties. They therefore designed a presidential election system that could narrow down a field of many candidates. (See Chapter 14 for a complete discussion of the modern presidential election cycle, including primary elections and national conventions.) The institution the

Framers created is called the Electoral College. This "college" has no campus and no students; its only function is to elect a President. Many attempts have been made to abolish it, in fact, since the special circumstances that inspired it no longer exist.

The Electoral College process. When American voters go to the polls in November of a presidential election year, they do not actually vote directly for the President. The small print on each ballot reads, "For electors pledged to Theodore Roosevelt," or whatever the candidate's name is that year. Each state receives a number of electors equal to the number of representatives plus the two senators from that state. The number varies with changing population patterns, as shown in each census. Alaska, with one representative and two senators, would merit three electoral votes; a populous state like Texas might have twenty-six. The slate of electors winning the highest number of votes in a given state (but not necessarily a majority, if the vote is split among three or more candidates) wins all of the electoral votes from that state.

On the first Monday after the second Wednesday in December of presidential election years, the winning electors gather at the state capitals to cast their ballots formally. In theory, the electors are free to vote for any of the candidates, but very few have chosen to do so. As a matter of course, most electors vote for their party's nominee. Each of the fifty Electoral College meetings sends a certificate to the President of the Senate confirming its selection. On January 6 of the following year, Congress meets in joint session to open these ballots. That congressional count of the 538 electoral votes brings the election to an official conclusion. The American people can now be officially informed of what they have known since the vote tallies indicated the winner on election night. In the deliberate manner required by the Constitution, a new President has been elected.

Weaknesses of the Electoral College system. The Electoral College has several times selected a candidate who did not receive the highest number of popular votes. Jackson (1824), Tilden (1876), and Cleveland (1888) all received the highest number of votes but lost the election—they did not receive a majority of electoral votes. By carrying the most populous states, a candidate can still win an election without gaining a majority of the total votes cast. It is this weakness of the Electoral College—which seems to deny the value of the popular vote—that has led to the most vigorous cries for its reform or abolition.

Another problem develops when no candidate wins a majority of the electoral vote. That has happened only twice, in 1801 and in 1824, although the 1968 election came within a key state or two of repeating the experience. The Constitution provides that if no clear majority exists, the election will be thrown into the House of Representatives. With each state having only one vote, the House must choose from the top three candidates. This procedure obviously favors the party that holds political control of the House, another strike against the Electoral College system.

TERM OF OFFICE

American presidents serve four-year terms following national elections, which take place in years divisible by four—1792, 1860, 1976, 1980, and so on (see Table 7.1 for a chart of the presidents). Washington began the tradition of not serving more than two terms, but before 1951, no law enforced this custom. Franklin Roosevelt first broke the pattern when he won a third term in 1940—and then a fourth term in 1944. The Twenty-

Table 7.1   **Presidents of the United States**

Name	Party	Native state	Born–Died	Served
1. George Washington	Fed.	Va.	1732–1799	1789–1797
2. John Adams	Fed.	Mass.	1735–1826	1797–1801
3. Thomas Jefferson	Dem.-Rep.	Va.	1743–1826	1801–1809
4. James Madison	Dem.-Rep.	Va.	1751–1836	1809–1817
5. James Monroe	Dem.-Rep.	Va.	1758–1831	1817–1825
6. John Quincy Adams	Dem.-Rep.	Mass.	1767–1848	1825–1829
7. Andrew Jackson	Dem.	S.C.	1767–1845	1829–1837
8. Martin Van Buren	Dem.	N.Y.	1782–1862	1837–1841
9. William H. Harrison	Whig	Va.	1773–1841	1841
10. John Tyler	Whig	Va.	1790–1862	1841–1845
11. James K. Polk	Dem.	N.C.	1795–1849	1845–1849
12. Zachary Taylor	Whig	Va.	1784–1850	1849–1850
13. Millard Fillmore	Whig	N.Y.	1800–1874	1850–1853
14. Franklin Pierce	Dem.	N.H.	1804–1869	1853–1857
15. James Buchanan	Dem.	Pa.	1791–1868	1857–1861
16. Abraham Lincoln	Rep.	Ky.	1809–1865	1861–1865
17. Andrew Johnson	Nat. Union	N.C.	1808–1875	1865–1869
18. Ulysses S. Grant	Rep.	Ohio	1822–1885	1869–1877
19. Rutherford B. Hayes	Rep.	Ohio	1822–1893	1877–1881
20. James A. Garfield	Rep.	Ohio	1831–1881	1881
21. Chester A. Arthur	Rep.	Vt.	1830–1886	1881–1885
22. Grover Cleveland	Dem.	N.J.	1837–1908	1885–1889
23. Benjamin Harrison	Rep.	Ohio	1833–1901	1889–1893
24. Grover Cleveland	Dem.	N.J.	1837–1908	1893–1897
25. William McKinley	Rep.	Ohio	1843–1901	1897–1901
26. Theodore Roosevelt	Rep.	N.Y.	1858–1919	1901–1909
27. William H. Taft	Rep.	Ohio	1857–1930	1909–1913
28. Woodrow Wilson	Dem.	Va.	1856–1924	1913–1921
29. Warren G. Harding	Rep.	Ohio	1865–1923	1921–1923
30. Calvin Coolidge	Rep.	Vt.	1872–1933	1923–1929
31. Herbert C. Hoover	Rep.	Iowa	1874–1964	1929–1933
32. Franklin D. Roosevelt	Dem.	N.Y.	1882–1945	1933–1945
33. Harry S Truman	Dem.	Mo.	1884–1972	1945–1953
34. Dwight D. Eisenhower	Rep.	Texas	1890–1969	1953–1961
35. John F. Kennedy	Dem.	Mass.	1917–1963	1961–1963
36. Lyndon B. Johnson	Dem.	Texas	1908–1973	1963–1969
37. Richard M. Nixon	Rep.	Calif.	1913–	1969–1974
38. Gerald R. Ford	Rep.	Neb.	1913–	1974–1977
39. Jimmy Carter	Dem.	Ga.	1924–	1977–1981
40. Ronald W. Reagan	Rep.	Ill.	1911–	1981–

second Amendment (ratified in 1951) now limits presidents to two terms. A Vice President who succeeds to the office may run for the presidency twice on his own—but only if his partial term was for less than two years. Under this rule, the maximum time in office is now ten years (two regular terms plus no more than one-half of the former President's term).

What are the duties of the President as chief of state?

Delegates to the 1787 Constitutional Convention debated at length on what the exact role of the head of government should be. A good deal of discussion centered on a proposal to create a *constitutional monarchy*, in which the king or queen represents the nation in ceremonial matters, but possesses no real political power. This system exists today in Great Britain, Sweden, and the Netherlands. The majority at the convention rejected that idea, however, and incorporated these ceremonial functions as one of the many roles that the President must play. (Figure 7.1 suggests the diversity of these responsibilities.)

A SYMBOL OF THE NATION

When the President acts as chief of state, he stands as the symbol of the United States, its power, and its policies. Not only do the American people look to him as a kind of embodiment of our way of life, but the rest of the world sees the United States reflected in his image. Because the President and Vice President are the only nationally elected officeholders, we turn to the President for leadership particularly in times of crisis.

The President spends much valuable time fulfilling his role as chief of state. He receives all high-level foreign visitors, sometimes housing them in the White House itself. Since World War II, presidential trips outside the country in quest of international agreements have become quite common. This form of personal diplomacy receives national attention, as do many of the President's more ceremonial activities. Every year he lights the national Christmas tree on the White House lawn. Time must also be found for attending the annual Easter Egg Roll, laying a wreath on the Tomb of the Unknown Soldier, being photographed buying stamps, seals, or poppies to publicize charity drives, and on and on. The President also signs all commissions of office under the United States, including those of junior-grade officers in the armed forces. Indeed, as early as the term of Thomas Jefferson, presidents were complaining about such time-consuming tasks. Just signing the stacks of formal documents that cross the presidential desk requires several hours a week.

A NECESSARY FUNCTION

Despite all of these apparently negative factors, the importance of having the President serve as a symbol for the ongoing life of the nation should not be overlooked. Even when standing in a reception line, the President is also serving as the country's chief legislator, chief executive, chief diplomat, chief politician, commander-in-chief, and chief jurist. He can never be ignored.

How does the President serve as chief legislator?

Despite the orderly separation of government into executive, legislative, and judicial powers, the President does exercise broad legislative powers and responsibilities. Most presidents enter office dedicated to enactment of a platform of specific programs, which must then be translated into legislation. At the same time, Congress continually looks to the President for suggestions and leadership for drafting programs to meet other legislative needs.

Figure 7.1
The seven "hats" of the President

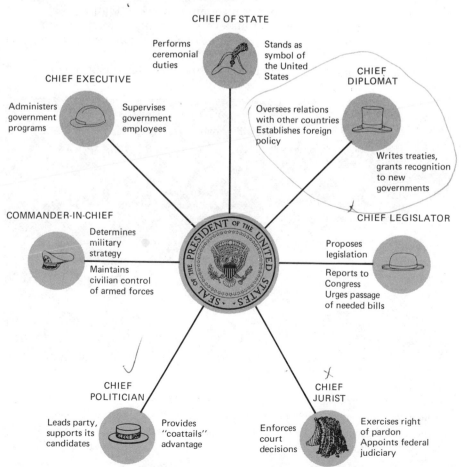

CHIEF OF STATE
Performs ceremonial duties
Stands as symbol of the United States

CHIEF EXECUTIVE
Administers government programs
Supervises government employees

CHIEF DIPLOMAT
Oversees relations with other countries
Establishes foreign policy
Writes treaties, grants recognition to new governments

COMMANDER-IN-CHIEF
Determines military strategy
Maintains civilian control of armed forces

CHIEF LEGISLATOR
Proposes legislation
Reports to Congress
Urges passage of needed bills

CHIEF POLITICIAN
Leads party, supports its candidates
Provides "coattails" advantage

CHIEF JURIST
Enforces court decisions
Exercises right of pardon
Appoints federal judiciary

SOURCE OF THE PRESIDENT'S LEGISLATIVE POWER

The President's legislative powers derive from the Constitution, which states that the President "shall from time to time give to the Congress information of the state of the Union, and recommend to their consideration such measures as he shall judge necessary and expedient." Each January, the President presents to Congress a formal State of the Union address, either in person or by special message. In this speech he outlines the economic and social problems of the country as he sees them, and suggests legislation to solve them. Early in the year, too, he submits a budget message asking Congress to appropriate the amount of money he believes will be required to run the federal government for the next fiscal year. Other presidential suggestions and requests follow throughout the legislative session.

INFLUENCE ON CONGRESS

Through his speeches, press conferences, and the weight of the entire executive branch, every President can bring tremendous pressure on Congress to pass the legislation he recommends (see Figure 7.2). With national press coverage carrying his every word into American homes, a President also finds it relatively easy to enlist public support for his programs.

Although the power has been used sparingly, the President may also call

Figure 7.2
President Ronald Reagan holds a press conference. By appealing directly to the public through the news media, a President can muster nationwide popular support for his views—a tactic that indirectly pressures Congress to go along with him, too. Source: Wide World Photos.

special sessions of Congress when emergency legislation is needed. Today's congressional sessions run almost year-round, however. In the past, when Congress often adjourned for the year by midsummer, the special session made more sense.

VETO POWER

Congress does not always pass legislation which meets with presidential favor. After weighing the merits of a bill, the President may refuse to sign it, thus exercising his veto power. Not only does the veto (described in more detail in Chapter 5) allow the President to kill a bill he doesn't like, it also gives him a bargaining item with Congress. Knowing that a bill faces a veto, congressional leaders will often modify the legislation to conform more closely with the White House's wishes. Even with a heavy Democratic majority in 1975–76, Congress scored less than one victory in seven when faced with the challenge of overriding President Ford's vetoes.

CHECKS AND BALANCES

The Framers of the Constitution did not adhere totally to the concept of separation of powers. The Constitution combines that philosophy with a more intricate idea called *checks and balances* (see Chapter 3). Each branch of government, they believed, should retain a strong influence on the actions of the other two. As described above, the President's legislative powers give him an important voice in legislative matters, without letting him dominate congressional activity.

What powers does the President exercise as chief executive?

As chief executive—head of the vast administrative machinery of the federal government—the President reaches into the lives of every American. The Constitution does not precisely outline how the President "shall take care that the laws be faithfully executed." In working out this problem, Congress has created the thirteen *Cabinet* offices (discussed in greater detail in Chapters 8 and 9). Branching out from that starting point, 2.8 million federal employees today enforce, administer, and direct the course of government—all under the President's supervision.

THE PRESIDENT'S CABINET

Acting without direct constitutional authority, Washington formed the first Cabinet in 1789 with three departments—State, War, and Treasury. The Constitution merely states that the President may "require the opinion, in writing, of the principal officer in each of the executive departments. . . ."

Each individual President stamps his Cabinet with his own personality and administrative concept; some Cabinets have had great influence, but others have served as little more than instruments of presidential policy. The top official of all but one of the Cabinet departments carries the title of Secretary, as in Secretary of State or Secretary of Defense (but the head of the Department of Justice is called the Attorney General). Each Cabinet department oversees a particular area of government as the direct representative of the President.

Selection of the Cabinet. Each new President selects his own Cabinet. Almost complete changeovers of Cabinet members occur at each change of administration, particularly when a new party takes over the White House. Presidents often appoint leading national figures to serve in the Cabinet, although most presidents also nominate their own key political advisors for several of the posts. Nominations require Senate approval before the new secretary can be sworn in, but few secretaries-designate do not pass this screening. If heavy Senate opposition develops, the President is more likely to withdraw the nomination than to risk the embarrassment of defeat on the Senate floor.

Duties of the Cabinet. Secretaries perform three main duties: (1) they manage the affairs of their departments; (2) they each represent their department in its relationship with Congress (writing legislation, testifying before committees); and (3) they advise the President on matters that concern the department. Conflicts over jurisdiction often arise between Cabinet members. Who, for instance, should have primary responsibility for the food stamp program—the Secretary of Agriculture or the Secretary of Health and Human Services?

No fixed schedule of meetings exists; the Cabinet gathers only at the call of the President. Some presidents, like Dwight Eisenhower, have used Cabinet meetings as times when important policy decisions can be debated. Other presidents have preferred to make Cabinet meetings largely ceremonial, with important matters reserved for private discussions with the individual secretaries.

EXECUTIVE AUTHORITY

The laws passed by Congress often establish broad guidelines, leaving the President and the executive branch to work out the details. The complex regulations written for this purpose are called *executive orders* and have the force of law. Over ten thousand executive orders now in effect regulate everything from aircraft flight patterns to the Peace Corps. As is pointed out in Chapter 12, the Supreme Court has sometimes intervened to strike down executive orders based on laws which the justices believe exceed constitutional limits.

The President also exercises his executive powers through his constitutional authority to appoint federal officials. Although Civil Service laws have limited this *patronage* power (see Chapter 20) to only the higher ranking positions, over 1,500 top executive branch employees owe their jobs to the President. As with Cabinet posts, most of these appointments require Senate approval.

The President's power extends to *dismissal* of these same high officials, with the exception of federal judges and officials of the regulatory agencies established by Congress (see Chapter 10). No constitutional basis for dismissal exists, except where impeachment is specified. Nevertheless, tradition requires that when the President asks for someone's resignation, that official promptly steps aside.

LET'S REVIEW FOR A MOMENT

According to folk tradition, all new parents look fondly upon their newborn child as a possible President of the United States. The constitutional requirements certainly eliminate few Americans—the President must merely be at least thirty-five years old, a natural-born citizen, and a fourteen-year resident of the United States. A look at history reveals other unwritten rules—experience gained in state or federal service, a legal or military background, and leadership of a major party.

Who elects our presidents? We all do, of course—or do we? Read the fine print on a presidential ballot—people are really voting for electors, not a President. Designed to meet eighteenth-century needs, the Electoral College system has a major flaw—a President still can be elected without gaining a majority of the popular vote.

As you've already gathered, the President wears many hats. As our chief of state, he shakes hands at White House receptions, welcomes foreign visitors, and speaks at the dedication of a new dam.

In the President's role as chief legislator, he can't pass a law, of course, but he has many ways of influencing Congress. Three major ways he puts pressure on Congress are (1) sending messages to Congress recommending new legislation, (2) mobilizing public pressure, and (3) using his veto power.

It is as chief executive that the President administers the nation's laws. With the aid of his Cabinet, the President conducts the nation's business, determines the priorities of government, and oversees the day-to-day conduct of the 2.8 million employees of the executive branch.

That sounds like a full-time job, doesn't it? Wait, there's more. Among many other duties, the President might be called on to work out a nuclear arms treaty with the Soviet Union. Let's see how our chief diplomat handles this important task along with his other roles.

How does the President represent us as chief diplomat?

When a President welcomes a visiting prime minister to Washington, he acts in his role as chief of state. Later that afternoon, when the two heads of government sit down to talk about a new trade treaty or a conflict over deep-sea fishing rights, the President switches to his job as our chief diplomat. The President's powers in the conduct of foreign affairs include (1) the initiation of foreign policy, (2) the recognition of new foreign governments, and (3) the making of treaties.

INITIATING FOREIGN POLICY

In his role as chief diplomat, the President stamps his personal philosophy on many aspects of American relations with other countries. A number of important foreign policy decisions from our past retain the name of their originator. These "doctrines" represent broad policy guidelines or statements of the U.S. government's attitudes. The Monroe Doctrine of 1823 and the Truman Doctrine of 1947 are two examples. The Monroe Doctrine concerned European influence in the Americas; the Truman Doctrine dedicated the United States to stopping the spread of international communism.

Beginning with Woodrow Wilson, American presidents have also traveled abroad to meet with foreign heads of state. These *summit conferences* give leaders a chance to meet each other personally and to work out agreements regarding war and peace, trade, boundary disputes, and other aspects of international relations. Technical advice on these trips comes from the Secretary of State and the State Department, which also handle the day-to-day problems of foreign affairs (see Chapter 8).

RECOGNIZING NEW FOREIGN GOVERNMENTS

Whenever a new government takes power in a foreign country—particularly if the change has taken place through a revolution or *coup d'état*—the United States must decide whether or not to "recognize" the new government as legitimate. If this *diplomatic recognition* is granted, formal relations between the two countries can be established. Diplomatic recognition (or nonrecognition) is a powerful political weapon. Only after a new government has been recognized can a country receive military or economic aid, participate in trade agreements with the United States, or have the right to establish diplomatic and consular ties with this country.

MAKING TREATIES

In the minds of some people, the term *treaty* suggests secret diplomatic maneuvers which bind nations to major war-and-peace commitments. That World War I concept seldom applies today; instead, the United States openly negotiates thousands of treaties with other countries, most of which involve mutual defense pacts, agreements on water rights, fishing grounds, international trade, military and economic aid, exchange of diplomats and cultural missions, and the like. As chief diplomat, the President takes final responsibility for all treaties, but must also present the signed document to the Senate for consideration. Unless two-thirds of the senators present vote to ratify it, the treaty must be considered invalid—even though the President has already signed it.

Emergency conditions sometimes require that a President negotiate a treaty quickly, without waiting for Senate approval. In such cases, he may sign an executive order, which carries the force of a formal treaty. Franklin Roosevelt made a famous agreement of that type just before World War II, when he committed the United States to provide military assistance to Great Britain in its war with Germany. Critics of presidential power have worried about this method of bypassing Senate control over treaties, but attempts to limit presidential authority through constitutional amendments have consistently failed in Congress.

How does the President serve as chief politician?

During each election year, some Americans seem to be surprised when the President takes an active role in national political affairs. Somehow, they have come to believe that the occupant of the White House should remain above the battle, immune to everyday, grubby politics. Such cannot be the case, however, for without political "muscle," a President could never provide the legislative leadership needed under our system. Even with the President's own party in control of Congress, passage of an administration's legislative program requires great political skill on the part of the President and his aides. If his party loses its congressional majority, the job doubles in difficulty.

Whether working with the majority or minority party in Congress, a President possesses an arsenal of weapons for persuading reluctant members of Congress. He may select from a variety of techniques. These include (1) personal contacts with key legislators, either by phone or in person, which allow the President to express his views on pending legislation; (2) suggestions that he might oppose "pet" bills greatly desired by a member of Congress; (3) the withholding of government spending or projects in the home districts of uncooperative legislators; (4) requests for loyalty and cooperation "for the good of the party"; or (5) direct appeals to the public, in which he asks the people to let their senators and representatives know that they approve of the President's position.

Whenever the people approve of a President, they tend to vote for other members of his party—members of Congress, governors, and even local officials. These politicians are said to ride into office on the President's coattails. While some political analysts warn that the "coattail effect" no longer has much validity, presidents still work hard at practical politics.

Using his built-in ability to make news, the President moves around the country giving speeches, posing for pictures with local politicians, handing out government jobs and money where the results will be politically profitable. Newspaper reporters and television cameras follow his every move. At election time, these activities pay off. Pollsters estimate that an incumbent President starts with an edge of 5 percentage points over any opponent, just by virtue of already holding office. With the single exception of Depression-plagued Herbert Hoover, every President elected in this century who has campaigned for a second term has won reelection. The 1976 election added a historical oddity to this record when a shaky economy and memories of the Watergate scandal contributed to the defeat of Gerald Ford—the only President to hold office without having first been elected either President or Vice President.

Why did the Constitution make the President commander-in-chief of the armed forces?

Imagine an Armed Forces Day review, with long lines of marching troops passing in front of the nation's top military commanders. Almost lost in the crowd of generals and admirals, one man in a business suit nevertheless holds center stage. That man, the President of the United States, returns his soldiers' salute as their commander-in-chief—a symbol of the Constitution's insistence that civilian control of the armed forces be unquestioned.

LESSONS OF HISTORY

History provides us with abundant reasons for placing the military forces under direction of civilian government. Our Declaration of Independence cites British attempts to "render the Military independent of, and superior to, the Civil power" as one of the causes of the Revolution. One need look no further than this hemisphere, in fact, to draw an object lesson from the Latin American military dictatorships. In those countries without a firm tradition of noninterference by the armed forces in civilian rule, government after government has fallen into the hands of military dictators who feel little regard for human rights.

A dramatic test of civilian versus military control of this country's armed forces came during the Korean War. General Douglas MacArthur, World War II hero and commander of the United Nations forces in Korea, pushed for expansion of the war into China—even though this brought him into direct conflict with the commander-in-chief, President Harry Truman (see Figure 7.3). Despite MacArthur's determination, Truman believed that political factors outweighed military considerations and decided against an invasion of China. When the general persisted in making public statements against this decision, Truman fired MacArthur for insubordination and ordered him home. The country welcomed the returning general with open arms—but no movement of any kind developed within the armed forces to oppose the will of their civilian commander-in-chief.

FINAL MILITARY AUTHORITY

As commander-in-chief, the President does much more than review Armed Forces Day parades. From the White House come far-reaching decisions of policy and strategy that direct the American military during times of war and peace. Woodrow Wilson, for example, tipped the scales toward the United States' entry into World War I. In 1944 Franklin Roosevelt overrode the wishes of the British government in ordering that the main attack on

Figure 7.3
President Harry Truman presents a medal to General Douglas MacArthur on Wake Island in October 1950. Six months later, Truman relieved the general of his command on grounds of insubordination.

Germany proceed through France, rather than through southern Europe. In 1945 Harry Truman made the decision to use the atomic bomb on Japan.

THE ROLE OF CONGRESS

A further constitutional safeguard requires that the President share his control over the military with Congress. The power to declare war belongs to Congress alone; Roosevelt appeared personally before the legislature to ask for a declaration of war on December 8, 1941, the day after Pearl Harbor was attacked.

Nevertheless, many of our wars have not been formally declared: the Barbary War and the Civil War in the 1800's, Korea and Vietnam in this century. Presidents in these cases believed that political considerations did not make a formal declaration of war desirable. This fine line between allowing a President too much freedom to "pull the trigger" and leaving him powerless to act in an emergency finally led to the War Powers Act of 1973. This law limits the President's ability to commit troops for long periods without congressional approval.

Such congressional controls have worried foreign policy experts in the White House, Pentagon, and State Department. Supporters of presidential freedom of action point to such successful examples as Eisenhower's use of marines in Lebanon in 1958 and to Kennedy's dispatch of troops to Thailand in 1962. In both cases, they argue, prompt United States action prevented communist takeovers in those countries. (The box on the next page outlines some other restrictions on presidential freedom of action.)

WARTIME POWERS

Along with directing battlefield strategy, the President holds extraordinary powers at home during any wartime emergency. With congressional ap-

Practical limitations on presidential power

Limitation	Discussion
Limits of permissibility	No President may do anything that is not acceptable to the great body of public opinion, is illegal, unworkable, or unenforceable.
Limits of available resources	Since resources are always limited, the President must establish priorities for the best use of existing money, manpower, time, brains, and material.
Limits of available time	Deadlines and schedules exist for presidents as well as everyone else. The budget is due by a certain date; an aircraft carrier takes years to build; his term lasts only four years.
Limits of previous commitments	A President cannot escape the precedents set by former presidents. Decisions made by Washington, Lincoln, FDR—all influence and bind him. Even his own actions become precedents. Once started, a course of action cannot easily be abandoned.
Limits of available information	Any presidential action is no better than the information on which it is based. How can he know that his briefing is accurate? Is it complete, giving both sides of an issue?
Limits of the President's personality	Every President cannot be a "man for all seasons." His likes and dislikes, his education, his political philosophy—all influence his conduct of the office. His capacity for work and decision also enter into the equation. He needs a political genius that enables him to know how far he can move his people.
Limits of political realities	Time and circumstances impose their own limits. FDR's New Deal would have died a quick death in the courts just a few years earlier. Johnson probably could not have recognized Red China; Nixon could and did.

Source: Adapted from Tom Wicker, "The President," *New York Times Election Handbook, 1968,* edited by Harold Faber. Copyright © 1968 by The New York Times. Reprinted by arrangement with The New American Library, Inc., New York, N.Y.

proval, the President is empowered to (1) control all industrial efforts related to the war; (2) place ceilings on wages and prices; (3) regulate or ration food, clothing, and manufactured items; and (4) suspend some personal freedoms when necessary to safeguard the war effort. These near-dictatorial powers must be given up once the emergency has passed.

When does the President function as chief jurist?

Just as the Constitution's system of checks and balances gives the executive branch a voice in legislative matters, so does it give the President a direct hand in some judicial matters. As provided by law, the President (1) appoints all judges of the federal judiciary, plus the marshals of the courts and all United States attorneys; (2) exercises the power of the pardon; and (3) takes responsibility for carrying out court orders and decisions.

JUDICIAL APPOINTMENTS

As with most presidential appointments, the Senate must confirm men and women selected to serve on the federal courts. To be chosen for a judicial post, an individual must normally meet two tests: (1) demonstrated competency in the law and (2) solid credentials as a member of the President's own party. Republican presidents customarily pick Republican judges; Democratic presidents traditionally select from qualified Democrats. White House staffers help the President make his choices by preparing lists of qualified people based on recommendations from bar associations, working judges, and party officials.

PARDON—THE FINAL APPEAL

President Ford made headlines and generated nationwide controversy in 1974 when he granted Richard Nixon a "full, free, and absolute pardon . . . for all offenses against the United States. . . ." Whatever the merits of that particular pardon, Ford's use of this constitutional privilege could not be challenged in Congress or the courts. Most presidential pardons are given after the courts have passed sentence, and provide full legal forgiveness; as with Nixon, however, a pardon can be given even before a trial is held.

When considering a pardon, the President has three choices: (1) he may grant a *full pardon*, which restores civil rights, ends punishment or prevents it, and grants legal forgiveness for any criminal acts; (2) if the individual has already served time in prison, the President may *commute* the sentence, either shortening it or cutting it off at the time served to date; (3) a *reprieve* postpones execution of a sentence, thus freeing the prisoner from fine or imprisonment. The pardoning power may be exercised only in federal criminal cases; it extends to the military as well as the civilian courts—but not to state courts. The President cannot pardon a federal official who has been impeached and convicted.

CARRYING OUT COURT ORDERS

The Constitution demands that the President carry out and enforce court decisions, even when he disagrees with those rulings. In 1831, Andrew Jackson directly challenged this requirement. When he opposed a Supreme Court decision involving Cherokee Indian lands, President Jackson blustered, "John Marshall [the Chief Justice] has made his decision; now let him enforce it." Despite the President's duty under the Constitution to "take care that the laws be faithfully executed," Jackson defied the Supreme Court's ruling. The Indians lost their land and were forced to make a long march west to Oklahoma.

Jackson's resistance, fortunately, did not set a precedent. In 1974, for example, President Nixon obeyed Supreme Court decisions involving the activities of the presidency itself. Ordered to surrender Watergate-related tapes and records, he bowed to the high court (and public opinion) and handed over the incriminating evidence.

What is the role of the Vice President?

The modern vice-presidency of the United States was born in 1804, when the Twelfth Amendment was added to the Constitution. Previously, electors had voted for two people for President; the man who came in second became Vice President. Starting with the election of 1804, the electors have voted separately for President and Vice President.

Opponents of the amendment predicted that future vice presidents would be "carried into the market to be exchanged for the votes of some large states for President." That cynical prediction has largely come true. Vice Presidents most often accept their nomination knowing that they have been selected to "balance the ticket"—a means of avoiding bitter disputes within the party and of appealing to a bigger segment of the electorate.

DUTIES OF THE VICE PRESIDENT

Given only a single constitutional duty—that of presiding over the Senate —vice presidents labor in a political vacuum. The first holder of the job suggested that his title should be "His Superfluous Excellency." Thomas Marshall, Vice President under Wilson, liked to tell this story:

There were once two brothers. One ran away to sea. The other was elected Vice President and neither was heard of again.

In recent years, presidents have made serious efforts to increase the importance of the Vice President. A 1949 law made him a statutory member of the National Security Council, and he often attends Cabinet meetings. Modern vice presidents such as Humphrey, Rockefeller, and Mondale have chaired important presidential councils and committees, including the President's Committee on Equal Employment Opportunities, the Peace Corps National Advisory Council, National Council on Marine Resources and Engineering Development, and the 1975 Commission on CIA Activities Within the United States.

ACCESSION TO THE PRESIDENCY

With all these increased duties, the Vice President still has only limited powers until the death or disability of the President. When President Eisenhower was asked in 1960 to name one major decision that Vice President Nixon had influenced, he was unable to do so; but during Eisenhower's recovery from a heart attack, Nixon had presided over Cabinet meetings as unofficial acting president. Eight of our presidents have died

in office and one has resigned; each time, the Vice President has assumed
the powers as well as the title of the presidency. With the increasing
physical and mental strain of the modern presidency, the casualty rate in
the White House has been mounting. Since 1900, seven presidents have
either died in office or spent long periods in the hospital. Because of this
uncertainty, today's vice-presidency is worth far more than (in Vice President John Nance Garner's inelegant phrase) "a bucket of warm spit."

THE TWENTY-FIFTH AMENDMENT

Serious constitutional questions regarding presidential disability and succession were the subject of the Twenty-fifth Amendment, ratified in 1967.

Presidential disability. Several times in our history, the President has
been disabled for long periods—Garfield, Wilson, and Eisenhower among
them. With no machinery or precedents available, the Vice President could
not assume, even temporarily, the duties of the presidency. Now, following
a procedure worked out by Nixon and Eisenhower in 1958, the amendment
provides that (1) the Vice President can take over when notified by a
letter from the President that he can no longer carry out his duties, or
(2) should the President be unable or unwilling to write this letter, the
Vice President, with the approval of a majority of the Cabinet officers, may
notify Congress that he is taking over. Should the President challenge
the Vice President's action, he may ask Congress to decide the issue. A
two-thirds vote of both houses is required to confirm the incapacity of the
President.

Presidential succession. The Constitution left it up to Congress to determine the presidential succession should the office of vice president become
vacant (through the death, resignation, or elevation to the presidency of
the Vice President). Originally, the succession passed to the President
pro tempore of the Senate, and then to the Speaker of the House; in
1886, the Cabinet was placed in the line of succession, beginning with the
Secretary of State; finally, in 1947, the succession reverted to Congress
and elected officials, beginning with the Speaker of the House.

In 1973, Gerald Ford became the first Vice President to serve under the
terms of the Twenty-fifth Amendment. When Vice President Spiro Agnew
resigned, President Nixon nominated Ford, who was confirmed by a
majority vote of both houses of Congress. The amendment was used a
second time less than a year later, after Nixon's resignation elevated Ford
to the presidency. Ford selected Nelson Rockefeller as the second nonelected Vice President in our history.

What is the job of the President's Executive Office?

As noted earlier, the President directs the activities of all the departments,
bureaus, agencies, and commissions which make up the executive branch
of the government. One agency, the Executive Office of the President,

coordinates the day-to-day flow of government business and advises the President on the most sensitive national and international matters. Established in 1939, the Executive Office really consists of a number of separate agencies, all directly responsible to the President (see Figure 7.4). Several of the most important agencies are discussed below.

AGENCIES IN THE EXECUTIVE OFFICE

1. White House Staff. The White House Staff serves the President much as a military staff serves a general. A host of special assistants, counselors, and secretaries handles the daily affairs of the White House. The staff also maintains communication with Congress, the executive departments and agencies, the press, and the general public.

2. Office of Management and Budget. Managing the immense federal budget is the duty of the OMB. Its economists and other specialists advise the President on fiscal matters, particularly in the areas of budgetary control and evaluation of program performance.

3. National Security Council. One of the key policymaking bodies in the federal government, the NSC coordinates military activities with other agencies of government and advises the President on all aspects of national security. Members, who meet weekly (more often during emergencies), include the President and Vice President, the Secretaries of State and Defense, and the Director of the Office of Emergency Preparedness. Research papers and plans prepared by the Department of Defense, the Nuclear Regulatory Commission, the Office of Management and Budget, and other specialized agencies supply the NSC with the information needed for its decision-making.

4. Domestic Council. The Domestic Council relates to home-grown problems as the NSC relates to foreign ones. The Council helps the President assess national needs, recommends policies and programs, and oversees ongoing programs. Working through a series of project committees, the Council may deal with broad program areas (national energy policy) or specific problems (strip-mining legislation).

5. Council of Economic Advisors. Highly respected economists advise the President on all matters relating to the national economy. The members analyze the economic health of the country, and develop policies and programs which the President may use to combat specific problems like inflation and unemployment.

THE BURDEN OF THE PRESIDENCY

Even with the aid of these specialized agencies, running the affairs of government remains an intensely demanding job. Harry Truman liked to say, "The buck stops here." He meant that after all the staff work has been done, the responsibility for final decisions rests with the man in the Oval Office. Warren G. Harding, overwhelmed by the office, could only moan, "My God, this is a hell of a job!" Many social scientists seriously doubt that any one man can fulfill all the responsibilities and expectations Americans

Figure 7.4
Organizational chart: Executive Office of the President

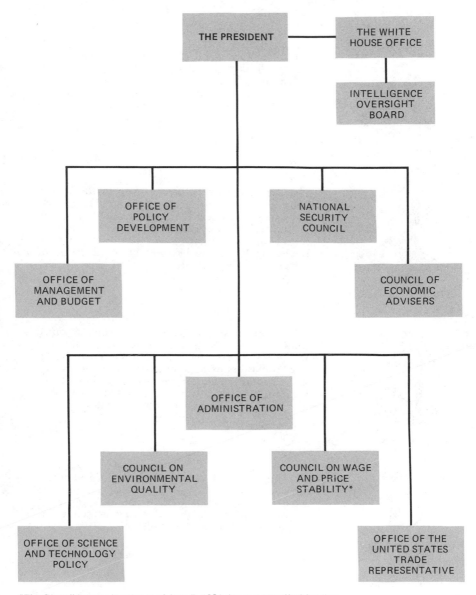

*The Council became inactive as of June 5, 1981 due to a cut-off of funding.

Source: *United States Government Organization Manual, 1981–82* (Washington, D.C.: Government Printing Office, 1981), p. 82.

have concentrated in this one office. We go on every four years, however, measuring a new incumbent against the challenge. Fortunately, the men elected to the office have almost always responded to that trust. (See the box on the next two pages for an overview of the contributions some presidents have made to the office.)

Development of the presidency

President   **Contributions**

George Washington

The first President's every action set precedents which built a firm foundation for later presidents. He brought dignity and authority to the office, and clarified the vague "executive power" as the President's right to take the initiative in both foreign and domestic affairs.

Thomas Jefferson

Not just a thoughtful contributor to the philosophy of American government, Jefferson left two practical legacies: (1) he was the first "party leader," thus providing the President with a source of political power; and (2) by making the Louisiana Purchase, he brought the doctrine of "implied powers" to life.

Andrew Jackson

The presidency first became a "people's" office under Jackson. By appealing to the public over the heads of Congress, and by vigorously wielding the powers of appointment and dismissal, he gained total control of the executive branch. In the nullification dispute, he asserted the federal government's supremacy over the states.

Abraham Lincoln

Lincoln did much more than save the Union. He showed that the President had the authority to master crisis, manage the nation's growing strength, and establish policy that he felt right, no matter what the opposition.

Theodore Roosevelt

Under TR, the presidency moved into the center spotlight of American life. By "carrying a big stick" and using executive powers fully, he helped create a sense of purpose and direction which added greatly to the institution of the presidency.

Under Wilson, the presidency came to dominate the legislative process. His programs came complete to the last comma, and he pushed them with all his power. He originated the press conference, demonstrating the appeal of forceful, eloquent presidential prose. And he took America into the world, for better or worse.

Woodrow Wilson

Roosevelt's New Deal restored heart to America when it was needed most. Under his leadership, the country survived the Great Depression and passed safely through World War II—but also gained new insight into the social and economic needs which a compassionate government must meet.

Franklin Roosevelt

Johnson's civil rights legislation did much to begin removal of generations of accumulated racial injustice. Because of high costs, however, many of Johnson's social programs have come under increasing attack in recent years.

Lyndon Johnson

Source: Adapted from Tom Wicker, "The President," *New York Times Election Handbook, 1968*, edited by Harold Faber. Copyright © 1968 by The New York Times. Reprinted by arrangement with The New American Library, Inc., New York, N.Y.

Ⓢummary and conclusions

1. Out of some 226 million Americans, one emerges each four years to serve as President. The qualifications, if we look only to the letter of the Constitution, are few: age thirty-five or over; a natural-born citizen; and resident in this country for at least fourteen years. In addition, we demand maturity, experience, and leadership ability; we hope for someone greater in moral and intellectual stature than other people.

2. In one of the few areas where the Constitution has been outmoded, election to the presidency still involves the Electoral College. Popular vote notwithstanding, the electors are not bound by the voters' ballots. It

is still quite possible that, as has happened in the past, the presidential candidate who receives the greatest popular vote might not be elected President.

3. The various jobs of the President require that at one moment he must be our *chief of state*, the ceremonial head of government, while later that morning he must work with Congress on an anti-crime bill as *chief legislator*. He also conducts the daily business of government as *chief executive*—signing commissions, meeting with his Cabinet, and overseeing the huge federal bureaucracy.

4. As *chief diplomat*, the President formulates and carries out the nation's foreign policy. He exchanges visits with foreign diplomats, writes treaties, establishes trade relations, and extends diplomatic recognition (with Senate approval). As *chief politician* and leader of his party, he tries to "sell" the party program to Congress and the public.

5. When military decisions must be made, the President becomes *commander-in-chief*, ready to issue orders involving troop movements, strategic battlefield decisions, and wartime emergency measures on the home front. Not the least of his duties in this role is that of maintaining strict civilian control of the armed forces.

6. Just as the President heads wearily toward bed, another phone call might alert him to a final task: he must use his authority as *chief jurist* to decide on a possible pardon—*full pardon*, *commutation*, or *reprieve*. The next day, he might also appoint a number of members to the federal judiciary, possibly even a member of the Supreme Court. Under the system of checks and balances, the President may also be asked to enforce court decisions.

7. Waiting in the wings will be the Vice President. The Constitution gives him little to do except preside over the Senate. Recent presidents have added duties to the vice-presidency, including attendance at Cabinet meetings, representing the President overseas, and overseeing the work of important federal agencies.

8. Like a good general, the President relies on his Executive Office to provide the information, coordination, and counsel needed to run the government. These agencies have a hand in almost all policy decisions made in the White House.

9. The presidency is more than the sum of its parts. Although it administers, legislates, makes policy, manages, and even commands, at best it offers the nation the closest thing we have to a symbol of our own identity. We look to the White House for moral leadership, a sense of purpose, and a ready response to the needs of all of us.

REVIEW QUESTIONS AND ACTIVITIES

TERMS YOU SHOULD KNOW

Cabinet

"coattail effect"

commuted sentence

constitutional monarchy

diplomatic recognition

dismissal

Electoral College
Executive Office of the President
executive order
full pardon
pardon

patronage
presidential succession
reprieve
summit conference
treaty

REVIEW QUESTIONS

The following multiple-choice questions are based on the important ideas presented in this chapter. Select the response that best completes each statement.

1. Which of the following people would *not* be able to run for President under the Constitution? (a) A thirty-seven-year-old black woman. (b) The governor of Hawaii, born in Japan of American parents. (c) An eighty-year-old man with only an elementary school education. (d) A well-known diplomat who has spent much time out of the country. (e) All would be eligible.

2. Under the Twenty-second Amendment, the maximum time a President may now serve is (a) four years. (b) eight years. (c) ten years. (d) twelve years. (e) no limit.

3. The ceremonial duties performed by the President as chief of state take little time; nor do they have much importance. This statement is (a) true. (b) false; as chief of state, the President serves as the symbol of U.S. power and policy. (c) false; the duties are important, but most have been given to the Vice President to perform.

4. When the President is actually administering the federal government and its many programs and employees, he is serving as (a) chief of state. (b) chief executive. (c) commander-in-chief. (d) chief politician. (e) none of these.

5. Which of the following officeholders could a President *not* dismiss? (a) A federal court of appeals judge. (b) The Secretary of State. (c) The director of the CIA. (d) The director of the Office of Management and Budget. (e) All can be dismissed by the President because all are appointed officials.

6. If a President believes that emergency conditions require a quick decision regarding a treaty question, he can make a decision without Senate approval via (a) a writ of mandamus. (b) the power of pardon. (c) an executive order. (d) a presidential proclamation. (e) the law of presidential succession.

7. A President might "persuade" Congress to pass a certain bill by (a) threatening to veto other bills. (b) withholding federal projects in the home districts of uncooperative legislators. (c) appealing to the public for support. (d) calling for party unity. (e) all of these.

8. When President Ford forgave Richard Nixon for any crimes he might have committed while in the White House, he was using the power to (a) commute a sentence. (b) grant a reprieve. (c) review a court-martial. (d) grant a pardon. (e) execute a court order.

9. Most presidential candidates traditionally choose their vice-presidential running mate because of his (a) stature as a possible President. (b)

ability to "balance the ticket" and carry a large number of regional and ethnic votes. (c) campaign to win the presidential nomination for himself. (d) contrast to the candidate in age, experience, and political philosophy. (e) photogenic good looks.

10. Should a President die in office, he would be succeeded first by the Vice President and then, if necessary, by (a) the Secretary of State. (b) the Attorney General. (c) a newly nominated Vice President chosen by the new President and confirmed by the Congress. (d) the President *pro tempore* of the Senate. (e) a new President chosen in a special national election.

CONCEPT DEVELOPMENT

This chapter has explored a number of significant concepts relating to the U.S. presidency. You can use your skills in thinking, researching, and writing to answer the following questions.

1. Summarize the major responsibilities of the President of the United States.

2. Should the President be relieved of his duties as ceremonial head of state? Summarize the arguments for this change, and explain how it could be accomplished.

3. Discuss the arguments for and against allowing a civilian President to serve as commander-in-chief of the nation's armed forces.

4. Evaluate the effect on American government of the Twenty-fifth Amendment, which provides for the appointment of a nonelected Vice President.

5. Agree or disagree with the statement: "No man is capable of doing a good job in all of the roles of the President."

ACTIVITIES

The following activities are designed to help you use the ideas developed in this chapter.

1. From all available news sources, chart the President's activities over a two-week period. You might also write to the White House for a copy of his schedule. Can you identify which roles the President is fulfilling as he moves from activity to activity? What conclusions can you draw about the pressures of his office?

2. Write a letter to the President, 1600 Pennsylvania Avenue NW, Washington, D.C. 20500. State your position on a current issue clearly and concisely. Share the response with the class.

3. Have each class member select a different President and prepare a poster illustrating the man and his major accomplishments.

4. Set up a debate between two teams from your class based on the topic: "Resolved, that the presidency has outgrown the checks and balances established by the Constitution, and should be limited in scope and authority before it becomes a virtual dictatorship." Many excellent articles on both sides of this question have appeared over the past few years; use the *Reader's Guide to Periodical Literature* to find them.

CHAPTER EIGHT

GETTING ALONG WITH THE REST OF THE WORLD: THE MAKING OF FOREIGN POLICY

The Panama riots of 1964 started over a missing flag. In the Canal Zone, a group of U.S. high school students raised the Stars and Stripes—but refused to fly the flag of Panama. Panamanian students answered with bricks and Molotov cocktails. Before order could be restored, twenty people lay dead and another three hundred had been wounded. American troops backed by tanks moved into position. Diplomatic cables crackled between the riot-torn country and Washington, D.C. Fears of a communist takeover obscured the basic issue—the Panamanian desire to reclaim sovereignty over the Canal Zone.

President Lyndon Johnson, scarcely sixty days in office, weighed his foreign policy options. Because this incident came so soon after the Kennedy assassination, Johnson knew that a diplomatic defeat would be devastating to his presidency. Johnson might be forgiven if he momentarily regretted this legacy from Theodore Roosevelt. After all, TR's quest for American imperial power had gained the Panama Canal for the United States in the first place.

Following the Spanish-American War of 1898, the United States had realized the need for a canal through Central America. With it, the navy could steam quickly from the Atlantic to the Pacific, eliminating the six-weeks voyage around the tip of South America. In 1903, the government of Colombia refused to sign a treaty which would have given the United States sovereignty over a six-mile strip of land across the Isthmus of Panama in exchange for $10 million and a $250,000 annual rental. Roosevelt, therefore, resolved to use less diplomatic means.

The President believed that the province of Panama, isolated by heavy

Figure 8.1

American soldiers watch Panamanian youths attach their country's flag to a lamp pole at the Canal Zone border in 1964. Source: Wide World Photos.

jungle from the rest of Colombia, would revolt if given any encouragement. Panamanians who favored the canal took the hint and launched a revolution. United States marines landed to support the revolutionaries. The Colombian troops quickly surrendered, and on November 4, 1903, Panama declared its independence. Two days later Roosevelt recognized the new country. On November 18 the Hay-Bunau-Varilla Treaty was signed, giving the United States control of a ten-mile-wide Canal Zone "in perpetuity" for the same price that Colombia had refused.

Over the years, the canal brought both prosperity and discontent to Panama. By agreement, the rental was increased to $1,930,000 yearly, and jobs and dollars helped support the local economy. Still, the sight of the 30,000 U.S. citizens who operated and protected the canal, snug and comfortable behind their wire fences, grated on Panamanian feelings. These growing irritations led in 1960 to an agreement that the flag of Panama would be flown along with the United States flag at specified places in the Canal Zone. When the U.S. students refused to honor that commitment in 1964, irate Panamanians exploded into violence.

Faced not only with bloodshed but with the real possibility that the canal could be lost, Johnson acted with characteristic directness. He called President Roberto F. Chiari of Panama on the phone, asking that the violence be stopped. The personal contact worked; an uneasy peace returned to the country, and diplomatic conversations took the place of gunfire. The following years brought lengthy negotiations that concluded in 1978. Amid great controversy, both countries ratified a treaty giving Panama control of the canal by the year 2000. Despite misgivings on both sides, the treaty went into effect without serious incident. The peaceful solution also improved U.S. relations with the rest of Latin America.

Several general conclusions can be drawn from this incident: (1) The roots of our current international problems reach deeply into the past. (2) Foreign policy cannot be separated from national defense requirements. (3) In a complex world, disagreements between any two nations almost certainly will involve other countries as well. (4) Diplomatic matters often drag out for many years without satisfactory settlement.

In this chapter, you will look at the interrelationship of the three major foreign policy functions of the United States government—diplomacy, national defense, and intelligence-gathering. The questions that will be answered include:

1. How has U.S. foreign policy developed over the years?
2. How does the government make foreign policy?
3. What is the role of the State Department?
4. What does the United States hope to accomplish with foreign aid?
5. What role do international organizations play in U.S. foreign policy?
6. What is the United Nations accomplishing?
7. How does the Department of Defense protect national security?
8. How does the Central Intelligence Agency contribute to U.S. foreign policy?
9. What progress is being made toward world disarmament?

How has U.S. foreign policy developed over the years?

United States national interests spread out from our borders like a worldwide network of nerve fibers. A copper miners' strike in Chile, a famine in the Sahara, revolution in Southeast Asia, an oil price increase in the Mideast—all affect our national well-being. American economic, political, and military decisions cannot be made in a vacuum, for they are limited by the realities of international relationships.

Foreign policy may be defined as the total package of policies through which the United States attempts to maintain satisfactory economic, political, and military relationships with other countries—both friendly and hostile. The "splendid isolation" once made possible by ocean barriers has vanished in an era of intercontinental missiles, international finance, and disappearing domestic natural resources. Few countries agree on the policies that will best promote mutual well-being; *diplomacy* is the art of establishing relationships that both sides can accept as useful and beneficial.

In aiming at that goal, U.S. foreign policy has gone through a series of historic changes.

ISOLATIONISM

The United States' first foreign policy was one of *isolationism*—separation from the rest of the world. The nation needed time to work out the tangles in its new government and to tame the wilderness at its back door. Washington, Adams, and Jefferson believed that the infant republic had little to gain from involvement in the European conflicts that were widespread at the turn of the century. Even so, Jefferson's embargo (designed to keep the United States out of the Napoleonic wars) failed, and in 1812 the United States ended up at war with Great Britain over the question of freedom of trade on the high seas.

By the 1820's, isolationist policy had been modified enough to allow for the Monroe Doctrine. Issued by President James Monroe in 1823, the doctrine proclaimed that both North and South America were off-limits to further European colonization. The makers of U.S. foreign policy did not wish to see renewed Spanish or French domination of any segment of the western hemisphere. Fortunately, the U.S. proclamation paralleled Britain's own policy at the time. U.S. military power could not have enforced such a ban, but the British navy could, and did.

IMPERIALISM

The second half of the 1800's found the United States edging toward a policy of *imperialism*, the belief that the United States was destined to rule over other parts of the world.

Expansion in the Pacific. With the nation now stretching from shore to shore, Americans looked westward into the Pacific. As early as the 1850's, Admiral Matthew Perry ended Japan's own period of isolation; a rich trade began moving across the Pacific between the United States and its new "sphere of influence." In 1867, the purchase of Alaska established American power in the northern Pacific. The central Pacific was secured by the annexation of Hawaii and the conquest of the Philippines in 1898. Secretary of State John Hay's Open Door policy helped save China from dismemberment by European countries in 1900—and guaranteed a share in the rich China trade for U.S. shipping. By the time Teddy Roosevelt offered to serve as peacemaker in the Russo–Japanese War of 1905, no one questioned the United States' role in international politics. For better or worse, the United States had joined the world outside its borders.

Intervention in Latin America. Latin America did not escape U.S. attention in the period after the Civil War. Still citing the Monroe Doctrine, the U.S. government forced the French to abandon their foothold in Mexico in 1867. U.S. diplomats mediated a dispute in 1902 over debts Venezuela owed Great Britain and Germany. The United States acquired Puerto Rico from Spain in 1898 and the Virgin Islands from Denmark in 1917.

The United States has, on occasion, intervened in the political and economic affairs of its southern neighbors. Haiti, Nicaragua, Costa Rica, and Mexico all witnessed the landing of U.S. marines when the United States government came to believe that these countries' internal affairs were not being carried on in the best interests of the United States. Interventions officially ended when Franklin D. Roosevelt spelled out the Good Neighbor policy in 1933. That did not prevent President Lyndon Johnson from dispatching marines to the Dominican Republic in 1965 to prevent what the government believed was a possible communist takeover.

INVOLVEMENT IN EUROPE

The dominant foreign policy question of this century has been the extent to which the United States should involve itself in European affairs. The United States' determination to stay out of Europe ended with its entry into

World War I. President Wilson's Fourteen Points were to have been the basis for a just peace, but France and Britain rejected most of them in writing the Treaty of Versailles. Wilson compromised many of his beliefs in return for creation of the League of Nations; the United States Senate responded by refusing to join the League. The period of renewed isolation that followed came to a close in the flames of World War II. With the Japanese attack on Pearl Harbor and Germany's declaration of war, the United States could no longer escape involvement in the savage struggle. The United States enthusiastically applied itself to the defeat of the Axis powers.

WORLD LEADERSHIP

After the war, the United States abandoned its tradition of isolationism in favor of a role requiring global leadership. This new policy developed because (1) our growing worldwide military and economic interests demanded it, and (2) the traditional world powers, Britain and France, had been greatly weakened by the war. The United Nations grew out of the United States' belief that the postwar world needed some sort of peace-keeping agency (see pages 184–85). The Marshall Plan poured billions of U.S. dollars into the shattered nations of Europe and Asia. At the same time, the Truman Doctrine created a new role for the United States—that of helping free people to maintain their national integrity against communist aggression.

The Truman decision to oppose communist expansion led to an increasingly bitter struggle for world supremacy between the Soviet Union and the United States. By virtue of their size, economic strength, and nuclear arsenals, the two superpowers came to dominate world affairs. Economically and politically, the United States fought to contain communism to those areas where it had existed before 1946. Economic and military aid was handed out to help our friends; U.S. dollars built roads and bridges, produced better crops, and established new industries. Unfortunately, dollars have not always been enough. Land wars in Korea and Vietnam claimed American lives and treasure in staggering amounts.

A POLICY FOR THE FUTURE

In the 1970's, a series of unexpected developments led to a rethinking of U.S. foreign policy. Withdrawal from Vietnam, the Arab oil embargo, growing impatience with the United Nations, and worldwide inflation erased any lingering optimism that United States manpower, money, and national purpose could make the world over in our image. At the same time, the threat of communist military expansion in Europe diminished, creating a better climate for *détente* (peaceful competition) with the Soviet Union.

Out of those events has emerged a more realistic foreign policy. While the United States cannot turn its back on dangerous situations like the Arab-Israeli conflict, the Greek-Turkish disputes over Cyprus, or the black liberation movement in South Africa, Washington's policymakers have come to realize that U.S. resources are limited. Today the nation steers a course somewhere between a retreat to the isolation of "Fortress America" and overly expensive foreign commitments it cannot afford.

How does the government make foreign policy?

As you learned in Chapter 7, one of the President's major responsibilities lies in the field of foreign affairs. Recent history has seen the President grow even more dominant. Several reasons exist for this: (1) greater interdependence among nations has increased the number and importance of the United States' contacts with other countries; (2) the executive branch possesses a near monopoly on sources of information about foreign affairs; and (3) the public and Congress have increasingly accepted strong presidential leadership in foreign affairs (although the disillusionment with presidential decision-making in Vietnam may have reversed this tendency to some degree).

The President does not, of course, make policy decisions without guidance. Three major forces influence the foreign policy of the United States: the Secretary of State and the State Department, Congress, and public opinion. (Other influences on presidential decision-making are shown in Figure 8.2.)

THE SECRETARY OF STATE

The Secretary of State ranks as the foremost presidential advisor on international affairs. How the President uses this advice depends on the personalities of the two men involved. Some presidents prefer to act on their own, leaving the Secretary of State to carry out policy rather than share in its formation. On the other hand, President Ford's experience when he took office in 1974 was largely in domestic matters; therefore, Secretary of State Henry Kissinger was allowed considerable freedom to develop foreign policy—but always subject to the President's approval.

A number of distinguished Americans have served as Secretary of State, including Thomas Jefferson (the first to hold the post), James Madison, Henry Clay, William Jennings Bryan, George C. Marshall, and Dean Rusk. Along with his primary role of advising the President, the Secretary oversees the work of the State Department. The Secretary also takes care of certain types of official correspondence within the United States. It was to Secretary of State Kissinger, for example, that Richard Nixon submitted his formal letter of resignation in 1974.

CONGRESS

The controversy between Congress and the President that almost every foreign policy proposal generates usually ends with the President getting what he wants. Congress does hold two formal powers in this area: the power of the purse and the Senate's right to approve or reject treaties.

The power of the purse. Most foreign policy decisions call for the spending of money somewhere along the line. If Congress does not approve of

Figure 8.2
The making of U.S. foreign policy

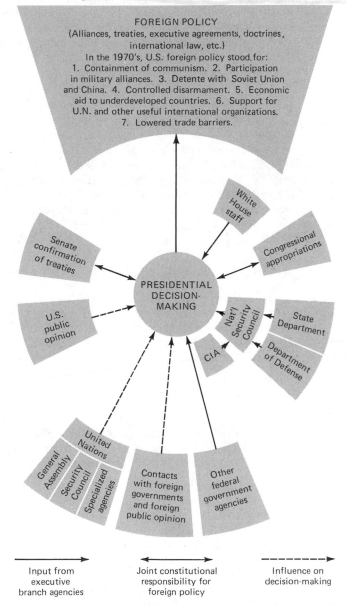

FOREIGN POLICY
(Alliances, treaties, executive agreements, doctrines,
international law, etc.)
In the 1970's, U.S. foreign policy stood for:
1. Containment of communism. 2. Participation
in military alliances. 3. Detente with Soviet Union
and China. 4. Controlled disarmament. 5. Economic
aid to underdeveloped countries. 6. Support for
U.N. and other useful international organizations.
7. Lowered trade barriers.

White House staff

Senate confirmation of treaties

Congressional appropriations

PRESIDENTIAL DECISION-MAKING

U.S. public opinion

Nat'l Security Council

State Department

CIA

Department of Defense

United Nations

General Assembly

Security Council

Specialized agencies

Contacts with foreign governments and foreign public opinion

Other federal government agencies

| Input from executive branch agencies | Joint constitutional responsibility for foreign policy | Influence on decision-making |

a particular decision—for example, to increase military aid to Latin America—it can refuse to appropriate the money. Usually the result is a compromise, with the President gaining a substantial percentage of his original request.

The power to ratify treaties. Every formal agreement signed by the President with a foreign country must be ratified (approved) by the Senate.

Even though the President has signed the treaty, it cannot take effect until the Senate acts. Recent presidents have sidestepped this requirement through the increased use of executive agreements, which have the force of law but do not require Senate approval. In any event, Congress has largely been content to delegate treaty-making authority to the White House. Four-fifths of all treaties submitted to the Senate have been ratified.

PUBLIC OPINION

Although the President guides our foreign policy, he cannot lead the nation where the people will not go. Presidents respond quickly to public pressures. Opinion polls, pickets on Pennsylvania Avenue, newspaper editorials, letters, personal conversations—all alert the White House to the mood of the country. Woodrow Wilson's attempt to sell the American people on joining the League of Nations failed in a nation which was quickly slipping back into isolationism. Likewise, public disapproval forced the United States to withdraw from Vietnam despite the wishes of Presidents Johnson and Nixon.

What is the role of the State Department?

The President and the Secretary of State decide the foreign policy of the United States; the State Department carries out that policy. Considered by many the elite branch of the federal civil service, the State Department employs 24,000 men and women, many of them quartered in a massive building in an area near the Potomac River that Washington calls Foggy Bottom.

THE FOREIGN SERVICE

The Foreign Service of the State Department represents the United States abroad. Two branches of the Foreign Service spread across the globe into every country with which the United States maintains diplomatic relations.

The diplomatic corps. The diplomatic corps deals mainly with political matters between the United States and other countries. The United States maintains an *embassy* (a diplomatic center) in the capital city of every country it recognizes—over 130 at last count. The chief diplomatic official at each embassy is an *ambassador*, who is appointed by the President and confirmed by the Senate. The law sets no fixed term of office, and many ambassadorships change hands when a different party takes power in Washington.

An embassy staff assists the ambassadors in the performance of their duties, which include (1) transmitting official communications between the two nations; (2) alerting the U.S. government to important happenings in the host country; (3) protecting U.S. citizens and U.S. interests in the host country; (4) arranging treaties, trade agreements, and other diplomatic matters; and (5) explaining U.S. laws, policies, and culture to the host country.

The consular service. The duty of protecting United States commercial interests overseas falls to the second branch of the Foreign Service, the consular service. A local United States *consul*, whose office is known as a *consulate*, resides in most major cities of the world. Consular officials must pass a civil service exam before they are appointed by the President and confirmed by the Senate. Their duties are to (1) promote U.S. trade and commerce; (2) aid U.S. citizens with passport or other problems; (3) enforce U.S. customs regulations; and (4) assist people who wish to emigrate to the United States.

STATE DEPARTMENT PERSONNEL

Most State Department officials have chosen service in the department as a rewarding professional career. Candidates must take highly competitive examinations to qualify for appointment. Historically, many ambassadors have been political appointees, better known for their party service than for their abilities as diplomats. This practice has lessened in recent years; most ambassadors work their way up through the Foreign Service.

STATE DEPARTMENT STRUCTURE

The State Department stands at the center of its own vast information network. Radio, wire, and courier services link Foggy Bottom with its embassies and consulates everywhere. Incoming reports from a particular country go to the proper *geographic* bureau (the Bureau of Near Eastern and South Asian Affairs, for example) for study and action by experts on that country. More important matters move upward to undersecretaries, and eventually to the Secretary of State himself. *Functional* bureaus handle specific types of problems, such as arms control and relations with international organizations.

OTHER FUNCTIONS

The State Department issues *passports* to Americans who wish to travel overseas. A passport extends the protection of international law to its holder, and identifies him or her as a U.S. citizen. Some countries also require that visitors obtain a *visa* (a permit to visit), which they issue as a means of controlling the visitors who cross their borders.

State Department reports provide the President and other government officials with information about events, conditions, and personalities in foreign countries. Without such insights, the making of foreign policy would be much more difficult.

What does the United States hope to accomplish with foreign aid?

One of the most important elements in the foreign policy of the United States since World War II has been the extension of aid to other countries.

Foreign aid may take the form of *grants* (outright gifts) or long-term loans, generally at low interest rates.

PROS AND CONS OF FOREIGN AID

Supporters of foreign aid state that these programs generally buy far more security for this country than any other use to which the money could be put. The United States' interests, the defenders continue, require a worldwide network of stable, noncommunist countries friendly to U.S. political and economic goals. Without the help of the United States, many of these underdeveloped countries might fall into communist hands.

Opponents of foreign aid call it a "giveaway program" that attempts to buy friends—with little success. They point out what they see as a general lack of appreciation by aid recipients. In truth, few countries receiving aid have allowed the United States to dictate their policies. Moreover, opponents add, with so many problems unsolved within our own country we cannot afford to feed and arm the rest of the world.

DEVELOPMENT OF FOREIGN AID PROGRAMS

Even though most loans made during World War I were never repaid, the United States began a massive military assistance program during World War II (called Lend-Lease). After the war, President Truman and Secretary of State Marshall convinced Congress that a program of assistance to rebuild the war-damaged countries of Europe and Asia would be in our own best interests. With the stimulus of billions of U.S. dollars they received under the Marshall Plan, Western Europe and Japan quickly constructed new factories, houses, rail lines, and other necessities.

In 1949, Truman extended the aid programs to Latin America, Africa, and Asia as a way of combating communist infiltration into these areas. Kennedy added an ambitious program for Latin America, the Alliance for Progress, in the early 1960's. Unlike the successful Marshall Plan for Europe, these aid programs (see Figure 8.3) in less-developed countries have not been totally successful. Most Third World countries live under unstable governments and lack the industrial base needed to compete in today's world. Many also have high birth rates. With these factors slowing economic growth, the return on aid given to developing countries has been disappointing to those who expected quick results.

U.S. FOREIGN AID TODAY

Since the end of World War II, U.S. foreign aid programs have cost over $250 billion. In recent years, changes in foreign policy and increased congressional opposition have altered the amount and type of aid presently being given. Most foreign aid now takes the form of (1) military assistance to those countries most vulnerable to communist takeover; (2) loans and credits distributed through international agencies; or (3) direct person-to-person aid of the type given by the Peace Corps.

1. Military assistance. United States money, equipment, and training help maintain strong military forces in friendly, noncommunist countries around the world. In recent years, much of this aid has gone to Southeast Asia and Israel, but many other countries also depend upon U.S. planes and guns for their defense.

2. *Loans and credits.* Much of the economic aid given today flows through international agencies like the World Bank, the Export-Import Bank, and the Inter-American Development Bank. Within the State Department, the Agency for International Development (AID) administers foreign development loans. AID officials study requests for help with projects like irrigation systems, electric power generation, highway networks, schools, and industrial plants. The agency evaluates loans on the basis of their usefulness to the recipient as well as the possibilities of repayment. Because most aid money must be spent in the United States, American industries benefit from increased orders.

3. *Person-to-person aid.* U.S. know-how has often worked wonders abroad. Engineering, agricultural, and educational skills have become a major export to underdeveloped countries. Peace Corps volunteers build schools, improve crops, develop water systems, plan housing, and conduct basic education classes in some fifty-five countries.

Figure 8.3
U.S. help for Third World countries

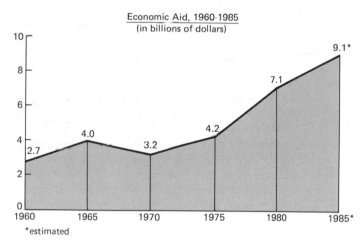

Economic Aid, 1960-1985
(in billions of dollars)

*estimated

Countries receiving the most economic aid, 1981		Countries receiving the most military aid, 1981	
1. Egypt	$1,189 million	1. Israel	$1,400 million
2. Israel	$785 million	2. Egypt	$551 million
3. India	$244 million	3. Turkey	$252 million
4. Turkey	$200 million	4. Greece	$177 million
5. Bangladesh	$155 million	5. Korea	$161 million
6. Indonesia	$128 million	6. Spain	$126 million
7. Sudan	$105 million	7. Philippines	$76 million
8. Nicaragua	$95 million	8. Portugal	$53 million
9. Philippines	$92 million	9. Thailand	$51 million
10. Peru	$81 million	10. Jordan	$43 million

LET'S REVIEW FOR A MOMENT

Have you ever felt that life would be simpler if we just ignored the rest of the world? The United States attempted to do just that in its early years, adopting a policy of *isolationism*. As we expanded, we took a more active interest in foreign affairs—the period of *imperialism*. Isolationism grew again in the years after World War I, but World War II forced us into a position of world leadership. Today we remain committed to encouraging democracy and resisting the spread of communism.

The President makes foreign policy, of course—but who helps him? The Secretary of State for one, then Congress. Who else? All of us together, the American people! No President can take us anywhere in foreign policy that we don't want to go (or at least he can't keep us there very long).

Assisting the President and Secretary of State is the State Department —an organization of thousands of people stationed all over the world to carry out U.S. foreign policy. A professional Foreign Service supplies the expert skills needed in this sensitive area.

Need a couple of million dollars? Organize your own country and apply for U.S. foreign aid. It's not really that simple, but the United States does give billions of dollars to help friendly governments develop their economies, improve education and health services, and maintain political stability.

What role do international organizations play in U.S. foreign policy?

The United States belongs to a number of international organizations as a necessary part of its foreign relations. These bodies gather members on a regional or worldwide basis in order to pursue one or more of three separate goals: (1) to provide a forum for discussion of international problems; (2) to provide military security; or (3) to promote international commerce and raise living standards.

RESOLVING INTERNATIONAL PROBLEMS

Two important organizations serve as examples of U.S. attempts to resolve problems without resort to warfare:

The United Nations. The best-known of international bodies formed to settle disputes is the United Nations. Largely the creation of President Franklin Roosevelt, the U.N. was established at San Francisco in 1945 as a successor to the League of Nations. No one intended the U.N. to serve as a world government; instead it was designed as a forum for settling disputes between nations in what everyone hoped would be a peaceful postwar world. The cold war and the recent tendency for nations to divide into competing power blocs have robbed the U.N. of much of its effectiveness. In spite of this, it remains a useful platform for airing international differences (see the following section for an evaluation of the U.N.'s successes and failures).

The United Nations Charter created an organization made up of six main bodies:

1. *General Assembly.* All member nations sit in the "town meeting of the world" called the General Assembly. Every member, regardless of size, has one vote. The 153 nations represented there debate matters concerning international politics, trade, and social welfare. General Assembly resolutions are not binding on the members, but do carry the weight of world opinion.

2. *Security Council.* Fifteen nations make up the Security Council, which is responsible for maintaining world peace. Five permanent members (the United States, the Soviet Union, Great Britain, France, and the People's Republic of China) each hold veto power over any Security Council action. Although the Charter permits the Security Council to take action against an aggressor nation in a breach of international peace, the veto power has often tied the Council's hands. Threats to peace can be dealt with by the General Assembly when the Security Council cannot act.

3. *International Court of Justice.* Judges from fifteen nations meet at The Hague in the Netherlands to resolve questions of international law. Unfortunately, the court can hear a dispute only when both parties agree to accept its jurisdiction.

4. *Trusteeship Council.* With colonialism out of favor after World War II, the Trusteeship Council was set up to protect the interests of "non–self-governing" territories. Only one trust territory remains of the original eleven administered by the council.

5. *Economic and Social Council (ECOSOC).* This council was established to promote the health, working conditions, education, and cultural development of people everywhere. It coordinates the work of thirteen specialized agencies, including the World Health Organization, the International Labor Organization, and the Food and Agriculture Organization.

6. *Secretariat.* Administration of U.N. business falls to the Secretariat, headed by the Secretary General. The second Secretary General, Dag Hammarskjöld, expanded the function of the office by making it an instrument for settling international disputes. Later Secretaries, however, have not always been as successful. The Secretariat also keeps the books on U.N. financial affairs, to which the United States is the largest single donor.

The Organization of American States (OAS). The U.N. Charter permits development of regional organizations. A long series of inter-American agreements on economic and military cooperation led finally to adoption of the OAS Charter in 1948. The OAS maintains programs designed to bring about closer political, cultural, economic, and social relations among its members. An older organization, the Pan American Union, now serves as its secretariat.

In practice, the United States has used the OAS as a league aimed chiefly at guarding against further communist penetration of the western hemisphere. U.S. intervention in the Dominican Republic in 1965 earned grudging OAS support, but most Latin American states remain suspicious of U.S. policies. Too often they have seen this country supporting conservative military dictatorships in order to stop what many Latin Americans believe is a largely imaginary communist threat (see Figure 8.4).

PROMOTING MILITARY SECURITY

Because no nation can stand completely alone in the event of war, the United States has taken the lead in organizing a series of mutual defense alliances outside the United Nations. Although the OAS Charter provides for such defense cooperation with Latin American nations, the main thrust of U.S. participation in military pacts has come in Europe and Asia.

North Atlantic Treaty Organization (NATO). Now over twenty-five years old, the North Atlantic Treaty Organization remains the cornerstone of American military alliances. The primary purpose of NATO is to provide for the mutual defense of Europe, particularly against the communist bloc. Members include the United States, Canada, Great Britain, France, Italy, Portugal, Belgium, the Netherlands, Luxembourg, Denmark, Norway, Iceland, Greece, Turkey, West Germany, and Spain. Political disputes have weakened the roles played by France, Greece, and Turkey in the alliance, but NATO membership still means that "an armed attack against one or more of them in Europe or North America shall be considered an attack against them all."

"You mean there's no other way to keep them from going Communist?"

Figure 8.4
Source: Bill Mauldin, Chicago *Sun-Times.*

Other defense treaties. The United States has mutual defense treaties with over forty countries, most of whom depend on the U.S. for military security. A dispute arose when President Carter canceled the treaty with Taiwan in favor of improved ties with mainland China. The Supreme Court affirmed in 1979 the President's right to end such treaties.

The United States tried to form other alliances to help contain the spread of communism in the 1950's. The Southeast Asia Treaty Organization (SEATO) could not prevent communist advances into Laos, Cambodia, and Vietnam, however. Similarly, the Central Treaty Organization (CENTO) lost its effectiveness in the Middle East after the withdrawal of Iran, Iraq, and Pakistan.

PROMOTING ECONOMIC COOPERATION

The United States has long been a major force in world economic affairs. For many years, the United States dollar (backed by both gold reserves and productive capacity) set the standard against which all the world's currencies were measured. This favorable condition no longer exists, for inflation, negative trade balances, and the growing strength of European and Middle Eastern capital reserves (the latter largely from oil income) have reduced the dollar in value and status. International economic cooperation has become a necessity.

The United States is a member of several economic agencies which have been established to help stabilize currency values and promote trade and development. The International Monetary Fund supports failing currencies (the British pound has needed help frequently). The World Bank (International Bank for Reconstruction and Development) was set up under the United Nations in 1945 with $10 billion in initial capital largely provided by the United States. The bank provides large-scale loans to countries short of funds for major industrial and agricultural projects. Regional development agencies (the Inter-American Development Bank serves Latin America) provide similar assistance to the underdeveloped nations caught in the desperate bind between scarce resources and hungry, jobless populations. In all of these organizations, the United States provides dollars and management skills to further world economic stability.

What is the United Nations accomplishing?

The United Nations was designed to deal with a world dominated by a desire for peace. A long series of limited wars has tended to conceal the very real accomplishments of this international body.

NEGATIVE FORCES

Several factors have kept the U.N. from fulfilling the high hopes with which it was launched in 1945.

Hostile new majority. The majority of U.N. members have joined since the organization was founded. Most of the original member countries belonged either to the Western European bloc or to the Latin American bloc —both friendly to the interests of the United States. By 1980, membership had increased to 153 countries, many of which were newly emerging nations of Africa and Asia. With their entry, the comfortable U.S. voting majority vanished. A new *coalition* (unified voting bloc) of small, underdeveloped countries, often joined by the communist nations, began to pass resolutions contrary to the national interests of the United States. The 1971 vote that ousted Nationalist China from the U.N. in favor of the People's Republic of China and the 1974 Charter of Economic Rights and Duties of States, which approved the takeover of foreign property without compensation, are two examples of actions by this new majority.

Security Council vetoes. Security Council action can be vetoed by any of the five permanent members. Since many of the conflicts brought to the Council have involved communist aggression, the Soviet Union has been quick to use its veto power to deny the United Nations a role in halting the fighting. The Soviets hold the record for use of the veto—over one hundred times; the United States cast its first veto in 1970, and has added only a few vetoes since then.

Inadequate financial support. As it has from the beginning, the United States contributes the largest single segment of the U.N. budget. Some other nations have fallen behind in their payments; still others, including the Soviet Union, refuse to pay their share for U.N. peacekeeping activities they dislike. The U.N.'s activities cost money, and the Secretary General has not had sufficient funds to meet the organization's increasing needs.

POSITIVE ACCOMPLISHMENTS

Even though the United Nations has not fulfilled the high hopes of its Charter, it should not be judged a failure. As long as delegates continue to meet and debate world issues, the possibility of better understanding among nations remains bright. In addition, the U.N.'s humanitarian agencies have contributed greatly to world health, education, and living conditions.

Food and Agriculture Organization (FAO). The FAO aims to raise levels of nutrition and food production. It has sponsored much of the research that has created "miracle" strains of rice, wheat, and other staple foods. FAO experts also teach farmers the new, more productive cultivation techniques required by the "green revolution."

World Health Organization (WHO). WHO specialists work to raise standards of health and sanitation in underdeveloped countries and to wipe out such long-dreaded illnesses as malaria and smallpox. One sign of WHO's effectiveness is the fact that Americans no longer need vaccinations prior to visiting most of the world's countries.

International Labor Organization (ILO). The ILO's goal is to raise living standards and working conditions of workers throughout the world.

Educational, Scientific, and Cultural Organization (UNESCO). The specialists of UNESCO have done valuable service in improving international relations by sponsoring cultural exchanges, education and training programs, and exchanges of scientific information.

Other programs. Children, disaster victims, and refugees all receive attention from specialized U.N. agencies. UNICEF, for example, supports long-range and emergency programs in developing countries in the fields of mother and child health, nutrition, education, and social welfare. Sales of UNICEF greeting cards and folk art help support this work. Many refugees from wars and natural disasters owe their lives to United Nations programs for the care and resettlement of displaced peoples. Other U.N. agencies work on such problems as international communications, world weather forecasting, improved safety standards for maritime traffic, and development of commercial air traffic.

How does the Department of Defense protect national security?

As you have learned in this chapter, U.S. foreign policy attempts to provide national security through diplomatic means. When diplomacy does not work, military strength may provide the only means of safeguarding the nation from attack. The Department of Defense (DOD) carries the responsibility for maintaining military competency and preparedness.

Established in 1789 as one of the four original Cabinet offices, the War Department divided its authority between rival Departments of the Army and Navy. A 1947 reorganization created the Department of Defense, headed by the Secretary of Defense; individual Secretaries now supervise army, navy, and air force activities. The worldwide responsibilities of the defense establishment are centered in a massive headquarters building, the Pentagon, located just outside Washington, D.C.

DEFENSE DEPARTMENT STRUCTURE

Firm civilian control of military plans and operations extends from the President through the Secretary of Defense, the Deputy Secretary, the Secretaries of the three armed services, and the Director of Defense Research and Engineering. All are civilians, as are their many assistants. As a group, these officials supervise all DOD activities, including finance, research and development of weapons, and public affairs.

Special DOD assistants meet with congressional committees to work out budgets and testify on legislative matters. Other specialists deal with the complex questions relating to military research, weapons development, and the like. The Department of Defense receives the single largest appropriation in the federal budget. The Pentagon defends heavy defense expenditures as necessary to national security, a point reinforced by the Soviet Union's rapid military buildup in recent years.

Figure 8.5
Major American foreign policy goals
from independence to the 1980's

Over the past two centuries, American foreign policy has been governed by several key goals. Each goal has grown out of the special circumstances that surround it. Can you predict the foreign policy goals that will guide this country in the coming years?

Isolationism
First spelled out in Washington's Farewell Address, 1796. Based on the desire to avoid alliances that would involve the U.S. in European wars. Contributed to the Monroe Doctrine in 1823. Gained strength in the 1930's as a reaction to World War I. Reborn again in the 1960's and 1970's after U.S. involvement in Vietnam.

Protection
The willingness of the U.S. to protect its own interests and those of its allies. First used in the Monroe Doctrine, which guaranteed independence to the nations of Latin America. The Open Door Policy (1899–1900) carried a similar guarantee to the mainland of Asia. In recent times, the U.S. fought in two world wars to protect democracy and freedom throughout the world.

Intervention
The use of U.S. military forces in foreign countries to further American political and economic goals. Used primarily in Latin America, a right reserved to the U.S. by the Roosevelt Corollary (1904–1905). Also used by President Eisenhower in the Middle East (1958) and by President Lyndon Johnson in the Dominican Republic (1965).

Imperialism
The addition of territory to the United States by means of force, either political, military, or economic. Most historians include the following as examples of imperialism: the Mexican Cession, the gains from the Spanish American War, the acquisition of the Panama Canal Zone, and the annexation of Hawaii.

Containment and Détente
President Harry Truman proclaimed an American commitment to contain the spread of communism after World War II. Uses economic, political, and military aid to help any country threatened by communist aggression. This led to the Cold War and an arms race. The dangers of that race in a nuclear age brought the U.S. and the Soviet Union together in a policy of détente, in which each country accepts the legitimate interests of the other. Peaceful competition under détente has not always worked, and containment remains a part of U.S. foreign policy.

Alliances
Despite isolationism, U.S. pursues military and economic partnerships with other countries. Policy began with efforts to build Good Neighbor policy in Latin America. Today is based on regional alliances such as NATO and other bilateral defense commitments with friendly countries such as Japan and Israel.

THE JOINT CHIEFS OF STAFF

The most important uniformed military advisors to the Secretary of Defense serve in the office of the Joint Chiefs of Staff. The President selects the Chairman of the Joint Chiefs of Staff, who automatically becomes the nation's top military officer. The Chairman joins the Army Chief of Staff, the Chief of Naval Operations, the Air Force Chief of Staff, and the Marine Corps Commandant in (1) formulating military plans and operations; (2) solving problems of supply, training, and future needs; and (3) coordinating the activities of the various services. The Joint Chiefs also advise the National Security Council (see Chapter 7) and sit in on meetings of the high-level Armed Forces Policy Council.

Membership in the Joint Chiefs creates a continuing conflict of interest for the generals and admirals promoted to that important group. During morning planning meetings, the members must unselfishly serve the national interest—but later that day, they return to their roles as champions for expansion of the budgets and missions of their respective services. As might be imagined, policy meetings of the Joint Chiefs can become intensely emotional, for military judgments must often give way to civilian political considerations.

THE DOD AS A CENTER OF CONTROVERSY

No less an authority than former General Dwight D. Eisenhower has warned of the dangers of a too-powerful military establishment. When he left the presidency in 1961, Eisenhower told the nation in his farewell address that the military's "total influence—economic, political, even spiritual—is felt in every city, every statehouse, every office of the federal government." Although the military has emerged from Vietnam with lowered prestige, and the conversion to an all-volunteer army has at least temporarily eliminated the emotional question of the draft, worries regarding military influence on the decisions of the federal government continue to trouble many thoughtful citizens. Criticisms of the military can be summarized as follows:

1. *The military-industrial complex.* Eisenhower's speech took note of what has been called the military-industrial complex. In this close relationship between Pentagon officials and defense industry leaders, critics charge, the arms race with the Soviet Union has been used as an excuse to build an oversized army, navy, and air force while at the same time enriching favored defense contractors. The relationship has been described by Senator William Proxmire, a frequent opponent of the defense establishment, who writes of the "fast-moving, revolving door between the Pentagon and its big suppliers." In a recent year, defense contractors hired over 1,000 high-ranking Pentagon officials and retired military officers.

Americans of all political beliefs are divided over the possible consequences of this combination. One side believes that the result has been to produce an influential lobby for ever-higher military budgets and a military-oriented foreign policy that Congress finds difficult to deny. Others, however, take the opposite view. These people charge that inadequate appropriations for the Defense Department have caused the United States to fall dangerously behind the Soviet Union in the battle for military supremacy.

2. *Waste and inefficiency.* One of the consequences of the special relationship between the military and defense industries, critics continue, has been gross inefficiency in spending taxpayers' money. Weapons systems are designed and put into production without apparent regard for how much they cost—or how well they work. The B–1 bomber, Sheridan light tank, and various quickly obsolete missiles have been pointed out by critics as only a few examples of the military-industrial complex's improper planning and inability to control costs. In the 1980's, increased military spending raised fears of further waste in the Pentagon's new and expensive weapons systems.

3. *Civilian control of the military.* Frequent charges were made during the Vietnam War that military officials ordered air strikes and other operations without presidential approval. In 1972, for example, it was revealed that the Air Force had carried out several bombing raids on North Vietnam in direct violation of presidential orders then in effect. Although the Constitution clearly establishes civilian control of the military, incidents such as these raise serious doubts about the willingness of the military to accept such controls when political decisions go against their strategic judgment.

4. *Congressional supervision of military spending.* Most members of Congress are reluctant to deny the funds which the military says are necessary for national security. Much of the waste in military spending, some observers contend, could be eliminated if Congress would require stricter accounting for every dollar spent. The military-industrial complex has many supporters in Congress, however.

REFORM OF THE DOD

Reform of the military establishment must be handled carefully. No major country can afford to disband its military; as a leader of the free world, the United States carries an even greater responsibility for providing security to its allies. Several reforms can logically be suggested, however, which would not diminish military preparedness:

1. *Reduce the power of the military-industrial complex.* At the present time, not only do DOD military personnel move into the defense industry when they leave the armed forces, but defense industry officials frequently are selected for sensitive posts at the Pentagon. As a result, a network of "contacts" has been established which creates favored treatment for those companies with the most influence. Rules against this exchange of personnel between the military and the defense industry should be established. New campaign financing laws have already cut back on the amount of money businesses can contribute to their political allies.

2. *Control escalating expenses.* Modern weapons will remain expensive, but careful cost-accounting practices could eliminate many cases where weapons end up costing hundreds of millions of dollars more than was

originally estimated. Wider use of competitive bidding for new weapons will often cut costs in half, according to a congressional staff study. Duplication of weapons by the various military services could also be curtailed.

3. *Strengthen civilian control.* Fortunately, the United States has never had to worry about a military takeover of the government. But every President must insist on close adherence to the civilian chain of command. As described in Chapter 7, President Truman upheld this principle when he fired General MacArthur during the Korean War; both the White House and the Pentagon must recognize the justice of that precedent.

How does the Central Intelligence Agency contribute to U.S. foreign policy?

The art of gathering information about foreign governments has come a long way since 1929. That was the year that Secretary of State Henry L. Stimson ordered the government to end spying activities, saying, "Gentlemen do not read each other's mail." That directive probably did not last long anyway, since the making of foreign policy cannot take place in a vacuum. As former CIA director Allen Dulles wrote, "When the fate of a nation and the lives of its soldiers are at stake, gentlemen do read each other's mail—if they can get their hands on it."*

The President relies primarily upon the Central Intelligence Agency for *foreign intelligence* (data about the activities of other governments). The CIA has recently become one of the most controversial of all agencies of the executive branch. The agency was established in 1947 to replace a hodgepodge of intelligence-gathering offices in both military and civilian departments of the federal government. Even so, the CIA shares intelligence-gathering responsibilities with several other lesser-known agencies, including the Defense Intelligence Agency, the National Security Agency (both under the DOD), the State Department's Bureau of Intelligence and Research, and the Justice Department's Federal Bureau of Investigation.

THE CIA'S MISSION

The CIA charter makes the agency responsible for (1) gathering and evaluating intelligence and (2) coordinating the other intelligence-collecting agencies of the United States. Until recently, CIA budgets were rarely questioned by Congress. Indeed, a sizable share of the millions needed each year to run the CIA is hidden in appropriations for other agencies.

CIA TECHNIQUES

Intelligence collection has lost a good amount of its romance since Mata Hari used her seductive dances to charm secrets out of Allied officers during World War I. CIA agents use a combination of new and old techniques.

* Allen Dulles, *The Craft of Intelligence* (New York: Harper & Row, 1963), p. 71.

(1) High-altitude photo-reconnaissance planes and Samos satellites fly over the Soviet Union, China, and other countries to check on missile sites, factory locations, troop movements, and similar activities. (2) Communications experts listen in on military transmissions across the globe, then use computers to crack the codes. (3) Ships bristling with electronic gear "snoop" in international waters off many countries, keeping track of ship movements, plane flights, and military communications. (4) Undercover agents penetrate foreign borders to gather data and contact friendly citizens willing to help the United States. (5) Other agents routinely attach themselves to American embassy and business staffs overseas, join suspected subversive organizations, and generally listen in on any activity relating to military or political decision-making. The Soviet Union and most other countries maintain similar foreign intelligence organizations.

CIA OPERATIONS

Most CIA operations never make the headlines. By their very nature, intelligence activities cannot survive the glare of publicity. Still, the agency has been credited with having a hand in the overthrow of communist-leaning governments from Iran and Guatemala to Chile and Indonesia (the fact that such operations violate the CIA's charter is discussed later in this section). United States disarmament talks with Russia could not take place without hard information on Soviet missile capabilities. Thanks to the CIA, foreign policy planners often know well in advance what a particular country will do when the United States proposes a certain course of action.

On the other hand, CIA failures have sometimes been spectacular. Faulty CIA execution of the Bay of Pigs invasion of Cuba resulted in a shattering defeat in 1961. The agency also encountered difficulties in Vietnam, where its agents frequently misjudged the communists' military plans, such as their successful Tet offensive of 1968. CIA infiltration of otherwise innocent American organizations made headlines in 1967 when the press disclosed that the National Student Association (a student-run organization with members from some three hundred universities) had received over $3.3 million in CIA funds. Similar subsidies have been received by other academic, labor, church, and cultural associations in exchange for serving as CIA "fronts" while operating abroad.

When CIA employees were found to be involved in the Watergate scandal, the agency received even greater criticism. Opponents fear that the use of the CIA in domestic spying activities (a violation of its legal authority, which is restricted to foreign intelligence-gathering) has endangered precious First Amendment rights. The 1975 investigation of CIA activities also turned up a number of unsavory stories, including the CIA's attempt to use the Mafia in assassination plots against Cuban Premier Fidel Castro.

REFORM OF THE CIA

Most critics of the CIA center their attacks on three areas: (1) lack of careful supervision of intelligence-gathering activities by Congress; (2)

intrusion by the CIA into domestic matters; and (3) the tendency of the CIA to hold itself above restraint, as a kind of invisible government deciding what is good for the rest of us. Reforms have been suggested in each of these areas.

1. *Better supervision.* CIA officials have been accused of lying to Congress in their reports and testimony. Suggested reforms would involve Congress in deep and continuing supervision of all CIA activities, including full disclosure of CIA budgets. Such knowledge would carry with it the responsibility of maintaining secrecy on sensitive material—a habit many publicity-seeking members of Congress have not fully developed.

2. *No domestic spying.* The CIA must stick to its legally assigned task— the gathering of intelligence *outside* the United States. The President, with the help of Congress, can supervise intelligence activities so as to ensure that "national security" does not come to include keeping tabs on everyone with unpopular views.

3. *No "elitist" tendencies.* Careful selection of CIA leadership can keep the agency dedicated to the difficult task of gathering intelligence while remaining within constitutional limits. No CIA director—and no President —can be allowed to use the CIA to enforce his own private view of what is good for the country.

Two steps toward implementing such reforms came in the spring of 1976. First, President Gerald Ford issued an executive order aimed at reorganizing the intelligence community. He placed overall supervision of intelligence policy in the hands of the National Security Council; day-to-day management of all intelligence-gathering agencies was given to a three-member Committee on Foreign Intelligence headed by the director of the CIA. Violations of the law, such as bugging or spying on United States citizens or plotting the assassination of foreign leaders during peacetime, were also forbidden.

Second, the Senate, stung by the accounts of past abuses uncovered during investigations of the CIA and other agencies, established a new "watchdog" committee—the Senate Select Committee on Intelligence. The committee chairman, Senator Daniel Inouye of Hawaii, pledged that "the CIA and other intelligence agencies will not violate the civil rights of any American."

In the end, the success of these reforms rests largely on the determination and character of the President himself. The complex network of intelligence agencies ultimately leads to the Oval Office. The President's willingness to use that power with restraint and a sense of fair play will tell the people of the United States that its intelligence-gathering operations still obey the rule of law.

What progress is being made toward world disarmament?

From the 1790's onward, the United States has traditionally favored small peacetime armies. Beginning in the 1920's, the United States led the way toward general *disarmament*, a plan for all nations to agree to reduce military forces to the minimum needed to maintain internal order. In 1921–22, this country hosted the Washington Conference, which attempted to limit the size of world navies. American diplomats also signed the 1928 Kellogg-Briand Pact, in which the major nations renounced war as a means of settling international disputes. Further disarmament conferences in the 1930's ended with the coming of World War II.

After the horrors of that war had climaxed with the dropping of the first atomic bomb on Hiroshima by the United States, this country proposed international control of atomic weapons. Although the plan received United Nations approval, the Soviet Union rejected it. The reason became clear in 1949, when Russia exploded its own nuclear device. The development of more powerful hydrogen warheads, coupled with accurate intercontinental ballistic missiles (ICBM's), now makes the arms competition between the United States and the Soviet Union a "race with death" for the entire planet.

ATMOSPHERIC TEST BAN

In 1963, a small step in the direction of nuclear arms control took place. The United States and the Soviet Union signed a treaty banning nuclear testing in the atmosphere. World concern over the dangers of radioactive fallout was growing, and ninety other nations voluntarily associated themselves with the pact. France, China, and India have not felt bound by the agreement, however, and have continued to test nuclear weapons in the atmosphere. Other atomic powers confine their testing to underground explosions.

THE SALT TALKS

The United States first proposed *strategic arms limitation* (mutual reduction of key weapons such as missiles and warheads) in the 1950's, but Russia refused to accept inspection teams on its soil (see Figure 8.6). Once accurate data on the Soviet Union's military strength became available through satellite surveillance, the United States began the Strategic Arms Limitation Talks (SALT) in the late 1960's.

SALT I. Years of hard bargaining ended in 1972 with passage of a preliminary agreement called SALT I. The treaty limited development of costly antiballistic missile systems by both sides. It also froze for up to five years the existing number of offensive strategic missiles; this gave the United States over 1,700 ICBM's, while Russia maintains around 2,300 ICBM's. Although smaller in number, the American missiles were considered to be more accurate, and many carried multiple warheads. The Senate approved the treaty only after passing a resolution ordering the President not to write any agreement that would give Russia military superiority over this country.

SALT II. Continuing talks, known as SALT II, have aimed at achieving a permanent limitation on the number and destructiveness of offensive strategic weapons. If possible, SALT II will also reduce the weapons in-

Figure 8.6
Guided missiles roll past the Kremlin in Moscow's annual May Day parade. Although some progress toward disarmament has been made by the two countries' diplomats at the SALT I and II conferences, competition for military superiority continues between the United States and the Soviet Union. Source: Magnum Photos.

ventory on both sides. Debate on SALT II in the Senate centered on the fear that the treaty would give the Russians superiority in some categories of weapons. If true, this would endanger the security of the United States. After the Soviets invaded Afghanistan in 1979, however, President Carter canceled efforts to ratify SALT II.

OTHER DISARMAMENT PROGRESS

Talks on further limitation of nuclear testing and of the development of weapons for chemical warfare drag on at Geneva with little hope for progress. Some advances have been made in banning biological warfare. President Nixon ordered all U.S. stocks of biological weapons for "germ warfare" to be destroyed in 1971. The United States, Russia, and a number of other nations have also agreed not to introduce weapons into their space exploration programs. A further sign of progress came in 1976, when the Soviet Union agreed for the first time to permit on-site inspection of its nuclear testing facilities by U.S. observers.

$\mathbb{S}$UMMARY AND CONCLUSIONS

1. Over the years, U.S. foreign policy has shifted back and forth between *isolationism* and involvement with the rest of the world. Today, even though isolationism holds an attraction for many people, no nation can endure without trade agreements and working political relationships with other

countries. As a leader of the Western democracies, the United States attempts to (1) contain communism, (2) promote democratic ideals, and (3) safeguard American interests.

2. The President must clear many of his foreign policy decisions with Congress: the Senate must approve treaties; and both houses must appropriate the funds for foreign and miiltary aid, our own armed forces, intelligence-gathering, and our worldwide diplomatic corps. The wishes of the American people also guide the President, for in the final analysis, he cannot approve policies the rest of us would not accept.

3. The Secretary of State assists the President and also administers the State Department. Professional, highly trained experts staff our Foreign Service, which is made up of the *diplomatic corps* (the political side) and the *consular service* (to aid business and travelers). In many of the poorer countries, extensive programs of foreign aid assist in feeding, educating, and training their people.

4. International economic organizations attempt to stabilize world currencies, make development loans to the poorer countries, and promote the free flow of world trade. American food surpluses and industrial products give this country a strong voice in international economic matters. The World Bank, the International Monetary Fund, and the Inter-American Development Bank are examples of agencies which keep world business going.

5. The United States belongs to NATO, a military alliance with Western European countries. NATO members have pledged to support each other in event of an attack. Similar alliances elsewhere have collapsed as world conditions have changed. Troubles in Asia and the Middle East have forced the U.S. to seek new partners in those critical areas.

6. The United Nations serves as a forum for discussion and a channel for worldwide programs in the areas of public health, betterment of working conditions, and development of higher living standards. The technical agencies like WHO, FAO, and UNESCO have achieved greater success than the political bodies. On balance, the world probably has been more peaceful with the U.N. than it would have been without it.

7. The Department of Defense does for military affairs what the State Department does for diplomatic matters. Civilian control of the armed forces is assured through the Secretary of Defense and his assistants. The highest-ranking military officers—the Joint Chiefs of Staff—advise the Secretaries of the Army, Navy, and Air Force, the National Security Council, and the President, but do not make final policy decisions.

8. The information necessary to make sound foreign policy comes from the Central Intelligence Agency. CIA agents gather raw intelligence from many countries through both modern and old-style spying techniques. Complaints about CIA involvement in domestic intelligence-gathering activities and its involvement in plots against foreign governments have sparked attempts to reform that secretive organization. A 1976 executive order took the first step in that direction by clarifying the lines of authority over U.S. intelligence operations.

9. Efforts at disarmament have long occupied foreign policy planners. Despite many obstacles, progress has been made, particularly in limiting nuclear testing and biological warfare. With the threat of nuclear destruc-

tion hanging over everyone's head, the United States and Russia have agreed to limit further development of ICBM's and antiballistic missiles. Further arms limitations talks, however, have not been successful. SALT I remains only a hopeful beginning in this vital process.

ℝEVIEW QUESTIONS AND ACTIVITIES

TERMS YOU SHOULD KNOW

ambassador

consul

consular service

consulate

détente

diplomacy

diplomatic corps

disarmament

embassy

foreign policy

imperialism

intelligence

isolationism

military-industrial complex

passport

strategic arms limitation

visa

REVIEW QUESTIONS

The following multiple-choice questions are based on the important ideas presented in this chapter. Select the response that best completes each statement.

1. The aspect of U.S. foreign policy represented by the acquisition of the Panama Canal Zone by Theodore Roosevelt is (a) isolationism. (b) imperialism. (c) world leadership. (d) containment of communism. (e) none of these.

2. The Monroe Doctrine attempted to (a) prevent further European interference in western hemisphere affairs. (b) involve the United States in the Napoleonic wars. (c) open China to trade and commerce. (d) set up joint British-U.S. domination of Latin America. (e) open the territory across the Mississippi to settlement.

3. The strongest voice in shaping foreign policy belongs to (a) Congress. (b) the State Department. (c) the CIA. (d) the President. (e) the Department of Defense.

4. The most effective way for both houses of Congress to prevent the President from following a particular foreign policy would be to (a) cut off budget support. (b) ask the courts to bring an injunction. (c) rally public opinion against that policy. (d) refuse to confirm a treaty. (e) pass a resolution against that policy.

5. The best argument for continuing foreign aid is that (a) giving away dollars buys good friends and allies. (b) Russia will take over any country we don't help. (c) we have more money than we know what to do with. (d) economic and military aid helps maintain stable

governments open to American influence. (e) it is good business; the loans bring in more money than we give out.

6. Within the United Nations, the United States can always count on support from (a) the General Assembly. (b) the Security Council. (c) UNESCO. (d) the Secretariat. (e) none of these.

7. The most important American military alliance is (a) NATO. (b) SEATO. (c) OAS. (d) FAO. (e) Marshall Plan.

8. The United Nations has more than lived up to the hopes of its founders. This statement is (a) true. (b) false; nothing important has been accomplished. (c) false, but the U.N. has worked effectively to keep the peace in some areas and has done much humanitarian work.

9. The Department of Defense operates completely under civilian control, from the President on down to the various Secretaries. This statement is (a) true. (b) false; in time of war the military heads of the Joint Chiefs of Staff take control of the DOD. (c) false; civilians control the DOD's relations with Congress and the civilian economy, but military men make all tactical and strategic decisions on use of the armed forces.

10. The CIA is forbidden to engage in spying on members of Congress because (a) the First Amendment prohibits it. (b) the CIA charter gives it authority to investigate only matters of foreign affairs. (c) the separation of powers doctrine prohibits it. (d) conflicts of interest might result when members of Congress must supervise the same agency that knows their secret activities. (e) all of these.

CONCEPT DEVELOPMENT

This chapter has explored a number of significant concepts relating to government formulation of U.S. foreign policy. You can use your skills in thinking, researching, and writing to answer the following questions.

1. What are the general objectives of United States foreign policy? How would you modify these objectives over the next ten years?

2. Foreign aid has been a major part of U.S. foreign policy since World War II. What does the United States hope to accomplish by giving food, machines, and military assistance to other countries?

3. What are the chief accomplishments of the United Nations? Why has the United States grown more unhappy with the U.N. in recent years?

4. Despite mistakes and misdeeds by the CIA and other intelligence agencies, no one seriously suggests that we do away with such organizations. Why is it so important that the United States maintain a strong intelligence capability?

5. What progress has been made in reaching international agreements on disarmament since World War II? Why has it been so difficult to move faster in this critical area?

ACTIVITIES

The following activities are designed to help you use the ideas developed in this chapter.

1. Join four other students in staging a mock conference of foreign ministers from the United States, France, Russia, China, and Saudi Arabia. The conference has been called to deal with the question of sharing the world's rapidly disappearing oil reserves. What position would each country take? What conflicts can you foresee? Can the five of you arrive at a formula for compromise that all can support? If your conference is presented before the class, allow the other students to ask questions of the "ministers," each of whom should answer in character.

2. Research the story of the Alliance for Progress. Try to discover what went wrong with this ambitious plan, and what it did accomplish. Can you find any guidelines for future foreign aid programs in this experiment? Prepare a paper or oral report on the topic. Remember that it will be easy to favor one side or the other; try to maintain an objective viewpoint.

3. Prepare a poster illustrating the relative military strengths of the United States and the Soviet Union. Can you discover any indication that either country has gained superiority over the other?

4. Investigate the possibility of a career in one of the government agencies that is involved in working out U.S. foreign policy. Jobs range from clerk-typist to ambassador, from army private to U.N. translator. Your school's career center or vocational counselor, or the public library, can help you find information on job openings, pay scales, training requirements, and other useful data.

CHAPTER NINE

Managing the Nation's Affairs: The Cabinet's Role in Domestic Policy

In his memoirs, President Harry S Truman wrote candidly about his ideas on government. Speaking of the Cabinet, he said:

> The Secretaries of the President's Cabinet are the civilian heads of the executive branch of the government. They are responsible to the President for carrying out the directions and the policies of the executive branch, as the law provides. . . .
>
> When a Cabinet member speaks publicly, he usually speaks on authorization of the President, in which case he speaks for the President. If he takes it upon himself to announce a policy that is contrary to the policy the President wants carried out, he can cause a great deal of trouble.*

The stormy career of Walter Hickel, Richard Nixon's first Secretary of the Interior, illustrates Truman's warning perfectly. A former governor of Alaska, Hickel filled the traditional qualifications for the Interior post: he was a Westerner, a strong Nixon campaigner, and an experienced administrator. Hickel's original nomination did arouse strong opposition from conservationists, who feared the Alaskan's friendly ties with the oil companies.

In the months that followed his confirmation by the Senate, however, the new Secretary converted his critics into avid supporters. Emerging as a new champion of conservation, Hickel halted oil drilling off California after a disastrous oil leak almost ruined local beaches. At his direction,

---

* Harry S Truman, *Year of Decisions* (Garden City, N.Y.: Doubleday, 1955), p. 328.

Interior brought suit against a Louisiana oil firm for not taking adequate precautions against leaks. He delayed issuance of a license for the Alaska oil pipeline.

Restless in the secondary role of Cabinet officer, the spirited Hickel soon found himself at war with the administration. He criticized the Vice President when he thought Spiro Agnew's speeches were harming the country. Even worse, he made policy without clearing it with the White House. The climax came in May of 1970 when his aides "leaked" a personal letter Hickel had written to the President after the Kent State University shootings, where National Guardsmen opened fire on unarmed students, killing four of them. In the letter, Hickel charged the President with alienating the young people of America.

A few days later, Nixon called Hickel into the Oval Office and asked for his resignation. Although many antiwar activists protested the firing, most students of government understood the issues involved. As a member of the presidential "team," Hickel had embarrassed the boss. In Truman's words, he had "caused a great deal of trouble," and no President can permit that situation to continue without losing some of his own authority.

In his own view, Truman said,

> Cabinet positions . . . are created by law at the request of the President to help him carry out his duties as chief executive under the Constitution. It is a very satisfactory arrangement if the President keeps his hands on the reins, and knows exactly what goes on in each department. That he has to do if he is to be successful.*

* *Ibid.*, pp. 328–29.

Figure 9.1

Although the Cabinet (pictured here with President Jimmy Carter in 1977) plays an important role in the management of the nation's domestic and foreign affairs, and meets often with the President, the burden of decision-making finally rests with the Chief Executive. Source: Wide World Photos.

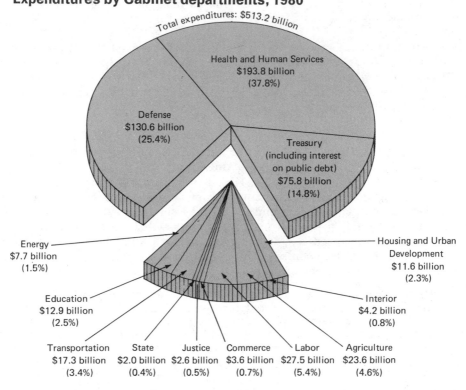

Figure 9.2

Expenditures by Cabinet departments, 1980

Total expenditures: $513.2 billion

Health and Human Services
$193.8 billion
(37.8%)

Defense
$130.6 billion
(25.4%)

Treasury
(including interest
on public debt)
$75.8 billion
(14.8%)

Energy
$7.7 billion
(1.5%)

Housing and Urban
Development
$11.6 billion
(2.3%)

Education
$12.9 billion
(2.5%)

Interior
$4.2 billion
(0.8%)

Transportation
$17.3 billion
(3.4%)

State
$2.0 billion
(0.4%)

Justice
$2.6 billion
(0.5%)

Commerce
$3.6 billion
(0.7%)

Labor
$27.5 billion
(5.4%)

Agriculture
$23.6 billion
(4.6%)

Source: U.S. Bureau of the Census, *Statistical Abstract of the United States: 1980*
(101st edition). Washington, D.C., 1980.

Truman's advice about keeping informed as to the activities of all the
Cabinet departments cannot be ignored, but neither is it easy to follow.
Today, the original four Cabinet members have increased to thirteen (the
Postal Service lost Cabinet status in 1970, but the Department of Energy
was added in 1977 and the Department of Education in 1979). The federal
government employs more civilian and military personnel than made up
the entire population during Washington's first term in 1789.

Chapter 8 described the headline-making task of the State and Defense
Departments in helping the President conduct U.S. foreign policy. In this
chapter you will learn about the ten other, equally important Cabinet
departments that work with the President in administering the domestic
affairs of the United States. As Daniel Webster said in 1824, "The country
is increasing; there is a great deal more work to be done." Figure 9.2
compares the expenditures of the departments during fiscal year 1980.

The questions to be answered about the work of the departments are:

1. How does the Treasury Department manage the nation's money?
2. How does the Justice Department administer the nation's legal
   system?
3. How does the Commerce Department aid businesses and consumers?

4. Why does the Department of Health and Human Services receive such large appropriations?
5. Why was the Department of Energy created?
6. How does the Department of Education influence the nation's schools?
7. What does the Department of Labor do for American workers?
8. How does the Department of Agriculture assist farmers?
9. How does the Department of the Interior manage the nation's natural resources?
10. How does the Department of Transportation oversee the movement of the nation's freight and passenger traffic?
11. Why was the Department of Housing and Urban Development added to the Cabinet?

How does the Treasury Department manage the nation's money?

The President appoints the Secretary of the Treasury, subject to confirmation by the Senate (as are all Cabinet posts). Alexander Hamilton served as the first in a long line of distinguished Americans who have held the job. Among a multitude of other tasks, the Treasury Department (1) advises the President on all matters of domestic and foreign economic policy; (2) performs a variety of fiscal services, including collecting taxes, coining and printing money, and issuing payment checks; and (3) provides certain law enforcement services. The Secretary often coordinates the Treasury's work on such economic problems as inflation and balance of payments deficits with the work of other agencies (the Federal Reserve Board and the Office of Management and Budget, for example). As Figure 9.3 demonstrates, the changing value of the dollar makes the Treasury Department increasingly important.

A number of important government agencies make up the Treasury Department. Some, such as the Internal Revenue Service, are familiar to every American; others, such as the Comptroller of the Currency, seldom appear in headlines despite the importance of their work.

INTERNAL REVENUE SERVICE (IRS)

Never anyone's favorite federal agency, the Internal Revenue Service collects the billions of dollars in tax money that each year pay for the operations of the federal government. In addition, the IRS guards against tax fraud by ensuring that all Americans pay their fair share. Seven regional commissioners oversee the work of fifty-eight district directors. (See Chapter 6 for further discussion of IRS organization.)

Congress has given the IRS authority to collect revenue from a number of other sources in addition to personal and corporate income taxes: (1) excise taxes (so-called luxury taxes on items like playing cards, liquor, cigarettes, gasoline, and television sets), (2) estate taxes (taxes on the value of the property and money people leave when they die), and (3) gift taxes (taxes on gifts and donations over a minimum amount).

Figure 9.3   **What inflation means to the consumer**

Consumer Price Index, 1954–1980
The dollar's changing value, 1940–1980

(1967 = 100¢)

Items	1954	1970	1980
ALL ITEMS	80.5 ¢	116.3 ¢	248.0 ¢
Food total	82.8	114.9	255.5
Apparel and upkeep	84.5	116.1	175.4
Housing total	81.7	118.9	265.1
Transportation	78.3	112.7	251.9
Medical care	63.4	120.6	267.8
Personal care	76.6	113.2	213.1
Reading and recreation	76.9	113.4	204.4

(1967 = $1.00)

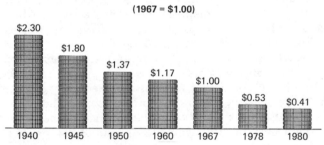

1940	1945	1950	1960	1967	1978	1980
$2.30	$1.80	$1.37	$1.17	$1.00	$0.53	$0.41

Source: U.S. Bureau of Labor Statistics.

CUSTOMS SERVICE

Officers of the Customs Service (1) collect duties and taxes on imported merchandise, (2) control the movement of goods in and out of the country, and (3) attempt to prevent smuggling and other frauds. Once a major source of government income, customs duties now provide less than 2 percent of the total annual federal budget. Customs inspectors work at all major harbors, airports, and border crossing points (about 300 in all).

Customs duties fall into one of three categories: (1) *specific* duties, set at a fixed amount per item imported; (2) *ad valorem* duties, set at a percentage of the item's value; and (3) *mixed* rates, a combination of the first two. Customs rates range as high as 80 percent of an item's value. High rates provide protection for U.S. industries.

TREASURER OF THE UNITED STATES

Many people confuse the Treasurer of the United States with the Secretary of the Treasury, but they hold separate jobs. The Office of the Treasurer (part of the *Fiscal Service*) receives, holds, and pays out the public's money for the federal government. The Treasurer's signature appears on every piece of currency and every government check (close to a billion checks per year). As the bookkeeping office for the Treasury Department, the Fiscal Service maintains federal accounts, keeps records, and deposits the government's cash. In recent years, the job of Treasurer of the United States has customarily been filled by a woman.

COMPTROLLER GENERAL

The Comptroller General heads an independent agency, the *General Accounting Office*. Known as "the watchdog of the Treasury," the GAO was established by Congress in 1921 to make sure that public money is spent in the way that the legislators intended. GAO accountants report back to Congress on management and efficiency in the executive branch. The Comptroller General is appointed by the President and confirmed by the Senate for a fifteen-year term.

BUREAU OF THE MINT

The coins that jingle in our pockets pour out of the three mints maintained by this bureau in Philadelphia, Denver, and San Francisco. The Bureau of the Mint also maintains depositories for gold at Fort Knox, Kentucky, and for silver at West Point, New York. From the time of the founding of the mints in 1792 until gold coinage ceased in 1934, the government produced gold, silver, and copper coins. The mints produced the last silver dollars in 1935; silver quarters, half-dollars, and dimes were discontinued for general circulation in 1965 because of increasing silver prices. Today's "silver" coins are made from an alloy of 75 percent copper and 25 percent nickel, bonded to a core of pure copper. The mints issue over 13 billion coins annually, with pennies making up almost 80 percent of the total.

BUREAU OF ENGRAVING AND PRINTING

The Bureau of Engraving and Printing designs and engraves or prints all United States paper money, postage stamps, Treasury bonds, revenue stamps, food stamps, and other government documents. Paper money runs in denominations from $1 to $10,000 (plus a few $100,000 notes for interbank transactions). Visitors to Washington, D.C., enjoy the tour through the Bureau's printing operation, where large presses turn out yard-high stacks of crisp new currency.

SECRET SERVICE

Two very different responsibilities keep the Secret Service busy. Its best-known job involves the prevention of counterfeiting. Treasury agents, popularly known as "T-men," take pride in their record—they seize almost 90 percent of all counterfeit money before it reaches the public.

The Director of the Secret Service also supervises a corps of agents who provide protection for leading government figures—the President and his family, the Vice President, presidential candidates, former presidents and their families, and visiting heads of state. A Secret Service agent gave his life defending President Truman from attack in 1950.

How does the Justice Department administer the nation's legal system?

As head of the Department of Justice, the Attorney General ranks as the top law enforcement officer of the United States. The only Cabinet member not given the title of secretary, the Attorney General (1) serves as the chief legal advisor to the federal government; (2) investigates and prosecutes offenses against federal law; (3) represents the United States in all its cases before the Supreme Court; (4) supervises the federal prison system; and (5) administers the immigration and naturalization laws. Another key official, the *Solicitor General*, heads a group of federal attorneys who decide when to prosecute a case and when to appeal to a higher court.

The various divisions of the Justice Department provide the Attorney General with the people and skills needed to enforce federal law.

BUREAU OF PRISONS

The Director of the Bureau of Prisons manages thirty-eight federal penal and correctional institutions. Some of the names will sound familiar to anyone who's ever watched old movies—Leavenworth, Kansas; Atlanta, Georgia; and Alcatraz ("the Rock") in San Francisco Bay, now closed. In addition to these and other penitentiaries for long-term civilian prisoners (convicted military personnel serve time in different prisons), the Bureau of Prisons runs youth centers, low-security facilities for short-term prisoners, reformatories, a National Training School for Boys, and a series of community treatment centers.

FEDERAL BUREAU OF INVESTIGATION (FBI)

The FBI investigates all violations of federal law not specifically assigned to other agencies. Over 180 kinds of federal crimes fall under FBI jurisdiction, including espionage, treason, kidnapping, bank robbery, many crimes involving interstate transport of stolen goods, election law violations, and assaulting or killing the President or a federal officer. Federal agents also cooperate with state and local police forces, maintain an extensive fingerprint file, do research in new crime-fighting technology, and run advanced training courses for police officers throughout the nation.

Following a 1934 reorganization, J. Edgar Hoover developed the FBI into one of the world's most efficient police forces. Hoover's death in 1972 after thirty-eight years on the job came at a time when Congress was taking a critical interest in the Bureau's methods. Of particular concern to civil rights activists have been illegal FBI wiretaps, secret information files, and break-ins.

IMMIGRATION AND NATURALIZATION SERVICE (INS)

The 395,000 foreigners who enter the United States each year to live, work, and eventually take out citizenship papers keep the Immigration and Naturalization Service busy. The INS has a twofold job: (1) to aid immigrants who legally enter and apply for naturalization and (2) to prevent the illegal entry of aliens and to deport those who have entered without proper permits.

Prior to the 1880's, the government encouraged waves of immigrants to come and help build the new nation. Immigration averaged over one million people a year even through the early part of this century. After World War I, however, Congress severely limited immigration by setting up quotas based on the immigrants' countries of origin. These quotas cut the number of entries to around 150,000 immigrants a year from countries outside the western hemisphere. The complex system, set up by laws passed in 1965 and 1976, allows 290,000 immigrants a year. Within this quota, each country is limited to 20,000 immigrants a year. The law gives preference to certain classes of immigrants. These categories include children of U.S. citizens, members of the professions or people of exceptional ability in the sciences and arts, skilled and unskilled workers needed in the U.S., and refugees from communist countries.

Congress has also lowered the barriers for groups such as the Hungarian Freedom Fighters of 1957, the Cubans who escaped from Castro's dictatorship, and the Vietnam refugees of 1975. On the other side of the coin, many thousands of illegal aliens enter the U.S. each year to seek better living conditions and higher wages.

ANTITRUST DIVISION

The Antitrust Division of the Justice Department spearheads the government's efforts to prevent large corporations from monopolizing all or most of the market in their particular product. Action against companies that try to eliminate competition dates back to the beginning of the century. After World War II, however, a new wave of mergers among giant corporations brought strong government response.

In many instances, the Antitrust Division notifies companies that it will oppose proposed mergers as being against the public interest. In other cases, the division's lawyers will take the companies into court in hopes of obtaining an order that will break the corporation into competing divisions. One of the most famous antitrust cases forced John D. Rockefeller's Standard Oil Company to split into smaller companies back in 1911.

BUREAU OF NARCOTICS AND DANGEROUS DRUGS (BNDD)

One of the Justice Department's newest bureaus, the Bureau of Narcotics and Dangerous Drugs (1) enforces federal laws dealing with the illegal use of narcotics and other dangerous drugs and (2) regulates the legal manufacture and import of these items. Agents of the BNDD cooperate with foreign narcotics police, state law enforcement agencies, and the Coast Guard to combat the smuggling of drugs across the country's borders. In coordination with the Public Health Service, the bureau controls the legitimate medical and research uses of all controlled drugs. The BNDD also sponsors a national drug abuse prevention program.

OTHER DIVISIONS

As one of the government's busiest departments, Justice runs a number of other important divisions in addition to those described. Among these are the *Civil Rights Division*, which enforces federal laws affecting an individual's right to live and work, free from racial or other forms of discrimination; the *Internal Security Division*, which prosecutes people suspected of subversive activities, including sabotage, treason, and espionage; and the *Law Enforcement Assistance Administration*, created in 1968 to help local law enforcement agencies to improve the nation's criminal justice system.

How does the Commerce Department aid businesses and consumers?

The Department of Commerce promotes full development of the economic resources of the United States. Specifically, Commerce renders aid to the mining, manufacturing, shipping, and fishing industries at home and in international trade. The Secretary of Commerce supervises a fairly new department created as the Department of Commerce and Labor in 1903, then split into two separate agencies in 1913. The work of the Commerce Department also touches the average American more directly through its weather, weights and measures, and statistical services.

CENSUS BUREAU

Every ten years (1970, 1980, and so forth) the Bureau of the Census sends its census takers out to check on the growth of the American population. The census is used as the basis for apportionment to the states of the 435 seats in the House of Representatives (see Chapter 4). Special censuses at shorter intervals also gather data on housing, agriculture, government activities, industrial and business growth, transportation, and construction.

NATIONAL BUREAU OF STANDARDS

Officials of the National Bureau of Standards maintain, develop, and safeguard the nation's standards of physical measurement. The original measures, which are calibrated with extreme accuracy and against which all others are tested and corrected, stay in the Bureau's laboratories in Washington, D.C. The NBS also maintains a testing and scientific research center.

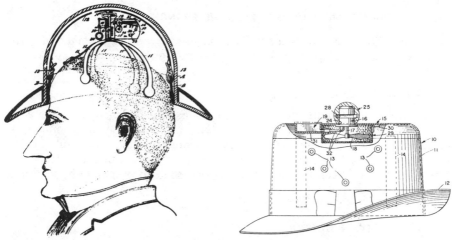

Figure 9.4
The inexhaustible ingenuity of the American inventor
At the turn of the century, good manners were a must: the patent diagram at left shows a self-tipping hat for a man with his arms full, invented by James C. Boyle in 1896 (patent number 556,248). Seventy years later, comfort seemed more desirable: the patent diagram at right shows a hat cooled by a fan driven by a solar-powered motor, invented by Harold W. Dahly in 1967 (patent number 3,353,191). Source: U.S. Patent and Trademark Office.

Anyone who has ever struggled with inches, feet, and yards knows that the United States uses the English system of measurement, which Congress officially adopted in 1836. Steps are now under way to convert to the metric system (kilograms, meters, and the like). This will bring the United States in line with most of the rest of the world.

PATENT OFFICE

The Commissioner of the Patent Office administers the laws which reserve to individuals or corporations the exclusive right to make, use, or sell their inventions and designs (see Figure 9.4). The Office grants patents for a period of seventeen years, but rarely renews them. The Office also registers trademarks, drawings, and slogans; these rights last for twenty years and are easily renewed. (Copyrights, which protect an author's rights to the books, essays, and music he or she writes, are administered through the Library of Congress.)

NATIONAL WEATHER SERVICE

Despite all the jokes about inaccurate forecasts, the National Weather Service's reports are invaluable to farmers, airlines, and the general public. Weather Service technicians make observations of climatic conditions throughout the world. Weather stations, planes, ships, and a network of satellites gather the data on wind, clouds, heat, and cold which provide the basis for increasingly accurate predictions. The aviation industry in particular relies on the Weather Service, and listens to special radio frequencies that report worldwide weather conditions around the clock.

COAST AND GEODETIC SURVEY

Detailed, accurate maps of the United States are the primary product of the Coast and Geodetic Survey. Pilots, city and highway planners, backpackers, and others who need exact information on rivers, mountains, roads, and other terrain features use Geodetic Survey maps extensively. The Bureau has recently begun surveys designed to pinpoint the locations of earthquake and flood areas.

MARITIME ADMINISTRATION

The Maritime Administration works to maintain a strong and up-to-date merchant marine. Because the United States needs a large number of cargo ships during both peace and war, the government pays a subsidy for the building of ships and the operation of American vessels. This support enables U.S. merchant ships to compete with the vessels of other nations, whose operating expenses (for crew salaries, safety standards, and construction) are often much lower. The Maritime Administration also operates a Merchant Marine Academy at King's Point, New York, where future officers receive their training.

(An independent agency, the *Federal Maritime Commission*, sets rates, fares, and charges for American ships engaged in foreign trade—in the same way that the Interstate Commerce Commission regulates domestic rates. The Commission also licenses and bonds shipowners, and investigates unfair shipping practices. See Chapter 10 for a full discussion of the independent regulatory agencies.)

OTHER AGENCIES

The widespread interests of the Department of Commerce include several other important agencies. The *Business and Defense Services Administration* makes plans for rapid conversion of industry to wartime production, and builds up stockpiles of critical raw materials. The *Office of Foreign Direct Investments* restricts the flow of American investment dollars overseas as a means of helping the balance of payments deficit. Finally, the *United States Travel Service* promotes visits to this country by foreign tourists; VISIT USA programs in many countries advertise Disneyland, the Grand Canyon, and American hospitality.

LET'S REVIEW FOR A MOMENT

Under the overall direction of the President, the departments that make up the Cabinet oversee the daily operations of government—from printing money to enforcing the law. Each department operates under the direction of a secretary, appointed by the President and confirmed by the Senate.

Treasury Department officials collect the government's taxes, pay its bills, and keep track of its bookkeeping. Major divisions include the *Internal Revenue Service* (tax collection), the *Customs Service* (duty collection), the *Bureau of the Mint* (coinage), the *Bureau of Engraving and Printing* (paper money and stamps), and the *Secret Service* (tracking down counterfeiters, guarding the President).

The *Justice Department* supervises the enforcement of federal law. As the nation's top law officer, the Attorney General provides legal advice to the President as well as administers the Department of Justice. The *Federal Bureau of Investigation* is probably the best-known division of Justice. Add the *Bureau of Prisons* for handling federal convicts, and the *Bureau of Narcotics and Dangerous Drugs*, which puts illegal drug users in those penitentiaries. The *Immigration and Naturalization Service* helps legal immigrants meet entry and citizenship requirements. If you think General Conglomerates has a stranglehold on the market in widgets, tell the *Antitrust Division*. Their lawyers will investigate the case and take antimonopoly action if necessary.

The *Department of Commerce* promotes the full development of the nation's economic resources. In practice, it can also tell you how many people live in your community (*Census Bureau*), whether your yardstick is accurate (*National Bureau of Standards*), how to protect your rights to your anti-gravity machine (*Patent Office*), and whether it will rain on graduation day (*National Weather Service*).

Why does the Department of Health and Human Services receive such large appropriations?

The varied programs of the Department of Health and Human Services (HHS), created in 1979 to replace the Department of Health, Education, and Welfare, receive approximately one-third of all federal appropriations (about $200 billion in 1980). These dollars reflect the popular belief that the federal government must accept a major role in promoting the health, education, and social welfare of every American. Hundreds of agencies administer HHS's widespread activities; only a few of the most important can be discussed here.

SOCIAL SECURITY ADMINISTRATION

Created as part of the New Deal legislation of the 1930's, the Social Security Administration (also discussed in Chapter 6) provides retirement, survivors, disability, and health insurance programs for many elderly or otherwise needy people. A Social Security number issued to every covered worker sets up an account; both worker and employer pay matching amounts to the fund, 8 percent of wages up to $29,700 in 1981. Typical benefits are shown in Figure 9.6. Since 1966, most Americans over sixty-

Figure 9.5

Why was the Department of Energy created?

When the energy crisis of the early 1970's hit, the federal government found itself poorly prepared to cope with the problems of the Arab oil embargo, lagging supplies of natural gas, the need for conservation, and a thousand related situations. As a result, Congress brought together some fifty federal energy agencies under a new Cabinet post—the Department of Energy (DOE). Once started, DOE found that its efforts to coordinate federal energy policies were hampered by a slow-moving Congress. By 1980, the Congress was still struggling to design an overall energy program acceptable to the White House, consumers, energy suppliers, and industry.

The DOE began life with two powerful independent agencies under its supervision—the *Energy Research and Development Administration* and the *Federal Energy Administration*. The Federal Power Commission, renamed the *Federal Energy Regulatory Commission* (see page 242), retains its independent status but works closely with DOE on regulation of hydroelectric power and natural gas.

One of DOE's most important jobs is to coordinate all federal activities related to energy research and development. DOE's *Energy Technology* staff supervises federal energy research centers and projects related to fossil fuel research, underground energy transmission, solar heating and cooling, geothermal power, alternative automotive power systems, and military and civilian activities in nuclear research and development. The *Defense Programs* branch works closely with the Department of Defense to develop and maintain the world's most powerful nuclear arsenal. Despite continued investment in peaceful uses of nuclear energy, the country still depends largely upon fossil fuels—oil, natural gas, and coal. The unlimited potential of wind, sun, tide, and geothermal energy sources is still largely untapped.

Two other important DOE offices are the *Economic Regulatory Administration* and the *Resource Applications* section. The Economic Regulatory Administration controls the pricing, importation, and transport of crude oil, petroleum products, and natural gas. Resource Applications markets and distributes the department's energy production, regulates government uranium policies, and watches over naval and oil shale reserves.

What will happen if the United States is hit by another energy crunch? The DOE has been given the job of preparing us for just such an emergency. The department believes that a mix of conservation, development of new energy sources, and better use of domestic supplies will see us through. Can the Department of Energy achieve the goal of preventing a severe energy shortage? This is a question all American citizens will be asking over the next few years.

Figure 9.6
Social Security benefits for a worker retiring in 1980

Avg. yearly earnings $6,000

Retirement at age 65

Social Security pays $723.22* monthly to retired worker with eligible spouse

Avg. yearly earnings $10,000

Retirement at age 65

Social Security pays $996.21* monthly to retired worker with eligible spouse

*Congress usually adds a cost-of-living increase each year.

five have also been eligible for a hospital insurance program known as Medicare. The federal Social Security system works with state governments in many related areas, including unemployment compensation, aid to dependent children, and vocational rehabilitation.

PUBLIC HEALTH SERVICE (PHS)

Under the direction of the Assistant Secretary for Health, the Public Health Service has the responsibility of (1) identifying health hazards in the environment; (2) aiding in development of proper physical and mental health services for all Americans; and (3) conducting research in public health problems. The PHS enforces quarantines, examines immigrants, and provides hospital care for Coast Guard personnel and a few other federal employees.

Much of the PHS's effort today goes into administering a program of federal health care grants to state and local governments, mostly for

Figure 9.7

Food and Drug Administration inspectors, one of whom is shown here checking sardines at a cannery, try to ensure that food processors maintain high standards of wholesomeness and cleanliness. Source: FDA.

hospital construction. Other grant programs help medical schools train the doctors and nurses needed to care for the nation's sick and disabled. Ten *National Institutes of Health* research centers provide facilities in which scientists can search for cures to such illnesses as cancer, heart disease, arthritis, and various communicable diseases.

FOOD AND DRUG ADMINISTRATION (FDA)

Early in this century, a group of "muckraking" journalists (notably Upton Sinclair in *The Jungle*) exposed the unhealthy conditions commonly found in many food processing plants. Congress responded by creating the Food and Drug Administration to guard the quality, purity, and safety of products purchased by the American consumer. The scientists and inspectors of the agency enforce truthfulness in advertising, standards of quality and cleanliness for foods, adequate proof of the safety and effectiveness of medicines, and proper labeling (see Figure 9.7). A recent FDA ruling, for example, requires that labels on food packages include a list of the product's nutritional values.

Now part of the Public Health Service, the FDA continues to work with a limited budget and staff. Consumer advocates, moreover, have accused it of moving too slowly in taking products off the market, particularly when suspected cancer-causing substances are found in food. These critics also point to what they regard as a too-friendly relationship between FDA officials and the drug industry. Even so, the agency has prevented many health disasters through its inspections, testing, and screening of new drugs and food additives. (See the introduction to Chapter 20 for a dramatic example of the FDA's scientists at work.)

How does the Department of Education influence the nation's schools?

Before 1979, 170 federal education programs were scattered among various agencies and departments. Congress established the Department of Education in 1979 to coordinate these programs. The new department started with a budget of $41 billion, an amount greater than the budgets of Commerce, Energy, Interior, Justice, and State. A new Cabinet-rank Secretary of Education was selected to run the department. Congress also simplified the making of rules, budgets, and legislative proposals by cutting the number of offices involved in such activities from twenty-five to ten.

Contrary to the fears expressed by opponents, the new department was not intended to increase federal control of education; in fact, Congress wrote restrictions on such activities into the legislation. As security, an Intergovernmental Advisory Council on Education was created, with membership drawn from state and local governments. The council's job is to evaluate the department's impact on education at the state and local levels. Congress also put strict limits on staff growth within the department.

The Department of Education will administer federal scholarships, loans, grants, and direct aid to state departments of education. Special funds aid gifted students, the mentally and physically handicapped, library development, and vocational education. The department supports educational research, compiles studies on education, and plans international teacher exchanges. It also runs schools for overseas dependents and migrant workers, and administers science education and college housing loan programs.

What does the Department of Labor do for American workers?

Even though most Americans work for a living, the Department of Labor remains one of the smallest departments in the Cabinet. The Secretary of Labor, whom the President often selects from among national labor leaders, promotes the well-being of wage earners by (1) improving working conditions, (2) providing better job opportunities, and (3) protecting workers' interests under minimum wage laws and similar legislation.

WAGE AND LABOR STANDARDS ADMINISTRATION

Any employer who engages in interstate commerce must obey the Fair Labor Standards Act of 1938. The Wage and Labor Standards Administration enforces provisions of the act relating to minimum wages, overtime pay, equal pay, and child labor restrictions. The Administration also supervises working conditions under federal contracts, such as those in construction firms building the Interstate Highway system.

BUREAU OF LABOR STATISTICS

Established as a statistical and fact-finding agency, the Bureau of Labor Statistics provides businesses and unions with information on employment, productivity, wages, prices, and hours of work. Its publications are often used as the basis for settlement of wage disputes, cost-of-living raises, and negotiations of new contracts.

U.S. TRAINING AND EMPLOYMENT SERVICE (USTES)

USTES arranges counseling, training, and employment for young people, veterans, and other people in need of special vocational help. One of USTES' best-known projects is the Neighborhood Youth Corps, which hires high school students for useful tasks in schools, parks, and other community services. USTES also administers other programs designed to solve the nation's hard-core unemployment problem.

NATIONAL LABOR RELATIONS BOARD

Although it is an independent agency not directly connected with the Department of Labor, the National Labor Relations Board deals with closely related matters. Created by the National Labor Relations (Wagner) Act of 1935, the NLRB conducts elections to determine whether or not employees of a particular business want to be represented by a union. The agency also enforces the unfair labor practices provisions of the Wagner Act, which forbid an employer to (1) refuse to bargain collectively; (2) interfere in union organization efforts; (3) place undue pressure on an employee in relation to union activities or membership; and (4) fire or mistreat a union member for union activities or membership.

How does the Department of Agriculture assist farmers?

The Department of Agriculture once represented the largest single vocation in the United States. Improved technology, however, has reduced the number of Americans working in agriculture from one in two people in 1900 to one in twenty today. At the same time, rising food costs have cut deeply into everyone's budget, and farmers often get the blame—though they receive only thirty-eight cents out of each dollar consumers spend on food.

AGRICULTURAL RESEARCH

The Department sponsors the world's largest agricultural research program. The *Agricultural Research Service* keeps more than 13,000 employees busy studying soil chemistry, animal diseases, improved crops, pest control, and antipollution techniques. The Service cooperates with the states in maintaining *experiment stations* throughout the country which specialize in studying the important farm products of their particular regions.

MARKETING HELP AND CREDIT

The days when farmers ate most of their produce and sold the rest locally have disappeared. Today Department of Agriculture consultants advise farmers and others in the food industry on the demand for their products, commodity prices, transportation conditions, and preservation of foods. Other experts help farmers sell their products overseas (grain sales to Russia made headlines in 1973 and 1975), and coordinate their efforts with the foreign aid agencies.

Through the *Farmers Home Administration*, the government lends money to farmers to buy family-size farms, purchase new equipment, buy livestock, and build irrigation systems. Through other agencies, farmers may borrow money to meet their operating expenses (the *Federal Land Bank*) and to bring electricity to their farms and ranches (the *Rural Electrification Agency*).

PRICE SUPPORTS

Since the 1930's, the federal government has followed a double policy of (1) supporting minimum prices for farm products and (2) limiting the acreage planted to particular crops. If the price of wheat, for example, falls so low as to threaten wheat farmers with ruin, the government will purchase huge quantities of the grain at a base price established by Congress. With less wheat available to the public, prices tend to return to higher levels. The government also supports prices by limiting the number of acres planted, thus keeping overproduction to a minimum. Farmers who reduce their planted acreage receive cash payments in compensation.

The Agriculture Department's *Commodity Credit Corporation* administers price support and acreage allotment payments; the *Agricultural Stabilization and Conservation Service* decides on the actual number of acres to be held out of production. As a further service, farmers may purchase insurance against crop failures from the *Federal Crop Insurance Corporation*.

CONSERVATION PROGRAMS

The preservation of the national forests and programs of soil conservation also lie within the Department of Agriculture's authority. The *Forest Service* manages the national forests and conducts extensive reforestation programs. The *Soil Conservation Service* administers 3,000 soil conservation districts, provides millions of seedlings, and assists farmers in bringing eroded land back into agricultural production.

EDUCATION

The Department's *Extension Service* (in cooperation with state and county governments) helps farmers learn about the latest agricultural technology. Area and county extension agents help with production and marketing, home economics and nutrition, 4-H youth development, and rural development. Even nonfarming homeowners profit from Extension Service assistance with lawn and garden care and the use of pesticides.

How does the Department of the Interior manage the nation's natural resources?

Officials of the Department of the Interior accept as their main task the management, conservation, and development of America's natural resources. The Department (1) watches over three-quarters of a billion acres of federal land, (2) promotes mine safety, (3) protects fish and wildlife, (4) manages federal hydroelectric systems, and (5) oversees the affairs of half a million people on Indian lands and in the United States' overseas territories.

BUREAU OF LAND MANAGEMENT

The Bureau of Land Management acts as landlord for government real estate—those 770 million acres mentioned above. Ninety-eight percent of Alaska and 86.1 percent of Nevada belong to the federal government; six other states have over 40 percent of their area tied up in this way. Today the Bureau develops grazing lands and leases acreage for mining of mineral deposits. Oil companies interested in offshore exploration and drilling must also lease their sites from the Bureau.

BUREAU OF RECLAMATION

Engineers of the Bureau of Reclamation work to turn arid western lands into productive recreational or agricultural areas. Irrigation and hydro-electric power projects such as those at Grand Coulee and Hoover dams illustrate the size and complexity of this job. Development of water resources also falls under the Bureau's supervision (the Bureau's Central Valley Project, for example, transports water five hundred miles from northern California to water-poor southern California).

NATIONAL PARK SERVICE

Rangers and naturalists of the National Park Service manage over two hundred national parks, recreation areas, and monuments, plus other historic or archeologically important sites. More than 100 million visitors a year enjoy the beauty and excitement of nature in such national parks as Yellowstone, Grand Canyon, and Crater Lake.

GEOLOGICAL SURVEY

Engineers and surveyors of the Geological Survey map the geographic and geologic face of the United States. Geological Survey maps indicate the location of mineral deposits, the height of mountains, and the flow of water in rivers. Private industry uses these charts to locate sites for mineral exploration or routes for roads and rail lines.

BUREAU OF MINES

The Bureau of Mines works to (1) develop the nation's mineral resources, (2) enforce mine safety standards, and (3) protect the environment from damage during mining operations. Bureau investigators study the causes of mine explosions and train mine-disaster rescue teams. Current work includes development of petroleum from oil shales. If oil can be recovered economically from this abundant source, much of the nation's energy crisis could be resolved.

FISH AND WILDLIFE SERVICE

Conservationists attached to the Fish and Wildlife Service protect American wild birds, mammals, fish, and reptiles. The Service conducts hunting and trapping campaigns against animals that prey on endangered species, manages wildlife refuges, and works with foreign governments to conserve migratory wild fowl. Hatcheries maintained by the Service stock the nation's streams and lakes with millions of fish each year for the benefit of sport fishers.

BUREAU OF INDIAN AFFAIRS (BIA)

Since 1933, the Bureau of Indian Affairs has attempted to help Indians living on reservations to develop a way of life within a framework of their own customs, culture, and traditions. The BIA's main responsibilities are (1) to assist Indians in wise use of their land and resources and (2) to provide health, education, and welfare services to Indians.

In 1953, the BIA set out to end the status of Indians as wards of the government, but without great success. Indian leaders resent what they consider the BIA's paternalistic attitudes. Like many other minority groups, they have begun demanding full self-government, jobs, and other rewards of mainstream American life—something the BIA has never been fully able to provide.

OFFICE OF TERRITORIES

The economic and political development of territories outside the United States is the job of the Office of Territories. Present-day U.S. territories include the Pacific Trust territories, Guam, Puerto Rico, and the Virgin Islands. Representatives offer advice and assistance to each territory's government. Residents of the Marianas Islands in the western Pacific voted to accept territorial status in 1975.

OTHER AGENCIES

Lists of Department of the Interior agencies take up a number of pages in government organizational manuals. Some of the most important are the *Federal Water Quality Administration*, created in 1970 to cope with increasing problems of water pollution and shortages; the *Bureau of Outdoor Recreation*, which surveys outdoor recreation needs and provides assistance to states and communities for establishing parks and recreation facilities; and a number of *power administrations*, set up to market low-cost electrical power produced at federal reservoir projects.

How does the Department of Transportation oversee the movement of the nation's freight and passenger traffic?

The newest department of the executive branch joined the Cabinet in 1967. Congress established the agency to ensure (1) the effective administration of federal transportation programs and (2) development of national policies leading to fast, safe, efficient, low-cost transportation systems.

FEDERAL AVIATION ADMINISTRATION (FAA)

All air travel in the United States falls under the jurisdiction of the FAA. The agency (1) writes and enforces safety rules; (2) promotes civil aviation and a system of national airports; and (3) operates a nationwide system of air traffic control and navigation for both civilian and military aircraft. FAA inspectors also certify aircraft and their pilots as part of the agency's air safety program.

FEDERAL HIGHWAY ADMINISTRATION

Officials of the Federal Highway Administration coordinate the nation's highways with other types of transportation. The agency administers the Federal Aid Highway Program, which includes the 42,500-mile Interstate Highway system. Other duties include (1) assisting the states in developing highway safety and beautification programs; (2) setting up training programs for major transport companies and government agencies; and (3) regulation of commercial carriers in interstate and foreign commerce.

NATIONAL HIGHWAY TRAFFIC SAFETY ADMINISTRATION (NHTSA)

The highway death rate, though dramatically reduced after the 1974 reduction of the speed limit, is the high-priority target of the NHTSA. Agency experts carry out programs related to the safety performance of motor vehicles, related equipment, and the drivers themselves. Research programs sponsored by the NHTSA aim at developing crash-proof vehicles capable of protecting their occupants and reducing repair costs. Educational programs, particularly in the areas of pedestrian safety and control of drunken driving, are also sponsored by the NHTSA regional offices.

FEDERAL RAILROAD ADMINISTRATION

Although U.S. railroads have fallen on financially difficult days, they still carry a large percentage of the nation's freight. In support of the rail lines, the Federal Railroad Administration (1) coordinates federal programs that promote rail transport, (2) enforces rail safety regulations, (3) administers financial aid programs for specified railroads, and (4) conducts research and development in support of improved intercity ground transportation.

URBAN MASS TRANSPORTATION ADMINISTRATION (UMTA)

The urgent need for improved mass transit facilities led to the creation of this agency in 1968. UMTA assists the states and cities in developing improved mass transportation facilities, equipment, and routes. The agency encourages development of regional transport systems which integrate existing facilities, as well as of new devices such as monorail trains and expressway lanes reserved for buses. The high cost of building new systems can be met in part with federal funds administered by UMTA.

ST. LAWRENCE SEAWAY DEVELOPMENT CORPORATION

The St. Lawrence Seaway Development Corporation, a government-owned company, operates the United States portion of the Seaway between Montreal and Lake Erie. The ports of inland Great Lakes cities, such as Chicago, Detroit, and Milwaukee, are now international harbors. Heavily traveled and self-supporting, the St. Lawrence Seaway provides a safe and efficient water link to the Atlantic Ocean for the upper Midwest.

COAST GUARD

During peacetime, the Coast Guard serves under the Department of Transportation; in time of war, it becomes part of the Navy under the Department of Defense. The Coast Guard is primarily a police agency that enforces maritime regulations, rather than a defense force. The Guard's mission includes (1) maintaining lighthouses, (2) watching for icebergs in the North Atlantic, (3) holding boating safety classes, (4) conducting safety inspections of commercial and pleasure boats, (5) patroling the coastal waters on the lookout for smugglers, pirates, and illegal gambling ships, and (6) providing emergency rescue service. Officers graduate from the Coast Guard Academy at New London, Connecticut, a school similar to the U.S. Army and Navy academies at West Point and Annapolis.

Why was the Department of Housing and Urban Development added to the Cabinet?

The addition of the Department of Housing and Urban Development (HUD) to the Cabinet in 1965 reflected the growing urban nature of the United States—and the problems which came with the rapid growth of U.S. cities (see Figure 9.8). Congress had set up so many programs aimed at helping the cities with their housing problems that it became necessary to consolidate them under one department. (The first Secretary of Housing and Urban Development, Robert C. Weaver, was also the first black person to hold Cabinet rank.)

COMMUNITY DEVELOPMENT CORPORATION

Planners and builders of new communities can go to HUD's Office of New Community Development for research data, planning help, and financing.

MODEL CITIES PROGRAM

Congress budgeted $600 million in 1974 to help cities rebuild their blighted central areas. When a Model Cities program is approved, federal money helps replace old, decayed neighborhoods so that business and cultural life can return to the heart of the city. HUD also provides money to help re-

"It Says Here We're Winning The Space Race"

Figure 9.8
The severe problems of America's cities have required increased attention from Cabinet departments like HUD, HHS, Justice, and Transportation. Source: From *Herblock's State of the Union* (Simon & Schuster, 1972).

Figure 9.9
These modern apartments are typical of the housing built with federal funds from the Department of Housing and Urban Development. Well-designed projects like this provide decent living quarters for low-income families. Source: HUD.

locate people who are uprooted by the redevelopment. The *Renewal Assistance Administration* concentrates similar efforts on slum clearance and other "urban renewal" projects (see Figure 9.9).

FEDERAL HOUSING ADMINISTRATION (FHA)

Because almost one out of every four new houses in the United States carries an FHA-guaranteed mortgage, the agency has become one of HUD's best-known departments. FHA does not make loans; instead, it guarantees banks, insurance companies, and other lenders against loss. With FHA protection behind the loan, lenders grant mortgages at lower interest rates and to higher-risk borrowers than they might do otherwise.

HOUSING ASSISTANCE ADMINISTRATION

The Housing Assistance Administration runs a public housing program which attempts to provide low-income families with decent, inexpensive apartments. A rent supplement program also helps families find private housing by paying the difference between the established rents and what the family can afford to pay.

COMMUNITY RESOURCES DEVELOPMENT ADMINISTRATION

Because communities need water, gas, electricity, and recreational facilities as well as housing, Congress set up the Community Resources Development

Administration. The agency makes loans and grants for the construction and improvement of utilities, parks, and landscaping.

OTHER AGENCIES

HUD administers a series of additional programs, all dedicated to making urban life richer, safer, and more comfortable. The *Office of Equal Housing Opportunity*, for example, tries to prevent discrimination in the sale or rental of private housing. Whenever natural disaster strikes, the *Federal Disaster Assistance Administration* moves in to furnish financial assistance to victims in the form of grants and low-interest loans.

§UMMARY AND CONCLUSIONS

1. Eleven Cabinet Secretaries manage the nation's domestic affairs. Cabinet appointments are made by the President, but require Senate confirmation. One of the newest Cabinet departments is the *Department of Energy*. Created in 1977, it coordinates the government's efforts to safeguard existing energy supplies and find new sources of power.

2. The *Treasury Department* collects the government's taxes, pays its bills, keeps the books, and prints its money. Major divisions include the *Internal Revenue Service*, the *Customs Service*, the *Bureau of the Mint*, the *Bureau of Engraving and Printing*, and the *Secret Service*.

3. The Attorney General ranks as the President's top legal advisor. The *Justice Department* also enforces federal laws through a variety of divisions: *Federal Bureau of Investigation*, *Bureau of Prisons*, *Bureau of Narcotics and Dangerous Drugs*, the *Immigration and Naturalization Service*, and the *Antitrust Division*.

4. Commercial activities of all kinds—mining, manufacturing, shipping, fishing—receive assistance from the *Department of Commerce*. The *Census Bureau* keeps track of the nation's population patterns, and the *National Weather Service* predicts changing climatic conditions. The *Bureau of Standards* maintains precise weights and measures, while the *Patent Office* protects the rights of inventors and writers. The *Coast and Geodetic Survey* publishes accurate maps, and the *Maritime Administration* tries to keep the merchant marine healthy.

5. The *Department of Health and Human Services* spends more than any other department except Defense. The *Social Security Administration* helps the retired, disabled, and sick. The *Public Health Service* and the *Food and Drug Administration* help HHS guard the nation's health.

6. The *Department of Education* was created in 1979 to coordinate all of the federal education programs formerly scattered among many departments. Its large budget reflects a wide variety of programs designed to improve education without imposing further federal controls.

7. American workers look to the *Department of Labor* to enforce federal laws governing working conditions, wage rates, and safety standards. The *Wage and Labor Standards Administration* checks on compliance with

minimum wage and child labor laws. The *U.S. Training and Employment Service* works to help the unemployed and untrained develop needed skills. Union activities are supervised by the *National Labor Relations Board*.

8. The *Department of Agriculture* helps farmers through its programs of research, marketing and credit assistance, price supports, and conservation. Important agencies include the *Agriculture Research Service*; *Farmers Home Administration* (loans); the *Commodity Credit Corporation* (price supports); *Forest Service* and *Soil Conservation Service* (reforestation and soil reclamation); and the *Extension Service* (educational and youth programs).

9. Management, conservation, and development of America's natural resources are the responsibility of the *Department of the Interior*. The *Bureau of Land Management* watches over 770 million acres of federal land. The *Bureau of Reclamation* irrigates and develops arid western land. The *National Park Service* welcomes visitors to the national parks and monuments it manages. The *Fish and Wildlife Service* protects the nation's wild animals, birds, and fish. The *Bureau of Indian Affairs* tries to help Indians gain a proper economic and social position in American society; the *Office of Territories* does the same for American overseas possessions.

10. The *Department of Transportation* wrestles with the nation's complex transportation problems. Air traffic moves under the supervision of the *Federal Aviation Administration*; similar agencies, the *Federal Highway Administration* and the *Federal Railroad Administration*, supervise the highways and railroads. The *National Highway Traffic Safety Administration* has helped cut down the death toll on our roads. The *Urban Mass Transportation Administration* encourages cities to develop better ways of moving large numbers of people. The *Coast Guard* rescues capsized sailors, patrols for icebergs, and chases smugglers.

11. The nation's housing problems, mostly concentrated in large metropolitan areas, led to creation of the *Department of Housing and Urban Development*. The *Community Development Corporation* and the *Model Cities Program* both help cities rebuild older sections of downtown areas. The *Federal Housing Administration* guarantees low-cost mortgages as a means of encouraging home ownership. Low-income families receive help from the *Housing Assistance Administration* in finding rental units they can afford. Other agencies work to end racial and sexual discrimination in housing and to provide financial assistance following natural disasters.

ℝEVIEW QUESTIONS AND ACTIVITIES

DOMESTIC AGENCIES YOU SHOULD KNOW

Agriculture Extension Service	*Bureau of Indian Affairs*
Agriculture Research Service	*Bureau of Land Management*
Antitrust Division (Justice Department)	*Bureau of the Mint*

Bureau of Narcotics and
  Dangerous Drugs
Bureau of Engraving and Printing
Bureau of Prisons
Census Bureau
Coast and Geodetic Survey
Coast Guard
Commodity Credit Corporation
Federal Aviation Administration
Federal Bureau of Investigation
Federal Housing Administration
Fish and Wildlife Service
Food and Drug Administration
Forest Service
Geological Survey
General Accounting Office
Housing Assistance Administration
Immigration and Naturalization
  Service
Internal Revenue Service

Maritime Administration
Model Cities Program
National Institutes of Health
National Highway Traffic Safety
  Administration
National Labor Relations Board
National Park Service
National Weather Service
Office of Education
Office of Territories
Patent Office
Public Health Service
Secret Service
Social Security Administration
Soil Conservation Service
Training and Education Service
  (USTES)
Urban Mass Transit Administration
Wage and Labor Standards
  Administration

REVIEW QUESTIONS

The following multiple-choice questions are based on the important ideas presented in this chapter. Select the response that best completes each statement.

1. High customs duties set on a particular manufactured product serve the purpose of (a) protecting American producers. (b) keeping large quantities of the product out of the country. (c) establishing a bargaining point with foreign countries over their high tariffs on American goods. (d) encouraging the development of an American industry in that product. (e) all of these are possible reasons for high duties.

2. The only pure, 100 percent silver coin still produced by the Bureau of the Mint is (a) the dime. (b) the quarter. (c) the half-dollar. (d) the Bicentennial dollar. (e) none of these.

3. The agency that guards the President and his family is the (a) FBI. (b) Border Patrol. (c) Secret Service. (d) Coast Guard. (e) Internal Security Division of the Justice Department.

4. The approximate number of immigrants from *all* other countries now allowed to enter the United States each year is (a) 20,000. (b) 290,000. (c) 450,000. (d) 1 million. (e) unlimited.

5. Which of the following has lost its status as a Cabinet department? (a) Housing and Urban Development. (b) Commerce. (c) Agriculture. (d) Postal Service. (e) Labor.

6. Maintaining the quality and purity of the American diet is the re-

sponsibility of the (a) Food and Drug Administration. (b) Public Health Service. (c) Social Security Administration. (d) Fish and Wildlife Service. (e) Bureau of Narcotics and Dangerous Drugs.

7. The practice of paying farmers *not* to grow a certain crop developed as a means of (a) rewarding political supporters in the farm states. (b) building up surpluses for foreign sales. (c) maintaining farm prices at reasonably profitable levels. (d) using up surplus federal funds. (e) none of these.

8. The type of transportation that is *not* under the jurisdiction of the Department of Transportation is (a) aviation. (b) shipping. (c) railroads. (d) automobile and truck traffic. (e) mass rapid transit.

9. Programs aimed at rebuilding the old, run-down sections of our cities fall under the jurisdiction of the Department of (a) the Interior. (b) Housing and Urban Development. (c) Commerce. (d) Energy. (e) Health, Education, and Welfare.

10. A member of the Cabinet serves (a) a four-year term. (b) for life. (c) as long as the President wants him or her to stay. (d) until dismissed by the Senate. (e) as long as allowed by the Civil Service Commission.

CONCEPT DEVELOPMENT

This chapter has explored a number of significant concepts relating to the domestic Cabinet departments of the executive branch. You can use your skills in thinking, researching, and writing to answer the following questions.

1. Why does the President need the advice and administrative services of the Cabinet Secretaries? Would it be better if the Secretaries were elected rather than appointed?

2. Name the eleven domestic Cabinet departments that provide services to the American people. Briefly describe the important activities of each department.

3. Federal departments have been created to aid labor, business and industry, but no Cabinet department has been established to protect consumer interests. List some arguments in favor of a Department of Consumer Affairs.

4. What factors in the changing American society have led to the rapid growth of the federal bureaucracy? What are the results when government increases in this way?

5. How does the role of a typical department—such as Agriculture— change as the nation's population moves to the cities and the economy becomes more industrialized?

ACTIVITIES

The following activities are designed to help you use the ideas developed in this chapter.

1. Consult the *United States Government Organization Manual* in your library for organization charts of the various departments of the Cabinet. Select one to transfer to a poster. Use the poster as a visual

aid while you describe to your class the activities of the many bureaus and offices which make up the department; point out specific department activities which can be seen in your own community.

2. Ask an official from any of the many federal agencies described in this chapter to visit your class to talk about the work carried on by the organization. Prepare questions ahead of time to ask after the official speaks—not only on the work of the agency, but also on career possibilities in government service.

3. Divide the class into small groups, each group assigned to write to a particular agency—FBI, FAA, FDA, Bureau of the Mint, Bureau of Indian Affairs, and the like. Ask the agency to comment on a specific question or problem the group has uncovered in its reading. For example, what is the FBI's position on wiretaps? Will the Mint start producing coins containing silver again? What degree of accuracy does the National Weather Service aim for? Report to the class on (a) the general work of the agency and (b) the responses to your particular questions.

4. Welfare programs often arouse strong feelings in a community. Locate the office or offices in your community that administer federal and state welfare programs. Interview officials there to determine the nature and extent of payments and services provided. Talk to some of the welfare recipients waiting in line at the office. You might also do some reading on the subject. Write a paper on your observations and research, stating your conclusions about the use or misuse of welfare.

CHAPTER TEN

THE "FOURTH BRANCH" OF GOVERNMENT: THE INDEPENDENT AGENCIES

Consider these situations for a moment:

—Your favorite radio station fades out several miles outside your home town. Other stations can be heard for hundreds of miles. Who determines the broadcasting power of a station?

—The marvelous, new and improved washday miracle soap you bought turns out to be the same old product in a different box—but at a higher price. Can't something be done about ripoffs like that?

—After the telephone company fouls up your bill for the hundredth time, you decide to change services. Unfortunately, there's no place to go. What happened to the antimonopoly laws?

—Twist the television dial to every channel available, and you won't find a cigarette or liquor ad. But pick up any newspaper or magazine, and those products jump off the page at you. Why should radio and television ignore such a rich source of advertising revenue?

—Try setting up a bus line to take people to the beach or lake during the summer. Sounds like a simple exercise in free enterprise, doesn't it? Wait until you've started cutting through all the red tape—you might have a different answer to that question.

—Compare your family's electric bill with one from two or three years ago. The increase in cost per kilowatt hour will probably astonish you. Who told the electric company it could raise its rates so quickly?

—With your graduation checks firmly in hand, you decide to shop around for the bank that pays the highest rate of interest on savings accounts. Eight phone calls later, you realize that all the savings banks pay the same rate. What happened to good old American competition?

Well, by now you probably have guessed that a common theme ties all of these everyday occurrences together—the federal government has been at work. More specifically, these situations grow out of the regulatory activities of the *independent agencies*. Congress created most of these agencies to *regulate* the actions of companies engaged in interstate commerce, like railroads or television stations. Other independent agencies *administer* important governmental programs like veterans' affairs, development of electrical power, and supervision of atomic energy.

The power of the independent agencies to affect national economic life has grown greatly in recent years. Certainly, an agency like the Federal Communications Commission has the power to enrich one company while bankrupting another. In any year, the volume of "administrative legislation" issued by these agencies easily equals the lawmaking output of Congress.

In this chapter, you will learn how the independent agencies came into being and how they have developed. Emphasis will be placed on the work of the regulatory agencies, which have greater impact than the administrative agencies on both businesses and individuals. The questions that will be answered include:

1. Why were the independent agencies established?
2. How do the independent agencies operate?
3. What is the role of the Interstate Commerce Commission?
4. How does the Federal Communications Commission supervise the broadcast and telephone industries?
5. How does the Civil Aeronautics Board regulate the aviation industry?
6. How does the Federal Trade Commission protect consumers?
7. What is the role of the Federal Energy Regulatory Commission?
8. How does the Securities and Exchange Commission protect investors?
9. Why were the independent administrative agencies established?
10. What are the duties of the United States Postal Service?
11. What do some of the other independent agencies accomplish?
12. Who regulates the regulators?

Why were the independent agencies established?

HISTORICAL BACKGROUND

President Woodrow Wilson recommended creation of the Federal Trade Commission as a means to "make men in a small way of business as free to succeed as men in a big way."

Wilson knew, as had presidents before him, that the Constitution made no specific provision for the organization of the executive branch of government. Instead, the Founders had wisely left the creation of administrative agencies to later congresses and presidents. Over the years, a workable system of administration emerged, centered around the major

Cabinet departments. Cabinet secretaries, as Chapters 8 and 9 described, carry a twofold responsibility: (1) to advise the President on matters related to the work of their departments and (2) to administer the day-to-day affairs of government.

In time, Congress came to believe that the mushrooming economic system needed more than the administrative authority of the Cabinet departments. The Department of Agriculture, for example, carries out policy relating to wheat production, but has no authority to regulate the transport of that wheat to market. Congress, therefore, delegated a portion of its constitutional power over interstate commerce in order to create independent, specialized agencies with wide *regulatory authority* in their special fields. These agencies have come to operate almost as a "fourth branch" of the federal government, combining some of the legislative, executive, and judicial powers of the other three branches.

EMPHASIS ON INDEPENDENCE

The independence of these agencies has always been carefully protected, for a variety of reasons:

1. The agency must be guarded from undue pressures brought by the industry it regulates. When farmers, for instance, lobbied the Interstate Commerce Commission into existence in 1887, it was obvious that the new agency could not set railroad freight rates unless it was protected from the political influence of the powerful railroad magnates.

2. The agency must be shielded from political pressure. The Federal Communications Commission cannot properly evaluate a television license application, for example, if Congress or the White House can step in and command favorable treatment for itself or its friends.

3. Some agencies deal with such sensitive matters that their independence should not be violated for reasons of national security. The Energy Research and Development Administration, which is responsible for nuclear research and development, fits that category exactly.

In all the controversy that presently surrounds the independent agencies, one objective remains clear—the majority were established to regulate American business and industry. The commercial and industrial revolution of the late 1800's and the early 1900's developed in a climate of "let the buyer beware." Gradually, the excesses of that philosophy became clear. The strong businesses strangled the weak; inferior, overpriced food and merchandise flooded the market. The American people, as individuals and in pressure groups, called upon Congress to regulate entire areas of economic activity.

The independent agencies are a peculiarly American institution. Socialist and communist theory claims that only full government ownership can properly regulate big business. The United States, however, chose government regulation instead of outright government ownership. This theory—that rates, prices, operating procedures, and profits of certain industries should be set by a regulatory authority—has become widely accepted by politicians and economists of all political viewpoints.

Figure 10.1
Consumers today can choose from a wide range of products with the knowledge that government regulations regarding labeling, packaging, and purity of ingredients provide a reasonable degree of safety and effectiveness. Source: FDA.

How do the independent agencies operate?

As was noted earlier, the independent agencies possess the combined features of the other three major branches of government. (1) They serve as *legislative* bodies when they enact their own regulations (for example, when the Federal Communications Commission sets the broadcasting power allowed a given radio station). (2) They assume *executive* powers when they enforce their own regulations (for example, when the Interstate Commerce Commission checks to be sure that trucks carry proper safety features). (3) They act as a *judicial* body when they hold hearings for accused violators and hand out fines or suspensions (for example, when the Securities and Exchange Commission suspends sales in a company's stock). These powers are sometimes called "quasi-legislative" or "quasi-judicial," *quasi* being a Latin word meaning "resembling."

ORGANIZATION

Congress writes the laws that create the independent agencies. The agency may be formed in response to a request from the President or in response to a need seen by Congress itself. Although their names vary (most are known as boards, commissions, or administrations), all receive yearly appropriations from Congress to support their work. Most independent agencies are headed by a board of commissioners. Members are appointed by the President, subject to confirmation by the Senate. Unlike members of the Cabinet, commissioners serve long terms (usually seven years) and may be removed only "for cause." This job security helps insulate the commissioners from White House and congressional pressure, but they are never totally immune.

Each agency's five to eleven commissioners establish policy, hold hearings, and make major decisions. A professional staff of economists, lawyers, investigators, accountants, clerks, and secretaries handles the day-to-day paper work, enforces agency regulations, and gathers data for the commissioners' use. Since these permanent employees tend to stay on the job through changes of the top administration, they exercise considerable influence on the work of the agency.

CONTROVERSY OVER POLICY

Given the combined freedom and authority described above, the independent agencies frequently find themselves working counter to the wishes of the President, Cabinet, and Congress. Serious difficulties generally arise when a new administration takes over the White House, only to find its policies blocked by agencies still committed to opposite ideas. Because commissioners' terms are staggered, only a few replacements can be made in any given year. Presidents find this fact extremely frustrating.

The Federal Reserve System, for example, may see its role in fighting inflation as that of restricting the money supply. The Secretary of the Treasury, on the other hand, may wish to stimulate business by increasing the flow of new money into the economy. The chairman of the Reserve Board almost always wins an argument like that; not even the President can order a change in board policy.

Despite this independence, the commissioners often respond to the wishes of Congress, the President, and the public. In fact, an agency's relationships with the industry it regulates sometimes become so close as to raise questions regarding conflict of interest (see the final section of this chapter for a discussion of reform proposals). Companies that object to an agency decision have the option of taking the case to the Federal Courts of Appeals, but the courts traditionally have supported the regulatory authority of the agencies.

What is the role of
the Interstate Commerce Commission?

A long-simmering feud between farmers and the railroads came to a head after the Civil War. Farmers claimed that the railroads (1) charged exorbitant freight rates, (2) discriminated against some towns and shippers, (3) cheated on billings, and (4) conspired to eliminate competition. State laws that attempted to regulate interstate railroad commerce (called *granger laws*) were overturned by the Supreme Court.

DEVELOPMENT OF THE ICC

Out of this battle came the Interstate Commerce Act of 1887, which set up the first regulatory agency, the Interstate Commerce Commission

(ICC). Although the ICC was weakened during its early years by adverse court decisions, the Hepburn Act of 1906 greatly strengthened the agency's regulatory power. Originally limited to supervision of the railroads, the ICC's charter was expanded to include the trucking industry in 1935. Today, the ICC regulates all overland interstate commerce which moves by bus, truck, train, pipeline, and inland waterway (but not private automobiles). ICC regulations cover the transport of people as well as freight. All transportation facilities, including waiting rooms, warehouses, and the vehicles themselves, come under agency jurisdiction. The ICC is moving toward deregulation of the trucking industry by the end of 1981. Opposition comes from large trucking companies and the Teamsters union, which fears nonunion competition.

ICC ORGANIZATION

ICC activities are directed by eleven commissioners (as with all independent agencies, the President nominates the commissioners and their chairman for confirmation by the Senate). Commissioners serve staggered seven-year terms, so that no more than two terms may expire in any given year. No more than six commissioners may be of the same political party. Widespread ICC functions are administered by six regional and seventy-six area offices.

REGULATING OVERLAND TRANSPORT

ICC regulators identify three classes of shippers: (1) common carriers with fixed routes and schedules of pickups and deliveries; (2) common carriers that operate under contract with shipping companies; and (3) private carriers owned by shipping companies. The ICC controls both common and private carriers in five main areas:

Setting rates. Rate hearings attract more attention than any other ICC activity. Rates set too low can ruin a carrier, while those set too high can be a hardship for the public. Rate schedules must be published; rebates are forbidden; and rates for short hauls may not be higher than for longer runs. ICC commissioners also use different rate schedules as a means of aiding hard-pressed carriers. The truck and bus lines, for instance, must charge higher freight rates than the railroads. Because the rail lines have long been losing business to the long-haul truckers, they need the rate advantage to stay in business.

Guaranteeing service. Transport companies cannot establish or drop routes without ICC approval. ICC examiners issue certificates of "convenience and necessity" to carriers which allow them to operate in specific areas. The ICC may refuse to allow a railroad or bus line to drop a money-losing route if that would harm a community. The agency may also refuse to certify a carrier for a new route if that would take business away from an existing company.

Setting safety standards. Both equipment and operators must meet ICC safety standards. These complex regulations establish maintenance procedures, safety equipment, and load limits for vehicles; drivers must satisfy requirements covering their physical condition, training, and age. Owners and operators must buy insurance for the protection of passengers, drivers, freight, and property.

Requiring standard accounting. ICC rules require all regulated companies to use standard accounting procedures, to send in regular reports, and to open their books to inspectors from the agency.

Regulating corporate securities. Companies in the transportation business need ICC approval before issuing stocks, bonds, or other financial instruments. This requirement carries over from the days when some railroads issued securities of dubious value.

How does the Federal Communications Commission supervise the broadcast and telephone industries?

The concept of independent regulatory agencies gave the federal government a means of dealing with new technological developments that did not exist when the Constitution was written. The rapid spread of the telegraph, followed by the telephone and radio, made regulation of the growing communications industry a necessity. Congress finally passed legislation in 1934 that established the Federal Communications Commission (FCC). It now also regulates the television industry.

FCC ORGANIZATION

Seven commissioners, including a chairman directly nominated by the President, set FCC policy under guidelines established by Congress. FCC employees staff thirty field offices, nineteen monitoring stations, and a mobile network, all designed to guard against violations of federal broadcasting standards.

REGULATING THE AIRWAVES

The airwaves are considered public property, and the FCC regulates their use "in the public interest." FCC regulations cover a number of key areas:

Broadcasting licenses. Because broadcasting channels are limited, FCC licenses are eagerly sought after. The right to operate a radio or television station can mean millions of dollars in revenue for the successful bidder. Licenses must be renewed every three years, at which time the station must prove that it has performed proper public service or its license can be taken away. The FCC also sets limits on a station's broadcasting power and hours of operation.

Influence on program content. The FCC may not act as a censor (broadcasters are expected to practice self-censorship), but the agency does affect program content through its licensing power. Limitations have been set on the number of commercials per hour, and a certain number of public service broadcasts are required. Concern over the quality of television entertainment has led the FCC to investigate the role of American broadcasters in such matters as violence, crime, and the slanting of political news.

Equal time requirement. The FCC requires that broadcasters remain nonpartisan in controversial matters. If free air time has been given to supporters of one candidate or political viewpoint, equal time must be offered to opposing candidates or points of view. Similarly, if a station takes an editorial position, equal time must be made available to spokespersons for opposing views.

Other areas of broadcasting. In addition to regulating radio (AM and FM) and television (VHF and UHF), the FCC supervises other areas of broadcasting: (1) Cable television now serves an increasing number of communities; the FCC awards franchises and regulates the material sent out over the cable. (2) FCC examiners monitor and license marine, amateur, police, fire, industrial, and citizen's band radio frequencies to prevent misuse. (3) Microwave and satellite transmission facilities also fall under FCC jurisdiction.

Telephone and telegraph. The FCC regulates all telephone and telegraph services. Because telephone companies have effective monopolies over the service in their franchise areas, they must accept FCC control of their rate structures, equipment maintenance, and other aspects of the business.

How does the Civil Aeronautics Board regulate the aviation industry?

The Civil Aeronautics Board (CAB) regulates air travel in the same way the ICC controls overland transport. First established in 1938, but extensively reorganized in 1958, the CAB is responsible for (1) regulating the civil air transport industry within the United States and between this country and foreign airports; (2) promoting air travel and commerce in this country and abroad; (3) supervising those air carriers used for mail delivery; and (4) coordinating the civil air industry with national defense needs. The rapid growth of air travel has made the CAB one of the most active regulatory agencies.

CAB ORGANIZATION

CAB's five board members serve six-year terms; no more than three members may be appointed from the same political party. As with most other independent agencies, CAB decisions are not subject to review by the executive or legislative branches of the federal government; anyone dissatisfied with a CAB action must turn to the United States Courts of Appeals. The CAB itself uses the courts to enforce its decisions when informal requests for compliance do not work.

CAB JURISDICTION

The CAB issues regulations in six major areas:

Authorizations. The Airline Deregulation Act of 1978 allowed airlines more freedom to drop routes and serve new ones. Domestic and foreign airlines still must gain CAB authorization before flying passengers in or out of any American airport.

Rates and fares. The CAB determines what fares will be charged on both domestic and foreign flights (the latter in coordination with international air agencies). Rate schedules may not be changed without CAB approval, but in recent years examiners have allowed airlines with too many empty seats to experiment with more cut-rate fares and discount plans.

Subsidies. The CAB sometimes grants *subsidies* (financial payments) to airlines that serve small communities. The Airline Deregulation Act of 1978 required the CAB to continue subsidizing essential air service to these low-population areas for at least ten more years.

Intercarrier relations. CAB control over the airlines extends into their business relationships. All mergers, agreements, and sharing of routes and facilities must receive CAB approval. Even advertising campaigns by airlines and travel agents must follow CAB rules.

Accounting and reporting. Uniform accounting and reporting methods are specified for all airlines. The CAB uses these reports and its own staff examiners to compile and publish statistical information useful to both government and the aviation industry.

International aviation. The CAB advises the State Department on the negotiation of international air agreements. Major international routes are awarded to a single airline, known as a *flag carrier.* Foreign flag carriers often receive subsidies from their governments, but American airlines are expected to show a profit from their international operations without help from the government.

LET'S REVIEW FOR A MOMENT

Are you still wondering why your hometown radio station fades out so quickly? It's not because the management can't afford a more powerful transmitter, but because the FCC restricts good ol' WPOW to only 500 watts. All those confusing airline fares, of course, result from efforts by the airlines to attract customers and yet stay within CAB regulations.

The *independent agencies* have earned their informal title of "the fourth branch of government." Given their authority by Congress, they have a hand in almost every commercial enterprise in this country. Wouldn't it be easier for the government simply to take over the railroads and the television stations? Not if you believe in free enterprise. The regulatory agencies represent a compromise between absolute government control and all-powerful corporations.

The *Interstate Commerce Commission* sets rates, enforces safety standards, checks offerings of securities, and regulates service by railroad trucks, buses, pipelines, and inland waterways. Still thinking about starting your own bus line? The red tape will be mostly state and local, unless you're going to cross a state line. That's when the ICC would come in.

The *Federal Communications Commission* regulates radio and television broadcasting along with telephone and telegraph communications. Did your local station recently air an editorial you didn't like? Ask for FCC-guaranteed air time to reply, if you think you're qualified to do so.

The aerial equivalent of the ICC is the *Civil Aeronautics Board*. CAB inspectors enforce fare and rate schedules, hold hearings on route applications, and generally oversee the operation of domestic airlines and foreign air carriers operating in this country.

Now, where would you go to complain about that misleadingly packaged laundry soap that was mentioned at the beginning of the chapter? Let's see—why not try the Federal Trade Commission?

How does the Federal Trade Commission protect consumers?

When Congress passed the Clayton Antitrust Act in 1914, the need for an agency to help enforce its provisions led to establishment of the Federal Trade Commission at the same time. The FTC was given two objectives: (1) to maintain the free enterprise system by helping companies comply with the antitrust laws and (2) to protect consumers from unfair trade practices.

FTC ORGANIZATION

Five FTC commissioners serve overlapping seven-year terms. As with most other agencies, an executive director supervises the staff of 1,600. This leaves the commissioners free to concentrate on writing policy and hearing important cases. The agency divides its work among three bureaus—Competition, Consumer Protection, and Economics.

FTC JURISDICTION

Federal Trade Commission activities seek to aid consumers in three areas:

Antitrust regulation. The FTC acts to promote free and fair competition in interstate commerce by preventing companies from acting in *restraint of trade.* FTC examiners watch for (1) illegal pricing structures, including price-fixing, price discrimination, and rebates or discounts for large buyers but not for smaller retailers; (2) illegal agreements, such as exclusive-dealing arrangements or interlocking management in competing industries; (3) illegal mergers, which join companies that otherwise would remain in competition.

Consumer protection. The FTC's most publicized efforts have come in the field of consumer protection. The agency requires (1) honest packaging that does away with deceptive sizes and shapes; (2) proper labeling of textile and fur products (rabbit was once sold under twenty or more different names); (3) true and complete statements to consumers of the cost of buying on credit; (4) accuracy in credit reports; and (5) safeguards for registered trademarks.

The most recent FTC consumer protection effort has been toward "truth in lending" for the benefit of borrowers and credit card holders. Lenders must clearly state the true interest rates and total interest costs of installment purchases at the time of purchase (see Figure 10.2). Finally, the Fair Credit Reporting Act gives consumers the right to examine their credit files and remove inaccurate information.

Economic reports. FTC statisticians publish economic studies on changing conditions of business competition in the United States. Quarterly summaries of the nation's business activities help the government's domestic policymakers choose the programs that will keep the economy healthy.

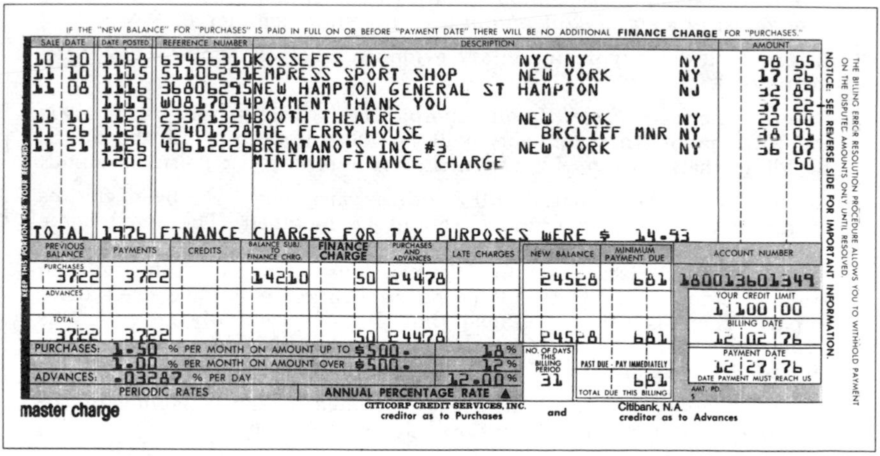
IF THE "NEW BALANCE" FOR "PURCHASES" IS PAID IN FULL ON OR BEFORE "PAYMENT DATE" THERE WILL BE NO ADDITIONAL **FINANCE CHARGE** FOR "PURCHASES."

SALE DATE	DATE POSTED	REFERENCE NUMBER	DESCRIPTION			AMOUNT
10 30	1108	63466310	KOSSEFFS INC	NYC NY	NY	98 55
11 10	1115	51106291	EMPRESS SPORT SHOP	NEW YORK	NY	17 26
11 08	1116	36806295	NEW HAMPTON GENERAL ST	HAMPTON	NJ	32 89
	1119	W0817094	PAYMENT THANK YOU			37 22-
11 10	1122	23371324	BOOTH THEATRE	NEW YORK	NY	22 00
11 26	1129	Z2401778	THE FERRY HOUSE	BRCLIFF MNR	NY	38 01
11 21	1126	40612226	BRENTANO'S INC #3	NEW YORK	NY	36 07
	1202		MINIMUM FINANCE CHARGE			50

TOTAL 1976 FINANCE CHARGES FOR TAX PURPOSES WERE $ 14.93

	PREVIOUS BALANCE	PAYMENTS	CREDITS	BALANCE SUBJ. TO FINANCE CHRG.	FINANCE CHARGE	PURCHASES AND ADVANCES	LATE CHARGES	NEW BALANCE	MINIMUM PAYMENT DUE
PURCHASES	37 22	37 22		142 10	50	244 78		245 28	6 81
ADVANCES									
TOTAL	37 22	37 22			50	244 78		245 28	6 81

ACCOUNT NUMBER 180013601349

YOUR CREDIT LIMIT 1 100 00

BILLING DATE 12 02 76

PAYMENT DATE 12 27 76 DATE PAYMENT MUST REACH US

AMT. PD. $

PERIODIC RATES	ANNUAL PERCENTAGE RATE ▲
PURCHASES: 1.50 % PER MONTH ON AMOUNT UP TO $500.	18 %
1.00 % PER MONTH ON AMOUNT OVER $500.	12 %
ADVANCES: .03287 % PER DAY	12.00 %

NO. OF DAYS THIS BILLING PERIOD 31

PAST DUE - PAY IMMEDIATELY

TOTAL DUE THIS BILLING 6 81

KEEP THIS PORTION FOR YOUR RECORDS

NOTICE: SEE REVERSE SIDE FOR IMPORTANT INFORMATION.

THE BILLING ERROR RESOLUTION PROCEDURE ALLOWS YOU TO WITHHOLD PAYMENT ON THE DISPUTED AMOUNTS ONLY UNTIL RESOLVED.

master charge

CITICORP CREDIT SERVICES, INC. creditor as to Purchases and Citibank, N.A. creditor as to Advances

Figure 10.2

"Truth-in-lending" laws require lenders to tell borrowers exactly what rate of interest they must pay

Use of the "revolving charge" option provided by bank credit cards is not cheap! On an average annual balance of $500 "borrowed" by using this credit card, 18 percent interest a year would come to $90.

ENFORCEMENT

Even more than most other agencies, the FTC actively enforces its decisions. Most companies will agree to stop a particular practice when FTC personnel recommend that they do so. Consumers can initiate this process through the simple steps outlined in the accompanying box. If the case goes to court, the FTC may ask for a court order telling the company to "cease and desist." If the company continues to violate the ruling, the FTC may bring suit in federal district court. A ruling against the company carries possible fines of up to $10,000 per day for continued violations.

What is the role of the Federal Energy Regulatory Commission?

In an era when the phrase "energy crisis" has become a very real part of our lives, the Federal Energy Regulatory Commission (FERC) has great importance. Two major energy sources are regulated by the FERC: (1) hydroelectric power and (2) the natural gas industry. It should be noted that

How to make a complaint to a federal regulatory agency

The National Consumer Law Center at Boston University Law School has listed five points which should be covered in a well-drawn application for complaint:

1. Include the name and address of the company you are complaining about. This should be accompanied by an explanation that the company is engaged in a significant amount of interstate commerce.

2. Attach copies of any documentary evidence involved, such as advertisements or letters.

3. Describe the facts as clearly and completely as you possibly can. This is the information that probably will be most important in the staff's deciding whether to investigate further or to send you a polite brush-off.

4. As much evidence as possible that other consumers have been victims of the same deceptive practice should be included. The greater the number of consumers victimized, the more likely it is that the commission will take some action. If other consumers are willing to sign affidavits [notarized statements], the application will have even more impact. There is little likelihood that they will actually be called as witnesses in formal hearings, but it is possible that they will be interviewed if the agency decides to conduct an investigation.

5. The application for complaint must be signed by the consumer or the consumer's attorney, with a return address provided.

Making an application for a complaint is the simplest means of gaining access to the regulatory process. Consumers who wish to become more deeply involved are invited to consult the source from which this advice was taken: *Working on the System: A Comprehensive Manual for Citizen Access to Federal Agencies*, edited by James R. Michael with Ruth C. Fort, © 1974 by Center for Study of Responsive Law, Basic Books, Inc., Publishers, New York.

the FERC's regulatory powers are restricted primarily to the *transmission* of electricity and natural gas; *production* and *distribution* processes fall under state regulation for the most part.

FERC ORGANIZATION

The FERC replaced the Federal Power Commission in 1977, when the Department of Energy was created. Five commissioners administer the work of the agency, aided by over 1,300 lawyers, engineers, and other technical experts.

FERC ACTIVITIES

Federal Energy Regulatory Commission personnel attempt to regulate the nation's power transmission needs in several ways:

Regulation of hydroelectric power. The FERC sets rates for transmission across state lines of all electric power produced by private or government generating stations. The agency's regulatory authority begins with granting approval for the building of dams on navigable waterways, even though construction is carried out by another government agency or a private utility company. Utility companies must also obtain FERC permission for the construction of new transmission lines.

The FERC requires companies under its jurisdiction to hook into one another's transmission lines. This power grid allows the utilities in one area to compensate for a failure in another system's generators. An unfortunate demonstration of the interdependence of modern transmission systems occurred in 1965, when an overloaded relay at a hydroelectric plant in Ontario caused a blackout that extended across New York State, through several other Northeastern states, and parts of Canada.

Regulation of natural gas. Clean-burning natural gas has become more important in an era of oil shortages and concern over air pollution. As with electric power, the FERC's authority centers on the transmission of natural gas from the producer to the consumer. FERC officials (1) establish interstate pipeline rates; (2) license the construction and operation of interstate pipelines, such as the proposed $43-billion, 4,800-mile Alaska-Canada pipeline; (3) make sure that enough gas is produced to meet the nation's future need for natural gas; and (4) insure that producing companies provide service to all qualified distributors.

Other functions. The FERC staff performs a number of other services related to the regulation of hydroelectric power and natural gas transmission: (1) Field workers have prepared studies of fifty-six river basins, revealing tens of millions of kilowatts waiting in undammed rivers. (2) Agency economists regulate the financial activities of companies in the energy field (reporting procedures and sales of securities, for example). (3) The FERC referees the long-standing conflict between private utility companies and government-owned power producers such as the Tennessee Valley Authority. Finally, (4) the agency regulates foreign sales of electrical energy and natural gas, first making sure that domestic needs are satisfied.

How does the Securities and Exchange Commission protect investors?

The great stock market crash of 1929 destroyed thousands of small investors, who saw their savings wiped out almost overnight. The stock market had become an uncharted sea in which the average person was at the mercy of financial sharks who promised quick profits. Despite attempts by state legislatures to control the worst excesses of these stock promoters, widespread misrepresentation of securities continued. That situation led in 1934 to formation of the Securities and Exchange Commission (SEC).

SEC ORGANIZATION

The SEC operates under the direction of five members, who are appointed to staggered five-year terms. The commissioners oversee the work of over 1,300 lawyers, economists, analysts, and other employees who work out of nine regional offices.

Figure 10.3

The nation's economic pulse can be felt on the trading floor of the New York Stock Exchange, whose operation is regulated by the Securities and Exchange Commission. Source: Wide World Photos.

SEC SAFEGUARDS

The SEC's commissioners cannot guarantee the safety of any investment. Honest companies may still go bankrupt, leaving stockholders with suddenly worthless securities. The SEC can, however, provide safeguards in two areas:

1. *Full disclosure.* SEC regulations require that all companies make full disclosure of financial information relating to new offerings of stocks and bonds. Any sale of securities not registered with the SEC is illegal. Registration of the stock with the SEC does not signify government approval or endorsement of the issue; the investor, however, can be certain that the information contained in the stock description (called a *prospectus*) is accurate under penalty of law.

2. *Market regulation.* SEC officials follow up on the disclosure rules by regulating the way in which stocks and bonds are traded after they are first offered. Elaborate rules govern the operation of stock exchanges (see Figure 10.3) and brokerage houses, and the conditions under which sales are made—including the brokers' fees. Agency inspectors investigate and prosecute illegal stock trades based on "inside" information (privileged data not available to the general public).

Sales on *margin* (stock sold on credit) and in *futures* (a commodity purchased now to be delivered later) are strictly regulated. The percentage of the stock's price that must be paid in cash varies according to the SEC's judgment of market conditions and the general national economy.

OTHER SEC CONCERNS

Any time a corporation's securities show a sudden change in value, the SEC takes an interest. The agency sits in on bankruptcy hearings in order to represent the interests of the investors who had purchased that company's securities. SEC studies look into market conditions and recommend new regulations to better protect investors. Two areas that have attracted particular attention have been holding companies and mutual funds.

1. *Holding companies.* A holding company exists to own stock in and control other companies. Antitrust elements of holding company activities are investigated by the Federal Trade Commission. The SEC's regulation of holding companies involves (1) requirements for full disclosure of their finances, (2) elimination or reorganization of poorly managed companies, and (3) supervision of holding companies in the electrical and natural gas industries.

2. *Mutual funds.* Mutual funds invest money received from the sale of their own securities in the stocks and bonds of other companies. In effect, a person who invests in a mutual fund buys the investment judgment of professional fund managers—for which an annual fee is usually charged. The SEC does not involve itself in the funds' investment decisions. Instead, the agency protects the mutual fund investor by controlling management fees, mergers, "inside" deals, and other practices relating to investment security.

Why were the independent administrative agencies established?

In addition to the regulatory agencies discussed so far, Congress has created a second type of independent agency. These administrative commissions provide a wide variety of services to the American people. Although many activities of this type are carried out by the traditional Cabinet departments (see Chapter 9), a number of politically sensitive duties have been assigned to agencies in the "fourth branch" of government. These administrative agencies—three of which are described below —normally pursue their goals without direct supervision by the legislative or executive branches.

VETERANS ADMINISTRATION

The United States has traditionally rewarded its veterans generously. Revolutionary soldiers, for example, received free homestead land. The many services for veterans were gathered together in 1930 under an independent administrative agency, the Veterans Administration (VA). This generosity has been extremely costly to the American taxpayer. Veterans' benefits for World War II alone have amounted to over one-half trillion dollars.

VA organization. The administrator of the VA supervises more than 239,000 medical, legal, and office personnel. With over 30 million Americans qualifying as veterans, the VA administers a wide variety of programs.

VA benefits and services. VA services may be divided into three types:
1. *Health care.* The VA operates 172 medical centers, 220 clinics, and 92 nursing homes in 193 cities. Eligible veterans receive general medical and dental services, nursing home care, surgery performed by highly qualified specialists, and extensive physical and psychological therapy.
2. *Financial benefits.* An extensive program of financial benefits includes (a) compensation and pension payments for disabled and retired veterans; (b) monthly checks for veterans who enroll in college or vocational training programs; (c) rehabilitation programs for disabled veterans; (d) loan guarantees and low-cost life insurance; and (e) educational aid for spouses and children of veterans killed or disabled in service.
3. *General assistance.* Through its offices and service centers across the country, the VA provides information, counseling, and assistance to veterans, their dependents, and their beneficiaries. A National Cemetery System provides free funeral services to veterans and other eligible government employees.

TENNESSEE VALLEY AUTHORITY

Socialists believe that government should own and manage major industrial complexes. In the Tennessee Valley Authority (TVA), the government of

Does government regulation help or hurt the economy?

No one escapes the long arm of government regulation these days. Your car, house, food, fuel, and even the air you breathe come under control of one agency or another. A lively debate over the effect of such regulation can be seen in the following paragraphs.

HENRY FORD II TALKS ABOUT THE HIGH COST OF REGULATION

"As I look at our country today, I see a powerful but uncertain giant being trussed up in a growing web of rules and regulations to the point where it can no longer exert its strength freely and effectively. . . .

"Perhaps it's only a coincidence that the recent period of rapidly rising government spending and roughshod regulation also has been a time of high unemployment, slow productivity improvement, soaring deficits and unprecedented peacetime inflation. But I don't believe it at all. Despite a mounting record of failure and frustration, our leaders have failed to grasp the fact that too much government inevitably leads to economic decay." *

SOME BUSINESSES HAVE BENEFITED FROM REGULATION

The paperwork generated by government regulations has created a number of new industries. Electronics companies are marketing computers tailored to the needs of companies that must keep up with personnel data required by agencies such as the Equal Employment Opportunity Commission. Almost fifty percent more personnel officers were hired in 1977 than in 1976 for the same reason.

At the same time, the microfilm industry is reaping profits from the demand for space-saving records. Similarly, microfiche (a system for keeping hundreds of pages on a single 6″ x 9″ card) is being widely adopted. Newsletters and seminars which tell business people how to comply with regulations are widespread. In fact, the need to influence regulatory agencies has increased the number of Washington lobbyists to over 5,000.

THE COSTS OF REGULATION CAN BE MEASURED IN TIME AND DOLLARS

The federal government prints almost 5,000 different forms. Filling them out takes Americans about 800 million hours every year. Of course, much of this time is spent filling out individual income tax returns (over 180 million hours), but employers spend over 195 million hours coping with wage and tax statements—before they start on any other reports.

One report alone, the request to operate a nuclear power plant, takes 55,000 hours to fill out. The Office of Management and Budget estimates that it would take the full-time efforts of 27 people working 40 hours a week for a full year. Processing this mountain of paperwork costs $100 billion a year. That breaks down to federal costs of over $43 billion (more than 10 percent of the budget) and industry costs of about $30 billion, with the remainder spread among individuals and other levels of government.

the United States has created a unique independent agency that does exactly that. Congress started the TVA in the Depression year of 1933 for "the orderly and proper physical, economic, and social development" of an entire region—the 41,000 square miles of the Tennessee River valley. Today, the seven-state system of dams, power stations, research labs, and recreational areas serves a population of about 4 million Americans (see Figure 10.4).

TVA organization. A three-member Board of Directors (appointed by the President to nine-year terms) sets policy for the massive TVA operation. Division managers direct some 26,000 workers at various administrative, technical, and operational facilities.

TVA's responsibilities. Two primary tasks occupy most of TVA's attention: (1) flood control and (2) development of hydroelectric power. Other TVA programs include maintenance of a 650-mile channel for navigation; reforestation and soil conservation programs; agricultural experimentation, particularly in fertilizers; and development of recreational areas.

Controversy. Angry controversy has swirled around the TVA since its beginning. The Supreme Court declared the project constitutional in 1936, but critics still urge that its facilities be sold to private enterprise. Tax-exempt government power stations, they claim, should not compete with taxpaying utility companies. In the late 1970's, a major controversy arose over the question of completing a dam that endangered a small fish, the snail darter. With energy needs growing, the snail darter lost.

The TVA's supporters answer these criticisms by listing the agency's accomplishments: (1) the formerly depressed region has gained greatly in per capita income; (2) yearly floods no longer wreck the valley's farms and towns; (3) most farms now have electricity; (4) extensive areas have been reforested; and (5) many new industries, attracted by the abundant power, have located in the valley. Without this progress, the region might have required much greater amounts of money for social welfare programs.

Figure 10.4
Norris Dam in Tennessee, the first dam built by the Tennessee Valley Authority. Completed in 1936, it provides flood control, electricity, drinking water, and recreation. Source: TVA.

What are the duties of
the United States Postal Service?

One of the nation's oldest public services, the Post Office Department was founded by the Second Continental Congress in 1775, before the Constitution was written. In the Postal Reorganization Act of 1970, Congress converted the Post Office Department into the United States Postal Service, an independent federal agency. Thus the Postmaster General no longer holds a Cabinet seat. Congressional sponsors of the reorganization hoped that the Postal Service would become more efficient as well as self-supporting. The old Post Office Department had always operated at a deficit, for the federal government believed that a low-cost postal system helped tie the country together. By the early 1980's, however, even dramatically increased postal rates had not provided sufficient revenue to overcome the red ink.

THE SERVICE

The United States Postal Service employs some 666,000 workers, which makes it second in size only to the Department of Defense among federal employers. Over 100 billion pieces of mail pass through the system every year—more than all the other postal systems of the world combined. The post office provides a number of services besides selling stamps and delivering mail; employees also take applications for passports, sell money orders and savings bonds, and distribute stamps used to validate hunting licenses that permit the taking of certain migratory birds.

CONTROVERSIES AND COMPLAINTS

The Postal Service has had its share of controversy. In the 1800's, for example, bitter political battles raged over the question of patronage. The party in power rewarded its supporters with appointments to post office jobs. The Department was placed under civil service late in the century, but presidents continued to name leading political supporters as Postmasters General well into the mid-1900's.

Of more recent concern have been rising complaints about high postage rates and slow mail service. The stamp that sent a one-ounce letter to any address in the United States cost three cents in 1958: it now costs twenty cents. Despite these increased charges and some progress toward mechanization, Americans found that mail deliveries were fewer and the mail was taking longer to reach its destination. One newspaper article charged that a colonial horse and rider could beat today's delivery time for a letter traveling from Philadelphia to New York.

DIMINISHING THE DEFICIT

Postal Service deficits run yearly into hundreds of millions of dollars. One important reason may be found in the rate schedule. Mail divides into various classes, depending on content and service desired. Personal and

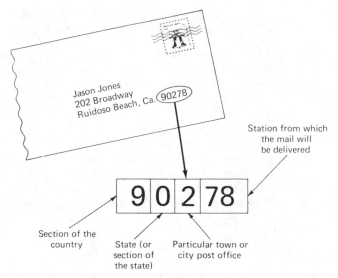

Figure 10.5

What the ZIP Code numbers mean

ZIP Code numbers provide a shortcut for sorting and shipping mail quickly and efficiently. Eventually, optical-scanning equipment that can read the numbers will eliminate the need for postal clerks to handle each letter individually.

business letters are known as first class mail, and cost the most. Books, newspapers, magazines, and other printed material can be mailed at lower rates per ounce. Obviously, the cost of handling these bulky materials must be greater than that of processing a first class letter, but Congress has traditionally used the mails to encourage the free flow of printed information. Postal Service officials say that the nation can have one or the other—a profitmaking system in which everyone pays what the service costs, or a deficit-ridden system that provides low-cost mail delivery.

A number of new developments have been added to improve mail service. Ziptronic machines take advantage of ZIP Codes (see Figure 10.5) to sort letters at a rate of one every second. Automated bulk mail plants near the big cities speed up handling of parcel post and magazine shipments. Guaranteed overnight mail delivery to major cities is now available for an extra fee.

What do some of the other independent agencies accomplish?

This chapter has so far considered only nine agencies out of almost four dozen federal commissions and boards that regulate industry and serve the American people (see the accompanying box). In almost every session, Congress creates new agencies or combines several existing agencies under a new name.

Independent agencies of the federal government, 1980

Action
American Battle Monuments
  Commission
Arms Control and Disarmament
  Agency
Board for International
  Broadcasting
Central Intelligence Agency
Civil Aeronautics Board
Civil Service Commission
Commission of Fine Arts
Commission on Civil Rights
Community Services
  Administration
Consumer Products Safety
  Commission
Environmental Protection Agency
Equal Employment Opportunity
  Commission
Export-Import Bank, U.S.
Farm Credit Administration
Federal Communications
  Commission
Federal Deposit Insurance
  Corporation
Federal Election Commission
Federal Energy Management
  Agency
Federal Home Loan Bank Board
Federal Maritime Commission
Federal Mediation and Conciliation
  Service
Federal Reserve System
Federal Savings and Loan
  Insurance Corporation

Federal Trade Commission
General Services Administration
Inter-American Foundation
International Commerce Agency
International Development
  Cooperation Agency
International Trade Commission
Interstate Commerce Commission
National Aeronautics and Space
  Administration
National Credit Union
  Administration
National Foundation on the Arts
  and Humanities
National Labor Relations Board
National Mediation Board
National Science Foundation
National Transportation Safety
  Board
Nuclear Regulatory Commission
Office of Personnel Management
Overseas Private Investment
  Corporation
Postal Rate Commission
Railroad Retirement Board
Securities and Exchange
  Commission
Small Business Administration
Smithsonian Institution
Tennessee Valley Authority
U.S. Information Agency
U.S. Postal Service
Veterans Administration

A sampling of other interesting and important independent agencies follows.

The *Environmental Protection Agency*, one of the newest regulatory agencies, was established by President Nixon in 1970. The EPA attempts to control pollution at its source, clean up existing conditions, and find better ways to protect the environment in the future. Major efforts presently aim at (1) attacking air and water pollution and (2) solving the problem of waste disposal.

The *Equal Employment Opportunity Commission* works to end job discrimination based on race, religion, sex, age, or national origin. The EEOC's *affirmative action program* requires that companies doing business with the federal government take positive steps to hire minority and female employees.

The *Federal Deposit Insurance Corporation* protects bank depositors by insuring individual savings accounts in banks that belong to the system. FDIC insurance covers accounts up to a maximum of $100,000.

The *Federal Reserve System* is responsible for (1) controlling the nation's credit, (2) regulating the amount of money in circulation, and (3) supervising the activities of the twelve Federal Reserve Banks. In the late 1970's, the Federal Reserve System Board of Governors tried to limit inflation by raising the rediscount rate (the interest rate charged banks that borrow from the FRS) to an all-time high. Economists hoped this high interest rate would cut down on the money supply and discourage unnecessary use of credit and borrowing. Federal Reserve Banks issue the bulk of the nation's paper currency, serve as banker for the federal government, and advance funds to member banks when they need ready cash.

The *National Aeronautics and Space Administration* plans, coordinates, and controls the national space program. NASA's successes include the moon landing (1969), a soft landing on Mars (1976), and the flight of the space shuttle (1981). Space exploration has slowed in recent years, however, because of cutbacks in NASA's budget.

The *Selective Service System* administers the military conscription system—the draft. Even though no one has been drafted since July 1, 1973, the Selective Service continues to register male Americans when they reach the age of eighteen. This controversial program is intended to provide a readily available supply of draftees should a war emergency arise.

The *Smithsonian Institution* manages a number of national museums as a means of (1) preserving the nation's historic and cultural heritage and (2) pursuing scientific research. Its museums include the National Museum of History and Technology, the National Gallery of Art, and the National Air and Space Museum.

The *United States Information Agency* promotes better understanding of the United States in other countries. USIA specialists use all means of communication—radio, television, films, books, newspapers, exhibitions, libraries, and instructional programs—to inform people overseas about the culture, politics, and foreign policy of this country.

Who regulates the regulators?

Richard Olney, chief legal counsel for several eastern railroads, once wrote to reassure a railroad company president who wanted the newly formed Interstate Commerce Commission to be abolished. Olney (who was later to serve as Attorney General and Secretary of State under Grover Cleveland) told the worried official that the ICC "can be made of great use to the railroads. . . . The older such a commission gets to be, the more inclined it will be found to take the business and railroad view of things."*

Olney wrote that letter in 1887. Critics of the ICC and the other regulatory agencies believe that little has happened to prove him wrong. The President's own economic advisors point out that ICC-controlled freight rates cost consumers $400 million a year in overcharges. Similarly, the Hoover Commission blasted the Federal Trade Commission, calling "its operations, programs and administrative methods . . . inadequate and its procedures cumbersome."† As Figure 10.6 suggests, it's possible that the federal "watchdogs" no longer guard the public's interests.

* Quoted in James R. Michael, ed., *Working on the System* (New York: Basic Books, 1974), p. 9.
† Quoted in *ibid.*

"Something went wrong here"

CRITICISMS OF REGULATORY AGENCIES

Although the charges against the independent regulatory agencies vary according to the nature of the agency's activities, the most common general criticisms include:

Regulators who don't regulate. Despite efforts to provide commissioners with immunity to pressure, the agencies cannot escape being influenced—particularly by the very industries they regulate. Because agency heads should be "experts," Presidents often reach into corporate offices for their appointees. Low budgets, small staffs, and natural sympathies all tend to tie the agency to the corporations it supposedly controls. At the other end of the cycle, agency personnel frequently leave their jobs for better-paying positions with the companies they formerly regulated—but maintain contacts with their old friends within the regulatory body.

Pressure from Capitol Hill and the White House also complicates the regulatory process. Examples abound in Washington of legislators who have seen to it that their television stations back home sail through FCC license hearings. If Congress holds the purse strings, the President holds the power of political life and death. Bureaucrats anxious to protect their jobs and chances of advancement cannot ignore the wishes of the Oval Office too often.

Indifference to the public interest. Regulatory agencies periodically hold hearings, but the public (consumers, poor people, minorities) is seldom heard. Consumer advocates like Ralph Nader believe that the antitrust laws have been almost forgotten, that "bigness" has become equal to "goodness" in the eyes of the regulatory agencies and of industry.

Over-regulation. Well-meaning bureaucrats, armed with restrictive regulations and governmental red tape, have sometimes caused needlessly high costs and inefficiency for industry. In such cases, rate schedules remain unchanged despite changing market conditions; new technology is unused because of outmoded work rules; and excessive paperwork prevents office workers from performing more productive tasks. According to the Chase Manhattan Bank, government regulation added more than $100 billion to the cost of goods and services in the U.S. in 1977 alone.

Regulation by compromise. Regulatory agencies move slowly and cautiously. Fearful of upsetting railroad presidents, auto industry directors, and congressional committee members, agency bureaucrats "study" issues to death. Court challenges can drag out a proposed regulation for years. When the agency finally does write a new rule, it usually ends up as one that business "can live with." While the textile industry and the FTC spent years debating the time and costs necessary to convert to making all children's sleepwear flame-retardant, thousands of children were burned.

PROPOSED REFORMS

Reform attempts have gathered steam since the 1946 Administrative Procedure Act tried to move the regulatory agencies in the direction of "fair and uniform procedures." Consumer groups have begun to open the agencies to public supervision (see Figure 10.7). From such studies, public and private, have come a number of recommendations for reform.

Abolish the agencies. The most drastic proposal urges that all regulatory agencies be disbanded. Where still needed, their functions could be given to the appropriate Cabinet departments.

Regulate the regulators. An independent agency already exists—the Administrative Conference of the United States—that could serve as general supervisor of the regulatory agencies. As presently established, the Administrative Conference can only study regulatory problems and suggest reforms. In order to truly accomplish its purpose, the ACUS would need (1) administrative authority over the independent agencies and (2) increased staff and budget.

Accelerate antitrust prosecution. The Justice Department should greatly speed up its prosecution of antitrust cases. General Motors, one argument claims, should long ago have been split into six smaller companies. Until the government actively seeks to prevent virtual monopolies by a few big companies, the regulatory agencies' hands are tied.

Increase congressional supervision. Critics contend that Congress should begin examining the regulatory agencies on a regular basis. Budget controls can keep the agencies tuned in on their primary job—that of pro-

```
Ralph Nader,                    :
                                :
            Petitioner          :
                                :
                                :
_____:
```

PETITION FOR RULEMAKING

Petitioner requests the Commission to establish a rule of general applicability for passenger motor carriers in interstate commerce, and to amend all certificates of convenience and necessity held by such carriers, to prohibit the smoking of cigars, cigarettes and pipes, by passengers or operating personnel, on all passenger carrying motor buses.

The authority of the Commission is found in the Interstate Commerce Act, part II, 49 U.S.C. 304(a)(1), which empowers the Commission to make "reasonable requirements with respect to continuous and adequate service," and 49 U.S.C. 308, which empowers the Commission to place conditions on certificates of convenience and necessity to carry out requirements established under 49 U.S.C. 304(a)(1).

Section 304(a)(3a) of Title 49 U.S.C., more particularly, empow-

~~rs the Commission to make "reasonable requirements~~

Figure 10.7
Can regulatory agencies be made more responsive to consumer needs?

Consumer organizations like those founded by Ralph Nader have learned the legal routes by which citizens must bring their complaints before the regulatory agencies. This petition to the ICC requests that smoking be prohibited on interstate buses. Source: James R. Michael, *Working on the System* (New York: Basic Books, 1974).

tecting consumers. At the same time, senators and representatives must stop using the agencies for selfish political and economic purposes.

Establish a consumer agency. Many consumer advocates insist that creation of a new agency dedicated to protecting consumer interests is long overdue. The Consumer Protection Agency would represent the public before other federal agencies and in the courts. In addition, the agency could serve as a clearinghouse for data on products of all types, thus putting the vast research facilities of the federal government to work for the individual consumer.

SUMMARY AND CONCLUSIONS

1. Independent agencies have come to be called the "fourth branch" of the federal government. Possessed of legislative, executive, and judicial powers, they exist relatively free of presidential and congressional control. The regulatory agencies represent a compromise between total government ownership of industry and the opposite pole of all-powerful private corporations.

2. Oldest of the independent agencies is the *Interstate Commerce Commission*. The ICC regulates all overland and river transport in the United States. Agency examiners set rates and safety standards, regulate securities, and guarantee service at "reasonable rates." The ICC hopes to increase competition and lower shipping costs by deregulating the trucking industry.

3. Radio and television broadcasting, along with telephone and telegraph communications, comes under control of the *Federal Communications Commission*. The FCC licenses the use of the public airwaves, sets broadcasting standards, and holds hearings on telephone rates. The FCC's "equal time" requirement guarantees all political views a chance to be heard on the air.

4. The *Civil Aeronautics Board* sets airline rates and makes route decisions that affect all air travelers. CAB examiners must approve all airline mergers, and the agency guarantees service to small communities by means of subsidies when necessary. The CAB also speaks for American aviation in negotiations with foreign governments.

5. Maintenance of the free enterprise system and elimination of unfair trade practices are responsibilities of the *Federal Trade Commission*. Although some consumer activists argue that the FTC hasn't moved fast enough, some progress has been made in the field of consumer protection. Recent "truth in lending" laws grew out of FTC efforts, as did the requirement that credit files be opened for the individual's inspection.

6. The *Federal Energy Regulatory Commission* supervises the transmission of electric power and natural gas. FERC rules (1) cover the construction of new generators and transmission lines; (2) set rates for electricity and natural gas delivered interstate; and (3) attempt to guarantee adequate supplies for all private and industrial users of power.

7. The *Securities and Exchange Commission* cannot guarantee that anyone's investment will make money, but it does require full disclosure of all financial information by a company that is selling securities. Investors also are protected by controls on margin buying, the futures market, holding companies, mutual funds, and the stock market itself.

8. The independent administrative agencies serve a particular group of citizens (such as veterans) or concentrate on control and production of a special product (such as atomic energy). The *Veterans Administration* keeps busy supplying hospital care, insurance, education, rehabilitation, and other benefits to more than 30 million veterans. Thanks to the flood control dams and hydroelectric power developed by the *Tennessee Valley*

Authority, the entire seven-state region served by that often controversial agency has achieved both economic and social growth.

9. Some business leaders believe that the economy has been over-regulated by the independent agencies. They point to unemployment, limited growth, inflation, and decreased productivity as results of excessive paperwork. But consumers have been protected, and a few new industries have developed because of the work of the independent agencies.

10. The *United States Postal Service* keeps the nation's mail moving—too slowly, some critics charge. Heavy labor costs account for most of the Postal Service's budget deficit, which independence has not enabled the Service to overcome. Increased mechanization holds out hope for eventual solution of the problem, but at the probable cost of higher postal rates.

11. Even as the number of independent agencies has increased, critics have charged that (1) regulators sometimes ignore the public interest; (2) discussions of serious situations are allowed to drag on for years; and (3) many agency heads seem to bend to outside pressures, either from Congress or from the industries they regulate. Reform proposals range from abolishing all regulatory agencies to pulling them together under the supervision of one "superagency." More careful supervision of the regulatory bodies by Congress would be a good starting point for reform.

REVIEW QUESTIONS AND ACTIVITIES

TERMS YOU SHOULD KNOW

affirmative action program
flag carrier
"fourth branch"
futures market
granger laws
holding company
independent agencies

margin
mutual funds
prospectus
regulatory authority
restraint of trade
subsidies

REVIEW QUESTIONS

The following multiple-choice questions are based on the important ideas presented in this chapter. Select the response that best completes each statement.

1. The independent agencies are sometimes spoken of as the "fourth branch" of government because (a) the Constitution created the first agencies to regulate the other three branches. (b) they combine legislative, executive, and judicial powers. (c) most of them have their own police forces. (d) politicians cannot be elected without their assistance. (e) they all regulate interstate commerce.

2. In creating the regulatory agencies, Congress delegated to them part of its power over (a) the executive branch. (b) the judicial branch.

(c) interstate commerce. (d) administration of the civil service. (e) the general welfare.

3. The method of overland transport that is *not* regulated by the Interstate Commerce Commission is (a) railroads. (b) trucks. (c) pipelines. (d) inland waterways (barges, tow boats). (e) private automobiles.

4. Despite the regulatory authority of the Interstate Commerce Commission and the Civil Aeronautics Board, a railroad or airline may discontinue any route that loses money. This statement is (a) true. (b) false, because the agencies require that routes be continued even if they bankrupt the carrier. (c) false, because the agencies require that service be continued in most cases, but will grant subsidies or rate increases to compensate for the losses.

5. The power that the Federal Communications Commission does *not* exercise is that of (a) censorship of program content. (b) regulation of broadcasting transmitter power. (c) denial of a new license. (d) supervision of ham radio broadcasting. (e) regulation of programs transmitted over cable TV.

6. The independent agency most directly involved in consumer protection is the (a) Interstate Commerce Commission. (b) Civil Aeronautics Board. (c) Veterans Administration. (d) Federal Trade Commission. (e) Securities and Exchange Commission.

7. The Securities and Exchange Commission protects investors by (a) keeping the mechanisms of the securities market honest. (b) denying companies that might lose money the right to sell stock. (c) taking over all aspects of the issuance and marketing of securities. (d) controlling stock prices so that they cannot fall. (e) keeping its hands off the stock market completely and letting free enterprise take its course.

8. The criticism of the Tennessee Valley Authority most often heard has been that (a) the TVA has not been successful in its development work. (b) the government should not compete with private power companies. (c) flood control projects have ruined the natural beauty of the area's rivers. (d) only the wealthy have profited from the agency's work. (e) no one has ever criticized the TVA.

9. The independent agencies often find their independence threatened by pressure from Congress, the White House, and the industries they regulate. This statement is (a) true. (b) false; the agencies are immune to outside pressures. (c) false; the public would never permit the agencies to be pressured by outside interests.

10. *Not* suggested as a means of reforming the regulatory agencies is the idea of (a) doing away with all regulatory agencies. (b) setting up a "superagency" to watch over all the others. (c) requiring that Congress supervise the agencies more closely. (d) setting up an agency to speak for the consumer before the regulatory agencies. (e) all of these are frequently advanced as means of reforming the independent regulatory agencies.

CONCEPT DEVELOPMENT

This chapter has explored a number of significant concepts relating to independent regulatory agencies. You can use your skills in thinking, researching, and writing to answer the following questions.

1. Why are the independent agencies often called the "fourth branch" of government?

2. Explain several important ways the independent agencies regulate the economic life of the United States.

3. Contrast the American system of regulation by agencies with the system commonly found in many other countries, where government owns key manufacturing, transport, and communications industries.

4. Select one of the federal regulatory agencies described in this chapter and evaluate its performance in detail.

5. What complaints are most often brought against the independent regulatory agencies? Suggest the reforms that you feel would be most effective in solving these problems.

ACTIVITIES

The following activities are designed to help you use the ideas developed in this chapter.

1. Use your library's copy of the *United States Government Organization Manual* to look up the major independent agencies described in this chapter. Prepare an information sheet that lists (a) name of the director, (b) agency name and address (including local offices), and (c) a brief listing of the agency's responsibilities. Distribute the information around your school (and in the community if you wish) as a means of encouraging people to write to appropriate agencies with complaints and suggestions about problems that need attention. Another useful source for this project is James R. Michael's *Working on the System: A Comprehensive Manual for Citizen Access to Federal Agencies* (New York: Basic Books, 1974).

2. The single agency most important to consumers is probably the Federal Trade Commission. Survey the customers in a local supermarket to collect a list of complaints about such problems as deceptive packaging, unfair pricing, misleading advertising, and other improper practices. Compile your results and recommendations for correction, and send them to

> Special Assistant Director for Rulemaking
> Federal Trade Commission
> Washington, D.C. 20580

It is through contact with the public that FTC examiners gather the data needed to improve trade standards.

3. Arrange a debate between two teams of students who will take the roles of (a) the directors of a heavily regulated company—such as a major trucking firm—and (b) the head of the appropriate regulating agency—such as the ICC. Let each side state its case for and against regulation (they'll need to do some research, perhaps including interviews with people in these fields). Let the class vote on whether regulation should be continued, lessened, or increased in this case.

4. Organize your class to conduct a careful survey of areas of pollution—air, water, noise, and waste disposal—in your community. Make accurate observations of your own, but also talk to city officials about

what they are doing to solve these problems. If enough interest can be generated, you might think of starting an environmental protection club in your school to assist in this important task. The Environmental Protection Agency will send you information on projects and procedures that have worked in other towns and cities.

5. Study the data compiled in the table below. Survey a representative group of people in your community to find out if they respond in the same percentages to this question. What do the lower ratings in Germany, Italy, and Mexico mean?

Question: "Suppose you had some question to take to a government office—for example, a tax question or housing regulation. Do you think you would be given equal treatment—I mean, would you be treated as well as anyone else?"

Percentage who say	U.S.	Germany	Italy	Mexico
They expect equal treatment	83	65	53	42
They don't expect equal treatment	9	9	13	50
Depends	4	19	17	5
Other	—	—	6	—
Don't know	4	7	11	3
Total percentage	100	100	100	100

Source: Table 2 (in abridged form) from Gabriel A. Almond and Sidney Verba, *The Civic Culture* (Princeton: Princeton University Press, 1963), p. 108.

THE JUDICIAL
BRANCH
DETERMINES
THE LAW

CHAPTER ELEVEN

THE U.S. COURT SYSTEM

At a time when Americans routinely question the integrity of Congress and the presidency, the nation's system of justice has retained a major share of its prestige. Across the land, from the marble halls of the Supreme Court to the crowded aisles of the municipal courts, judges and juries sit in judgment. Their verdicts, we'd like to believe, always reflect a fair application of the law.

Consider for a moment, however, the case of the German farmer's mule.

Texas law requires that landowners in rural areas fence their property in order to keep livestock from wandering onto the highways. If a stray animal causes an accident, moreover, its owner must accept liability for damages.

One day in the late 1940's, a Dallas motorist was driving rapidly along a stretch of country highway. He topped a slight rise and, before he could use his brakes, smashed into a stray mule. The driver's wife suffered severe facial injuries. In order to recover damages, the motorist sued the farmer whose land adjoined the scene of the accident.

When the suit came up for trial, the farmer did not appear in court. Without the defendant there to speak for himself, the judge had no choice but to award substantial damages to the injured woman. Weeks later, the sheriff of the county sent a deputy to the farm to serve a warrant of attachment. This legal notice informed the thunderstruck farmer that his land must be sold to satisfy the judgment of the court.

When he finally understood the meaning of the warrant, the farmer explained what had happened. Because he was a German immigrant, he did not read English well. Yes, he remembered receiving notice of the suit.

Yes, he had gone to the courthouse—but on the wrong day. Finding the courtroom empty, he had returned home.

The deputy explained that the court had awarded the damages because one of the farmer's mules had caused the accident. Now the farmer was not only angry, he was incredulous. "What mule?" he roared. "I don't even own a mule!" Investigation proved that he was telling the truth. The ill-fated animal had strayed from another, nearby farm.

Despite this new information, the judge's decision could not be challenged. The farmer lost his property in a court sale. Having been offered his day in court—and having failed to appear—the farmer was forced to accept the bitter fruits of his negligence.

Fortunately, history wrote a happy ending for this story. Alerted by the widespread newspaper publicity, students at the University of Texas collected enough money to buy new land for the luckless farmer.

The verdict, however, still offends our sense of fair play. Should an innocent man—even a careless one—suffer such severe punishment for a matter beyond his control? Granted, this was an unusual case—but Justice does stand blindfolded on her pedestal. Any citizen who does not understand his or her legal rights and obligations can be caught in a similar legal predicament.

With that concern in mind, this chapter will attempt to provide answers to some basic questions about the American system of justice and the courts which administer that system:

1. How were the federal courts established?
2. How does the system of state courts operate?
3. When does a court have the right to hear a case?
4. How are judges selected, and what do they do?
5. What happens when a case goes to trial?
6. How well does the U.S. jury system work?
7. What powers do the courts exercise?

How were the federal courts established?

When the delegates to the Constitutional Convention met in 1787, they were aware that the courts created under the Articles of Confederation had worked poorly. Each state had been left to interpret the laws of the United States as it saw fit. Disputes between the states could not be resolved in court, and decisions made in one state had no legal force in any other state.

This judicial anarchy led to the creation of the federal court system. Article III of the Constitution states:

> The judicial power of the United States shall be vested in one Supreme Court, and in such inferior courts as the Congress may from time to time ordain and establish.

Congress had already received the expressed power to establish these courts in Article I, Section 8, Clause 9 (see Chapter 4, page 94). Out of that congressional mandate emerged a three-level federal court system—the district courts, the courts of appeals, and the Supreme Court.

DISTRICT COURTS

The first-level federal courts—the district courts—were established in the first year of Washington's administration (1789). The district courts exercise *original jurisdiction* in federal matters. That is, they serve as trial courts for all cases arising under the laws of the United States, except in the few instances where the Supreme Court retains original jurisdiction.

The law divides the fifty states into eighty-nine districts, with at least one district allocated to each state and the District of Columbia. Large states like California and New York have four districts. Each district keeps several judges busy. Unlike the higher federal courts, the district courts use grand and petit juries (see page 279) to assist the trial judges in making their decisions.

COURTS OF APPEALS

The courts of appeals were created by Congress in 1891 to relieve the burden on the Supreme Court caused by the large number of appeals from the district courts. Courts of appeals stand midway between the district courts and the highest court of the land. Only when a lower court has declared an act of Congress unconstitutional may a case be appealed directly to the Supreme Court.

Ten judicial circuits serve the fifty states. An eleventh court hears cases on appeal for the District of Columbia. One justice of the Supreme Court is also assigned in an advisory role to each circuit, but most cases are heard by a three-judge "bench." Either the defense or the prosecution may appeal a case to the courts of appeals, as long as federal jurisdiction is involved. Appeals, however, are normally made only on the basis of (1) alleged improper courtroom procedure or (2) incorrect application of law—not on the basis of the evidence presented at the original trial.

Because the Supreme Court agrees to review only about 4 percent of the cases brought before it, the courts of appeals serve as the last court of appeal for most district court decisions.

SUPREME COURT

The judiciary ranks as a powerful equal of the legislative and executive branches of government. Under the American system of checks and balances, the power of the Supreme Court cannot be overemphasized. The nine judges who occupy the Supreme Court bench serve as the final decision-makers on all questions of federal law; they also serve as the court of final resort for any lower court decisions that involve federal jurisdiction (see page 270). The path by which a case reaches the Supreme Court can be seen graphically in Figure 11.1

Figure 11.1
The path to the Supreme Court

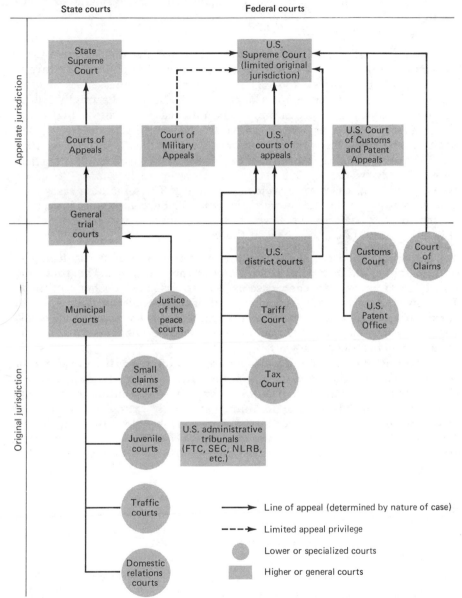

Supreme Court justices. A Chief Justice presides over the Supreme Court, assisted by eight associate justices. Congress has the power to change the number of associate justices; the total has varied from a low of four to as many as nine. The Court's present number was established in 1869.

Supreme Court justices are appointed by the President, but must be confirmed by the Senate. Because the justices hold their positions for life (unless they resign, retire, or are impeached), a President fortunate enough to fill several Supreme Court vacancies can change the Court's philosophy for a generation.

Supreme Court jurisdiction. The Constitution limits the Supreme Court to original jurisdiction over only two types of cases: (1) those that involve two or more of the states and (2) those that affect ambassadors or other public ministers. Although the Court may choose to take original jurisdiction in a few other special situations, most cases reach the high court on an appeal called a *writ of certiorari.* Of the several thousand writs filed each year, only about 4 percent are accepted by the Court. In the 1979 term, for example, the Court faced a docket of 4,781 cases. The justices agreed to review only 199 cases, while denying review to 1,776 cases. Seventy-five other cases were decided summarily. The remaining cases were carried forward to the next term. It is usual for Supreme Court justices to return most appeals to the lower courts because they feel that no significant point of law is involved in the case.

The Supreme Court at work. The nine justices hear arguments during an eight-month term that runs from October through June. The time allocated for arguments in each case is limited, usually one hour per side. Extensive *briefs* (written summaries of legal precedents and other information) are filed to support the oral arguments. The justices then take the case under advisement, beginning a period of deliberation and discussion held in strict privacy.

The voting majority that decides a case may offer a written explanation of their decision called a *majority opinion.* Any justice who dissents from the majority view may write a *minority opinion.* A dissenting opinion may represent the beliefs of one to four justices; in extreme instances, as many as four separate minority opinions may be filed. In many cases, however, the Court simply announces its decision, without presenting written opinions. Because of the controversial nature of the cases heard by the Court, close votes are common.

OTHER FEDERAL COURTS

A number of special courts established by Congress complete the federal court system. These lower-level courts include:

Territorial courts. United States overseas possessions (Guam, the Virgin Islands, the Marianas, and Puerto Rico) use territorial courts in place of district courts for matters involving federal law.

Courts of the District of Columbia. Because of its unique legal position, the District of Columbia has its own district-level federal courts.

Court of Military Appeals. Military personnel who violate military law must be tried by a military court. Court-martial decisions involving imprisonment or other severe penalties are reviewed by the Court of Military Appeals. This court may confirm the severe punishment of the lower court, but more often it reduces the penalty.

Tax Court. A panel of sixteen judges, appointed by the President, serves as a court of last appeal in tax cases. Tax Court judges hear cases involving decisions of the Internal Revenue Service throughout the country.

How does the system of state courts operate?

Even more clearly than in the federal courts, the state tribunals exist to settle disputes between individuals or between private citizens and government.

COMMON LAW AND EQUITY

Not only do the state courts interpret state and local laws and regulations, they also can utilize two other kinds of law in making their decisions—common law and equity.

Not all law has been written by the country's lawmaking bodies. Dating back to early Anglo-Saxon England, a body of unwritten law has developed that is called the *common law*. Customs, usages, and previous decisions by judges when applying the common law make up this important segment of our legal heritage. Even though *statutory law* (laws as written by government bodies) may override the common law in specific cases, the *precedents* (similar decisions made in the past) established under common law often guide judges in making their decisions. Only Louisiana, with its French heritage, does not officially recognize the English common law. But even there, the precedents of common law have gradually become part of the state's legal foundation.

The laws of *equity* provide fairness and justice when neither statutory nor common law can protect a citizen's rights. Statutory and common law, in other words, provide means for resolving a matter after the event; equity attempts to prevent an injury from happening. The most common cases in equity involve requests for *injunctions*—legal documents which either prohibit or require a certain action.

MINOR STATE COURTS

Most states have developed four types of minor courts designed to handle less serious problems. Many cases heard in these lowest-level courts do not require a jury trial. Even though the legal problem involved may be relatively simple, few people take their appearance in one of these courtrooms lightly.

Justice of the peace courts. In some states, the court system begins with the justice of the peace, an official elected by the community to resolve minor legal matters. A JP hears cases involving traffic violations, for example, except in larger cities which have established special *traffic courts*. The JP court often is called upon to resolve family and neighborhood disputes, or to settle simple matters of public drunkenness or other minor violations. Most JP's serve without salary, but receive their income by collecting court costs from the parties to the cases they hear.

Small claims courts. What happens when your neighbor's dog digs up your garden but the owner refuses to pay for the damages? Or what if a department store refuses to refund the $12.45 it owes you? When minor amounts of money are involved, the small claims court provides a low-cost means of resolving civil conflicts. Not only does this leave the higher courts free to consider more serious matters, but it gives the citizen a place to seek inexpensive justice for the small injuries we all suffer in our daily lives.

Juvenile courts. The law provides special courts for juveniles (young people under either sixteen or eighteen years of age, depending on the state). Generally, the juvenile court attempts to correct the young person's behavior before more serious offenses can occur. The juvenile court judge, sometimes aided by court-appointed experts in psychology and child welfare, makes decisions without the use of a jury. The judge has the power to (1) dismiss charges, (2) suspend sentences, (3) place the offender on probation, (4) assess fines, or (5) sentence the individual to a reform school or work camp. Because of this far-reaching power, recent court rulings have provided juveniles with more protection, including the right to an attorney.

Domestic relations courts. Because the community has a stake in keeping families together, domestic relations courts (called family courts in some states) are provided to settle family disputes. Trained counselors work with the judges, who use their experience and authority to help families cope with their sometimes overwhelming problems.

MUNICIPAL COURTS

The municipal courts rank a step above the minor courts. Many municipal courts consist of divisions that handle specific types of cases, such as (1) *probate* (the hearings that settle questions involved in a dead person's estate); (2) civil suits (disputes between two parties over legal rights or duties); and (3) minor criminal offenses (misdemeanor violations). The municipal courts have generally replaced the older police and magistrates' courts in many larger communities.

GENERAL TRIAL COURTS

The first level of state court empowered to hear all types of cases without restriction is the general trial court. Different states give different names to these courts: circuit courts, superior courts, district courts, courts of common pleas, and county courts. General trial courts have wide jurisdiction, including both original jurisdiction and appellate jurisdiction (see the following section). Individuals bringing a case to this court may either request a jury trial or waive their right to a jury trial and leave the decision to the presiding judge.

STATE APPEALS COURTS

Like the federal courts of appeals, the state appeals courts exist to lighten the case load of the state supreme courts. Where they have been established (in just over one-fourth of the states), the appeals courts are known by a variety of names. Except in the rare cases where they possess original jurisdiction, the appeals courts do not hear witnesses or judge evidence. The judges, who are elected in most states, review the legal points and courtroom procedures used by the lower courts and make their decisions on that basis.

STATE SUPREME COURTS

Standing atop the pyramid of state courts is the state supreme court. This court serves as (1) the final interpreter of a state's laws and constitution and (2) a final court of appeal for lower court decisions. In most cases, this court's decisions are final. Parties to a legal matter may appeal to the United States Supreme Court only when a federal question (interpretation of the Constitution or application of a federal law) is involved.

When does a court have the right to hear a case?

As the previous section has described, courts are often limited in their *jurisdiction*; that is, they may try only certain types of cases. The legislation that establishes the particular court normally spells out its jurisdiction.

TYPES OF JURISDICTION

The four types of jurisdiction are as follows:

1. *Exclusive jurisdiction.* Exclusive jurisdiction applies when a case may be brought only in a certain court. The federal Tax Court, for example, holds exclusive jurisdiction over appeals from decisions of Internal Revenue Service tax referees.

2. *Concurrent jurisdiction.* A case may involve matters within the jurisdiction of both federal and state courts—a situation known as concurrent jurisdiction. When concurrent jurisdiction applies, the *plaintiff* (the person bringing the suit) may usually choose between the two court systems. In some cases of concurrent jurisdiction, however, the *defendant* (the person accused and summoned into court) is allowed to make this choice.

3. *Original jurisdiction.* When a court may hear a case *de novo* (for

the first time), that court has original jurisdiction. Municipal and general trial courts hold original jurisdiction over the great majority of civil and criminal actions tried in the United States.

4. *Appellate jurisdiction.* A court holds appellate jurisdiction when it receives cases on appeal from a lower court. As the name implies, the appeals courts exist to exercise this type of jurisdiction.

STATE AND FEDERAL JURISDICTIONS

State and federal courts divide their jurisdictions according to the circumstances of the case. A large percentage of cases heard by the courts fall under the jurisdiction of the state courts. Most legal matters, after all, involve violations of state or local laws and conflicts between citizens living in the same state.

Federal courts exercise jurisdiction when the case involves any of the following:

1. All cases in law and equity arising under the Constitution.
2. All cases in law and equity arising under the laws of the United States.
3. All cases in law and equity arising under treaties made under the authority of the United States.
4. All cases of admiralty and maritime jurisdiction.
5. Controversies to which the United States is a party.
6. Controversies between two or more states.
7. Controversies between a state and citizens of another state.
8. Controversies between citizens of different states.
9. Controversies between a state (or the citizens of that state) and a foreign country (or citizens of that country).
10. All cases affecting ambassadors, other public ministers, and consuls.

CIVIL AND CRIMINAL JURISDICTIONS

A court's jurisdiction may also depend upon whether the case falls under the civil or criminal code of laws.

Civil cases. A case heard under *civil procedure* usually involves a dispute between two or more people. Most civil cases center on property and personal rights. Typical civil suits include divorce cases, property-line controversies, disputes over debts, bankruptcy, and personal injury cases. The state takes no sides in civil cases, but provides the courtroom and officials needed to settle the conflict. The private parties (which may be companies as well as individuals) hire attorneys to represent them. Civil cases are usually heard before a judge and jury. If both parties agree, however, the judge may hear the case without a jury.

Criminal cases. A *criminal procedure* must be brought when an individual is accused of committing an act prohibited by law. Criminal codes establish two types of crimes: (1) *misdemeanors,* less serious offenses

Figure 11.2

Judge Oliver J. Carter presides over the armed robbery trial of Patty Hearst in San Francisco in 1976. Sketches like this one are frequently used by the media because in recent years the courts have severely restricted the presence of cameras in courtrooms to preserve order and to protect the defendant's right to privacy. Source: Wide World Photos; sketch by Bill Lignante, ABC-TV.

punishable by a small fine or imprisonment of less than a year and (2) *felonies*, offenses serious enough to warrant heavy fines, long prison terms, or even the death penalty. Felonies usually involve crimes against people and property, such as grand theft, aggravated assault, arson, kidnapping, rape, and murder. Petty theft, drunkenness, cruelty to animals, gambling, and speeding are examples of misdemeanors.

How are judges selected, and what do they do?

Black-robed judges, whether they sit on the Supreme Court bench or in a small-town municipal courtroom, represent all the impressive dignity of the law (see Figure 11.2). Given their prestige and power, one would guess that society takes extreme care in selecting the men and women who fill these positions. Such is not always the case, however.

ELECTION VERSUS APPOINTMENT

Judges who serve in the state courts may gain their office either by election or by appointment, depending on the state in which they serve. The appointment method requires that either the governor of the state or the state legislature fill any open judgeships. Until the 1860's, almost all judges owed their positions to appointment. Most states then began changing to direct election of judges, in the belief that democracy was better served when the people voted for their officials. In about three-fourths of the states, for example, trial court judges are elected by their community or district.

Both direct election and appointment are only partly satisfactory selection procedures. Most voters have little knowledge of a candidate's true qualifications. Everyone agrees that a judge should possess such virtues as extensive legal training, experience in courtroom procedures and law enforcement, an even temperament, and total honesty. A political campaign seldom reveals whether a candidate has such qualities, however.

To some degree, the appointment process provides a means by which candidates can be studied more carefully. The governor's staff, or the legislature, can question the candidate. The prospective judge's record and qualifications are given public attention, and both supporters and opponents can express their opinions.

All federal court judges owe their appointments to the President. Neither the Constitution nor Congress has established qualifications for service in the federal judiciary; as a consequence, the President may select anyone he believes the Senate will confirm. As was mentioned previously, presidents tend to select prospective judges who share their own political philosophy. Professional qualifications also count. Most federal judges are drawn from the state courts, the law profession, and the faculties of the leading law schools.

TERM OF OFFICE

Long terms in office protect many judges from the need to worry about popularity or running for reelection. Federal appointments carry a life term, for the period of the judge's "good behavior." Only four federal judges have been removed from office by impeachment; most vacancies occur through resignation, retirement, or death. Three states also give their judges a tenure for life, but six years is the most common term in the state courts.

SALARIES

The Chief Justice of the United States receives $85,000 a year in salary. Other judicial salaries scale down from that high point, with the average running around $45,000. Pay must be kept high, for many men and women who accept judicial appointments could earn even greater income in private law practice. Generous pension plans also make service on the bench a desirable career. Federal judges, for example, may retire at full salary at age sixty-five after a minimum fifteen years of service.

THE JUDGE'S JOB

Few observers would deny the demanding nature of a judge's work, yet as Figure 11.3 points out, even the most precise enforcement of the law

"How Are We Going To Stop Lawlessness If You Fellows Insist On Observing The Laws?"

Figure 11.3
The courts engage in a perpetual balancing act, applying the law so as to protect society without taking away individual rights guaranteed by the Constitution. Source: From *The Herblock Gallery* (Simon & Schuster, 1968).

does not make everyone happy. Always burdened by a heavy caseload, the judge must not rush the business of the court, for to do so might be to deny justice. Among the many specific duties which come with the robes of office are (1) ruling on points of law; (2) determining admissibility of evidence; (3) conducting the complex mechanisms of a trial; (4) studying legal briefs (most of which are far from brief); (5) balancing the rights and needs of society against those of the defendant; (6) setting a reasonable sentence; (7) choosing between conflicting precedents; (8) giving clear and proper instructions to the jury; and (9) maintaining a calm and dignified manner in every imaginable courtroom situation.

LET'S REVIEW FOR A MOMENT

Suppose you've discovered that the CIA has placed a "bug" on your phone, or maybe you want to bring suit against the Postal Service for nondelivery of your mail. Where in the U.S. court system would you begin? Since federal laws and federal agencies are involved, your federal *district court* would be the proper starting point. If you lose there, the *court of appeals* may rule on the questions of law or procedure (but not evidence) that arose at your trial. What are your chances of carrying your case to the *Supreme Court*? Not very good. The high court hears only about 4 percent of the cases brought before it.

Most Americans, however, gain their first courtroom experience (whether as defendant, plaintiff, or juror) in a *state court*. Your state's pyramid-shaped system begins with a cluster of minor courts—*small claims, traffic, juvenile, domestic relations*. More serious cases move upward into the *municipal* and *general trial* courts. Appeals from these courts are heard by the *state appeals court* or the *state supreme court*.

The right to bring a case to a particular court depends on the parties to the case and the subject matter of the suit. *Original jurisdiction* authorizes a court to hear a case for the first time; *appellate jurisdiction* allows a higher court to hear the same case on appeal; *exclusive jurisdiction* limits a case to one specific court, while *concurrent jurisdiction* means that the parties involved have a choice of either a state or federal court. Cases also may be divided into civil and criminal jurisdictions. *Civil* suits involve disputes between two parties; *criminal* cases try a defendant for breaking the law.

Ever think it might be fun to be a judge? The rewards are great—in pay, prestige, and tenure—but the workload and the responsibilities are heavy. Many judges, including the entire federal judiciary, are appointed to the bench; state courts often require that judges run for office, like any other candidate.

What happens when a case goes to trial?

On the television screen, all courtrooms look much alike (see Figure 11.4 for a typical floor plan). Major differences separate trial procedures in civil and criminal cases, however. While not all of the steps outlined below need occur in every case, the general process applies to almost every state court.

TRYING A CIVIL SUIT

A civil suit begins when the plaintiff files suit in trial court with the help of a lawyer. Court officials notify the defendant of the suit (remember the German farmer?) so that he or she may prepare a defense. From that point, a well-established pattern takes over.

1. Summoning witnesses. If witnesses are needed, both parties to the suit may ask the court to require their presence at the trial through legal orders called *subpoenas.* Judges have the power to declare persons who refuse to honor a subpoena in *contempt of court*—a criminal offense.

2. Setting a trial date. With the preliminaries out of the way, the suit takes its place on the court calendar, or *docket.* Heavy caseloads in many courts may delay the actual trial date by as long as two years. Because of this frustrating wait, as well as the cost of a court trial, many cases are settled out of court.

3. Selecting a jury. When the trial date finally arrives, either side has the right to demand a jury trial. Court officials select citizens for jury duty from the list of registered voters. The attorneys choose the twelve-member petit jury (see page 279) from a panel of prospective jurors. Careful questioning eliminates those individuals who reveal any bias about the

Figure 11.4
Floor plan of a typical courtroom (general trial court)

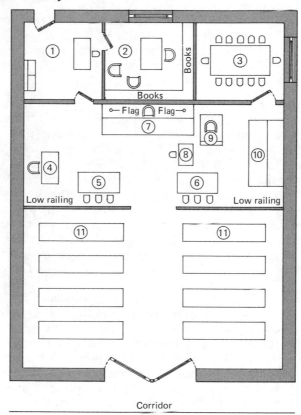

1 Entry chamber	5 Plaintiff or prosecutor	9 Witness stand
2 Judge's chamber	6 Defendant and attorneys	10 Jury box
3 Jury room	7 Judge's bench	11 Spectators' benches
4 Marshal (bailiff)	8 Court reporter	

case; the attorneys are also allowed to dismiss a certain number of jurors without having to state a reason.

4. Conducting the trial. Once the jury has been seated, the attorneys make their opening statements. Witnesses are then called to testify under oath. The plaintiff's attorney establishes the facts of the case by asking questions of the witnesses. A major and sometimes dramatic privilege of attorneys for both the plaintiff and the defendant is the *cross-examination* of witnesses. The lawyers probe for weaknesses in the testimony, hoping to discredit the accuracy of each witness's memory or truthfulness.

Sometimes, before a civil trial begins, the attorneys present briefs to the judge which summarize court decisions handed down in earlier and similar cases. This process of citing precedents is called *stare decisis*, a Latin phrase meaning "it stands decided." Since both sides will usually be able to find precedents that support their arguments, the briefs do not necessarily simplify the case.

During the trial, a *court reporter* takes down all of the testimony, word for word. This record, which also includes the lawyers' final pleas, is known as the *transcript*. The transcript provides a permanent record of the trial and serves as the basis for possible appeals court action at a later time.

5. *Reaching a verdict.* With all arguments completed, the judge submits the case to the jury. The judge's instructions, called the *charge*, summarize the major points of law raised by the case and pinpoint the questions of fact to be decided. If the evidence appears overwhelmingly favorable to one side, the judge may order the jury to bring in a directed *verdict.* This means that the judge believes no other decision could reasonably be returned. After the charge, the jury retires to discuss the case in strict privacy; not even the judge may listen in on the jury's deliberations. While the jury is attempting to reach a *verdict,* it remains in custody of the court. Fearing that a jury may be influenced by media publicity or by contacts with other people, the judge sometimes orders that the jury be *sequestered*—that is, locked up in hotel rooms while not in court.

The jury's efforts to reach a verdict may continue for several days. One member is elected to preside over its meetings as *foreman,* but every juror's vote counts equally. Two-thirds of the states require a unanimous verdict in civil cases (a 12–0 majority), while the others accept 8–4 or 10–2 majorities. If the jury cannot reach agreement, the foreman reports this fact to the judge. A "hung jury" requires that a *mistrial* be declared; if the plaintiff wishes to pursue the matter, a new trial must be heard.

In most trials, however, the jury does reach a verdict. The foreman, as directed by the judge, reads the jury's findings in open court. Once the jury's decision has been read, the judge usually approves the verdict and announces the terms of its execution. If a jury has found the defendant guilty of negligence, for example, it may also establish the money damages to be paid to the plaintiff.

6. *Establishing judgment.* The judge has the final word. In cases where plaintiff and defendant waived a jury trial, the judge arrives at a verdict after careful study of the evidence and precedents. On the other hand, if a jury has made what the judge considers an excessive award for damages, the figure may be reduced to a lesser amount. At this time the judge also may establish time limits for payment of damages and court costs, issue court orders to ensure compliance with the decision, or take other steps to ensure that the court's judgment will be carried out.

TRYING A CRIMINAL CASE

Criminal court procedures are different from those of civil courts. With some differences relating to state law and special circumstances, the

Table 11.1

Stages in a criminal trial following commission of a felony

Stage	Agencies involved	Action taken	Other possible actions
1. *Apprehension*	*Police*	*Investigation*	*Case dropped for insufficient evidence*
	Court may furnish warrants	*Apprehension*	
		Arrest	
		Booking	
2. *Indictment*	*Magistrate*	*Preliminary hearing*	*Charges reduced*
	Court	*Setting of bail*	
	Prosecuting attorney	*Evidence considered by grand jury*	*Case dismissed*
	Grand jury	*Indictment handed down*	
		Case placed on docket	
3. *Trial*	*General trial court*	*Arraignment*	*Court accepts a lesser plea*
		Plea	
		Jury selection	*Mistrial declared*
		Witnesses testify	*Defendant acquitted*
		Prosecution and defense argue the case	
		Jury returns a verdict	*Appeal to higher court*
4. *Sentencing*	*General trial court*	*Judge and/or jury pronounce sentence: fine, imprisonment, or both*	*Suspended sentence*
			Probation
	State penal system	*Sentence begins*	*Pardon*
			Parole

criminal case follows a pattern that begins with apprehension and continues through indictment, trial, and sentencing (see Table 11.1).

1. Apprehending the suspect. Unless an individual has been caught in the act of committing a crime, or arrested in suspicious circumstances, police need an *arrest warrant* to take a suspect into custody. This legal document describes the suspected criminal, the nature of the offense, and the magistrate (or judge) before whom the individual is to be brought. Any trial court judge may issue a warrant. Law enforcement officials normally make all arrests, of course, but under special circumstances any person may make a *citizen's arrest*—though he or she becomes liable for a lawsuit if the arrest is made without just cause.

2. *Indicting the accused.* After arrest, police or court officials bring the accused before a magistrate. If the crime is a misdemeanor (such as a traffic violation), the accused may be tried at once, or released to return later for trial. In felony cases, however, the court holds a *preliminary hearing* to establish a reasonable probability of guilt. If this probability is found to exist, the judge ensures that the accused will return to stand trial by one of three methods: (a) The accused may be released on his or her promise to return on the trial date. (b) The accused may be required to post *bail*—a sum of money ranging from less than $100 to many thousands of dollars—as a condition of release from jail. Bail may be posted by the accused, by the family or friends, or by a professional bail bondsman. This money is forfeited if the accused fails to return when scheduled. (c) The accused may be held without bail in special cases— those involving capital crimes or where the suspicion exists that the accused would "jump bail" and disappear.

At this point, the *prosecuting attorney,* a law enforcement official found in both federal and state court systems, examines the testimony given at the preliminary hearing. If the evidence of guilt seems sufficient, he or she prepares a *bill of indictment* which summarizes the state's case. A grand jury (see page 279) hears the bill of indictment and studies the evidence presented. If the members of the grand jury agree with the prosecuting attorney, the foreman writes the words "a true bill" across the face of the indictment. Court officials then place the case on the docket of the appropriate trial court.

3. *Conducting the trial.* When the court date arrives, the defendant makes a *plea* before the court; this process is called *arraignment.* If the accused enters a guilty plea, the court normally takes quick action. Various sentences may be handed down, including imprisonment, fine, or probation. If the defendant pleads not guilty, the trial judge then sets a new date for the trial to begin.

All defendants have the right to be represented by an attorney. For those who cannot afford to hire one, the court provides a *public defender.* Because of crowded courts and high trial costs, both public and private attorneys often engage in a process called *plea bargaining.* This is an agreement between prosecutor and the defense to accept a guilty plea, usually to a lesser charge, rather than go through the trial itself.

The criminal trial itself begins with selection of the jury. This process closely resembles that of the civil trial previously described. Once the jury has been seated, the defense and prosecuting attorneys present their opening statements. The state makes its case first, using physical evidence and witnesses to establish the proof required under the law. If the prosecutor does not make a strong case, the defense may move for a directed verdict of not guilty. Failing in this, the defense then offers its case. Both prosecution and defense witnesses are subject to cross-examination. Any witness who commits *perjury* (lying under oath) faces fine or imprisonment. No defendant can be made to take the stand. The judge must instruct the jury that the defendant's refusal to testify does not constitute evidence of guilt.

After both prosecution and defense complete their presentation of evidence, each side makes a *summation*—a final speech to the jury that ties together all the arguments in the case. The judge then instructs the jury as to the possible verdicts they can return, and explains the laws that apply to the case.

4. *Sentencing the criminal.* Jury deliberations proceed as in a civil trial, until a unanimous verdict is reached or disagreement becomes definite. In some states, a guilty verdict leads directly to a separate hearing to determine fine or prison sentence. In other states, the jury itself recommends the punishment. In still other states, the judge decides the penalty.

A defendant who has been found guilty may appeal the verdict to a higher court, but only if the defendant and his or her attorneys believe that grounds exist for an appeal. During the appeal process, the defendant may remain free on bail under conditions similar to those described earlier. A verdict of not guilty releases the defendant from custody immediately.

How well does the U.S. jury system work?

Few legal traditions were considered more important by the Founders than the right to trial by a jury of one's peers. The Fifth, Sixth, and Seventh Amendments to the Constitution all touch upon the guarantees that underlie the American system of justice. Still, criticism of the jury system itself has grown in recent years.

KINDS OF JURIES

Juries are of two kinds: the *grand jury* and the *petit jury*. Each plays an important role in the American court system.

Grand jury. Before the petit jury can try a case, the grand jury must decide whether or not the accused should be brought to trial at all. In short, the grand jury studies the evidence, hears witnesses, questions law enforcement officials, and finally hands down the bill of indictment if it is justified. In different states, the size of a grand jury may range from six to twenty-three; unlike the petit jury, the grand jury usually serves for a full year before retiring.

Another role of the grand jury is that of investigation. If suspicion of wrongdoing exists in any area of community life, a vigorous probe by a grand jury may bring the facts to light.

Petit jury. As was described on page 274, the petit jury weighs the evidence presented during the course of the trial, deliberates, and finally arrives at a verdict. Members of the trial jury are expected to set aside their prejudices and previous thoughts on the case. Sometimes a trial may drag on for many weeks, but the jury must remain alert to all the subtle turns of the testimony. Compensation for this difficult service includes meals, lodging (if the jury is sequestered), and a modest *per diem* payment to cover daily expenses.

Figure 11.5

The process of jury selection lies at the heart of the American system of justice. In this photograph (taken in 1957, before photographers were virtually barred from courtrooms), the prosecuting attorneys, the defendants, and the defense lawyers face the newly selected jurors in the jury box. Prospective jurors, called *veniremen*, wait at the far left to be called for questioning by the attorneys for both sides. Source: Wide World Photos.

CRITICISMS OF THE JURY SYSTEM

Many critics attack the day-to-day operation of American juries rather than the jury system itself. Most criticism fits under one of two headings:

1. *Faulty jury selection procedures.* American juries were originally designed to ensure that accused people would be tried by their peers—friends and neighbors who could weigh personal factors when considering their verdict. Today, the procedures for selecting jurors (see Figure 11.5) tend to work against this purpose, for these reasons: (a) people who are not registered to vote are automatically excluded; (b) many people are exempted from jury duty, including teachers, lawyers, and other professionals; (c) challenges for bias tend to exclude from any jury the concerned citizens who follow the news and think deeply about community problems; (d) minority groups seldom receive fair representation on the lists from which jurors are drawn. So juries in most parts of the country tend to be heavily weighted with older people, ethnic majorities, and housewives.

2. *Compromised verdicts.* No matter how carefully a jury has been prepared for its deliberations, human nature always influences the verdict. After a long and perhaps dull trial, full of pauses and recesses, the jury settles into its final task with relief. Immediately, differences of opinion develop. Conflicts arise over interpretation of testimony. Political and philosophical positions color each juror's perception. Finally, with one eye on the clock, a move toward compromise usually develops. No one wants to report a "hung jury," to admit that the trial has been in vain because

the jury cannot agree on a verdict. So the final verdict may sometimes have more to do with fatigue and emotion than with reason and justice.

PROPOSALS FOR JURY REFORM

Proposals for reform of the jury system have received limited acceptance. The most successful change has come in the area of minority representation; many cities now make a serious effort to provide a true cross section of the community on the jury selection lists. Other reforms that have been discussed include (1) reducing jury size, (2) relaxing requirements for unanimous verdicts, and (3) replacing juries with panels of judges. Despite evident weaknesses, however, most Americans still look on the jury trial as their best protection against the awesome power of the government and its courts.

What powers do the courts exercise?

DECIDING GUILT OR INNOCENCE

Courts have been established primarily to hand down decisions in cases of civil or criminal law. Custom and statutes have given the courts other responsibilities, however, beyond establishing individual guilt, innocence, or liability.

OTHER COURT POWERS

1. Judicial review. Federal courts, as well as the higher state courts, are often called upon to review the legality of actions taken by the executive and legislative branches of government. Does a new city law regulating pornographic movie houses violate the state constitution? Did the police exceed their power in conducting undercover drug busts on a high school campus? Any citizen may petition the courts to conduct a judicial review of the actions of any local, state, or federal agency. Furthermore, the decision of the courts in such matters must be accepted as final.

2. Habeas corpus. A basic right carefully protected by the courts is that of *habeas corpus*. Under this legal doctrine, an imprisoned person has the constitutional right to know why he or she was jailed and to have a speedy trial (although overcrowded dockets often make a mockery of the latter safeguard, particularly in the high-crime areas of our big cities). *Habeas corpus* thus warns officials holding someone in custody that if they cannot show cause before a judge as to why that person should not be freed, they must release the prisoner.

3. Injunction. Most often used in civil cases, an injunction is a legal order that either (a) forbids a certain action or (b) orders that a particular action be taken. For example, an injunction might require that a factory stop polluting a river, or it might demand that a school accept suspended students back into class.

4. *Writ of mandamus*. A court order that forces government officials to fulfill their public duty is called a writ of *mandamus*. An example of such a writ would be an order requiring a police department to protect a minority group during a flareup of racial tensions.

5. *Warrants*. Many law enforcement procedures require court permission before action can be taken. *Arrest warrants* and *search warrants*, for example, not only permit the actions described in their titles, but also limit the conditions under which those actions may be carried out.

6. *Contempt of court*. Courts possess an enforcement power which ensures that court orders will be obeyed. A contempt of court citation may be issued against a witness who refuses to testify, a lawyer who consistently violates court procedures, or a company that ignores an injunction. Contempt citations carry the threat of fine or imprisonment.

LIMITATIONS ON ADVISORY OPINIONS

When the executive branch asked the Supreme Court to rule on pending legislation during Washington's first administration, the Court refused. That tradition, based on the belief that the Court could rule only on cases at law, holds firm to this day. Congress cannot know in advance whether a given law, especially one that raises a constitutional question, will be accepted or struck down by the judiciary.

In the state courts, by contrast, about one-fourth of the states allow the legislature or the governor to request an opinion about the constitutionality of proposed legislation before it is passed. That opinion need not bind the court later—the legislation may be altered, or the court may simply change its mind—but it is a helpful practice that prevents obviously unconstitutional laws from being enacted.

SUMMARY AND CONCLUSIONS

1. The *federal court* system begins at the *district court* level, where cases involving federal jurisdiction are tried. Appeals move upward to the *courts of appeals*, whose decisions carry great weight, since the Supreme Court seldom overturns them. The *Supreme Court* itself stands as the ultimate check on the powers of the executive and legislative branches of government.

2. Like the federal courts, the *state courts* have been organized in a pyramid of authority. The minor courts in each community handle *traffic, juvenile, domestic relations,* and *small claims* cases; *municipal* and *general trial* courts accept more serious cases involving large sums of money or felony crimes. The *state appeals court* and the *state supreme court* function much like their federal counterparts, accepting cases on appeal and interpreting state and local laws.

3. Along with statutory law, the courts are guided by common law and

equity. Legal and social traditions, plus the precedents established by judges in earlier decisions, make up the *common law*. *Equity* provides a means of protecting a citizen's rights even when no violation has yet been committed.

4. *Jurisdiction* refers to the right of a particular court to hear a case. The most important kinds of jurisdiction are (1) *original jurisdiction*, which means that the court has the right to hear the case for the first time, and (2) *appellate jurisdiction*, which means that a court receives a case on appeal from a lower court. Other kinds of jurisdictions are *exclusive* and *concurrent*. Appeals may normally be made only on the basis of points of law.

5. *Civil cases* generally involve disputes between two parties, although either party may be a company or government agency. *Criminal cases* begin with the alleged violation of a law. *Misdemeanors* are minor offenses which carry short prison terms or light fines; *felonies* are crimes serious enough to require long prison terms or heavy fines if the defendant is found guilty.

6. At the heart of the court system sit the judges in their traditional black robes. On their honesty, knowledge of the law, and ability to maintain proper courtroom procedures rests our nation's ability to provide equal justice for all. Some state court judges must be elected to office; many others, including all federal judges, receive their jobs by appointment.

7. Once a case comes to trial, the procedure varies between civil and criminal courts. In a civil case, once the suit has been filed, *subpoenas* are issued to witnesses and the trial date is set. At the trial, jury selection comes first; an alternative choice would be to have the judge hear the case without a jury. Attorneys for plaintiff and defendant present their cases to the court. After deliberating, the jury returns a verdict if agreement can be reached; if not, a hung jury results and a new trial must be scheduled. Either the judge or the jury sets the amount of damages to be paid if the verdict found for the plaintiff.

8. Criminal cases begin with the apprehension of the accused. An *indictment* must be obtained before he or she may be tried, however; a *preliminary hearing* establishes this probability of guilt. *Bail* may be allowed, if the judge believes it wise. The trial itself begins with jury selection, then moves on to examine possible guilt or innocence through the testimony given by prosecution and defense witnesses. The jury's deliberations result finally in a verdict of guilty or not guilty. Sentence may be set by the jury or by the judge, depending upon the state in which the trial is held.

9. *Grand juries* attempt to establish possible wrongdoing; *petit juries* render verdicts of guilt or innocence. Critics fear that neither jury is truly representative of the community and that minority defendants in particular do not receive fair hearings. Forcing a jury to reach a unanimous verdict may also result in "compromised verdicts."

10. Courts possess a number of powers beyond that of trying cases. Judges may issue a *writ of habeas corpus* or a *writ of mandamus*; a judge must sign *arrest warrants* and *search warrants* before police officers can take action; and they issue *injunctions* to protect the public welfare. *Contempt of court* citations allow courts to enforce their orders with

threats of fine or imprisonment. *Judicial review* provides the courts with a powerful check on government, for no law can be maintained which the courts have struck down as unconstitutional.

REVIEW QUESTIONS AND ACTIVITIES

TERMS YOU SHOULD KNOW

appellate jurisdiction	*majority opinion*
arraignment	*minority opinion*
arrest warrant	*misdemeanor*
bail	*mistrial*
bill of indictment	*municipal court*
charge	*original jurisdiction*
citizen's arrest	*perjury*
civil procedure	*petit jury*
common law	*plea*
concurrent jurisdiction	*precedents*
contempt of court	*preliminary hearing*
court of appeals	*probate*
court reporter	*prosecuting attorney*
criminal procedure	*public defender*
directed verdict	*search warrant*
district court	*small claims court*
docket	*state appeals court*
domestic relations court	*state supreme court*
equity	*statutory law*
exclusive jurisdiction	*subpoena*
felony	*summation*
foreman	*territorial courts*
general trial court	*traffic court*
grand jury	*transcript*
injunction	*writ of* certiorari
judicial review	*writ of* habeas corpus
juvenile court	*writ of* mandamus

REVIEW QUESTIONS

The following multiple-choice questions are based on the important ideas presented in this chapter. Select the response that best completes each statement.

1. The Constitution provides full and complete details on how the federal court system should be organized and administered. This statement is (a) true. (b) false; no mention is made in the Constitution of a federal court system. (c) false; the Constitution states that a court system shall be established, but leaves it up to Congress to fill in the details.

2. The proper path for a typical case through the federal courts would be from (a) court of appeals to district court to Supreme Court. (b) district court to court of appeals to Supreme Court. (c) Supreme Court to district court to court of appeals. (d) the plaintiff may begin at any level if he or she can afford it. (e) none of these.

3. Final authority for deciding on the constitutionality of a federal law lies with the (a) Supreme Court. (b) courts of appeals. (c) U.S. district courts. (d) state supreme courts. (e) Congress of the United States.

4. As in many civil and criminal courts, the decisions of Supreme Court judges must be unanimous (9–0). This statement is (a) true. (b) false; only a 7–2 majority is required. (c) false; any majority is enough to establish a court decision.

5. A typical case that would be heard in a civil suit would be: (a) two neighbors argue over the exact dividing line between their properties. (b) the town sot is arrested for public drunkenness. (c) a driver is arrested for felony hit-and-run. (d) a politician violates the law that regulates campaign contributions. (e) all of these.

6. If you wished to prevent the police in your town from going on strike, your suit would be filed under (a) the common law. (b) equity. (c) criminal law codes. (d) appellate jurisdiction. (e) none of these; everyone has the right to strike if it seems necessary.

7. The local cleaning store ruined your best outfit, but has refused to replace it. The best place for you to file suit would be in (a) domestic relations court. (b) justice of the peace court. (c) general trial court. (d) small claims court. (e) municipal court.

8. Along with a knowledge of the law, a good judge should have (a) strong political connections. (b) an independent income because judges' salaries are quite low. (c) absolute personal honesty and an understanding of human nature. (d) a good hobby, because judges seldom work very hard. (e) all of these.

9. In order to control behavior of lawyers, spectators, and defendants in the courtroom, a judge might issue (a) a writ of *habeas corpus*. (b) an injunction. (c) a writ of *certiorari*. (d) a contempt of court citation. (e) a writ of *mandamus*.

10. "The foreman of the grand jury read the verdict: 'Guilty as charged, your honor.'" This statement is faulty because (a) a grand jury establishes only the indictment, never the verdict. (b) the verdict should be announced by the judge. (c) a grand jury sits only for civil cases, where no guilt is in question. (d) grand juries work only with the federal courts on appeals cases, where interpretations of the law are in question. (e) the foreman of a grand jury never reads the verdict.

CONCEPT DEVELOPMENT

This chapter has explored a number of significant concepts relating to the American court system. You can use your skills in thinking, researching, and writing to answer the following questions.

1. What qualifications should a federal judge bring to the bench?

2. Discuss the various types of jurisdiction: (a) state v. federal, (b) civil v. criminal, and (c) original v. appellate.

3. Create an imaginary bank robbery. Trace the case through the court system, from arrest through final sentencing. Point out how the defendant's rights are protected at every step of the process.

4. Summarize the strengths and weaknesses of the jury system. Suggest at least two reforms that might make it work even better.

5. Critics frequently accuse judges of being too easy on criminals. Explain why this accusation is made, and evaluate the conflict between those who believe in punishment and those who favor rehabilitation.

ACTIVITIES

The following activities are designed to help you use the ideas developed in this chapter.

1. How fair are the jury selection procedures in your community? First research the actual procedure used. Then interview several lawyers, a judge, and a cross section of people you find in the corridors of your local court building. Report to your class on the results of your study. Is the system equitable? Are all racial, ethnic, and social groups fairly represented? What could be done to improve the process?

2. Help your teacher arrange a field trip for your class to a local courtroom. If the entire class can't go, make the visit yourself. Study the courtroom procedures, the types of cases being tried, the attitudes and reactions of the various people in the courtroom. Do you sense any of the dignity and power of the law? Put yourself in the role of the judge; would you have done anything differently? Write a report on your experience.

3. Organize your classroom to stage a mock trial. Select a civil or criminal case related to your own community. Appoint a judge, attorneys, plaintiff and defendant, a jury, and other court officials. Structure the trial enough so that it is not a game, but allow the participants to play their roles freely. Witnesses can be subpoenaed (teachers make good witnesses), and the attorneys can conduct a stiff cross-examination. After the jury has given its verdict, find out what people have learned.

4. Do some extra reading on the Supreme Court and its role in our governmental system. Check out some of its recent decisions. What kinds of cases has it been working on? What blocs of conservatives, liberals, and moderates can you discover on the court? Report back to your class on your research.

5. Invite a local judge to speak to your class. He or she might want to choose a topic, but ask him or her to include remarks on such subjects as (a) the law as a profession, (b) the citizen's role in law enforcement, and (c) the "view from the bench."

CHAPTER TWELVE

THE COURTS SPEAK: LANDMARK CASES THAT HAVE ALTERED THE COURSE OF AMERICAN LIFE

Once or twice in a generation, the courts hand down a landmark decision, one that has a lasting effect on American life. Like the baseball umpire who says, "No pitch is a ball or strike until I call it," the courts occasionally remind Congress and the President that no law can be considered final until judged against the "strike zone" established by the Constitution. One such case involved a fair trade law . . . and a sick chicken.

In the Depression year of 1933, President Franklin Roosevelt organized the business men and women of the country under the National Recovery Administration (NRA). Business leaders joined hands to write codes of proper commercial practices for all manufacturing, wholesale, and retail enterprises throughout a particular industry. With one eye on the Depression and the other on their falling profits, the cooperating businesses hoped that the NRA codes would eliminate wage and price cuts—and restore prosperity.

Four brothers in Brooklyn, New York, came into conflict with the NRA code for the live poultry industry. Their firm, the Schechter Live Poultry Market, was charged with a number of violations under the code, including the charge that caught the public's attention—that of the "sick chicken." The Live Poultry Market, the suit claimed, had allowed a customer to select an individual live chicken from a crate of other chickens, thus violating the NRA code regulation which required that all customers take "the luck of the draw." The chicken, moreover, turned out to be "egg-bound"—that is, unable to lay eggs—another violation of NRA rules.

Taken to federal district court, the Schechter brothers were found guilty, given brief jail sentences, and fined $7,425. Unwilling to accept the verdict, the Schechters appealed, only to lose again in the court of appeals. The appellate court judges upheld the lower court's decision on the charges of unfair trade practices. Still determined, the brothers took their appeal to the Supreme Court.

The case touched upon several constitutional questions. One, for example, asked whether the Schechters were really engaged in interstate commerce, and were thus under the regulatory powers of Congress. The chickens, as a matter of fact, did come from outside New York. However, the defense claimed that interstate commerce ended once the chickens were delivered to the dealers, since the further resale of the fowl took place within the state. A second, and more critical question, struck at the NRA itself. Did Congress have the right to delegate its power to regulate interstate commerce to the NRA? That body, after all, was under the control of the President and the executive branch.

When the Supreme Court announced its decision on May 27, 1935, the worst fears of the Roosevelt administration were confirmed. Led by Chief Justice Charles Evans Hughes, the Court declared that this particular poultry sale was not interstate commerce; the delegation of powers to the NRA, moreover, was struck down as unconstitutional. The NRA was dead, killed by a sick chicken.

Telegrams were sent out suspending the enforcement of NRA codes for all industries. The decision, however, did the Schechters little good financially. By 1936, the Depression had wiped out their business, and they were forced to sell their home. A few NRA codes were later reenacted as individual laws, but the effort to halt the Depression by informal agreements and industry-wide codes died with the high court's decision.

With the NRA withering away, an angry Roosevelt turned on the Supreme Court, which he considered too old and too conservative. He drafted legislation that would enable him to appoint an additional justice to the court for every justice then over seventy years of age. Congress rejected this "court-packing" scheme, handing Roosevelt one of his few legislative defeats of the 1930's. Ironically, the views of the justices also changed. The Court eventually found most New Deal legislation to be constitutional after all.

In the last two chapter introductions, you've seen how cases involving a mule and a chicken have illustrated major principles of the U.S. judicial system. In this chapter you will read about a number of additional cases that have had lasting impact on the nation's history. These court decisions, and the questions they answer, are:

1. How did the courts gain the power of judicial review? (*Marbury v. Madison*)
2. Are there any limitations on the implied powers of Congress? (*McCulloch v. Maryland*)
3. How far may Congress go in regulating interstate commerce? (*Gibbons v. Ogden*)
4. How did a case involving slavery help lead to the Civil War? (*Dred Scott v. Sandford*)
5. How far may state laws go in limiting a corporation's activities? (*Munn v. Illinois*)

6. Which is stronger—business monopolies or the federal government? (*Northern Securities Company* et al. *v. United States*)
7. Are segregated schools automatically unequal? (*Brown v. Board of Education of Topeka*)
8. Should any restrictions be placed on the police when making arrests? (*Miranda v. Arizona*)

How did the courts gain the power of judicial review? (Marbury v. Madison)

The Supreme Court has not always reigned as the powerful and respected third branch of government Americans know today. One man—the fourth Chief Justice, John Marshall—perhaps had as much to do with the creation of the modern Supreme Court as did the Constitution. The case that most clearly established the strength of the Court grew out of a seemingly trivial matter.

FACTS OF THE CASE

In the election of 1800, the Federalist candidate, John Adams, lost his bid for reelection to the presidency to Thomas Jefferson and his Democratic-Republicans. On the evening of March 3, 1801, his last day in office under the old inauguration schedule, President Adams was still making appointments. Loyal Federalists were to be rewarded with federal judgeships.

Now, on this last night, Adams had worked his way down to the least important of federal judicial posts, the forty-two justices of the peace for the District of Columbia. After Adams signed the commissions, Secretary of State John Marshall (see Figure 12.1) should have affixed the Great

Figure 12.1

Under the leadership of John Marshall, Chief Justice from 1801 to 1835, the Supreme Court gained equal status with the executive and legislative branches of the federal government. Source: Brown Brothers.

Seal of the United States before sending the documents to the recipients. In the haste of the moment, Marshall neglected to see to this final detail.

When President Jefferson later realized how many federal judges had been appointed by the outgoing President, he angrily refused to deliver the incomplete commissions. Federalist William Marbury, suddenly deprived of his new position, brought suit in the Supreme Court, along with three other men similarly "robbed" of their offices. The suit asked for a writ of *mandamus*, a court order that would require the new Secretary of State, James Madison, to affix the seal and deliver the commissions. The suit came before the Supreme Court in December 1801. Marshall (now Chief Justice) eagerly accepted jurisdiction over the case.

LEGAL STEPS IN THE CASE

As the case developed, it became apparent that the implications involved far more than Marbury and his place on the federal bench.

1. *Jurisdiction.* Marbury asked the Supreme Court to take original jurisdiction under a provision of the Judiciary Act of 1789. Section 13 of this law stated that the Supreme Court could issue writs of *mandamus* in cases involving "persons holding office under the authority of the United States."

2. *Marshall's dilemma.* Marshall knew that if he issued the writ, Madison would ignore it. Jefferson would then back up his Secretary of State, and public opinion would support the highly popular President. The Court would then end up out on a limb with no means of enforcing its decision.

3. *The solution.* Marshall's eventual solution was a masterpiece of judicial logic. First, he pointed out the obvious fact that the original jurisdiction of the Supreme Court was limited by the Constitution to two types of cases: (a) those involving foreign diplomats and (b) those involving the states. When the Judiciary Act added another original jurisdiction to the Court's powers, Congress had, in effect, amended the Constitution.

4. *Marbury's case thrown out of court.* The Constitution, Marshall pointed out, cannot be changed by an act of Congress. Therefore, he concluded, the Judiciary Act of 1789 must be declared unconstitutional. Marbury's case was thus thrown out of court. If he wished to pursue his suit, he would have to begin with a lower court.

RESULTS OF THE CASE

Marbury never did receive his commission. His unsuccessful lawsuit, however, was the most important case in American legal history. In declaring an act of Congress unconstitutional, Marshall had claimed for the Court a power not given (nor denied, for that matter) in the Constitution. Thus emerged the doctrine of *judicial review*: any act of Congress, as well as any act of the President (or his administration), can be tested by the courts to see if those acts conform to the Constitution, the basic law of the land. Judicial review gave the courts the tool needed to make them a co-equal branch of government.

Figure 12.2
The Bank of the United States became the focus of a stormy political battle which led to the Supreme Court's landmark *McCulloch v. Maryland* decision. Source: The Bettmann Archive, Inc.

Are there any limitations on the implied powers of Congress? (McCulloch v. Maryland)

The case of *McCulloch v. Maryland* centered on the leading financial institution of a young and growing country—the Bank of the United States. What was really at stake, however, was something even more important: a liberal interpretation of the *implied powers* clause of the Constitution. How far could Congress go in fulfilling its legislative responsibilities? In the early 1800's, the Supreme Court finally resolved the issue.

FACTS OF THE CASE

In 1791, Alexander Hamilton, the first Secretary of the Treasury, supported the creation of the Bank of the United States (see Figure 12.2). He designed the bank as the agency through which federal funds would be spent and through which tax collections would be made. The government owned only part of the bank; control was placed in private hands. The Jeffersonians opposed the bank as an unwanted federal invasion of *states' rights* as guaranteed by the Ninth and Tenth Amendments.

Although the bank was allowed to lapse in 1811 at the end of its twenty-year charter, five years later a second national bank received a similar charter. The new bank remained a private institution. With headquarters in Philadelphia, the bank's eighteen branch offices spread from Portsmouth and Boston in the north to Savannah and New Orleans in the south.

LEGAL STEPS IN THE CASE

Despite the conflicts generated by the existence of the bank, it was only after a suit was brought against the national bank that the Supreme Court could hear the arguments.

1. *Maryland passes a law.* In February 1818, the state of Maryland passed a law that left the Baltimore branch of the Bank of the United States in a difficult spot. Under the law, the bank was ordered to buy stamped paper (paper with an expensive tax stamp affixed) on which to issue its notes, and to pay the state a franchise fee of $15,000 a year (roughly $165,000 today), or it would have to go out of business.

2. *The bank ignores the law.* The new law became effective on May 1, 1818. When the date passed without any sign that the Baltimore branch intended to obey the regulations, the state of Maryland brought suit against James W. McCulloch, the bank's Baltimore cashier.

3. *Appeal to the Supreme Court.* The Baltimore County Court passed judgment in favor of the state, and the Maryland Court of Appeals confirmed the lower court's findings. The bank appealed to the United States Supreme Court, where attorneys argued the case in February 1819.

4. *Arguments.* Both sides marshaled their best talent. Joseph Hopkinson, Walter Jones, and Luther Martin (an active dissenter at the Constitutional Convention) spoke for the state of Maryland. They argued that Maryland, as a sovereign state, had the right to tax the national bank. Moreover, they contended, Congress had created the bank without proper constitutional authority. Daniel Webster, William Pinckney, and U.S. Attorney General William Wirt defended the bank. The defense contended that the Constitution gave Congress the necessary authority to carry out its expressed powers. Since Congress had the expressed power to regulate money, they argued, then Congress could choose reasonable means of accomplishing that task. Therefore, chartering a bank fell well within the reasonable exercise of the implied powers granted by the Constitution.

5. *Decision.* The Court handed down a unanimous decision in favor of the bank. The ruling caused great bitterness among the Jeffersonian Republicans, for of the seven judges, they had expected to lose only the votes of the two Federalists.

RESULTS OF THE CASE

Two important constitutional traditions emerged from *McCulloch v. Maryland.* First, the decision confirmed the power of Congress to decide what actions are reasonable and necessary to fulfill its constitutional responsibilities. Few real limits exist on what Congress may do, as long as the legislation falls under the "necessary and proper" clause—and as long as the action survives judicial review by the courts.

Second, in its decision the Court rejected the idea that one level of

Figure 12.3

Steamboats and sailboats crisscross the waters of New York Harbor. At the upper left is the Hudson River, across which lay the ferry route disputed in *Gibbons v. Ogden.* Source: The Bettmann Archive, Inc.

government has the right to tax any other level of government, or any of its agencies. The federal government may not tax the income of the states, nor may the states tax the activities of their cities, schools, counties, or other governmental bodies.

How far may Congress go in regulating interstate commerce? (Gibbons v. Ogden)

Gibbons v. Ogden gave John Marshall the chance to make what was perhaps his only truly popular decision in all his many years on the bench. By 1824, the new nation was expanding rapidly westward. Quarrels between the states and the federal government over the extent of federal powers, however, still hampered development. *Gibbons v. Ogden* would settle the conflict once and for all.

FACTS OF THE CASE

In 1789 the state of New York transferred an exclusive monopoly to run steamboats on state waters from the inventor, John Fitch, to the wealthy chancellor of the state, Robert Livingston. By 1807, Livingston had joined forces with Robert Fulton and had launched service up the Hudson from New York City to Albany.

After the deaths of Livingston and Fulton, the monopoly passed to Livingston's brother, John. Competition developed in 1819, when Aaron Ogden and Thomas Gibbons of New Jersey began a steamboat service across the Hudson from New York City to Elizabethtown, New Jersey (see Figure 12.3). The partners soon fell out, however, over the need to cooperate with the New York monopoly, which claimed to dominate harbor traffic as well as the river route. A tangled bramble of lawsuits followed, but Ogden was determined to control the New York river and harbor traffic. He invested most of his wealth in the Livingston monopoly.

Gibbons, denied the right to operate in New York waters, was determined to break Ogden's new monopoly. Aided by financier Cornelius Vanderbilt, Gibbons filed suit against the restrictive state laws. In support of his right to operate his passenger service, he pointed to a coasting license he had obtained from the United States government under a federal statute of 1793.

LEGAL STEPS IN THE CASE

The country quickly sensed that the issues in the case involved far more than the question of Gibbons and his steamboat. The future of the federal government's power to regulate *interstate commerce* lay in the hands of the courts. The arguments developed in this fashion:

1. States' rights upheld. In October 1819, the New York Court of Chancery ruled that the federal law did not authorize interstate commerce, but merely gave an American identity to licensed vessels. Did the federal license grant ships the right to travel from port to port within a state as well as from port to port between different states? The court said no.

2. Appeal denied. New York's Court of Errors upheld the lower court. The decision denied that Gibbons' coasting license from the federal government was superior to the New York laws which had granted the steamboat monopoly now held by Ogden. Although Gibbons' lawyers tried to show that the coasting license had been issued under the power of Congress to regulate interstate commerce, the appeals court rejected their argument. Gibbons took his case to the Supreme Court.

3. Webster argues for federal control. After several delays, the Supreme Court heard the case in February 1824. Daniel Webster and U.S. Attorney General Wirt served as attorneys for Gibbons. They argued that New York's monopoly laws conflicted with federal law, and must therefore be struck down. Webster's logic went to the heart of the matter. The power of Congress to regulate interstate commerce, he said, permitted the federal government to regulate commerce of any kind on any waters involved in the passage of goods or people between the states.

4. Decision. Chief Justice Marshall declared, and the other justices unanimously agreed, that interstate commerce included not only mere buying and selling, but any and all intercourse between the states. Since the passage of Gibbons' steamboat between New York and New Jersey obviously met this definition, the Coasting Licensing Act of 1793 was held to be superior to the statutes of the state of New York. Marshall thus set the steamboat free to travel where it would, without restriction by the monopolistic laws of any state.

RESULTS OF THE CASE

Gibbons died a millionaire, Ogden a bankrupt. Beyond personal gain or loss, however, the decision foreshadowed federal regulation over all types of interstate traffic. In a rapidly mechanizing America, this meant that not only would trains, airplanes, and buses travel under federal rules, but telecommunications, pipelines, and private cars would also be subject to federal regulation. Marshall's ruling has been called "the emancipation of American commerce," because it forever removed interstate commerce from interference by state legislatures and by the special interests that so often dominate them.

How did a case involving slavery help lead to the Civil War? (Dred Scott v. Sandford)

The pages of judicial history are filled with cases that were apparently filed to bring justice to an individual, but in reality were meant to settle a point of law. The famous Dred Scott decision illustrates the practice perfectly. By the time the courts finally decided his case, Scott was a frail old man, destined to die within the year. For the divided young country, however, the court's decision that slavery could not be contained by compromise and federal law soon led to secession and civil war.

FACTS OF THE CASE

Dred Scott (see Figure 12.4) was born into slavery in Virginia sometime around 1795. After his owner took him to Missouri in 1827, Scott passed

Figure 12.4

The decision in the case of Dred Scott (1795?–1858) permitted slavery to expand into free territory and led indirectly to the Civil War. Source: New York Public Library Picture Collection.

through the hands of several other slaveholders. He lived with one of them, an army surgeon, for almost five years in the territories of Illinois and Wisconsin, where slavery had been prohibited by the Missouri Compromise of 1820. Returned to Missouri in 1838, Scott became the property of Mrs. Irene Emerson. When Mrs. Emerson moved to New York, she left her slave in Missouri. Nothing much might have come of that, except that in 1846 an abolitionist, Henry Blow, filed a lawsuit in the Missouri courts. Because of Scott's residence in free territory, the suit asked the court to declare him a free man.

Although the lower court found for Scott, in 1852 the Missouri Supreme Court reversed the decision; Scott remained a slave. Title to Scott eventually fell to Mrs. Emerson's brother, John Sanford of New York.

Meanwhile, the national argument over slavery was revived by the passage of the Kansas–Nebraska Bill in 1854, which permitted those two territories to choose for themselves whether to be free or slave. Abolitionists revived the Scott suit, charging Sanford with "assault and battery" in carrying Scott off to his new home. The case was heard in a federal district court in Missouri as *Dred Scott v. Sandford* (a misspelling, but only one of many errors in the case).

LEGAL STEPS IN THE CASE

A federal circuit court decided against Scott, but the United States Supreme Court took the case on appeal in 1856. Everyone understood that the case contained political dynamite. A new party, the Republican, had run its first national campaign that same year, losing to the Democrats and James Buchanan. In a move of doubtful political ethics, the President-elect wrote to the Court in February 1857, asking the justices to decide the question of the spread of slavery one way or the other.

1. *Legal questions.* The case hinged on three legal issues:

a. Was Scott legally a citizen of Missouri, and therefore entitled to sue Sanford, a New York resident, in a federal court?

b. Did Scott's years of residence in free territory entitle him to his freedom?

c. Was the Missouri Compromise of 1820 unconstitutional? If so, the status of Wisconsin and Illinois as free territories became irrelevant.

2. *Decision.* The Supreme Court announced its decision on March 6, 1857, with only two justices dissenting. The ruling held that Scott was a slave, and therefore not qualified to bring suit. Had the Court stopped there, little serious harm might have resulted on the national political scene. Instead, partly in response to the new President's urging, the Court went much further. In his written opinion, Chief Justice Taney stated that the holding of slaves was recognized by the Constitution as a legitimate practice. Since the Compromises of 1820 and 1850 had attempted to make this type of private property illegal in certain states and territories, these acts of Congress were, in effect, amendments to the Constitution. Therefore, the ruling continued, the compromises were unconstitutional; slavery could legally exist in any state.

RESULTS OF THE CASE

The Court's action brought great satisfaction to the South, but Northerners of both parties reacted angrily. Free-soil supporters had begun a campaign for the total abolition of slavery. Democratic hopes for retaining the White House fell sharply under the swelling abolitionist feeling. When the Republicans elected Lincoln in 1860, the Southern states felt they had no choice but to secede. The nation stood on the edge of civil war.

LET'S REVIEW FOR A MOMENT

If you have ever doubted the ability of the courts to make a lasting impact on the course of American history, these cases should have helped change your mind. Did you see the common thread that tied the first three together? Under John Marshall, the Supreme Court established the lasting legacy of a strong central government and a co-equal court system.

Marbury v. Madison began with the plea of an unhappy man who felt that his federal judgeship had been unfairly denied him. Out of this case, however, came the concept of *judicial review*, which gives the courts the power to decide the constitutionality of congressional and presidential actions.

McCulloch v. Maryland apparently favored the creation of a national bank. More to the point, the case established the right of Congress to exercise fully its implied powers.

Gibbons v. Ogden gave Marshall the opportunity to free interstate commerce from state interference. Without his broad definition of interstate commerce, every state border today might be a formidable barrier to the free passage of people and goods.

The final case, *Dred Scott v. Sandford*, however, led the nation into the bloody Civil War. The Supreme Court's decision ended efforts to reach political compromises over slavery, efforts that stretched from the writing of the Constitution itself through the Compromise of 1850.

After the Civil War, giant corporations began to create new problems for the rapidly industrializing country. Could the courts take effective action in this new situation? Let's find out.

How far may states go in limiting a corporation's activities? (Munn v. Illinois)

Within twenty years after the first train chugged slowly out of Chicago in 1848, that city had grown tenfold. As the city grew, so did the wheat and grain shipping and storage businesses that based their operations there. These giant concerns operated in seemingly open defiance of the laws of Illinois.

FACTS OF THE CASE

Millions of bushels of grain flowed into Chicago each year (see Figure 12.5). Midwestern farmers, who had no choice but to market their grain through Chicago, found themselves at the mercy of the railroads and warehouse owners. Some of these profit-hungry middlemen employed underhanded practices, which included (1) delivering grain to warehouses other than those specified by the farmer; (2) grading high-quality grain as low; (3) charging excessively high storage fees; (4) spreading rumors that grain was spoiling, thus forcing distress sales of quality wheat to speculators; (5) mixing poor grain with good and selling the mixture as premium; and (6) signing false receipts that indicated storage of nonexistent grain.

Figure 12.5
Grain elevators in the bustling port of Chicago during the mid-1800's played a key role in the case of *Munn v. Illinois*. Source: The Bettmann Archive, Inc.

Among the most extreme of the dishonest companies was Munn & Scott. After an investigation centered on their activities, the company built false bottoms in their silos, covered them with a few feet of grain, and claimed that they were full. The trick was discovered only when an employee told authorities the truth.

LEGAL STEPS IN THE CASE

Even today, despite strict laws, similar illegal practices still happen (as was demonstrated by the discovery in 1975 that grain wholesalers were adding dirty, spoiled wheat to their overseas shipments). In the 1870's, the right of government to "interfere" with business by forbidding such acts was very much in question; *laissez-faire* capitalism still ruled. The legal process developed like this:

1. Farmers rebel. In 1870, a new farmers' organization, the National Grange of the Patrons of Husbandry, began to speak for its members. The Grange supported those warehouse owners in Illinois who refused to follow the dishonest practices of companies like Munn & Scott. Political pressure led to amendments to the state constitution which authorized the regulation of warehouses and railroads.

2. New laws. In 1871, the same groups secured passage of state laws which forbade railroad rate discrimination, prescribed maximum freight and passenger rates, banned certain shady warehouse practices, and set a limit on storage rates. A Railroad and Warehouse Commission was established to enforce the regulations.

3. The state brings suit. Munn & Scott, however, refused to take out a state-required license, or to admit state officials to their grain elevators. The company claimed that the state laws were unconstitutional. The state brought suit and won a judgment in a lower court; in 1872, the Illinois Supreme Court accepted the case on appeal. (In the meantime, Munn & Scott went bankrupt in a grain speculation deal. George Armour & Company absorbed the smaller business, but the case went on.)

4. The court finds for the public welfare. Arguments in the state supreme court centered on the constitutional issue. Munn & Scott lost, with the court ruling that a state clearly had the right to regulate all activities concerned with the public welfare.

5. The railroads appeal. The spread of state regulation disturbed the powerful railroad interests. The rail companies appealed the Munn & Scott case (along with a number of similar cases from other states) to the United States Supreme Court. Now known as *Munn v. Illinois*, the suit reached the Court in 1876.

6. State laws upheld. By a 7–2 vote, the high court upheld the Grange-inspired laws. Munn & Scott's business did not involve interstate commerce, the Court pointed out, which meant that they could not claim that federal jurisdiction overrode the power of the state to regulate them. The state legislatures clearly possessed the power to regulate state commerce, the majority opinion continued. If the people didn't like a state law, they should go to the polls, not to the courts.

RESULTS OF THE CASE

The Supreme Court's unwillingness to examine the content of the Illinois regulations provides an excellent example of *judicial restraint*. The courts, the decision reminds us, are not interested in taking over the power of the legislatures.

Munn v. Illinois has never been overruled. During one period in history (1895–1937), later justices who were more committed to industrial capitalism than were those of 1876 did invalidate some state regulatory laws as violations of the *due process clauses* of the Fifth and Fourteenth Amendments (which state that no one shall be deprived of life, liberty, or property without due process of law). Today the courts regularly approve such legislation when it regulates commerce so as to "promote the greatest good for the greatest number."

Which is stronger, business monopolies or the federal government? (Northern Securities Company et al. v. United States)

The Northern Securities trial of 1903 attracted public attention like no case since the Dred Scott decision. The ingredients were surefire box office: the glamor of big names (J. P. Morgan, the nation's top financier— see Figure 12.6; Jim Hill, western railroad tycoon; and Ned Harriman, a

Figure 12.6

J. P. Morgan, the foremost financier of his day, was prevented from forming a giant railroad monopoly by the Supreme Court's decision in the *Northern Securities* case.

millionaire rival railroader); an issue most people could understand (did government have the power to regulate the growth of huge interstate trusts?), and a specific case involving hundreds of millions of dollars.

FACTS OF THE CASE

Piratical business practices abounded at the turn of the century. The great corporations and their colorful owners competed for the tremendous profits available in the rich and growing country. The railroads stood in the front ranks of such enterprises.

Two railroads—the Northern Pacific, owned by Morgan, and the Great Northern, owned by Hill—ran almost parallel from Minnesota to the Pacific. Harriman's Union Pacific followed the same route farther south. All three lines connected with the Chicago, Burlington & Quincy Railroad, which linked the three western roads with the rich Chicago market. All railroad men knew that whoever controlled the Burlington would gain a distinct advantage over the competition. In 1900, Hill tried for a takeover but failed. The next year, however, Morgan succeeded in buying a majority interest in the smaller line.

In response, Harriman plotted a financial raid on Morgan's Northern Pacific. When Morgan and Hill (who ran their two railroads in close cooperation) were both away from New York, Harriman managed to buy up 370,000 of the 800,000 shares of common stock and a majority of the preferred stock. Both stocks carried voting rights. The Morgan forces awoke in time, and prevented a complete takeover. A compromise was worked out that elected Harriman and several supporters to the Northern Pacific's governing board.

A few months later, Morgan attempted to prevent any future raids by creating a corporation too large to be taken over by anyone. He announced the formation of a new *holding company* (a corporation that exists only to own stock in other companies) called the Northern Securities Company. Capitalized at $400 million, the new company inherited voting control of the three Morgan and Hill railroads—the Northern Pacific, the Great Northern, and the Burlington.

The new concentration of power did not escape notice in Washington, where a new and untested President occupied the White House. Theodore Roosevelt had become President in 1901 after William McKinley, "the businessman's friend," had fallen victim to an assassin's bullet. Early in 1902, Roosevelt ordered an investigation of the Northern Securities Company. In March, the government filed a federal suit in St. Paul, Minnesota, charging the company with violation of the Sherman Antitrust Act of 1890.

LEGAL STEPS IN THE CASE

Largely unused for a dozen years, the vaguely worded Sherman Antitrust Act's main intent was to forbid illegal combinations of businesses in *restraint of trade*. In other words, the Sherman Act gave the government authority to prevent monopolies from restricting the free flow of interstate commerce by reducing or eliminating competition. The arguments at the heart of the case would determine whether the Northern Securities Company was such a monopoly within the meaning of the law.

1. *Sherman Act upheld in lower court.* The four-judge federal circuit court found against Northern Securities in April 1903. The judges ruled that the railroads were, in fact, competing companies; to place them under one management would have the effect of reducing competition. The antitrust law had passed its first test.

2. *Appeal to Supreme Court.* Morgan and his lawyers carried their appeal to the Supreme Court. The defense argument claimed that the merger had not restrained trade—that it only had the potential to do so. Should a company be penalized for size alone? The government's attorneys retorted that by combining the rail lines, Northern Securities effectively controlled transportation across a major segment of the country.

3. *Decision.* The Supreme Court reported a 5–4 decision against the Northern Securities Company. Justice John Marshall Harlan wrote that no scheme or device could more clearly come within the meaning of the Sherman Act. Oliver Wendell Holmes joined the dissenters with a bitter minority opinion. Nevertheless, the Sherman Antitrust Act survived as a means of limiting "unreasonable" restraints of trade.

RESULTS OF THE CASE

The long-range importance of the case had little to do with the railroads themselves. Hill and Morgan continued to run their parallel rail lines as a team. The government, however, had established its right to regulate business for the common good. Teddy Roosevelt now had the "big stick" he needed to maintain stricter control over other big corporations.

Are segregated schools automatically unequal?
(Brown v. Board of Education of Topeka)

In the 1950's, many Americans joined in an attack on school segregation practices which they believed shackled the minds of black people as surely as chains had once imprisoned their bodies. The decision of the Supreme Court in *Brown v. Board of Education of Topeka*, which grew out of that concern, still echoes in the classrooms and streets of American cities over twenty years later (see Figure 12.7).

FACTS OF THE CASE

The case of *Brown v. Board of Education* began with a long string of precedents to overcome. In May 1896, the United States Supreme Court announced a decision in a Louisiana railroad suit known as *Plessy v. Ferguson.* The ruling supported the *Jim Crow laws* by which some thirty states segregated public facilities—schools, restaurants, beaches, railroads

Figure 12.7
The impact of the Supreme Court's 1954 decision in the *Brown v. Topeka Board of Education* case continued to be felt decades later. Vehement protests by some parents like these in Louisville, Kentucky, against federally ordered busing of children to achieve racial balance in the schools created headlines and controversy year after year. Source: Wide World Photos.

—under the doctrine of *separate but equal*. This meant that separation by race was legal as long as the public facilities for blacks and whites were substantially the same. *Plessy* did not specifically mention schools, but they were covered in a later decision handed down in 1927, *Gong Lum v. Lee.*

The social climate of the 1950's brought the "separate but equal" doctrine under increasing attack. Under the leadership of the National Association for the Advancement of Colored People (NAACP), several suits were brought that struck successfully at Jim Crow.

LEGAL STEPS IN THE CASE

The case called *Brown v. Board of Education* actually combined several suits that questioned the legality of segregated schools. Four states and the District of Columbia were represented, and although the local conditions differed slightly, the basic arguments ran in parallel.

1. "Separate but equal" doctrine upheld. In Topeka, Kansas, where the *Brown* case originated, a three-judge federal panel ruled that *Plessy v. Ferguson* and its "separate but equal" doctrine was still the law of the land.

2. Appeal to Supreme Court. In December 1952, the Supreme Court agreed to review all five school segregation cases. Thurgood Marshall, an

Figure 12.8
Earl Warren, Chief Justice from 1953 to 1969, led the Supreme Court in a series of landmark decisions that broadened the interpretation of the civil rights amendments to the Constitution.

eminent black attorney, argued the plaintiffs' case. (In 1967, Marshall was appointed by President Johnson to the high court as an associate justice.)

3. Basic questions. In June 1953, the Court broke a six-month silence to ask that both sides answer four questions:

a. Did the Fourteenth Amendment, as passed by Congress and ratified by the states, intend to abolish school segregation? The amendment, after all, guarantees equal protection under the law.

b. If no such intent existed, did those who wrote the amendment think that it entitled Congress or the Supreme Court to act on school segregation?

c. If the intent of the amendment was unclear, did the Court itself have the power to abolish segregated schools?

d. If the Court did declare an end to segregation, would such a declaration take immediate effect, or could integration proceed on a gradual basis?

The NAACP lawyers consulted with legal scholars, sociologists, and educators from every section of the country before filing their response in November 1953. The court heard the oral arguments that December.

4. Decision. In May 1954, Chief Justice Earl Warren (see Figure 12.8) read a unanimous decision that ruled against racially separate schools as "inherently unequal." Citing sociological evidence, the Court stated that separate schools automatically gave black children a "feeling of inferiority as to their status in the community that may affect their hearts and minds in a way unlikely ever to be undone." With those words, the Supreme Court formally overturned *Plessy v. Ferguson.*

RESULTS OF THE CASE

Political scientists consider *Brown v. Board of Education* a modern landmark in the history of American justice. The Warren Court clearly took upon itself the responsibility of acting decisively in what it considered to be the public interest. Opponents of the Court called the decision "political"—which indeed it was, since court decisions always carry political implications. Judges do not work in a vacuum, but must always be aware of the changing needs of the society they serve.

Enforcement of the desegregation decision began in the heavily segregated South, but later spread to other sections of the country. Correcting racial segregation or imbalance in the schools has created heated controversies over busing and community control of schools. Whatever the social turmoil it created, however, the *Brown* decision demonstrated clearly that our Constitution is still capable of growth and evolution.

Should any restrictions be placed on the police when making arrests? (Miranda v. Arizona)

Rising crime rates in the 1960's focused attention on two opposing viewpoints regarding police authority. On one hand, the public was demanding that the police take vigorous action to protect American communities from criminal violence. On the other hand, concern was growing that heavy-handed police activities could do harm to cherished constitutional rights (see Figure 12.9). The conflict reached its peak in the case of *Miranda v. Arizona.*

FACTS OF THE CASE

In March 1963, an eighteen-year-old girl was kidnapped and attacked near Phoenix, Arizona. Ten days later, Ernesto Miranda, age twenty-three, was arrested for the crime. Taken to the police station, he was questioned without being told that he had the right to remain silent and to have a lawyer present. The victim picked him out of a police lineup. After two hours of further interrogation, Miranda made a detailed oral confession.

Miranda's confession was admitted as evidence at his trial, despite his attorney's objection. Found guilty, he was sentenced to a prison term of twenty to thirty-nine years. The verdict was upheld on appeal by the Arizona Supreme Court. That decision ruled that the defendant's constitutional rights had not been violated, as Miranda had never specifically

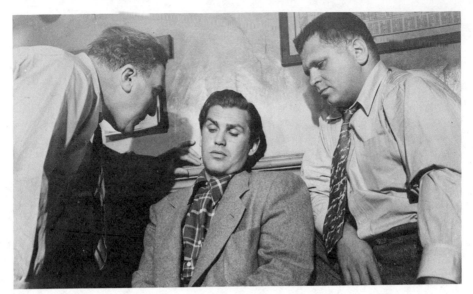

Figure 12.9

The *Miranda v. Arizona* decision, which protected the rights of individuals accused of crimes, has eliminated the "third degree" grilling of suspects so beloved by Hollywood filmmakers. Scenes like this one from the 1951 film *Detective Story* are now as out of date as the clothing styles of the actors. Source: Culver Pictures.

requested a lawyer. Miranda and his attorney then sought review of the case by the United States Supreme Court.

LEGAL STEPS IN THE CASE

In 1964, the Supreme Court had already begun to concern itself with the extension of Bill of Rights guarantees to state court trials. The well-publicized Miranda case continued this movement.

1. Right to counsel. In the 1964 case of *Escobedo v. Illinois,* the Court had held by a 5–4 majority that the defendant had been denied his constitutional rights when authorities refused him access to a lawyer until after he confessed.

2. Negative precedents. Escobedo and *Miranda* both centered on the question of whether the Fourteenth Amendment (through either the due process clause or the privileges and immunities clause) incorporated the Bill of Rights into cases tried under state laws. The amendment had always applied to the federal courts, but since the question was first asked in 1873, a total of fifty-three justices had ruled against extending the Fourteenth Amendment protections to the state courts and only one justice had ruled in favor of it.

3. Changing Supreme Court rulings. Beginning in the early 1960's, however, the Court began to decide such appeals on the basis of *selective incorporation*—that is, picking individual guarantees from the Bill of

Rights and applying them to state cases. Previous decisions had already been made involving (a) protection against self-incrimination (*Malloy v. Hogan*, 1961); (b) the right of the poor to free legal counsel (*Gideon v. Wainwright*, 1963); and (c) protection against unreasonable search and seizure (*Mapp v. Ohio*, 1961).

4. *Decision.* Chief Justice Warren delivered the majority opinion, from which three justices dissented. Warren took note of the stresses that arrest and interrogation place on a suspect. Under these conditions, he wrote, the person held in custody must be informed in clear terms that (a) he or she has the right to remain silent and (b) he or she has the right to consult with an attorney. The *Miranda* decision thus placed constitutional protections between every citizen and the power of the state.

RESULTS OF THE CASE

As with every controversial Supreme Court decision, *Miranda* left a legacy of discontent. From people involved in law enforcement has come a steady chorus of complaints claiming that police work has been severely hampered. Confessions are almost impossible to obtain, the argument continues, and guilty individuals walk unscathed out of the station houses. Defenders of the ruling reply that no noticeable decrease in the number of confessions has developed, and that convictions can still be obtained through solid police investigation. As a matter of fact, Miranda himself was later found guilty when his common-law wife testified that he had told her of committing the crime.

In brief, the *Miranda* debate involves a question that goes to the heart of a free society: Have the rights of citizens to be protected from criminals been lost in the rush to safeguard the rights of the criminals themselves? Whatever the answer turns out to be, the results of *Miranda* can be seen on every television crime show. As soon as any suspects are placed under arrest, the police inform them of their rights according to the formula established by the *Miranda* decision. Rising crime rates seem to result from much broader social forces than the requirement that a suspect's right to legal counsel must be safeguarded.

§UMMARY AND CONCLUSIONS

1. The courts of the United States have remained responsive to the social, political, and economic problems of the country. Where the original decisions discussed in this chapter concerned themselves with the exercise of federal power, later cases gave the Supreme Court the chance to protect the individual—first against big corporations and then against big government.

2. *Marbury v. Madison* established the principle of *judicial review,* forever confirming the courts as a co-equal branch of government. Con-

gressional power under the concept of implied powers was secured by *McCulloch v. Maryland,* while *Gibbons v. Ogden* released interstate commerce from narrow-interest state controls.

3. A debate over individual rights began to surface when the slavery question split the country. *Dred Scott v. Sandford,* by striking down the compromise legislation of the 1820's and 1850's, made the Civil War inevitable. Still, despite the Union victory, segregation laws haunted the nation's sense of justice. Almost a hundred years passed, however, before the Supreme Court, in *Brown v. Board of Education of Topeka,* finally ended the "separate but equal" doctrine that had been used to justify school segregation.

4. The Supreme Court also moved against the big corporations. In *Munn v. Illinois,* the states gained the right to regulate corporations for the public benefit, even though private companies lose some freedom as a result. On a national level, the Sherman Antitrust Act became an effective government weapon against monopoly combinations only after *Northern Securities Company* et al. *v. United States* confirmed its usefulness.

5. In *Miranda v. Arizona,* the Supreme Court brought state courts into line with federal guarantees of the right to counsel and against self-incrimination for persons accused of a crime. Faced with a choice between police power and individual rights, the Court came down on the side of the individual.

REVIEW QUESTIONS AND ACTIVITIES

TERMS YOU SHOULD KNOW

due process clause

holding company

implied powers

industrial monopoly

interstate commerce

Jim Crow laws

judicial restraint

judicial review

public welfare

restraint of trade

selective incorporation

"separate but equal" doctrine

states' rights

MATCHING QUESTIONS

From the list of court cases below, pick the case that best illustrates the legal principle embodied in each of the following statements.

a. *Marbury v. Madison*

b. *McCulloch v. Maryland*

c. *Gibbons v. Ogden*

d. *Dred Scott v. Sandford*

e. *Munn v. Illinois*

f. *Northern Securities v. U.S.*

g. *Brown v. Board of Education*

h. *Miranda v. Arizona*

1. A federal judge orders the city of Los Angeles to bus students between neighborhood schools in order to achieve racial balance.

2. IBM is taken to court and charged with monopolizing the sale of computers to business and industry.

3. A new federal "no-knock" law that authorizes search and seizure without a warrant in criminal investigations is struck down in the federal courts.

4. The state of Arkansas attempts to pass a law taxing the income of cities and counties within the state.

5. The district attorney in Minneapolis loses a murder conviction when the court discovers that the defendant did not know he was entitled to counsel despite his inability to pay a lawyer's fee.

6. The Supreme Court upholds a Louisiana law that places a ceiling on the rates an insurance company can charge doctors for malpractice insurance.

7. The Supreme Court refuses to hear an appeal from a well-known film star who was prosecuted for nonpayment of state taxes. The star said that she would not pay taxes to support the state welfare system.

8. The state of Arizona attempts to enforce a law banning the import of California oranges as a means of protecting the Arizona citrus industry.

9. The Justice Department takes action when the three largest oil companies agree to establish uniform prices for their petroleum products.

10. A federal court rules that the President must spend funds appropriated by Congress for a low-income housing project, even though he believes the project will cause additional inflation.

CONCEPT DEVELOPMENT

This chapter has explored a number of landmark Supreme Court cases. You can use your skills in thinking, researching, and writing to answer the following questions.

1. Explain the role taken by the court system in opposing the executive branch in *Marbury v. Madison*.

2. Evaluate the contributions of Chief Justice John Marshall to the development of the federal court system.

3. Discuss the concept of implied powers as interpreted by the courts. Are there any areas left in which government cannot act?

4. List the current members of the Supreme Court, along with their political philosophy—liberal, moderate, or conservative. Where does the balance of power appear to lie? What would you say the social implications of that balance of power will be in the next few years?

5. What do critics mean when they charge that the Supreme Court is "making law, not interpreting it"?

ACTIVITIES

The following activities are designed to help you use the ideas developed in this chapter.

1. This chapter has selected only eight out of literally thousands of Supreme Court decisions. Use one of your library reference books to locate some of the other major decisions handed down over the years. Select one or two to report on, either in a paper or in an oral presentation to the class. A few possibilities, all relating to the First Amendment, are *Near v. Minnesota*, 1931 (censorship), *Sheppard v. Maxwell*, 1966 (unfair publicity in a court trial), *New York Times v. Sullivan*, 1964 (newspaper libel), *A Book v. Attorney General of Massachusetts* (pornography), *Pierce v. Society of Sisters*, 1925 (religious education). The list is endless; can you find a case of even greater interest?

2. Select one of the cases described in this chapter to dramatize for your class. An effective technique is to do it in the form of a reading, with well-rehearsed actors reading their parts from a prepared script. A narrator can fill in the background and provide transitions from one event to the next; individual voices can take the roles of plaintiffs and defendants, judges, the President of the United States, and other participants. An effective variation would be to record the scene on tape with sound effects, like a radio show of the 1940's. A college textbook on constitutional law will furnish additional details.

3. Organize a debate on the topic, "Resolved: that the Supreme Court of the United States should confine itself to its constitutionally defined tasks, and should leave legislation and its enforcement to Congress and the executive branch." The debate teams will need to research this controversial topic, but the audience will find the contrasting points of view interesting and highly relevant to the future of the Supreme Court.

4. Conduct a survey among members of your community to discover how many people can (a) name any or all members of the Supreme Court and (b) name or describe any recent Court rulings. If you come up with rather negative results, to what do you ascribe this ignorance of our most important court? Is there any danger in this, given the apparent distance of the Supreme Court from most of us? (You may wish to argue that last point.)

CHAPTER THIRTEEN

DEFINING INDIVIDUAL RIGHTS: THE AMERICAN CITIZEN TODAY

So protective of American freedoms is the Constitution that some Americans are surprised when they discover limits on any particular activity. Even as simple an act as asking school children to say a short prayer can find the will of the majority contested by a determined minority. Consider the case of the New York Board of Regents' classroom prayer.

Since 1837, New York State had followed a policy of permitting prayer in the public schools. In 1951, the State Board of Regents adopted a nondenominational prayer that they recommended for classroom use. To be recited after the flag salute each school day, the prayer stated:

> Almighty God, we acknowledge our dependence upon Thee, as we beg Thy blessings upon us, our parents, our teachers, and our country.

Use of the prayer was not mandatory—a local school board could vote to adopt it or not. The Union Free School District Number Nine, Town of North Hempstead, Long Island, did agree in 1958 to require the daily recitation of the prayer. The decision did not go unchallenged. Five parents filed suit against the board the following year, charging that adoption and use of the prayer constituted "establishment of religion" in violation of the First Amendment to the Constitution. The plaintiffs represented several different religious beliefs: two were Jewish, one was Unitarian, one belonged to the Society of Ethical Culture, and one was a nonbeliever.

Because the case involved provisions of the state constitution as well as that of the United States, a state court accepted jurisdiction. The lower court ruled in favor of the school board and the use of the prayer. The decision noted that since neither the Constitution nor its writers discussed the use of prayer in public schools, court precedents provided the only means of resolving the suit.

Analyzing the case further, the judges noted that the prayer did not fall into the same category as Bible readings in public schools (already declared unconstitutional) or religious instruction. No one was compelled to recite the prayer, nor were those who did not participate discriminated against. Therefore, the court concluded, the prayer was permissible so long as it did not become compulsory or sectarian.

The New York Court of Appeals reviewed the case and upheld the lower court. In a 5–2 decision, the court said that the ban on establishment of a state religion in the United States Constitution was never intended to forbid a simple declaration of belief in God.

When this decision was appealed to the United States Supreme Court, the defense based its case on the lower court rulings, as well as on custom and tradition. Attorneys pointed out that the United States had been built by God-fearing, religiously oriented people. They pointed to the use of "In God We Trust" on the nation's coinage and the phrase "one nation, under God" in the Pledge of Allegiance.

Despite these arguments, a 6–1 Supreme Court majority declared in June 1962 that the New York prayer was in violation of the First Amendment. No matter how brief, the decision stated, a prayer must be defined as a religious activity. Neither the nonsectarian nature of the prayer nor the lack of compulsion mattered. Not even the smallest intrusion on First Amendment protections could be permitted. Although the ruling came in a New York case, school districts across the country were affected. There would be no prayers in the American public schools.

Those who opposed the school prayer decision claimed that under the cover of religious liberty, the minority exercised a veto over the wishes of the majority. Should that be permitted in a democracy? This chapter will explore that basic problem. It might be stated in this way: What rights do individuals possess that cannot be denied by a majority vote of their fellow citizens or by the powers of government?

In particular, the following questions will be explored:

1. What civil rights are guaranteed to all citizens by the Bill of Rights?
2. Where did American civil rights originate?
3. What basic rights does the Constitution itself guarantee?
4. How do the states guarantee individual rights?
5. How did the "civil liberties" amendments enlarge individual rights?
6. How does a person gain—and keep—citizenship?
7. When may civil liberties be limited or suspended?

What civil rights are guaranteed to all citizens by the Bill of Rights?

Although a few individual rights are listed in the Constitution itself (see pages 324–26), the first ten amendments—the Bill of Rights—are the primary shield between the individual and the impersonal power of society.

When the Constitution was written in 1787, its authors attempted to lay down a framework for federal government that was general enough to gain wide acceptance. This brevity has proved to be one of the strengths of the Constitution; we have relied upon statute law to deal with specific situations. The Founders believed that the American people would have faith in their national government. With that in mind, they thought it unnecessary to spell out every safeguard and liberty.

PROMISE OF A BILL OF RIGHTS

In the struggle for ratification of the Constitution in 1787–1788, opponents attacked this omission as a serious flaw. After all, they argued, hadn't Americans fought the Revolutionary War because their traditional rights as English subjects had been ignored? A compromise developed, based on the promise that once the Constitution was adopted, the new government would add a Bill of Rights as one of its first orders of business. The promise was kept.

The Bill of Rights was largely the work of James Madison. Proposed in the first year of Washington's administration (1789), these ten amendments were ratified by the states and became part of the Constitution in 1791.

FREEDOM OF RELIGION (FIRST AMENDMENT)

In a few words, the Constitution says all it has to say on the subject of religion: "Congress shall make no law respecting an establishment of religion, or prohibiting the free exercise thereof." By "establishing a religion" the amendment means that government may not make any specific religion, any religious activity, or any religious qualification a part of its official functions. Thus, Congress may not adopt an official church, as Great Britain has done with the Church of England. Neither may government funds be spent to support church activities, as is often done in the Scandinavian countries.

Despite this apparently clear-cut restriction, the relationship between church and state still raises many constitutional questions.

Does religious belief take precedence over federal authority? For example, should the government draft a pacifist who bases his antiwar feelings on religious beliefs? Or can the state force Christian Scientists to allow a hospital to administer a life-saving blood transfusion to their child? (The courts have answered "no" to the drafting of pacifists, "yes" to the question of the dying child's constitutional right to life.)

Should church income be exempt from taxation? Organized religious groups—such as churches, monasteries, and religious schools—do not have to pay income taxes. Many people believe that this exemption constitutes a type of government "establishment" of organized religion, requiring other citizens to pay higher taxes as a consequence.

Should government help support church schools? Rising educational costs have led many church schools to seek financial support from local

Figure 13.1

Freedom of speech, a basic right guaranteed by the Constitution, is loudly exercised in demonstrations and meetings throughout the country. This Student Free Speech Forum was held at Louisiana State University in Baton Rouge. Source: Wide World Photos.

and state governments. Even if local voters wish to provide this subsidy (usually in the form of textbooks or transportation), does the Constitution allow such payment? The Supreme Court has drawn a strict limitation on state support of church schools, although lending of state textbooks has been permitted in certain cases.

FREEDOM OF SPEECH (FIRST AMENDMENT)

Freedom of speech, like every other freedom, is not absolute. As Oliver Wendell Holmes pointed out, "The most stringent protection of free speech would not protect a man in falsely shouting fire in a theater and causing a panic."

Individuals must accept legal responsibility for what they say or write. Oral statements that damage someone else's reputation may lead to a lawsuit for *slander*, in which the injured party attempts to collect damages. If a newspaper or magazine publishes the slanderous statement, it may be sued for *libel*. The best defense in libel and slander suits is to show that the statements were true.

A revolutionary may advocate overthrow of the government only so long as the speech does not become an actual attempt to promote violence or revolution. The courts have the responsibility of deciding the point at which unpopular beliefs become a "clear and present danger" to public safety—such as philosophies that would lead to an attempted takeover of the government at gunpoint.

Outside of these obvious limitations, the constitutional guarantees on freedom of speech are absolute. Under no circumstances may the government pass laws or take action against people who express opinions that are merely unpopular or contrary to governmental policy (see Figure 13.1).

FREEDOM OF THE PRESS (FIRST AMENDMENT)

One of the oldest of American freedoms, the right of the press to publish freely without fear of government censorship was severely tested during the colonial period. The case of John Peter Zenger illustrates the nature of the struggle. The royal governor of New York charged Zenger in 1735 with printing seditious statements that might well lead to rebellion. Zenger replied that what he had printed was the truth. The jury found him not guilty, thus establishing the tradition of the free press in this country.

FREEDOM OF ASSEMBLY AND PETITION (FIRST AMENDMENT)

The First Amendment also guarantees Americans the right "peaceably to assemble" in order to exchange opinions and ideas. The key word is "peaceably." Should a meeting clearly show signs of turning into a riot or threatening the public safety, the police have the responsibility of breaking it up. If people wish to challenge the police interpretation, they may refuse to disperse and take their chances with the courts. Common sense should dictate the reasonable limits of this freedom—and all others.

Right to petition. The right "to petition the government for a redress of grievances" includes far more than the word "petition" seems to indicate. Any citizen may circulate a petition for signatures, then send it to the proper government official for consideration. An individual letter, or a request to testify before a governmental body, also counts as a petition. When people knock on any official door to ask for help or advice, or to suggest action in the public good—that is also a form of petition.

Picketing. Long lines of pickets marching in front of government buildings symbolized the protest movements of the 1960's and early 1970's. Picketing combines the right of assembly with the right of petition. Most city governments have established procedures that pickets must follow—take out a permit, don't block public walkways, obey lawful orders of the police. First Amendment guarantees fully protect the act of picketing itself.

RIGHT TO BEAR ARMS (SECOND AMENDMENT)

The right to bear arms made good sense when many Americans needed guns for hunting or for defense against Indians and wild animals. The Founders also believed that the new country should depend upon a civilian militia rather than a permanent standing army. Neither of those conditions holds true today: the frontier has disappeared, and the armed forces maintain a full-time, highly professional corps of combat and support troops.

Does the Second Amendment right to bear arms still apply under these changed conditions? The federal government already forbids ownership of many categories of automatic and heavy weapons. Most states (the amendment does not apply to state law) require permits to own firearms, and regulate the carrying of concealed weapons through special permits. Despite

'PARDON ME, SIR! WE'RE DOING A SURVEY ON FEAR IN AMERICA...'

Figure 13.2
Growing rates of violent crime in American cities have made many citizens fearful. In such a climate, people find it easier to accept restrictions on their civil rights in return for more protection against crime. Source: Jeff MacNelly, courtesy of the Chicago Tribune–New York News Syndicate, Inc.

these existing restrictions, the question of further gun control still sparks regular national debates (see Figure 13.2).

FREEDOM FROM QUARTERING TROOPS (THIRD AMENDMENT)

Time has robbed the Third Amendment of its significance. In colonial times, private citizens were often required to take British troops into their homes, mostly because suitable barracks were not available. Members of the armed forces today live on military bases, or find quarters in the civilian communities nearby like any other renter or homeowner.

FREEDOM FROM UNREASONABLE SEARCH AND SEIZURE (FOURTH AMENDMENT)

The Constitution guarantees that everyone's person, home, papers, and possessions should be secure. In practice, however, the courts do not deny police the right of "search and seizure"—as long as the action is *reasonable*. Common sense requires that the authorities sometimes must stop a suspect or search a home in the interest of public safety. When sufficient evidence exists to charge a suspect with a crime, the court may issue a warrant for that person's arrest.

Even so, cases questioning the legality of police searches abound in the courts today. Many arrests for violations of narcotics laws, for example, are thrown out because the arresting officer failed to follow court-ordered limitations on searches of homes, cars, or individuals. Police officials argue in favor of "no-knock" laws, claiming that if they must first obtain a search warrant, the suspects will have time to destroy essential evidence. Despite these complaints, the courts still consider this constitutional safeguard more important than the possible apprehension of a lawbreaker who hides behind it.

FREEDOM TO OWN PROPERTY (FIFTH AMENDMENT)

The right to own and use private property forms the keystone of the capitalist system. As with other freedoms, this right is not absolute. An individual's private property may be taken away through *due process*— that is, by means of the proper legal procedures. For example, a bank or other mortgage holder may legally foreclose on a home, farm, or business when the mortgagee falls behind in the payments.

Another restriction on the right to own property often develops when a community decides to build a freeway, school, or other public convenience. Under the *right of eminent domain*, private property may be taken when needed for the greater public good. The Fifth Amendment guarantees that, in return for giving up their land, the property owners will receive "just compensation."

FREEDOM FROM PROSECUTION WITHOUT INDICTMENT (FIFTH AMENDMENT)

When someone is arrested and charged with a major crime, the Constitution protects that individual from having to stand trial unless an *indictment*—a formal charge—is made. This power to hold a person for trial belongs to a citizens' panel called a grand jury (further described in Chapter 12). Unless the grand jury can be convinced that sufficient evidence exists to provide a reasonable chance of conviction, they will not hand down the indictment. This procedure is intended to protect accused persons from being brought to trial on the basis of flimsy, inadequate proof or careless police work.

FREEDOM FROM DOUBLE JEOPARDY (FIFTH AMENDMENT)

The Fifth Amendment states that no person shall for the same offense "be twice put in jeopardy of life or limb." Should a defendant be found not guilty by a judge or jury, he or she may not be tried again for the same crime.

GUARANTEE OF PRESUMED INNOCENCE (FIFTH AMENDMENT)

No matter how serious the nature of a crime, or how overwhelming the evidence, a person charged with an offense must be presumed to be innocent until proven guilty. The Bill of Rights spells out this protection, a heritage from the common law, in the due process clause of the Fifth Amendment. The courts have severely limited the ways in which the police may gather evidence; any facts or testimony gained by nonlegal means are barred from use, no matter how damaging to the accused.

FREEDOM FROM SELF-INCRIMINATION (FIFTH AMENDMENT)

No one may be forced to testify against himself or herself. The use of the "third degree" and other intensive questioning techniques is forbidden. Defendants need not testify in their own behalf, nor may their silence be interpreted by the judge or jury as a sign of guilt.

In complex prosecutions like those involving leaders of organized crime, the courts have worked out a system known as *immunity from prosecution.* Once immunity is granted, the normal rules relating to self-incrimination no longer apply. The individual must testify under oath about the case. Any witness who refuses to testify under these conditions faces contempt of court charges.

Figure 13.3 summarizes the various protections provided by the U.S. system of justice against misuse of police or judicial power.

GUARANTEE OF DUE PROCESS (FIFTH AMENDMENT)

The Fifth Amendment states that no person shall be "deprived of life, liberty, or property without due process of law." This due process clause originated centuries ago in English common law. Despite those hundreds of years of established precedent, the courts have not yet reached a final definition of the exact rights included under due process.

Today the main emphasis falls on the rights of an individual accused of a crime and facing trial. As illustrated in *Miranda v. Arizona* (see Chapter 12), police action that denies court-defined rights makes all further judicial consideration impossible. In recent years, the courts have also set aside many local and state regulatory laws because the laws denied owners of businesses the right of due process. A state regulation that taxed away all possible profits of a legitimate business would fall into this category.

GUARANTEE OF JURY TRIAL
(SIXTH AND SEVENTH AMENDMENTS)

Guilt or innocence in a criminal case must be decided by the twelve men and women of the petit jury. Whether the offense is first-degree murder or jaywalking, everyone has the right to request a jury trial. Almost all civil cases except for the most minor (those heard in small claims court, for example) may be tried before juries as well. Defendants have the right to a jury that is free of bias and partiality; the goal is to seat a jury that will make its verdict only on the facts presented in the courtroom.

A trial, moreover, must be both "speedy and public." The law also requires that the trial be held in the city or county where the crime

Figure 13.3

Innocent until proven guilty: constitutional protections that stand between the accused and the power of government

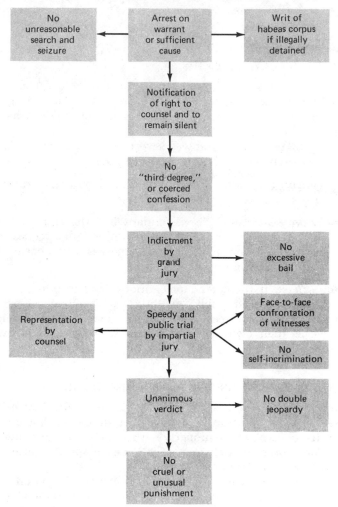

Source: Adapted from William Ebenstein *et al., American Democracy in World Perspective*, 3rd ed. (New York: Harper & Row, 1973), p. 134.

was committed. Should a defendant believe that extensive publicity has made a fair hearing impossible, however, the defense attorney may ask that the trial site be changed. In some cases the judge may refuse to admit the public and the press if the welfare of any participant—the defendant, the witnesses, or the jury—appears to be threatened.

The right to a "speedy" trial does not require that the trial itself move quickly. Rather, it means that the trial should begin as soon as possible after the indictment has been handed up. Moving quickly to trial works to the advantage of the defendant in several ways: witnesses remember their stories more clearly; and should bail not be granted, the defendant need not spend months in jail waiting for trial. Despite this constitutional protection, heavy caseloads in many courts have created waits of a year or more before trial begins.

RIGHT TO BE INFORMED
OF CHARGES (SIXTH AMENDMENT)

A defendant in a civil or criminal action must be told the nature of the charges so that a proper defense can be prepared. The charge must be spelled out in detail. The defense also has a right to know what evidence will be used at the trial.

The Sixth Amendment guarantees several related rights, which add to the protections included in this general safeguard:

Right to confront witnesses. All accusers and witnesses must face the defendant in open court.

Right to secure witnesses. The defendant has the right to secure witnesses to testify in his or her behalf. At the defendant's request, the court will issue subpoenas to ensure that the witnesses will appear. A sample subpoena is shown in Figure 13.4.

Right to counsel. If the defendant cannot afford to pay attorney's fees, the court will appoint a public defender, with expenses paid by the government. A 1975 Supreme Court decision also granted defendants the right to serve as their own attorneys—even at the risk of having "a fool for a client."

GUARANTEE OF RELEASE ON BAIL (EIGHTH AMENDMENT)

Without provision for the posting of bail, the accused might be forced to spend months in jail waiting for trial to begin. By putting up a sum of money (or its equivalent in property), the defendant guarantees his or her appearance for trial. Release on bail also gives the accused an opportunity to prepare a defense for the coming trial.

In many minor traffic cases, the court establishes the amount of the bail as equal to the fine; if the defendant fails to appear, the bail is forfeited and that ends the case. In the most serious felonies, or where the defendant has a long record of unreliability, the judge may deny the right to post bail.

FREEDOM FROM CRUEL AND UNUSUAL
PUNISHMENT (EIGHTH AMENDMENT)

The writers of the Bill of Rights forbade "cruel and unusual punishment" of convicted criminals in order to prevent torture, whipping, and other eighteenth-century excesses. Modern court decisions have broadened the Eighth Amendment to forbid the death penalty, unless certain legislative actions are taken that make its application uniform. Excessively severe punishments, such as a twenty-year prison term for petty theft, are also forbidden by this amendment.

Figure 13.4
Sample subpoena used in a criminal case

<table>
<tr>
<td>
NAME, ADDRESS, AND TELEPHONE NUMBER OF ATTORNEY(S)

Harry Doe
456 Main Street
Big Town, Ca. 90028
(213) 456-0000

ATTORNEY(S) FOR

John Doe
</td>
<td></td>
</tr>
</table>

SUPERIOR COURT OF CALIFORNIA, COUNTY OF LOS ANGELES

<table>
<tr>
<td>
The People of the State of California

JOHN DOE PLAINTIFF(S)

VS

SAMUEL DOE

DEFENDANT(S)
</td>
<td>
Criminal Case Number

SP - 0000

SUBPOENA, in Criminal Case
</td>
</tr>
</table>

PEOPLE OF THE STATE OF CALIFORNIA TO:

JEREMIAH K. DOE

We command you to attend a session of this Superior Court to be held at the Court Room of Department No. **24** at the **Municipal Court Building** in the County of Los Angeles, on **27 Sept.** 19-- , at 9:00 o'clock A.M., then and there to testify in the above action now pending in said Superior Court, on the part of the defendant.
For failure to attend you will be deemed guilty of a contempt of Court, liable to pay all losses and damages sustained thereby by the party aggrieved, and forfeit one hundred dollars in addition thereto.

Dated: **1 September** , 19--

Given under my hand, with the Seal of said Court by order of said Court:

CLARENCE E. CABELL, County Clerk and Clerk of the Superior Court of California, County of Los Angeles

(Seal)

By _[signature]_ Deputy

785807 - (8/72) - CDB 10-73   SUBPOENA

LIMITATIONS ON THE POWER OF THE FEDERAL GOVERNMENT (NINTH AND TENTH AMENDMENTS)

The final two amendments of the Bill of Rights establish limits on the power of the federal government. The Ninth Amendment reminds the federal authorities that even though the Constitution does not specifically mention a particular right, that right still exists and must be protected. While the Ninth Amendment defines the noninclusive nature of the Constitution, the Tenth Amendment speaks to the limited nature of the federal government. The last amendment of the Bill of Rights states that all powers not delegated to the federal government are reserved to the states or to the people.

LET'S REVIEW FOR A MOMENT

Without a doubt, the Framers of the Constitution strongly believed that the individual citizens must be protected from the abuse of power by government. The absolute guarantees hammered out in the Bill of Rights (and in the court decisions that have broadened them) shelter all Americans under a broad and almost rainproof umbrella. But nothing is truly absolute. Abuses of power still exist in this country, as witness the recent disclosures of illegal CIA and IRS intelligence-gathering operations, or the painfully slow progress of black people toward equal treatment by white-dominated courts and police forces.

How many of the eighteen rights described in this chapter can you remember? Close your eyes for a moment and try to count them off. How many was that—eight, nine? Not bad. Here's the full list:

1. Freedom of RELIGION
2. Freedom of SPEECH
3. Freedom of the PRESS
4. Freedom of ASSEMBLY AND PETITION
5. Right to bear ARMS
6. Freedom from QUARTERING TROOPS in your home
7. Freedom from unreasonable SEARCH AND SEIZURE
8. Right to own PROPERTY
9. Freedom from prosecution without an INDICTMENT
10. Freedom from DOUBLE JEOPARDY
11. Guarantee of DUE PROCESS OF LAW
12. Guarantee of PRESUMPTION OF INNOCENCE
13. Freedom from SELF-INCRIMINATION
14. Guarantee of a JURY TRIAL
15. Guarantee of being INFORMED OF CHARGES
16. Guarantee of reasonable BAIL
17. Freedom from CRUEL AND UNUSUAL PUNISHMENT
18. Limitations on the POWER OF THE FEDERAL GOVERNMENT

Let's try a mnemonic device (a fancy name for memory-jogger) that may help you remember all the protections guaranteed by the Bill of Rights.

One popular memory system asks that you begin by picking out the first letter of each key word in the listing. In this case, the letters would be:

R * S * P * A
A * Q * S * P
I * D * D * P
S * J * I * B
C * P

Now write a short poem whose words begin with the same letters as each of the eighteen key words above. Here's a sample, with a British theme:

Ringo Starr, Pubs Abound;
Ancient Queens, Sinking Pound
In Decline; Devon Pride,
Silly Jokes, Irish Bride.
Chaucer's Provoked.

Now it's your turn. However you go about remembering these ideas, you should also remember that your basic civil rights do not depend upon the whim of a local police officer or a Washington bureaucrat. They're yours— for keeps.

Where did these rights originate? Let's take a look.

Where did American civil rights originate?

As you learned in Chapter 2, the U.S. legal system and its stress on individual rights developed during the colonial period. In the years between 1607 and 1787, the British colonists—unlike their French and Spanish counterparts—lived under a government that accepted centuries-old limitations on its power. As early as 1215, Magna Carta had placed the king under the rule of law. The British people received their own Bill of Rights in 1689, passed by Parliament when the Stuart king fled the country. William and Mary were forced to accept the throne under terms of a limited monarchy. The charter of the Jamestown colony, in fact, granted to British colonists in the New World all the rights, liberties, and privileges of English subjects—just as if they had been born and were living in Great Britain.

SALUTARY NEGLECT

The long colonial period, coupled with the difficulty of transatlantic communication, gave the thirteen colonies the chance to add a growing tradition of self-government to the rights granted under their charters. Colonial legislatures interpreted and modified the laws of Parliament, much to the dismay of the royal governors. Not only was Great Britain far away, but its wars with France, Spain, and the Netherlands prevented it from closely supervising the colonies. Civil war in England, which resulted in the strengthening of Parliament, also helped create the climate of *salutary neglect* which allowed Americans the opportunity to conduct their own affairs.

RESISTANCE TO BRITISH RULE

By the time the wars with France ended in 1763, Americans were accustomed to passing their own tax legislation, regulating their own courts, and safeguarding their own liberties. When Parliament passed a series of revenue bills (believing it only fair that the colonists should pay their fair share of the wars' costs), American opposition stiffened.

When troops were stationed in the colonies to enforce the tax laws, the colonists treated the soldiers like foreign invaders. When the British tried tax-law violators in colonial courts, the juries refused to convict their fellow Americans. When special search warrants and other legal maneuvers seemed to be chipping away at long-cherished liberties, Americans began to organize a resistance movement.

THE DECLARATION OF INDEPENDENCE

In 1776, this growing discontent led a group of colonial leaders to write the Declaration of Independence. The document summarized the grievances that the colonists believed the king had inflicted upon them. They objected to the dissolving of colonial legislatures, the keeping of British troops in the colonies in time of peace, the denial of trial by jury, the lack of representation in Parliament, and other acts considered to be threats to colonial liberties. The Declaration reached the conclusion that when these rights were denied—rights that Americans believed were natural rights given by God to all people—the only option was revolution against British rule.

What basic rights does the Constitution itself guarantee?

Even though a Bill of Rights was needed to complete the Constitution, the writers of that document did not neglect the subject of individual rights. Five important safeguards are included in the body of the Constitution itself.

WRIT OF *HABEAS CORPUS*
(ARTICLE I, SECTION 9)

Without the protection of the right to a writ of *habeas corpus*, a prisoner might be held indefinitely without being arraigned (charged with the crime)—as often happens in a dictatorship. A writ of *habeas corpus* leaves the arresting agency with only two choices: (1) to bring the prisoner into court to be arraigned or (2) to release the prisoner. The restriction is absolute, and the interval between arrest and arraignment cannot

Figure 13.5
Sample writ of habeas corpus

SUPERIOR COURT OF THE STATE OF CALIFORNIA
FOR THE COUNTY OF LOS ANGELES

In the Matter of the Application of

CASE NUMBER

H. C.   0000-00

JOHN DOE,   Petitioner

WRIT OF HABEAS CORPUS
1474 Penal Code
Criminal

On Behalf of   **SAM DOE**

THE PEOPLE OF THE STATE OF CALIFORNIA, TO:

_____**HARRY DOE**_____SHERIFF. CHIEF OF POLICE.

GREETINGS:

We command you to have the body of _____**Sam Doe**_____ _____

---

who is now imprisoned and detained by you, together with the reasons for such imprisonment and detention

and the length of time imprisoned, by whatever name said prisoner shall be called or charged before the

Honorable _____**Peter Doe**_____ , Judge of the Superior Court, for the

County of Los Angeles, State of California, in Department No. **24**_____ , located at **Big**_____

_____**Town, USA**_____ , on__ **June 20**____ , 19 **--**, at **10 A** M.,

for proceedings concerning the said prisoner; and have with you this writ.

Said prisoner may be released upon the posting of $____**500.00**____ Bail plus penalty assessment of

$____**none**____.

NO BAIL FIXED.

Dated: **June 19, 19--**

WILLIAM G. SHARP, County Clerk and Clerk
of the Superior Court of the State of California
for the County of Los Angeles.

By_____ Deputy

exceed a day or two. The writ may be asked for by the prisoner or an
attorney, and is issued by the appropriate court (a sample writ is reproduced in Figure 13.5). This protection against lengthy imprisonment
without a trial can be suspended only in time of rebellion or invasion.

NO BILL OF ATTAINDER
(ARTICLE I, SECTION 9)

Passage of any *bill of attainder* is expressly forbidden by the Constitution.
Under this type of law, an individual may be found guilty of an offense

without ever having gone through a court trial. Such laws were common in the colonial period, and violated the American concept of limited government and the right to trial by jury. A traffic law that gave a police officer the right to fine a speeder on the spot would be a bill of attainder.

NO *EX POST FACTO* LAWS
(ARTICLE I, SECTION 9)

An *ex post facto* law makes a crime of an act that was not illegal at the time it was performed. Let's say that the city council's new parking ordinance goes into effect on Wednesday. Any tickets given to cars parked in the newly restricted areas before Wednesday would be *ex post facto* and therefore illegal.

Three factors define an *ex post facto* law: (1) it must be retroactive (it applies to acts that were performed before the law took effect); (2) it must impose harsher penalties than existing laws do; and (3) it must deal with a criminal matter (as opposed to a civil procedure). For example, a new law making the penalties for arson—a criminal offense— more severe could apply only to offenses committed after the new law became valid. In a civil matter such as a zoning change, however, a dairy farm might be forced to leave a residential area even though the farm was there long before the houses were built.

NARROW DEFINITION OF TREASON
(ARTICLE III, SECTION 3)

The Constitution defines *treason* (betrayal of one's country) very narrowly. After all, the Framers knew that had the revolutionary forces lost the war, many of them would have been considered traitors by the British government. Since the crime then carried the death penalty, three limitations on conviction were established: (1) two or more witnesses must testify to knowledge of the act; (2) the treasonous act must be a definite physical action, as opposed to attendance at a meeting or mere talk about treason; and (3) a confession is admissible only if the accused person admits his or her guilt in open court.

RIGHT TO TRIAL BY JURY
(ARTICLE III, SECTION 2)

Except in cases of impeachment, the Constitution guarantees a trial by jury in all criminal cases. As was described earlier in this chapter, the Bill of Rights defines this protection more fully (see pages 318–20).

How do the states guarantee individual rights?

Each state operates under a contract with its people defined by a state constitution. Indeed, Congress examines the constitution of a prospective state as part of the process by which it decides if a territory is ready for statehood. Although every state constitution is different, each one spells out such matters as legislative organization, separation of powers, educational rights, voting regulations, and tax procedures.

Many of the rights established in the national Constitution are not necessarily binding upon the states. Each state, therefore, includes a bill of rights in its own constitution specifically aimed at protecting its citizens from abuses of power by state or city government. Most—but not all—of the same freedoms defined by the national Bill of Rights appear in these state constitutions.

Through the federal courts, however, the basic freedoms contained in the national Constitution have been extended to the state level. With the ratification of the Fourteenth Amendment, the means of extending constitutional guarantees became available. Federal judges have found the necessary authority in the statement, "No state shall make or enforce any law which shall abridge the privileges or immunities of citizens of the United States" (Fourteenth Amendment, Section 1).

How did the "civil liberties" amendments enlarge individual rights?

Even though the Constitution and the Bill of Rights apparently resolved all questions regarding civil rights, new circumstances in the years following the Civil War required further constitutional amendments. The Thirteenth, Fourteenth, and Fifteenth Amendments tackled the problems faced by the newly freed blacks; the Nineteenth Amendment extended the franchise to women; the Twenty-fourth Amendment ended the use of the poll tax as a means of restricting voting rights; the Twenty-sixth Amendment gave the vote to eighteen-year-olds; and in the 1970's, the proposed Twenty-seventh Amendment sought to provide equal rights to women in all areas of American life.

THIRTEENTH AMENDMENT (1865)

This brief amendment formally abolished slavery and involuntary servitude in the United States. The restriction on involuntary servitude does not apply when a court sentences a convicted criminal to jail as punishment for his or her crime.

FOURTEENTH AMENDMENT (1868)

Southern resistance to acceptance of black people as full citizens under the law did not end with the Civil War. Congress passed the first section of the Fourteenth Amendment as a means of eliminating "black codes" and other postwar restrictions on the civil rights of the former slaves. The amendment promised that no state may deprive its inhabitants of "life, liberty, or property, without due process of law." This phrase was then interpreted as applying all Fifth Amendment protections to every citizen. More recently, as discussed earlier in this chapter, it has been used to apply all constitutional guarantees to every American, whatever the individual's color, religion, wealth, or place of residence.

This amendment forbids any state to deny its citizens "the equal protection of the laws"; but this does not compel government to treat all people alike. Age restrictions on the purchase of tobacco or alcohol, for example, remain perfectly legal. Rather, *equal protection of the laws* means that the rights given to any citizens within a certain category will not be denied to others in that same category because of arbitrary state standards. This philosophy led the Supreme Court in 1978 to issue the Bakke decision, which prohibited universities from using quotas as a way of guaranteeing minority admissions. The court described quotas as reverse discrimination.

FIFTEENTH AMENDMENT (1870)

Another brief amendment, the Fifteenth specifically extended state and federal voting privileges to all male Americans. Minimum requirements of age and residence set by the individual states are still permitted, but the right to vote cannot be denied "on account of race, color, or previous condition of servitude."

NINETEENTH AMENDMENT (1920)

Previous extensions of voting rights had guaranteed the franchise for all American men, but women remained powerless observers of the political scene. The suffrage movement of the late 1800's and early 1900's finally resulted in ratification of the Nineteenth Amendment, which states that the right to vote shall not be denied in any federal or state election "on account of sex."

TWENTY-SIXTH AMENDMENT (1971)

A long-standing dispute over the age at which minors should receive full citizenship privileges ended in 1971 with the ratification of the Twenty-sixth Amendment. Under the terms of this amendment, citizens who are eighteen years of age or older may not be denied the vote in federal or state elections "on account of age."

EQUAL RIGHTS AMENDMENT

Full equality under the law for American women moved closer to reality in the 1970's. Congress passed the Equal Rights Amendment (ERA) in 1972, forty-nine years after it was first introduced, and sent it to the states for ratification as the Twenty-seventh Amendment. Under the ERA, "equality of rights under the law shall not be denied or abridged by the United States or by any state on account of sex." Even though Congress extended the deadline for ratification in 1979 for three years, the amendment still did not gain approval by the required number of states.

How does a person gain—and keep—citizenship?

The Fourteenth Amendment defines *citizenship* quite precisely: "All persons born or naturalized in the United States . . . are citizens of the United

States and of the state wherein they reside." The main body of the Constitution does not define the term, although the word "citizen" is used several times. In any event, a legal definition gives only part of the meaning.

RIGHTS AND PRIVILEGES

United States citizenship carries with it a number of rights and privileges. Only citizens may vote in state and national elections, or serve on juries. Many jobs are open only to citizens, including elective offices and sensitive positions in defense industries. *Aliens* (noncitizens living in the United States) do qualify for most of the same constitutional protections enjoyed by citizens—freedom of speech and religion, trial by jury, and ownership of property. By the same token, aliens must accept many responsibilities— obeying the laws of the land, paying taxes, serving in the armed forces, and the like.

ACQUIRING CITIZENSHIP

Citizenship may be acquired in any of three ways:

1. Birth to American parents. If either of a child's parents holds United States citizenship, the child is automatically an American citizen at birth. This rule applies even though the child is born outside the United States.

2. Birth within United States to alien parents. A fairly common sight at international airports or border crossing points is that of a pregnant woman entering the United States to give birth to her child. By doing so, she gives her baby the right to United States citizenship, no matter where she and her husband were born. These children usually hold *dual citizenship*, which means that they are citizens of two countries at the same time. In most cases, dual citizenship lasts only until the age of twenty-eight, when these people must decide which country they wish to claim as their native land.

3. Naturalization. Any alien who wishes to become a citizen of this country may do so through a process called *naturalization*. When the candidate is already a resident of the United States, the process of naturalization involves three steps:

a. *Statement of intent.* The citizen-to-be first files a statement of intent (called "first papers"), which declares that the individual is over eighteen years of age, is ready to give up his or her former citizenship, and intends to become a United States citizen.

b. *Second statement.* After five years of residence in this country (three years for foreign-born spouses of American citizens), the prospective citizen files a second statement. These papers include personal data, two statements from citizens testifying to the person's good character, a statement renouncing the former citizenship, and a statement swearing that he or she has never belonged to any group advocating the violent overthrow of the government of the United States.

Figure 13.6

On July 4, 1976, America's two-hundredth birthday, more than 7,000 new citizens solemnly swear allegiance to the United States at a mass naturalization ceremony in Miami Beach, Florida. Source: Wide World Photos.

c. *Taking the oath.* Finally, the applicants appear before a federal judge, to whom they demonstrate their ability to read and write English and their knowledge of the American system of government. After passing this test, the aliens recite the oath of allegiance to their new country (see Figure 13.6). In a formal but always emotional ceremony, the judge awards a certificate of citizenship to each new American. Children under the age of sixteen automatically become citizens at the same time their parents are naturalized. The new citizens have equal status with natural-born citizens in every way except one—no one not born to United States citizenship may become President of this country.

LOSS OF CITIZENSHIP

United States citizens may lose their citizenship (1) by deliberately renouncing it; (2) upon conviction of treason or of attempting to overthrow the United States government by force; (3) by serving in the armed forces of a foreign country without the written permission of the Secretary of State or the Secretary of Defense; or (4) by becoming a naturalized citizen of another country. Americans with dual citizenship may lose their United States citizenship by choosing the other country over this one, or by not maintaining residence in this country.

Partial loss of citizenship privileges follows a felony conviction (see page 363). Even after "paying their debt to society" by serving a prison term, convicted felons may not vote, serve on juries, or hold most public offices. Recent court decisions have tended to restore most citizenship rights formerly lost through criminal convictions.

When may civil liberties
be limited or suspended?

The civil liberties guaranteed by the Constitution and the Bill of Rights stand as a firm shield against the misuse of governmental power. Overriding requirements related to the maintenance of public safety sometimes demand that civil liberties be temporarily suspended, however. In times of emergency, the governors of the individual states have the power to declare *martial law*, which places a designated area under military control. National emergencies similarly allow the President to suspend individual freedoms, including the rights of *habeas corpus* and freedom of movement.

THE "CLEAR AND PRESENT DANGER" DOCTRINE

Justice Oliver Wendell Holmes wrote the formula by which the courts determine when suspension of liberties is justified. Holmes specified that a "clear and present danger" to public safety or to national security must exist before the government may move to restrict any freedom. The Smith Act of 1940, for example, makes it illegal for any person to teach or advocate violent overthrow of the government of the United States. The law bases its restriction of the First Amendment right of free speech on the belief that "words can be weapons" in any effort to arouse people to violent revolutionary actions.

APPEAL TO THE COURTS

Any suspension of civil liberties may be appealed in the courts. President Lincoln's suspension of *habeas corpus* at the onset of the Civil War was overthrown in the case of *Ex parte Milligan* (1866) soon after the war ended. Convictions under the Smith Act are allowed to stand only if a defendant has actually urged people to *do* something; an attempt to change the way someone *thinks* does not constitute a violation of this law.

===

Summary and Conclusions

1. The Bill of Rights provides an enduring heritage upon which American citizens may depend. The first ten amendments to the Constitution secure for us such important rights as freedom of religion, speech, and the press; the right to assemble and petition for change; freedom from unreasonable search and seizure of one's person or property; guarantee of a fair trial before a jury of one's peers; and protection from cruel and unusual punishment.

2. With a tradition of English common law and of self-rule, the American colonists gradually developed clear and workable concepts of the role of government and its relationship to individual rights. The Constitution defined such rights in five areas—guaranteeing the right to a writ of

habeas corpus, banning bills of attainder and *ex post facto* laws, restricting the definition of treason, and guaranteeing the right to trial by jury.

3. State constitutions also carry their own bills of rights. In most cases, these repeat the federal guarantees, but may also include statements on the right to education and restrictions on police or legislative power. The federal Constitution's civil rights guarantees did not originally apply to Americans in their relations with the individual states. The Fourteenth Amendment's guarantees of due process of law and of equal protection under the law, however, have now been extended to bring all violations of individual rights under the federal law.

4. Not only have the courts continued to extend personal freedoms, but the Constitution itself has been amended to meet new problems. The Thirteenth, Fourteenth, and Fifteenth Amendments granted full citizenship privileges to the former black slaves after the Civil War. Voting rights have also been broadened. The Nineteenth Amendment extended the franchise to women, while the Twenty-sixth did the same for people eighteen to twenty years of age.

5. The rights and privileges of American citizenship are given to all persons born or naturalized in this country. Most Americans gain their citizenship by being born to American parents, but a child born in this country to alien parents also qualifies for citizenship. The foreign-born may elect to become naturalized citizens after meeting residence, language, and loyalty requirements.

6. The rights of citizenship may be suspended under certain circumstances, such as natural disaster, foreign invasion, or rebellion. The rise of totalitarian systems such as communism have also led the courts to confirm certain restrictions Congress has placed on First Amendment freedoms. The rule established by the Supreme Court permits suspension of these rights if a "clear and present danger" can be proven.

REVIEW QUESTIONS AND ACTIVITIES

TERMS YOU SHOULD KNOW

alien	*libel*
bill of attainder	*martial law*
citizenship	*naturalization*
dual citizenship	*right of eminent domain*
due process	*salutary neglect*
equal protection of the laws	*slander*
ex post facto *law*	*treason*
immunity from prosecution	*writ of* habeas corpus
indictment	

REVIEW QUESTIONS

The following multiple-choice questions are based on the important ideas presented in this chapter. Select the response that best completes each statement.

1. In a democracy like the United States, the wishes of the majority must always outweigh the wishes of a minority. This statement is (a) true. (b) false; the minority must always come first. (c) false; certain basic rights must be safeguarded, no matter how unpopular their expression might be.

2. Statements printed in a newspaper that maliciously injure someone's good name may be cause for a lawsuit under the laws against (a) slander. (b) sedition. (c) libel. (d) treason. (e) malicious mischief.

3. In order for a revolutionary speech to be considered cause for arrest, the government must prove that it constituted (a) a clear and present danger. (b) a violation of public morality. (c) a view contrary to that held by the majority of U.S. citizens. (d) an offense against tradition or custom. (e) a promotion of a foreign system of government.

4. The right to "keep and bear arms" is an absolute privilege granted under the Bill of Rights. This statement is (a) true. (b) false; the government already places many restrictions upon the use of arms. (c) false; the government has the right to decide upon all matters of public safety without worry about constitutional restrictions.

5. Police may legally invade the security of a private home (a) when invited to do so by the occupant. (b) when in possession of a valid search warrant. (c) when in "hot pursuit" of a fleeing lawbreaker. (d) when required to do so in a situation of extreme emergency, such as a fire or explosion. (e) all of these are legal situations.

6. The due process clause in the Fifth and Fourteenth Amendments defines a citizen's right to fair and equal protection under state and federal laws. This statement is (a) true. (b) false; "due process" refers to the process by which an alien becomes a citizen. (c) false; the Constitution makes no mention of "due process" in any amendment.

7. The American colonists based their decision to revolt against British rule on (a) their dislike of being English subjects. (b) the belief that they were being denied their rights as English subjects. (c) their desire to do away with all government controls over their lives. (d) the wish to do away with all taxation. (e) the wish to become part of the French possessions in the New World.

8. Federal protections written into the Bill of Rights have always applied to state law as well. This statement is (a) true. (b) false; the Constitution forbids the federal government to interfere with state laws. (c) false; not until 1868 did the due process clause of the Fourteenth Amendment give the courts the legal means of extending federal civil rights guarantees to cases involving state laws.

9. Noncitizens living in the United States receive equal protection under the guarantees of the Constitution. This statement is (a) true. (b) false; aliens may be tried in special government courts that do not follow the usual procedures for trial by jury. (c) false; aliens do not pay taxes, so they do not receive civil rights protections.

10. A child would *not* have United States citizenship who was born to (a) U.S. citizens living in Russia. (b) Mexican citizens living in San Diego, California. (c) an American citizen married to a Japanese citizen and living in Afghanistan. (d) parents who had become naturalized citizens two years before. (e) all would be U.S. citizens.

CONCEPT DEVELOPMENT

This chapter has explored a number of significant concepts relating to individual rights. You can use your skills in thinking, researching, and writing to answer the following questions.

1. Why did Americans demand the addition of a Bill of Rights to the Constitution? Are any further protections needed today?

2. Discuss Lincoln's suspension of *habeas corpus* in the opening days of the Civil War. Do you believe that this was justified? Why or why not?

3. Which four constitutional rights are most important to you? Why?

4. Why does the American system of government work so hard to maintain the separation of church and state? What are your own feelings about the questions of school prayer and federal aid to religious schools?

5. The struggle for civil rights by minority groups in the United States has been a long and difficult one. Summarize the conflicts involved in obtaining full civil rights by one minority group—blacks, Chicanos, Oriental Americans, or any other.

ACTIVITIES

The following activities are designed to help you use the ideas developed in this chapter.

1. Do Americans really believe in the Bill of Rights? You can conduct an interesting experiment to investigate that question. Write up the Bill of Rights guarantees in the form of a petition demanding that these freedoms be granted to spokespersons for unpopular causes in your community. Circulate the petition in a local shopping center, asking people to read and sign if they agree with it. Keep a record of each person's response to the request to sign. Write a report on your data.

2. Ask your parents, relatives, and friends to help you locate several naturalized citizens. Interview these people, recording (a) their experiences in immigrating to this country and obtaining citizenship and (b) their attitudes toward the United States and the value of their citizenship.

3. Invite a member of a local civil rights organization to speak to your class on the work the group does in the community. Typical groups that you are likely to find in your area are the American Civil Liberties Union (ACLU), the NAACP, the National Organization for Women, Common Cause, and the Anti-Defamation League of B'nai B'rith.

4. Research a number of civil rights cases (see that listing in the card catalog), extracting the basic facts of each case. Present these to your class, either orally or in written form. Ask the class to judge the cases. How do the results compare with the actual decisions? What factors make it so difficult to predict consistently the direction the courts will take?

5

THE AMERICAN
POLITICAL
PROCESS

CHAPTER FOURTEEN

THE AMERICAN POLITICAL SYSTEM

The scene: The icy streets of the towns and cities of New Hampshire.

The date: Spring, 1968. New Hampshire's presidential primary election, the first in the nation.

The plot: Can an army of college students, political novices all, unseat an incumbent President of the United States?

Only a movie script writer would have dared develop such a scenario. Still, the conditions were right. The American people no longer believed that democracy's future depended on events in Vietnam. Lyndon Johnson, the Democratic President, had become the symbol for a growing national tragedy.

When Senator Eugene McCarthy, Democrat from Minnesota, stepped forward as an antiwar candidate, more than 3,000 enthusiastic college students joined him in New Hampshire for that election year's first primary campaign. They cranked up their mimeograph machines, knocked on doors, and laid their beliefs on the line. In the two weeks before the election, they spoke to 30,000 voters and left leaflets for 10,000 more. By election eve, their personal appeals had reached over one-half the homes in the state.

Political polls traced the growing impact of this youth-oriented campaign. In January, the Gallup poll scorned McCarthy's chances, awarding him a scant 12 percent of the state's Democratic vote. In February, President Johnson's private poll revealed that the antiwar vote had increased to 18 percent. Just before the election, New Hampshire's governor predicted that McCarthy's strength would peak at 25 percent. Only Eugene

McCarthy and his "kids" believed that Johnson's presidency had begun to collapse.

Election night proved that the polls had misjudged the mood of the voters. When precinct workers added Republican write-in ballots to the Democratic tally, President Johnson's lead over McCarthy shrank to a razor-thin margin of 230 votes. The McCarthy forces celebrated briefly, then headed for Wisconsin, site of the next primary.

All through March, the college students continued to work their political magic. In the hard, daily grind of the American election process, their energy and determination struck sparks. The new polls forecast an overwhelming McCarthy victory. What would the President do?

The answer came with dramatic suddenness. On Sunday, March 31, the President electrified the nation by announcing, "I shall not seek and I will not accept the nomination of my party for another term as your President."

The thousands of antiwar students had succeeded in mobilizing public opinion against the war and the President who was blamed for it. They had demonstrated that citizens who understand the workings of the American political system can win a major victory—even when opposing that most powerful of all political animals, an incumbent President.

Unfortunately, the end of this story does not match its upbeat opening. The bitterly contested Democratic convention turned away from Eugene McCarthy and nominated Hubert Humphrey. Four years later, George McGovern carried the antiwar banner to a convention victory, to the joy of the old McCarthy supporters. Both men lost to Richard Nixon—Humphrey by a narrow margin in the 1968 election, McGovern by a landslide in 1972.

This chapter will attempt to give you some answers to the following questions about the workings of the American political system:

1. What is a political party?
2. What do political parties accomplish?
3. Why does the United States retain the two-party system?
4. How did the American two-party system develop?
5. How have third parties affected the American political system?
6. What do political labels really stand for?
7. How is a political party organized?
8. What happens at a party convention?
9. What are the steps in the presidential election cycle?

What is a political party?

In a democracy, the people select their government and influence its policies through their vote. Those same people differ greatly, however, when deciding the direction that government should take on any given issue. When like-minded people join together to achieve common political goals, a *political party* results.

REQUIREMENTS FOR A POLITICAL PARTY

Before a group of citizens may be considered a true political party (as opposed to a pressure group), three elements must be present:

1. *Shared beliefs.* All members must hold some degree of belief in the same political philosophy and be willing to work for the same goals.

2. *Program.* All members must agree upon a program for translating their beliefs into law once they have obtained political office.

3. *Chance of success.* The membership must have a realistic chance of winning an election or implementing its programs, either now or at some future time.

Lacking these qualifications, the organization should properly be classified as a *pressure group* (see Chapters 5 and 16). The American political system extends power only to organized parties which can deliver votes on election day.

HISTORICAL DEVELOPMENT

Political parties are a relatively new invention. Parties did not exist in England before the American Revolution in a form that we would recognize today, even though politicians divided themselves into Whigs and Tories. George Washington, in fact, warned against the development of political parties in his Farewell Address:

> Let me now . . . warn you in the most solemn manner against the baneful effects of the spirit of party generally. . . . It serves to distract public councils and enfeebles the public administration. It agitates the community with ill-founded jealousies and false alarms. [It] kindles the animosity of one part against another.

The advice went unheeded. By the end of Washington's term of office in 1797, the United States had already established the pattern for a two-party system. Since then the American political party has become the model for similar political associations in almost all other democratically governed countries.

What do political parties accomplish?

In a democracy, the needs of many competing interests must be balanced before even the most worthwhile idea can be enacted into law. There are five ways in which political parties provide the vehicle needed to convert goals into law.

1. ORGANIZE A POLITICAL MAJORITY

People join the political party that best reflects their own ideas about economics, foreign affairs, social welfare, personal freedom, and the like. In a two-party system, neither political party could possibly hold positions

identical with the beliefs of every individual voter. Political power, therefore, falls to the party that comes closest to representing the majority's
wishes at any given time.

2. PROVIDE REASONABLE CHOICES

Political parties serve as a screening device. Each party's candidates must
appear before the public and state their positions on the issues. Public
opinion, the media, and the party leadership combine to eliminate candidates with unpopular, unworkable, or extremist views. When election time
arrives, the party and its candidates have usually adjusted their positions
to meet the wishes of what they hope will be a majority of the voters.

3. EDUCATE VOTERS

American election campaigns provide prolonged periods during which
candidates circulate widely, publicizing their views on important questions
of the day (see Figure 14.1). The party writes a *platform* that summarizes
its position on national priorities. Candidates list the specific steps they
will take if they are elected. Ideally, by the time voters reach the polling
place, they have heard and read enough information to make logical
choices.

Figure 14.1

Presidential campaigners
travel widely during the long
election campaign in order to
assess the grass-roots sentiments of voters, to excite the
public, and to strengthen the
appeal of all the party's candidates—like Lyndon Johnson,
one of the greatest campaigners of recent times. Source:
Lyndon Baines Johnson Library.

4. MAKE ELECTION TO OFFICE POSSIBLE

A political party endures as a continuing institution even after it has suffered years of defeat. National in scope, parties can raise the large sums of money needed to conduct an election campaign. Few candidates, even the wealthiest, could raise the millions of dollars eaten up by advertising, television, travel, staff, and the other requirements of a modern campaign. Candidates in local elections, despite their smaller budgets, also need the organization, loyalties, and financing a party can provide.

5. PROVIDE PEOPLE TO RUN THE GOVERNMENT

Once a party wins control of the presidency or Congress, it staffs most high government positions with its own members. The civil service laws prevent a repetition of the spoils system developed during the 1800's, but many executive and judicial jobs fall naturally into the hands of the winners.

In England, when the ruling party in Parliament loses a vote on an important issue, it must resign immediately. American law does not require such abrupt changes of government, but the public does tend to hold a party responsible for what happens during its term of office. Herbert Hoover and the Republican party, for example, received the blame for the Great Depression that followed the stock market crash of 1929. When such a disaster strikes, the party in power almost always loses the next election.

Why does the United States retain the two-party system?

Despite some obvious flaws, such as the difficulty of encompassing all political beliefs within two major parties, the two-party system seems destined to endure in the United States. Four reasons for the long life of this system are as follows:

1. DESIRE FOR STABILITY

Many countries, Italy and Israel among them, support numerous political parties. With the vote split six or eight ways, it often happens that no single party gains control of the government. When this occurs, a *coalition*, or combination of parties, must be formed before a chief executive can be chosen. This multi-party system, which may result in rapidly changing, unstable governments, never became part of American politics.

2. NATIONAL ELECTION LAWS

American election laws favor the two-party system. Most elected positions are decided on the basis of "winner take all." A major party's candidates might win all the congressional seats in a given state with only 51 percent of the vote in each district. Smaller parties, therefore, stand little chance of gaining national representation.

3. SIZE OF THE FEDERAL SYSTEM

The very size of the United States has helped create the two-party system. Many *third parties* (also known as *minority parties*), despite strong local support, have discovered that their regional appeal cannot command national attention. Third parties have occasionally carried cities, and even states. But before a minority party can grow big and powerful enough to succeed on the national level, one of the major parties usually takes over its ideas and issues.

4. TRADITION OF ALTERNATION IN OFFICE

No American political party has ever "owned" the national government. Democrats and Republicans have each enjoyed long periods of success, but inevitably the voters tire of the same old policies and return the other party to power. Although the Democrats held the balance of power for most of the years from Jefferson's presidency until the Civil War, the Republicans came back to win fourteen of the next eighteen national elections between 1860 and 1928.

How did the American two-party system develop?

Modern political parties began to develop in the United States in 1787, during the campaign to ratify the Constitution. One faction of the new country's leadership wanted a strong federal government. Calling themselves *Federalists*, they took on a political selling job aimed at convincing the legislatures of the thirteen states that they should ratify the Constitution. The opposition, known as the *Anti-Federalists*, believed that the state governments should retain more independence. The Anti-Federalists also objected to the absence of specific guarantees of personal freedom in the Constitution. The ratification of the Constitution in 1788, along with the Bill of Rights, failed to end this division.

Early in the 1790's, the two factions clashed again. This time, the issue grew out of the Federalist proposal for a national bank that would control the country's currency. By 1794, seats in Congress were regularly being contested on a party basis.

DEVELOPMENT OF THE DEMOCRATIC PARTY

Thomas Jefferson led the Anti-Federalists, who by 1800 had changed their name to the *Democratic-Republican party*. Jefferson's political ideas appealed to the country, and he defeated John Adams, the second and last Federalist President. The Federalist belief in government by an aristocracy, plus a continuing distrust of strong national government, helped ensure Adams' defeat.

The Era of Good Feeling, dominated by the Democratic-Republican presidency of James Monroe, lasted until 1824. In the 1830's, Andrew Jackson restructured the *Democratic party* ("Republican" had been dropped from the name in 1825). Unable to hold on to the White House consistently between 1860 and 1932, the Democrats gradually changed from a states' rights party to one that believes in a strong federal authority. The modern Democratic party, with its emphasis on "the common people," dedicates itself to using government to solve the problems that neither the individual nor the states can solve for themselves.

DEVELOPMENT OF THE REPUBLICAN PARTY

Today's Republican party traces its history back to the original Federalists. The Federalist party had largely broken up by the end of the War of 1812. The short-lived *National Republican party* took its place, only to be absorbed by the *Whig party* in the 1830's. The Whigs won with William Henry Harrison in 1840 and with Zachary Taylor in 1848, but divided and disappeared in the 1850's over the slavery question.

The heritage of the Federalist-Whig party fell to a minority party that was organized in 1854 on a platform of opposition to slavery. Abraham Lincoln led the new *Republican party* to its first national victory in 1860, beginning a domination of American politics that ended with the election of Franklin Roosevelt in 1932.

Like the Democratic party, the Republicans have undergone a major transformation in basic political philosophy. The original Federalists believed in a strong federal authority, but modern Republicans favor states' rights and individual freedom from government control.

DANGERS OF HISTORICAL COMPARISONS

A word of caution should be added regarding the dangers of comparing political beliefs over a span of two centuries. Despite the apparent shift in philosophy noted above, most Republicans today accept much more involvement by the federal government in everyday affairs than any Federalist would have believed possible. Times change, and so does politics.

How have third parties affected the American political system?

The modern Republican party began as a minority, sectional party. In 1860, however, it emerged as the country's second major party. No other minority party has ever made that leap. Most of the third parties in our history have had to be content with a satellite role relative to the majority parties. Minority party candidates have little hope of election in their own right.

The American campaign trail has been well traveled by third parties,

Table 14.1
A sampling of third parties in American politics

Party	Dates	Description
Liberal party	1840–48	First antislavery party.
Free-Soil party	1848–56	Favored free territories in the West.
American party (Know-Nothings)	1852–60	Anti-immigrant, anti-Catholic party. Nickname grew out of members' claim, when questioned, to "know nothing" about the party.
Prohibition party	1869–	Based on opposition to use of alcohol. Worked for Eighteenth Amendment.
Greenback party	1876–84	Supported paper money, extension of federal power, and the income tax.
Socialist party	1890–	Favors government ownership of natural resources and of major industries.
Populist party	1891–96	Farmer and worker party; antimonopoly.
Progressive Bull Moose party	1912–16	Teddy Roosevelt's split from conservative Republicanism.
Progressive party	1924–46	LaFollette's semi-socialistic party; promoted government ownership and regulation of business and resources.
States' Rights party (Dixiecrats)	1948	Southern Democratic split over civil rights question.
American Independent party	1968–	George Wallace's states'-rights party.
Peace and Freedom party	1968–	Antiwar, antidraft, left-wing movement.

however, as Table 14.1 demonstrates. In those states where few require-ments exist for adding a party's candidates to the ballot, voters may be faced with six or more choices for President. Once their candidates qualify to be put on the ballot, most minority parties do not make a serious campaign effort. Instead, they use the publicity generated by their campaign to advance some special cause. Their goals may be as special-ized as vegetarianism, or as basic as constitutional revision.

ECONOMIC GOALS

A few third parties have done more than satisfy private enthusiasms. The *Populist party*, active in the 1880's and 1890's, consisted mainly of dis-contented farmers in the West and South who felt ignored by the major parties. The Populists wanted federal ownership of the railroads, a grad-uated income tax, and unlimited coinage of silver and gold at a 16-to-1 ratio. On this platform, the Populist party won some city elections, elected state legislators, and sent representatives to Congress. Nevertheless, the Populists disappeared when many of their ideas were incorporated into the Democratic party platform.

Malice in Wonderland

Figure 14.2

Extremist movements of the far right bring their own brand of malice to the American political tea party. Source: Bill Mauldin, Chicago *Sun-Times*.

SECTIONAL DISCONTENT

Some third parties have reflected sectional discontent rather than economic ideas. The *States' Rights party* polled more than a million votes in the 1948 national election. Its membership was composed of Southern Democrats who were unhappy with the liberal civil rights platform supported by the regular Democratic candidate, Harry S Truman.

A similar Southern movement produced the *American Independent party* of George Wallace in 1968. Heavy Southern support for the AIP stripped enough votes from the Democrats to send Richard Nixon to the White House with less than 50 percent of the popular vote.

RADICAL POLITICS

Pursuit of radical political philosophies has often created third-party movements. The *Socialist party* has participated in national elections for many years. The *Peace and Freedom party* became active in 1968, primarily in opposition to the war in Vietnam. At the conservative end of the political spectrum, the *Know-Nothings* and the *American Nazi party* have at times attempted to use political means to promote their limited goals, but with little success (see Figure 14.2).

SINGLE–ISSUE PARTIES

Occasionally, a party emerges to focus attention on a single issue. The *Prohibition party*, which helped promote the Eighteenth Amendment, drew its entire strength from its opposition to the sale and use of alcoholic beverages. Teddy Roosevelt created the *Progressive Bull Moose party* in 1912 largely through the force of his own vigorous personality.

LET'S REVIEW FOR A MOMENT

A political party may be defined as an organization of people who attempt to elect government officials and influence government policies. To be a true party, as distinct from a pressure group, the party must demonstrate (1) common beliefs, (2) a program of action should they be elected, and (3) a reasonable chance of success.

Can you remember the five functions of political parties in a democracy? They serve to (1) organize a political majority, (2) provide reasonable choices, (3) educate the public, (4) make election to office possible, and (5) provide personnel for government service.

The two-party system took hold largely because the United States elects its officials on a "winner-take-all" basis. The desire for stability, the size of the federal system, and changes in policy by the major parties to keep themselves in power have also helped restrict the growth of minority parties. Can you remember the different names the Republicans and Democrats have been known by during their history? Let's see. Federalists → National Republicans → Whigs → Republicans → the modern Republican party. The Democratic genealogy reads like this: Anti-Federalists → Democratic-Republicans → Democrats → the modern Democratic party.

Now let's look at some of the political labels that are frequently pasted on the various members of our major parties.

What do political labels really stand for?

Can you imagine shopping in a market where none of the cans, bottles, and packages were labeled? Without some type of identifying markings, you couldn't tell a can of peas from a tin of sauerkraut. While the country hasn't yet required that its politicians wear identifying tags, people are always more comfortable when they can fit candidates into pigeonholes neatly labeled with their political philosophy.

The use of political labels can never be totally precise, of course. As the issues change, and as the society's values shift, the meaning of political labels changes as well. Many people see terms like "liberal" and "conservative" as carrying judgments of good or bad; in reality, these value standards depend almost totally on one's own political beliefs.

Figure 14.3 shows how the most common political labels relate to one another. In general, groups who want more government action are called *left wing*; thus they are placed on the left side of the diagram. Those who

Figure 14.3
The American political spectrum

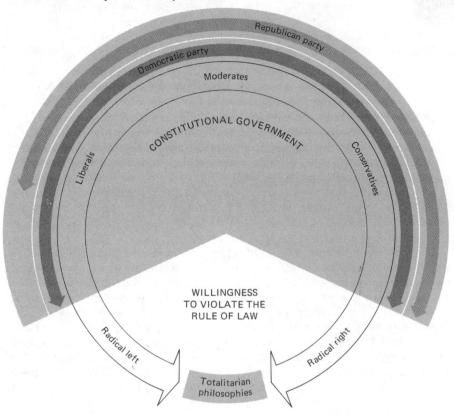

want less government control are called *right wing*; they appear on the right side of the diagram. The terms date back to the French Revolution, when the members of the National Convention seated themselves on the left or right side of the presiding officer's podium, according to their political philosophy—liberal or conservative. Now let's discuss the political labels shown in the diagram.

RADICAL

A *radical* might be described as someone who believes (1) that the problems of the country can be solved only through extreme measures and (2) that the change should take place immediately. Some radical groups are content to work within the structure of the democratic process. Others believe in revolutionary change.

The *radical right* consists of groups that sometimes gather under the flag of zealous anticommunism. Often known as *reactionaries*, they denounce most forms of government regulation, including welfare payments, progressive taxation, and restrictions on business and industry. Strangely enough, these radicals would not hesitate to use government or police power to enforce the changes they desire. Examples of political groups on the radical right are the John Birch Society, the National States' Rights Party, and the Christian Crusade.

The *radical left*, on the other hand, often marches under the banner of socialism. Groups like the Socialist Workers party and Students for a Democratic Society believe that the problems of poverty, race relations, and unequal distribution of wealth can best be solved by government takeover of the country's natural and industrial resources.

LIBERAL

Liberals look to the government for solutions to the many problems of modern life. They accept increased government regulation as a price to be paid in return for providing everyone with basic human necessities. Liberals advocate gradual change by democratic means, rather than by revolution. Most liberals, for example, would not favor government take-over of the medical profession. Instead, they would vote for government-guaranteed health insurance, extended Medicare programs, and greater supervision of the entire health industry.

MODERATE

A *moderate* occupies that political position called "the middle of the road." Politicians do not dare ignore the moderate vote, for the great majority of Americans can usually be found voting under this label. Although moderates largely accept government as they find it, they often favor new and better laws. Their loyalties, however, may shift to the liberal or conservative side, depending on the issue to be decided.

CONSERVATIVE

Conservatives believe that "that government governs best which governs least." They hold that most regulation by the federal government should be transferred to the state or local level. The conservatives' ultimate goal would be to give each individual a maximum amount of freedom to attend to his or her own affairs. In this way, responsibility for the public welfare could be taken out of what they see as government's costly and inefficient hands.

INADEQUACY OF LABELS

Even though terms like "liberal" and "conservative" are convenient to use, they can never fully describe a person's total political beliefs. Sharp breaks do not exist between one philosophy and the next; instead, moderate gradually merges with conservative on the right, and with liberal on the left (as Figure 14.3 indicates). The label applied may well depend on the viewpoint of the person who applies it.

To make matters more confusing, Americans wear their party labels rather lightly. A party never knows until after the election how many of its members will use the secrecy of the voting booth to cast a vote for the other side. Political independence may take the form of voting a *split ticket* (supporting candidates from both parties) or *crossover voting* (supporting the full slate of candidates of the opposition party).

How is a political party organized?

Today approximately one voter in five says that he or she is a Republican. About two in five call themselves Democrats. Except for a scattering of minority party members, the remaining 40 percent of the electorate think of themselves as *independents*. Independent voters do not always vote in predictable patterns—and neither do registered Democrats and Republicans. The major parties, therefore, cannot win an election unless they have a party organization strong enough to gain maximum support for their candidates at every level of government. Figure 14.4 outlines a typical party structure.

NATIONAL COMMITTEE

American political parties maintain a national organization, but they are most active at the state level. The activities of the national committee reach a peak during every presidential election year. The role of the committee includes (1) planning the national convention (held every four years); (2) raising money to finance party election activities; (3) writing the party platform; and (4) running the presidential election campaign. State committees select the members of the national committee, which then elects its own national party chairman or chairwoman. National committee members, who often include the chairmen of the state committees, must be confirmed by action of the delegates to the national convention.

STATE CENTRAL COMMITTEE

Party structure reflects federal–state government relationships. Within each state, however, the party develops policies independent of the national committee. Members of the powerful state central committee gain their positions by (1) election in a state primary; (2) appointment by county and city committees; or (3) election at a state convention.

The state central committee and its chairman supervise the writing of party policies and programs. The chairman tries to keep county organizations working together. Other duties of the state central committee include (1) supervising the selection of candidates; (2) fundraising; (3) organizing conventions; (4) coordinating the work of county committees; and (5) supervising party political activities throughout the state. The state central committee also oversees the distribution of party *patronage*, handing out jobs, contracts, and other favors to party supporters.

COUNTY COMMITTEE

The county committee is the basic organizational unit below the state

Figure 14.4
Organization of a political party

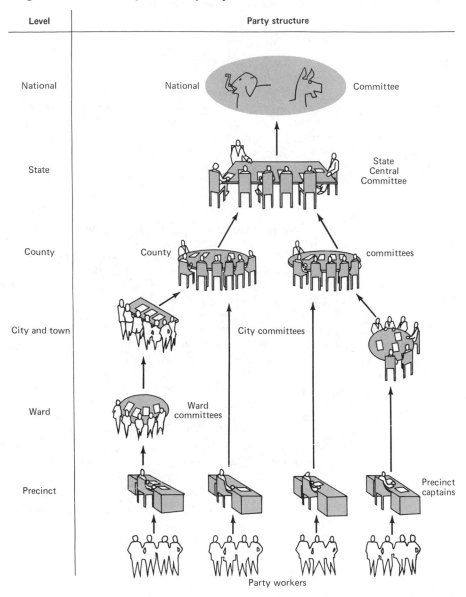

Level	Party structure
National	National ... Committee
State	State Central Committee
County	County ... committees
City and town	City committees
Ward	Ward committees
Precinct	Precinct captains
	Party workers

level. Led by a county chairman, the committee members supervise the daily political life of their district. Not only does the committee direct party workers during election campaigns, it also expects to influence zoning decisions, business licensing, and other sensitive political matters. Many county chairmen build up disciplined party followings, called *political machines,* through the calculated distribution of county jobs and political favors. A smoothly running political machine provides cooperative politicians with the support they need to remain in office.

PRECINCT ORGANIZATION

In some states, there is a city or town committee below the county committee. The most common party organization below the county level, however, is the *ward committee* or *precinct committee.* If a ward committee exists, it supervises the work of the precinct captains. These "grass roots" workers have the important job of ensuring a strong voter turnout on election day. For average voters, their precinct committee represents the party; their loyalty may well be determined by the precinct captain's ability to help them work out any difficulties they might have with local government agencies.

What happens at a party convention?

Every four years, the major parties hold a widely publicized convention. State committees meet in convention more frequently, but without the same attention from the press. Whether they are at the state or national level, conventions engage in three important political activities: (1) the convention nominates candidates for political office, often after vigorous debate; (2) the convention hammers together a *platform,* which spells out the positions the party will support in coming elections; and (3) the convention votes on regulations for the operation of the party.

CONTROL OF THE CONVENTION

The convention system replaced the *party caucus,* which was a closed meeting run by party officials. In the "smoke-filled rooms" of the caucus, political bosses selected candidates and established party policy. Faced with the loss of voter confidence, party leaders in most states finally abandoned this undemocratic process in favor of the open convention.

Delegates to the national convention are selected in two ways. (1) Many states hold statewide elections, called *primaries;* in these special elections, voters select slates of delegates, each pledged to support a particular candidate for the party's nomination. (2) Other states hold a *nominating convention,* which selects the delegates to the national convention. In many cases, these delegates are not required to commit themselves to support any particular candidate.

Despite these reforms, powerful political leaders still control many aspects of the convention. Mayors, governors, senators, state central committee leaders, special-interest groups, and candidates all attempt to use their influence to accomplish their own political ends. Groups of uncommitted delegates from non-primary states can often be pressured to support a particular candidate or sectional interest. If no one candidate gains an early victory in convention voting, the professional party leaders begin to maneuver, trading their delegate strength for favors to be collected at a later date.

EARLY CONVENTION BUSINESS

In the early days of the convention, two seldom-noticed activities take place.

Committee on credentials. The committee on credentials settles disputes over which slate of delegates from a particular state should be seated. Credentials disputes arise when rival camps within the state party each send their own delegates to the convention.

Platform committee. The platform committee decides what positions on various issues the party will support in the coming election. Sharply opposing views often make agreement or compromise impossible. When that happens, the committee may send both a majority and a minority report to the floor of the convention, so that the entire body of delegates can make the final decision.

CONVENTION BALLOTING

The drama of the convention reaches its peak with the balloting on nominations. A series of speakers nominate the candidates; the chairman or chairwoman then asks for a roll-call vote of the states. Some state delegations vote as a bloc, while others split their votes. The roll calls continue until one candidate attains a majority. At that point, the delegations scramble to switch their votes so that the nomination will appear to be unanimous. In this way, the party can present a unified image to the voters in the coming campaign.

What are the steps in the presidential election cycle?

The conventions are only one point in the election cycle. Before any citizens step into the voting booth early in November of each even-numbered year, the parties must invest months of expensive effort. The length of local and state campaigns varies widely from state to state and from election to election. Presidential election campaigns, however, dominate the nation's political life for a full ten months. Within the long campaign, the voter can expect certain traditional milestones.

1. THE ANNOUNCEMENT

Despite the polite fiction that the office seeks the person, ambitious politicians seldom wait to be selected. Candidates often decide a year or more in advance of an election whether or not they will run. There is some danger in starting out this early. A front-runner often becomes a highly visible target, sniped at by enemies within his or her own party as well as by the opposition.

2. NOMINATING CONVENTIONS AND PRIMARIES

In states without primary elections, the party organization holds a nominating convention in the spring. At the convention, state political leaders play a major role in selecting candidates for local, state, and national office. In this century, the presidential primary has continued to grow in popularity. In 1976, thirty states and the District of Columbia held primaries to select candidates for that year's presidential election campaign.

Primary elections allow voters registered as members of a particular party to select their party's candidate for the general election. Primaries open only to registered members of the particular party are called *closed primaries*. A few states hold *open primaries*, in which voters do not declare their choice of party until they are in the privacy of the voting booth, where they mark only the appropriate party ballot. To make matters even more complicated, some states permit *crossover voting*, which allows Democrats to vote in the Republican primary and vice versa. Finally, a few states run *presidential preference primaries* (sometimes called "beauty contests"), in which the election of delegates is separate from the voting for a presidential candidate. These contests give candidates useful publicity, but the results are not binding on the delegates—they are not required to vote for the winner of the "beauty contest" at the national convention.

Where direct primaries are held, state laws differ widely. In some states, if no candidate gains a *majority* (more than 50 percent) of the votes, the party holds a runoff election between the two top vote-getters. In other states, a *plurality* (more votes than anyone else, but not necessarily a majority) is enough to give a candidate the support of that state's delegates to the national convention. Winning the primary does not always ensure a candidate of a state party's full support. In some states, whoever receives a plurality walks off with the entire state delegation. Other states, however, split their delegate vote either by district or in a proportional arrangement.

3. NATIONAL CONVENTION

One of the great spectacles in American politics, national conventions bring candidates and delegates together for a week or two of summer madness (see Figure 14.5). Large cities bid for the conventions, which bring them publicity as well as business; to cut expenses, both parties often choose the same location. The political tensions built up during the long campaign for delegate support are worked out in wild floor demonstrations and a sometimes frenzied search for the additional votes needed to secure the nomination.

After oratory and demonstrations, promises and much political bloodletting, the party delegates finally choose their presidential candidate. Incumbent presidents and highly popular candidates are often nominated

Figure 14.5
Just nominated for President and Vice President, Ronald Reagan and George Bush and their wives, Nancy Reagan and Barbara Bush, acknowledge the cheers of the delegates to the 1980 Republican national convention in Detroit. Source: Wide World Photos.

on the first ballot. In the event of a deadlock, however, the convention may be forced to take many separate votes before agreeing on a candidate; in such cases, a compromise "dark horse" candidate often emerges as the party's nominee.

By custom, the choice of a party's vice-presidential candidate belongs to the newly nominated candidate for President. No one can publicly run for the office of Vice President. Instead, without time or energy for a careful search—even though the nation's second-highest elected position is at stake —the presidential candidate and his advisors must hurriedly select someone to "balance the ticket."

Once selected, the nominees for President and Vice President set to work to heal the wounds inflicted by the rivalry between candidates within their party during the primary campaigns.

4. THE CAMPAIGN

Presidential campaigns traditionally begin on Labor Day, when the American public ends its summer vacation and returns to work. In truth, the campaign starts on the day the national convention makes its choice, but the pace steps up during September and October. With the two major candidates now supported by their respective parties, and with the White House as the prize, the tiring, expensive campaign dominates national attention until Election Day. (The campaign and the election itself are discussed in greater detail in Chapter 15.)

5. ELECTION DAY

On the first Tuesday after the first Monday in November of an election year, Americans go to their polling places across the nation. After all the excitement and controversy of the campaign, the decisive moment comes when each voter marks his or her secret ballot. Government agencies, whether city, county, or state, manage the election process. Voting may be by machine, computer punch card, or hand-marked ballot. The counting takes only a short time; officials frequently announce preliminary results within a few hours after the polls close.

6. INAUGURATION

The election cycle ends when victorious candidates take their oath of office. The weeks between the election and the swearing-in ceremonies are called the outgoing administration's "lame duck" period. A newly elected President must wait more than two months to be inaugurated—until the new Congress meets and certifies the vote of the Electoral College (see Chapter 7). The interim period between November and January allows the President-elect to assemble his administration, particularly his executive staff and Cabinet. Cooperation between the outgoing, "lame duck" President and his incoming successor, not often found after earlier elections, has been a growing—and welcome—trend in recent years.

$\mathbb{S}$UMMARY AND CONCLUSIONS

1. Whenever a large number of people join together and successfully elect candidates or promote their political beliefs, a *political party* is born. Parties serve to organize a political majority, provide reasonable choices at election time, educate voters, make election to office possible, and provide personnel to run the government.

2. The Democratic and Republican parties trace their ancestry back to our country's beginnings. The *Democratic party* grew out of the strict constructionism of Thomas Jefferson; Andrew Jackson rebuilt the party in the 1830's, and gradually the Democratic philosophy moved from belief in states' rights to today's emphasis on using government to solve our society's problems. The *Republican party* was born out of the antislavery movement of the Civil War period, but its heritage leads back to the Federalist and Whig parties. Like the Democrats, Republicans have revised their philosophy, changing from a belief in the expanded powers of the federal system to their modern dislike of "big government."

3. *Third parties* have made little impression on American politics. Although they often appear on state ballots, they do not achieve national importance because their most popular goals are often adopted by one of the major parties. When third parties do arise, it is usually to promote a particular economic, sectional, or political goal.

4. Political labels often serve as a shorthand method of id
candidates and issues. Labels like *reactionary, conservative, r_____,*
liberal, and *radical left,* however, possess limited usefulness. No completely accurate political label exists, for meanings and beliefs change as
the times change. American voters, moreover, wear party labels lightly,
sometimes changing them on their way to the voting booth.

5. Power within a political party concentrates at the state level. The
party's *national committee,* made up of representatives from each state,
emerges every four years to stage the national convention and to run
the election campaign. *State central committees* work year-round, coordinating party activities, raising money, and mending political fences.
County, city, ward, and *precinct* committees complete the party structure.

6. *Primary elections,* which allow the voters to select their party's
candidates for office, capture most of the headlines. Party *nominating
conventions,* however, still pick many state-level candidates and delegates
to the national convention. Political pressure pays off at these conventions,
where special-interest groups, political bosses, and powerful elected officials compete for the privilege of choosing the party's nominees.

7. Election Day in November climaxes the long cycle of the political
campaign. State primaries and conventions take place in the spring of a
presidential election year, followed by the national convention in the summer, at which delegates make the final choice of the party's presidential
candidate. The fall campaign runs through September and October, with
the election taking place, by law, in early November. *Inauguration* of the
newly elected President takes place in January of the next year.

REVIEW QUESTIONS AND ACTIVITIES

TERMS YOU SHOULD KNOW

American Independent party	*independent voter*
Anti-Federalists	*left wing*
closed primary	*liberal*
coalition	*majority vote*
committee on credentials	*minority party*
conservative	*moderate*
county committee	*national committee*
crossover voting	*nominating convention*
Democratic-Republican party	*open primary*
Democratic party	*party caucus*
Federalists	*patronage*
inauguration	**Peace and Freedom party**

platform   radical left

platform committee   radical right

plurality   reactionary

political party   Republican party

political machine   right wing

Populist party   Socialist party

precinct   split-ticket voting

presidential preference primary   state central committee

pressure group   States' Rights party

primary election   third party

Prohibition party   ward

radical   Whig party

REVIEW QUESTIONS

The following multiple-choice questions are based on the important ideas presented in this chapter. Select the response that best completes each statement.

1. Political parties are needed in a democracy in order to (a) organize the political majority. (b) educate the people about the issues of the day. (c) provide personnel to run the government. (d) provide candidates with a means to run for office. (e) all of these.

2. A two-party system holds an advantage over the multi-party European systems in that (a) it makes coalition governments possible. (b) it provides stable governments which change only at election time. (c) all minority parties receive equal representation. (d) multi-party governments work well only when people don't care about their form of government. (e) all of these.

3. The modern Republican party inherited the political traditions of the (a) Federalists and Democratic-Republicans. (b) Anti-federalists and Whigs. (c) Federalists and Progressives. (d) Federalists and Whigs. (e) none of these.

4. The failure of third parties to win national elections can be traced to (a) the tendency of the major parties to take over the ideas of third parties once those ideas become popular. (b) their failure to present programs that appeal to American voters. (c) laws that prevent third parties from appearing on the ballot. (d) voter dislike of parties that have a great deal of money to spend. (e) all of these.

5. A right-wing politician would most likely believe in (a) increased welfare payments to the poor. (b) a program of national health care. (c) less government control over auto manufacturers. (d) government takover of the arms and munitions industry. (e) stricter controls over industrial pollution of the environment.

6. Most American voters can usually be found in the political camp of

the (a) radical left. (b) liberals. (c) moderates. (d) conservatives. (e) reactionaries.

7. Unlike the federal government, most power in a political party is concentrated (a) at the national level. (b) in the state central committees. (c) in the county committees. (d) at the precinct level. (e) in local political machines.

8. Of the following party procedures, the most democratic is the (a) party caucus. (b) distribution of party patronage. (c) primary election. (d) state convention. (e) national convention.

9. The biggest responsibility of the national convention is to (a) select the party's candidate for President. (b) raise money to run the campaign. (c) write a platform that states the party's position on important issues. (d) check the credentials of the delegates. (e) select the party leaders who will guide party policy for the next four years.

10. A "lame duck" politician is one who (a) was careless while on a hunting trip. (b) is waiting to take office after winning an election. (c) lost his or her party's nomination at the convention. (d) is waiting to leave office after his or her successor has been elected. (e) none of these.

CONCEPT DEVELOPMENT

This chapter has explored a number of significant concepts relating to the American political system. You can use your skills in thinking, researching, and writing to answer the following questions.

1. Why do most Americans prefer not to become involved in politics? What are the long-range consequences of this attitude?

2. What differences can you find in the viewpoints supported by the Republican and Democratic parties today?

3. Why have third parties traditionally failed to establish themselves as lasting political forces in the United States? Would our country be better off with more than two major parties?

4. Describe the structure of a typical political party. Why are the "grass roots" so important to the success of a party's candidates?

5. What reforms would you suggest for the American political system? How might such changes be brought about?

ACTIVITIES

The following activities are designed to help you use the ideas developed in this chapter.

1. "Grass roots" politics begins with the local party officials. Invite both the Republicans and Democrats to send staff members to your class to talk about their jobs and their party. Ask that they emphasize the role individual voters can play in the political process at the community level. Political party headquarters are usually listed in the telephone book—and they'll be happy to talk to new voters like you and your classmates.

2. Set up a round-table discussion among five students from your class, with each individual assigned to speak as a reactionary, conservative, moderate, liberal, or radical leftist. Use a currently controversial topic that will bring out contrasting viewpoints; for example, "How do you feel about legalized abortion?" "Should the United States nationalize the railroads and airlines?" or "In the event of another oil embargo, should the United States invade and occupy the Middle East oil fields?"

3. Arrange to visit a meeting of the Republican or Democratic central committee (county or city). Report back to your class on the business conducted by the committee, its membership, and its reaction to your visit. If that's not possible, try to attend a ward or precinct meeting.

4. Dramatize a scene from a "smoke-filled room" at a national political convention. Through the dialogue, show how powerful politicians trade votes in order to gain influence over a candidate's policies. Useful background material can be found in such books as Edwin O'Connor's *The Last Hurrah*, Robert Penn Warren's *All the King's Men*, and Allen Drury's *Advise and Consent*.

5. Involve yourself (and your class, if possible) in a local political campaign. Volunteer for precinct work: stuff envelopes, ring doorbells, answer phones. All the while, note what is going on around you. Write up your experiences for the class or the school paper, including an honest appraisal of the value of joining in the political process at the grass roots level.

CHAPTER FIFTEEN

THE AMERICAN VOTER'S ROLE IN THE ELECTORAL PROCESS

Over 80 million Americans cast ballots in the 1980 presidential election; millions more will vote for future Presidents. Does your vote really count among all those others? Even if you do take the trouble to go to the polls, how can you be sure that political bosses won't "steal" the election?

One guarantee can be given: elections often turn on a handful of votes. On the national level, political scientists point out that if one or two more Republicans in each precinct had voted in 1960, John Kennedy would never have been elected. Richard Nixon lost by only 118,000 votes—less than two-tenths of one percent of the 68 million votes cast. Many elections, it becomes obvious, depend on the number of nonvoters who never leave the comfort of their easy chairs.

Voting, important as it is, may not be enough. It is also essential that your ballot be accurately counted. Lyndon Johnson, for example, found himself on both the winning and losing sides in different recounts during his quest for a Senate seat in the 1940's.

In 1941, Johnson apparently led Governor W. Lee "Pappy" O'Daniel by a safe 5,000 votes in a special senatorial election. By the next day, however, "corrected" votes had poured in from rural counties controlled by the governor's party organization. O'Daniel eventually rolled into the Senate by a margin of 1,311 out of more than 600,000 votes cast.

Seven years later, Johnson opposed another Texas governor, Coke Stevenson, in the Democratic primary. Again the election was close. Election day returns favored Stevenson, and it looked as though Johnson's Senate bid had been denied a second time. A few days later, however, the tiny town of Alice, in Jim Wells County, "found" 202 additional votes, 201 of them for Johnson. The county's political boss, Archie Parr, was a Johnson supporter. Despite this unusual coincidence, the revised count stood up in court. "Landslide" Lyndon's edge of 87 votes out of 988,000 cast paved the way for his later victory in the general election.

These examples of close elections, even when distorted by electoral hanky-panky, serve to underline a major thesis in American politics: *Individual votes do matter.* Our system depends on every citizen's participation. Every time we vote, count ballots, or report honest election returns, we renew the vitality of our government and its ability to serve the needs of all its people.

Where do you fit into the electoral process? Your responsibilities and limitations as an American voter are explored in this chapter. You'll learn the answers to such questions as:

1. What limitations have historically been placed on the right to vote?
2. What limitations on the right to vote remain today?
3. What does party membership have to do with voting?
4. How does the American secret ballot work?
5. How do Americans select their party and candidates?
6. Why do so many Americans choose not to vote?
7. How are American election campaigns paid for?

What limitations have historically been placed on the right to vote?

Today's American citizen enjoys the *franchise* (the right to vote) with fewer limitations than at any time in the country's history. Many of the restrictions that were accepted in colonial times have been eliminated by constitutional amendments, congressional action, or court decisions.

Voting limitations during our early years as a nation grew out of the laws established by the individual colonies. Probably less than one American in fifteen qualified to vote for Washington in 1789. At various times, one or more states adopted the following restrictions on the franchise.

PROPERTY OWNERSHIP

All thirteen colonies required property ownership as a qualification for voting. The reasoning was that men without property lacked the independence, judgment, and virtue to make proper decisions regarding government in a free republic.

RELIGIOUS BELIEF

Not surprisingly, since many colonies were founded by religious groups, prospective voters were required to swear an oath that they believed in a Supreme Being. Others, like the Massachusetts Bay Colony, went a step further and required church membership.

Figure 15.1

The passage of the Nineteenth Amendment giving women the right to vote came after a decades-long, highly organized campaign by suffragists like Elizabeth Blackwell (the first woman doctor in the United States), shown here riding in a suffrage parade in New York City. That long struggle continues today in the drive for ratification of the Equal Rights Amendment. Source: Brown Brothers.

POLL TAX

A tax on the right to vote, called a *poll tax*, produced revenue for some states, much as a property tax does today. Sometimes the tax was cumulative; if not paid one year, it was doubled the next. When added up year after year, it effectively served to take the vote away from the poor. Many Southern states used poll taxes in this way until they were abolished by the Twenty-fourth Amendment in 1964.

SEX DISCRIMINATION

Until 1869, when Wyoming gave women the right to vote, the female half of the country's population had no voice in political affairs—local, state, or national. The popular belief was that women were not interested in politics, that women could not vote wisely because they were not as well educated as men, and that married women would vote as ordered by their husbands.

Suffragist leaders began the struggle before the Civil War, led by Elizabeth Cady Stanton and Susan B. Anthony. Slowly, following Wyoming's lead, more states joined the suffrage movement. The debate ended in 1920, when the Nineteenth Amendment awarded the vote to women on the same basis as men (see Figure 15.1).

CONDITION OF SERVITUDE

The question of slavery bedeviled the country for many years. The famous Three-fifths Compromise in the Constitution allowed a state to count three-fifths of its slaves as part of its population when seats were allocated for the House of Representatives. The slaves themselves could not vote, of course, a situation that was finally corrected by the Fourteenth and Fifteenth Amendments. After 1870, a previous condition of servitude (slavery) could no longer bar a man from voting.

INDIRECT ELECTIONS

Because the Founders believed that full democracy could lead to rash and impulsive action, they adopted the Electoral College and also specified that senators should be elected by the various state legislatures. Not until the Seventeenth Amendment was ratified in 1913 did Americans vote directly for their state's two senators.

What limitations on the right to vote remain today?

Even though the franchise today has been extended to all American citizens of voting age, the Constitution permits the individual states to enact specific voting regulations.

CONSTITUTIONAL PROTECTION OF VOTING RIGHTS

A state's voting regulations, however, may not violate four major constitutional guarantees:

1. *Voting equality.* Any voter allowed by the state to vote in an election for its larger house (the state assembly, for example) must also be allowed to vote in federal elections.

2. *No racial discrimination.* No state may deny the right to vote on the basis of race, color, or previous condition of servitude.

3. *No sex discrimination.* No state may deny the right to vote on the basis of sex.

4. *No poll tax.* No state may require the payment of a poll tax or any other tax as a requirement for voting in a federal election. Supreme Court decisions have applied this principle to local and state elections, as well.

REMAINING LIMITATIONS

Working within the restrictions written into the Constitution, the states have imposed a number of realistic limitations on the right to vote.

1. *Citizenship.* Every state requires that voters must be citizens before they may take part in local, state, or national elections. At one time, aliens were allowed to vote; but Arkansas, the last state to permit it, barred noncitizens from voting in 1926. Voting laws make no distinction between naturalized and native-born citizens.

2. *Residency.* Every state requires that new voters must live within the state for a specified length of time. Shorter periods of residency are often required for local elections. One year's residence within a state and thirty days within a precinct are the most common requirements, but these vary greatly from state to state.

Residency requirements have two major purposes: (a) to prevent political bosses from "importing" voters into their districts in order to win a close election and (b) to ensure that voters will be familiar with the local issues and candidates. Almost all states bar temporary residents from voting, such as members of the Armed Forces on active duty, and out-of-state college students. These voters must obtain absentee ballots from their home precincts if they wish to vote.

3. *Age.* In 1971, the Twenty-sixth Amendment made it illegal for any state to restrict the right to vote of any American over eighteen years of age. Supporters of this action had argued that if young people could legally marry and be drafted at eighteen, they should be considered adults and allowed to vote. The movement began in Georgia (which changed its law in 1943) and Kentucky (1955). The effects of extending the vote to eighteen-year-olds remain unclear. A study of the 1974 congressional election showed that a much smaller percentage of people aged eighteen to twenty-one voted in that election than people over twenty-one.

4. *Registration.* Even though citizens meet all other requirements, they may not vote until they have *registered*—gone to election officials and formally added their names to the list of voters. Registration prevents people from voting more than once. Precinct workers post the voting list outside the polling place; as people vote, their names are crossed off.

A new voter may register at any time. To vote in a certain election, however, the new voter must complete registration a specified number of days before the election. This gives registrars time to check the voting lists to ensure that all requirements have been met. In some states, a voter's registration may stay in force as long as he or she takes part in all general elections or does not move to a new voting district. In other states, registration must be renewed every few years.

5. *Legal disfranchisement.* Some citizens may be legally *disfranchised* (not allowed to vote). Many states disfranchise paupers, vagrants, idiots, convicted felons, and other inmates of public institutions. Voting rights lost for any of these reasons can be restored only by an act of the state legislature or by a pardon from the governor of the state.

What does party membership
have to do with voting?

General elections, held in November of even-numbered years, select the officials who run our state, local, and national governments. All eligible voters, whether or not they belong to a political party, may also take part in *special elections*, which are called to meet specific state or local needs— to pass revenue bonds, raise tax rates, or elect city council and school board members.

Although all registered voters may vote in general and special elections, *primary elections* are often restricted to voters who have registered as members of organized political parties (see Chapter 14 for a full discussion of primary elections). With the growing emphasis on primary elections as a means of choosing candidates for office, citizens who desire a voice in this process must register as members of one of the nation's political parties.

In most states, new voters state their party preference when they first register to vote. Political parties count on their registered members as reasonably certain supporters, and they spend much time and money to attract and hold them. Voter registration drives seek out nonvoters at home, at work, and in public places—even shopping centers.

Many Americans change their party registration as candidates and issues change. A change of party registration requires only a ten-minute visit to the Registrar of Voters, and may be done at any time except immediately before an election. A typical registration form is shown in Figure 15.2.

Voters may decline to state their party preference, or may list themselves as independents. These choices restrict the citizen from voting in *closed primaries*—which, as you recall from Chapter 14, are closed to all voters who are not members of the particular party. Although approximately 40 percent of the voting public consider themselves independents, most people declare a party choice because they want to be eligible to vote in closed primaries.

How does the American secret ballot work?

When Americans step into a voting booth, they use one of a wide variety of ballots. Small towns still use paper ballots, on which voters indicate their choices by marking an "X" with a rubber stamp or a pen. Larger cities may own voting machines, which allow each voter to flip down levers next to the printed names of his or her selections; the machine then records all the votes automatically when the curtain is opened. Other cities have adopted computer punch cards, which speed up vote-counting by many hours.

AUSTRALIAN SECRET BALLOT

Whatever system a local precinct uses, however, it will include features of the *secret ballot*, which was first developed in Australia. Secret ballots have

Figure 15.2
Sample voter registration form

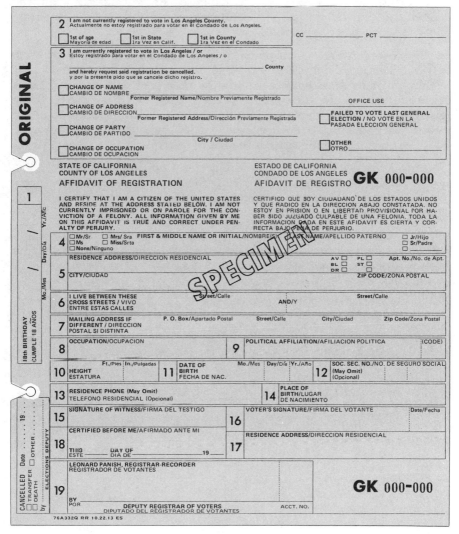

not always been part of the American electoral process. In the early years of the republic, people called out their votes in public. When paper ballots came into use, the parties printed ballots of different sizes and shapes. This allowed an observer to note which party's ballot a voter selected, and pressure could be exerted by powerful politicians to make sure that people picked the "right" ballot.

The current system guarantees that the voter's privacy will not be violated, and goes a long way toward ensuring an honest vote count. Common features of the secret ballot today include:

1. Uniform ballots. Election officials have all ballots printed in identical sizes, shapes, and colors at public expense. Each ballot lists all the candidates of all the parties (except in primary elections, when separate ballots for each party are printed).

2. Numbered ballots. Each polling place receives a series of consecutively numbered ballots. The number of votes cast must match exactly the number of registered voters signing the tally book. All voters sign this book when they receive their ballots. Their names are then crossed off the registry book, in order to prevent multiple voting. When a voting machine is used, election officials do not issue ballots, but check the number of votes cast on the machine against the list of voters.

3. Detachable ballot numbers. Before voters drop their completed ballots into the ballot box, an official tears off the identifying numbers and returns it to them. From that point on, every ballot looks like the next one. It thus becomes impossible to determine how any individual voted.

4. Write-in votes. Most ballots provide space for write-in votes for candidates whose names are not printed on the ballot. If someone using a voting machine wishes to vote for a candidate not listed on the machine, he or she may ask for a special paper ballot.

SUPERVISING THE POLLS

Every county elects or appoints a *Registrar of Voters.* This official prepares the ballots, supervises the election, and oversees the counting of the ballots. By law, voters must be notified (usually by mail) of the location of their polling place well before the election. The voter's packet may also include sample ballots and summaries of the arguments for and against issues to be decided at the election.

Every party has the right to place observers in each polling place and at the locations where votes are counted.

CONTESTED ELECTIONS

If an individual or a party believes that the vote count has been dishonest, they may appeal to the courts to investigate. A candidate who loses a close election may also pay for a *recount* of the ballots. A number of elections have been won because of a few ballots that were originally overlooked or miscounted, so recounts are fairly common. In cases of contested congressional elections, each house maintains a committee to investigate and make recommendations on the dispute. The full house must vote on the matter before a winning candidate may be seated.

Most observers believe that American elections accurately report the wishes of the voters. That has not always been so. *Vote frauds* mocked the democratic process fairly often during the last century. These frauds included such tricks as registration of dead or nonexistent persons, multiple voting, ballot-box stuffing, and questionable counting of ballots. Irregularities still happen, but safeguards in the system have made the rigged election increasingly rare.

LET'S REVIEW FOR A MOMENT

The privilege of voting, which so many Americans take for granted, existed for only a few citizens when the country was founded. Property requirements, religious qualifications, poll taxes, and discrimination on the basis of age, sex, and race limited the franchise. How do you qualify to vote today? If you meet the age, residency, citizenship, and registration requirements of your state, you're a potential voter.

The *general election* held every two years gives you an opportunity to vote for local, state, and national government officials. From time to time, you will also find notices in your mailbox for *special elections*. Perhaps in March, you can vote for the local school board; in June, the balloting might be for the city council, along with a bond issue to build a new city library. If you registered as a member of a specific party, you will also be eligible to vote in the *primary elections* to help select your party's candidates.

Many colorful stories can be told of historic *vote frauds*, but these have almost disappeared. The Australian *secret ballot*, with its careful double-checks of each step in the voting process, makes certain that only one ballot is cast—and counted—per voter.

What can you do if you detect some improper activity at the polling place? Report your suspicions to the *Registrar of Voters*, or to one of your party's poll watchers. All candidates who lose a close election are entitled to call for a *recount*. They still may not win, but they will have the satisfaction of knowing that the tally was accurate.

How do Americans select their party and candidates?

Scientists and politicians alike have studied the behavior of that strange species, *voter Americanus*. Their findings show that Americans often exhibit *bloc voting* tendencies. This means that people with similar characteristics tend to vote the same way.

CHARACTERISTICS OF BLOC VOTING

Some of the qualities that lead to bloc voting include:

1. Parents' voting patterns. Two out of three Americans express the same political preferences as their parents.

2. *Place of residence.* Traditionally, rural and small-town voters tend to support Republican candidates, while city dwellers vote Democratic. Suburban residents tend to be about equally divided between the two major parties.

3. *Section of the country.* Certain regions have traditionally expressed a preference for one party over the other. For instance, the South remained almost solidly Democratic for a century after the Civil War.

4. *Religion.* Although many variables exist in this category, Catholic and Jewish voters are more likely to vote Democratic; Protestants vote more frequently in the Republican column.

5. *Race.* Although white voters divide their loyalties about equally between the two major parties, they are much more likely to vote Republican than are nonwhites. Blacks and Mexican-Americans overwhelmingly prefer the Democratic party.

6. *Age.* Voting preferences sometimes divide along lines of age rather than family tradition. Younger voters (under thirty-five) tend to register and vote Democratic; their parents (over fifty-five) often support Republican candidates.

7. *Income level.* Many low-income voters believe that the Democratic party supports their interests. People with higher incomes, by contrast, tend to identify with Republican candidates and ideals.

8. *Education.* Americans who ended their education at the elementary or high school level tend to register as Democrats. The college-educated are more likely to call themselves Republicans.

9. *Occupation.* Business people, farmers, professional people, and white-collar workers tend to support the Republican party. Blue-collar workers, whether skilled or unskilled, usually stay with the Democratic party.

VALUE OF STUDYING VOTER TENDENCIES

In spite of these generalizations about voting patterns, many Americans will deny that their party choice was influenced by parents, age, income, or any other bloc characteristic. You probably know many voters who cannot be jammed into such neat categories. A voter may be under thirty, college-educated, Jewish, live in a suburb, make $20,000 a year, and belong to a labor union, all at the same time.

The key idea, in any case, is the concept of *voter tendencies.* The preference may amount to only a few percentage points, but these electoral patterns do repeat themselves in election after election.

NEW TRENDS IN AMERICAN VOTING

Politicians cannot always count on familiar voting patterns. Several new trends in American politics have begun to blur the old certainties.

Voting a split ticket. Individual Americans increasingly vote a *split ticket*; that is, they may vote for a Republican candidate for President, but for a Democrat to represent them in Congress. New voting machines (with a separate lever for each candidate) and computer punch cards make it easy to ignore party labels. As a consequence, a President or state governor often represents one party, while the national or state legislature is controlled by the opposition.

Voting for the person. Ticket splitting frequently results when voters disregard party positions in favor of a candidate's public personality. The voter, who may be confused by party platforms and political controversy, selects a candidate on the basis of the "image" he or she projects. Politicians who can appear dynamic, sincere, honest, dedicated, and likeable in the election campaign may ride into office on that combination of inspiring personal qualities that has come to be called *charisma*.

Political campaigns, therefore, have increasingly been taken over by "image-makers." Advertising agencies carefully mold a candidate's public image, disregarding the real political issues. This emphasis on speaking voice, physical appearance, an attractive family, and a something-for-everybody philosophy has turned many elections into a sort of popularity contest. Figure 15.3 reminds us that this approach does not always work.

Another negative outcome of voting for the person lies in the substitution of personal image for hard political issues. A well-known actor or astronaut may not prove equally successful in the demanding job of writing legislation or running a state. Historically, major American wars have produced at least one President from among the generals who gained

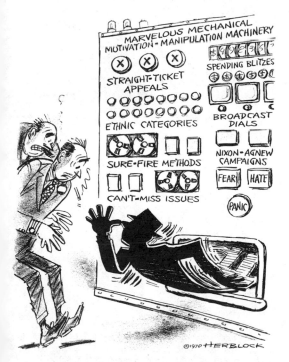

Figure 15.3
"Voter profile"
Shortly before the 1970 elections, this Herblock cartoon predicted that American voters would defy the strategists who had manipulated them and "packaged" the candidates. Well-informed voters who insist on workable solutions to problems can make this prediction come true. Source: From *Herblock's State of the Union* (Simon & Schuster, 1972).

public attention. Good generals may make good presidents—as Washington proved; but the opposite may also happen—as Grant's scandal-ridden administration reminds us.

Why do so many Americans choose not to vote?

How many people voted in the last election held in your community? If your neighbors followed the usual pattern, about 56 percent voted in the general election, and far fewer in special elections. As Table 15.1 shows, Americans run dead last among Western democracies in the voting derby.

GENERAL ELECTION TURNOUT

Every four years, the excitement of the presidential sweepstakes creates the highest voter turnout Americans generally muster. When the returns flash across our television screens, the millions of votes look impressive. Even so, the figures are misleading. Let's break down the results of the 1976 presidential election:

—150 million Americans were eligible to vote.
—Of these, only 97.7 million (66.7 percent) bothered to register to vote. One potential voter in three, therefore, was lost before election day.
—81.7 million people voted—about 54.5 percent of those eligible. (Jimmy Carter was elected by a narrow margin—51 percent of the vote to Gerald Ford's 48 percent. The low voter turnout, therefore, meant that the President was chosen by only 28 percent of the eligible voters.)

Table 15.1

Approximate percentage of the eligible population voting in national elections

Country	Percent voting
Australia	*93.3 (compulsory)*
Belgium	*91.5 (compulsory)*
Austria	*91.4*
West Germany	*91.1*
Sweden	*88.3*
Netherlands	*83.5*
France	*80*
Canada	*77.2*
United Kingdom (Great Britain)	*72.2*
Switzerland	*56.8*
United States	*55.7*

Source: Thomas T. Mackie and Richard Rose, *The International Almanac of Electoral History* (New York: The Free Press, 1974). Reprinted with permission of Macmillan Publishing Company, Inc. Copyright © 1974 by Thomas T. Mackie and Richard Rose.

OFF-YEAR AND SPECIAL ELECTION TURNOUT

Congressional elections held in *off years* (when no presidential race is scheduled) attract even lower percentages. In 1970, only 44 percent of the registered voters participated. Special elections at the local level (even when taxes are involved) often find less than 20 percent of the eligible voters going to the polls.

CAUSES OF LOW VOTER TURNOUT

Ask any nonvoter why he or she didn't make it to the polls, and you'll receive one of several basic answers:

1. Reasons beyond voter's control. Experts estimate that as many as 10 percent of otherwise eligible citizens do not vote because of reasons beyond their control. They may be ill, on a vacation or business trip, or unable to take time off from work or school (although polls stay open in many states from 7:00 a.m. to 8:00 or 9:00 p.m.). Many of these ill or on-the-move people could have applied for and mailed in an *absentee ballot* if they had cared enough. As the application in Figure 15.4 demonstrates, a voter might have waited as late as five days prior to this primary election before submitting a request for an absentee ballot.

2. Difficult registration procedures. Difficult registration procedures in some states create hardships for citizens who wish to sign up to vote. Election officials sometimes deliberately make it hard to register, as when

Figure 15.4
Sample application for an absentee ballot

Application for Absent Voters Ballot—Primary Nominating Election—APRIL 1, 1975
Do not use this form if you have already requested an absent ballot for this election

I, _____, am a registered voter in the
(Print full name — women use own first name and Miss or Mrs.)

City of Los Angeles, the Los Angeles Unified School District, or the Los Angeles Community College District.
I am registered at my present home address, which is

_____ _____ _____ _____
(Number and Street)   (City)   (Zip Code)   (Phone: Res. or Bus.)

The only reasons a voter may vote an absent voters ballot are the following:

(Check the reason applicable to you.)

☐ 1. Because of physical disability I will be unable to go to the polls on the day of election.
☐ 2. The tenets of my religion will prevent me from attending the polls throughout the day.
☐ 3. I reside more than 10 miles from polling place by the most direct route for public travel.
☐ 4. I expect to be absent from my election precinct. I will be leaving _____ ;
(Date)

after this date mail my ballot to: _____

Mail to: **Los Angeles City Clerk**
Election Division
P.O. Box 54377, Terminal Annex
Los Angeles, California 90054

_____
(Signature of Applicant as Registered — DO NOT PRINT)

_____
(Date of Signing)

APPLICATION MUST BE MADE NO LATER THAN MARCH 25, 1975

they use unfair literacy tests. In other cases, the registrar's office may be difficult to reach, or it may stay open only during the hours when most people are at work or school.

3. *Complex election issues.* Some voters are intimidated by the long, complicated ballot frequently found in general elections. Others listen to the barrage of arguments that assault their ears as the election approaches, and become confused. Some voters ignore the election until the last minute, then decide not to vote on the grounds that they haven't had time to make a proper judgment on the issues or candidates.

4. *One-party domination.* In the South or Midwest, where one party has long dominated Congressional races, some people miss the excitement of a hot campaign. Seeing little chance that their party will lose—or that their minority views will win—they either forget to register, or don't take the time to vote.

5. *Voter alienation.* Many Americans today believe that no matter who wins an election, it cannot make any difference in their lives. This feeling reveals a deep and growing distrust of politics and politicians by people who feel powerless to change things: *alienated voters.* Some of these nonvoters simply drop out of the political process. Others believe themselves morally superior to those who do vote. Casting a ballot, they claim, implies an approval of the existing system.

WHAT EFFECT DOES NONVOTING HAVE?

Edmund Burke, an Englishman, told us very clearly what nonvoting means to our democracy. "The only thing necessary for the triumph of evil," he warned, "is for good men to do nothing." The strength of the United States lies in its ability to provide peaceful change without destroying what has already been built.

Nonvoters who refuse to seek change within the system leave themselves only two choices: (1) they must continue to suffer the conditions they believe are unjust or (2) they must join a revolutionary movement, even though violent change challenges the American tradition.

If citizens who do not exercise their rights harmed only themselves, we could leave the matter to their own consciences. Nonvoters, however, endanger the freedom of us all. History proves that without the full participation of all citizens, governments soon fall into the hands of strong and ambitious people who wish to use power for their own purposes.

How are American election campaigns paid for?

The visible costs of holding an election—printing voter information and ballots, paying workers at the polling places and vote-counting centers— are paid for by state and local government. Like the tip of an iceberg, however, these relatively small sums tend to conceal the massive expenses run up by office seekers during their campaigns. National campaigns for the presidency require the investment of many millions of dollars; but even at the local level, a city council race calls for candidates to spend thousands of dollars. Television spots, campaign literature, postage, office rent, billboards, bumper stickers, telephone lines, opinion polls—these and dozens of other expenses make running for office an increasingly costly luxury.

Because most Americans feel little passionate loyalty to their party, the European system of collecting dues from party members would probably not work in the United States. An optional $1 check-off contribution included on federal income tax forms, beginning in 1974, gives taxpayers an opportunity to help finance presidential election campaigns. Until now, the burden of campaign costs has fallen heavily on the parties—and often on the candidates themselves. Campaign debts have often remained long after the election itself has been decided.

The enormous increase in the cost of running for office has raised fears that (1) soon only rich people or those with the support of wealthy special interests will be able to seek an elected position; (2) payment of the huge debts run up in the campaign—particularly for the losers—may drive a party into bankruptcy.

SOURCES OF CAMPAIGN FUNDS

Aside from the experimental check-off contribution plan, four traditional sources have been tapped for most of a party's campaign expenses:

1. *Families and individual supporters.* Tax laws permit individual taxpayers to deduct a political contribution of up to $100 from their taxable income; larger gifts are not tax deductible. The Federal Election Campaign Law of 1974 also sets a $1,000 limit on gifts to an individual candidate. By using family and friends to make the contributions for them, however, wealthy candidates can evade this ceiling.

2. *Office holders and office seekers.* So powerful is the lure of public office that some politicians willingly pay most or all of their own campaign expenses. Primary campaigns, where a would-be candidate may have no political following, often cannot be financed in any other way. Officials running for reelection, despite the advantages of already holding office, may also find themselves forced to pay many of their own expenses. In 1976, the Supreme Court struck down a provision of the 1974 law that prevented presidential candidates or their families from giving more than $50,000 to their own campaigns.

3. *Special-interest groups.* Many special-interest groups donate large sums to the candidates most favorable to their needs. Labor groups (such as the AFL-CIO), business and industrial associations (such as the National Association of Manufacturers), and professional groups (such as the American Medical Association) contribute heavily to both major parties. Even the most dedicated and fair-minded politician finds it difficult to ignore such gifts when decisions must be made on legislation favorable to special-interest organizations.

Figure 15.5
Political fund-raising dinners have become a fixture in the American electoral process. Candidates welcome the chance to raise money for their campaigns, and the party faithful enjoy seeing their candidates in person. Here, Lyndon Johnson speaks at a fund-raising dinner in 1964. Source: Lyndon Baines Johnson Library.

4. *Fund-raising events.* Campaign committees, often formed only for the purpose of raising money, hold special events to support their candidate. Banquets and dinners—with tickets selling for $100 a plate and up—bring the candidate and his or her supporters together for an evening of entertainment and speechmaking (see Figure 15.5). Sports and entertainment figures often contribute their talents, thus ensuring a bigger turnout and more publicity for their candidate.

REGULATION OF CAMPAIGN SPENDING

Large sums of money sometimes bring out the worst in people. With that in mind, federal law has attempted to prevent the misuse of party campaign funds. Controls deal with three areas:

1. *Financial reports.* Campaign committees must file extensive reports on all financial matters. These reports go to Congress in federal elections and to the appropriate state officials in state and local elections.

2. *Limits on spending.* Attempts have been made to set limits on the amount candidates may spend in running for many federal offices. The 1974 campaign law, for example, limited presidential candidates to a maximum expenditure of $20 million during the general election campaign. Even when the law restricts a candidate's spending, however, no means exist to limit the amount others may spend on the same campaign.

3. Limits on sources of funds. Since 1907, corporations have been forbidden to contribute to a candidate for federal office; labor unions have operated under a similar ban since 1943. Some company presidents and special union election committees have evaded the intent of the law, however. For example, many corporations contributed heavily—and illegally—to the Nixon reelection campaign in 1972. The courts have imposed fines and suspended sentences on a number of business executives as a result of such activities.

REFORM OF CAMPAIGN SPENDING

As long as campaigns continue to grow more expensive, abuses of campaign funds will probably continue. A number of reforms have been suggested that would ease the worst problems. Some of these were originally developed in the early 1960's by a commission set up by President Kennedy. Other suggested reforms are based on more recent studies. They include: (1) free air time for candidates on radio and television; (2) federal funding of all campaigns (perhaps based on the taxpayer check-off system); (3) strict limitations on the amount spent per voter; (4) government printing of voter information pamphlets; (5) stricter financial reporting procedures for campaign committees; and (6) creation of a nonpartisan body to raise and distribute funds equally to all qualified candidates.

SUMMARY AND CONCLUSIONS

1. Despite voter apathy, campaign funding scandals, and occasional vote frauds, the American electoral system works. Old limitations on the franchise have been gradually removed. Today's voters are not hindered by limitations based on property ownership, religion, race, or sex. Restrictions like poll taxes and literacy tests have also largely been removed by federal law. Any person who qualifies on the basis of citizenship, residency, and age may register to vote.

2. Most voters join a political party. Some do so out of party loyalty, others in order to vote in *primary elections*. Party labels mean little, however, when voters step into the privacy of the voting booth. There, protected by the *secret ballot*, they freely choose the candidates and issues they wish to support. Later, if a voter believes that *vote fraud* has taken place, he or she may request an investigation. The *recount* process also allows a defeated candidate to double-check the accuracy of the tally.

3. Researchers have discovered that Americans with similar backgrounds tend to vote alike. Many exceptions to this pattern exist, of course, but the politics of one's parents seem to have the strongest influence on young voters. Other influences include place of residence (rural, urban, or suburban), section of the country, religious background, race, age, income, education, and occupation. The influence of any single factor on an individual's voting tendencies varies greatly from person to person.

4. Americans in recent years have tended to separate the candidate from his or her party. This habit of "voting for the person" has led candidates to substitute an attractive public image for specific stands on the issues. Advertising and public relations agencies that manage this "packaging" process have emerged as potent political forces.

5. American nonvoters trouble many observers of our society. Whether their reason lies in forgetfulness or alienation, their lack of participation spells trouble for a democracy. Change and improvement can take place in our system only when all citizens accept their share of the responsibility for decision-making.

6. The growing cost of American elections has led to many problems. Some qualified candidates cannot afford the high cost of running for office; others end up owing favors to powerful individuals or special-interest groups. Fund raisers accept checks from special-interest groups, hold fund-raising dinners, and dig into the pockets of the candidates themselves if necessary. Federal laws have attempted to limit campaign spending, tighten financial reporting, and limit the amount individuals can contribute.

REVIEW QUESTIONS AND ACTIVITIES

TERMS YOU SHOULD KNOW

absentee ballot	*open primary*
alienated voter	*poll tax*
Australian secret ballot	*primary election*
bloc voting	*recount*
charisma	*registration*
disfranchisement	*special election*
franchise	*split ticket*
general election	*vote fraud*
off-year election	*write-in vote*

REVIEW QUESTIONS

The following multiple-choice questions are based on the important ideas presented in this chapter. Select the response that best completes each statement.

1. A requirement that citizens in the early 1800's did *not* have to meet in order to qualify for the franchise was (a) belief in God. (b) ownership of property. (c) a minimum bank balance. (d) membership in the male sex. (e) all of these were required.

2. A residency requirement for voting is intended to ensure that (a) voters will pay local taxes. (b) voters will be familiar with local issues

and candidates. (c) local candidates will have a better chance of winning. (d) nonresidents will be prevented from coming into a neighborhood precinct on election day just to vote. (e) all of these.

3. Disfranchisement would most likely result if a citizen (a) were found guilty of a felony. (b) filed for bankruptcy. (c) lost a civil suit for damages resulting from an auto accident. (d) consistently failed to vote in local elections. (e) all of these.

4. Many independent voters decide to register as members of a party because (a) registration procedures require them to make a party choice after a certain number of years. (b) as independents they cannot vote in closed primary elections. (c) party membership gives them special tax advantages. (d) general elections are open only to registered party members. (e) many government jobs require party membership.

5. The Australian ballot attempts to guarantee that (a) every voter's ballot remains totally private. (b) all candidates will receive a minimum percentage of the vote. (c) vote-counting will be fast and efficient. (d) voters will not make any mistakes in filling out their ballots. (e) minority parties do not receive the same ballot space as the major parties.

6. The most important factor influencing an American voter would probably be his or her (a) place of residence. (b) occupation. (c) parents' politics. (d) income level. (e) religion.

7. Low-income, young, minority voters would most likely support (a) Republican candidates. (b) Communist candidates. (c) Conservative candidates. (d) Prohibition candidates. (e) Democratic candidates.

8. The increasing tendency to "vote for the person" creates a problem because (a) charisma does not guarantee a good performance in office. (b) a candidate may be "packaged" to appear different than he or she really is. (c) important issues are often overlooked. (d) all of these create problems. (e) none of these is a serious problem.

9. In a typical general election, the percentage of eligible American voters that can be expected to go to the polls is about (a) 20 percent. (b) 40 percent. (c) 60 percent. (d) 80 percent. (e) 90 percent.

10. When a candidate must rely upon large campaign contributions from individuals and special interests, a problem may result because (a) the candidate may feel obligated to return the favor by voting for legislation desired by the donors. (b) only wealthy, well-known candidates have a chance to find the money needed to run a campaign. (c) people lose faith in a government that seems too indebted to special interests. (d) all of these are possible problems. (e) none of these will happen.

CONCEPT DEVELOPMENT

This chapter has explored a number of significant concepts relating to the electoral process. You can use your skills in thinking, researching, and writing to answer the following questions.

1. How does a citizen become a registered voter? Do you believe that restrictions on voting should be increased or further decreased? How?

2. What factors tend to influence the way American voters cast their ballots?

3. What is the purpose of a presidential primary? Do the primaries usually make possible the nomination of the best available candidate? Why?

4. Do you believe that the typical American voter can be "sold" a candidate by a high-powered public relations firm? Why have modern campaign tactics increased the tendency to "vote for the person"?

5. How important should party labels be in influencing your vote for a particular candidate?

ACTIVITIES

The following activities are designed to help you use the ideas developed in this chapter.

1. How good a job of voter registration does your town or city do? Contact the Registrar of Voters and arrange for an interview. You might ask about registration procedures, limitations and requirements, and voter turnout percentages. Report to the class on your findings.

2. A surprising number of eighteen-year-olds have not been registering to vote. Perhaps your class could organize a voter-registration drive in your school. Ask the local registrar's office to send someone out to sign up your eligible juniors and seniors. Your social studies teacher and your principal can help you set up and publicize this important service.

3. Survey a representative number of voters in your community. How many voted in the last general election? How many in the last special election? Compile the reasons people give for not voting. Can you think of any ways to increase the percentage of people who register and vote?

4. Organize a debate to be presented before your class on the topic, "Resolved: that the United States should follow the lead of Australia and establish a system of compulsory voting in all state and national elections." You will find it interesting to research the Australian and Belgian experience with compulsory voting. If your library does not provide sufficient information, ask the nearest Australian and Belgian consulates for help.

5. Make a poster for your classroom showing the amount of money spent by the winning and losing candidates for office in the most recent election (President, member of Congress, governor, state legislators, and city council). Do you find any matchups between victors and big spenders? If so, what dangers does this factor present to our democracy?

CHAPTER SIXTEEN

AMERICAN VOTERS: HOW THEY INFLUENCE THE GOVERNMENT

On December 1, 1955, Rosa Parks boarded the Cleveland Avenue bus in downtown Montgomery, Alabama. Mrs. Parks, a seamstress in a big department store, settled wearily into a seat in the first row of the section in the rear reserved for black passengers. As the bus filled up, however, driver J. F. Blake prepared to enforce the city bus line's seating regulations: when the white section in the front of the bus was full, black passengers in the next row back must vacate their seats so that whites could sit down. Three of the black people sitting in the row moved back at his request. Only Mrs. Parks remained where she was. Faced with her determined refusal to move, Blake called for police assistance. Officers Day and Mixon arrested Mrs. Parks.

Ordinarily, the courts defused such protests as this by calling them "disorderly conduct." Mrs. Parks, however, insisted on being tried for breaking the segregation law. A judge heard the arguments, found her guilty, and fined her ten dollars plus court costs. Throughout her ordeal, Mrs. Parks displayed great courage and dignity.

Meanwhile, the growing civil rights movement in Montgomery decided to support its new heroine by refusing to ride the buses until they were desegregated. A young Baptist preacher, Martin Luther King, Jr., emerged as the leader of the organized bus boycott. Inspired by Dr. King's words, the Montgomery Improvement Association publicized the boycott, formed car pools, and cheered as the almost-empty buses rolled past.

As the months dragged on, the two sides fought a bitter battle on two levels. Within the city, black people crowded into car pools or walked miles to work. The bus company suffered severe financial losses. Violence flared as white segregationists fought back with rifle fire and dynamite. At the same time, the battle was also waged in the courts. Appeals carried the case to Washington. When the Supreme Court confirmed an appeals court judgment that had struck down Montgomery's segregation laws, the city had no choice but to give in.

On December 21, 1956, Dr. King and some of his supporters stepped onto a desegregated bus in a ceremony witnessed by the entire nation through its television sets and newspapers. By the 1960's, what had begun as one woman's demand for dignity and equality had grown into a series of national laws guaranteeing all American citizens equal treatment under the law.

This story illustrates three important stages in correcting a social injustice. First, one person took a stand, but found herself powerless to bring about any change or improvement. Second, a special-interest group took up the cause, and used legal means to bring pressure to bear on local and national government. Finally, the American political system translated the protest into laws designed to end the injustices that had motivated Rosa Parks in the beginning.

Can you, as an individual citizen, influence the course of government in this country? Part 2 showed you how to deal directly with your representatives in Congress, but in this chapter you will learn how public opinion, pressure groups, and other techniques operate to influence all levels of government. You will find answers to such questions as:

1. What is public opinion?
2. What forces create public opinion?
3. How are pressure groups created?
4. Are pressure groups effective?
5. How can the people themselves create new laws?
6. How can voters confirm or reject new laws?
7. How can voters fire an elected official?
8. How else can voters take part in the political process?

What is public opinion?

Political scientists use the term *public opinion* to mean the public's attitudes toward all aspects of life in the United States. In this chapter, we will use the term to mean the attitudes of citizens toward issues involving our government.

ASPECTS OF PUBLIC OPINION

Three factors affect our understanding of public opinion:

1. *Shifting public concerns.* The issues that Americans worry about change as the political, economic, and social climate changes. Surveys taken during the 1960's showed that most people were worried about the dangers of world war, crime, and narcotics. By the mid-1970's, crime was

still a major concern, but new issues had also appeared: inflation, energy shortages, and conservation of natural resources. The other problems of the 1960's had not disappeared, of course, but even as government struggled with them, new ones had arisen to occupy the public's attention.

2. *Lack of consensus.* Even when public opinion spotlights an issue of great concern, wide disagreement remains over what to do about it. Many people worry about inflation, for example, without having any practical solutions to offer. Most of us expect others to make the sacrifices that will bring prices under control. Name an issue—capital punishment, abortion, foreign aid, environmentalism, or whatever—and about as many Americans will be against it as will support it.

3. *Time lag.* A long time often passes between the creation of strong public opinion and the enactment of this consensus into law. A majority of the American people wanted an end to U.S. involvement in the Vietnam War long before the government could achieve political and military withdrawal. On the other hand, the government often believes that the public's wishes are impractical. A shift in public opinion may leave the party in power opposed to a newly emerging policy. This type of conflict can be resolved only at the next election.

MEASURING PUBLIC OPINION

The taking of the public pulse has become something of a science in recent years. Polltakers not only attempt to measure current opinions but also try to chart changes and make predictions. Their most commonly used techniques are straw polls and scientific sampling.

Straw polls. Measurement of public opinion originally took the form of the *straw poll.* With this method, magazine or newspaper readers or radio audiences were asked to send in ballots for or against a candidate or issue. Some papers and stations still use straw polls to find out listeners' opinions on everything from politicians to football games. Since only those who feel strongly about the issue bother to respond to the poll, however, the results tend to be inaccurate.

Scientific sampling. In the 1930's, commercial firms began to take polls based on a scientific *cross-sample* of the American population. Using census data, the polltakers first determine how many people make up each major segment of the population. They know, for example, how many Southerners, white-collar workers, Methodists, married couples, forty-year-olds, and other groups they must include in the survey. In this way, a sampling of only a few thousand people can produce a prediction accurate for all Americans.

Improving polltaking techniques. No matter how carefully the polltakers calculate their sampling, they can still make embarrassing mistakes. The outstanding example took place during the presidential election of 1948,

Figure 16.1
Pioneer polltaker Louis Harris demonstrates that the highly computerized business of interpreting public opinion still depends on the data gathered in the person-to-person interview. Source: Louis Harris & Associates, Inc.

when the Gallup poll predicted an overwhelming victory for Thomas E. Dewey. A late voter swing to Truman went unnoticed by the Gallup surveys. When Harry Truman returned in triumph to the White House, the polls experienced a period of national ridicule.

Today, better polling techniques have been developed that use computers, follow-up surveys, and cross-checks on voter responses (see Figure 16.1). No polling company, however, claims to be accurate by more than a margin of 2 percent. In a close election, that leeway could prove to be significant. Table 16.1 reviews the growing accuracy of the Gallup poll in pinpointing voter decisions for the twelve presidential elections between 1936 and 1980.

DIFFICULTY OF PINNING DOWN PUBLIC OPINION

Many people see themselves as typical Americans. They believe that their own solutions to national problems, therefore, reflect public opinion nationally. With so many "publics" determining American political and social views, it is difficult to achieve the consensus needed to transform a hundred competing ideas into effective new legislation.

Public opinion thus has many components. Voters' beliefs are conditioned not only by where they live and how they make a living, but by such changing factors as recent news stories. Many people hold no particular opinions at all, or remain unaware of serious issues. Like a chameleon, public opinion constantly changes its colors, defying even the best efforts to capture it.

Table 16.1   **Record of accuracy for Gallup polls
in presidential elections**

Year	Election winner	Gallup prediction of winner's percentage	Winner's actual percentage	Percentage of error
1936	Roosevelt	55.7	62.5	6.8
1940	Roosevelt	52.0	55.0	3.0
1944	Roosevelt	51.5	53.9	1.8
1948	Truman	44.5	49.9	5.5
1952	Eisenhower	51.0	55.4	4.4
1956	Eisenhower	59.5	57.8	1.7
1960	Kennedy	51.0	50.1	0.9
1964	Johnson	64.0	61.3	2.7
1968	Nixon	43.0	43.4	0.4
1972	Nixon	62.0	60.7	1.3
1976	Carter	46.0	51.0	5.0
1980	Reagan	42.0	51.7	9.7*

In the five elections between 1936 and 1952, the polls produced an average error of 4.3 percent. Between 1956 and 1968, the Gallup organization cut its prediction error to an average of 1.2 percent. The improvement could be credited mostly to improved polling techniques. *The three-way race of 1980 complicated the polling greatly. People who expressed support for the third party candidate did not always vote for him.

Source: Louis H. Bean, *How to Predict the 1972 Election* (New York: Quadrangle Books, 1972), p. 146. Figures for 1972, 1976, and 1980 elections from *U.S. News and World Report*.

What forces create public opinion?

Individual Americans base their opinions on many different influences and experiences. Gradually they develop a series of attitudes that they believe are right. Many of these feelings can be translated into opinions about the problems facing government.

The experiences and data that become public opinion are drawn from three major influences on the lives of all of us: propaganda, economic forces, and cultural patterns.

PROPAGANDA

Information designed to persuade people to think a certain way is called *propaganda.* Depending upon your point of view, propaganda may be either bad or good. The cigarette ad designed to encourage people to smoke would be considered evil by those who are worried about the public health. People in the tobacco industry, however, would see that same ad as innocent and profitable.

1. Mass media. Much of our information regarding the world comes to us through the *mass media.* Designed to reach large numbers of people quickly and cheaply, the mass media are composed of the broadcast media (radio and television) and the *print media* (newspapers, magazines, and other publications).

Tens of millions of Americans hear radio and television news programs daily. Today, more people say that they receive news from the broadcast media than from the press. Although radio and television news programs claim to present information fairly, even the best broadcasters cannot maintain a perfect balance. Conservatives, for example, have charged repeatedly that the broadcast media have a liberal slant, whether intentional or not. In any event, pressures of time and the need to entertain viewers tend to limit the depth and judgment of television news. Programs that give a full hour to a particular issue (mental retardation, for instance) have little success competing against popular entertainment shows (such as the Super Bowl or a favorite comedy hour).

Newspapers and magazines claim to provide the in-depth news analysis impossible to find on television. The traditional ethics of the press demands that news stories be reported "straight," without distortion. Selecting the stories to be covered, placing an item on a back page, or leaving out unpleasant facts, however, are all opportunities for an editor to "slant" the news. Information directly designed to convince or persuade the public normally runs on the *editorial pages*. These pages, despite their editorial cartoons and human-interest columns, attract mainly the better-educated and more influential readers. For this reason, newspaper editorials have an influence beyond the size of their readership.

Most major cities once supported several highly competitive newspapers. Rising production costs, mergers, and bankruptcies have reduced the number of papers available. A few national chains now control a number of large newspaper markets. This means that many newspaper readers are exposed in print to only a single editorial viewpoint.

With so many incomplete or slanted news sources around, a reader must work hard to gain a truly informed opinion. Many citizens find this a difficult chore. It takes time to read more than one newspaper or magazine, and to follow several television news programs—yet American voters must do just that if they are to be properly prepared for decision-making.

2. *Motion pictures.* Many films spotlight controversial subjects. Filmmakers, who deal primarily in entertainment, do not exercise the same balance and self-restraint expected of the news media. Viewers may become so involved with the action on the screen that they do not realize how deeply their opinions are being influenced. Television entertainment—whether a TV movie, situation comedy, or variety program—may also carry the same impact.

3. *Advertising.* The advertising industry, by definition, openly promotes a point of view. Most often, the message tries to sell the public on the merits of buying Kwispy Kwackers or the new Torpedo-8. A growing number of commercials and advertisements, however, attempt to "sell" political viewpoints. Political candidates praise themselves and push their programs. Uncle Sam tells us to invest our money in Savings Bonds. Not to be

outdone, a public utility, such as the telephone company, buys air time to tell us what a marvelous job it does for us.

4. *Government.* Politicians also attempt to mold public opinion. Presidents, governors, members of Congress, and civil servants all use press conferences, press releases, public appearances, and televised speeches to promote themselves and their causes. A public appearance may be used to announce a senator's decision to seek another term; a press conference may be used to line up support for a new bill aimed at lowering the crime rate.

5. *Other sources of propaganda.* Propaganda designed to influence public opinion also comes from business, industrial, charitable, and professional organizations. Pressure groups (see the following section) conduct local and national campaigns via mailings, telephone calls, and media publicity.

ECONOMIC FORCES

People tend to support those viewpoints which add to their own sense of economic security. Conflict arises when policies that help one group seem to deny equal advantages to another. Sponsors of competing programs use all of the propaganda outlets described above to convince voters that only they have the answers to the country's economic problems—inflation, recession, poverty, and high taxes. The general public has been conditioned to support affirmative-action hiring programs for women and minority groups—until such programs affect an individual's own job opportunities.

CULTURAL INFLUENCES

A third major factor in forming your opinions relates to the people you meet every day. Research shows that most Americans tend to reflect the opinions of their own geographic, religious, social, or educational group. For example, Oregonians may look and dress like Georgians, but the distance between their political attitudes is often wider than the continent that separates them—as demonstrated by Oregon's more liberal attitude toward the use of marijuana.

Why are pressure groups created?

Citizens who join together to attempt to influence public policy form what is known as a *pressure group.* Such a group may have anywhere from a few dozen members to more than a million. Pressure groups are most active in the state and national capitals, but they may be found anywhere that a governmental body meets. Pressure groups support political parties, candidates, and officeholders at all levels in return for favorable action on their own interests.

Many of the most influential pressure groups represent economic interests: labor groups (the AFL-CIO), professional organizations (the

American Association of University Professors), Chambers of Commerce, farm and business organizations (the Associated Milk Producers). Political pressure groups also compete for public attention: the League of Women Voters, Common Cause, and the American Civil Liberties Union are examples. Specific issues, such as ecology, may give birth to other groups: the National Air Pollution Committee, the Sierra Club. Religious, racial, and ethnic groups often form their own organizations if they feel the need of public support: the NAACP, the B'nai B'rith Anti-Defamation League, the National Association of Arab Americans.

REASONS FOR THE GROWTH OF PRESSURE GROUPS

Several factors have led to the growth of pressure groups in the United States:

1. *Guarantees of free speech and assembly.* The Constitution guarantees the rights of free speech and assembly. These safeguards remove many barriers to setting up a pressure group. No legitimate groups need fear official government opposition or repression (although in 1976 it was revealed that a number of organizations like the Black Panthers and the Socialist Workers party had been harassed by FBI and police interference in their affairs). If two or more people believe as you do about an issue, you are free to form a new group.

2. *Responsive political system.* In many countries, pressure groups may gain influence by forming their own political party. Under the American two-party system, people who have strong opinions about an issue find it more effective to work under the broad umbrella of one of the major parties. Politicians, for their part, welcome the support of the various pressure groups for two main reasons: (1) such organizations often give generously to election campaigns, and (2) listening to the leaders of such groups is one means by which politicians keep themselves informed about the wishes of the people.

3. *Growing size of government.* As government grows larger, it touches our lives more frequently. Almost powerless alone, individual citizens find that by joining a pressure group, they can increase their influence. Instead of letting others decide on policy and legislative matters, they become active participants in national debate.

THE EFFECTIVENESS OF PRESSURE GROUPS

Most Americans realize that pressure groups play a useful role in the democratic process. Still, the suspicion remains (as Figure 16.2 reminds us) that there is something underhanded about the way some pressure groups promote their own special interests.

Historical abuses by pressure groups. In the 1800's, pressure groups sometimes deserved this distrust. Big business trusts and monopolies hired *lobbyists* to influence government officials illegally and thus corrupt the

"It's Awful The Way They're Trying To Influence Congress. Why Don't They Serve Cocktails And Make Campaign Contributions Like We Do?"

Figure 16.2

Source: From *The Herblock Gallery* (Simon & Schuster, 1968).

political process. (See Chapter 5 for a full discussion of lobbyists and their activities.) Some politicians were openly elected by special interests. Once in office, they sold their votes and ignored the public welfare.

Modern limits on pressure groups. Many laws now limit the activities of pressure groups. Generally (although state laws may vary), lobbyists for such a group may entertain a legislator at golf or dinner; they may also provide limited secretarial and publicity services. On the other hand, they may not pay legislators for their votes (which would be bribery), contribute money for their private use, or (as was mentioned in Chapter 15) make excessively large donations to their campaign funds. Strict reporting procedures have been set up to enforce these restrictions on financial dealings between lawmakers and pressure groups.

The law also requires that many government officials make public *disclosure* of their personal wealth. A lawmaker who owns stock in a coal company, for example, might find it difficult to vote objectively on a law restricting strip-mining operations. Such *conflicts of interest* destroy public confidence in elected representatives.

Success of pressure groups. Despite continued suspicion, pressure groups play a useful role in our system. Not surprisingly, they frequently win important benefits for their members. In addition, they provide information, research, and guidance at all levels of government. Faced with a bill that would benefit farmers, for example, a member of Congress will also be reminded that the same law may harm food processors, retailers, and consumers. By listening carefully to representatives from all sides of the issue, the lawmaker can modify the legislation to achieve the greatest good for all.

LET'S REVIEW FOR A MOMENT

Can you really change anything in this country? Rosa Parks did, as you learned at the beginning of this chapter. She didn't do it alone, however, and that's the major point. Find enough dedicated supporters, and you can make things happen.

The term *public opinion* evades easy definition. Usually, it refers to the sum of all views held by Americans on any given issue. If different groups believe A, B, and C about oil conservation policy, for example, then public opinion on oil conservation probably equals something like (A + ½B − ¼C); everyone's views count, but in varying degrees. To further complicate matters, the public's priorities change, and not everyone cares about every issue.

Where do your own opinions come from? No one likes to think that they're strongly influenced by others, but many different forces affect you every day. Scientific public *polls* measure the degree to which your own economic and cultural background helps form your opinions. What else? The broadcast media, along with the press, bombard you daily with *propaganda* designed to influence your thinking. Motion pictures, the advertising industry, government, and even your own friends also contribute to your point of view.

Pressure groups mobilize public opinion through the actions of their own members and by hiring representatives called *lobbyists*. You don't have to travel to Washington or your state capital to find such groups at work. A local homeowners' association, working to keep apartments out of a residential area, would demonstrate the principle very well. Given the increasing size of government, such group action seems unavoidable. The Constitution guarantees us the right to join groups of our own choosing, and our government does respond to our wishes.

How can the people themselves create new laws?

Most people think of "writing to their senator" when they want a new law. At the national level, this would be the proper procedure. In some states, however, citizens can make their own laws. This practice of direct democracy dates back to colonial times and the New England town meeting. Today's cities have too many people to permit town meetings, but in about one-third of the states (and in many cities and counties), general election ballots often list new laws suggested by the people. These proposed laws, which take effect if approved by the voters, are called *initiatives* (or, in some states, *propositions*).

THE INITIATIVE PROCEDURE

In a time when many people believe government has grown too remote, the initiative process holds great appeal. Today voters are using the initiative to bypass slow-moving legislatures in matters of tax relief, educational reform, and limiting government spending. A group that wishes to pass an initiative usually follows a seven-step procedure:

1. *Drafting the proposal.* Any individual or group may write an initiative. The language of the proposed law, however, must meet legal requirements and satisfy constitutional standards.

2. *Preliminary filing.* Sponsors must file the proposal with a designated official. The secretary of state usually handles the processing if a state law or constitutional amendment is involved. At this time, specific requirements are spelled out.

3. *Circulation of petitions.* Before the initiative is placed before the voters, all states require that *petitions* be circulated and submitted within a specified time. The signatures of a given number of registered voters on printed copies of the proposed law confirm the people's interest in the new legislation. The states vary widely as to the number of signatures required. Some call for 3 to 10 percent of the vote cast for governor in the last general election; others set a fixed number, running from 10,000 to 50,000 signatures.

4. *Verification of petition signatures.* As the deadline for filing approaches, election officials check the signatures on the petitions. Initiative sponsors must expect to lose a number of signatures through (a) duplication, (b) faulty completion of the petition, or (c) discovery that a voter was not properly registered. This *shrinkage* must be allowed for by gathering more signatures than the actual number required. If the petitions pass this check, state officials certify the initiative for the next general election ballot.

5. *Educating the public.* Circulating petitions only begins the battle to pass an initiative. Individuals and groups supporting (or opposing) the measure must try to convince the public that they should vote for (or against) it. Billboards, television spots, and direct mailings assault the public with urgent appeals. In several states, balanced arguments for and against initiatives are included in information packets mailed to voters.

6. *Decision by the voters.* All qualified initiatives receive a place on the ballot. When election day arrives, voters indicate their choices on the same ballot used for selecting the candidates for office. In most cases, a simple majority vote either passes or rejects the initiative.

7. *Promulgation of the new law.* Following a successful vote count, officials *promulgate* the new law—that is, they issue a proclamation that establishes the initiative measure as law in the state or locality where the election took place.

ARGUMENTS AGAINST THE INITIATIVE

Opponents of the initiative process point to a number of possible abuses. These include (1) the possibility of heavily financed special-interest legislation being passed by confused voters; (2) the possibility of dishonest practices by firms hired to circulate petitions; (3) interference with the normal procedures of representative government; (4) the confusion of voters resulting from long and complicated ballots; (5) the high cost of circulating petitions and publicizing the proposal; and (6) the possibility that widely misunderstood or poorly drafted legislation will be passed.

ARGUMENTS FOR THE INITIATIVE

Supporters of the initiative process admit that some problems exist, but believe that the merits outweigh the dangers. Their arguments suggest that the initiative (1) strengthens *popular sovereignty* (rule by the people); (2) counteracts the influence of special-interest groups, which might otherwise dominate a legislative body; (3) awakens the public to important issues; and (4) forces the legislature to consider new laws that would otherwise be ignored. If a poorly written initiative is passed, they argue, the city council or state legislature can amend or repeal it later.

How can voters confirm or reject new laws?

A number of states grant additional direct power to their citizens. Certain types of laws, even though passed by city councils or state legislatures, may not be enforced until they are ratified by the voters. This process of voter approval or rejection of proposed legislation is called the *referendum*. Like the initiative, the referendum began almost two hundred years ago. The state of Massachusetts, for example, submitted its own constitution to the voters for approval in 1780.

THREE TYPES OF REFERENDUMS

Where permitted by law, three types of referendums exist:

1. *Mandatory referendum.* Mandatory referendums are those required by law. Amendments to the state constitution must be submitted to the voters in all states except Delaware. Bond elections in most cities and states also fall into this category.

2. *Optional referendum.* In some cases, a legislature may call on the people to vote on exceptionally important or controversial legislation. This

optional referendum would be appropriate when issues such as capital punishment or marijuana laws are involved.

3. *Petition (or protest) referendum.* Even though a law has passed the legislature, some states still allow the voters to approve or disapprove. Usually, a law does not take effect until a definite time period has passed (usually sixty or ninety days after the legislature adjourns). During this time, any interested group may initiate a petition referendum (sometimes called a protest referendum) leading to a popular vote on the law.

QUALIFYING FOR A REFERENDUM

In almost all states, the petition for a referendum requires fewer signatures than for an initiative. A common figure for a petition referendum to qualify to appear on the ballot is 5 percent of the vote for governor in the last general election. The steps necessary to pass a referendum (except for the qualifying process itself) usually repeat those of the initiative. All states that utilize the referendum accept a simple majority vote as binding, except for some bond issues, which require a two-thirds majority.

How can voters fire an elected official?

What can you do when public officials don't satisfy your expectations? If guilty of "high crimes and misdemeanors," many federal and state officials—both elected and appointed—can be removed from office through impeachment (see Chapter 4). Even if a state or local official hasn't committed a serious offense, however, he or she can still be sent back to private life. This process, used to dismiss a politician who has lost the confidence of the electorate, is known as the *recall.*

The recall appeared well after the initiative and referendum. Oregon first used the procedure on a state level in 1908; by 1914, ten other states had adopted it. Today, about three-fourths of the states permit the use of the recall process.

STEPS IN THE RECALL PROCESS

The legal steps leading to a recall election parallel those for the initiative. Many more signatures are needed on the recall petition, however—as many as 25 percent of the number who voted for candidates for a designated office in the previous election. Once the signatures have been certified, the recall vote must be held within a specified time—unless the official being recalled resigns first.

The voters simply mark their recall ballots "yes" or "no." Sometimes the people vote for a possible successor in the same election. In other cases, a second election is held, usually within thirty days. Only once has the recall successfully removed a state governor from office—Governor Lynn J. Frazier of North Dakota, in 1921. Recall elections for mayors, city council members, and school board trustees, however, have frequently ended the careers of corrupt or incompetent officials.

DEBATE ON THE USEFULNESS OF RECALL

The recall process has always created controversy. Some observers fear that every public official who takes an unpopular stand will be recalled. In the states where the recall is used, however, no officeholder can normally be recalled until he or she has been in office for six months or longer. Further protection exists in the provision that only one attempt at recall may be made during an official's term in office.

Fears that minority and special-interest groups would overuse the recall privilege have not been justified. Voters, in fact, have proven generally reluctant to resort to the recall. Instead, they have preferred to wait until the next regular election to remove an official. Perhaps, in the American tradition of fair play, most voters prefer to give even the worst of our leaders the benefit of the doubt.

How else can voters take part in the political process?

As Chapters 14, 15, and 16 have revealed, alert citizens can make their political presence felt in a number of ways. The key word has been participation: joining in the activities of a political party or pressure group; voting in general and special elections; taking part in initiative, referendum, or recall campaigns. The exceptionally committed person can go the final distance and become a candidate for office.

Short of running for office, however, other ways of influencing government decisions remain, as outlined in Figure 16.3. Of course, every time you express an opinion, it exerts an influence on others—but little noticeable change results from such private debates. Making your voice heard in a larger forum, surprisingly enough, requires little extra effort.

WRITE TO YOUR REPRESENTATIVES

A letter directed to any elected local, state, or federal official almost always receives a prompt reply. Personally written letters, expressing your opinions in your own words, work best. Those mass mailings run off by pressure groups are usually tallied by a clerk, and only the totals reach the legislator.

When you write to your representative in Congress, address yourself to a specific subject; explain what concerns you, and what you want done about it. Letters may deal with any matter involving you and your government. Not only will a representative provide information about any governmental matter, he or she will also refer your requests to the appropriate agency. If you need help in dealing with the Veterans Administration, for example, a nudge from your representative or senator may hurry up the process considerably.

Tradition suggests that telegrams carry a greater impact than letters. If you wish to take advantage of this, the telegraph company provides an inexpensive night letter service with next-day delivery.

Figure 16.3
What can you do to influence Congress?

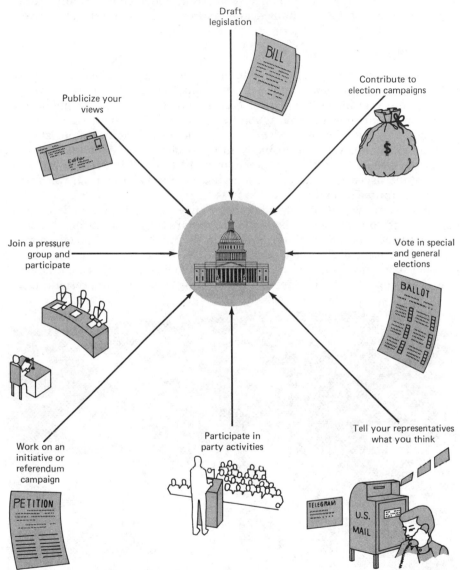

Draft legislation

Contribute to election campaigns

Publicize your views

Join a pressure group and participate

Vote in special and general elections

Work on an initiative or referendum campaign

Participate in party activities

Tell your representatives what you think

Don't be upset if you receive a form letter in reply. When a major issue touches off a large volume of mail, a busy official cannot respond individually to everyone. Most letters are answered by legislative assistants, in any event. While that may not seem very personal, you must remember that the demands of legislative activity must come first with your representative in Congress.

What is true in Washington is even more true at state and local levels of government. A member of the House of Representatives speaks for almost 500,000 people—but a state legislator or a city council member is responsible to far fewer voters. Your letters to these officials, therefore, may carry even greater influence. For your convenience, many newspapers regularly print the names and addresses of your representatives.

VISIT YOUR ELECTION OFFICIALS

Your personal visit may gain immediate results. A trip to Washington may not be necessary; every member of the House of Representatives maintains an office in his or her district (see Figure 16.4). Write or phone for an appointment. If your request merits his or her attention, time will be set aside for you. You may also be asked to testify before a legislative committee, if your views seem likely to contribute to a better understanding of the issues. A member of the committee staff will interview you, and you may be asked to write down your testimony ahead of time for study by the committee members.

Within your own city or town, boards of supervisors, city councils, school boards, and other elected bodies are required by law to hold open, scheduled meetings. Sometimes anyone in the audience may speak; often, however, you must request a place on the agenda ahead of time. As a political newcomer, you will be surprised at how few citizens take advantage of this opportunity for face-to-face meetings with their representatives.

Figure 16.4

On a walking tour of New York City's Lower East Side, then Democratic Representative Ed Koch listened to his constituents in person. In 1977, Koch's supporters responded by electing him Mayor of New York. Source: Courtesy of Mayor Edward I. Koch.

SPEAK OUT IN THE MASS MEDIA

Most newspapers and many radio and television stations provide space or time for you to air your views. Almost all newspapers print a cross section of the letters they receive, whether or not the letters agree with the paper's editorial position. If a radio or television station takes an editorial stand, the Federal Communications Commission requires that the station provide free time for qualified speakers for opposing views. The increasing number of radio talk shows also provides the average person with a chance to tell the community how he or she feels about any subject under the sun.

§UMMARY AND CONCLUSIONS

1. Once public opinion has been mobilized behind a cause, the American political process responds. Given proper leadership, pressure groups can work within the system to achieve their goals. *Public opinion* represents the public's attitude about all aspects of life in this country. Public opinion changes frequently, however, and many citizens disagree strongly about the proper methods for solving almost every problem imaginable.

2. The task of measuring public opinion falls to the polltakers. *Straw polls*, with their built-in inaccuracies, have given way to *scientific sampling*, using a statistically derived *cross-sample* of the population. The polltakers still find that shifting tides of public opinion make exact predictions almost impossible.

3. Public opinion is shaped by the many forces which surround every American citizen. The mass media bombard us with *propaganda*, information designed to influence our views. Movies, the advertising industry, and government also spend time and money attempting to persuade us to accept their viewpoints. Economic forces and cultural influences also build public opinion.

4. Many Americans join *pressure groups* with other people who share their opinions. The Constitution protects such organizations, and our political system responds to them. Most pressure groups represent economic, political, religious, or racial interests. Others support specific issues, such as ecology or consumer interests.

5. Past abuses by pressure groups and their hired *lobbyists* have led to stricter laws controlling their activities. Despite scandals and conflicts of interest growing out of lobbying practices, pressure groups still serve a useful purpose. Not only do they give individual citizens a voice in national affairs, but they also provide useful information upon which legislators can build better laws.

6. In a number of states, voters can create their own laws through the *initiative* process. Once the initiative has been drafted, signatures must be gathered on petitions. When the signatures are verified, the petitions are filed and the proposed law appears on the general election ballot. A *referendum* is a means by which voters can approve or reject a new law.

A referendum measure appears on the ballot when mandated by law or when either the legislature or the people have asked for public approval of a particular piece of legislation. Public officials who do not properly serve their constituents may be removed from office in a *recall* election.

7. Members of Congress and other public officials take letters and telegrams from constituents seriously. When schedules permit, citizens may be given appointments with their elected officials. Local and national publications welcome letters to the editor; broadcasters are required by law to air views that oppose their own editorial position.

8. Voting in a general election is only the minimum participation expected of concerned Americans. Anything less than full and active participation creates the possibility that a few powerful leaders will speak for all of us. A democracy cannot afford to run that risk.

REVIEW QUESTIONS AND ACTIVITIES

TERMS YOU SHOULD KNOW

broadcast media

conflict of interest

cross-sample

disclosure

editorial page

initiative

lobbyist

mandatory referendum

mass media

optional referendum

petition

petition referendum

popular sovereignty

pressure group

promulgation

propaganda

proposition

protest referendum

public opinion

recall

referendum

shrinkage

straw poll

REVIEW QUESTIONS

The following multiple-choice questions are based on the important ideas presented in this chapter. Select the response that best completes each statement.

1. The Montgomery bus boycott illustrates the essential principle of American democracy that (a) all bad laws will eventually be changed. (b) conflict between blacks and whites cannot be avoided. (c) the American system responds to a strong expression of public opinion. (d) when their economic interests are threatened, the rich and powerful always win. (e) violence is required if unjust laws are to be changed.

2. The most accurate poll on a major question of national policy would be (a) a straw poll taken among listeners to a popular radio station. (b) an interview survey of people in a shopping center. (c) a cross-sampling of the population of a big city. (d) a cross-sampling of people from several widely scattered states. (e) all are about equally accurate.

3. The biggest problem with conducting an accurate poll lies in the fact that (a) people's opinions change rather rapidly. (b) a good cross-sample is impossible to obtain. (c) most people never tell the truth to a polltaker. (d) no one really pays any attention to the results of a poll. (e) all of these have an equally bad effect on a poll's accuracy.

4. The best place to look in a newspaper for articles designed to both inform and persuade would be (a) the front page. (b) the editorial page. (c) the society page. (d) the entertainment section. (e) all of these.

5. The primary job of a pressure group is to (a) elect its members to public office. (b) obtain favorable action from government for its members. (c) furnish campaign money to candidates running for office. (d) change the political system to reflect some extremist philosophy like communism or fascism. (e) all of these.

6. An example of improper conduct by a pressure group or its lobbyist would be (a) making a large, secret donation to a candidate's congressional campaign fund. (b) sponsoring a dinner for a political candidate. (c) providing expert testimony before a congressional committee. (d) helping its members obtain appointments to see an important legislator. (e) all of these are improper.

7. An initiative permits the people of a state to (a) approve or reject a law passed by the legislature. (b) remove an unpopular official from office. (c) approve or reject a state bond issue for new highways. (d) propose and pass a law without the action of the legislature. (e) write an *ex post facto* law into the state criminal code.

8. The most common kinds of measures submitted to voter approval by referendum are (a) laws involving the daily affairs of government. (b) constitutional amendments and revenue bonds. (c) confirmation of general election results. (d) bills relating to business practices, such as fair trade laws and health and safety codes. (e) none of these.

9. The public official who is most likely to be removed from office by a recall vote is (a) a state governor. (b) a justice of the state supreme court. (c) a mayor of a large city. (d) a member of a school board. (e) any appointed official of a small town.

10. Persistent low voter turnout at election time poses a threat to the American system because (a) public officials cannot legally take office unless they are approved by more than 50 percent of the eligible voters. (b) a democracy cannot survive without the support and participation of all its people. (c) failure to vote is a violation of federal election laws. (d) strong leaders will not run for office if people don't care about their government. (e) none of these.

CONCEPT DEVELOPMENT

This chapter has explored a number of significant concepts relating to the ways American voters can influence their government. You can use your

skills in thinking, researching, and writing to answer the following questions.

1. What is a lobbyist? Discuss the positive and negative results of allowing lobbyists to influence legislation.

2. How can the voters remove incompetent or corrupt officials from public
   office? Why aren't these procedures used more often?

3. What do we mean by the phrase "public opinion"? Why do people and
   groups spend so much time and money attempting to influence it?

4. Write out a list of the alternatives open to a person who wishes to
   change a government policy. Evaluate the effectiveness of each method
   listed.

5. Pick out a social issue that you feel is important to most Americans—
   the cost of living, civil rights, crime, or any similar topic. How has
   public opinion on this issue been formed?

ACTIVITIES

The following activities are designed to help you use the ideas developed in
this chapter.

1. Forming a pressure group isn't as difficult as you might think. Select
   an issue that currently concerns your community. Organize a letter-
   writing campaign to the appropriate public officials, asking for prompt
   and effective action on the problem. Visit their offices to reinforce your
   ideas. If you zero in on a situation that is (a) local and (b) immediate,
   you can accomplish something. Examples might be (a) installation of
   traffic control devices at a dangerous intersection near the school; (b)
   provision of summer recreation programs at local parks; (c) addition
   of long-needed courses to your school's curriculum.

2. Select a current national or local issue that has aroused controversy in
   your school. Organize your class to conduct a scientific survey of the
   student body to obtain a valid sampling of opinion. This will mean
   analyzing students on a number of criteria—sex, age, social groups,
   ethnic background (if appropriate to the issue), economic status, and so
   on (Your registrar or attendance office can help you develop an accurate
   sampling.) Can you find differences of opinion that seem to be based
   on these economic and social factors?

3. Ask to have your name placed on the agenda of the next school board
   meeting. Use your allotted time either (a) to speak for a project you
   feel is important to you and your school or (b) to question the board
   about policies and decisions you wish to know more about. Afterward,
   report to your class on the experience. (Board meetings are generally
   serious affairs; do not use valuable meeting time to pursue frivolous
   questions.)

4. Research the history of protest movements in the United States. You
   will discover that the early labor movement vibrated to the sound of
   violence; even Martin Luther King's nonviolent philosophy sometimes
   could not prevent bloody conflict. Do you feel that true change can
   come about only through violent confrontation, or do peaceful channels
   still exist? Discuss this with your class, perhaps in the form of a panel
   report and debate.

THE AMERICAN
FEDERAL
SYSTEM
AT WORK

CHAPTER SEVENTEEN

GOVERNMENT IN THE FIFTY STATES

The proclamation was phrased in language strong enough to scorch the ears of the President:

> We, the People of South Carolina . . . do further declare that we will not submit to the application of force, on the part of the Federal Government, to reduce this State to obedience; but that we will consider the passage, by Congress, of any act . . . to coerce the State, shut up her ports, destroy or harass her commerce, or to enforce the acts hereby declared null and void . . . as inconsistent with the longer continuance of South Carolina in the Union: and that the people of this State . . . will forthwith proceed to organize a separate Government, and do all other acts and things which sovereign and independent States may do.

Today the document rings with echoes of the Civil War, but when written, that terrible conflict was almost thirty years in the future. The "tariff of abominations" in 1828 angered the South; the Tariff of 1832 eased the rates slightly, but failed to defuse the protest that was building toward an explosion in South Carolina. Tariffs of 30 to 45 percent inflated prices on imported cotton goods, woolens, iron, hemp, flax, raw wool, molasses, and sailcloth. The agricultural South believed that the tariffs it paid served only to protect Northern industries from European competition. Unable to win on the floor of Congress, South Carolina decided to make a stand by using the hotly debated doctrine of nullification, by which a state claimed the right to declare federal legislation null and void.

John C. Calhoun, former Vice President and now senator from South Carolina, and President Andrew Jackson stood out as the leaders of the opposing sides. Calhoun championed the doctrine of nullification to prevent what he saw as Northern plundering of Southern pocketbooks. President Jackson, once a states' rights advocate, had come to believe deeply in national sovereignty. Jackson knew that if South Carolina was allowed to declare a national law null and void, the federal union would be in great danger. Laws would become enforceable only at the whim of individual states.

In 1830, the clash between Calhoun and Jackson had surfaced at a banquet on the anniversary of Jefferson's birthday. Calhoun attempted to trap Jackson into endorsing nullification with a toast: "To the Union! next to our liberty, most dear."

When Jackson's turn came to reply, he looked straight at Calhoun: "Our Federal Union—it *must* be preserved!"

Jackson was as good as his word. He refused to back down before the threat of nullification. But he was also a skillful politician who knew better than to push South Carolina into a corner. He helped write the Compromise Tariff Bill of 1833, which established a reduced schedule of tariffs that would fall to a maximum of 20 percent by 1842. Then, to show that he would not allow a state to challenge the power of the national government, Jackson issued a "Proclamation to the People of South Carolina." He pointed out that nullification meant disunion, and disunion meant treason. On the same day that Jackson signed the tariff bill, he also signed a Force Bill. He now had the authority to use the military to collect customs duties if necessary.

Both sides were thus able to save face. The South found the Compromise Tariff of 1833 acceptable; the state of South Carolina repealed its nullification of the tariff, but kept its dignity by quickly nullifying the Force Bill. No one minded, however, since customs were being collected normally. Armed action was never necessary.

The challenge of the federal union by a state was over. Civil war had been avoided. But Jackson knew that deeper issues remained; the "next pretext," he predicted, "will be the Negro, or slavery, question." In light of the events of the 1860's, he proved to be an accurate prophet.

Today, the states no longer question the supremacy of the federal government. Nullification and secession have fallen into the dustbin of American history. State governments, however, still play a major role in the political life of the American people. Many of the basic features of the federal government were first tried out in the state constitutions of the original thirteen colonies. In this chapter, you will read about the responsibilities and problems of state government. The questions that will be examined include:

1. Why did the states write their own constitutions?
2. What are the major powers exercised by the states?
3. How do governors administer their states?
4. What role does the legislature play in state government?
5. How do the states use their powers of law enforcement?
6. How do the states pay the costs of government?
7. How do the states regulate corporations?

8. What is the role of the states in educating their citizens?
9. How does the federal government cooperate with the states?

Why did the states write their own constitutions?

A state constitution is the supreme law of the state; all other acts of the state, its counties, and its cities must be measured against it. At the same time, the state constitution must conform to the requirements of the United States Constitution. Like the federal Constitution, the state constitutions established governments based on separation of powers and popular sovereignty. Two-house (bicameral) legislatures were set up in all states but one. Only Nebraska chose a unicameral legislature, although other states periodically study the possibility of adopting that system.

ORGANIZATION

Most state constitutions divide into seven basic sections: (1) a preamble, or general statement of the powers and purposes of state government; (2) a bill of rights; (3) provisions for the three separate branches of state government, describing terms in office, powers, and duties; (4) a description of the political subdivisions of the state, including the powers held by local government; (5) general provisions regarding voting, taxes, appropriations, elections, schools, and other aspects of state business; (6) provision for an amendment process; and (7) the amendments themselves. By the time these seven areas are covered, most constitutions run to hundreds of pages. Louisiana's constitution, for example, has grown to more than thirty times the length of the 7,000-word federal Constitution.

REASONS FOR LENGTH AND SPECIFIC CONTENT

Several factors combine to make state constitutions both longer and more specific than the national Constitution.

1. Ease of amendment. Most states allow amendments to be made through a relatively simple procedure. Once an amendment has been proposed, either by the legislature or by the people of the state, ratification requires only a majority vote in the next general election. Special-interest groups find that procedure easier than pushing a new law through the legislature. Supporters of a new law also know that their law is less likely to be repealed if it becomes a part of the state constitution.

2. Distrust of state government. Rightly or wrongly, many people distrust their state governments. Fearful that basic rights will be abused by the legislature or the governor's office, they insist that specific rules for business and personal conduct be written into the constitution. A proposal that Congress would pass as statute law might well become a constitutional amendment in any given state.

3. *Outmaneuvering the courts.* State supreme courts frequently find state laws unconstitutional. In response, legislatures may rewrite the law and ask the voters to incorporate it into the constitution. Once that is done, the matter is out of the hands of the courts. Louisiana and California each have added several hundred amendments to their basic constitutions, many for that reason.

What are the major powers exercised by the states?

All powers not granted to the federal government are specifically reserved to the states by the Ninth Amendment in the Bill of Rights. Figure 17.1 outlines the distinction between the powers of federal and state governments. Even as the federal government has grown to meet the demands of the twentieth century, state governments have experienced a similar expansion in the scope and cost of their activities. State budgets now total billions of dollars a year. California and New York administer state budgets that exceed those of many major nations of the world.

BASIC STATE AUTHORITY

The basic authority of an individual state lies in three areas:

1. *Public safety.* States exercise law enforcement authority, of course, but the authority to ensure public safety also means that the state has the power to make laws affecting the health, safety, morals, and education of the communities within its boundaries.

2. *Regulation of business.* All states regulate the conduct of business within their borders in order to promote the general welfare. Chartering corporations, licensing and regulating businesses, and collecting sales and income taxes are accepted as normal concerns of the state.

3. *Regulation of political subdivisions.* The states regulate many aspects of the economic and political life of the counties, cities, and towns that form their geographic subdivisions. The states can revise county lines, raise sales taxes, or require unification of school districts as part of their constitutional duties.

SPECIFIC STATE RESPONSIBILITIES

Out of the three basic powers described above has developed a long list of specific state responsibilities. Their impact on the lives of every American can be seen from the following:

1. *Agriculture.* The state works with the U.S. Department of Agriculture; maintains state programs of information, pest control, and crop improvement.

2. *Banking.* The state issues charters to state banks; maintains a system of bank examiners; writes banking regulations.

Figure 17.1
How the Constitution divides power between the federal government and the states

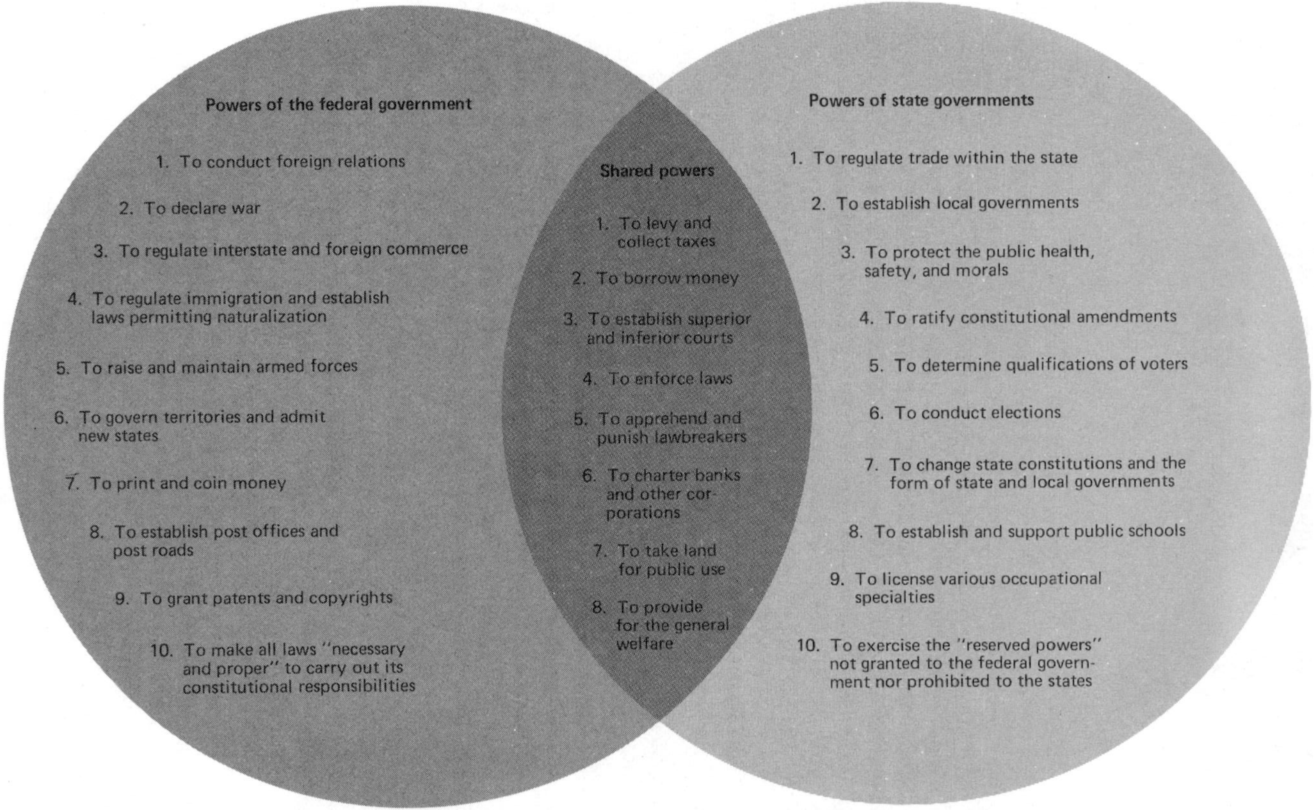

Powers of the federal government

1. To conduct foreign relations

2. To declare war

3. To regulate interstate and foreign commerce

4. To regulate immigration and establish laws permitting naturalization

5. To raise and maintain armed forces

6. To govern territories and admit new states

7. To print and coin money

8. To establish post offices and post roads

9. To grant patents and copyrights

10. To make all laws "necessary and proper" to carry out its constitutional responsibilities

Shared powers

1. To levy and collect taxes

2. To borrow money

3. To establish superior and inferior courts

4. To enforce laws

5. To apprehend and punish lawbreakers

6. To charter banks and other corporations

7. To take land for public use

8. To provide for the general welfare

Powers of state governments

1. To regulate trade within the state

2. To establish local governments

3. To protect the public health, safety, and morals

4. To ratify constitutional amendments

5. To determine qualifications of voters

6. To conduct elections

7. To change state constitutions and the form of state and local governments

8. To establish and support public schools

9. To license various occupational specialties

10. To exercise the "reserved powers" not granted to the federal government nor prohibited to the states

3. *Civil defense.* The state coordinates programs for wartime and natural disasters with national agencies.

4. *Commerce.* The state regulates and grants charters to corporations; aids businesses; issues licenses; regulates certain prices.

5. *Conservation.* The state preserves natural resources and wildlife; cooperates with federal conservation agencies.

6. *Education.* The state finances and administers state colleges and universities; works with local school boards in financing and establishing curriculums for the public elementary and secondary schools.

7. *Elections.* The state establishes boundaries for federal and state legislative districts; writes rules for voting and conduct of elections.

8. *Family relations.* The state makes laws regarding marriage, divorce, child support, and abortion.

9. *Food and drugs.* The state licenses pharmacists; sets up standards for inspection and sale of raw and processed foods; inspects retail stores and restaurants for sanitary conditions, honest weights and measures.

10. *Health.* The state licenses doctors and nurses; maintains state hospitals for those in need of institutional care.

11. *Highways.* The state builds and maintains state highways; oversees design and construction of the Interstate Highway system.

12. *Insurance.* The state regulates types of policies sold within the state; sets standards of coverage and payment.

13. *Labor.* The state maintains an employment service; establishes standards for working conditions and employment of minors; provides mediation service for labor disputes.

14. *Law enforcement.* The state runs its own prison system; polices state highways; aids communities in law enforcement.

15. *Local government.* The state approves boundaries for new towns and subdivisions; provides funds for operation of local government through refund of sales tax collections.

16. *Motor vehicles.* The state licenses drivers and vehicles; sets standards for operation of commercial and private cars, trucks, and buses.

17. *Welfare.* The state provides funding for welfare programs; coordinates welfare programs between local and federal agencies.

How do governors administer their states?

Colonial governors, thanks to their association with the king, ranked low on the list of public officials admired by the American people. Today, that has changed to the point where state governors can accurately be called the "presidents" of their states. In fact, a number of governors have used their state *gubernatorial* (from the Latin word for governor) experiences for later advancement to the White House.

QUALIFICATIONS

Minimum age requirements for a governor range from twenty-one to thirty-four; thirty-six states set a minimum age of thirty. Candidates must be United States citizens, qualified voters, and residents of the state (usually for at least five years). Membership in a political party is not required, but political common sense suggests that it is easier to win a gubernatorial election with party backing.

TERMS OF OFFICE

All states elect their governors by direct vote of the people. Governors were originally elected for one-year terms, but since 1920 all governors serve terms of at least two years. Most states now allow a four-year term, with elections set in "off years," when no presidential election competes for voters' attention. About one-fifth of the states have constitutional restrictions that prevent a governor from serving two consecutive terms. Several governors have evaded this limitation by running their wives for the office, thus keeping the governorship "in the family."

RESPONSIBILITIES

The governor's job closely resembles that of the President, if the responsibilities of foreign affairs and national security are subtracted. Generally, the governor may be thought of as (1) commander of the state's law enforcement, military (national guard), and emergency forces; (2) a ceremonial figure who provides civic leadership; (3) the leader of a political party; (4) a key figure in passing legislation; and (5) the chief administrative officer of the state. The requirements a strong governor must meet are outlined in the accompanying box. Two of the governor's jobs call for further discussion—legislative leadership and administrative responsibilities.

Legislative leadership. Like the President, governors propose legislative programs, work for their passage, attempt to defeat bills they dislike, and veto those which they feel should not have been passed. Governors support their programs with speeches and messages that receive widespread attention in the newspapers and on television. If public pressure does not produce results, governors use standard techniques of persuasion—phone calls, political threats and promises, or even a friendly breakfast in the governor's mansion.

Governors also serve on many influential state boards. These seldom-seen but important bodies regulate higher education, the penal system, corporations, and state medical institutions. Many states also allow the governor to call special sessions of the legislature to deal with pressing public issues.

A key part of every governor's program is the yearly state budget. By

Requirements for a strong governor

Requirement	Description
1. Constitutional authority	The great responsibility given a governor should be matched by constitutional powers—control of the executive branch, the veto, and the right to call special sessions of the legislature.
2. Adequate personal staff	A governor needs loyal, qualified staffers to handle the many administrative details of office.
3. Competent department directors	A governor cannot plan and carry out a program unless the people in positions of executive authority can do the job.
4. Modern administrative organization	Many states try to handle twentieth-century problems with nineteenth-century government organization.
5. Fiscal responsibility	Expenditures should be matched by income; the governor should control the budget process.
6. Legislative majority	The governor needs a working majority in both houses of the legislature to ensure passage of the administration's programs.
7. Party control	By achieving party leadership, the governor can maintain pressure on the legislature to approve the administration's programs.
8. Good press relations	Without good press contacts, no governor can achieve the public support needed to get things done.
9. Planning program	A good governor plans for the future growth and development of the state.
10. Social consciousness	A governor must be aware of the needs of all people in the state—minorities, the poor, and other groups in need of special attention.

Source: Adapted from Sherrill D. Luke, "The Need for Strength," *National Civic Review*, March 1964.

establishing spending goals, the governor effectively sets state priorities. In forty-two states the governors possess a power denied to the President—the *item veto*. This means that they may strike out individual items from the total budget; four states (Massachusetts, Tennessee, Pennsylvania, and California) allow the governor to reduce amounts as well as to eliminate specific appropriations.

Administrative responsibilities. No governor enjoys the total executive authority given the President. Most must share their administrative responsibilities with other elected officials (discussed below). A governor's law enforcement power, for example, is shared with the state attorney general. Most states allow their governors to pardon or reprieve convicted criminals and to commute sentences. A state's provisions for *extradition* (returning fugitives or suspected lawbreakers to other states) require the governor's approval before the transfer can be made.

Another source of gubernatorial strength lies in the power of appointment. Many state officials owe their jobs to the governor—judges, members of state boards and commissions, and some personnel in administrative departments. States differ in their methods of confirming appointments— some require legislative approval, others do not. Once appointed, officials can usually be removed only after legislative or judicial hearings.

REMOVAL FROM OFFICE

Forty-nine states have constitutional provisions for impeaching a governor; four have been impeached and convicted in this century. About one-fourth of the states allow voters to remove a governor by the recall, but only one has had his term cut short in this way (see page 391). As with presidents, the wrath of the voters is usually withheld until election time.

OTHER STATE EXECUTIVE OFFICIALS

Governors receive administrative assistance from a number of state officials, some elected and some appointed. The recent trend has been toward a unified executive branch, with fewer elected officials; Alaska elects only two, compared to North Dakota's eleven.

1. *Lieutenant governor.* Three-quarters of the states elect a lieutenant governor. Most lieutenant governors preside over the state senate and sit as acting governor when the governor is out of the state. While serving as acting governor, they may veto or sign bills, make appointments, and perform other official duties. The lieutenant governor succeeds to the higher office upon the death, retirement, or impeachment of the governor.

2. *Attorney general.* All but ten states elect their chief law enforcement officer. Many political scientists consider this office the second most important in the state. The attorney general has three major responsibilities: (a) to see that state laws are enforced; (b) to represent the state in court, either as chief prosecutor or defense attorney; and (c) to serve as legal advisor to state government. These duties give the attorney general great public visibility and considerable political muscle.

3. *Secretary of state.* As chief clerk and recording officer, the secretary of state supervises the state's official business. Most secretaries of state (a) supervise elections and certify their results; (b) safeguard the state's official papers; (c) issue certificates of incorporation and register trademarks; and (d) use the state seal to authenticate official documents.

4. *State treasurer.* The state treasurer collects state tax revenues and pays bills that have been approved by the state auditor. The treasurer deposits state money in bank accounts until needed, and supervises the sale of state bonds.

5. *State auditor.* States differ in their approaches to the office of auditor (or comptroller, as the office is sometimes called). Basically, an auditor examines the accounts of state agencies and authorizes the expenditure of state funds for legitimate purposes. Some auditors are authorized to conduct post-audits designed to ensure that public agencies are using their funds properly.

6. *Superintendent of public instruction.* Over thirty states elect their top state school official. The superintendent of public instruction oversees the administration of the public schools and enforces the state education code. Through their influence on textbook adoptions, curriculum frameworks, and teacher certification (licensing), superintendents can greatly influence the instructional programs of the local school districts.

LET'S REVIEW FOR A MOMENT

Many Americans take notice of their state governments only when the governor or legislature does something they don't like. An increase in the sales tax, a cut in school funding, a change in the welfare program— these arouse strong emotions. Day by day, it is federal activities that grab the headlines. The men and women who run each state's government, however, make decisions just as vital to the lives of every citizen of their state—but they seem to work behind a curtain of invisibility.

Do you disagree with that statement? Good—now name the elected officials who serve in your state capital. Let's see, there's Governor So-and-so. And Lieutenant Governor What's-his-name. And Attorney General . . . well, you get the idea.

And, of course, you're up to date on your state constitution, aren't you? If not, don't worry. You're not alone. The fact is, though, that your state constitution forms the basis for all state government. Typically, your state constitution will contain many of the same provisions as the United States Constitution—separation of powers, checks and balances, a bill of rights, a plan for executive, legislative, and judicial branches—but it will be longer, with many amendments.

State authority touches your life in three major areas. The citizens of your state have given their government the right to (1) protect public safety (the police power), (2) regulate business and commerce, and (3) supervise the state's political subdivisions. Talk to a member of your city council, and it won't take long to discover how many local activities are tied into state regulation—highway maintenance, law enforcement, and tax collection, to name a few.

The governor and other administrative officials of the state have the executive authority. Lawmaking responsibilities, of course, belong to the state legislature, discussed below.

What role does the legislature
play in state government?

Most citizens find that their closest contact with state government comes through their local representative to the state legislature. Most members of a state senate and house of representatives live and work within the community they serve. In many states, their offices are not considered full-time positions, and salaries run as low as $200 a session in New Hampshire. Other states recognize the importance of attracting highly qualified legislators, and pay accordingly. Several states now pay over $25,000 a year. Most states also provide additional payments for office expenses and for travel and mailing costs associated with the office. (See Table 17.1 on pages 412–13 for a summary of salaries, terms, and memberships of all the state governments.)

ORGANIZATION

All states except Nebraska elect representatives to a bicameral legislature. The upper house is known as the senate, and the lower house is most often called the house of representatives. Five states name their lower house the assembly, and three call it the house of delegates. Some twenty states summon their legislatures into session every year; the others meet every other year unless the governor calls a special session.

Leadership. The internal organization of most state legislatures resembles that of Congress. A speaker elected by the majority party usually presides over the lower house. Three-quarters of the states give the lieutenant governor the job of chairing the senate. Each house utilizes a number of standing committees. Committee members specialize in writing the bills that will regulate state finance, taxation, agriculture, labor, business, and the like.

This committee system carries even more authority than does that of Congress. Because much legislation comes out of meetings among the governor, powerful committee chairmen, and party leaders, the average legislator has relatively little influence. Party discipline keeps individual lawmakers in line; the unspoken rule says that if you don't follow orders, your own bills will never be reported out of committee.

Legislative councils. Because the legislature meets infrequently in many states, legislative councils have been established to keep work moving. Members chosen from both houses meet several times during the period between sessions to prepare a legislative program. Members of the council (or of standing committees, in other states) hold meetings across the state to listen to the public's opinions and study state problems. A professional staff of legislative experts supports the legislators by supplying research data, writing bills, and scheduling hearings.

Direct democracy. Several states allow voters to legislate for themselves through use of the referendum and initiative. These forms of direct democracy (see Chapter 16) bypass the state legislature.

PROBLEMS WITH STATE LEGISLATURES

Even though state law governs the people of a state as surely as federal law governs all Americans, state legislatures have seldom earned great public confidence. Some of the reasons are as follows:

1. Political games. Politics plays an important role in the work of state legislatures. Members may speak out in public for or against a particular bill, but party discipline usually takes over when the votes are counted. Stalemates often develop when the governor is of one party and the opposition party controls the legislature. If a compromise cannot be worked out, the legislation dies—or emerges greatly weakened.

2. Non-party splits. Legislatures may also split along regional, liberal v. conservative, or rural v. urban lines. This happens more frequently where one party consistently controls the legislature, as has been true in the South. Again, stalemate results, with urban lawmakers refusing to support farm programs, and vice versa.

3. Lobbyists. Lobbyists and special-interest groups frequently find state legislatures receptive to their arguments. With many legislators poorly paid and inexperienced, unscrupulous lobbyists "wheel and deal" by offering special favors, information, and even money in return for votes. A state that receives much of its income from a particular industry (agriculture, oil, steel, or aerospace, for example) will often enact laws favorable to that activity. Attempts to regulate lobbying have not proven particularly successful.

4. Last-minute laws. In many states, the approach of the deadline for the end of a legislative session brings on a rush of last-minute bills. The entire legislative process, normally slow and orderly, moves faster. Bills receive quick hearings, and debate is held to a minimum. As a result, the people of the state end up with hastily enacted, ill-considered laws, many of which benefit only special-interest groups.

REFORM PROPOSALS

Suggestions for improving the state legislatures have always been easy to find; the problem has been in putting reforms into effect. Some of the most common proposals have called for (1) removing limits on length of sessions; (2) attracting better-qualified legislators by raising salaries and benefits; (3) enlarging professional staffs to aid overworked legislators; (4) limiting the time during which new bills can be introduced in order to end the last-minute jam; and (5) preventing lawmakers from voting on bills in which they have a personal financial interest.

How do the states use their powers of law enforcement?

Protecting the public safety is one of the most basic of governmental responsibilities. The state must guard its citizens from the dangers of natural

Table 17.1

State governments: terms, salaries, and memberships of the executive, legislative, and judicial branches

State	Governor		Legislature					Highest court		
	Term, years	Annual salary	Membership Upper house	Lower house	Term, yrs. Upper house	Lower house	Salaries of members	Members	Term, years	Annual salary
Alabama	4†	$50,000	35	105	4	4	$ 6,800/yr.	9	6	$39,500
Alaska	4	70,068	20	40	4	2	17,280/yr.	5	3/10	70,068
Arizona	4	50,000	30	60	2	2	6,000/yr.	5	6	47,500
Arkansas	2	35,000	35	100	4	2	7,500/yr.	7	8	41,243
California	4	49,100	40	80	4	2	25,555/yr.	7	12	62,935
Colorado	4	50,000	35	65	4	2	12,000/yr.	7	10	45,600
Connecticut	4	42,000	36	151	2	2	17,000/2 yrs.	6	8	42,400
Delaware	4†	35,000	21	41	4	2	9,600/yr.	3	12	42,000
Florida	4‡	50,000	40	120	4	2	12,000/yr.	7	6	49,380
Georgia	4‡	61,050	56	180	2	2	7,200/yr.	7	6	48,530
Hawaii	4	50,000	25	51	4	2	12,000/sess.	5	10	45,000
Idaho	4	33,000	35	70	2	2	4,200/yr.	5	6	38,000
Illinois	4	58,000	59	177	4–2	2	28,000/yr.	7	10	58,000
Indiana	4‡	48,000	50	100	4	2	9,600/2 yrs.	5	2/10	42,000
Iowa	4	60,000	50	100	4	2	12,000/yr.	9	8	49,000
Kansas	4	45,000	40	125	4	2	35/day	7	6	47,500
Kentucky	4*	45,000	38	100	4	2	50/day	7	8	49,000
Louisiana	4	52,400	39	105	4	4	50/day	7	10	56,200
Maine	4	35,000	33	151	2	2	7,000/2 yrs.	6	7	26,000
Maryland	4‡	60,000	47	141	4	4	17,600/yr.	7	10	56,200
Massachusetts	4	60,000	40	160	2	2	20,335/yr.	7	Life	50,000
Michigan	4	61,500	38	110	4	2	25,500/yr.	7	8	56,500
Minnesota	4	58,000	67	134	4	2	16,500/yr.	9	6	49,000
Mississippi	4*	53,000	52	122	4	4	8,100/sess.	9	8	46,000

State										
Missouri	4‡	$55,000	34	163	4	2	$15,000/yr.	7	12	$50,000
Montana	4	37,500	50	100	4	2	40/day	7	8	38,000
Nebraska	4‡	40,000	49	—	4	—	4,800/yr.	7	6	43,000
Nevada	4	50,000	20	40	4	2	4,800/2 yrs.	5	6	47,250
New Hampshire	2	44,520	24	375–400	2	2	200/2 yrs.	5	to age 70	42,400
New Jersey	4‡	65,000	40	80	4	2	18,000/yr.	7	7	56,000
New Mexico	4*	50,000	42	70	4	2	40/day	5	8	44,000
New York	4	85,000	60	150	2	2	23,500/yr.	7	14	69,352
North Carolina	4*	50,085	50	120	2	2	6,400/yr.	7	8	50,400
North Dakota	4	42,000	50	100	4	2	5/day	5	10	41,700
Ohio	4	50,000	33	99	4	2	22,500/yr.	7	6	51,000
Oklahoma	4	48,000	48	101	4	2	12,948/yr.	9	6	40,700
Oregon	4‡	53,394	30	60	4	2	8,400/yr.	7	6	51,356
Pennsylvania	4	66,000	50	203	4	2	25,000/yr.	7	10	64,500
Rhode Island	2	42,500	50	100	2	2	5/day	5	§	42,198
South Carolina	4‡	39,500	46	124	4	2	10,000/yr.	5	10	47,000
South Dakota	4‡	45,500	35	70	2	2	6,000/2 yrs.	5	8	43,000
Tennessee	4	68,226	33	99	4	2	8,308/yr.	5	8	62,616
Texas	4	71,400	31	150	4	2	7,200/yr.	9	6	59,600
Utah	4	40,000	29	75	4	2	25/day	5	10	36,000
Vermont	2	44,850	30	150	2	2	225/wk.	5	6	35,500
Virginia	4*	60,000	40	100	4	2	8,000/yr.	7	12	54,000
Washington	4	63,000	49	98	4	2	11,200/yr.	9	6	51,500
West Virginia	4	50,000	34	100	4	2	5,136/yr.	5	12	40,000
Wisconsin	4	65,801	33	99	4	2	22,632/yr.	7	10	56,016
Wyoming	4	55,000	30	62	4	2	74/day	5	8	48,500

* Cannot succeed self in office.
† May serve only two terms, consecutive or otherwise.
‡ May not serve third consecutive term.
§ Term of good behavior.

Source: Adapted from *Information Please Almanac, 1981,* p. 701.

disaster, fire, and crime. In the United States, law enforcement and prosecution of crime usually remain in the hands of local authorities, unless a federal law has been violated. The state does, however, take a direct hand in maintaining public safety in a number of other areas:

STATE POLICE

State police forces began with the founding of the Texas Rangers in 1835. In this century, the automobile soon overwhelmed the abilities of local police to cope with the twin problems of traffic and fast-moving criminals. In response, modern state police forces were developed. Many of them are composed of two segments: (1) the highway patrol, which enforces traffic safety on the state's highways, and (2) an administrative authority, which coordinates law enforcement activities among the local police forces across the state.

SPECIALIZED ENFORCEMENT OFFICIALS

Most states also support a number of specialized enforcement officials, such as (1) fish and game wardens, (2) fire wardens, (3) weights and measures inspectors, and (4) liquor control officers. Even some forestry officials have begun carrying weapons and making arrests in overcrowded state parks, where urban problems have moved outdoors.

PENAL INSTITUTIONS

One of the principal—and most controversial—law enforcement responsibilities is the management of the nation's prison system. Federal penitentiaries hold prisoners convicted of crimes by federal courts. Minor offenders against state laws are held in city jails, while those serving a year or less usually stay in county jails. Serious offenders against state laws are housed in state-run penal institutions.

Federal and state prisons held over 300,000 inmates in 1980 at a cost running into billions of dollars a year. Nine out of ten of these prisoners are held in state prisons. As prison sentences have increased in length, prisons have become overcrowded. One study estimated that the average state prison was packed 58 percent above its safe capacity. This overcrowding has often led to prison riots and other deadly violence.

Failure of rehabilitation. The major trend in prison management throughout the past century has been to replace punishment with *rehabilitation* efforts. Rehabilitation means helping prisoners recover their self-respect, learn new skills, and return to society as productive, lawabiding citizens.

Now, almost everyone connected with the criminal justice system— judges, lawyers, penologists, and even convicts themselves—acknowledges that rehabilitation in prison does not work for most inmates. As former Governor Edmund G. Brown of California stated, "[Prisons] don't rehabilitate, they don't deter, they don't punish, and they don't protect." More than one-half of all prisoners released after serving their sentences end up behind bars again.

Some penologists urge the elimination of prisons altogether, except to isolate the 10 to 20 percent of criminals whose potential for violence threatens the public safety. All other offenders, they suggest, should be handled within the community in halfway houses, social welfare facilities, drug treatment centers, and mental health institutions. Experiments in which nonviolent prisoners are allowed to continue working at their regular jobs, returning to prison each night, have generally been successful on a small scale.

Prison as punishment. A consensus seems to be emerging among prison experts and politicians that prison systems should be geared to a single task—punishment by confinement (see Figure 17.2). This return to an earlier view of prisons—born of rising prison costs and crime rates and the failure of rehabilitation efforts—upholds public safety as a first priority. Conviction for certain offenses, these critics say, should carry an automatic

Figure 17.2
Although rehabilitation is the primary goal of the prison system, the bleakness and boredom found in most prisons serve more to punish than to reform criminals.
Source: Magnum Photos.

prison sentence. Crimes most frequently mentioned in this regard are murder, rape, robbery, burglary, arson, and aggravated assault. Since the parole system hasn't prevented repeated offenses, the argument continues, convicts should serve their full sentences.

This side of the debate claims that enforced sentences will deter other would-be criminals from committing crimes. Released convicts, moreover, would stay "straight" in order to avoid a second term in prison. An equal amount of research can be found on the other side of this theory; as with many other social problems, no final answer has yet been found.

NATIONAL GUARD

The National Guard exists primarily as a trained reserve of combat troops for use in event of war. Until activated by the President, however, each state's National Guard units remain under the control of the governor. Although Guard units are available to help in any natural disaster or civil disorder, state officials prefer to use regular law enforcement personnel whenever possible. This preference results from the uneven quality of leadership and training in many guard units. Americans will long remember the tragedy at Kent State University in 1970, when Guardsmen opened fire on demonstrating students, killing four. On the other hand, in natural disasters, Guard personnel have performed well. Uniformed troops under military discipline have often been used to prevent looting and other crimes during the critical period immediately following a tornado, flood, or earthquake.

How do the states pay the costs of government?

State governments are no strangers to the rise in the cost of living. Increased costs for everything from salaries to paper clips have led to state and local tax bills that eat up one-fourth of all taxes paid by the American people. Both the national Constitution and individual state constitutions limit the ability of states to raise tax revenue. States cannot tax imports, for example, nor can they borrow from foreign governments.

WHERE THE MONEY COMES FROM

States once received most of their tax collections from the general property tax. That tax now accounts for less than 4 percent of total state revenues; the great bulk of property taxes goes to support counties, cities, and towns. The major sources of state income are:

State income taxes. Forty-four states collect an average of almost 30 percent of their tax revenues from a state income tax. Individual taxpayers pay state income taxes based on a percentage of their taxable incomes; corporations pay state corporation income taxes based on a percentage of their profits. Like the federal income tax, state income taxes are usually *progressive*—the rates increase as net income increases. Rates range from a flat 2 percent in Indiana and Pennsylvania to a maximum of 16 percent on income over $27,500 in Minnesota. Florida and South Dakota have no personal income tax; Nevada, Texas, Washington, and Wyoming collect neither personal nor corporate income taxes.

State sales taxes. The single most important source of tax revenue is the *general sales tax.* A general sales tax is a fixed percentage levied on retail sales of most products purchased by consumers. Some items may be exempted from the tax—food and medicine, for example. Forty-five states collect a general sales tax, with rates running from 2 percent (Oklahoma) to 7.5 percent (Connecticut). Because everyone pays the same sales tax, economists call it a *regressive tax*—that is, it hits hardest at those with the least money.

All states also levy *selected sales taxes* on items such as gasoline, tobacco products, and alcoholic beverages. Sales taxes are popular with state officials because (1) they are easy to collect and (2) the state can depend on the income they produce.

Other state revenues. The states have learned to find revenues in a number of areas. Some of these additional sources are (1) vehicle registration and license fees, (2) inheritance and estate taxes, (3) business license fees, (4) toll bridges and toll roads, (5) state-operated industries (utility companies, bus lines, harbor facilities, and the like), and (6) state-run lotteries (presently operating in thirteen states).

Federal contributions. The federal government hands over almost $50 billion a year for the use of state and local governments. Federal money is usually earmarked for particular projects—freeways, housing projects, urban renewal, hospital construction, improvement of law enforcement, education, and social welfare programs.

State borrowing. A number of states issue state bonds as a means of raising the large sums needed for major construction projects. Other states must operate on a "pay-as-you-go" basis—their constitutions prohibit borrowing.

WHERE THE MONEY GOES

About sixty cents out of every state tax dollar returns to the cities and counties. This money supports essential services such as education, public health, social welfare, housing, recreation, and public roads. By far the largest percentage goes to the schools, although the amount spent on welfare programs is the fastest-growing segment of the budget.

About thirty cents of each dollar pays for state activities—state government, hospitals, universities and colleges, parks, prisons, and other state institutions. The remaining ten cents goes for construction (mostly highways, hospitals, and other public facilities), plus a small amount for interest on state debts.

How do the states regulate corporations?

Like friendly enemies, the states and the corporations that do business within their boundaries play a continual game of tug-of-war. The states have the responsibility of collecting corporate income taxes and of protecting their citizens from economic and environmental abuse by the powerful corporations. The size and economic power of today's giant corporations, however, make this difficult. Because they are so important to the financial health of the state—in terms of jobs as well as revenues—the major companies can often bring strong political influence to bear on any attempt to raise taxes or increase controls over business operations. (Figure 17.3 compares the revenues of five large states with those of a typical large corporation.)

THE CORPORATIONS' "MAGNA CARTA"

In 1819, Chief Justice John Marshall issued a ruling in the case of *Dartmouth College v. Woodward* that has been called "the Magna Carta of the corporation." The state of New Hampshire had passed a law revising the private college's charter to bring it under state control. After hearing Daniel Webster's defense of his alma mater's independence, Marshall decided that once a state gave a charter to a corporation (whether a college or a business), that agreement was thereafter protected by the federal Constitution's provision that no state may enact a "law impairing the obligation of contracts." Thus, a state legislature could not unilaterally change what amounted to a contract between the state and the business that had been granted incorporation.

The meaning of the decision was clear: once a charter had been issued, the state's power to regulate a corporation's activities was limited. The Fourteenth Amendment later expanded this protection by including corporations in the definition of the word "persons." Corporations thus have all the legal rights (except for political rights such as voting) that individuals have within a state.

HOW TO FORM A CORPORATION

A business that wishes to form itself into a corporation must obtain a certificate of incorporation from the state. This *corporate charter* is usually issued by the office of the secretary of state. The charter describes the type of business the corporation may engage in; rules and regulations limiting corporate activities are also listed.

Three general requirements must normally be met before a charter will be issued: (1) The corporation must have a legitimate and reasonable purpose for incorporation. (2) The corporation must possess tangible assets, such as capital, a patent, land, or technical know-how in a particular area. (3) Most states also specify the minimum number of people who may participate in ownership. Only after it has been incorporated does the business have the right to sell securities.

Rules and standards for corporate behavior vary widely from state to state. Many corporations with headquarters in one state take out their charter in another state, in order to benefit from more liberal laws in the

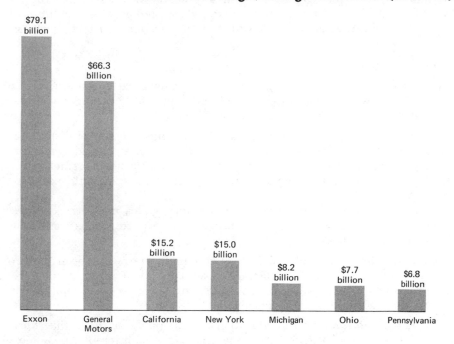

Figure 17.3   **Comparison of corporation revenues with those of five large state governments (1979–80)**

Exxon	$79.1 billion
General Motors	$66.3 billion
California	$15.2 billion
New York	$15.0 billion
Michigan	$8.2 billion
Ohio	$7.7 billion
Pennsylvania	$6.8 billion

second state. Once incorporated in that one state, they may operate in all states under the protection of Article IV of the Constitution.

ADVANTAGES OF INCORPORATION

The advantages of incorporation are many. Most importantly, the ownership of stock in a corporation carries *limited liability*. If the business fails, the stockholders cannot lose any more money than they have invested. In addition, the corporation has a life of its own; even though the founders die, the business continues. Finally, by issuing stocks and bonds, the corporation can raise the huge sums of money needed to build plants, develop new products, and open untapped markets.

BENEFITS TO THE STATE

By allowing corporations to operate, the people of a state benefit through increased job opportunities, greater tax revenues, and development of natural resources. Against these benefits must be balanced the problems of industrialization—creation of crowded urban areas and environmental pollution.

What is the role of the states in educating their citizens?

Every state constitution requires that state government provide a system of free public education. In 1980, that meant over 47 million public school students between the ages of five and seventeen, with state expenditures of some $43 billion (and a total federal, state, and local expenditure of $107.1 billion). Education in the United States has become a big business.

ORGANIZATION

State *education codes* (laws passed by the legislature pertaining to the schools) allocate to varying levels of local government the day-to-day responsibility for operating the public schools.

Local school districts. Over one-half of the states use school districts as the basic unit of school administration. A district may include an entire town or city, or even several incorporated communities; a single community may also contain separate districts for elementary and secondary schools.

By contrast, some Southeastern and Western states make the counties responsible for local education. Northeastern states often place control of the schools in the townships.

Consolidation of school districts. A general pattern has been to consolidate smaller districts into larger, more economical units, particularly in rural areas. The little red schoolhouse has largely been replaced by larger, more efficient unified schools.

Line of authority. The top education official in all states is the *superintendent of public instruction* (some states use a different title). Most states also have a policy-making body called the state board of education. The superintendent and the board carry out state laws regarding all aspects of education—curriculum, compulsory attendance laws, textbook adoption, training and licensing of teachers, and the like. Even though the state has shown a tendency to assume greater control over education, local boards of education still retain considerable authority. School curriculum, discipline, and philosophy may differ greatly in two apparently similar districts within the same state.

FINANCING THE SCHOOLS

Schools receive financial support from three main sources: local property taxes, state allocations, and federal funding. Nationally, state aid contributes an average of 20 percent of a school district's yearly budget. Some states contribute less, while in others the percentage runs as high as 60 percent. Federal assistance generally funds specific programs, such as language help for non–English-speaking students, vocational training courses, and efforts to improve instruction.

Critics of the American schools have long complained that an accident of geography may determine the quality of a person's education. Because a school district's income from local property taxes varies with the value of land, housing, and business in the community, a well-to-do district may be able to spend $2,000 a year per pupil, while a poorer district a few miles away may have only $1,000 to spend. Recent court decisions have ordered the states to begin revising the system so that all students in a state receive equal educational opportunities.

HIGHER EDUCATION

In addition to its public elementary and secondary schools, each state supports a system of colleges and universities. Out of some 8 million students enrolled in institutions of higher education nationwide, over 6 million attend state-supported schools. Many states have established a system of two-year colleges (called junior or community colleges) as a means of reaching more post-secondary students of all ages. Junior colleges also take some of the financial burden off the colleges. State tax dollars must take up the difference between low tuition charges and the actual cost of a higher education.

ISSUES IN PUBLIC EDUCATION

No area in American life today can be considered problem-free. Public education, however, attracts an overload of critics and self-proclaimed experts.

Federal aid. As more and more federal funds flow into local schools (see Figure 17.4), the debate over this form of aid increases. Those who oppose federal aid fear that it will bring federal control and standardization of school curriculums and programs. This group believes strongly in *local*

Figure 17.4

The magnitude of federal involvement in all levels of education can be seen in the total grants and loans distributed in 1980—more than $25 billion.

control of the schools, a concept summed up by the question, "Why let Washington tell us how to educate our children?"

Supporters of federal aid believe it can help end the vast differences in the amounts spent per pupil in the various states. That argument becomes clearer when the range of state spending per pupil in the 1978–79 school year is considered: Arkansas, $1,218 per student; New York, $2,645; national average, $1,816. Proponents also claim that federal assistance can raise the general quality of education in all states by paying for new programs that otherwise could not be funded.

Aid to church-supported schools. State legislatures almost yearly pass bills that authorize aid to church-supported schools for tuition reimbursement, transportation, textbooks, and other needs. Just as regularly, the courts strike down the laws as violations of the traditional separation of church and state. Religious groups make two practical points: (1) parents who send their children to church-supported schools also pay for the support of the public schools through their property taxes, and (2) if all students currently enrolled in such schools were suddenly to switch to the public schools, the system would be overloaded. In New York, for example, 20 percent of the state's student population attend church-supported schools.

Upgrading education. A number of recent best-selling books have told the American people that "Johnny can't read." The argument over the quality of education offered by the public schools has caused a great deal of bitter community debate. Supporters of the system admit that the schools are not perfect, but blame most of the problems on crowded classrooms, low budgets, and a society more tuned in to television than to the great books. Opponents blame the schools for lower test scores in reading and mathematics, increased truancy, violence on the campus, and other signs of unrest. The schools themselves, confused as to exactly what their communities want, have developed liberal programs featuring electives and "survival skills" at the same time that many parents have decided that increased emphasis on academic disciplines is needed. Even teachers, once the most timid of professional groups, now go out on strike regularly over salary and job conditions. As with many complex social issues, the conflict rages on, with no solution in sight.

How does the federal government cooperate with the states?

When the Founders of our country chose a federal system, they guaranteed that the national government and the states would be forced into a close working relationship. As the nullification and secession arguments of the mid-1800's demonstrated, that association has not always been a peaceful one. In this century, disagreements have arisen over such questions as (1) ownership of offshore oil deposits; (2) division of tax revenues between the states and Washington; (3) responsibility for providing funds

Figure 17.5

The federal government, two states (Maryland and Virginia), and the District of Columbia jointly constructed this sewage treatment plant. The Environmental Protection Agency has pledged billions of dollars to assist states and communities in purifying their rivers and lakes through similar joint projects. Source: EPA.

for specific services, particularly in the area of welfare; and (4) environmental controls.

AREAS OF COOPERATION

Despite these and other disputes, federal–state cooperation has been achieved in the areas of technical agreements and financial assistance.

Technical agreements. State and federal officials have worked out agreements on such matters as (1) regulation of interstate commerce; (2) joint ventures that involve both state and federal agencies—for example, flood control, hydroelectric and nuclear power, and sewage treatment projects (see Figure 17.5) and coordinated law enforcement programs; (3) sharing of research data; and (4) joint conferences that bring together officials from both government levels to share views and problems.

Financial assistance. An increasing amount of federal money has begun to find its way back to the states. This aid comes in four categories: grants-in-aid, revenue-sharing, aid to impacted areas, and shared-revenue arrangements.

1. *Grants-in-aid.* Grants-in-aid are given for specific purposes as defined by the federal government—highway construction, unemployment and welfare benefits, and about sixty other purposes. Grants come complete with "strings" tied to the money by Congress. These restrictions include controls on what the money is spent for, a requirement that the state put up a specified share of the costs, and acceptance of federal supervision over the spending of the money.

2. *Revenue-sharing.* Almost the opposite of grants-in-aid, revenue-sharing

operates on the belief that the states know best how to solve their own problems. In support of that philosophy, the federal government returns about $6.9 billion of its tax revenues each year to the states, in much the same way that the states return their sales-tax revenues to local governments.

3. *Aid to impacted areas.* The presence of a large military base or defense industry, along with its personnel and their families, often places heavy demands on public services in that particular area. In recognition of this problem, the federal government provides aid to such *impacted areas* in the form of funds for schools, utilities, housing, and other local needs. The state usually administers this form of aid.

4. *Shared-revenue arrangements.* State and local governments cannot tax federal lands. To help compensate for this lack of income, the federal government shares with state and local governments its revenues from the lease or sale of such lands.

TOWARD INCREASED FEDERAL CONTROL

Historically, the long-term trend has been toward increased federal control at the expense of state autonomy. The two main reasons for this have been (1) the growth of the federal budget and the taxing power that goes with it and (2) court rulings that have consistently added to federal power. Recent moves by the federal government toward revenue-sharing and greater cooperation in the planning of state projects have not reversed the trend. In turn, the states have increased their own control of local government. Political power in the United States has grown more and more centralized; whether or not to try to decentralize it has become one of the nation's most important questions.

SUMMARY AND CONCLUSIONS

1. The nature and powers of state governments are defined by the state constitutions. All state constitutions contain the same separation of powers and system of checks and balances found in the national Constitution. Most state constitutions contain many provisions which would normally be passed as statute laws. This practice reflects the people's distrust of state legislatures, as well as the ease with which special-interest groups can obtain constitutional amendments.

2. State government touches the lives of its people in three major areas: (1) enforcement of laws regarding the public safety, (2) regulation of business and industry, and (3) supervision of county and city government. From aeronautics to welfare, the state administers and regulates the affairs of private citizens and giant corporations.

3. State governors perform many of the same jobs as the President.

Elected for a four-year term in most states, they act as the state's chief executive officer, supervise law enforcement, promote legislation, take part in public ceremonies, and provide political leadership. Other important members of the state administration include the *lieutenant governor*, the *attorney general*, and the *secretary of state*.

4. State legislatures themselves have undergone many changes. Legislative sessions have grown longer, and the membership has been reapportioned on the basis of population in both houses. The committee system has grown in importance as legislation has become more complex. Many state legislatures meet only every other year, making it necessary to set up *legislative councils*, which plan for future meetings.

5. State protection of the *public safety* is divided between state and local authorities. State responsibilities include (1) maintenance of a state police force and other specialized law enforcement agencies; (2) running a state penal system; and (3) joining the federal government in supporting National Guard units for use in emergency situations. Most experts believe the penal system has failed to deter crime and *rehabilitate* criminals. They call for reforms that include longer, fixed terms, speedier trials, and an end to parole.

6. State and local governments consume one-fourth of the money Americans pay in taxes. State tax revenues are drawn from a variety of sources, the most important of which are (1) state income taxes levied on individuals and corporations, (2) *general* and *selective sales taxes*, (3) miscellaneous sources, including license fees and state-operated businesses, (4) federal sources, and (5) state borrowing. Most state revenues go to support local government, particularly education, social welfare, and highways.

7. Once a *corporate charter* has been granted to a corporation, the state's ability to regulate the business is limited by the terms of the charter. States vary in their treatment of corporations; some are lenient, others regulate strictly. Corporations bring more jobs and tax revenues to a state, but they also require increased public services.

8. Each state assumes responsibility for the free public education of its citizens. A state board of education oversees general standards of curriculum, recommends textbooks, and sets graduation requirements. Under each state's *education code*, local boards retain considerable authority over elementary and secondary schools. State colleges and universities complete the system of public education. The problems of federal aid (and increasing federal control), state aid to religious schools (denied by court decisions), and improving education (lots of theories but no hard answers) also complicate the education business.

9. Under the federal system, the states have been drawn into a close relationship with the national government. Federal money—*grants-in-aid, revenue-sharing, aid to impacted areas,* and *shared-revenue arrangements* —helps solve state financial difficulties, but brings with it federal leverage over decisions many people believe should be made by state and local governments.

REVIEW QUESTIONS AND ACTIVITIES

TERMS YOU SHOULD KNOW

aid to impacted areas

attorney general

auditor

corporate charter

education code

extradition

general sales tax

grants-in-aid

gubernatorial

item veto

legislative council

lieutenant governor

limited liability

local control

progressive tax

public safety

regressive tax

rehabilitation

revenue-sharing

secretary of state

selective sales tax

shared-revenue arrangements

superintendent of public instruction

treasurer

REVIEW QUESTIONS

The following multiple-choice questions are based on the important ideas presented in this chapter. Select the response that best completes each statement.

1. If South Carolina had been successful in establishing the doctrine of nullification, (a) many bad laws would have been set aside. (b) the United States would have returned to British control. (c) the Union would have been strengthened. (d) federalism would have been badly damaged. (e) nothing important would have happened.

2. The activities of state government have an effect on almost everything an individual American does in daily life. This statement is (a) true. (b) false; state governments have little impact on individual citizens. (c) false; state governments affect only an individual's education, taxes, and safety.

3. To influence legislative actions, a governor could *not* use (a) the item veto. (b) public messages, press conferences, and speeches. (c) political armtwisting. (d) private meetings with chairpersons of key committees. (e) a declaration that a law is unconstitutional.

4. Next to the governor, the most important state official is probably the (a) lieutenant governor. (b) attorney general. (c) treasurer. (d) secretary of state. (e) auditor.

5. The only way to remove incompetent or dishonest governors from office is to impeach them. This statement is (a) true. (b) false; the federal government can remove a governor from office if the federal

courts request it. (c) false; in some states, a governor may be removed by a recall election.

6. The biggest recent change in state legislatures has been in the trend toward unicameral organization. This statement is (a) true. (b) false; the biggest change has been the reapportionment of the upper house strictly on the basis of population. (c) false; the biggest change has been the passage of new laws that effectively prevent lobbyists from influencing legislation.

7. The largest single source of income for the states is (a) the property tax. (b) the sales tax. (c) the individual and corporate income tax. (d) federal grants-in-aid. (e) state-operated businesses.

8. The biggest single item in the budget of state and local governments is for (a) welfare. (b) public roads and highways. (c) the operating expenses of state government. (d) prisons and other law enforcement activities. (e) public schools and state-supported colleges.

9. The advantage of incorporating a business is that no one can lose more than the amount invested. This concept is known as (a) corporate charter. (b) limited liability. (c) issuing securities. (d) having the legal status of a "person." (e) exemption from corporate income taxes.

10. Federal aid to schools is welcomed by many educators, but others object because they fear that federal money also means that the government will (a) take away their jobs. (b) force the schools to teach religious subjects. (c) gain greater control of school curriculum and policy. (d) impose higher property taxes. (e) all of these are possible outcomes.

CONCEPT DEVELOPMENT

This chapter has explored a number of significant concepts relating to state government. You can use your skills in thinking, researching, and writing to answer the following questions.

1. Describe the organization of your state government. What reforms are needed to improve it?

2. Why have Americans increasingly looked to Washington rather than to their state capitals for solutions to individual and community problems? Why do many people believe that this is a trend that should be reversed?

3. Under the American federal system, divorce laws, voting qualifications, regulation of business, and similar areas differ from state to state. Is this desirable? Why or why not?

4. From what sources does your state government draw its budget? What are the major services it provides with these funds?

5. Most public schools are regulated by local, county, state, and federal government agencies. Which governing body holds the balance of power? If you had the authority, what would you change in your schools?

ACTIVITIES

The following activities are designed to help you use the ideas developed in this chapter.

1. Invite your local representative in the state legislature to speak to your class the next time he or she is in town (or to send a staff member). The talk might be broken into two segments: (a) a discussion of current issues in the state legislature and (b) a look at the job of a legislator—how to run for office, rewards of serving, careers in state politics.

2. Make a poster that compares your state with three or four states in different regions of the country on the basis of (a) population, (b) per capita income, (c) amount spent per student in public schools, (d) governor's salary, (e) legislative salaries, (e) percentage of registered voters among eligible citizens, (f) any other factors you consider important or interesting. Use illustrations with your figures to make this poster more attractive. The handiest source for this type of data is the almanac (but be sure it's a current edition).

3. You may remember that this chapter described the sales tax as a regressive form of taxation. In other words, rich and poor alike must pay the same amount of tax—an average of four cents on the dollar—in addition to the selling price of most products they buy. If you can, find out how many dollars your state collects in sales taxes each year. Now, think of ways this money might be obtained without using the sales tax. You might want to involve your class in this search. What about going in the opposite direction and cutting down on the state budget? What current programs should the state stop funding?

4. Discuss the problem of federal and state control in the schools with your principal or superintendent. You might ask (a) how much your district receives from these two sources, (b) how much control they actually exercise, and (c) what trends are visible in the future. Report the results of your interviews to your classmates. Do they believe strongly enough in local control to pass up federal money?

CHAPTER EIGHTEEN

The COUNTY: LARGEST DIVISION OF LOCAL GOVERNMENT

COUNTY (koun' tĭ), noun. 1. Obsolete except historically: an earldom. 2. In Great Britain and Northern Ireland, one of the territorial divisions constituting the chief units for administrative, judicial, and political purposes. 3. In the United States, the largest division of local government.

This dictionary definition makes obvious the origins of American counties. Medieval earldoms served as the basis of local administration for British kings who wanted to centralize their government. Americans brought the idea with them to the New World.

But the dictionary definition leaves out too much. What roles does the county play in the lives of people today? How many different ways of life, how many different forms of government can be found in the 3,044 counties that make up this country? The years have brought great changes, but smaller, rural counties have changed least of all.

Let's look at one of them.

Springfield with its 1,500 inhabitants in 1837 was the big town of Sangamon County, selling to the 18,000 people of the county a large part of their supplies, tools, groceries, handling grain, pork, beef, and produce, with stores, churches, schools, banks, newspapers, courts, lawyers, offices of government, taverns, saloons, places of entertainment. It was a city, its people ready to say that there was no more wilderness in that part of the country; the land had been surveyed and allotted.

The farm women who came to town wore shoes where they used to go barefooted; the men had changed from moccasins to rawhide boots and shoes. Farmers no longer spent time killing deer, tanning the hide and making leather breeches to tie at the ankles: it was cheaper and quicker to raise corn and buy pantaloons which had come from Massachusetts over the Ohio or the Mississippi River or the Great Lakes. Stores advertised "velvets, silks, satin, and Marseilles vestings . . . for gentlemen," and for ladies, "silks, crepe lisse, lace veils, thread lace, Thibet shawls, lace handkerchiefs, fine prunella shoes."

Carriages held men riding in top-boots and ruffled silk shirts, and women in silks and laces. It was civilization which Abraham Lincoln, twenty-eight years old, saw as he rode into Springfield that March day in 1837—to be a lawyer. Its people were mostly from Kentucky, coming by horse, wagon, and boat across country not yet cleared of wolves, wildcats, and horse thieves. And there were in Sangamon County 78 free negroes, 20 registered indentured servants, and six slaves.

The center of the town was a public square, with the courthouse, jails, stores, churches, banks, harness-makers, and blacksmiths lined about the square. The streets and sidewalks were plain black Illinois soil underfoot, except for gravel here and there for dry footing in rain or snow, and stones and sticks for street crossings.

Lincoln pulled in his horse at the general store of Joshua Speed. He asked the price of bedclothes for a single bedstead, which Speed figured at $17.00. "Cheap as it is, I have not the money to pay," he told Speed. "But if you will credit me until Christmas, and my experiment here as a lawyer is a success, I will pay you then. If I fail in that I will probably never pay you at all."

Speed said afterward, "The tone of his voice was so melancholy that I felt for him. I looked up at him and thought that I had never seen so gloomy and melancholy a face in my life." Speed offered to share his own big double bed upstairs over the store. Lincoln took his saddlebags upstairs, came down with his face lit up and said, "Well, Speed, I'm moved."*

Since Lincoln's time, the roads have been paved, electricity brings lights and power to comfortable homes, and rapid communications link previously isolated communities with the rest of the nation. Yet, should Lincoln find himself transported to a courthouse square in many of America's rural communities today, he would recognize more similarities than differences. The courtrooms, the officials, the politics of county government have not changed very much from those he knew in his beloved Illinois.

Earlier in this century, some political scientists predicted that counties would eventually disappear from American life. Nothing of the kind has occurred. Today's counties, large and small, still play an important part in the complex pattern of local government. This chapter will examine these questions about county government:

---

* From *Abraham Lincoln: The Prairie Years*, Volume I, pp. 215–17, by Carl Sandburg, copyright, 1926, by Harcourt Brace Jovanovich, Inc.; copyright, 1954, by Carl Sandburg. Reprinted by permission of Harcourt Brace Jovanovich, Inc.

1. What is the relationship of the county to the state?
2. How do counties differ in power and purpose?
3. How are the counties governed?
4. What are the jobs of county government?
5. How are the counties financed?
6. What problems face county government—and what can be done about them?

What is the relationship
of the county to the state?

The states cannot possibly conduct all the business of government from offices in a state capital. As a consequence, states have created a variety of subdivisions to administer state laws, serve the public welfare, and guard public safety. The states generally do this in two ways: (1) state agencies set up branches in the local communities—for example, the Department of Motor Vehicles operates a series of offices throughout the state; or (2) the state divides itself into permanent subdivisions that are given the authority to administer the law and provide needed public services.

These permanent political units are called *counties* in every state except Alaska ("boroughs") and Louisiana ("parishes"). Supreme Court Chief Justice Roger B. Taney once emphasized that the counties are creations of the state: "Counties are nothing more than certain portions of territory into which the state is divided for the convenient exercise of the powers of government."

Because they are creatures of the state, counties can exercise only the authority given them by state legislatures—and that authority varies greatly. The trend earlier in the century to ignore county government in favor of transferring power to the cities has been reversed. Today, many states have attempted to streamline and strengthen the county government—not always successfully. At the same time, state legislatures have had their hands tied by state constitutional amendments aimed at protecting the rights of county government from further legislative alteration.

HISTORICAL BACKGROUND

As was noted earlier, the concept of the county came to this country as part of our British heritage. By the time the first colonists left for the New World, British counties (or shires) had been established for centuries as administrative departments of the national government. The title of county sheriff, for example, can be traced back to the medieval English "shire-reeve." In time, the name was shortened to its modern form, but the job remains the same today—enforcing the laws, guarding prisoners, and carrying out the decisions of the courts.

Many American political leaders began their careers in county government. New York's Tammany Hall, the nation's oldest political "machine," rose to power by capturing control of the county courthouse. Only later, when the cities increased in wealth and population, did ambitious politicians shift their attention to city hall.

NUMBER AND SIZE OF COUNTIES

The fifty states have divided themselves into 3,042 counties. The number of counties per state ranges from 254 in Texas to three in Delaware. In geographical size, counties range from California's San Bernardino County (20,119 square miles) to New York County (less than 23 square miles).

Populations show similar contrasts. Los Angeles County has 7 million residents in its 4,069 square miles; and Cook County (Chicago), Illinois, bulges at the seams with over 5 million people in 954 square miles. At the other end of the scale, Alpine County in California's mountainous north has just over 1,000 people (see Figure 18.1).

COUNTIES STILL USEFUL

State legislatures drew most of the original county lines with the horse and buggy in mind. They believed that county residents should be able to travel to the county seat, conduct their business, and return home the same day. States find in counties a convenient unit for administering state-supported programs of education, welfare, recreation, library services, and the like.

In rural areas, the *county seat* still serves as the center of regional government. The town within the county that is made the county seat usually attracts additional business and industry.

Why do counties differ in power and purpose?

Counties differ not only in size and population, but also in basic structure. Early in U.S. history, the states of each region designed their counties to fit their particular economic and geographical situation.

SOUTHERN COUNTIES

The early South geared its administrative setup to the large plantations required for growing tobacco and cotton. Political power lay in the hands of the wealthy plantation owners. They often served as county officials, and met regularly at the call of the state governor as a "county court." In this capacity, they raised and collected taxes, laid out roads, maintained the jail, and constructed a county courthouse to serve as an administrative center.

Gradually, increased county business required the addition of more county officials—a sheriff, a coroner, a clerk of the county court, and constables to uphold the law. The sheriff supervised law enforcement activities and doubled as tax collector and county treasurer. The county clerk maintained court records, registered land titles, and kept the archives

Figure 18.1   **Counties vary greatly in geographic size and population: California's counties**

of the county. This Southern model, with its aristocratic features, was patterned closely after the British model.

NEW ENGLAND COUNTIES

Counties never developed into significant political structures in the New England states. The people engaged in fishing, shipbuilding, and trade, or worked small farms that produced little more than a bare living. Threats of French and Indian attack bound the colonists together in small towns.

In these communities they developed a township government that fulfilled many of the tasks which the Southern colonies allotted to the counties.

Even today, the New England counties typically have few administrative powers. Rhode Island and Connecticut, for example, hardly have county government at all; the Rhode Island counties are merely divisions of the state courts. In all New England states, the county boards exist mainly to administer welfare, maintain roads, and operate the county jails. They may not levy taxes, own property in the name of the county, or elect county officials.

MIDDLE STATES COUNTIES

Counties in the middle colonies (New York, New Jersey, and Pennsylvania) served as models for most of the remaining states. The counties of the middle states combined features of the Southern county and the New England township. As a result, county governments were given powers that overlapped those of the cities. Voters elect county officials to carry out a wide variety of duties, from keeping birth and death records to organizing the annual county fair. In return, elected officials (see the following section) must account to the people for the way in which they perform their duties.

How are the counties governed?

Most counties are governed by a group of public officials elected by the voters; after that, the differences tend to outnumber the similarities. The variations can be seen in the different titles given to the governing bodies of counties: the most common are boards of commissioners and boards of supervisors; others are levy courts, fiscal courts, commissioners' courts, commissioners of roads and revenues, and police juries. Very seldom does a county have a chief executive, however. Members of the governing bodies must share the authority.

COUNTY GOVERNING BODIES

Most county governing bodies are organized as either a board of commissioners or a board of supervisors.

Board of commissioners. Over two-thirds of the nation's counties are governed by a board of commissioners (see Figure 18.2). Voters elect three to seven commissioners to terms of four years (although in a few counties, terms vary from two to eight years). Commissioners may represent election districts within the county, or may be elected at large by all of the voters.

Board of supervisors. Roughly a third of the states have adopted the type of governing body known as a board of supervisors. Because supervisors are first chosen as township trustees or city council members, board membership may run anywhere from twelve to fifty; Wayne County,

Figure 18.2
A typical county government

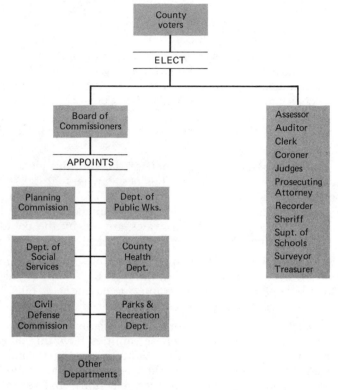

Michigan, has over one hundred supervisors. The size of the board requires that much of the work be done by committees. This works well enough with legislative matters, but smaller boards are more efficient where administrative details are concerned.

POWERS OF COUNTY GOVERNING BODIES

The principle of separation of powers was ignored when most county boards were created. Members exercise legislative, executive, and limited judicial functions in performing their regular daily duties.

Legislative powers. As legislative bodies, the county boards (1) regulate use of county property; (2) levy taxes; (3) issue bonds; (4) establish zoning regulations; (5) set requirements for business licenses; and (6) appropriate funds for county operations.

Executive powers. County boards demonstrate their executive authority when they (1) administer welfare programs, hospitals, schools, and jails; (2) collect taxes; (3) maintain roads; (4) keep records of births, deaths, and land transfers; (5) conduct elections; (6) build county facilities; and (7) enforce county regulations.

Judicial powers. Many county boards take on a judicial function when they sit as a tax review board for local taxpayers dissatisfied with the assessments on their properties.

OTHER COUNTY OFFICIALS

County business demands the services of a large number of public officials. Some counties require that candidates for many of these offices face the voters in a general election; others elect only the county board and perhaps a few key officials (often the sheriff, assessor, prosecuting attorney, and county judge).

Some of the most important county officials (listed in alphabetical order) are:

1. *County assessor.* More than one-half of the counties elect an official who becomes familiar to home and business owners at tax time. The county assessor studies each piece of property in the county and attempts to establish its fair market value; this evaluation becomes the basis on which the property will be taxed. Tax rates are set by the county board and by other taxing agencies, such as school boards and water districts.

2. *County auditor.* The county auditor (also known as the comptroller, or controller) oversees the financial affairs of the county. The auditor examines county accounts, issues warrants for payment of bills, and prepares balance sheets that summarize county finances.

3. *County clerk.* The office of county clerk carries more responsibility than the name suggests. The states whose counties have this office assign the clerk to serve as secretary to the county board, and sometimes as business manager for the county. The clerk issues marriage, hunting, and fishing licenses, records divorces, supervises elections, and records claims against the state. Some clerks compile the transcripts of court trials.

4. *County coroner.* A county official known to all followers of television crime shows, the coroner determines the cause of death when people have died under unusual circumstances. If evidence of death by criminal action is discovered, the coroner may issue a warrant for the arrest of suspected individuals. In many counties, the elected office of coroner has been replaced by an appointed county medical examiner.

5. *Prosecuting attorney.* The counties of all but three states elect a prosecuting attorney (more popularly known as the district attorney). As the name suggests, the prosecuting attorney tries to obtain convictions in criminal cases under the jurisdiction of the county courts. In addition, these officials present evidence of suspected wrongdoing to county grand juries.

6. *County recorder.* About one-half of the counties elect a county recorder to maintain property records and deeds. The job is an important one, for transfer of land titles can involve complex legal questions. Another name for this official is registrar of deeds.

7. *County sheriff.* Although they have traded in their horses for patrol

cars, county sheriffs still serve as the chief law enforcement officers for American counties. The sheriff's activities are usually confined to unincorporated areas within the county, for most cities maintain their own police forces. With the help of other county police officers, the sheriff supervises the arrest of lawbreakers, keeps the peace, carries out county court orders, serves warrants and subpoenas, and manages county prison and detention facilities. Almost all states elect their sheriffs for two- to four-year terms. Most receive a salary, but a few states allow county sheriffs to collect fees for their services—the more arrests made, the more fees received. As might be expected, this procedure has often led to corruption and an uneven administration of justice.

8. County superintendent of schools. All but nine states have a superintendent of schools in each county. Most counties elect the official who holds the office. The superintendent manages the county's own schools; cities and towns usually maintain separate school districts. In either case, the county superintendent (a) furnishes advisory services to all schools in the county, (b) distributes state funds, and (c) enforces the state education code.

9. County surveyor. The county surveyor is responsible for accurately surveying and recording county lands and boundaries. Sometimes called the county engineer, the surveyor may also oversee the construction and maintenance of public works—roads, bridges, sewer systems, and the like.

10. Other officials. Counties create other offices as needed. A typical county would also have a *county treasurer* to receive and collect county funds; *public health officers* to conduct clinics, give inoculations, and keep health records; and *county agricultural agents* to assist farmers and home gardeners.

LET'S REVIEW FOR A MOMENT

Counties have little to do with geography. The states needed convenient subdivisions to handle details of law enforcement, tax collection, and the like, so they borrowed a standard British administrative unit. Along the way, just about every state gave its counties a slightly different form of government. In the same spirit, counties also vary immensely in size and population.

The Southern colonies set up their counties as part of an agricultural way of life and made them administrative agencies of the state. New England took an opposite tack. Because the townships there took over many of the functions normally given to counties, the New England county remained limited in its powers. As other states joined the Union, they adopted a combined county-township form of county government first used in the middle states.

The governing body in most American counties is known as either a *board of commissioners* or a *board of supervisors*. Either way, the county board never worries about separation of powers. Under most state constitutions, it exercises legislative, executive, and limited judicial powers.

Other county officials keep tabs on you from birth to the grave, although you may never see them. The *county clerk* records your birth and later issues your marriage license. The *county recorder* keeps your property title straight, and the *sheriff* serves a court order on you if you neglect the mortgage payments. The *assessor* establishes the fair market value of your house for tax purposes. And, at the end of the line, the *coroner* may examine your body to make sure that your sudden death wasn't due to foul play.

What are the jobs of county government?

County government operates within strict limitations established by the state constitution and state law. In this respect, the relationship between state and county is unitary rather than federal. (See Chapter 1 for a discussion of unitary systems of government.) Even so, as the listing of county officials suggests, the county has a number of important jobs to do.

WELFARE

English tradition has always called upon the county to provide care for the poor and needy within its borders. Today's U.S. county follows in that

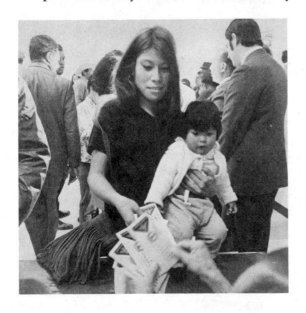

Figure 18.3

A migrant family in Florida receives food stamps under a federal program administered by the counties. Source: Wide World Photos.

Figure 18.4

The expanding cost of welfare at every level of government (1950–1981)

(California aid to families with dependent children
and general relief subsistence grants)
(in millions of dollars)

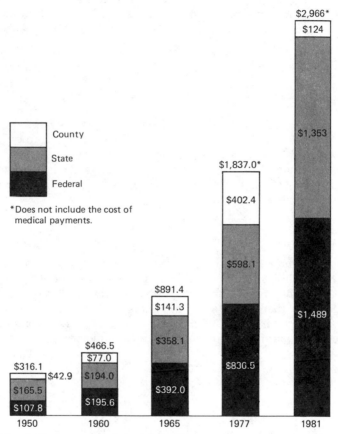

Source: California Department of Social Services.

tradition. Officials coordinate welfare programs funded by the state and federal governments with their own welfare services. The twin features of county relief in the past—the poor farm and the workhouse—have largely disappeared. The old belief that to be poor was a sign of moral weakness has also been erased, replaced by social security, aid for dependent children, unemployment insurance, food stamps, and other welfare programs (see Figure 18.3).

Homeless and delinquent children receive shelter in county juvenile halls, or in foster homes under county supervision. Most larger counties also maintain hospitals for the insane, the elderly, and the handicapped. The costs of these services have become one of the major problems facing the county—and the other levels of government (see Figure 18.4).

HEALTH

The public health depends on a delicate balance of good diet, clean water, control of disease, and proper medical care. County health officers work to keep the balance intact. Smaller counties often place that burden on a single doctor. Larger counties are more likely to fund a complete range of services—water quality inspection, programs of mental and physical hygiene, education in proper dental care, public health nurses, and inspection of waste disposal facilities. For the poor, or those without medical insurance, the county hospital may provide modern clinical and surgical services at little or no cost.

EDUCATION

As was noted earlier, the county superintendent of schools has little control over local school districts. For the most part, county educational services are restricted to (1) programs for exceptional children, (2) advisory and teacher-training services for local school districts, and (3) clearinghouse services for financial matters—distributing state aid, issuing checks, and the like.

HIGHWAYS

Construction and maintenance of roads and highways takes a bigger bite of the county budget than any other program except welfare. The trend toward state and federal highway systems has reduced the importance of the county road system as a means of long-distance travel. Many counties build their roads with money voted in bond elections. Members of the county board sometimes act as road supervisors for their districts.

ADMINISTRATION OF JUSTICE

The county serves as a basic unit within the state system of justice. County court buildings often house a full range of court facilities, from juvenile hearing rooms to the county jail. The sheriff and his officers, although employed by the county, enforce state laws and carry out court decisions. Because crime does not recognize county lines and city boundaries, the sheriff also coordinates law enforcement activities with state and city police authorities.

ELECTIONS

In state general elections, the county serves as a key administrative unit. Governing boards establish the political divisions of the county (precincts, wards, and other election districts). Additional responsibilities include choosing election judges, tabulating returns, printing ballots, distributing supplies, and hiring election workers. In many metropolitan areas, county computers also count ballots and provide rapid election results.

TAXATION

The counties generally operate a dual tax system. On one track, the county collects fees for the state and acts as disbursing agent for state-funded programs. In some states, for example, the county collects automobile licensing and registration fees, and distributes state funds to local school districts.

On the second track, the county collects its own property taxes, license fees, sales taxes, and the like. With *property taxes* (an *ad valorem* tax on real property) making up the single largest part of county income, the county board must establish tax rates high enough to pay the costs of government. The amount of property tax paid by an individual homeowner depends on the tax rate, usually expressed in dollars per hundred dollars of the assessed valuation of the property; when the rate is multiplied by the assessor's valuation of the property, the result is the tax bill (see Table 18.1).

OTHER COUNTY FUNCTIONS

As populations grow and the demand for services increases, many counties have added other functions to the list. A partial list includes (1) parks and

Table 18.1

The property tax: where does the money go?

(A sample county tax bill)

County government agency from which property owner receives services	Tax rate per $100 of assessed valuation of property	Typical property owner's yearly tax bill
County	3.8652	$390.38
County School Services	.0429	4.33
Handicapped Education	.1258	12.71
Unified Schools	6.3404	640.38
Community College	.6687	67.54
Road District	.0712	7.19
Fire Protection	.7499	75.74
Public Library	.4011	40.51
Flood Control	.4001	47.41
Lighting Maintenance	.1573	18.64
Sewer Maintenance	.0734	8.70
Sanitation District	.2386	28.27
Water Replenishment	.0040	.47
Metropolitan Water District	.1500	15.15
TOTAL	13.2886	$1,357.42

recreational activities, (2) construction of airports, (3) supervision of forest areas, (4) maintenance of firefighting facilities, (5) water and sewage systems, (6) public housing projects, (7) master planning of county development, and (8) conservation activities.

How are the counties financed?

With budgets in the larger counties running into the hundreds of millions of dollars, finances have become a major concern. A typical county governing board has authority to make the following financial decisions: (1) to levy and collect taxes for support of county and state government operations; (2) to place bond issues before the voters; (3) to arrange loans; (4) to equalize taxes throughout the county; (5) to negotiate salaries and compensation for county employees; and (6) to budget county funds for necessary services, salaries, and construction.

SOURCES OF COUNTY INCOME

As was noted earlier, the major source of county income (over 50 percent in most counties) is the property tax. Governing boards may not set tax rates as high as they might wish, however. Public pressure, especially during an election year, tends to keep tax increases down. In addition, many states have established legal maximums for property taxes; some states even divide the maximum property tax into amounts that may be assessed for specific purposes—the general fund, roads and bridges, court costs, construction, education, bond retirement, and similar budget items.

Other major sources of county revenue are (1) state and federal contributions for welfare, education, and other specific programs; (2) revenues shared with the state, such as sales taxes and auto license fees; (3) business license fees; (4) fines collected for traffic violations and other court-ordered penalties; (5) forfeitures of bail; and (6) county-operated businesses—toll bridges, harbor facilities, and office buildings.

What problems face county government— and what can be done about them?

Political scientists, economists, and urban planners all look with dismay at the erratic, inefficient, and costly mechanism of county government. At its heart, the problem comes to this: the United States has changed into an urban society, but county government is still organized for the horse and buggy.

Look at the case of Los Angeles County. County government there employs almost 80,000 people; the powerful five-member Board of Supervisors administers three hundred special districts, eighty boards and commissions, and fifty-three departments (refer back to Figure 18.2). Eighty-one cities lie within the county's boundaries, and over seven million people live there—but only one million look directly to the county for services. This overlap leads to the estimate that in 1980 the taxpayers of the city of Los Angeles paid 40 percent of the county's taxes—many millions of dollars—and received almost no county services in return.

Similar situations across the country, along with a host of other problems, have led to a growing demand for reform of county government. Some of the most pressing issues are summarized below, along with possible reforms.

TOO MANY COUNTIES

County lines drawn in days when travel moved on foot or on horseback have little real meaning today. Population shifts away from rural areas have left many counties with little reason for existence—yet all are required under state constitutions to provide full services. Most counties with a population of less than 50,000 lack the tax resources to support an adequate county government. Sixty million Americans—almost 30 percent of the population—live in such counties.

Possible solutions. Small counties should be consolidated into larger, more efficient units. However, local pride and the vested interests of officeholders who would lose their jobs would make this reform difficult to accomplish. An alternate proposal calls for the formation of multi-county districts that could share the costs of needed services without sacrificing individual county identity. Without such action, the states might very well move in and take over the service in question. If that happens, control of local matters falls into the hands of state politicians and bureaucrats.

LIMITED AUTHORITY

Many state constitutions give the county governing boards too little power to do a satisfactory job. They lack sufficient authority in three areas: (1) taxation, (2) supervision of elected officials, and (3) enactment of legislation needed to solve county problems.

Possible solution. One answer to this problem proposes establishment of *county home rule.* Under this plan, the county would establish its own charter or constitution. The county could then assume much the same independence as that presently enjoyed by city governments.

LACK OF A CHIEF EXECUTIVE

Try to visualize the United States without a President, or a state without a governor. The idea seems silly, of course—yet county governments traditionally have operated without a chief executive. Much of the inefficiency, logrolling politics, and lack of coordination found in county affairs can be traced to this problem.

Possible solutions. The simplest solution would be for county boards to amend their rules to give one member of the board sufficient authority to serve a term as "president" of the board (or whatever title seems appropriate). The board president would serve in much the same capacity as a city mayor, taking over administrative duties while leaving the rest of the board free to concentrate on policy.

An alternative solution involves hiring a professional administrator to serve as *county manager*. Many cities already use these trained officials, who handle the daily affairs of the city under the direct guidance of the city council. The plan has the advantage of establishing clear lines of responsibility: the county department heads report to the manager; the manager takes orders from the governing board; the commissioners face the voters at election time (see Figure 18.5). Administrative efficiency increases; the political spoils system dies a welcome death. Only a handful of counties have adopted the county manager plan (a larger number of counties use county administrators, who are given less authority than a manager), but those that have tried it report good results.

TOO MANY ELECTED OFFICIALS

The county manager plan works only when a county replaces its roster of elected officials with appointed department heads. The long list of candidates for county offices confuses voters and reduces administrative responsibility.

Figure 18.5
County manager form of county government

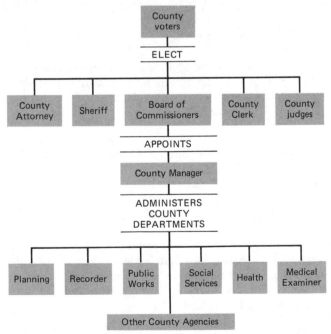

Possible solutions. A first step would be to abolish a number of offices that are no longer needed. Others could easily be made appointive with no real decrease in representative government.

An alternate proposal is to place jobs that involve state functions (the sheriff, prosecuting attorney, and county judges) under state control. As with other state officials, they would be appointed and paid by state government. Positions below that of department head should be filled under the state civil service system as further protection against the spoils system. Eighty percent of the nation's counties do not presently use civil service examinations.

DUPLICATION OF CITY AND COUNTY SERVICES

As the Los Angeles example illustrates, city taxpayers often pay double for police, fire protection, and other services. Attempts to consolidate services often bog down in political power struggles between city and county officials.

Possible solutions. A number of possible solutions exist, none easy to achieve. (1) County–state relations could be straightened out by restricting county government to those simple administrative tasks it does best—record-keeping, health services, recreation programs.

(2) City–county duplication could be resolved by merging city and county governments, as Nashville and Davidson County, Tennessee, did in 1962. Because urban areas often spill over into adjoining counties, some redrawing of county boundaries would also be necessary.

(3) A third plan aims at a less complex shifting of traditional city–county relations. Duplicate city and county departments would be merged, while separate governing bodies would stay in force; residents would pay only the costs of services received.

NEED FOR NEW REVENUES

Property tax rates have risen to the point where a taxpayers' rebellion seems possible. Worthwhile school tax increases and general county construction bonds are voted down because that is one of the few opportunities property owners have to voice their dissent. In 1978, California voters passed Proposition 13, an amendment to the state constitution that limited property taxes to one percent of the 1975 assessed value. Schools, libraries, and other governmental services lost up to 60 percent of their income, although the state used its own surplus to replace most of the losses. Similar tax revolts are under way in a number of other states.

Possible solutions. Counties are not alone in their search for new tax revenue. Every level of government finds itself trapped between rising costs and demands for additional services on the one hand and unhappy taxpayers on the other. A rescue operation will require three phases:

1. New money in any quantity can come to the counties only from the state and federal governments. The terms of such funding remain to be worked out (federal revenue-sharing has been a step in that direction)—

Figure 18.6
County employees spend so much time on the paperwork required by the federal
and state governments that they often cannot provide efficient services to county
residents. Source: Courtesy of Barnstable County, Mass.

but it should be accomplished without increased state and federal control
over the counties.

2. County government must be reorganized to weed out inefficient and
overlapping programs. Payrolls could be cut by firing nonessential employees and by ending local spoils systems. The consolidation plans discussed earlier would do away with duplicate departments. Next would
come elimination of waste and extravagance in administration. Some
states have begun to send in their own auditors in an attempt to reform
faulty accounting procedures by the counties.

3. Finally, the American people must understand that government is
not a magic carpet that can furnish a free ride for all of us. If every
community made a careful study of its real needs and did away with
unnecessary services, all government budgets would shrink immediately.

HIGH ADMINISTRATIVE COSTS

A common complaint about county government is that too large a share
of state and federal funds for social welfare programs go to pay county
administrative expenses. By the time funds trickle down to needy people
in the county, the charge states, little remains to buy food, pay teachers,
or build decent housing. In their own defense, county officials point to the
mountains of paperwork required by federal agencies (see Figure 18.6).
Conflicting state and federal regulations also complicate clerical work
immensely.

Possible solutions. The first step in solving this problem would be for the federal government to simplify the administration of its programs. Fewer reports, less complex regulations, and fewer strings on grants— these would bring about a quick improvement. Second, all levels of government should coordinate their programs. Too often, federal, state, and local agencies try to help the same people with programs that work at cross-purposes. A single national policy on medical assistance for the poor and elderly, for example, could replace the present jungle of conflicting federal, state, and county programs. Everyone would benefit—including the taxpayers who foot the bills.

Summary and Conclusions

1. County government has stumbled into the twentieth century seemingly without clear purpose. The state legislatures established the counties. Today, the same states are taking over many county functions. That slow process of centralization, however, moves government further away from the people. The demand for local control that helped create the counties hundreds of years ago has not lost its meaning.

2. The original counties grew out of British administrative units of the same name and general purpose. Southern counties came closest to the British model; they placed administrative authority in the hands of the aristocracy, but real political control remained with the state government. New England's counties, by contrast, were given severely limited powers; townships retained many of the powers customarily associated with county governments. The middle colonies borrowed from North and South to create a county that served as a model for the rest of the country. Today's typical county grew from that example; overlapping jurisdictions between city and county were part of the heritage.

3. County governing bodies vary as greatly as county size and population. *Boards of supervisors* and *boards of commissioners* are the most common types; both exercise legislative, executive, and limited judicial powers. Few counties elect or appoint a chief executive; part of their inefficiency results from this lack of strong administrative leadership. Many counties also elect a long list of additional officials. The most important are the *assessor, auditor, clerk, coroner, prosecuting attorney, recorder, sheriff, superintendent of schools,* and *surveyor.*

4. The states delegate a number of important service functions to the counties. Most counties administer a full range of welfare programs. Many counties also offer dental, hygiene, water quality, and medical services. State requirements and financial support for the local schools are administered through the office of the county superintendent of education. Other county responsibilities include highway maintenance, administration of the courts and jails, supervision of elections, assessment of property, and collection of taxes.

5. Various tax sources support most county governments, but the *property tax* remains the most important. Statutory limits set by the state, as well as increased public resistance, have combined to restrict the county's ability to increase revenues through property taxes. Other major county revenues come from state and federal funding, vehicle and business license fees, and court fines.

6. County government still lags behind in adjusting to the changing conditions of American life. The most needed reforms would (1) consolidate smaller counties into larger, more efficient units; (2) create stronger executive authority in county government—either through an elected board president or an appointed *county manager*; (3) further centralize authority by eliminating many elective offices, thus replacing the political spoils system with proper management; (4) end duplication of city and county services; (5) find new state and federal sources of revenue that would ease the burden on property owners while cutting down on waste and inefficiency at the same time.

REVIEW QUESTIONS AND ACTIVITIES

TERMS YOU SHOULD KNOW

board of commissioners

board of supervisors

coroner

county

county agricultural agent

county assessor

county auditor

county clerk

county home rule

county manager

county recorder

county seat

county superintendent of schools

county surveyor

county treasurer

property tax

prosecuting attorney

public health officer

sheriff

REVIEW QUESTIONS

The following multiple-choice questions are based on the important ideas presented in this chapter. Select the response that best completes each statement.

1. Counties have the same powers in relation to the states that the states have in relation to the federal government. This statement is (a) true. (b) false; the counties operate almost completely independently of state government. (c) false; because counties were created by state government, they exist only for the convenience of the state.

2. Which of the following is a *true* statement about American counties?

(a) Most counties have a strong executive as head of county government. (b) Counties vary greatly in size, population, and form of government. (c) County and city governments have generally worked out solutions to the problem of duplicated services such as fire and police protection. (d) County government is a leftover from the past and should be done away with as it is no longer needed. (e) None of these statements is true.

3. The most common kind of county governing body is the (a) board of commissioners. (b) board of supervisors. (c) county manager. (d) county administrator. (e) levy court.

4. The county official who is responsible for establishing the value of homes and businesses so that taxes can be levied is the county (a) clerk. (b) recorder. (c) sheriff. (d) auditor. (e) assessor.

5. A couple applying for a marriage license would go to the office of the county (a) clerk. (b) recorder. (c) coroner. (d) auditor. (e) assessor.

6. The fastest-growing and most costly of county services is (a) education. (b) maintenance of roads. (c) welfare. (d) administration of justice. (e) recreation.

7. The main source of county revenues is (a) auto and business license fees. (b) state revenue-sharing. (c) federal grants-in-aid. (d) property taxes. (e) fines for traffic violations.

8. Many city taxpayers resent the costs of county government because (a) county residents receive better services than city inhabitants. (b) the county assessor gives favored treatment to county areas outside city limits. (c) federal money bypasses the cities and goes to the counties. (d) county politicians are generally more honest than city politicians. (e) they often pay for duplicate county services that they do not receive.

9. It would *not* be a useful reform measure for a typical county government to (a) reorganize the county with a strong executive, as in the county manager plan. (b) consolidate city and county services to avoid duplication and waste. (c) simplify federal and state regulations regarding welfare, education, and other basic county services. (d) reduce the number of elected officials and centralize administrative authority. (e) subdivide itself into smaller counties.

10. The best answer to the need for additional money in county government would be for the federal government to give whatever is needed. This statement is (a) true. (b) false; not even the federal government can supply every need, because its money also comes from the taxpayers. (c) false; more money would be automatically wasted by inefficient county government.

CONCEPT DEVELOPMENT

This chapter has explored a number of significant concepts relating to county government. You can use your skills in thinking, researching, and writing to answer the following questions.

1. Discuss the traditional services offered by most county governments in the United States.

2. Describe the form of government that exists in your own county. How well does this system work?

3. Duplication of city and county services exists in many metropolitan areas. What can be done to end this waste of tax dollars? Why weren't these reforms enacted long ago?

4. How does the system of property assessment work? What abuses are often found in the assessment of private property?

5. How would you be affected if your county were abolished entirely, or combined with another county? What benefits can be gained from such consolidation?

ACTIVITIES

The following activities are designed to help you use the ideas developed in this chapter.

1. Prepare a poster for display in your classroom that shows your county and the incorporated cities within it. Also include basic statistical data about the county: area, population, income, tax revenues, and the like. If the library does not have this information, telephone the office of the county clerk.

2. Do a little checking to find out if there is any duplication of services between your county and the cities within its borders. The most visible overlaps are usually in public safety services—police, fire, lifeguard, and similar programs. How much coordination and consolidation have taken place? You might have to talk to both city and county officials to learn the full story. Report to your class on the results of your survey.

3. Attend a meeting of your county's governing body. At such a meeting you will quickly learn a great deal about the workings of government in your particular county. Pay particular attention to (a) the issues discussed and voted on, (b) the roles taken by various officials, (c) the amount of public participation, and (d) the personalities of the board members. Write up your experience for the school newspaper or a class report.

4. How do people in your community feel about county government? Prepare a brief questionnaire and survey a random sampling of your fellow students. Include easily answered questions on taxes, adequacy of welfare and health services, and other important topics. The best method is to word each question as a statement that can be answered on a rating scale. For example, "On a scale of 1 to 10, how would you rate the quality of police protection in this county?"

5. Since county officials usually live and work fairly close to you, invite one or two of them to visit your class for a discussion of county government. Such talks work best if the class has prepared specific questions ahead of time. Officials such as the sheriff or the assessor can talk about their own jobs; commissioners and supervisors can talk more generally about the problems of the county.

CHAPTER NINETEEN

GOVERNING THE CITIES: THE PROBLEM ON AMERICA'S DOORSTEP

The 1960's and 1970's drained some of the traditional self-confidence of Americans. The world no longer jumped at our command. Diplomats from remote African countries blistered our ears in the United Nations. Vietnam sapped our manpower, treasure, and national will in staggering amounts. The Arabs placed a boycott on oil, and sent gasoline prices soaring. Worst of all, America's great cities continued to drift into growing confusion and ugliness. Faced with problems so immense that the potential costs in money and resources totaled literally trillions of dollars, governmental planners began to doubt that acceptable solutions existed for big-city problems.

Many of the nation's biggest cities today face bankruptcy. Inefficient government and increasing demands for public services eat into budgets already strained by falling tax revenues and inflationary pressures. . . .

Kevin Roberts handed in his badge today. He'd worn a New York City police uniform for only six months, and now he's been laid off. His face reveals both anger and bewilderment as he walks the streets. "How could a whole city go broke?" he asks, but there's no answer. New York's gaudy, giddy life pulses on every side, but Kevin Roberts doesn't feel it. He's out of a job, and his wife is pregnant. "They can't do this to me!" he rages. "I'm a cop—they need me!"

Kevin Roberts knows what he is talking about. Big-city crime, once thought to be under control, again shows a frightening rise. More than 20,000 Americans died at the hands of their fellow citizens in 1974. A climate of brutal violence makes people fearful of strangers, afraid to go out at night. . . .

Mary Tomaso opens her door carefully. In the dim light of the dingy hallway, the visitor can see the heavy chains that guard her apartment against intruders. Does Mrs. Tomaso know about the tragedy in the apartment building down the block? Yes, she's heard. Bad news travels fast. Three children burned to death in a ground-floor apartment—trapped by steel bars on the windows, and a security lock they couldn't open. Won't she think about making her own apartment easier to escape from in case of fire? No, she tells the fire marshall, she'll take her chances. Mary Tomaso is alone, and old, and very frightened of what could happen if someone broke in. . . .

Within sight of towering glass skyscrapers, decaying slums fester in the humid summer nights. Well-meaning politicians and sociologists talk about urban blight, but that evades the issue. The reality of the cities lies in the long, desperate blocks of cheerless apartments, where mothers keep a vigil for rats. . . .

David Jimenez tells his grim story: "Sometimes they don't even wait for night. I seen one the other day while I was watching television—a big one. And at night, we hear them scratching in the walls. My little girl was bitten, and now she screams and screams whenever I put her to bed. We put out a trap, but the rat pulled it away with him, and died in the walls. That don't smell good. It smells, smells, smells."

Most big cities have been forced to stand helpless while white middle-class citizens fled to the suburbs. With them have gone business, jobs, and taxes. Chicago has lost 211,000 jobs in the last ten years. Perhaps worst of all, the cities are losing their humanity. A sense of unimportance blunts the feelings of love and respect for one's fellow human beings. Caught up in the grinding life of the city, people turn away from one another. They don't want to get involved. . . .

At least thirty-eight people saw Kitty Genovese die. The young New Yorker, walking home one evening in March 1964, screamed as a knife-wielding man grabbed her. The deserted street echoed with her cries, but no one came to help. Desperately, Kitty broke away, ran, screamed again. The assailant chased her, slashed at her with the knife under the shocked, curious gaze of her neighbors. Again the panic-stricken woman escaped. Running for her life, she must have felt that the silent windows of the apartments were mocking her. When the man caught her the last time, in the vestibule of her building, he raped her as she lay dying. Later, when asked why no one had come to Kitty's aid—or even called the police—the witnesses shrugged and looked embarrassed. Some said they had felt sure "someone else was taking care of it." A few said, in a shame-faced way, "We didn't want to get involved."

How did Kevin, Mary, David, and Kitty get trapped in this no-win game? What has happened to the billions of public and private dollars that have been spent in the cities over the past twenty years? Urban renewal projects, new expressways, housing projects, school integration, expanded welfare programs—nothing has seemed capable of halting the decay of city life. True, a handful of cities do show signs of renewed vigor. Denver,

Indianapolis, Dallas, Portland, Seattle, Milwaukee, and San Diego have combined reasonable financial health with creative programs aimed at revitalizing downtown areas.

To understand the problems of the cities, it is necessary to go back to the way they developed, and to consider the types of government they chose. This chapter will focus on both historical background and present-day problems by considering the following questions:

1. How did big cities develop in the United States?
2. What is the legal basis for city government?
3. What are the different forms of city government?
4. How are America's smaller towns and villages governed?
5. How do cities pay the costs of government and public services?
6. What are the goals of city planning and zoning?
7. How does the growth of the suburbs create problems for the cities?
8. How do cities deal with the critical problems of traffic, air pollution, and regulation of utilities?
9. Why has big-city crime increased?

How did big cities develop in the United States?

The Americans who fought and won the War for Independence were citizens of a country of farms and small towns. When the nation's first census was taken, in fact, no city had reached a population of 50,000— and only two (New York and Philadelphia) were over 20,000. Only a little more than 3 percent of the people lived in communities of 8,000 or more. By contrast, in 1978, the country had 164 cities with more than 100,000 residents. For most Americans, rural life had become a nostalgic part of the past.

When the percentage of the population living in urban areas is considered, the picture becomes even clearer (see Figure 19.1). The census defines *urban areas* as those communities having more than 2,500 inhabitants. In 1800, only 6.1 percent of the population lived in such communities. By 1900, the percentage had risen to 39.7, and in 1980, three out of four Americans—76.6 percent—were classified as urban dwellers. Movement out of rural areas had not stopped; ghost towns dot the back country.

WHY PEOPLE MOVED TO THE CITIES

People flocked to the cities for a number of reasons. Perhaps the most important were—and still are—the availability of jobs and the excitement of city life.

Jobs. After the Industrial Revolution took hold in the United States, many people chose city life over rural life. New farm machinery made it possible for fewer farmers to feed many more people. At the same time, the expanding factories had begun to offer better wages to attract workers. Farmhands moved to the cities and learned to cope with the noise and

Figure 19.1
Growth of America's urban population

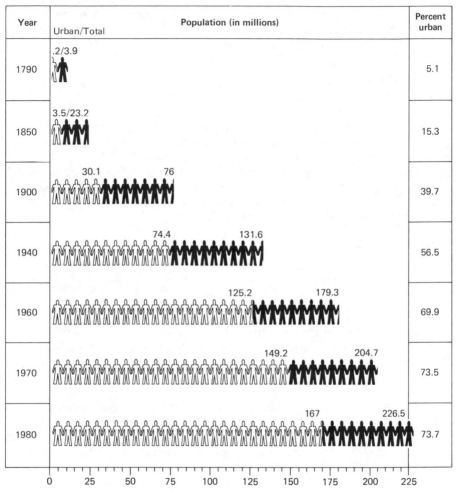

Year	Population (in millions) Urban/Total	Percent urban
1790	.2/3.9	5.1
1850	3.5/23.2	15.3
1900	30.1 76	39.7
1940	74.4 131.6	56.5
1960	125.2 179.3	69.9
1970	149.2 204.7	73.5
1980	167 226.5	73.7

Source: U.S. Census Bureau.

dangers of city life. By the end of the nineteenth century, vast numbers of immigrants were pouring into the cities. They settled down, found jobs in trade and industry, and built new lives for themselves and their children.

Excitement of city life. City life runs at a faster tempo than does rural existence. Americans found that they liked the availability of restaurants, shops, theaters, schools, museums, professional sports, and other features of urban living. Cities also rewarded their inhabitants with a freedom and privacy that conservative small-town America could not accept. The World War I song about returning soldiers summed up the situation nicely:

> How you gonna keep 'em down on the farm,
> After they've seen Paree?

GROWTH BROUGHT PROBLEMS

The modern problems of the big cities have their roots in the past. Populations grew too rapidly for housing construction to keep up. Sanitation facilities and water supplies could not meet the demand. Disease raced through cold-water tenements with terrible speed. Crime increased by geometric ratios. Political bosses grabbed control of city government; graft and corruption ruled many city halls.

Caught up in forces that they could not control, people became more dependent than ever on government services. But social services cost money, and the costs of government per capita increased faster than the tax base. Law enforcement, public utilities, schools, libraries, health services, sewage systems, fire protection, garbage collection—all must be furnished to families whose incomes average only 77 percent of those earned by suburban wage earners. Too often today, the very attractions that brought people to the cities—jobs, housing, shopping, even restaurants and cultural institutions—are located in the suburbs. As George Sternlieb, an urban affairs expert, noted, "Our society has decided it's cheaper to turn over our old cities to the poor and buy them off with welfare." (Figure 19.2 places the issue of urban decay in dramatic perspective.)

What is the legal basis for city government?

Like counties (described in Chapter 18), cities are established by the states. City government owes its powers to provisions of the state constitu-

Figure 19.2

"Double, double toil and trouble; Fire burn and cauldron bubble." Source: Bruce Shanks, Buffalo *Evening News.*

tions and actions of the legislatures. Despite this close legal relationship, big cities do not always live at peace with state government. New York City officials, for example, have long demanded that state lawmakers authorize a greater state contribution to the city budget.

SCOPE OF CITY CHARTERS

By law, a city holds the status of a legal corporation within the state. It possesses the rights to (1) acquire, hold, and dispose of property; (2) enact ordinances; (3) raise money by taxation; (4) sue and be sued (under certain circumstances); and (5) exercise the right of eminent domain. The source of this authority lies in the *city charter*, which defines the city's powers, its method of government, and the duties of city officials. In effect, a charter serves as a city's constitution.

All state legislatures have the right to issue city charters. In 1977, the United States had over 35,600 incorporated (that is, chartered) cities. Many of them are very small: Illinois has over 1,200 *municipalities* (towns or cities having the right of self-government), Iowa almost 1,000. State legislatures have been protective of state powers, and have limited the rights given to the cities. By the same token, state courts generally interpret city charters very narrowly. Even so, the charters contain the same express and implied powers that are found in the state constitutions.

TYPES OF CHARTERS

City charters can be divided into five types:

1. Special charter. In some states, the legislature issues an individual charter to every city that meets the legal requirements for incorporation. The special charter allows the lawmakers to design charters that meet the special conditions found in each community. On the other hand, it encourages interference by the state in purely local affairs.

2. General charter. Originally, states issued the same general charter to all cities within their borders. The needs of small mountain towns, however, are very different from those of large manufacturing centers. As a consequence, no state today issues general charters to all of its cities.

3. Classified charter. Some states group cities by population, and issue classified charters to all cities within a particular category. Although it is an improvement over the general charter, the classified charter may cause problems for two cities of similar size but contrasting economies. A St. Louis suburb, for example, faces urban problems far removed from those of a southern Missouri farming community.

4. Optional charter. By writing a series of optional charters geared to specific city needs, the state attempts to give cities greater freedom in matching a charter to their individual needs. New York offers its cities a choice of six optional charters, Massachusetts has five, and New Jersey provides fourteen. City voters are often asked to choose their city's charter by a direct election.

5. *Home rule charter.* Thirty-six states now give each qualified city the opportunity of writing, adopting, and amending its own charter. The home rule charter allows the people of a community to choose the form of city government best suited to local conditions. In some of these states, a city must have a minimum population to qualify for home rule; for instance, California requires a population of at least 3,500.

What are the different forms of city government?

Although there are more than 35,000 municipalities and townships in the United States, most city governments fall into one of three general categories (see Figure 19.3).

MAYOR–COUNCIL FORM

The oldest form of city government and the most widely used, the mayor–council system provides a separation of powers similar to that of the state and federal models. The mayor administers the daily affairs of city government and enforces the *ordinances* (city laws) passed by the council. As the city's legislators, the council members hold hearings, write and pass ordinances, and establish city policy. Both the mayor and the council are popularly elected. The voters in each of the city's council districts select their own representative for a term that usually runs from two to four years. The mayor runs for election "at large" (as a representative of the entire city).

This form of city government permits wide variations in the power given to the mayor under the city charter. Although not a member of the city council, the mayor in some cities presides over its meetings and votes in case of a tie. Two more important variations involve the mayor's executive powers:

Strong-mayor system. Cities that use the strong-mayor plan allow the city's chief executive to veto ordinances, appoint department heads, and prepare the budget. Most big cities in the United States use this form of government.

Weak-mayor system. The weak-mayor form of city government concentrates power in the hands of the council, leaving the mayor largely a ceremonial figure. Political scientists believe that this plan tends to spread responsibility among too many people (council members and appointed department heads). Good government can still result, however, as Los Angeles has demonstrated.

COMMISSION FORM

Following the disastrous 1901 flood that nearly destroyed Galveston, Texas, the residents of that city were anxious to reform their government so that it could take prompt, efficient action during an emergency. They also

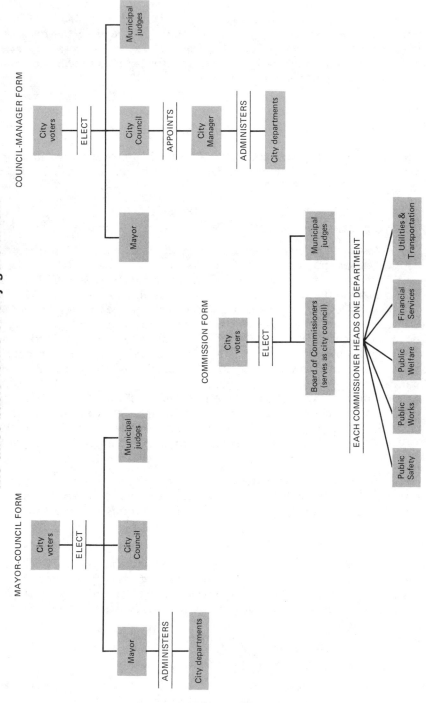

Figure 19.3
The three basic forms of city government

MAYOR-COUNCIL FORM

City voters → ELECT → City Council / Mayor / Municipal judges

Mayor → ADMINISTERS → City departments

COUNCIL-MANAGER FORM

City voters → ELECT → Mayor / City Council / Municipal judges

City Council → APPOINTS → City Manager → ADMINISTERS → City departments

COMMISSION FORM

City voters → ELECT → Board of Commissioners (serves as city council) / Municipal judges

EACH COMMISSIONER HEADS ONE DEPARTMENT

Public Safety / Public Works / Public Welfare / Financial Services / Utilities & Transportation wanted a simple system that would place administrative authority in the hands of elected officials. The result was the commission form of city government. Under this system, voters elect commissioners (five is the most common number) who (1) individually head the major departments of the city and (2) collectively sit as the city council. The system thus combines executive and legislative powers in a single body.

Responsibilities. The commission determines what departments each commissioner will administer. A typical list of city departments might be (1) public safety (police and fire), (2) public works, (3) public welfare and health, (4) financial services, and (5) utilities and transportation. Some cities allow one of the commissioners to be designated as mayor, but the office does not carry any additional authority. All decisions must be made by majority vote of the commissioners.

Pros and cons. Advantages of the commission form include: (1) the number of elected officials is kept to a minimum; (2) the commissioners have the power to act promptly and decisively; (3) the voters know exactly who is responsible for running the city's business. The disadvantages grow out of the fact that commissioners combine legislative and executive authority. Without checks and balances, the commissioners sometimes rule their districts and departments like medieval barons. Because they also appoint many of the city officials, the temptation to operate a spoils system is always there.

COUNCIL–MANAGER FORM

As city governments grew in complexity and budgets reached into the millions of dollars, the need for professional administrators became apparent. The council–manager form of government began in the South, and is really a modification of the mayor–council plan. Three elements make up the system: (1) a strong council, (2) a weak mayor, and (3) a *city manager* appointed by the council. The city manager, who is often university-trained in municipal affairs, takes over from the mayor the administration of the city's departments.

Advantages. Over 2,300 cities now use the city manager plan, with more adopting it every year. Its chief advantage lies in the ease with which responsibility can be fixed. The council sets policy; the manager carries it out. Politics and administration are kept separate. In smaller cities, the reduced council work load also allows concerned citizens to serve as part-time council members.

A difficult job. City managers often find themselves caught between opposing political factions in the community. Another problem may develop when inexperienced council members expect miracles from the professional they've hired to pull their city out of trouble. Some city problems cannot be solved, given limited community resources. This is particularly true where serious racial conflict has developed, or where the city tax base can no longer support needed public services.

How are America's smaller
towns and villages governed?

Many of America's smaller communities govern themselves under the *township* form of government that originated in New England during the colonial period. As small congregations moved out from Boston and other ports, they often set up a combined church and community government. The people called their settlements towns, after the English tradition. The term "township" is more frequently used outside New England, and refers not only to the central cluster of buildings, but to the surrounding territory as well. Early townships were small, irregular in shape, and averaged about twenty square miles each.

The township concept moved west with the settlers, eventually extending in a belt from the Atlantic to Nebraska. The township never took root in the South and West. Smaller communities in these regions remain unincorporated and under county control until they are incorporated as cities.

POWERS OF THE TOWNSHIP

The original townships had little contact with central government—the king and his royal agents. As late as the Revolution, townships were show-

Figure 19.4
Direct democracy, typified by this Vermont town meeting, is becoming less feasible as the population grows and concentrates in large cities.

ing their independence by appropriating money to help wage the war. As the nation developed, the townships became part of the centralized systems of state government established under state constitutions.

As a consequence, most townships have been left with only limited powers. Voters and their representatives deal largely with local matters— roads, schools, welfare, property taxes. In a few townships, officials also administer public works and enforce local police ordinances.

ADMINISTRATION OF THE TOWNSHIP

A noteworthy feature of township government is the *town meeting*, one of the last examples of direct democracy left at any level of government (see Figure 19.4). Citizens can make their voices heard by attending a well-publicized annual meeting, where they debate and vote on important local matters. If political parties wish to take a stand at the town meeting, they work out their positions at party caucuses.

Normally, township government rests in the hands of *selectmen*, a small group of elected officials who serve, usually for three-year terms, in much the same capacity as commissioners or city council members. A town clerk often acts as combined city manager, recorder, secretary, and license clerk. Police authority is vested in the town constables. Many townships also employ a town treasurer, justices of the peace, a school committee, road commissioners, and overseers of the poor.

How do cities pay the costs of government and public services?

In the early 1980's, cities were spending at a rate of over $65 billion a year. In 1978, for example, New York City's budget soared to $16 billion. Many cities came close to bankruptcy, as expenses far exceeded revenues and banks refused to advance further loans (see the box on page 462).

SOURCES OF REVENUE

Hard-pressed city councils depend on a variety of tax sources to meet their obligations: (1) direct taxes, levied on real and personal property at rates set by the council (sometimes limited by state-ordered maximums); (2) taxes on public service corporations; (3) license fees; (4) state and federal grants and revenue-sharing; (5) income from municipal enterprises (water and power companies, bus lines, and the like); (6) endowments and trust funds; (7) city income and sales taxes; and (8) special assessments on property owners for local improvements such as parks, streets, and storm drains.

When permitted by law, cities turn to bonded debt to meet demands on the treasury. Before bonds can be issued, voters must give their approval at a general or special election. Enough bond issues have been passed to build up a total debt of over $564 billion for America's cities. Much of the

What do the mayors say about their cities' problems?

Mayor and city	"This is the way I see it . . ."
Abraham D. Beame, New York City	Revenue fall-offs and cost increases have forced elimination of thousands of city jobs. To help close this gap, we're seeking emergency federal aid. . . . [New York] City residents and businesses pay over $14 billion in federal taxes annually; federal aid to the city has leveled off at about $2 billion annually.
Kenneth A. Gibson, Newark, New Jersey	All cutbacks in services in Newark are a direct result of the high cost of education—a cost the city of Newark can bear no longer. . . . We have had to limit services to the point of absolute need.
Thomas C. Maloney, Wilmington, Delaware	I believe that cities can do more for themselves, and, in fact, many have already. Cities are beleaguered by the fact that they are the major areas for our aged, uneducated and unskilled. They also house the majority of our hospitals and other similar property-tax-exempt organizations.
John P. Rousakis, Savannah, Georgia	[The states] saddle us with tax systems that are unresponsive to urban realities. They impose statutory restrictions that make difficult . . . the restructuring of city governments to respond to suburbanization and urban sprawl. . . . They mandate new responsibilities for city governments, often without the advice or consent of these governments, and frequently without supplying the financial means needed to finance the new responsibilities.
Stanley A. Cmich, Canton, Ohio	Inflation, unemployment, and drug abuse have a definite effect on the crime rate. Inflationary costs have cut deep into our city budget and the pocketbooks of our citizens.
Thomas Bradley, Los Angeles, California	Los Angeles—like other cities—is trying to tackle today's tough problems using antiquated revenue-raising mechanisms which just can't handle the job. Our municipal revenue is increasing only 5 percent a year, while the cost of living is rolling along at 11 percent. Each year we fall deeper into a bottomless hole.

Source: Adapted from *U.S. News & World Report,* April 7, 1975, pp. 43–46. Copyright 1975 U.S. News & World Report, Inc.

debt is in long-term securities, which taxpayers will be paying off ten and twenty years from now.

WHERE THE MONEY GOES

The services offered by city government differ little from those provided by the states or counties. Beginning with the largest expenditures, cities must budget for (1) education, (2) police and fire protection, (3) sewage and garbage disposal, (4) public welfare, (5) health and hospital services,

(6) highways and roads, (7) public utilities (when not provided by private enterprise), (8) parks and recreation, (9) interest on the city's debt, and (10) housing and urban renewal.

WHO SPENDS THE MONEY

The annual city budget begins with the city council or commission. City departments, often under the direction of the mayor or city manager, submit estimates of their needs for the coming year. The council must then perform a neat juggling act which involves several difficult steps: (1) revenues must be estimated as accurately as possible; (2) spending priorities must be established; (3) tax rates must be established; and (4) the final budget must be adopted—ideally, one that provides needed city services and fair wages for city employees at a minimum cost in taxes. When given federal funds to spend on immediate city needs, one Ohio city chose the projects outlined in the accompanying box.

LET'S REVIEW FOR A MOMENT

If you live in a medium-sized or big city, look around you. Perhaps you're fortunate, and the view is a pleasant one of clean streets, well-kept houses,

How Dayton, Ohio, spent its federal revenue-sharing funds

No two cities spend their revenue-sharing money in exactly the same way, since each has different problems. Here's what one city—Dayton, Ohio—did with its money in 1974. After hearings to determine community priorities, the following objectives were established for use of revenue-sharing funds:

- Provide free ambulance service.
- Clean streets on a monthly schedule.
- Employ 25 additional uniformed patrolmen.
- Install 600 residential-area street lights.
- Tear down 100 nuisance structures.
- Hire an "ombudsman" for those in small businesses dealing with city agencies.
- Launch a public-service careers program.
- Finance downtown improvements—such as a hotel—to attract private business.
- Improve park and street maintenance, park security, and fire protection.
- Maintain the present level of essential services.

Source: *U.S. News & World Report,* April 7, 1975, p. 48. Copyright 1975 U.S. News & World Report, Inc.

and green parks. Far too many Americans, however, see only the decaying remains of a once-proud urban environment.

Behind the problems lies the structure of city governments. The states charter the cities as legal corporations. The powers allotted to the city government come from that *charter*. Of the five types of charters, *home rule* charters have become the most popular, for they give citizens the right to adopt and amend their own city constitutions.

What type of government does your city have? Most cities divide legislative and administrative responsibilities between the *mayor* and the *city council*; in the *commission* form, however, the commissioners combine the two functions. Urban planners often recommend a third type of city government—the *manager–council* form. This provides good separation of powers: the elected council sets policy while the city manager (a professional administrator) conducts the daily business of the city. If you live in a small town in New England or the Midwest, you may be more familiar with *township* government. That may mean a chance to experience direct democracy at the annual town meeting.

Mention the costs of city government to your parents, and they'll probably grumble a lot—or explode. As costs of public services go up, property taxes, sales taxes, license fees, and state and federal grants must rise to keep pace. Where does the money go? A lot of it ends up supporting schools. Public safety—police and fire departments—takes a big bite, as do sanitation services, welfare services, highway maintenance, public utilities, recreation, interest on city debt, and housing.

What are the goals of city planning and zoning?

With few exceptions, American cities have grown rapidly and formlessly. That combination has created a situation in which people, cars, and pollution have overwhelmed the available facilities. Rush-hour traffic stalls on impossibly crowded streets. Parks and libraries are in short supply. Drivers fight for hard-to-find parking spaces. Public buildings are difficult to reach. A dense cloud of smog spreads over the city like an evil blanket.

ROLE OF CITY PLANNING

To help combat the menace of overcrowding and careless growth, almost all cities of 500,000 or more people have established permanent *city planning commissions*. The idea is not new: Savannah, Georgia, founded in 1733, was laid out with downtown parkways, and Washington, D.C., still follows the master plan designed by Pierre-Charles L'Enfant in 1790. Most city planning commissions are small, with three to five members appointed by the city council or mayor. Many universities offer specialized training in this vital field.

CONCERNS OF THE CITY PLANNER

City planners organize their efforts into three broad areas: physical layout and resources, city zoning, and urban renewal.

1. *Physical layout and resources.* Planning for the future must take into account such factors as population growth rates, water and electrical power needs, revenue sources, residential housing needs, and incentives for attracting business and industry. Problems of air and water pollution and waste disposal also present today's planners with serious problems, which must be solved if the cities are to survive.

2. *Zoning decisions.* City planners rely on zoning as a primary tool in their day-to-day work. Every city in the United States of over 100,000 population (except Houston, where voters have rejected the idea) has adopted a zoning plan. *Zoning* is the practice of enacting ordinances that divide the city into residential, commercial, industrial, and other special districts. Only specified types of buildings are permitted in a particular zone. In an R–1 zone, for example, property owners are restrcted to construction of single-family dwellings. Building heights, lot sizes, and other restrictions may also be included in the zoning plan.

Zoning hearings often spark vigorous public controversy. Any citizen has the right to apply for a variance to the local zoning ordinance. Zoning commissions hesitate to grant such requests, for too many exceptions can destroy the entire plan. Political pressures often become extremely heavy when a zoning change means increased value for a piece of land. Farm-land rezoned for manufacturing, for example, can make its owners wealthy overnight.

3. *Urban renewal.* Urban renewal projects have become a common feature of many downtown areas. *Urban blight* occurs when changing business patterns make it impossible for owners to earn sufficient income from their property to pay for taxes and upkeep. Once-handsome houses are subdivided into crowded, poorly maintained apartments; other buildings are abandoned, vacant lots fill with debris, and the streets fall into disrepair. The problem becomes a vicious cycle—businesses and middle-class residents move out, property values fall still lower, profits disappear, and conditions worsen.

Congress passed the Housing Act of 1949 as a way of interrupting the cycle of urban blight. Federal money was made available to assist the cities in rebuilding the central shopping areas, restoring residential streets, and literally rebuilding entire blocks where the old structures could not be saved. Urban renewal includes three types of programs: (a) planning for overall land use, (b) preventing further blight, and (c) providing financial assistance to private developers. Renewal projects must also fit in with overall city plans for the area.

How does the growth of the suburbs create problems for the cities?

The map of a typical metropolitan area resembles a crazy jigsaw puzzle. The incorporated central city is surrounded by a multitude of incorporated suburbs. Within the metropolitan area of New York City, for example, are more than 1,400 distinct political bodies, each with its own power to tax and spend. These smaller, suburban municipalities have grown more by chance than by design. They prize their status as cities, and only rarely cooperate as a cohesive unit.

PROBLEMS CREATED BY SUBURBS

The existence of suburban cities causes at least three major problems for the central cities:

1. Urban problems cross city lines. Major problems—air pollution, traffic congestion, and unemployment, for example—don't stop at city boundaries. It does little good for a city to clean up its factory emissions if the oil refinery in a neighboring suburb doesn't take similar action.

2. Services are duplicated. Despite their relatively small size and close proximity to one another and to the central city, most suburban cities maintain their own fire, police, water, and other departments. Costs to the taxpayers run high for this inefficient duplication.

3. Services are unequal. Metropolitan areas, sometimes fragmented into "have" and "have-not" communities, frequently show wide inequalities in the services provided to area residents. Modern, elaborately equipped school systems sometimes exist within a few miles of rundown schools in central-city districts. In the Cleveland area, for example, two neighboring districts show a 1,000-to-1 difference in per capita assessed valuation (the basis on which taxes are collected to pay for city services).

4. Central cities are caught in a tax bind. Many people live—and pay taxes—in suburbs and go to the central cities only to work or for recreation. While they're in the city, they demand a full range of city services—trash collection, police and fire protection, clean streets. The residents of the central city are forced to pick up a heavier tax burden in order to provide these extra services for commuters. Faced with escalating city taxes as well as the other problems of modern city life, more inner-city inhabitants flee to the suburbs, and the vicious cycle of urban decay grinds on.

PROPOSED SOLUTIONS

Five main solutions have been proposed for dealing with these problems. All involve far-reaching changes in the present structure of city and county government.

1. Annexation of suburbs by the city. A number of cities have reached out to annex surrounding communities for miles in all directions. Jacksonville, Florida, has grown to be the nation's largest city in geographic area, with over 800 square miles. Los Angeles sprawls over 463 square miles, but still takes in little more than 30 percent of the population of its metropolitan area. Annexation involves a number of legal steps, which differ according to the laws in each state. As might be expected, existing municipalities usually refuse to accept annexation by a major city, because they enjoy their relative freedom from big-city problems and big-city taxes.

2. *Consolidation of city and county.* Where city and county have nearly identical boundaries, a move to consolidate can end duplicate services and provide a better tax base. Such neat accidents of geography seldom happen. Most metropolitan areas spread across several county lines. Voters, moreover, usually resist city–county consolidation as vigorously as they resist city–suburb annexation.

3. *Forming special districts.* Cities and suburbs have learned that by joining together in special districts they can begin to tackle area-wide problems. These special districts usually deal with a particular public need—water supply, mass transit, hospitals, or a similar service. Each city and suburb in the district sends an elected or appointed representative to the governing board of the special district. Unfortunately, these boards often escape public attention, and may grow into private kingdoms free of voter control. Even so, they combine two vital ingredients for solving the problems of a metropolitan area: area-wide planning and a broad tax base.

4. *Intercity cooperation.* Some communities have combined to form metropolitan councils which combat common problems, such as traffic congestion, pollution, and crime. Intercity cooperation is also a requirement that must be met before many types of federal aid can be allocated to the cities. Through the intercity council, individual cities may also contract with their counties to provide services at a specified fee so that costly duplication of services can be avoided. This voluntary plan has at least one major shortcoming, which usually appears when one of the member cities refuses to accept the result of a vote taken by the council: since the organization has no legal power of its own, members cannot be forced to abide by its decisions.

5. *Metropolitan government.* The ambitious concept of a metropolitan government, pioneered by Toronto, Canada, calls for creation of two levels of government. In effect, the upper level serves as a miniature legislature, with each city represented. This legislature takes over those departments and services that are of regional concern—transportation, sewage, planning, traffic flow. City governments retain control over purely local affairs. Such "supergovernments" have not been adopted in great numbers, because voters apparently fear the concentration of power at the regional level.

How do cities deal with the critical problems of traffic, environmental pollution, and regulation of utilities?

Traffic problems, environmental problems, and regulation of public utilities represent the types of city problems that are sometimes ignored in the greater concern over poverty, crime, and failing budgets. Some progress is being made in these areas, however, despite the widespread pessimism reflected in Figure 19.5.

© 1975 by NEA, Inc. Jim Berry

"Dad, could we go to New York City for a visit sometime soon, so we can see it while it's still there?"

Figure 19.5
Source: Jim Berry, reprinted by permission of Newspaper Enterprise Association.

TRAFFIC PROBLEMS

Most American city centers were laid out before the development of the automobile, and before city populations expanded into the millions. Traffic jams cost more than lost time and strained nerves: the inability to move people and goods quickly drives businesses out of the city, subtracting further from the tax base.

Good ideas don't always work. During the 1960's, many cities believed that freeways were the answer. Instead, the high-speed roads only increased inner-city congestion by dumping more cars and trucks upon already crowded local streets. At rush hours, the freeways slowed to a frustrating crawl.

Traffic engineers have come up with a number of other solutions: (1) parking has been banned on major streets; (2) computer-controlled signals keep traffic moving more smoothly; (3) low-cost bus transport has been provided; (4) vehicles have been banned entirely from some streets, while other streets have been redesigned for one-way traffic; and (5) new, wider streets have been constructed. Such measures have helped a little, but no real cure has been found; the great cities are still dying of hardened traffic arteries.

Rapid transit. Most city planners now believe that only rapid transit systems will solve the traffic problem. Monorails, subways, and other people-movers can break the jams by taking Americans out of their cars. Progress has been slow; for every successful project, such as San Francisco's BART or Washington's new subway system, dozens of others remain stuck in the talking stage.

The reasons for the failure to move ahead on rapid transit include these: (1) many metropolitan areas sprawl over so many square miles that building adequate transit lines would cost billions of dollars; (2) Americans are reluctant to give up the convenience and prestige of the automobile; (3) the costs of even modest transit systems require expensive bond issues that voters will not approve. Despite these obstacles, the national government has moved strongly into the rapid transit field. Federal money has given cities the incentive to move ahead with their plans.

POLLUTION

Americans belatedly awoke to the dangers of environmental pollution during the 1960's. Air, water, and noise pollution have all become national headaches, with no easy remedies in sight (see Figure 19.6).

Air pollution. Los Angeles smog, once a local trademark, has become a subject of concern in cities across the country. Scientists estimate that 2.5 million tons of chemicals fall on New England with every year's rain

"Name Your Poison"

Figure 19.6
Source: From *Herblock's State of the Union* (Simon & Schuster, 1972).

and snow, including—for each square mile each day—nine pounds of chlorides, eleven pounds of calcium, and seventy-six pounds of sulphates. Factories, cars, furnaces, open burning, and other sources of pollutants release 260 million tons of material into the atmosphere every year, or more than a ton for every American.

This smog-filled air has been recognized as a health hazard. During "smog alerts," people are advised to stay indoors and to cut back on their physical activities so that they will inhale as little polluted air as possible.

Water pollution. American cities are faced with a second, equally dangerous form of pollution—the contamination of the water we drink, wash with, swim in, and travel on. Industrial waste, sewage, and runoffs of pesticides and fertilizers have poisoned rivers, lakes, and ocean beaches. So great has been the volume of toxic material released that fires have been reported on the surface of polluted rivers. Lake Erie was for a time considered to be a "dead" lake; only heroic rescue efforts are slowly restoring it to health. As if the problem of fish kills, polluted beaches, and unsafe drinking water were not enough, cities are often handcuffed in their efforts to control water pollution because the sources of the waste products are located outside their boundaries.

Noise pollution. Headlines during 1976 debated the future of the SST, or supersonic transport: In the name of progress, should the American public be forced to endure the added noise levels caused by the European-made Concorde passenger plane during takeoff and landing? Research has shown that noise is not simply a nuisance; exposure to high noise levels can lead to increased stress, damaged hearing, and loss of work efficiency. The courts have recognized this by granting residents of houses near airports financial compensation for being exposed to the excessive noise of jet traffic.

Airplanes are not the only offenders, however. Construction work, rush-hour traffic, highly amplified rock bands, and the multitude of whirring, banging, clattering machines that operate around us every day all add to the increasing din of urban life.

Counterattack on pollution. Faced with an estimated annual loss of $20 billion in health, property, and crop damage caused by pollution, cities have begun to fight back. Among the more useful techniques have been (1) banning of backyard incinerators; (2) control of factory emissions; (3) establishment of air quality control boards on a regional basis; (4) stricter control of waste disposal systems; (5) noise monitoring systems and anti-noise ordinances designed to locate and to control sources of excessive noise; and (6) extensive public education campaigns.

The necessary cooperation from state and federal officials has resulted in such steps as (1) national exhaust emission standards for cars; (2) state regulations specifying the nature and amount of wastes that may be discharged into the water; and (3) regional agencies for control of interstate waterways. Progress has been slow and costly, but some improvements can be measured: for example, salmon are again being caught in rivers that were once clogged by chemical debris, and the number of yearly smog alerts has decreased in Los Angeles.

REGULATING PUBLIC UTILITIES

Public utilities—gas, water, electricity, and transportation—are the city's lifeline. An electrical blackout or an interruption in water service disrupts urban life as surely as would an epidemic or revolution. Utility services are usually provided by private enterprise. Cities allow these companies to act as *natural monopolies;* that is, their services do not lend themselves to effective competition. Two phone companies serving the same street would only create higher costs and poorer service. As monopolies, however, the utility companies must accept government regulation in the interest of the consumer.

Some larger cities have their own public utility commissions. In most metropolitan areas, state regulatory agencies set utility rates and conditions of service. Because the companies usually extend beyond individual city borders, state agencies can do a more effective job of regulating their activities—and the companies find it more difficult to influence state commissioners than they might a city board.

Not all cities depend upon private utility companies. A number of large and small cities own and operate their own public utilities, particularly in the transportation field. The record of these bus lines and power departments suggests that city ownership does not automatically bring efficient management or low costs. Well-governed cities tend to have well-managed utilities; inefficient, poorly governed cities usually find that political maneuvering and bureaucratic bumbling have invaded their public services as well as their government.

Why has big-city crime increased?

Between 1961 and 1978, the rate of violent crime in the United States more than tripled, from over 150 per 100,000 population to 508 per 100,000. Robberies almost quadrupled in the same period, from 58 to 203. The murder rate doubled; forcible rapes tripled. A 1979 Gallup Poll revealed that one out of every five U.S. families had been hit by crime at least once during the year. Four out of ten people said they were afraid to walk alone in their neighborhoods at night.

THEORIES ABOUT THE INCREASE

Law enforcement officers have their own theories about the skyrocketing crime statistics. They relate the increase in crime to (1) high unemployment among racial minorities; (2) poverty; (3) courts that treat criminals too gently; (4) easy access to weapons; and (5) a decrease in police authority.

Serious students of urban society agree only in part with these points, adding a number of other possible causes: (1) Most Americans are led to expect society to reward them with the "good life," and when this expectation goes unfulfilled, crime and violence often result. (2) A climate of permissiveness tolerates antisocial behavior ("doing your own thing"). (3) Rapid shifts in technology also include the stresses that come with change. (4) Juvenile unemployment rates are high. (5) There is widespread abuse of drugs and alcohol, along with the development of a drug subculture that cares little for normal social restraints. (6) Poor slum-dwellers have little reason to support the existing social order. (7) The portrayal of casual violence on television and in movies seems to suggest that human life has little value or meaning. (8) The breakdown in the family structure leaves people rootless and lacking in basic values. (9) There is a lessening likelihood of capture and punishment when a crime is committed.

COSTS OF CRIME

Many of these possible causes of the increase in crime are so deeply embedded in the society that it will take decades to correct them. For the moment, most cities rely on the police to attempt to hold back the tidal wave of crime and violence. New York City employs 30,000 full-time police officers, Chicago over 14,000. Nationally, police made 10.3 million arrests in 1978 (not including arrests for traffic offenses).

The actual dollar cost of crime runs into the billions. Juvenile offenders who are sent to training schools cost $20,000 a year to house and feed— ironically, about the cost of four years at a private university—yet 80 percent are later arrested again for new offenses. Out of every hundred crimes, only twenty persons are arrested; of these, seventeen are charged, and only three are sent to prison. If police pick up a juvenile for burglary, the chances are only one in 659 that a jail sentence will be handed down. The odds for adults on the same offense are one in 412.

COPING WITH CRIME

Beginning in the late 1960's, the federal government began pouring large sums of money into local law enforcement. The cities responded by experimenting with a number of new police techniques: combined foot and car patrols, community rumor-control and information centers, volunteer and ride-along programs, better training of police officers, recruitment programs for female and minority police officers, increased mechanization and improved crime detection methods, and a number of similar improvements.

Despite these efforts, the crime statistics have continued their upward climb. Many experts now believe that the changes must come from within the American society. Until the causes of crime are erased, the police must continue to try to cope with increasing numbers of murders, rapes, robberies, and assaults.

$\mathbb{S}$UMMARY AND CONCLUSIONS

1. As colonial America's population moved from the farms into the great cities, the rapid growth, crowding, and lack of planning took their toll. Still, urban life offers jobs, cultural advantages, and the convenience of easy access to medical, educational, and other services. Today, about 75 percent of the American population lives in *urban areas*—communities of 2,500 or more people.

2. Cities have a legal existence guaranteed by state law. The rights and duties of city government are described by any one of five types of state-issued *charters*. Three major types of city government have been developed: (a) The *mayor–council* form is most common, with its division of executive and legislative functions. (b) The *commission* form elects a board of commissioners who combine executive and legislative functions. (c) In the *council–manager* form, voters elect a council and a mayor, but administrative authority is placed in the hands of a trained manager appointed by the council. Many smaller communities in New England have kept the *township* form of government. The township's most notable feature is the *town meeting*, where citizens gather to speak and vote directly on community affairs.

3. The most important sources of city revenue are property taxes, sales taxes, license fees, and state and federal grants. The bulk of city expenditures go to pay for schools, public safety services, welfare, highway maintenance, and recreation.

4. Most large cities now rely on *planning commissions* to develop master plans for future expansion and an orderly development of services. *Zoning* regulations limit land use and keep residential, business, and manufacturing areas separate. With financial help from the federal government, *urban renewal* projects have begun the expensive task of rebuilding blighted inner city areas.

5. Not the least of city problems has been the rapid flight of city residents to the suburbs. The cities are left without the taxes once paid by suburban commuters, but still must provide services. To deal with the problem, cities may attempt to (a) annex suburban areas, (b) consolidate city and county governments, (c) create *special districts* that cross city lines, (d) establish regional commissions to work on common problems, or (e) create area-wide *metropolitan governments*.

6. Traffic, pollution, and regulation of public utilities also trouble city government. With traffic congestion increasing, planners are turning from freeways to *rapid transit* systems as the only way to take cars off the road. Environmental controls are starting to make inroads on air, water, and noise pollution, but the problem still requires large investments of money, effort, and cooperation at all levels of government. Cities usually allow private utilities to furnish water, gas, electricity, telephone, and transportation services. Because these companies operate as *natural*

monopolies, they must accept city (or state) regulation of their rates and conditions of service.

7. Of all the major problems faced by the cities today, crime may be the worst. The causes include unemployment, poverty, family breakdown, ineffectual court action, and a growing climate of violence which seems to be overwhelming the old moral code. More police have been hired, and officials have experimented with new law enforcement techniques, but crime and its costs continue to rise.

REVIEW QUESTIONS AND ACTIVITIES

TERMS YOU SHOULD KNOW

city charter

city manager

city planning commission

classified charter

commission system

general charter

home rule charter

manager–council system

mayor–council system

metropolitan government

municipality

natural monopoly

optional charter

ordinance

rapid transit

selectmen

special charter

special district

strong-mayor system

township

urban area

urban blight

urban renewal

weak-mayor system

zoning

REVIEW QUESTIONS

The following multiple-choice questions are based on the important ideas presented in this chapter. Select the response that best completes each statement.

1. Out of every hundred Americans, the approximate number who live in urban areas is (a) twenty-five. (b) fifty. (c) seventy-five. (d) ninety. (e) one hundred.

2. The most important single reason that people move to urban areas is a desire to (a) take part in cultural activities. (b) go on welfare. (c) find a more exciting night life. (d) find better jobs and raise their standard of living. (e) leave their farms in response to government pressure.

3. The type of city charter that permits a city's voters to write, adopt, and amend their own charter is the (a) special charter. (b) general charter. (c) classified charter. (d) optional charter. (e) home rule charter.

4. The form of city government that combines executive and legislative power in a single body is the (a) mayor–council form. (b) commission form. (c) council–manager form. (d) strong-mayor form. (e) none of these.

5. The source of new money for the cities that would place the lightest burden on local taxpayers would be (a) increased property taxes. (b) increased state and federal aid. (c) higher business taxes. (d) more city-owned utility companies and bus lines. (e) increased sales taxes.

6. The cities' biggest single expenditure is for (a) education. (b) welfare. (c) roads. (d) sewage and sanitation. (e) parks and recreation.

7. To get permission to build an apartment building in a single-family residential area of a city, a property owner would go to the (a) city council. (b) mayor. (c) state senator or representative. (d) zoning commission. (e) police department.

8. The factor that is *not* a primary cause of urban blight is (a) the flight of the middle class to the suburbs. (b) the high costs of maintaining older sections of the city. (c) absentee landlords and high profits from renting to poor families. (d) the movement of business and industry out of the central city. (e) the fact that many inner-city residents are members of minority groups.

9. Voters frequently turn down plans for consolidation of city and county services and governments because (a) they distrust regional governments, which tend to be remote from their own communities. (b) such plans cost more. (c) regional governments are unconstitutional. (d) no examples of regional cooperation have ever been shown to be successful. (e) none of these.

10. Rising crime rates can be traced to (a) widespread abuse of drugs. (b) a reduced respect for human life. (c) unemployment and poverty. (d) changing social values, which leave individuals confused about right and wrong. (e) all of these probably contribute to the high crime rate.

CONCEPT DEVELOPMENT

This chapter has explored a number of significant concepts relating to city government. You can use your skills in thinking, researching, and writing to answer the following questions.

1. Explain what politicians mean when they say that big cities have become "ungovernable." List the reasons why you agree or disagree with the statement.

2. What steps can the cities take to cope with the problems caused by the flight of middle-class residents to the suburbs?

3. Why have cities adopted zoning ordinances? How has zoning worked to improve city life? How has zoning sometimes been abused?

4. Direct democracy (as seen in the New England town meeting) impresses many people who feel cut off from their own city governments. What are the strengths and weaknesses of such a system?

5. What forces have contributed to the dramatic increases in big-city crime? What can be done to make our homes and streets safe once again?

ACTIVITIES

The following activities are designed to help you use the ideas developed in this chapter.

1. You can easily get involved in the process of city government. Visit the city offices, listen to the city council debate local issues, talk to the mayor or city manager. Try to identify the most serious problems of your city and check to see what the government is doing about them. Would your city spend extra money on the same kinds of projects as Dayton, Ohio, did (see page 463)? Report to your class on your discoveries. How good a job does your city government do? How could it be improved?

2. The gap that often exists between young people and the police needs to be narrowed. One of the most imaginative programs in that respect is the "ride-along" plan operated by some police departments, in which citizens spend a day or evening observing police officers at work. If your local police have such a program, take advantage of it. You'll come away with a better appreciation for the job done by the police, and for police officers as real people with real feelings.

3. Plan a class debate on the question raised by the quotation used in this chapter: "Our society has decided it's cheaper to turn over our old cities to the poor and buy them off with welfare." Let one team support the quotation and the other attack the attitude it suggests. You may use library research material, but firsthand observation and interviews with city officials will be even more interesting. After the debate, let the class members ask questions and present their own views.

4. Make a poster showing the organization of your city government. Show which officials are elected and which are appointed. Label each position with the name of the present incumbent. How efficient is this form of city government? How could it be improved?

5. Many city governments allow eighteen-year-olds to run for public office. People just like you are serving on city councils, planning commissions, and school boards. Would you be interested? Even if you don't want to run for office yourself, you will find that getting involved in an election can be an exciting and educational experience. Watch for a chance to take part in your city's next election campaign.

7

FOR THE FUTURE

CHAPTER TWENTY

ℭAREER OPPORTUNITIES IN PUBLIC SERVICE

For most Americans, heroism is something to watch on the 10 o'clock news. Most jobs—even those in public service—seldom provide us with the opportunity of saving lives or preventing disaster. When the application for the new drug arrived on Dr. Frances Kelsey's desk at the Food and Drug Administration one day in 1960, she simply began the standard review that was part of her daily routine.

The application came from the William S. Merrill Company of Cincinnati, Ohio, and asked for the FDA's permission to market a tranquilizer with the trade name of Kevadon. Following twenty months of testing, Merrill felt confident in describing the drug as "a very safe and effective new drug for the symptomatic treatment of nervous tension and insomnia."

Kevadon—better known by the generic name thalidomide—had been introduced in Europe during 1957, the latest in a growing family of sedative and tranquilizing drugs. The new medicines had helped to quiet down troublesome mental patients. Many people in the general public had also come to depend on them as an effective, safe method of easing the tensions of modern living. Profits from the pills ran into millions of dollars, and the drug companies pressed the FDA for quick examination and certification of dozens of newly discovered products.

No one expected the FDA to delay approval of the thalidomide application. The agency had earned a reputation for close and friendly cooperation with the drug industry. Dr. Kelsey, however, refused to be hurried. After studying the test data submitted by Merrill scientists, she recommended that certification be delayed pending further studies.

Her decision rocked the agency, and the drug company filed an appeal. For the next fourteen months, the controversy dragged on. Dr. Kelsey was subjected to constant political and professional criticism, but she held fast to her decision. At the same time, a number of American doctors were receiving samples of thalidomide for testing on their patients. Of the nearly 16,000 Americans who eventually used the drug, about 200 were pregnant women—a fact all parties to the debate were soon to regret deeply.

Dr. Kelsey's hesitation was based in part on a tragic medical phenomenon that first appeared in West Germany in 1958. First dozens, then hundreds of babies were born with arms and legs missing, shortened, or otherwise deformed. The strange epidemic spread across the continent. Estimates place the final total of crippled infants at well over 7,000—about four-fifths of them in West Germany. A Hamburg University pediatrician, Dr. Widukind Lenz, finally solved the mystery in 1961. When taken by pregnant women, thalidomide caused the "seal-limb" deformity in the unborn child (described medically as phocomelia) that had so horrified the Continent.

Thanks to Dr. Kelsey's brave, stubborn stand, the epidemic of deformed children did not sweep over the United States. In 1962, President Kennedy awarded her the nation's highest honor for government workers—the gold medal for public service. Later that same year, Congress tightened controls on the experimental use of new drugs in humans, because those "thalidomide babies" who had been born in the United States resulted from the premature field use of the sedative. That amendment to the basic Food, Drug, and Cosmetic Act of 1938 might also be credited to Dr. Kelsey.

Not all government workers have the chance to make such a dramatic contribution, of course. But millions of unseen workers safeguard our daily well-being—men and women such as the flight control supervisor who guides a giant airliner down through heavy fog, or the meat inspector whose USDA stamp tells us that our steak is safe to eat. Public service offers the opportunity of combining well-paid, interesting work with useful service to the general public.

Surprisingly enough, many jobseekers turn to government employment only as a last resort. To help you think through this possible career choice, this chapter will examine the opportunities, requirements, and rewards of government jobs. The following questions will be examined:

1. What opportunities exist in government employment?
2. How does civil service work at the various levels of government?
3. How does the system of competitive examinations function?
4. How do colleges and other educational institutions train people for government service?
5. What are the advantages and disadvantages of working for government?
6. What are the pay scales and advancement opportunities in government service?
7. How do you apply for a government job?

What opportunities exist
in government employment?

If you are presently sitting in a typical class of thirty-five people, the odds are that six of you will become full-time government employees. Put another way, of the 103 million people employed full-time in the United States in 1979, more than one in six (15.6 million) civilian workers received their paychecks from some level of government. Given the present trend toward increased government services, that figure seems destined to grow even larger.

GOVERNMENT EMPLOYEES ARE FOUND EVERYWHERE

Government service extends far beyond Washington, D.C., as you learned in the preceding three chapters. Not counting members of the armed forces, the federal government employs over 2.8 million people. The remainder of the nation's public employees work for the fifty state governments, the 3,042 county governing bodies, the more than 35,500 municipalities and townships, and the more than 39,600 school and special districts. That's more than 78,000 individual government bodies, each of which hires an average of 130 men and women.

Government employment, therefore, does not require a move away from home. California, for example, had more federal, state, and local government employees in 1979 than did Washington, D.C. (1,729,000 vs. 289,000). Think about the people you pass by every day—postal employees, police officers, firefighters, sanitation workers, groundskeepers at the city park, the secretary at city hall. They're all government employees—as is your teacher, in all probability.

GOVERNMENT REQUIRES MANY SKILLS

Few limitations exist on the types of jobs required by government (see Figure 20.1). Over 15,000 occupational specialties have been defined at the various levels of American government. Blue-collar and white-collar jobs occupy about an equal number of workers; in 1978, professional employment in the federal government alone included 154,000 engineers and architects, 52,000 biologists, 15,000 mathematicians, and 68,000 lawyers.

As citizens have begun to demand increased services from government, the number of employees has risen dramatically. In the twenty years after World War II, when the nation's population increased by 38 percent, federal employment kept pace with the increase—but state and local governments boosted their work forces by 130 percent. State employment opportunities have also been stimulated by the growth of federal grant-in-aid and revenue-sharing programs; the increase in federal funds has enabled state governments to hire more workers. Public employment ranks as the fastest-growing segment of the American job market.

How does civil service work at the various levels of government?

As American government grew in size, political leaders finally accepted the necessity of regulating the hiring of government employees. Early presidents filled their administrations with loyal supporters. With the federal government limited in size and authority (George Washington had run the country with only 1,000 federal workers), the practice of political patronage seemed to cause little harm. By the mid-1800's, however, the abuse of this power to hand out federal, state, and local jobs had mushroomed into a national scandal. Corrupt political "machines" dominated the major cities, and the federal payroll was padded with elected officials' cronies, many of whom knew little more about public service employment than how to collect their salaries.

GROWTH OF CIVIL SERVICE

The assassination of President James A. Garfield by a disappointed office seeker led to the creation of a federal civil service in 1883. From the beginning, the *civil service system* established two basic criteria for federal employment: (1) job selection on the basis of merit as determined by competitive examinations and (2) protection from political pressure. When first enacted, the civil service law applied to only 10 percent of the nation's 133,000 federal employees. Major extensions of the coverage were added under Grover Cleveland and Theodore Roosevelt. By the seventy-fifth anniversary of the Pendleton Act in 1953, approximately 90 percent of federal jobs fell under civil service control.

STATE AND LOCAL GOVERNMENTS LAG BEHIND

State and local governments have not universally adopted the federal example. Only thirty states have civil service systems for their own employees, even though many federal grant-in-aid programs require merit standards as a condition for receiving funds.

Although all major cities and 60 percent of all municipalities have full or partial merit systems, only a few counties, townships, and special districts have adopted such programs. This means that some 1.5 million public employees still work under the modern equivalent of the old "spoils system," with the party in power using the jobs it controls as a means of paying off political debts. The inability of these government bodies to develop an effective corps of civil servants has been one of the factors leading to expanded federal intervention in local affairs.

CONDITIONS OF EMPLOYMENT

Those state and local governments which operate civil service systems usually model them after the federal example. Typical criteria for employ-

Figure 20.1
Typical government jobs as listed in

MISCELLANEOUS (Continued)

```
9000   Film Processing Work
8200   Fluid Systems Work
4700   General Maintenance and Operations Work
3200   Glass Work
8300   Instrumentation Work
6700   Manufacturing and Repair Shop Work
6200   Marine Maintenance Work
7500   Medical Services Work
7600   Merchandising and Personal Services Work
5200   Miscellaneous Occupations (Specify Job)
3900   Motion Picture, Radio, Television and
           Sound Recording Work
4000   Optical Work
4900   Plastic Materials Manufacturing Work
4300   Plastic Work
2700   Quartz Crystal Work
6100   Railroad Maintenance Work
6000   Railroad Operation Work
8400   Reclamation Work
5210   Rigger
4500   Rubber Work
```

MOBILE INDUSTRIAL EQUIPMENT MAINTENANCE

```
5823   Automotive Mechanic
5803   Heavy Mobile Equipment Mechanic
5878   Powered Ground Equipment Mechanic
5806   Service Station Attendant
5801   Other (specify job)
```

MOBILE INDUSTRIAL EQUIPMENT OPERATION

```
5725   Crane Operator
5716   Engineering Equipment Operator
5704   Fork Lift Operator
5703   Motor Vehicle Operator
5732   Pneumatic Tool Operator
5705   Tractor Operator
5701   Other (specify job)
```

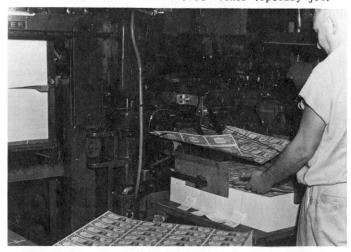

a single "Trades and Crafts" bulletin

PACKING AND PROCESSING

7009   Equipment Cleaner
7004   Preservation Packer
7001   Other (specify job)

PAINTING

4102A General Painter
4102B Marine Painter
4104   Sign Painter
4101   Other (specify job)

PIPEFITTING

4203   Pipecovering
4204   Pipefitter
4206   Plumber
4201   Other (specify job)

PRINTING AND REPRODUCTION

4402   Bindery Worker
4461   Blueprint Equipment Operator
4460   Diazo Equipment Operator
4417   Offset Press Operator
4414   Photographer, Halftone
4401   Other (specify job)

QUARRY WORK

5504   Blaster
5501   Other (specify job)

WIRE COMMUNICATIONS EQUIPMENT INSTALLATION
  AND MAINTENANCE

2513   Cryptographic Equipment Mechanic
2508   Telephone Lineman
2502A Telephone Mechanic, Outside
2502B Telephone Mechanic, Central Office
2509   Teletypewriter Mechanic
2504   Wire Communications Cable Splicer

ment include (1) open competition, (2) equal opportunity without reference to race, sex, or age, and (3) freedom from political interference.
Most state, county, and city civil service positions do not receive the full
range of federal fringe and pension benefits. Some cities also add restrictive qualifications, the most common being (1) a requirement that employees live in or near the city that employs them, (2) rules against moon-
lighting (holding a second job), (3) rules forbidding the employment of
relatives within the same department, and (4) miscellaneous regulations
regarding clothing, hair styles, beards, and other personal matters.

How does the system of competitive examinations function?

A person interested in applying for a federal, state, or local job will
normally be required to take a *competitive examination*. The process
usually begins when government employment officials announce the
openings through public notices. In cities and towns, the printed announcements will appear on town hall, courthouse, or post office bulletin boards.
Newspapers, radio and television stations, schools, employment offices,
placement bureaus, and federal job information centers also publicize the
date and location for the exams. Announcements can generally be found
for (1) local positions in the immediate area or (2) state and national
jobs, which would require successful applicants to move to other cities.

READING THE JOB ANNOUNCEMENT

Typical job announcements (see Figure 20.2) provide the applicant with
important information on the job and the examination: (1) the job title
and description, (2) the agency of government seeking applicants and
the location of the position, (3) the filing deadline and examination dates,
(4) the eligibility requirements, and (5) a description of the examination.
    Anyone interested in applying for the job should read the announcement
with great care. Applicants who do not meet the job requirements will not
be allowed to take the examination. Work experience and education are
the two most common requirements, either separately or in combination.
Specific skills, such as the ability to drive a truck or to type a minimum
number of words per minute, are mandatory for many positions. Hiring
agents are sometimes permitted to give credit for unrelated experience,
such as service in the armed forces or unpaid community volunteer work.

BASIC REQUIREMENTS FOR APPLICANTS

Government regulations normally require that applicants reach their
eighteenth birthday before taking a competitive examination. Only American citizens may apply for federal openings. A physical handicap does not
normally bar people from applying, provided they can meet the physical
requirements of the job. The government, in fact, is the country's largest
employer of the handicapped.

Young people out of school at sixteen or seventeen can be hired only if they have been out of school for three months and have completed a specific training program. Some special programs provide summer work for those over sixteen. Part-time employment is available for a few high school students, but only if they (1) remain in school, (2) receive school certification that they can maintain their studies while working, and (3) can meet the job schedule without missing their classes.

TAKING THE EXAM

If the job announcement states that a written test in required, the applicant submits an employment request form (see Figure 20.3). If the application meets the job requirements, the civil service office notifies the applicant as to the times and places where the examination will be held.

Anyone who fails the test may continue to retake it as long as the position remains open. Those who pass the exam, but wish to improve their scores, may retake the test as long as applications for the position are still being taken.

LIST OF ELIGIBLES

Civil service personnel notify the applicants as to whether or not they passed the test, and with what score. Those people who meet the minimum requirements are placed on a *list of eligibles*. Even at this point, the job-seeker is not guaranteed a position. Job chances depend upon (1) the applicant's relative position on the list, (2) how well the applicant meets the requirements for any specific position, and (3) how fast the various agencies are filling jobs from the list.

How do colleges and other educational institutions train people for government service?

Almost any type of career training will apply to one or more civil service positions. One researcher looked through a dictionary of occupations, trying to find vocational skills that could not be utilized by the government. After a long search, one job title turned up—"stripteaser."

With government service attracting more and more young people, most junior and senior colleges have organized practical programs that prepare their students for government employment. Obvious courses in this category include police and fire science, engineering, law, education, and social work. Political science—which deals with the theory and structure of government—is a major department in almost all universities.

SPECIAL FEDERAL PROGRAMS

The federal government has developed two interesting programs that reward the individual who has stuck it out for those additional years of education.

Figure 20.2
Typical federal job announcement

OPEN <u>CONTINUOUSLY</u> FOR TYPISTS/STENOGRAPHERS   ANNOUNCEMENT NO. FL-306
DICTATING MACHINE TRANSCRIBERS -- OPEN   ISSUED: APRIL 23, 1973
DURING THE MONTHS OF <u>JANUARY, MAY,</u> AND   REVISED: NOVEMBER 13, 1974
<u>OCTOBER</u> FOR CLERKS

<u>THIS IS A UNITED STATES CIVIL SERVICE COMMISSION ANNOUNCEMENT</u>

AN EQUAL OPPORTUNITY EMPLOYER

OPPORTUNITIES FOR

STENOGRAPHERS -- GS-3/5

CLERKS -- GS-2/4   TYPISTS -- GS-2/4

DICTATING MACHINE TRANSCRIBERS -- GS-3/4

<u>STARTING SALARIES:</u>

GS-2 -   2.88   PER HOUR
GS-3 -   3.25   PER HOUR
GS-4 -   3.65   PER HOUR
GS-5 -   4.09   PER HOUR

WRITTEN TEST REQUIRED

_____   X-118 MODIFIED

LOS ANGELES AREA OFFICE
U.S. CIVIL SERVICE COMMISSION
Serving Los Angeles, Kern, Orange,
San Luis Obispo, Santa Barbara
and Ventura Counties

Typical city job announcement

CITY OF TORRANCE

TORRANCE, CALIFORNIA 90503

INVITES APPLICATIONS
FOR

LIGHT EQUIPMENT OPERATOR

PROMOTIONAL - EXAM. NO. 092108

SALARY: $5.320 - $5.586 - $5.866 per hour.

FINAL FILING: Thursday, September 11, 1975 - 5 p.m.

TEST DATE: Saturday, September 27, 1975.

POSITION: Under general supervision, to operate light, power-driven main-tenance or construction equipment; performs a variety of semi-skilled manual tasks; and does related work as required.

REQUIREMENTS: One year of full time experience operating vehicular equipment. License: A valid California Motor Vehicle Operator's License of the appropriate class.

EXAMINATION: The written test will be weighted 40% and may include -

Knowledge of:
    a. The operation and maintenance of power-driven equipment, including trucks, loaders, rollers, compressors and related equipment;
    b. Methods, practices and materials used in public works construction and maintenance;
    c. The uses and purposes of hand tools;
    d. Safe driving practices and State and local laws per-taining to the operation of motor vehicles on streets, roads and highways.

Ability to:
    a. Operate assigned equipment with skill and safety;
    b. Perform heavy and manual labor;
    c. Work cooperatively with others;
    d. Follow oral and written directions.

The performance test will be weighted 60% and will evaluate ex-perience and training. The time and place of the performance test will be announced at a later date.

DATE - PLACE: The written test will be administered at 9:00 a.m., Saturday September 27, 1975 at the Main Cafeteria, Torrance High School, first building north of School District Offices at 2335 Plaza Del Amo, Torrance, California.

SPECIAL NOTE: The representatives of management wish to give notice that in accordance with the Memorandum of Understanding between AFL-CIO Local 1117, AFSCME, and the City of Torrance, new employees covered under that memorandum shall become members in good standing or pay the required service fee to said Local 1117.

THE CITY OF TORRANCE IS AN EQUAL OPPORTUNITY/AFFIRMATIVE ACTION EMPLOYER.

For further information: Telephone 328-5310 — Ext. 227 or 228

APPLY PERSONNEL DEPARTMENT, TORRANCE CITY HALL, 3031 TORRANCE BOULEVARD 90503

See Applicant Information on Reverse Side

8-20-75

1. *Junior college graduates.* Graduates who have taken the proper courses at a junior college (or who have completed two years at a four-year college) can qualify for a long list of responsible, well-paying federal government jobs. Positions included on this list are accounting assistants, claims and voucher examiners, general administrative management technicians, personnel technicians, purchasing and supply assistants, statistical assistants, tax examiners, and law enforcement technicians. Sixty semester hours or ninety quarter hours are considered to be equal to two years of college. Two years of experience in appropriate administrative or technical work may sometimes be accepted in place of college training. Successful applicants for these and similar positions start with a rating of GS–4 (GS stands simply for "general schedule"; see pages 491–492 for a discussion of government salaries).

2. *College graduates.* The federal government also needs highly qualified people with potential for advancement into administrative and professional positions. Eighty-five percent of these jobs lie outside Washington, D.C., and do not require specialized education or experience. Trainees for these upper-level posts need a college degree plus a passing grade (70 percent) on a four-hour written examination. Here, too, work experience can be substituted for all or part of the college training. Applicants who qualify receive a GS–5 rating. Those who have an additional year of graduate work, a law degree, or who score 90 or above on the test and have maintained a 2.9 grade average (out of a possible 4.0) begin at the GS–7 rank.

LET'S REVIEW FOR A MOMENT

The law of averages tells us that you or one of your close friends will choose a career in government service. How can we be so sure? Well, one out of six Americans already works for a local, state, or federal government agency.

Expanding government responsibilities require qualified workers of almost every imaginable skill. With most federal positions filled by the *civil service system* according to merit rather than through patronage, the civil servant is no longer considered to be a political hack. States and cities have been slower to switch from the political spoils system, but many now use *competitive examinations* modeled on the federal example.

Let's assume that you are interested in a government job. Perhaps you'd like to work as a safety inspector for the Federal Aviation Administration. How do you get started? First, check the qualifications for the position. You may need additional schooling before you qualify. Next, watch for the announcement bulletins that tell you about the available jobs, the dates for filing and taking the examination, and the requirements for the position. If the agency accepts your application, you will be notified of the date for the test. Congratulations! You passed with high marks. Now your name will be placed on the *list of eligibles*. As soon as a position opens up, you will be notified to report for work.

What are the advantages and disadvantages of working for government?

The job has not yet been invented that yields total satisfaction to those who hold it. Government service is no exception. All government employees, from the youngest secretary in a small-town city hall to the powerful politicians in the White House, must weigh advantages against disadvantages. For most people, however, the positive benefits outnumber the negative.

ADVANTAGES

The days when government service meant starvation wages and low prestige have long vanished. The advantages of working for almost any governing body now include:

1. *Good salaries.* Typically, people think in terms of one simple question when considering a new job: "How much does it pay?" Most government bodies now follow the policy of paying salaries that are comparable to those paid by private enterprise for work of a similar type. Legislators and administrators review salary schedules frequently, and make adjustments as needed. Observers note that government pay at the lower levels is somewhat higher than in private industry, but that the upper-level administrators and professionals fall behind their counterparts outside of government. Because of this difference, each year many high-ranking government employees leave their jobs for better-paying positions with business or industry.

Civil service employees receive annual raises (promotion within grade) for the first three years of federal employment. Less frequent raises continue after that time until the employee reaches the top of any particular GS level. Most workers will be promoted to a higher GS grade long before reaching that top pay category, however.

2. *Job security.* In the years when government salaries trailed well behind those of private industry, job security stood out as the chief attraction of government service. Once hired, and having successfully completed the probationary period, most government workers can count on having a job as long as they want it. Administrators conduct regular reviews of employee efficiency, however, to ensure that each worker remains productive. Examiners award ratings of outstanding, satisfactory, and unsatisfactory. Even an unsatisfactory rating usually results in nothing more severe than a transfer to a less demanding job.

During periods of inflation and tight budgets, reductions in government work forces have become more common—as New York's police officers, firefighters, teachers, and sanitation workers discovered in 1975. When layoffs occur, the workers affected are usually those who (a) lack seniority, (b) have low performance ratings, (c) hold only a temporary appointment, or (d) lack previous government experience, such as service in the armed forces. Unfortunately, women and members of racial minorities are often hit hardest by such layoffs, for few of them have the seniority necessary to protect their jobs.

3. *Job satisfaction.* For people who want to perform useful work that directly benefits their community or society, government service yields large rewards. This job satisfaction consists of the chance to provide assistance to those in need and participation in decision-making that contributes directly to improving the quality of life.

4. *Fringe benefits.* Most civil service jobs provide liberal fringe benefits. Salary checks are supplemented by cumulative sick leave, paid vacation time, paid holidays, group life and medical insurance, generous retirement programs, and unemployment compensation. Some jobs also include travel opportunities, on-the-job training, contact with influential politicians, and —at the higher levels—free use of an automobile.

DISADVANTAGES

The negative aspects of government service are harder to define, but anyone who is thinking about applying for a civil service position must be aware of them.

1. *Lack of recognition.* Perhaps the most important disadvantage is the relative invisibility of many employees. As tiny cogs in a huge, impersonal machine, they feel powerless and faceless. Complaints by the public about bureaucratic inefficiency often stem from the work habits of employees who have lost interest in their jobs for this reason.

2. *Restrictions on political activities.* The Hatch Act of 1939 forbids federal employees from taking part in certain political activities: campaigning for a particular candidate, collecting campaign contributions, or serving as delegate to a political convention. The right to vote is not restricted, of course, nor is the basic right to speak out on public issues. Most state and local government employees work under similar restrictions.

3. *Restrictions on bargaining rights.* Unions of government employees occupy a gray area in American labor relations. Laws and court decisions have generally forbidden these groups the right to strike. As the unions have grown more militant, however, "job actions" have grown in frequency. Strikes by firefighters, police officers, teachers, and postal employees have become almost routine, even though such actions defy the very law most employees have sworn to uphold.

4. *Other limitations.* Most government employees must swear loyalty to the United States before accepting employment. Some agencies restrict the employment of members of the same family. Forced moves from one

city to another do not occur frequently, but many FBI and State Department jobs, for example, require extensive travel and periodic transfers.

What are the pay scales and advancement opportunities in government service?

As was noted earlier in this chapter, public servants are no longer forced to sacrifice their own and their family's well-being for the honor of serving as government employees. That philosophy died in 1923, when the federal government ended a salary and classification schedule that had remained unchanged for seventy years. The Federal Salary Reform Act of 1962 went even further. In that legislation, Congress established a definite policy for defining and adjusting federal salaries.

Even if government policymakers did not recognize the justice of paying competitive salaries, worker organizations would have enforced such a philosophy. Government employees at every level have organized themselves in order to speak out in support of their annual salary demands. Presented with job offers from both government and private industry, today's average worker would find little difference in the basic salary scales.

FEDERAL PAY SCALES

A single salary schedule now governs civil service compensation (see Table 20.1). Every effort has been made to reward equal work with equal pay, regardless of the job or agency. In 1980, the average salaries of each of the fifteen main federal pay grades ranged from $7,960 at GS–1 to $44,547 at GS–15. One out of four federal employees rated as GS–4 or GS–5, with an average salary of $11,100. One out of five was paid as a GS–11 or GS–12, where the average came to $24,700. GS–4's and 5's generally work at clerical jobs, while GS–11's and 12's occupy managerial and administrative positions.

Salary figures do not include fringe benefits such as vacation time, medical care, and retirement plans. The federal retirement program predates Social Security by fifteen years, and offers roughly similar payments. Seventy has been set as the mandatory retirement age for civil service employees.

CHANCES FOR PROMOTION

Government service offers excellent advancement opportunities. Many of the men and women now serving at GS–11 and above began at the bottom of the ladder. Because most agencies fill vacancies by promoting their own employees, workers with high efficiency ratings and proper training can move upward. In keeping with civil service policy, promotion is based on merit—the worker's demonstrated ability to perform. Employees taking examinations for *merit promotions* possess a built-in advantage over outsiders, for their experience has been built up over months and years of on-the-job effort.

Table 20.1

Federal salary schedule, 1978

Grade	Percent of federal employment pool	Average salary
GS–1	.2	$ 7,960
GS–2	2.2	8,951
GS–3	7.9	9,766
GS–4	12.9	10,963
GS–5	13.5	12,266
GS–6	6.2	13,672
GS–7	9.6	15,193
GS–8	2.0	16,826
GS–9	9.9	18,585
GS–10	1.6	20,467
GS–11	10.5	22,486
GS–12	10.0	26,951
GS–13	7.8	32,048
GS–14	3.8	37,871
GS–15	1.8	44,547
GS–16	.3	*These positions are filled by presidential appointment only.*
GS–17	.1	
GS–18	.02	

Speed of promotion depends upon (1) the size of the agency or department, (2) retirements, resignations, and promotions at the higher positions, (3) the employee's alertness to opportunities in other agencies within the same government body, and (4) the employee's ability and energy. Workers who learn new skills through continued education usually receive prompt recognition. Many government agencies provide on-the-job training for advancement. Other possibilities for advanced training can often be found at nearby colleges and vocational schools, or in home study.

How do you apply for a government job?

Looking for a job—the right job—requires organization, patience, and determination. The following steps will help ensure you a fair chance at whatever positions are open.

1. FIND OUT WHAT JOBS ARE AVAILABLE

Begin your job search by locating the various hiring centers nearest you. Logical places include city hall, the county courthouse, a federal job information center, or any of the other government offices nearby. Your school counselors or career center can help point you in the proper direction. Check the phone directory for listings of city, county, state, and federal offices, then visit them to see what jobs are open. State employment offices maintain full listings of current job notices, and their counselors will help you with aptitude testing and career guidance.

2. CONSIDER YOUR QUALIFICATIONS

Once you know what jobs are available, match the job description against your own abilities and training. Realistically, it makes sense to sit down and write out a summary of your personal background, education, and work experience. This document is called a *résumé*. A well-written résumé helps you evaluate your own job prospects, and placement officers can use it to compare your qualifications with those of other applicants.

3. FILL OUT THE APPLICATION

Think of the application as your personal letter to a prospective employer (Figure 20.3 shows a typical federal job application form). Since the personnel officer will not be talking to you in person at this time, your application must speak for you. Answer all questions fully and honestly. Write carefully and legibly; type the application if possible. Pick up two application forms if you can—one for practice, the second for the final mailing. Do not hesitate to put your experience in the best possible light. A job selling brushes door-to-door sounds more impressive if described as "direct sales representative"! Don't hesitate to apply for more than one position if you are qualified. Competition for government jobs is intense, and increasing.

4. PREPARE FOR THE EXAM

Competitive examinations require careful preparation. The fact that you have worked at a similar job is not a guarantee of success. Visit the public library or a local bookstore to look over the available study guides, sample examinations, and other helpful publications. Talk to people who hold similar jobs in government for advice on taking the exam. Many adult schools and vocational schools offer courses geared to preparing people for civil service tests. Although such preparation is useful, the government does not require it; more important, no school can guarantee that its students will be offered a job. Regardless of how you prepare yourself, use the exam to show your future employers that you understand the concepts and operations involved in the job.

5. BE TEST-WISE

You will receive notification by mail of the time and place of the exam. Take this "ticket" with you to the test site—and be on time. Be prepared, too: pencils do break, and pens do run dry. Follow directions exactly as given by the test proctor. Answer truthfully any questions about the

Figure 20.3
Typical federal job application form

Test Date _____

Form Approved
OMB No. 50-R0444

QUALIFICATIONS BRIEF

DO NOT WRITE IN THIS BLOCK—FOR USE BY EXAMINING OFFICE ONLY

Options	Grade	Earned Rating	Preference	Aug. Rating
			☐ 5-points (tent.)	
			☐ 10-points	

IDENTIFICATION NUMBER: (To be assigned)

1. Name (Last, First, Middle) (Maiden, if any) ☐ Mr. ☐ Miss ☐ Mrs.

2. Mailing address, including ZIP Code (if not permanent address, address until—date......................).

Registration Date:

Notations

3. Telephone number (include area code)

HOME: OFFICE:

Form Reviewed: Form Approved:

4. Permanent address, including ZIP Code and phone number (if different from 2 or 3).

THIS SPACE FOR USE OF APPOINTING OFFICER ONLY
☐ 5-point
☐ 10-point comp. disab.
☐ 10-point other

5. Legal or voting residence (state):   6. Birth Date (Month, Day, Year)

Preference has been verified through proof that the separation was under honorable conditions, and other proof as required.

Signature

7. Social Security Account No.:

Title

8. Dates of Military Service, if any
From: To:
Branch of Service:
Serial Number:

9. Veteran Preference
☐ 5-point
☐ 10-point

Agency   Date

10. Indicate languages other than English in which you are proficient in reading, writing, and speaking:

15. Position(s) for which applying:

11. Are you a United States citizen?
☐ Yes ☐ No

12. Are you a high school graduate?
☐ Yes ☐ No

16. Primary geographic location(s) where you will work:

13. Lowest acceptable salary: 14. Earliest date available:

17. If you will accept a job only in certain agencies, list here:

18. Name and location (City and State) of College or University	Courses Studied		Dates Attended		Credits Completed		Type of Degree	Year of Degree
	Major	Minor	From	To	Semester	Quarter		

19. In the spaces below, show coursework taken in junior colleges, business schools, technical institutes, or other institutions above the high school level, including courses which you expect to complete within the next 9 months. For each of the subject areas listed indicate the number of semester or quarter credits, or classroom hours, as applicable.

Fields of Study	Sem.	Qtr.	Class-room hrs.	Fields of Study	Sem.	Qtr.	Class-room hrs.
Accounting and Bookkeeping				Home Economics			
Biological Sciences				Industrial Management			
Business Administration				Library Science			
Business Education				Mathematics			
Criminology and Law Enforcement				Modern Languages			
Data Processing (list total)				Personnel			
__EAM Operation				Physical Sciences			
__Console Operation (hands on)				Political Science			
__Peripheral Equip. Oper. (hands on)				Psychology			
__Programing				Recreation			
Economics				Secretarial Procedures			
Education				Sociology			
Engineering				Statistics			
English and Journalism				Traffic Management			
Fine and Applied Arts				Other (specify)			
Geography							
History							

(OVER)   CSC Form 994 November 1972

20. Qualifying experience only. List most recent experience first. Attach additional sheets if you need more space.

May inquiry be made of your present employer regarding your character, qualifications, and record of employment? ☐ Yes ☐ No

A

Dates of employment (month, year)	Exact title of position	If Federal service, civilian or military grade
From To PRESENT TIME		

Salary or earnings		Avg. hrs. per week	Place of employment	Number and kind of employees supervised	Kind of business or organization (manufacturing, accounting, insurance, etc.)
Starting $	per		City:		
Present $	per		State:		

Name of immediate supervisor | Name of employer (firm, organization, etc.) and address (include ZIP code)

Area code and phone No. if known | Reason for leaving

Description of work

B

Dates of employment (month, year)	Exact title of position	If Federal service, civilian or military grade
From To		

Salary or earnings		Avg. hrs. per week	Place of employment	Number and kind of employees supervised	Kind of business or organization (manufacturing, accounting, insurance, etc.)
Starting $	per		City:		
Final $	per		State:		

Name of immediate supervisor | Name of employer (firm, organization, etc.) and address (include ZIP code)

Area code and phone No. if known | Reason for leaving

Description of work

C

Dates of employment (month, year)	Exact title of position	If Federal service, civilian or military grade
From To		

Salary or earnings		Avg. hrs. per week	Place of employment	Number and kind of employees supervised	Kind of business or organization (manufacturing, accounting, insurance, etc.)
Starting $	per		City:		
Final $	per		State:		

Name of immediate supervisor | Name of employer (firm, organization, etc.) and address (include ZIP code)

Area code and phone No. if known | Reason for leaving

Description of work

Answer the following questions. If you answer "Yes" to any of these questions, give details on a separate sheet of paper. | Yes | No

21. Within the last 10 years, have you been a member of the Communist Party, USA, or any of its subdivisions?

22. Within the last 10 years, have you been a member of an organization that, to your present knowledge, seeks the overthrow of the constitutional form of the U.S. Government by force or other unlawful means?

23. Have you had heart disease, a nervous breakdown, epilepsy, tuberculosis, or diabetes?

24. Within the last 5 years, have you been fired from any job, or quit after being notified that you would be fired?

25. Have you been convicted of any offense against the law or forfeited collateral, or are you now under charges for any offense against the law (omit traffic fines of $30 or less and any offense committed prior to your 21st birthday which was finally adjudicated in juvenile court or under a Youth Offender law)?

26. While in the military service, were you convicted by general court-martial or discharged under other than honorable conditions?

27. Have you ever worked for the Federal Government (other than military service)?

28. I CERTIFY THAT ALL OF THE STATEMENTS MADE IN THIS BRIEF ARE TRUE, COMPLETE AND CORRECT TO THE BEST OF MY KNOWLEDGE AND BELIEF AND ARE MADE IN GOOD FAITH. A FALSE STATEMENT OR DISHONEST ANSWER TO ANY QUESTION MAY BE GROUNDS FOR DISMISSAL AFTER APPOINTMENT OR CONVERSION AND IS PUNISHABLE BY LAW. | Signature (sign in ink) | Date

THE FEDERAL GOVERNMENT IS AN EQUAL OPPORTUNITY EMPLOYER

minimum salary you will accept, and whether you would accept a job in another city.

If you're test-wise, you will begin with an advantage over the other applicants. Keep these simple guidelines in mind:

(a) Plan your work carefully. You may not have enough time to answer all the questions if you do not budget your time. On a one-hour, hundred-question exam, for instance, you would aim at completing twenty-five items each fifteen minutes.

(b) Most examinations are graded by electronic scoring machines; essay questions are seldom used today. Be careful to mark your answers in the proper column, and erase thoroughly.

(c) Answer easy questions first; go back to the harder ones if time permits. If you finish early, recheck your answers.

(d) Wrong answers are seldom subtracted from your score, so it pays to make intelligent guesses rather than to leave tougher questions blank.

Civil service examinations are designed as practical tests of (a) an individual's ability to perform the skills required by the job applied for, or (b) a person's aptitude for learning how to do the job with reasonable efficiency. Occasionally, applicants for a particular job will also be asked to take an appropriate performance test in addition to a pencil-and-paper exam. Typical performance tests would involve exercises in shorthand dictation, machine maintenance, or tractor operation.

6. UNCLE SAM WANTS YOU

If you have chosen the right job and prepared carefully—and if you relax and do your best on the exam—the chances are good that you will make the list of eligibles. The government needs qualified, reliable, hard-working people; why not give it a try?

$\mathcal{S}$UMMARY AND CONCLUSIONS

1. Vocational counselors list a career in public service as a desirable ambition for anyone who has not decided upon a life's work. Most government agencies—whether at the local, state, or federal level—offer attractive salaries, and the opportunities for promotion and job satisfaction are excellent. Government jobs call for almost every possible skill. With demand for government services constantly increasing, about 17 percent of the nation's work force now earns a government paycheck.

2. Most federal and many state and city positions are earned by merit under the *civil service system*. Jobs under civil service are announced through bulletins, which describe the work to be done, the agency seeking the employee, and the dates for the competitive examination. Applicants for these positions should be sure that they are properly qualified for the work—in education, experience, and aptitude—before submitting an

application. Examiners notify the successful applicants of their test scores, and place them on a *list of eligibles* in order of their rated competency as measured by the examination.

3. Government pay scales compare favorably with those for similar jobs in private industry. Individual employees are placed on a salary schedule according to the job they perform and the time they have spent in government service. Fringe benefits often surpass those of private industry, and include paid holidays, annual vacations, a retirement system, and medical coverage. The major disadvantages of government service lie in two areas: the public's lack of appreciation for the work done by its own employees, and the tough restrictions on political activities by public employees. Openings exist in public service for employees with little or no educational background, but the better positions are reserved for people with extensive preparation.

4. Applicants wishing to investigate the possibility of obtaining a government job should begin by checking into available openings. Job announcement bulletins and government hiring offices can help provide this information. Applicants should match their qualifications to the positions listed; a well-written résumé helps greatly in this task. After submitting the application, qualified people are notified as to the date of the *competitive examination* for the job they are seeking. Most exams are objective, written tests, but sometimes performance tests are also given. Tests can be taken several times, either to erase a failing score or to improve a passing one. It helps to prepare for the exam—through reading, trial tests, course work in school, and conversation with people who have already been through the process.

REVIEW QUESTIONS AND ACTIVITIES

TERMS YOU SHOULD KNOW

civil service system	*list of eligibles*
collective bargaining	*merit promotion*
competitive examination	*résumé*

REVIEW QUESTIONS

The following multiple-choice questions are based on the important ideas presented in this chapter. Select the response that best completes each statement.

1. The example of Dr. Frances Kelsey and her brave stand during the thalidomide controversy shows that public employees (a) completely control the free enterprise system in the United States. (b) are never subject to political or professional pressure by private business. (c) sometimes have a chance to perform service that literally involves

questions of life and death. (d) are concerned mostly with their paychecks and the right to strike. (e) are better and more efficient than workers in private industry.

2. Out of a hundred American workers, the number who might be expected to be employed by some level of government is (a) six. (b) twelve. (c) seventeen. (d) twenty-five. (e) thirty-two.

3. In the near future, opportunities in public employment will probably (a) increase. (b) decrease. (c) remain about the same.

4. The goal of the civil service system is to (a) protect public employees from political pressures. (b) ensure that properly qualified people are hired for government jobs. (c) provide job security for competent workers. (d) establish a system of merit promotions. (e) all of these.

5. Announcement of government job openings would *not* be likely to appear (a) on a city hall bulletin board. (b) in an individual's private mailbox. (c) in the newspaper. (d) at a state employment office. (e) at a school counseling office.

6. Passing the competitive examination for a government job guarantees that the applicant will be hired. This statement is (a) true. (b) false; the applicant must still be approved by the political party in power. (c) false; applicants are placed on a list of eligibles, from which they are hired as jobs open up.

7. When compared to jobs in private industry, government service provides (a) higher salaries at all levels of employment. (b) greater freedom to engage in political campaigns. (c) greater job security. (d) little or no supervision by bosses or managers. (e) more frequent transfers from job to job and from place to place.

8. Promotion in government jobs usually depends upon (a) knowing the right people. (b) playing office politics. (c) competitive examinations. (d) making political contributions to the right party. (e) promotions are so rare as to be almost nonexistent.

9. Which of these statements is *not* good advice for a job applicant taking a competitive examination? (a) Attract the proctor's attention by coming in late for the test. (b) Don't study beforehand; a clear mind is best when taking a test. (c) Finish the tough questions first, then do the easy ones if time permits. (d) Answer any questions about salary and job location in a way that will make your new employers happy; you can always argue about those things later on. (e) None of these will help you pass the exam; do just the opposite.

10. Starting salaries for the lower-level federal government jobs are lower, on the average, than salaries paid for similar jobs in private industry. This statement is (a) true. (b) false; even though the law requires that government salaries be less, fringe benefits make up for the difference in salaries. (c) false; starting salaries in the lower-level GS positions are generally above those paid in private industry.

CONCEPT DEVELOPMENT

This chapter has explored a number of significant concepts relating to career opportunities in government service. You can use your skills in thinking, researching, and writing to answer the following questions.

1. Compare the advantages and disadvantages of government service and private employment.

2. How would you go about applying for a government job? List all the necessary steps leading to your first day on the job.

3. How can extra years of schooling pay off for anyone planning a career in government service?

4. Contrast the traditional spoils system with the present civil service merit system. What "contributions" were made by Thomas Jefferson, Andrew Jackson, and Boss Tweed?

5. Why do many people have a negative image of government employees? What can be done to change this feeling?

ACTIVITIES

The following activities are designed to help you use the ideas developed in this chapter.

1. Organize your class to investigate all the sources of government job information in your community. Have each person in the group bring in whatever information he or she can discover—job titles, pay scales, educational requirements, and the like. Make salary and benefits comparisons with jobs in private industry that have the same requirements. Post the results on your bulletin board. You'll probably find some interesting jobs well within your own qualifications.

2. Invite a school counselor or a career guidance officer to speak to your class on current employment opportunities in your area. They will have firsthand information on current openings, and can advise you on educational requirements, chances for foreign travel, and other specific aspects of choosing government work as a career.

3. Although this chapter has been primarily concerned with civil service jobs, careers in politics are attracting larger numbers of young Americans. What does politics have to offer as a career? Do some research on your own, and share the results with your class. Check through the library resources; write to your representatives at state and federal levels; interview local members of the city council or county board. Try to find out about the rewards and job satisfactions of service in elective office—but don't ignore the negative aspects of the political life, either.

4. Visit some government offices and pick up job application forms. Ask your teacher to duplicate some of them so that everyone in the class can have the experience of filling out these somewhat complicated forms. Perhaps your school's guidance department would evaluate the completed applications as a test of your ability to follow directions and present yourself in the best possible light.

5. Organize a class debate on the topic, "Resolved: government employees should be denied the right to strike against the public interest under penalty of fines or imprisonment." The debate teams will find ample background information in the library, but they can also contact government and union officials for additional material. How does your class react to this current issue?

CHAPTER TWENTY–ONE

ᴾROMISE OR THREAT? THE FUTURE OF AMERICAN GOVERNMENT

Future shock: Alvin Toffler's diagnosis of the current state of American society. Too much change, too quickly. The result: shattering stress and disorientation for the individual. Can humans adjust to the change that vexes and complicates their lives? No one really knows.

We do know that Spaceship Earth carries a limited cargo of resources for its ever-growing passenger list. Threat of nuclear extinction always rides with us. Scientists have programmed their computers with current data on resource depletion, population growth, pollution factors, and other politico-economic possibilities. A number of these readouts flatly predict worldwide disaster in the first quarter of the next century when supplies of fossil fuels run out.

Whether that future holds promise or threat may be measured by the ability of government to adjust to change in the years to come. Men and women of courage and vision must be found to chart the nation's course, so that we may become masters of the future, rather than its victims. Toffler puts the issue this way:

> Can one live in a society that is out of control? That is the question posed for us by the concept of *future shock*. For that is the situation we find ourselves in. If it were the technology alone that had broken loose, our problems would be serious enough. The deadly fact is, however, that many other social processes have also begun to run free, oscillating wildly, resisting our best efforts to guide them.
>
> Urbanization, ethnic conflict, migration, population, crime—a thousand examples spring to mind of fields in which our efforts to shape change seem increasingly inept and futile. Some of these are strongly related to the breakaway of technology; others partially independent of it. The uneven, rocketing rates of change; the shifts

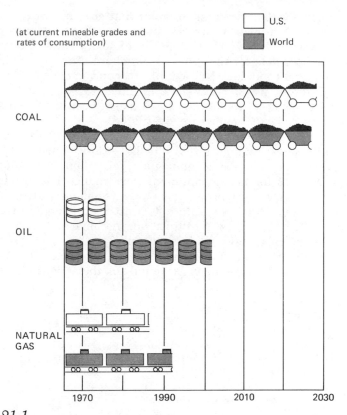

(at current mineable grades and rates of consumption)

☐ U.S.

▩ World

COAL

OIL

NATURAL GAS

1970   1990   2010   2030

Figure 21.1
Lifetimes of fossil fuel supplies
Source: Reprinted with permission of Macmillan Publishing Company, Inc., from John McHale, *World Facts and Trends,* p. 63. Copyright © 1972 by John McHale.

and jerks in direction, compel us to ask whether the techno-societies, even comparatively small ones like Sweden and Belgium, have grown too complex, too fast to manage.

How can we prevent mass future shock, selectively adjusting the tempos of change, raising or lowering levels of stimulation, when governments—including those with the best intentions—seem unable to point change in the right direction?

Thus a leading American urbanologist writes with unconcealed disgust: "At a cost of more than three billion dollars, the Urban Renewal Agency has succeeded in materially reducing the supply of low cost housing in American cities." Similar debacles could be cited in a dozen fields. Why do welfare programs today cripple rather than help their clients? . . . Why do expressways add to traffic congestion rather than reduce it? In short, why do so many well-intentioned liberal programs turn rancid so rapidly, producing side effects that cancel out their central effects?*

* Alvin Toffler, *Future Shock* (New York: Random House, 1970), pp. 446–47.

Toffler concludes that the problem is not that government does not plan sufficiently, but that it plans poorly. He points out that government aims at maximizing material welfare through technology and industry. The bureaucrats responsible for this process, he charges, are too remote, lack knowledge of local conditions, and cannot respond to change. People have reacted in different ways; many have decided to stop participating in society. This growing alienation brings with it a host of related problems that threaten to make the country ungovernable.

Alvin Toffler, in any event, looks past the search for goals to the balance wheels of the society. He argues that our first priority must be to regulate the rate of change that the technological revolution has brought with it (see Figure 21.2 for an indication of how change has accelerated in this century). People must have roots, he says, along with a feeling of security and a belief that the future is worth working for. Until then, government will be powerless to direct our national activities in a way satisfactory to the great majority of its citizens.

The future, then, is too important to be left solely to the politicians. Even though no final answers can be found for the serious challenges we

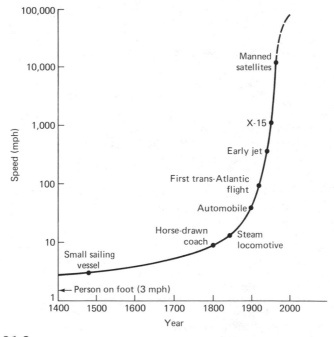

Figure 21.2
Increase in travel speed
Change of this magnitude leaves people with little or no time to adapt to new stresses. Source: Reprinted with permission of Macmillan Publishing Company, Inc., from John McHale, *World Facts and Trends*, p. 1. Copyright © 1972 by John McHale.

Figure 21.3

Films such as *The Manchurian Candidate* (left) and *1984* (right) warn about the dangers of totalitarian governments that use modern technology to modify behavior and to spy on their citizens. Unfortunately, the frightening developments shown in these films are based on trends already evident in society today. Sources: Springer/ Bettmann Film Archive (left); Culver Pictures (right).

face, some possibilities can be studied. This final chapter, therefore, will examine the following questions:

1. What positive changes may take place in the future?
2. What negative developments may occur in the future?
3. What will the future bring for the federal government?
4. What does the future hold for state and local governments?
5. What does the American trend toward polyculturalism mean?
6. What role will future citizens play in guiding government activities?
7. What further challenges will citizens of tomorrow face?

What positive changes may take place in the future?

Most writers in the second half of this century have adopted a pessimistic view of the future. Novels and films foresee a world dominated by giant corporate states that have reduced people to economic and political slavery. Almost all of these writers (see Ray Bradbury's *Fahrenheit 451*, Anthony Burgess's *A Clockwork Orange*, George Orwell's *1984*, and Aldous Huxley's *Brave New World*) describe a government that plays an overwhelming role in making choices for the individual (see Figure 21.3).

A number of thoughtful writers, however, have taken an opposite position. Confident that the human race has always managed to avoid impending chaos, the optimists base their predictions on current measurable trends. Their views suggest that:

1. A culture will be developed based on humanistic, workable values. Extremes of poverty, illness, and oppression will be erased.

2. Change will be brought under control, so that people will have time to adjust to new patterns of life.

3. The industrial nations will share their technology and wealth with the underdeveloped countries, so that all of humanity can share in the benefits of proper diet, medicine, housing, and recreation.

4. Increased amounts of leisure will give individuals the chance to develop constructive artistic and recreational interests.

5. Population will continue to grow, but at a slower rate. Food and other resources will keep pace with the increased demand.

6. People will continue to move into urban centers. Supercities will grow upward rather than outward, so that "green belts" can be left around the metropolitan centers of population.

7. Machines will do more and more of the manual labor; low-paid, unrewarding service occupations will decrease in importance.

8. Education will become a lifelong process, with entry into the schools encouraged at any stage of a person's life.

9. People will move toward a universal acceptance of individual differences; national and racial divisions will become unimportant.

10. Life expectancy will continue to increase as medical care improves and research conquers the traditional killers—cancer, heart disease, and the various communicable illnesses.

What negative developments may occur in the future?

Future governments will face hard decisions unknown to today's public officials. If population pressures increase, for example, the time may come when government must decide which couples may have children, and how many. Scientific experiments with (1) the creation of life outside the human body and (2) the alteration of behavior by chemical means will create whole new areas for regulation. A society that believes in democratic institutions and humanistic values may be forced to cope with a number of negative possibilities:

1. As society becomes more interdependent, organized minorities will gain greater ability to disrupt the orderly process of daily life.

2. Consumer products will become scarce as resources are diverted to higher priority uses.

3. Government will gain a greater degree of control over the individual through additional regulation and increased taxation.

4. Mental illness and random violence will increase as people feel the pressures of alienation, stress, and the loss of personal identity.

5. The individual will find it difficult to make a positive contribution to society; spectator sports and meaningless leisure activities will increase.

6. Inflationary pressures will send incomes and prices soaring to levels almost impossible to imagine today (see Table 21.1).

7. Present-day values will become outmoded as institutions crumble. The family, the church, and moral codes will either disappear or take on radically revised forms.

8. Continued despoilation of the environment will make the planet almost unliveable.

9. Giant international corporations and cartels will overshadow national governments.

10. International conflicts that escalate into nuclear war will bring about the final destruction of the human race.

None of these negative predictions is any more inevitable than the positive forecasts discussed earlier. But both pessimists and optimists agree that the time for determining the future is now. In May 1969, U Thant, then the Secretary General of the United Nations, warned:

> I do not wish to be overdramatic, but I can only conclude from the information that is available to me . . . that the members of the United Nations have perhaps ten years left in which to subordinate their ancient quarrels and launch a global partnership to curb the

Table 21.1

What will prices be like in the year 2000?

Cost of typical goods and services (based on average annual inflation rate of 9 percent)

New home		Year in private college		Hospital room, semi-private (per day)	
1975	$40,000	1975	$3,750	1975	$78
2000	$622,000	2000	$45,500	2000	$290
Physician's fee, house visit		Having a tooth filled		Drafting a simple will	
1975	$16.30	1975	$11	1975	$53
2000	$61	2000	$50	2000	$460
Man's suit		Woman's wool skirt		Man's shoes	
1975	$88	1975	$11	1975	$28
2000	$213	2000	$53	2000	$167
Cigarettes		Movie admission, adult		Man's haircut	
1975	52¢	1975	$2.25	1975	$3.20
2000	$1.35	2000	$8.00	2000	$20.50

AVERAGE FAMILY INCOME

1975	$14,200
2000	$112,000

Source: *U.S. News & World Report,* March 17, 1975, pp. 38–39. Copyright 1975 U.S. News & World Report, Inc.

arms race, to improve the human environment, to defuse the population explosion, and to supply the required momentum to development efforts. If such a global partnership is not forged within the next decade, then I have very much fear that the problems I have mentioned will have reached such staggering proportions that they will be beyond our capacity to control.

As individuals, most of us are powerless to make the decisions called for in the Secretary's speech. Only through the mechanism of government can a nation's strength and determination be focused on these challenges.

What will the future bring for the federal government?

Tomorrow's federal government will probably face three overriding concerns: (1) protection of individual rights and encouragement of individual self-direction; (2) preservation of environmental quality in both rural and urban areas; and (3) maintenance of civil order and political unity. Accomplishment of these goals will require careful governmental planning and coordination among the three branches of the federal system. The executive, legislative, and judicial branches will probably be forced to modify both their structure and procedures.

EXECUTIVE BRANCH

Most political scientists expect the presidency to continue to grow in strength and influence. With Congress divided politically and handicapped by lack of staff resources, only the President has the ability to move quickly and decisively when fast-moving events demand immediate action. Several changes would better equip the executive branch to handle its foreign and domestic responsibilities:

1. *Superdepartments.* Proposals have already been made which would combine the functions of related executive departments into several superdepartments. If all related agencies, bureaus, and administrations were brought together under a single administrator, overlapping programs could be eliminated and useful programs made more efficient.

Such would be the power of these superdepartments that critics have suggested that their directors would be acting as executive vice presidents. In the field of foreign affairs, for example, a Secretary of Foreign Affairs would formulate policy, develop programs, and direct every aspect of American relations with foreign countries. Day-to-day administration of the Department of State would be given to an Assistant Secretary of State. Domestic agencies, on the other hand, would consolidate their operations. Regional headquarters in major cities would be established to bring federal decision-making closer to the people served.

2. *Reorganization of independent agencies.* The independent administrative agencies would be reorganized, and overlapping jurisdictions would be eliminated. The policy-making powers of the independent agen-

cies would be returned to the President and Congress. The streamlined agencies would then serve primarily as enforcement bureaus clearly dedicated to serving the public interest.

3. New head of state. Many political scientists agree that the President can no longer properly fulfill all the duties of the office. Purely ceremonial tasks would be handed over to a Head of State, who would be elected solely for that purpose. Precedents for this reform already exist in a number of countries, including France, West Germany, and the Soviet Union. While the office would carry no administrative authority, its holder (perhaps an older, honored statesman) could well speak as the conscience of the American people.

LEGISLATIVE BRANCH

When the 106th Congress meets in the year 2000, the need for truly representative government will be greater than ever. Several proposals have been advanced to help the legislative branch meet that obligation:

1. Increased citizen involvement in lawmaking. Congress will attempt to incorporate more information on the wishes and opinions of citizens into the legislative process. Neighborhood advisory councils will forward summaries of voter wishes to their representatives. Special-service units will be organized to represent special-interest groups of all types in Washington, much as lobbyists now speak for the powerful corporations and unions. The technology could be developed to allow instant electronic surveys of individual preferences on major issues (see page 513).

2. Establishment of national goals. Congress will continue to seek a consensus on national goals. Three-year and five-year plans will be established to ensure that progress is made in major target areas, just as President Kennedy in the early 1960's set a high priority on landing an American astronaut on the moon by 1970. Such efforts at consensus will grow increasingly important as the nation becomes more diverse. Americans will need to be reminded that their similarities far outweigh their differences.

3. Greater power to balance the executive branch. In the future, as now, Congress must appraise, criticize, and oversee the administration of public policy. To do so, the legislature must gain power to match the growing strength of the presidency. Congress will come to see itself as the protector of the individual against bureaucratic fumbling and the insensitivity of big government. With the executive branch capable of gathering and storing a complete life history on every citizen, the day of Big Brother is no longer a remote threat.

Congress will probably gain increased strength from three sources:

Changes in the political environment. As the two major political parties adjust to changing conditions, representation from the cities and suburbs will be increased. The votes of younger Americans and minority groups will help elect a Congress that is more representative of the actual population.

Internal reform of Congress. A younger, more liberal Congress will put an end to the seniority system and reduce the power of the House Rules Committee. In turn, more highly qualified young people will be attracted to political careers when they see that there is a possibility of making their voices heard in a more responsive Congress.

Greater access to information. Congress will finally begin to match the executive branch's access to computer data. Of the approximately 5,000 data-processing units in use by the federal government in the early 1970's, only three were available to the members of the legislative branch. With its own computers and data banks, Congress will no longer be forced to rely on the White House for information about the background and possible effects of proposed legislation.

JUDICIAL BRANCH

Changes and reforms in the judicial branch will center on the work of the Supreme Court.

1. New courts. The Supreme Court can no longer deal effectively with the volume of cases it receives each year. New federal courts could be established to deal with (a) adversary actions (where two parties dispute the facts in a case); (b) administrative controversies over enforcement of government regulations; and (c) definition of individual and corporate rights and duties under the law.

2. Restriction of the Court's power. The Supreme Court would continue to exercise its right to interpret the Constitution. However, it would be deprived of its power to issue broad directives to the legislative and executive branches. Further, some critics suggest that the Constitution should be reviewed and revised once every twenty years. This action would greatly reduce the high court's tendency to "write" constitutional law through its decisions.

What does the future hold for state and local governments?

The creaky mechanism of federal–state–local relations will need major reforms if the American federal system is to regain its vitality. A combination of state constitutional amendments and passage by Congress of a national Modernization of State and Local Governments Act could bring about a number of changes.

1. REGIONAL GOVERNING BODIES

Regional governing bodies would be created to deal with common problems of health, education, welfare, and environmental pollution (see Figure 21.4). These interstate plans are unlikely to lead to complete consolidation of existing states, however, because if that happened, the resulting "super-

Figure 21.4

Because it can spread and cause damage in neighboring cities and states, pollution cannot be regarded as the problem only of the place where it originates: (left) an oil spill in New York Harbor poses a threat to both New York and New Jersey. Nor is pollution a problem only for the biggest cities: (right) smog in Knoxville, Tennessee. Sources: EPA (left); TVA (right).

state" would be forced to give up some of its representation in the Senate. Candidates for some form of regional government include such closely related states as the Dakotas, the Carolinas, Arizona–New Mexico, New Hampshire–Vermont, Connecticut–Rhode Island, and Montana–Wyoming–Idaho.

2. MODERNIZATION OF STATE GOVERNMENT

Modernization of state governments would provide better services at lower cost. Reforms include (a) shorter ballots, (b) longer terms for constitutional officers, (c) annual sessions for state legislatures, (d) better pay for legislators, (e) increased state borrowing power, (f) reorganization of boards and commissions so that they can properly fulfill their purposes, and (g) increased assistance to local governments.

3. IMPROVEMENT OF LOCAL SERVICES

Better service to communities would result from (a) consolidation of counties, towns, and other local municipalities; (b) decentralization of state administration through neighborhood service centers; and (c) increased home rule.

4. EQUALIZATION OF THE TAX BASE

Urban problems would be attacked through large grants-in-aid from state funds. This would help to narrow the existing gulf between have and have-not communities. All states would be encouraged to establish progressive income tax plans in order to relieve the burden of present property and sales taxes.

5. RESTRICTION OF ZONING POWER

City zoning authority would be restricted to prevent passage of ordinances that ruled out construction of low-cost housing. At the same time, cities would be encouraged to draw up rational, comprehensive growth plans in order to eliminate the eyesores caused by "urban sprawl."

Funding for all these major revisions of American political structures would come from federal taxes appropriated by Congress. Economists have estimated that $50 billion annually would be needed to finance the program. Half would be given directly to the states, with the rest going directly to cities, counties, and townships.

LET'S REVIEW FOR A MOMENT

The future contains the promise of greatness—or disaster. People working through responsive government units have the opportunity of improving the quality of life for everyone. Cities can be rebuilt as places of beauty and centers of culture and commerce. Mechanization can give us the leisure in which to create beauty in the environment and find peace within our own souls.

We cannot ignore the pessimists, however. In our own time, patterns have been established that may lead to further alienation, a ravaged environment, the collapse of social institutions, and international conflict. Whatever happens, government will be at the forefront of the change that is certain to come.

What can government do to prove the pessimists wrong? Individual rights must be protected, the quality of life must be improved, and civil order must be maintained. The three branches of the federal system can reorganize themselves in various ways to become more responsive to the needs of individuals.

State and local governments will move in two apparently opposite directions. On the one hand, governmental units at every level will consolidate their administrative and policy-making functions in order to eliminate duplication and provide better service to people. On the other hand, individual citizens will be given a bigger role in decision-making. Neighborhood offices will be established to meet with citizen groups so that each of us can directly influence our elected representatives.

What does the American trend toward polyculturalism mean?

A standard myth of the American experience died in the middle years of this century. As the old idea of the *melting pot* gave way to a new acceptance of *polyculturalism*, this country was forced to reexamine a number of long-accepted assumptions.

THEORY OF THE MELTING POT

The concept of the United States as a cultural melting pot dominated social thinking for a hundred years. Promoters of the theory held that a distinct American culture existed, with one set of standards. Immigrants to this country were expected to turn away from their own cultural patterns and conform to the beliefs, life style, and values of this standard way of life. Few people argued against these pressures. Children of new immigrants quickly discarded the ways of the old country; few even bothered to learn the language their parents spoke. Schools concentrated on teaching people to be Americans; non-Western cultures were largely ignored.

POLYCULTURALISM REVIVED

About twenty years ago, however, people began to doubt the old wisdom. Segments of American society came to reject the melting pot theory in favor of a polycultural approach that accepted all cultural backgrounds as valid and valuable. Negro groups now proclaim that "black is beautiful," and activists with Hispanic surnames promote "la raza." The diverse cultures of American Indians and Oriental Americans are considered with new respect. Universities offer degrees in ethnic studies; some states require the inclusion of such courses in public school curriculums.

STANDARD VALUES QUESTIONED

Polyculturalism is not limited to ethnic or racial minorities. With roots in the hippie movement of the early 1960's, a counterculture has developed that opposes the politics, life style, and legal system of the majority. Toffler views this as a logical development of the super-industrial revolution. Society splinters under the hammer blows of future shock. Social enclaves, tribes, and mini-cults multiply almost as fast as cigarette brands or automobile options.

Alternate life styles include a wide diversity of values—including many that reject the Puritan work ethic, so important to traditional American culture. Some surfers and skiers, for example, commit themselves to a life defined by the pursuit of pleasure. Other groups identify with youth, as in the "swinging singles" subculture. Still other people join psychic-mystical groups, narcotics-oriented subcults, or back-to-nature communes.

Futurists who predict a state-imposed uniformity have not given full weight to the phenomenon of polyculturalism. Toffler points out that although many people today are still locked into an almost choiceless way of life, the people of the near future will select their life styles and values from a multitude of socially acceptable alternatives.

ROLE OF GOVERNMENT

The problem for government will be that of implementing a social code that can accommodate all the new ways of thinking. Many of these alternative life styles will come into direct conflict with majority concepts of morality, property rights, and social justice. The present-day reform of marijuana laws illustrates an instance where the subculture has forced its values upon the majority. Government, for its part, must design new educational programs, political systems, and a unifying culture. If this effort is successful, our polycultural society will be tied together into a functioning whole. If it is not, the nation will be likely to turn to a totalitarian system of government under which all personal freedoms are crushed in the name of uniformity and discipline.

What role will future citizens play in guiding government activities?

Few problems exist today that youth is not willing to tackle: war, ecology, civil rights, poverty, morality, drugs, education, and many others. America's young people do not stop at raising the issues—they insist on doing something about them. Graduation speakers have long called upon their audiences to remake and improve the world. Today, young people take that charge literally. Indeed, many of them feel that unless they do, tomorrow's world may not be worth living in.

Unfortunately, a generation gap often divides the young and the old. Idealistic young people tend to be preoccupied with what is bad in the current system; older people, who have a greater stake in the existing society, are more anxious to preserve what is worthwhile from the past. Those who expect government to resolve this conflict will be disappointed. All Americans must join in a cooperative effort aimed at building a political and economic system that is capable of meeting urgent social needs.

INCREASED CITIZEN PARTICIPATION

The role of tomorrow's citizens will not change dramatically. Two political avenues will remain open—the opportunity to vote and the opportunity to play a direct role in political decision-making. In this second area, room exists for considerable improvement; several suggestions have been made:

1. *Ombudsman.* A few governmental units in the United States have already adopted the Swedish concept of the ombudsman (see Figure 21.5). This official's only responsibility is to help the individual citizen obtain fair treatment from government. Overlapping government bureaucracies

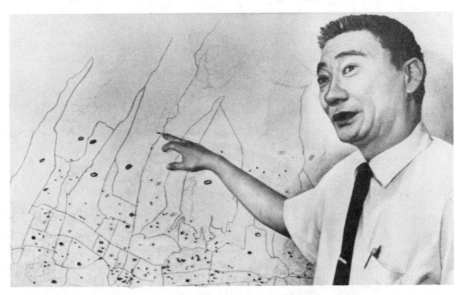

Figure 21.5

Hawaii's first ombudsman, Herman S. Doi, points to the location of a complaint received by his office when the program began in 1971. Like all ombudsmen, Mr. Doi investigates complaints by citizens against government officials and agencies. Source: Wide World Photos.

have become so complex and distant that the individual needs the help of this "friend at court" when dealing with almost any level of government.

2. *Neighborhood government.* As was mentioned earlier, many government agencies will open branch offices at the community level. By speaking to these officials through their *neighborhood councils,* citizens will know that their voices are heard by those in power. In time, the current feeling of alienation will diminish.

3. *National plebiscites.* A polycultural society cannot rely on today's slow-moving bureaucracy. To set future goals, the *plebiscite*—a nationwide direct ballot on a political issue—represents a mechanism through which members of all subgroups can be heard; people will have a yes-or-no vote on public decisions that will affect both their private and public lives. After holding a country-wide debate on the major issues, people will vote to accept or reject each proposal through a series of national plebiscites.

4. *Return to direct democracy.* Another solution would be to establish a series of *social future assemblies.* These assemblies would represent both geographical areas and socio-economic groups—labor, business, churches, the intellectual community, women, ethnic groups, the poor, and students. Service on such committees would be different from today's concept of jury duty—*everyone* would serve when called upon. By returning to this "town meeting" concept of direct democracy, citizens would be stimulated to take active roles in government—an absolute necessity for a free society to survive.

Figure 21.6
With 6 percent of the world's population, the United States consumes or produces . . .

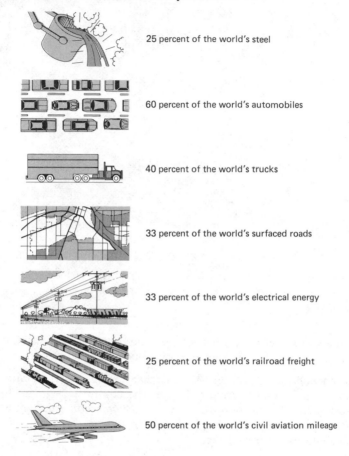

25 percent of the world's steel

60 percent of the world's automobiles

40 percent of the world's trucks

33 percent of the world's surfaced roads

33 percent of the world's electrical energy

25 percent of the world's railroad freight

50 percent of the world's civil aviation mileage

AMERICANS AS WORLD CITIZENS

Tomorrow's citizens will also be involved with affairs outside the boundaries of their own country. In an increasingly interdependent world, a number of truths will make themselves felt: (1) Industrial technology requires access to raw materials worldwide. (2) Depletion of resources and environmental pollution affect all nations. (3) Many industries already operate on a global scale. (4) Modern communications make an international exchange of cultural influences inevitable. (5) World regulatory agencies, perhaps based on the United Nations model, will take on greater importance. (6) A war anywhere on the globe affects people everywhere. The citizen of the future cannot escape the obligation of membership in a world community; as consumers of a disproportionate share of the world's natural resources (see Figure 21.6), Americans will have a particular responsibility to share the planet's increasingly scarce raw materials with all peoples.

What further challenges will
citizens of tomorrow face?

On any scale of physical specialization, the human race ranks far down the list. Our bodies do not have such useful adaptations as the tiger's jaws, the porcupine's quills, or the elephant's thick hide. The dolphin outswims us, the antelope outruns us, and the baboon outclimbs us. Only a single physiological attribute raises us above our fellow creatures. *Homo sapiens* has the largest and most complex brain in relation to body size in the animal kingdom. Even so, scientists tell us that we use only a fraction of the potential of this magnificent gift. The growing rate of mental illness in our society suggests that future challenges may make more demands on our adaptive abilities than we are physically and psychologically able to accommodate.

Most American social institutions have also undergone evolutionary change. Chapter 1 of this text traced the development of government, which began as an outgrowth of family and tribal organization. Today, it is obvious that the basic social unit we call the family is also in transition—and futurists argue that the splintering of society into new subcultures constitutes a return to ancient tribal structures (see Figure 21.7).

Figure 21.7

The constant pressures of modern life and the increasing acceptance of polyculturalism have led to a return to one of the earliest forms of social organization—the tribe. Primitive peoples such as the Tasaday (left), a Philippine Islands tribe, still live in Stone Age isolation. Some Americans (right) have chosen to search for new values in a communal life style that is strikingly similar to that of the Tasaday. Source: Magnum Photos.

EFFECTS OF CHANGE

Those who understand the concept of future shock know that many people react to change by negative behavior: anxiety, hostility to authority, senseless violence, physical illness, depression, and apathy. Victims of too much rapid change feel harassed; they want desperately to reduce the number of decisions they must make.

Social scientists have developed a rating system that assigns point values to those life changes which seem to cause stress. The death of a spouse rates a maximum score of 100 points, for example, while moving to a new home counts 20. Psychologists can now predict that anyone with a high score on the life-change scale—anyone who undergoes a great deal of stress—will almost certainly come down with a serious illness. Change, therefore, carries a physiological price tag; the more radical the change, the more severe the effect on the human body.

The many demands that face tomorrow's politicians make it obvious that change will occur in government, too. Governmental change also carries a price tag. The American public will pay that price in (1) additional tax dollars, (2) increased involvement in governmental decision-making, and (3) the physical stress caused by life changes.

Change, however, need not be thought of only in negative terms. To eliminate change would be to stop growth, progress, self-development, and maturation. The old saying "A change is as good as a vacation" has much merit. People who think about the future worry that the *rate* of change will leave people unable to make the needed adjustments to new life situations.

AN APPEAL FROM THE AUTHORS

An infamous criminal was once asked on the witness stand to name one contribution he had made to society. His response: "I paid my taxes." The judge was not impressed, and rightly so. If your future role as an American citizen consists only of paying taxes, voting, and occasionally griping about things you don't like, someone else will make tomorrow's decisions. Unfortunately, that "someone else" will probably be the representatives of organized pressure groups—who may or may not represent the real needs of our society.

It seems fitting, therefore, to conclude this text with an urgent appeal. We ask that you make a commitment to participate in government decision-making. Few young people today would identify their future goals with the statement, "I want to become a politician." But nothing less is needed than an army of young Americans willing to devote a part of their lives to building new and better political institutions.

Where do you start? Some young people are already running for school boards, city councils, and various commissions across the country—and they're winning some of those elections. Examine your own views, particularly those values you hold most deeply. Investigate the political structure of your community, and find the governing bodies that have the power to change the way things are done. Then speak up. Write letters, ask for a place on the agenda during public hearings. In short, learn what it means to be an *activist*—a concerned, involved participant in public affairs.

The opposite of active is passive, of course. Passive people let others make the decisions. They don't make things happen; rather, things happen to them. The future of the United States—your future—demands improvement in the quality of life. Without more involvement, more activism, and fewer spectators and fence-sitters, this great country will inevitably join the other cultures that have failed the test of history, and exist no more.

$\mathbb{S}$UMMARY AND CONCLUSIONS

1. Writers of science fiction have long based their predictions about future societies on existing trends and technological developments. The optimists point out that humanity has always risen to the challenge of the future, and that improved technology and greater psychological insight will enable us to greatly improve the quality of life. Pessimists, by contrast, forecast a future disrupted by alienated minorities, authoritarian government, collapse of social institutions, and further destruction of the environment.

2. Future development of the federal government will commit national resources to a threefold goal: protection of individual rights, enhancement of the quality of life, and maintenance of civil order. Many executive departments will be consolidated into *superdepartments*. The independent agencies will be reorganized to increase their effectiveness. A new, ceremonial position of Head of State will be created. Congress will do more to encourage involvement by individual citizens in legislative procedures, to establish national goals, and to oversee the actions of the powerful executive branch. New federal courts will relieve some of the Supreme Court's workload, but the high court will also be restricted in its ability to issue broad executive orders.

3. State and local governments will undergo major reforms: creation of *regional governing bodies* to deal with states' common problems; modernization of state government; improvement of local services; equalization of the tax base; and restriction of cities' zoning power. Much of the expense involved in these massive changes will be paid out of the federal budget.

4. American society has already begun to reject the idea of the United States as a *melting pot* in which everyone must conform to a single, dominant culture. In response to this increased acceptance of *polyculturalism*, a growing number of subcultures have emerged, based on race or nationality, moral values, or economic interests. These countercultures are fragmenting the traditional social order.

5. The citizen of the future will be more willing to attempt to reform society, and less interested in preserving old political and social institu-

tions. The cost of government will continue to increase. Citizens will still register their political will through voting, but their voices will become more important as *ombudsmen, neighborhood councils, plebiscites,* and *social future assemblies* emerge as channels for the national dialogue on goals and priorities. International affairs will increasingly affect each person, and the day of true "world citizenship" may finally arrive.

6. Change will occur in a beneficial, controlled way only if a maximum number of citizens become social and political *activists.* Only when a significant percentage of the American population gets involved in political life can we be assured that the United States of the year 2000 will fulfill the promise of its founding. In that great quest, all Americans must participate.

REVIEW QUESTIONS AND ACTIVITIES

TERMS YOU SHOULD KNOW

activist	*polyculturalism*
future shock	*problem-solving process*
melting pot	*regional governing bodies*
neighborhood councils	*social future assemblies*
ombudsman	*superdepartments*
plebiscite	

REVIEW QUESTIONS

The following multiple-choice questions are based on the important ideas presented in this chapter. Select the response that best completes each statement.

1. "Future shock" refers most specifically to (a) the development of electronic technology. (b) the accelerating rate of change and the stress it causes in society. (c) the possibility of future nuclear wars. (d) the rise of totalitarian systems of government. (e) the failure of government to solve the problems of urban life.

2. An *optimistic* view of the future would suggest that (a) population growth will outstrip the world food supply. (b) governments will grow steadily more restrictive of personal freedoms. (c) nations will be unable to settle their conflicts peacefully. (d) increased leisure time will turn most people into television addicts and violence freaks. (e) none of these is an optimistic viewpoint.

3. The American government of the future will probably *not* have as a goal (a) the expansion of American influence in and control over underdeveloped countries. (b) the protection of individual rights. (c) the preservation of environmental quality. (d) the maintenance of civil order. (e) the greater involvement of citizens in political decision-making.

4. The purpose of a plebiscite on national goals would be to (a) reach unanimous public agreement on a particular issue. (b) give the President an opportunity to bypass Congress in obtaining new legislation. (c) offer all citizens a chance to vote on basic issues facing the country. (d) bypass the Supreme Court's power of judicial review. (e) enable Congress to reduce the executive branch's authority over the federal bureaucracy.

5. One important advantage of consolidating country or state governments would lie in the possibility of (a) levying new taxes on interstate commerce. (b) eliminating duplicated services and handling regional problems that cross political boundaries. (c) bringing government closer to the people. (d) ending regional traditions and cultural patterns. (e) none of these would be an advantage.

6. The rise of polyculturalism in American society means the end of democratic institutions. This statement is (a) true. (b) false; polyculturalism has had little impact on American society and will soon die out. (c) false; a culturally diverse society can retain democratic institutions as long as all subcultures are given a voice in the decision-making process and accept the decisions of the majority.

7. A public official whose only job is to help individuals cope with problems involving government agencies is the (a) bureaucrat. (b) plebiscite. (c) world citizen. (d) delegate to the neighborhood council. (e) ombudsman.

8. Each of the following is a possible result of rapid changes in a person's life situation *except* (a) depression. (b) physical illness. (c) senseless violence. (d) inability to make decisions. (e) all of these are possible results.

9. The future of a free society depends largely upon the willingness of all American citizens to take an active role in local, state, and national government. This statement is (a) true. (b) false; the Constitution will protect American citizens, no matter what governments do. (c) false; the opportunity for citizens to influence political decisions is already closed off at most levels of government.

10. The creation of the office of Head of State would (a) increase the overall effectiveness of the President. (b) permit the officeholder to serve as the conscience of the American people. (c) relieve the President of purely ceremonial duties. (d) provide a suitable position for an older, widely respected national leader. (e) all of these.

CONCEPT DEVELOPMENT

This chapter has explored a number of significant concepts relating to the future of American government. You can use your skills in thinking, researching, and writing to answer the following questions.

1. What is meant by the term "future shock"? Can you find any examples of future shock in your own life?

2. Pick out a major problem faced by American government today. What do you think will have been done about this problem in ten years? In the year 2000?

3. Is polyculturalism a positive or negative development in the United States? How will we resolve this tendency for society to split into competing subcultures?

4. Explain how you would develop mechanisms for involving people more directly in government affairs at local, state, and national levels.

5. Will citizens of the next century look on this decade as a "golden age"? Why or why not?

ACTIVITIES

The following activities are designed to help you use the ideas developed in this chapter.

1. Throughout history, thoughtful writers have explored the possibility of building a perfect society. In 1516, Sir Thomas More gave us the name "Utopia" for such a peaceful, happy place. Suppose you had the power to construct your own utopia. What would it be like? How would you balance the desire to provide a maximum amount of personal freedom with the need to protect individuals from harming one another? Would your government be democratic? Would your economy be capitalistic? Remember, anyone can imagine a lovely world of sweetness and light. Can you construct a society based on realities—human nature, limited resources, international rivalries—and still devise a utopia? See what you can do, then share your results with your classmates.

2. If you're eighteen, you're probably eligible to run for a number of local civic offices. You may not feel ready for that sort of challenge, but it would be interesting to see what other young people across the country are doing. Research the question in your library (try the *Readers' Guide to Periodical Literature* for sources), and share the information with your classmates. If any young people in your community are serving on governing boards, invite them in to speak to your class about their experiences.

3. If you've never read any of the futuristic novels mentioned earlier (*Fahrenheit 451, A Clockwork Orange, 1984,* or *Brave New World*), give one or more of them a try. They're good reading, but they all project existing social trends into a terrifying future.

4. An interesting class project would be for each of you to write to a different public figure—state and federal politicians, high-ranking bureaucrats, military leaders, corporation presidents, entertainers, eminent educators, and the like. Ask each of them the same question: "What future do you foresee for American society?" Compile the results in a mimeographed booklet for distribution in your school. Not everyone will respond, of course, but you should receive enough answers to stimulate some interesting discussions.

5. How do you feel about this book? The authors welcome your comments. Write to us in care of the publisher: Amsco School Publications, 315 Hudson Street, New York, N.Y. 10013. Tell us what you liked, but also what you found difficult, boring, or useless. If you wish, talk about the level of vocabulary, the illustrations, the organization—in short, anything that either interested or annoyed you. We promise that when the book is revised, your suggestions will guide our decisions on what to change, what to delete, and what to add.

APPENDIX

THE DECLARATION OF INDEPENDENCE

(Adopted in Congress July 4, 1776)

The Unanimous Declaration of the Thirteen United States of America

When, in the course of human events, it becomes necessary for one people to dissolve the political bands which have connected them with another, and to assume among the powers of the earth, the separate and equal station to which the laws of nature and of nature's God entitle them, a decent respect to the opinions of mankind requires that they should declare the causes which impel them to the separation.

We hold these truths to be self-evident, that all men are created equal, that they are endowed by their Creator with certain unalienable rights, that among these are life, liberty and the pursuit of happiness. That to secure these rights, governments are instituted among men, deriving their just powers from the consent of the governed. That whenever any form of government becomes destructive of these ends, it is the right of the people to alter or to abolish it, and to institute new government, laying its foundation on such principles and organizing its powers in such form, as to them shall seem most likely to effect their safety and happiness. Prudence, indeed, will dictate that governments long established should not be changed for light and transient causes; and accordingly all experience hath shown that mankind are more disposed to suffer, while evils are sufferable, than to right themselves by abolishing the forms to which they are accustomed. But when a long train of abuses and usurpations, pursuing invariably the same object evinces a design to reduce them under absolute despotism, it is their right, it is their duty, to throw off such government, and to provide new guards for their future security.—Such has been the patient sufferance of these colonies; and such is now the necessity which constrains them to alter their former systems of government. The history of the present King of Great Britain is a history of repeated injuries and usurpations, all having in direct object the establishment of an absolute tyranny over these states. To prove this, let facts be submitted to a candid world.

He has refused his assent to laws, the most wholesome and necessary for the public good.

He has forbidden his governors to pass laws of immediate and pressing importance, unless suspended in their operation till his assent should be obtained; and when so suspended, he has utterly neglected to attend to them.

He has refused to pass other laws for the accommodation of large districts of people, unless those people would relinquish the right of representation in the legislature, a right inestimable to them and formidable to tyrants only.

He has called together legislative bodies at places unusual, uncomfortable, and distant from the depository of their public records, for the sole purpose of fatiguing them into compliance with his measures.

He has dissolved representative houses and repeatedly, for opposing with manly firmness his invasions on the rights of the people.

He has refused for a long time, after such dissolutions, to cause others to be elected; whereby the legislative powers, incapable of annihilation, have returned to the people at large for their exercise; the state remaining in the meantime exposed to all the dangers of invasion from without, and convulsions within.

He has endeavored to prevent the population of these states; for that purpose obstructing the laws for naturalization of foreigners, refusing to pass others to encourage their migration hither, and raising the conditions of new appropriations of lands.

He has obstructed the administration of justice, by refusing his assent to laws for establishing judiciary powers.

He has made judges dependent on his will alone, for the tenure of their offices, and the amount and payment of their salaries.

He has erected a multitude of new offices, and sent hither swarms of officers to harass our people, and eat out their substance.

He has kept among us, in times of peace, standing armies without the consent of our legislature.

He has affected to render the military independent of and superior to the civil power.

He has combined with others to subject us to a jurisdiction foreign to our constitution, and unacknowledged by our laws; giving his assent to their acts of pretended legislation:

For quartering large bodies of armed troops among us;

For protecting them, by a mock trial, from punishment for any murders which they should commit on the inhabitants of these states;

For cutting off our trade with all parts of the world;

For imposing taxes on us without our consent;

For depriving us in many cases, of the benefits of trial by jury;

For transporting us beyond seas to be tried for pretended offenses;

For abolishing the free system of English laws in a neighboring province, establishing therein an arbitrary government, and enlarging its boundaries so as to render it at once an example and fit instrument for introducing the same absolute rule into these colonies;

For taking away our charters, abolishing our most valuable laws, and altering fundamentally the forms of our governments;

For suspending our own legislatures, and declaring themselves invested with power to legislate for us in all cases whatsoever.

He has abdicated government here, by declaring us out of his protection and waging war against us.

He has plundered our seas, ravaged our coasts, burned our towns, and destroyed the lives of our people.

He is at this time transporting large armies of foreign mercenaries to complete the works of death, desolation and tyranny, already begun with circumstances of cruelty and perfidy scarcely paralleled in the most barbarous ages, and totally unworthy the head of a civilized nation.

He has constrained our fellow citizens taken captive on the high seas to bear arms against their country, to become the executioners of their friends and brethren, or to fall themselves by their hands.

He has excited domestic insurrections amongst us, and has endeavored to bring on the inhabitants of our frontiers, the merciless Indian savages, whose known rule of warfare, is an undistinguished destruction of all ages, sexes and conditions.

In every stage of these oppressions we have petitioned for redress in the most humble terms: our repeated petitions have been answered only by repeated injury. A prince whose character is thus marked by every act which may define a tyrant is unfit to be the ruler of a free people.

Nor have we been wanting in attention to our British brethren. We have warned them from time to time of attempts by their legislature to extend an unwarrantable jurisdiction over us. We have reminded them of the circumstances of our emigration and settlement here. We have appealed to their native justice and magnanimity, and we have conjured them by the ties of our common kindred to disavow these usurpations, which would inevitably interrupt our connections and correspondence. They too have been deaf to the voice of justice and of consanguinity. We must, therefore, acquiesce in the necessity, which denounces our separation, and hold them, as we hold the rest of mankind, enemies in war, in peace friends.

We, therefore, the representatives of the United States of America, in General Congress, assembled, appealing to the Supreme Judge of the world for the rectitude of our intentions, do, in the name, and by the authority of the good people of these colonies, solemnly publish and declare, that these united colonies are, and of right ought to be free and independent states; that they are absolved from all allegiance to the British Crown, and that all political connection between them and the state of Great Britain, is and ought to be totally dissolved; and that as free and independent states, they have full power to levy war, conclude peace, contract alliances, establish commerce, and to do all other acts and things which independent states may of right do. And for the support of this declaration, with a firm reliance on the protection of Divine Providence, we mutually pledge to each other our lives, our fortunes and our sacred honor.

Signed by John Hancock of Massachusetts as President of the Congress and by the fifty-five other Representatives of the thirteen United States of America.

CONSTITUTION OF THE UNITED STATES

(In Convention, September 17, 1787)

PREAMBLE

We, the people of the United States, in order to form a more perfect union, establish justice, insure domestic tranquility, provide for the common defense, promote the general welfare, and secure the blessings of liberty to ourselves and our posterity, do ordain and establish this Constitution for the United States of America.

ARTICLE I. LEGISLATIVE DEPARTMENT*

Section 1. Congress*

*Legislative Powers Vested in Senate and House.** All legislative powers herein granted shall be vested in a Congress of the United States, which shall consist of a Senate and House of Representatives.

Section 2. House of Representatives

1. Election of Representatives. The House of Representatives shall be composed of members chosen every second year by the people of the several states, and the electors in each state shall have the qualifications requisite for electors of the most numerous branch of the State legislature.

2. Qualifications of Representatives. No person shall be a Representative who shall not have attained to the age of twenty-five years, and been seven years a citizen of the United States, and who shall not, when elected, be an inhabitant of that state in which he shall be chosen.

3. Apportionment of Representatives. Representatives and direct taxes shall be apportioned among the several States which may be included within this Union, according to their respective numbers, [which shall be determined by adding to the whole number of free persons, including those bound to service for a term of years, and excluding Indians not taxed, three-fifths of all other persons.] The actual enumeration shall be made within three years after the first meeting of the Congress of the United States, and within every subsequent term of ten years, in such manner as they shall by law direct. The number of Representatives shall not exceed

---

* Headings and paragraph numbers have been inserted to assist the reader. The original Constitution contains only article and section numbers. Modern capitalization and punctuation have been used, and obsolete spelling of such words as "chuse" and "controul" has been changed to conform to modern spelling. Clauses that appear in brackets have been modified or made obsolete by later amendments.

one for every thirty thousand, but each State shall have at least one Representative; [and until such enumeration shall be made, the State of New Hampshire shall be entitled to choose three, Massachusetts eight, Rhode Island and Providence plantations one, Connecticut five, New York six, New Jersey four, Pennsylvania eight, Delaware one, Maryland six, Virginia ten, North Carolina five, South Carolina five, and Georgia three.]*

4. *Vacancies.* When vacancies happen in the representation from any state, the executive authority thereof shall issue writs of election to fill such vacancies.

5. *Officers of the House—Impeachment.* The House of Representatives shall choose their Speaker and other officers; and shall have the sole power of impeachment.

Section 3. The Senate

1. *Number of Senators.* The Senate of the United States shall be composed of two Senators from each State, [chosen by the legislature thereof,]† for six years; and each Senator shall have one vote.

2. *Classification of Senators.* Immediately after they shall be assembled in consequence of the first election, they shall be divided as equally as may be into three classes. [The seats of the Senators of the first class shall be vacated at the expiration of the second year, of the second class at the expiration of the fourth year, and of the third class at the expiration of the sixth year,] so that one-third may be chosen every second year; [and if vacancies happen by resignation, or otherwise, during the recess of the legislature of any State, the executive thereof may make temporary appointments until the next meeting of the legislature, which shall then fill such vacancies.]‡

3. *Qualifications of Senators.* No person shall be a Senator who shall not have attained to the age of thirty years, and been nine years a citizen of the United States, and who shall not, when elected, be an inhabitant of that State for which he shall be chosen.

4. *President of Senate.* The Vice President of the United States shall be President of the Senate, but shall have no vote, unless they be equally divided.

5. *Officers of Senate.* The Senate shall choose their other officers, and also a President *pro tempore*, in the absence of the Vice President or when he shall exercise the office of President of the United States.

6. *Trial of Impeachment.* The Senate shall have the sole power to try all impeachments. When sitting for that purpose, they shall be on oath or affirmation. When the President of the United States is tried, the Chief Justice shall preside: And no person shall be convicted without the concurrence of two-thirds of the members present.

---

* The bracketed parts of this clause, relating to representation, were superseded by Section 2 of the Fourteenth Amendment to the Constitution.
† Superseded by Amendment XVII.
‡ Modified by Amendment XVII.

7. *Judgment on Conviction of Impeachment.* Judgment in cases of impeachment shall not extend further than to removal from office, and disqualification to hold and enjoy any office of honor, trust or profit under the United States: but the party convicted shall nevertheless be liable and subject to indictment, trial, judgment and punishment, according to law.

Section 4. Election of Senators and Representatives; Meetings of Congress

1. *Election of Members of Congress.* The times, places, and manner of holding elections for Senators and Representatives, shall be prescribed in each State by the legislature thereof; but the Congress may at any time by law make or alter such regulations, except as to the places of choosing Senators.*

[2. *Congress to Meet Annually.* The Congress shall assemble at least once in every year, and such meeting shall be on the first Monday in December, unless they shall by law appoint a different day.]†

Section 5. Powers and Duties of Each House of Congress

1. *Sole Judge of Qualifications of Members.* Each House shall be the judge of the elections, returns, and qualifications of its own members, and a majority of each shall constitute a quorum to do business; but a smaller number may adjourn from day to day, and may be authorized to compel the attendance of absent members, in such manner, and under such penalties, as each House may provide.

2. *Rules of Proceedings; Punishment of Members.* Each House may determine the rules of its proceedings, punish its members for disorderly behavior, and, with the concurrence of two-thirds, expel a member.

3. *Journals.* Each House shall keep a journal of its proceedings,‡ and from time to time publish the same, excepting such parts as may in their judgment require secrecy; and the yeas and nays of the members of either House on any question shall, at the desire of one-fifth of those present, be entered on the journal.

4. *Adjournment.* Neither House, during the session of Congress, shall, without the consent of the other, adjourn for more than three days, nor to any other place than that in which the two Houses shall be sitting.

Section 6. Compensation, Privileges, and Disability of Senators and Representatives

1. *Compensation and Privileges.* The Senators and Representatives shall receive a compensation for their services, to be ascertained by law, and paid out of the Treasury of the United States. They shall in all cases, except treason, felony, and breach of the peace, be privileged from arrest during their attendance at the session of their respective Houses, and in

---

* See Amendment XX.
† Changed to January 3 by Amendment XX.
‡ This journal is published as the *Congressional Record.*

going to and returning from the same; and for any speech or debate in either House, they shall not be questioned in any other place.

2. *Disability to Hold Other Offices.* No Senator or Representative shall, during the time for which he was elected, be appointed to any civil office under the authority of the United States, which shall have been created, or the emoluments whereof shall have been increased during such time; and no person holding any office under the United States shall be a member of either House during his continuance in office.*

Section 7. Mode of Passing Laws

1. *Special Provision as to Revenue Laws.* All bills for raising revenue shall originate in the House of Representatives; but the Senate may propose or concur with amendments as on other bills.

2. *Enactment of Laws.* Every bill which shall have passed the House of Representatives and the Senate, shall, before it become a law, be presented to the President of the United States; if he approve he shall sign it, but if not he shall return it, with his objections, to that House in which it shall have originated, who shall enter the objections at large on their journal, and proceed to reconsider it. If after such reconsideration two-thirds of that House shall agree to pass the bill, it shall be sent, together with the objections, to the other House, by which it shall likewise be reconsidered, and if approved by two-thirds of that House, it shall become a law. But in all such cases the votes of both Houses shall be determined by yeas and nays, and the names of the persons voting for and against the bill shall be entered on the journal of each House respectively. If any bill shall not be returned by the President within ten days (Sundays excepted) after it shall have been presented to him, the same shall be a law, in like manner as if he had signed it, unless the Congress by their adjournment prevent its return, in which case it shall not be a law.

3. *Resolutions, Etc.* Every order, resolution, or vote to which the concurrence of the Senate and House of Representatives may be necessary (except on a question of adjournment) shall be presented to the President of the United States; and before the same shall take effect, shall be approved by him, or being disapproved by him, shall be repassed by two-thirds of the Senate and House of Representatives, according to the rules and limitations prescribed in the case of a bill.

Section 8. Powers Granted to Congress

The Congress shall have power:

1. *Taxation.* To lay and collect taxes, duties, imposts, and excises, to pay the debts and provide for the common defense and general welfare of the United States; but all duties, imposts, and excises shall be uniform throughout the United States;

2. *Loans.* To borrow money on the credit of the United States;

3. *Regulation of Commerce.* To regulate commerce with foreign nations, and among the several States, and with the Indian tribes;

* See also Section 3 of Amendment XIV.

4. *Naturalization and Bankruptcies.* To establish a uniform rule of naturalization, and uniform laws on the subject of bankruptcies throughout the United States;

5. *Coinage of money.* To coin money, regulate the value thereof, and of foreign coin, and fix the standard of weights and measures;

6. *Counterfeiting.* To provide for the punishment of counterfeiting the securities and current coin of the United States;

7. *Post Office.* To establish post offices and post roads;

8. *Patents and Copyrights.* To promote the progress of science and useful arts, by securing for limited times to authors and inventors the exclusive right to their respective writings and discoveries;

9. *Courts.* To constitute tribunals inferior to the Supreme Court;

10. *Piracies.* To define and punish piracies and felonies committed on the high seas, and offenses against the law of nations;

11. *War.* To declare war, grant letters of marque and reprisal, and make rules concerning captures on land and water;

12. *Army.* To raise and support armies, but no appropriation of money to that use shall be for a longer term than two years;

13. *Navy.* To provide and maintain a navy;

14. *Military and Naval Rules.* To make rules for the government and regulation of the land and naval forces;

15. *Calling Forth Militia.* To provide for calling forth the militia to execute the laws of the Union, suppress insurrections, and repel invasions;

16. *Organizing and Arming Militia.* To provide for organizing, arming, and disciplining the militia, and for governing such part of them as may be employed in the service of the United States, reserving to the States respectively the appointment of the officers, and the authority of training the militia according to the discipline prescribed by Congress;

17. *Federal District and Other Places.* To exercise exclusive legislation in all cases whatsoever, over such district (not exceeding ten miles square) as may, by cession of particular States, and the acceptance of Congress, become the seat of the government of the United States, and to exercise like authority over all places purchased by the consent of the legislature of the State in which the same shall be, for the erection of forts, magazines, arsenals, dockyards, and other needful buildings;—And

18. *Make Laws to Carry Out Foregoing Powers.* To make all laws which shall be necessary and proper for carrying into execution the foregoing powers, and all other powers vested by this Constitution in the Government of the United States, or in any department or officer thereof.*

---

* This is the "elastic clause." For other powers of Congress, see Article II, Section 1; Article III, Sections 2 and 3; Article IV, Sections 1–3; Article V; and Amendments XIII–XVI and XIX–XXI.

Section 9. Limitations on Powers Granted to the United States*

[*1. Slave Trade.* The migration or importation of such persons as any of the States now existing shall think proper to admit, shall not be prohibited by the Congress prior to the year one thousand eight hundred and eight, but a tax or duty may be imposed on such importation, not exceeding ten dollars for each person.]†

2. Habeas Corpus. The privilege of the writ of habeas corpus shall not be suspended, unless when in cases of rebellion or invasion the public safety may require it.

3. No Ex Post Facto Laws. No bill of attainder or ex post facto law shall be passed.

4. Direct Taxes. No capitation, or other direct, tax shall be laid, unless in proportion to the census or enumeration hereinbefore directed to be taken.

5. No Duties on Exports. No tax or duty shall be laid on articles exported from any State.

6. No Commercial Discrimination Between States. No preference shall be given by any regulation of commerce or revenue to the ports of one State over those of another; nor shall vessels bound to, or from, one State, be obliged to enter, clear, or pay duties in another.

7. Spending of Federal Funds. No money shall be drawn from the Treasury, but in consequence of appropriations made by law; and a regular statement and account of the receipts and expenditures of all public money shall be published from time to time.

8. No Titles of Nobility. No title of nobility shall be granted by the United States; and no person holding any office of profit or trust under them shall, without the consent of the Congress, accept of any present, emolument, office, or title, of any kind whatever, from any king, prince, or foreign state.

Section 10. Powers Prohibited to the States

1. Powers Prohibited Absolutely. No State shall enter into any treaty, alliance, or confederation; grant letters of marque and reprisal; coin money; emit bills of credit; make anything but gold and silver coin a tender in payment of debts; pass any bill of attainder, ex post facto law, or law impairing the obligation of contracts, or grant any title of nobility.

2. Powers Concerning Duties on Imports or Exports. No State shall, without the consent of the Congress, lay any imposts or duties on imports or exports, except what may be absolutely necessary for executing its inspection laws; and the net produce of all duties and imposts, laid by any State on imports or exports, shall be for the use of the Treasury of the United States; and all such laws shall be subject to the revision and control of the Congress.

---

* For other limitations, see Amendments I–X.
† Congress did end the slave trade in 1808. See also Amendment XIII.

3. Powers Permitted with Consent of Congress. No State shall, without the consent of Congress, lay any duty of tonnage, keep troops, or ships of war in time of peace, enter into any agreement or compact with another State, or with a foreign power, or engage in war, unless actually invaded, or in such imminent danger as will not admit of delay.

ARTICLE II. EXECUTIVE DEPARTMENT

Section 1. The President

1. Executive Power Vested in President; Term of Office. The executive power shall be vested in a President of the United States of America. He shall hold his office during the term of four years,* and together with the Vice President, chosen for the same term, be elected as follows:

2. Appointment and Number of Presidential Electors. Each State shall appoint, in such manner as the legislature thereof may direct, a number of Electors, equal to the whole number of Senators and Representatives to which the State may be entitled in the Congress; but no Senator or Representative, or person holding an office of trust or profit under the United States, shall be appointed an elector.

[*3. Mode of Electing President and Vice President.* The Electors shall meet in their respective States, and vote by ballot for two persons, of whom one at least shall not be an inhabitant of the same State with themselves. And they shall make a list of all the persons voted for, and of the number of votes for each; which list they shall sign and certify, and transmit sealed to the seat of the Government of the United States, directed to the President of the Senate. The President of the Senate shall, in the presence of the Senate and House of Representatives, open all the certificates, and the votes shall then be counted. The person having the greatest number of votes shall be the President, if such number be a majority of the whole number of Electors appointed; and if there be more than one who have such majority, and have an equal number of votes, then the House of Representatives shall immediately choose by ballot one of them for President; and if no person have a majority, then from the five highest on the list the said House shall in like manner choose the President. But in choosing the President, the vote shall be taken by States, the representation from each State having one vote; a quorum for this purpose shall consist of a member or members from two-thirds of the States, and a majority of all the States shall be necessary to a choice. In every case, after the choice of the President, the person having the greatest number of votes of the Electors shall be the Vice President. But if there should remain two or more who have equal votes, the Senate shall choose from them by ballot the Vice President.]†

4. Time of Choosing Electors and Casting Electoral Vote. The Congress may determine the time of choosing the Electors, and the day on which they shall give their votes; which day shall be the same throughout the United States.

---

* Amendment XXII limited the President to two four-year terms.
† This paragraph has been superseded by Amendment XII. See also Amendment XX.

5. *Qualifications of President.* No person except a natural-born citizen, or a citizen of the United States at the time of the adoption of this Constitution, shall be eligible to the office of President; neither shall any person be eligible to that office who shall not have attained to the age of thirty-five years, and been fourteen years a resident within the United States.*

6. *Presidential Succession.* In case of the removal of the President from office, or of his death, resignation, or inability to discharge the powers and duties of the said office, the same shall devolve on the Vice President, and the Congress may by law provide for the case of removal, death, resignation, or inability, both of the President and Vice President, declaring what officer shall then act as President, and such officer shall act accordingly, until the disability be removed, or a President shall be elected.†

7. *Salary of President.* The President shall, at stated times, receive for his services, a compensation, which shall neither be increased nor diminished during the period for which he shall have been elected, and he shall not receive within that period any other emolument from the United States, or any of them.

8. *Oath of Office of President.* Before he enter on the execution of his office, he shall take the following oath or affirmation: —"I do solemnly swear (or affirm) that I will faithfully execute the office of President of the United States, and will to the best of my ability, preserve, protect, and defend the Constitution of the United States."

Section 2. Powers of the President

1. *Commander-in-Chief.* The President shall be commander-in-chief of the Army and Navy of the United States, and of the militia of the several

---

* See also Article II, Section 1, and Amendment XIV.
† Modified by Amendment XXV. Also, *United States Code Annotated, Title 3, Sec. 19,* provides as follows:

(a) (1) If, by reason of death, resignation, removal from office, inability, or failure to qualify, there is neither a President nor Vice President to discharge the powers and duties of the office of President, then the Speaker of the House of Representatives shall, upon his resignation as Speaker and as Representative in Congress, act as President.

(2) The same rule shall apply in the case of the death, resignation, removal from office, or inability of an individual acting as President under this subsection.

(b) If, at the time when under subsection (a) of this section a Speaker is to begin the discharge of the powers and duties of the office of President, there is no Speaker, or the Speaker fails to qualify as Acting President, then the President *pro tempore* of the Senate shall, upon his resignation as President *pro tempore* and as Senator, act as President. . . .

(d) (1) If, by reason of death, resignation, removal from office, inability, or failure to qualify, there is no President *pro tempore* to act as President under subsection (b) of this section, then the officer of the United States who is highest on the following list, and who is not under disability to discharge the powers and duties of the office of President, shall act as President: Secretary of State, Secretary of the Treasury, Secretary of Defense, Attorney General, Postmaster General, Secretary of the Interior, Secretary of Agriculture, Secretary of Commerce, Secretary of Labor, Secretary of Health, Education, and Welfare, Secretary of Housing and Urban Development.

States, when called into the actual service of the United States; he may require the opinion, in writing, of the principal officer in each of the executive departments,* upon any subject relating to the duties of their respective offices, and he shall have power to grant reprieves and pardons for offenses against the United States, except in cases of impeachment.

2. *Treaties and Appointments.* He shall have power, by and with the advice and consent of the Senate, to make treaties, provided two-thirds of the Senators present concur; and he shall nominate, and by and with the advice and consent of the Senate, shall appoint ambassadors, other public ministers, and consuls, Judges of the Supreme Court, and all other officers of the United States, whose appointments are not herein otherwise provided for, and which shall be established by law; but the Congress may by law vest the appointment of such inferior officers, as they think proper, in the President alone, in the courts of law, or in the heads of departments.

3. *Filling Vacancies.* The President shall have power to fill up all vacancies that may happen during the recess of the Senate, by granting commissions which shall expire at the end of their next session.

Section 3. Duties of the President

He shall from time to time give to the Congress information of the state of the Union, and recommend to their consideration such measures as he shall judge necessary and expedient; he may, on extraordinary occasions, convene both Houses, or either of them, and in case of disagreement between them, with respect to the time of adjournment, he may adjourn them to such time as he shall think proper; he shall receive ambassadors and other public ministers; he shall take care that the laws be faithfully executed, and shall commission all the officers of the United States.†

Section 4. Impeachment

The President, Vice President, and all civil officers of the United States, shall be removed from office on impeachment for, and conviction of, treason, bribery, or other high crimes and misdemeanors.‡

ARTICLE III. JUDICIAL DEPARTMENT

Section 1. Judicial Powers Vested in Federal Courts

The judicial power of the United States shall be vested in one Supreme Court, and in such inferior courts as the Congress may from time to time ordain and establish. The judges, both of the Supreme and inferior courts, shall hold their offices during good behavior, and shall, at stated times, receive for their services a compensation, which shall not be diminished during their continuance in office.

---

* This phrase provides the constitutional basis for the President's Cabinet.
† See also Article I, Section 5.
‡ See also Article I, Sections 2 and 3.

Section 2. Jurisdiction of United States Courts

1. Cases That May Come Before United States Courts. The judicial power shall extend to all cases, in law and equity, arising under this Constitution, the laws of the United States, and treaties made, or which shall be made, under their authority; to all cases affecting ambassadors, other public ministers and consuls; to all cases of admiralty and maritime jurisdiction; to controversies to which the United States shall be a party; to controversies between two or more States; [between a State and citizens of another State;]* between citizens of different States; between citizens of the same State claiming lands under grants of different States, and between a State, or the citizens thereof, and foreign States, citizens or subjects.

2. Jurisdiction of Supreme and Appellate Courts. In all cases affecting ambassadors, other public ministers and consuls, and those in which a State shall be party, the Supreme Court shall have original jurisdiction. In all the other cases before mentioned, the Supreme Court shall have appellate jurisdiction, both as to law and fact, with such exceptions, and under such regulations as the Congress shall make.

3. Trial of Crimes. The trial of all crimes, except in cases of impeachment, shall be by jury; and such trial shall be held in the State where the said crimes shall have been committed; but when not committed within any State, the trial shall be at such place or places as the Congress may by law have directed.†

Section 3. Treason

1. Treason Defined. Treason against the United States, shall consist only in levying war against them, or in adhering to their enemies, giving them aid and comfort.

2. Conviction. No person shall be convicted of treason unless on the testimony of two witnesses to the same overt act, or on confession in open court.

3. Punishment. The Congress shall have power to declare the punishment of treason, but no attainder of treason shall work corruption of blood or forfeiture except during the life of the person attainted.

ARTICLE IV. THE STATES AND THE FEDERAL GOVERNMENT

Section 1. Full Faith and Credit

Full faith and credit shall be given in each State to the public acts, records, and judicial proceedings of every other State. And the Congress may by general laws prescribe the manner in which such acts, records, and proceedings shall be proved, and the effect thereof.‡

---

* Restricted by Amendment XI.
† See also Amendments V, VI, VII, and VIII.
‡ See also Amendment XIV.

Section 2. Citizens of the States

1. Interstate Privileges of Citizens. The citizens of each State shall be entitled to all privileges and immunities of citizens in the several States.

2. Fugitives from Justice. A person charged in any State with treason, felony, or other crime, who shall flee from justice, and be found in another State, shall on demand of the executive authority of the State from which he fled, be delivered up, to be removed to the State having jurisdiction of the crime.

[*3. Fugitives from Service.* No person held to service or labor in one State, under the laws thereof, escaping into another, shall, in consequence of any law or regulation therein, be discharged from such service or labor, but shall be delivered up on claim of the party to whom such service or labor may be due.]*

Section 3. New States and Territories

1. Admission of New States; No Division. New States may be admitted by the Congress into this Union; but no new State shall be formed or erected within the jurisdiction of any other State; nor any State be formed by the junction of two or more States, or parts of States, without the consent of the legislatures of the States concerned as well as of the Congress.

2. Control of the Property and Territory of the Union. The Congress shall have power to dispose of and make all needful rules and regulations respecting the territory or other property belonging to the United States; and nothing in this Constitution shall be so construed as to prejudice any claims of the United States, or of any particular State.

Section 4. Protection of States Guaranteed

The United States shall guarantee to every State in this Union a republican form of government, and shall protect each of them against invasion; and on application of the legislature, or of the executive (when the legislature cannot be convened), against domestic violence.

ARTICLE V. AMENDMENTS

The Congress, whenever two-thirds of both Houses shall deem it necessary, shall propose amendments to this Constitution, or, on the application of the legislatures of two-thirds of the several States, shall call a convention for proposing amendments, which, in either case, shall be valid to all intents and purposes, as part of this Constitution, when ratified by the legislatures of three-fourths of the several States, or by conventions in three-fourths thereof, as the one or the other mode of ratification may be proposed by the Congress; provided [that no amendment which may be made prior to the year one thousand eight hundred and eight shall in any manner affect the first and fourth clauses in the ninth section of

---

* "Person" here includes slave. This was the basis of the Fugitive Slave Laws of 1793 and 1850. It is now superseded by Amendment XIII, by which slavery is prohibited.

the first article; and] that no State, without its consent, shall be deprived of its equal suffrage in the Senate.

ARTICLE VI. GENERAL PROVISIONS

1. The Public Debt. All debts contracted and engagements entered into, before the adoption of this Constitution, shall be as valid against the United States under this Constitution, as under the Confederation.*

2. Supreme Law of the Land. This Constitution, and the laws of the United States which shall be made in pursuance thereof, and all treaties made, or which shall be made, under the authority of the United States, shall be the supreme law of the land; and the judges in every State shall be bound thereby, anything in the Constitution or laws of any State to the contrary notwithstanding.

3. Oath of Office; No Religious Test Required. The Senators and Representatives before mentioned, and the members of the several State legislatures, and all executive and judicial officers, both of the United States and of the several States, shall be bound by oath or affirmation, to support this Constitution; but no religious test shall ever be required as a qualification to any office or public trust under the United States.

ARTICLE VII. RATIFICATION OF THE CONSTITUTION

The ratification of the conventions of nine States, shall be sufficient for the establishment of this Constitution between the States so ratifying the same.

Done in convention by the unanimous consent of the States present the seventeenth day of September in the year of our Lord one thousand seven hundred and eighty-seven, and of the Independence of the United States of America the twelfth. In witness whereof we have hereunto subscribed our names.

Signed by George Washington as President of the Convention and deputy from Virginia and by the thirty-eight other representatives of twelve states.

AMENDMENTS

Amendment I: Freedom of Religion, Speech, Press, Assembly, and Petition†

Congress shall make no law respecting an establishment of religion, or prohibiting the free exercise thereof; or abridging the freedom of speech,

---

* Extended by Amendment XIV, Section 4.
† The first ten amendments make up the Bill of Rights. They were each proposed by Congress on September 25, 1789, and ratified by the necessary three-fourths of the states on December 15, 1791.

or of the press; or the right of the people peaceably to assemble, and to petition the Government for a redress of grievances.

Amendment II: Right to Bear Arms

A well-regulated militia being necessary to the security of a free State, the right of the people to keep and bear arms shall not be infringed.

Amendment III: Billeting of Soldiers

No soldier shall, in time of peace, be quartered in any house, without the consent of the owner, nor in time of war, but in a manner to be prescribed by law.

Amendent IV: Seizures, Searches, and Warrants

The right of the people to be secure in their persons, houses, papers, and effects, against unreasonable searches and seizures, shall not be violated, and no warrants shall issue, but upon probable cause, supported by oath or affirmation, and particularly describing the place to be searched, and the persons or things to be seized.

Amendment V: Criminal Proceedings
and Condemnation of Property

No person shall be held to answer for a capital, or otherwise infamous, crime, unless on a presentment or indictment of a grand jury, except in cases arising in the land or naval forces, or in the militia, when in actual service in time of war or public danger; nor shall any person be subject for the same offense to be twice put in jeopardy of life or limb; nor shall be compelled, in any criminal case, to be a witness against himself; nor be deprived of life, liberty, or property, without due process of law; nor shall private property be taken for public use, without just compensation.

Amendment VI: Mode of Trial in Criminal Proceedings

In all criminal prosecutions, the accused shall enjoy the right to a speedy and public trial by an impartial jury of the State and district wherein the crime shall have been committed, which district shall have been previously ascertained by law, and to be informed of the nature and cause of the accusation; to be confronted with the witnesses against him; to have compulsory process for obtaining witnesses in his favor, and to have the assistance of counsel for his defense.

Amendment VII: Trial by Jury

In suits at common law, where the value in controversy shall exceed twenty dollars, the right of trial by jury shall be preserved, and no fact tried by a jury shall be otherwise re-examined in any court of the United States, than according to the rules of the common law.

Amendment VIII: No Excessive Punishments

Excessive bail shall not be required, nor excessive fines imposed, nor cruel and unusual punishments inflicted.

Amendment IX: Other Rights Not Denied to the People

The enumeration in the Constitution, of certain rights, shall not be construed to deny or disparage others retained by the people.

Amendment X: Powers Reserved
to the States or People

The powers not delegated to the United States by the Constitution, nor prohibited by it to the States, are reserved to the States respectively, or to the people.

Amendment XI: Suits Against States*

The judicial power of the United States shall not be construed to extend to any suit in law or equity, commenced or prosecuted against one of the United States by citizens of another State, or by citizens or subjects of any foreign State.

Amendment XII: Revised Procedures for Election
of President and Vice President†

The Electors shall meet in their respective States and vote by ballot for President and Vice President, one of whom, at least, shall not be an inhabitant of the same State with themselves; they shall name in their ballots the person voted for as President, and in distinct ballots the person voted for as Vice President, and they shall make distinct lists of all persons voted for as President, and of all persons voted for as Vice President, and of the number of votes for each, which lists they shall sign and certify, and transmit sealed to the seat of the government of the United States, directed to the President of the Senate; the President of the Senate shall, in the presence of the Senate and House of Representatives, open all the certificates and the votes shall then be counted; the person having the greatest number of votes for President shall be the President, if such number be a majority of the whole number of Electors appointed; and if no person have such majority, then from the persons having the highest numbers not exceeding three on the list of those voted for as President, the House of Representatives shall choose immediately, by ballot, the President.‡ But in choosing the President, the votes shall be taken by States, the representation from each State having one vote; a quorum for this purpose shall consist of a member or members from two-thirds of the States, and a majority of all the States shall be necessary to a choice. And if the House of Representatives shall not choose a President whenever the right of choice shall devolve upon them, [before the fourth day of March next following,]§ then the Vice President shall act as President, as in the case of the death or other constitutional disability of the President. The person having the greatest number of votes as Vice President, shall be the Vice President, if such number be a majority of the whole number of Electors

* Proposed by Congress March 4, 1794; ratified February 7, 1795; not officially declared ratified until January 8, 1798.
† Proposed by Congress December 12, 1803; ratified June 15, 1804.
‡ Only twice has the House of Representatives chosen the President: Thomas Jefferson in 1801 and John Quincy Adams in 1825.
§ Amendment XX sets the date for presidential inaugurations at January 20.

appointed, and if no person have a majority, then, from the two highest numbers on the list, the Senate shall choose the Vice President; a quorum for the purpose shall consist of two-thirds of the whole number of Senators, and a majority of the whole number shall be necessary to a choice. But no person constitutionally ineligible to the office of President shall be eligible to that of Vice President of the United States.

Amendment XIII: Slavery Abolished*

Section 1. Neither slavery nor involuntary servitude, except as a punishment for crime whereof the party shall have been duly convicted, shall exist within the United States, or any place subject to their jurisdiction.

Section 2. Congress shall have power to enforce this article by appropriate legislation.

Amendment XIV: Citizenship, Due Process, Representation, and Payment of Public Debt†

Section 1. Citizenship and Due Process. All persons born or naturalized in the United States, and subject to the jurisdiction thereof, are citizens of the United States and of the State wherein they reside. No State shall make or enforce any law which shall abridge the privileges or immunities of citizens of the United States; nor shall any State deprive any person of life, liberty, or property, without due process of law; nor deny to any person within its jurisdiction the equal protection of the laws.

Section 2. Apportionment of Representatives. Representatives shall be apportioned among the several States according to their respective numbers, counting the whole number of persons in each State, excluding Indians not taxed. But when the right to vote at any election for the choice of Electors for President and Vice President of the United States, Representatives in Congress, the executive and judicial officers of a State, or the members of the legislature thereof, is denied to any of the male inhabitants of such State, being twenty-one years of age, and citizens of the United States, or in any way abridged, except for participation in rebellion, or other crime, the basis of representation therein shall be reduced in the proportion which the number of such male citizens shall bear to the whole number of male citizens twenty-one years of age in such State.

Section 3. Exclusion of Rebels from Public Office. No person shall be a Senator or Representative in Congress, or Elector of President and Vice President, or hold any office, civil or military, under the United States, or under any State, who, having previously taken an oath, as a member of Congress, or as an officer of the United States, or as a member of any State legislature, or as an executive or judicial officer of any State, to support the Constitution of the United States, shall have engaged in insurrection or rebellion against the same, or given aid or comfort to the enemies thereof. But Congress may, by a vote of two-thirds of each House, remove such disability.

* Proposed by Congress January 31, 1865; ratified December 6, 1865.
† Proposed by Congress June 16, 1866; ratified July 9, 1868.

Section 4. No Repayment of the Confederacy's Debt. The validity of the public debt of the United States, authorized by law, including debts incurred for payment of pensions and bounties for services in suppressing insurrection or rebellion, shall not be questioned. But neither the United States nor any State shall assume or pay any debt or obligation incurred in aid of insurrection or rebellion against the United States, or any claim for the loss or emancipation of any slave; but all such debts, obligations, and claims shall be held illegal and void.

Section 5. Enforcement Power of Congress. The Congress shall have power to enforce, by appropriate legislation, the provisions of this article.

Amendment XV: Right of Citizens to Vote*

Section 1. The right of citizens of the United States to vote shall not be denied or abridged by the United States or by any State on account of race, color, or previous condition of servitude.

Section 2. The Congress shall have power to enforce this article by appropriate legislation.

Amendment XVI: Income Tax†

The Congress shall have power to lay and collect taxes on incomes, from whatever source derived, without apportionment among the several States, and without regard to any census or enumeration.

Amendment XVII: Popular Election of Senators‡

Section 1. The Senate of the United States shall be composed of two Senators from each State, elected by the people thereof, for six years; and each Senator shall have one vote. The electors in each State shall have the qualifications requisite for electors of the most numerous branch of the State Legislatures.

Section 2. When vacancies happen in the representation of any State in the Senate, the executive authority of such State shall issue writs of election to fill such vacancies: *Provided,* That the legislature of any State may empower the executive thereof to make temporary appointments until the people fill the vacancies by election as the legislature may direct.

[*Section 3.* This amendment shall not be so construed as to affect the election or term of any Senator chosen before it becomes valid as part of the Constitution.]

Amendment XVIII: Prohibition§

[*Section 1.* After one year from the ratification of this article the manufacture, sale, or transportation of intoxicating liquors within, the importation thereof into, or the exportation thereof from the United States and

* Proposed by Congress February 26, 1869; ratified February 3, 1870.
† Proposed by Congress July 2, 1909; ratified February 3, 1913.
‡ Proposed by Congress May 13, 1912; ratified April 8, 1913. This amendment modifies Article I, Section 3, Clauses 1 and 2.
§ Proposed by Congress December 18, 1917; ratified January 16, 1919; certified January 29, 1919; went into effect January 29, 1920; repealed in 1933 by Amendment XXI.

all territory subject to the jurisdiction thereof for beverage purposes is hereby prohibited.]

[*Section 2.* The Congress and the several S'ates shall have concurrent power to enforce this article by appropriate legislation.]

[*Section 3.* This article shall be inoperative unless it shall have been ratified as an amendment to the Constitution by the legislatures of the several States, as provided in the Constitution, within seven years from the date of the submission hereof to the States by the Congress.]

Amendment XIX: Right of Women to Vote*

Section 1. The right of citizens of the United States to vote shall not be denied or abridged by the United States or by any State on account of sex.

Section 2. Congress shall have power to enforce this article by appropriate legislation.

Amendment XX: Presidential and Vice Presidential Terms, Interim Succession, Sessions of Congress†

Section 1. End of Terms. The terms of the President and Vice President shall end at noon on the 20th day of January, and the terms of Senators and Representatives at noon on the 3d day of January, of the years in which such terms would have ended if this article had not been ratified; and the terms of their successors shall then begin.

Section 2. Assembling of Congress. The Congress shall assemble at least once in every year, and such meeting shall begin at noon on the 3d day of January, unless they shall by law appoint a different day.

Section 3. Congress Provides for Acting President. If at the time fixed for the beginning of the term of the President, the President-elect shall have died, the Vice-President-elect shall become President. If a President shall not have been chosen before the time fixed for the beginning of his term, or if the President-elect shall have failed to qualify, then the Vice-President-elect shall act as President until a President shall have qualified; and the Congress may by law provide for the case wherein neither a President-elect nor a Vice-President-elect shall have qualified, declaring who shall then act as President, or the manner in which one who is to act shall be selected, and such person shall act accordingly until a President or Vice President shall have qualified.

Section 4. Congress Has Power Over Unusual Elections. The Congress may by law provide for the case of the death of any of the persons from whom the House of Representatives may choose a President whenever the right of choice shall have devolved upon them, and for the case of the death of any of the persons from whom the Senate may choose a Vice President whenever the right of choice shall have devolved upon them.

* Proposed by Congress June 4, 1919; ratified August 18, 1920.
† Proposed March 2, 1932; ratified January 23, 1933.

[*Section 5. Date in Effect.* Sections 1 and 2 shall take effect on the 15th day of October following the ratification of this article.]

[*Section 6. Conditions of Ratification.* This article shall be inoperative unless it shall have been ratified as an amendment to the Constitution by the legislatures of three-fourths of the several States within seven years from the date of its submission.]

Amendment XXI: Repeal of Prohibition*

Section 1. Repeal of Amendment XVIII. The eighteenth article of amendment to the Constitution of the United States is hereby repealed.

Section 2. Control of Liquor Transportation. The transportation or importation into any State, Territory, or possession of the United States for delivery or use therein of intoxicating liquors, in violation of the laws thereof, is hereby prohibited.

[*Section 3. Condition of Ratification.* This article shall be inoperative unless it shall have been ratified as an amendment to the Constitution by conventions in the several States, as provided in the Constitution, within seven years from the date of the submission hereof to the States by the Congress.]

Amendment XXII: Limitation of Presidential Terms†

Section 1. Limitation on Number of Terms. No person shall be elected to the office of the President more than twice, and no person who has held the office of President, or acted as President, for more than two years of a term to which some other person was elected President shall be elected to the office of the President more than once. But this article shall not apply to any person holding the office of President when this article was proposed by the Congress, and shall not prevent any person who may be holding the office of President, or acting as President, during the term within which this article becomes operative from holding the office of President or acting as President during the remainder of such term.

[*Section 2. Condition of Ratification.* This article shall be inoperative unless it shall have been ratified as an amendment to the Constitution by the legislatures of three-fourths of the several States within seven years from the date of its submission to the States by the Congress.]

Amendment XXIII: Presidential Electors
for the District of Columbia‡

Section 1. The District constituting the seat of Government of the United States shall appoint in such manner as the Congress may direct:
A number of Electors of President and Vice President equal to the whole number of Senators and Representatives in Congress to which the District would be entitled if it were a State, but in no event more than the least populous State; they shall be in addition to those appointed by the States,

---

* Proposed by Congress February 20, 1933; ratified December 5, 1933.
† Proposed by Congress March 24, 1947; ratified February 27, 1951.
‡ Proposed by Congress June 16, 1960; ratified March 29, 1961.

but they shall be considered, for the purposes of the election of President and Vice President, to be Electors appointed by a State; and they shall meet in the District and perform such duties as provided by the twelfth article of amendment.

Section 2. The Congress shall have power to enforce this article by appropriate legislation.

Amendment XXIV: No Poll Tax*

Section 1. The right of citizens of the United States to vote in any primary or other election for President or Vice President, for Electors for President or Vice President, or for Senator or Representative in Congress, shall not be denied or abridged by the United States or any State by reason of failure to pay any poll tax or other tax.

Section 2. The Congress shall have power to enforce this article by appropriate legislation.

Amendment XXV: Succession to Presidency
and Vice Presidency; Disability of President†

Section 1. Presidential Succession. In case of the removal of the President from office or of his death or resignation, the Vice President shall become President.

Section 2. Vice Presidential Succession. Whenever there is a vacancy in the office of the Vice President, the President shall nominate a Vice President who shall take office upon confirmation by a majority vote of both Houses of Congress.

Section 3. Presidential Disability. Whenever the President transmits to the President *pro tempore* of the Senate and the Speaker of the House of Representatives his written declaration that he is unable to discharge the powers and duties of his office, and until he transmits to them a written declaration to the contrary, such powers and duties shall be discharged by the Vice President as Acting President.

Section 4. Resumption of Power by the President. Whenever the Vice President and a majority of either the principal officers of the executive departments or of such other body as Congress may by law provide, transmit to the President *pro tempore* of the Senate and the Speaker of the House of Representatives their written declaration that the President is unable to discharge the powers and duties of his office, the Vice President shall immediately assume the powers and duties of the office as Acting President.

Thereafter, when the President transmits to the President *pro tempore* of the Senate and the Speaker of the House of Representatives his written declaration that no inability exists, he shall resume the powers and duties of his office unless the Vice President and a majority of either the principal officers of the executive department or of such other body as Congress may by law provide, transmit within four days to the President *pro tempore*

---

* Proposed by Congress September 14, 1962; ratified January 23, 1964.
† Proposed by Congress July 6, 1965; ratified February 10, 1967.

of the Senate and the Speaker of the House of Representatives their written declaration that the President is unable to discharge the powers and duties of his office. Thereupon Congress shall decide the issue, assembling within forty-eight hours for that purpose if not in session. If the Congress, within twenty-one days after receipt of the latter written declaration, or, if Congress is not in session, within twenty-one days after Congress is required to assemble, determines by two-thirds vote of both Houses that the President is unable to discharge the powers and duties of his office, the Vice President shall continue to discharge the same as Acting President; otherwise, the President shall resume the powers and duties of his office.

Amendment XXVI: Voting Age Set at Eighteen*

Section 1. The right of citizens of the United States, who are eighteen years of age or older, to vote shall not be denied or abridged by the United States or by any State on account of age.

Section 2. The Congress shall have power to enforce this article by appropriate legislation.

* Proposed March 23, 1971; ratified July 1, 1971.

INDEX